Christ's Associations

Christ's Associations

Connecting and Belonging in the Ancient City

John S. Kloppenborg

Yale
UNIVERSITY
PRESS
New Haven and London

Published with assistance from the Mary Cady Tew Memorial Fund.

Yale University Press books may be purchased in quantity for educational, business, or promotional use. For information, please e-mail sales.press@yale.edu (U.S. office) or sales@yaleup.co.uk (U.K. office).

Set in PostScript Electra type by Newgen North America, Austin, Texas.
Printed in the United States of America.

Library of Congress Control Number: 2019936636
ISBN 978-0-300-21704-9 (hardcover : alk. paper)

A catalogue record for this book is available from the British Library.

This paper meets the requirements of ANSI/NISO Z39.48-1992 (Permanence of Paper).

10 9 8 7 6 5 4 3 2 1

To M.
in gratitude

Contents

Preface

More than thirty years ago, in *The First Urban Christians*, Wayne Meeks struck a new note in the study of early Christ assemblies, focusing attention on devotees of Christ as residents in the major cities of the Roman Empire. This brought an engagement with what I call the "materiality" of the early Christ cult—the demographics of the Jesus movement, the main social and economic catchments of its members, models of governance, and the practices in which Christ followers engaged, including water rituals, communal meals, and collection of funds. Only in his last chapter did Meeks engage with what up to that point had been the major preoccupation of the study of the Jesus movement: its beliefs and confessions.

Since Meeks wrote his book we know much more about the associative practices of other small, face-to-face groups in Greek and Roman antiquity. These associations organized around the workplace, the cult of a deity, a diasporic identity, an extended family, or a neighborhood and could be found in practically every city and town of the Mediterranean. For the nonelite population, associations were the principal context for social, cultic, and other forms of interaction beyond the family on one hand and the citizen assembly in free Greek cities on the other.

Data about these groups have never been employed systematically and carefully as *comparanda* for early Christ assemblies, although since the late nineteenth century there have been a few gestures in this direction. While knowledge about Greek and Roman associations does not in itself produce any new data about Christ groups, comparison offers two benefits. First, since much is known about a variety of features and practices of those groups that is *not* known about Christ groups—membership size and profile, recruitment practices, governance, finances, and the relation to the cities in which they were resident—we can use data from associations heuristically to raise questions about Christ assemblies: What options were available for monitoring membership? Were membership lists kept, as they were in most other associations? When early texts speak of someone leaving a group or being expelled, what concretely is imagined? How were meals financed? In Christ assemblies that included elite or subelite individuals, how do we imagine their relationships to others in the group? Why do Christ groups imitate political language, calling the group an *ekklēsia*, the standard Greek term for a citizen assembly, or addressing Jesus as *kyrios* and speaking of his parousia? The use of *comparanda* from the rich data set supplied from associations allows the scholar to ask questions that hitherto have not been asked about Christ groups and to at least sketch the parameters of answers to these questions.

A second benefit of careful comparison is the ability to set some boundaries to our imagination of what was possible and likely for Christ assemblies. If the mean membership size of Greek and Roman cultic associations was about thirty people, how much larger can we reasonably imagine Christ groups to have been? What models are attested for financing the communal meals of associations, and how then might we reconstruct the financing of Christ groups? Having knowledge of the practices of other small face-to-face associations allows us to move from speculative scenarios about what *might* have been the case to documented possibilities. This is a matter of "normalizing" our reconstructions of the earliest Christ assemblies—that is, treating them as phenomena that belong to the spectrum of social practices of the ancient Mediterranean instead of exoticizing them as something unparalleled, incomparable, and sui generis.

Some readers will find this book irritating, for at least three reasons. First, in contrast to many works on the earliest Christ assemblies, I emphasize the ways in which Christ assemblies were comparable with other small face-to-face groups. The habit of much scholarship has been to dramatize the extent to which Christ assemblies (and Judean assemblies) were unique. Anxiety over identity is only heightened when pagan analogies are adduced. Hence, some readers may be distressed to learn that these assemblies were not as unusual, either demographically or in terms of their practices, as is often supposed.

It is not that I claim that Christ assemblies were just like other associations. That would be silly. Guilds and associations were extremely diverse, with hardly two of them exactly alike. But the claim that Christ groups were incomparable and incommensurable is not only historically untrue, it probably disguises a theological rather than a historical presumption that Christ devotees must have been up to something that was completely new and unparalleled and ultimately the result of divine causality. There are indeed some very interesting innovations of Christ assemblies and ways that their practices stood out from the practices of other comparable groups. The benefit of careful comparison that identifies similarities is that it in fact allows the differences to stand out with special prominence. But to ignore similarities and exaggerate differences obscures the many ways that Christ assemblies were also like other groups. It risks turning historiography into apologetics.

Second, it is common to insist that the most proximate *comparanda*—sometimes the only salient ones—for early Christ groups are Judean synagogues and their practices, from which Christ groups derived most of their practices and beliefs. This, as Jonathan Z. Smith observed in *Drudgery Divine,* is often a strategy to isolate the early Christ cult from its Greco-Roman environment, from which is was supposedly "overwhelmingly different." But then it is claimed that early Christ groups swiftly outstripped their Judean roots or even consciously distinguished themselves from those roots. Hence, in two swift moves the Christ cult becomes sui generis.

This too is apologetics, not historiography. I will avoid this approach, not because Judean synagogues were not important in the world in which Christ groups operated. Various iterations of the Christ cult owed much to Judean synagogues. The letter of James, for example, calls its meeting a *synagōgē,* a common term used by Judean assemblies, and it reflects a version of the Christ cult that saw itself as fully embedded in diasporic Judaism. Paul's identity as a diasporic Judean and his frequent interactions with other Judeans meant that the shape of his thought is influenced by Judean conceptual frameworks. Others still, such as the author of the letter to the Hebrews, invoked models of priesthood and sacrifice from the Hebrew Bible in order to advance the claim that a more perfect form of priesthood and sacrifice had appeared in Christ. Meanwhile, the author of the Letter of Barnabas constructed much of his letter around the thesis that the true meaning of the Hebrew Bible had been misunderstood by Judeans and was available only to Christ followers. Thus, the Hebrew Bible and Judaism loom large in the construction and self-understanding of Christ assemblies.

Despite these factors, I avoid the habit of privileging Judaism and Judean forms as the "closest" or "best" parallels for Christ groups. In some cases, they are not. For some of the arguments in this book membership lists and data on the financial practices of groups will be important. These are simply unavailable for Judean assemblies. Those assemblies doubtless had membership lists, and they certainly had practices to finance their meetings, meals, and burials. But we don't have those records, probably for reasons of preservation. The physical remains of synagogues may provide a rough index to group size, and these will be considered alongside the physical remains of buildings used by Greek and Roman associations, without necessarily privileging one *comparandum* over another (chapter 3). The presence of *triclinia* associated with some synagogues suggests that like Greek and Roman associations, Judean assemblies engaged in communal dining.

A second reason that I avoid privileging Judean assemblies as the "closest" *comparanda* is because this is not a book about origins and "influence." The point of comparison is heuristic—to allow us to see interpretive possibilities and to establish some boundaries for our historical imaginations. As the Introduction shows, useful *comparanda* may have no genealogical relationship at all to the feature under scrutiny and may yet let us see helpful interpretive possibilities.

The tendency to divide data into three piles—"Christ assemblies," "Judean assemblies," and "Greco-Roman associations"—invites the temptation to play one group off against another. Yet as I have said, "Greco-Roman" associations are extremely diverse. I propose some loose and broad heuristic categories, including "occupational guilds" and "cultic associations." For analytic purposes, many Judean assemblies can be treated as an instance of the latter category, although they could also be treated as "diasporic associations," and as Thomas Kraabel has shown, there are significant differences among Judean assemblies. It is absurd to set Judean assemblies contrastively against "Greco-Roman associations" as if these were natural and self-evident categories, since there is so much variation within each group. Comparative analysis looks for *limited* and *local* comparisons that enlighten particular features of a Christ group. Useful *comparanda* will sometimes be found in a feature of an Attic association that has no conceivable genealogical relation to the Christ group, sometimes in a particular Judean assembly, and sometimes in a Roman collegium. To reiterate the main point: the goal of comparison is heuristic, not genealogical.

The third feature that might irritate readers is the lack of attention that I pay to the theology of Christ assemblies, for surely, the argument might go, the successes and lasting importance of Christ groups had everything to do with the ideas that they espoused—the proclamation of the crucified Messiah, the message of God's grace, and the expectations of a dramatic eschatological transformation of the cosmos. It is not that such ideas are not important and noteworthy. The historical question is whether they have any demonstrable relation to many of the questions with which this book is concerned: the demographics of early Christ assemblies, the size and venues of these groups, an understanding of social dynamics involved in the rituals in which they engaged, and their financing. It might be supposed that beliefs played a critical role in recruitment: Who would not be attracted to a group that promised redemption from the world, transformation in an afterlife, and participation in the judgment of the world? Yet as Ramsay MacMullen has shown, conversion had little to do with persuading converts of the truth of doctrines and beliefs and much more to do with witnessing wonders and establishing trust. Rodney Stark has persuasively documented in relation to the recruitment strategies of modern cults that the particular—even peculiar—beliefs of modern cults are usually *not* the reasons for the initial attraction of recruits to the group, although converts routinely report *after* conversion that they joined having recognized that those beliefs were obviously true. Recruitment has more to do with affect and the sense of belonging and trust that these groups generate and advertise to potential recruits.

This is not to dismiss or denigrate the ideas purveyed by Christ assemblies as epiphenomenal. As I suggest in chapter 11, the intellectual activities of Christ assemblies are clearly one of their signal *differentiae*. These groups were early adopters of bookish practices—preserving and creating knowledge derived from books, at first the Jewish Scriptures and then their own writings, and forming what Brian Stock in his discussion of medieval groups has called textual communities. The bookish practices of early Christ groups may have had special appeal to the literate elite, who treated the possession and use of reading materials as a marker of elite culture. For the majority, the greatest appeal that Christ groups had was the "trust network" that they represented, the offer of a strong sense of belonging, and group recognition and esteem for moral and other forms of achievement.

A Note on Locations

Locations in Ostia are referred to by one of the five *regiones*, then the *insula* number, and finally locations within *insulae* (e.g., *Regio* III,II,1–2). For a map of the Ostian sites, see http://www.ostia-antica.org/dict.htm and Carlo Pavolini, *Ostia*, 3rd ed. (Rome: Editori laterza, 1989).

Similarly, the site of Pompeii is divided into nine *regiones*, and locations are arranged by *regio*, *insula*, entrance, and room, e.g., I,X,7,1 = *Regio* I, *Insula* X, House 7, Room 1. See http://www.pompeiiinpictures.org/ and the Board of Cultural Heritage of Pompeii, A *Guide to the Pompeii Excavations* ([Naples]: Board of Cultural Heritage of Pompeii, 2015).

Epigraphic Conventions

The following standard sigla are used in presenting epigraphic texts:

[ ]	fam[ ]a	lacuna (unrestored)
[ ]	fam[ili]a	lacuna (restored)
[ ]	[±?]	lacuna with uncertain number of missing letters
( )	M(arcus)	an editor's resolution of an abbreviation
‹ ›	co‹l›legio	letters omitted by accident and supplied by editor
{ }	sal{o}ute	superfluous or erroneous letters or words
⟦—⟧	⟦—⟧icius	erasure

ACKNOWLEDGMENTS

The author gratefully acknowledges invitations to present some of these chapters to colleagues and the opportunities to benefit from comment and critique: the Lutheran School of Theology at Chicago, the Divinity School of the University of Chicago, the Universités of Geneva and Lausanne, the Centro Italiano di Studi Superiori sulle Religioni, the Ancient Documentary Research Centre (Macquarie University), the Humboldt University of Berlin, the Meals in the Greco-Roman World Section and the Ancient Economy Group of the Society of Biblical Literature, the Epigraphy and Papyrology Group of the Studiorum Novi Testamenti Societas, and the Columbia-Union New Testament Seminar.

My colleagues in the Context Group read parts of this book and generously provided many suggestions and criticism: Scott Bartchy, Richard DeMaris, Harry Maier, Steven Muir, Douglas Oakman, Stephen Patterson, Sarah Rollens, and Daniel Ullucci. I am also grateful to the numerous kindnesses of William E. Arnal, Richard S. Ascough, David L. Balch, Giovanni Bazzana, Brigidda Bell, Andreas Bendlin, Christer Bruun, Callie Callon, Alison Cleverley, Christopher Cornthwaite, Zeba Crook, Philip Harland, Albert Harrill, Emily Hemilrijk, Marsha Hewitt, Edwin Judge, Connor Kokot, Christina Kreinecker, Richard Last, Kirill Lepekhin, Jinyu Liu, Bruce Longenecker, Mariana Mastagar, Anna Miller, Stephen Mitchell, Mark Mueller, Markus Öhler, Ryan Olfert, Steven Payne, Mauro Pesce, Anders Runesson, Colleen Shantz, Patrick Stange, Jason Yuh, Larry Welborn, Michael White, and Arjan Zuiderhoek. The two anonymous readers for Yale University Press provided many helpful suggestions for improvements.

A special note of thanks is due to Pasquale Manilo, Custode di Necropoli di Porto, who graciously allowed me access to the Isola Sacra, and to Dr. Giorgio

Filippi, curator of the Musei Vaticani's epigraphic collection, who arranged access to see the Lex collegi Aesculapi et Hygiae in the Museo Pio Clementino, Gabinetto dell'Apoxyomenos, normally closed to the public. Through the kind permission of Claudio Parisi Presicce, Sovrintendente di Archivio Fotografico dei Musei Capitolini, I have been able to print the photographs of NCE 2594 (fig. 3) and NCE 7080 (fig. 4). Dr. Federico Frasson graciously provided permission to use his photographs of CIL 11.1355a,b (fig. 7).

This book draws on research already published and under way: a five-volume edition of primary texts, J. S. Kloppenborg, R. S. Ascough, and P. A. Harland, *Greco-Roman Associations: Texts, Translations, and Commentary* (Berlin: Walter de Gruyter, 2011–), the first two volumes of which are now in print (GRA I, II); and a teaching-oriented English edition of more than three hundred association inscriptions and papyri, *Associations in the Greco-Roman World: A Sourcebook* (AGRW). Waco, Tex.: Baylor University Press, 2012. The English translations from AGRW are reproduced by permission of Carey Newman and Baylor University Press.

Finally, thanks are due to Heather Gold, who has shepherded this volume through production, and to Jessie Dolch and Susan Laity, for their careful copy- and production editing of the manuscript. Christina Gousopoulos read through the proofs, saving me from various errors and oversights.

ABBREVIATIONS

The abbreviations for periodicals and series can be found in *The SBL Handbook of Style: For Biblical Studies and Related Disciplines*, 2nd ed. (Atlanta: SBL Press, 2014). In addition, the following abbreviations are used.

CATALOGUES, GRAMMARS, LEXICA, PERIODICALS, TOOLS, JOURNALS, AND SERIALS

ABSA	*Annual of the British School at Athens*. London: Macmillan, 1894–.
AD	*Ἀρχαιολογικόν Δελτίον*. Athens: Hypourgeio Politismou, 1915–.
AE	*L'année épigraphique*
ASAA	*Annuario della Scuola Archeologica di Atene e delle Missioni Italiane in Oriente*. Bergamo, Rome: 1914–.
BCH	*Bulletin de correspondance hellénique*
CSEL	Corpus Scriptorum Ecclesiasticorum Latinorum
EDCS	Epigraphik-Datenbank Clauss/Slaby: http://www.manfredclauss.de/
IRD	Hatzfeld, Jean. "Les Italiens résidant à Délos." BCH 36 (1912): 5–218.
JJMJS	*Journal of the Jesus Movement in Its Jewish Setting*
JRA	*Journal of Roman Archaeology*
NCE	Nuovo catalogo epigrafico, schedario ms. presso la sezione epigrafica dei Musei Capitolini
NSA	*Notizie degli scavi di antichità*. Rome: Accademia nazionale dei Lincei, 1876–.

NRSV	New Revised Standard Version
PIR[1]	Klebs, E., P. de Rohden, and H. Dessau, eds. *Prosopographia Imperii Romani.* Berlin: Georg Reimer, 1897–1898.
PIR[2]	Groag, Edmund, Werner Eck, Arthur Stein, and Leiva Petersen, eds. *Prosopographia Imperii Romani saec. I. II. III.* 5 vols. Berlin: Walter de Gruyter, 1933–2015.
RAC	Rivista di archeologia cristiana
RSV	Revised Standard Version
TM	Trismegistos: An interdisciplinary portal of papyrological and epigraphic resources: https://www.trismegistos.org/

INSCRIPTIONS, PAPYRI, AND OTHER SOURCES

Agora	The *Athenian Agora.* Princeton: American School of Classical Studies at Athens, 1953–.
AGRW	Ascough, Richard S., Philip A. Harland, and John S. Kloppenborg. *Associations in the Greco-Roman World: A Sourcebook.* Waco, Tex.: Baylor University Press, 2012.
AM	*Mitteilungen des deutschen Archäologischen Instituts. Athenische Abteilung.* Berlin: Deutsches archäologisches Institut, 1876–.
BGU	*Ägyptische Urkunden aus den königlichen [staatlichen] Museen zu Berlin, Griechische Urkunden.* 15 vols. Berlin: Weidmann, 1895–1937.
CCCA	Vermaseren, Maarten Jozef. *Corpus cultus Cybelae Attidisque.* 7 vols. Leiden: Brill, 1977–1989.
CCID	Hörig, Monika, and E. Schwertheim. *Corpus cultus Iovis Dolicheni.* EPRO 106. Leiden: Brill, 1987.
CIG	Boeckh, August, ed. *Corpus inscriptionum graecarum.* 4 vols. Berlin: Georg Reimer, 1828–1877.
CIIP I–III	*Corpus inscriptionum Iudaeae/Palestinae.* Berlin: Walter de Gruyter, 2010–2014.
CIL	*Corpus Inscriptionum Latinarum.* Berlin: Georg Reimer, Walter de Gruyter, 1863–.
CIMRM	Vermaseren, Maarten Jozef. *Corpus Inscriptionum et Monumentorum Religionis Mithriacae.* 2 vols. The Hague: Martin Nijhoff, 1956–1960.

CIRB	Struve, V. V. *Corpus inscriptionum Regni Bosporani: Korpus bosporskikh nadpisei.* Moscow: Nauka, 1965.
CJZC	Lüderitz, G., and Joyce M. Reynolds, eds. *Corpus jüdischer Zeugnisse aus der Cyrenaika.* Weisbaden: Reichert, 1983.
Clara Rhodos	Jacopi, Giulio, Amedeo Maiuri, and Luciano Laurenzi, eds. *Clara Rhodos: Studi e materiali pubblicati a cura dell'Istituto storico-archeologico di Rodi.* Rhodes: Istituto Storico-Archeologico, 1928–1941.
D	Mommsen, Theodor, Paul Krueger, and Alan Watson. *The Digest of Justinian.* Philadelphia: University of Pennsylvania Press, 1985.
Dura-Europos	Rostovtzeff, Mikhail I., F. E. Brown, and C. Bradford Welles, eds. *The Excavations at Dura-Europos Conducted by Yale University and the French Academy of Inscriptions and Letters. Preliminary Report of the Seventh and Eighth Seasons of Work, 1933–1934 and 1934–1935.* New Haven: Yale University Press, 1939.
FIRA	Riccobono, S., G. Baviera, F. Ferrini, and V. Arangio-Ruiz. *Fontes iuris romani antejustiniani.* 3 vols. Florence: G. Barbera, 1940–1943.
GRA I	Kloppenborg, John S., and Richard S. Ascough. *Attica, Central Greece, Macedonia, Thrace.* Vol. 1 of *Greco-Roman Associations: Texts, Translations, and Commentary.* BZNW 181. Berlin: Walter de Gruyter, 2011.
GRA II	Harland, Philip A. *North Coast of the Black Sea, Asia Minor.* Vol. 2 of *Greco-Roman Associations: Texts, Translations, and Commentary.* BZNW 204. Berlin: Walter de Gruyter, 2014.
GRA III	Kloppenborg, John S. *Ptolemaic and Early Roman Egypt.* Vol. 3 of *Greco-Roman Associations: Texts, Translations, and Commentary.* BZNW. Berlin: Walter de Gruyter, forthcoming.
I.Alex.imp.	Kayser, François. *Recueil des inscriptions grecques et latines (non funéraires) d'Alexandrie Impériale (Ier–III^er^ s. apr. J.-C.).* Bibliothèque d'Étude 108. Cairo: L'Institut français d'archéologie orientale du Caire, 1994.

I.ApamBith — Corsten, Thomas, ed. *Die Inschriften von Apameia (Bithynien) und Pylai.* IGSK 32. Bonn: Habelt, 1987.

I.AphrodArchive — Reynolds, J. M. *Aphrodisias and Rome.* London: Society for the Promotion of Roman Studies, 1982.

I.AphrodJud — Reynolds, J. M., R. Tannenbaum, and K. T. Erim, eds. *Jews and God-Fearers at Aphrodisias: Greek Inscriptions with Commentary.* Cambridge: Cambridge Philological Society, 1987.

I.Beroia — Gounaropoulou, Loukrētias, and M. V. Chatzopoulou, eds. *Epigraphes kato Makedonias.* Athens: Hypourgeio Politismou, Ethnikon Hidryma Ereunōn, 1998–.

ICG — Inscriptiones Christianae Graecae. http://www.epigraph.topoi.org/ica/icamainapp/inscription/

I.CiliciaDF — Dagron, G., and D. Feissel, eds. *Inscriptions de Cilicie.* Paris: de Boccard, 1987.

I.Corinth.Kent — Kent, J. H., ed. *Corinth: Inscriptions, 1926–1950.* Corinth 8/3. Princeton: American School of Classical Studies at Athens, 1966.

I.Corinth.Meritt — Meritt, B. D., ed. *Greek Inscriptions, 1896–1927.* Corinth 8/1. Cambridge, Mass.: American School of Classical Studies at Athens and Harvard University Press, 1931.

I.CosED — Segre, Mario. *Iscrizioni di Cos.* Monografie della Scuola archeologica di Atene e delle missioni italiane in Oriente, 6. 2 vols. Roma: "L'Erma" di Bretschneider, 1993.

I.CosPH — Paton, W. R., and E. L. Hicks. *The Inscriptions of Cos.* Oxford: Clarendon, 1891.

ICUR — de Rossi, Iohannes Baptista, Angelus Silvagni, and Antonius Ferrua, eds. *Inscriptiones Christianae urbis Romae septimo saeculo antiquiores. Nova series.* Rome: Pont. Institutum Archaeologiae Christianae, 1922–.

ID — Dürrbach, F., P. Roussel, M. Launey, A. Plassart, and J. Coupry. *Inscriptions de Délos.* 7 vols. Paris: Librairie Ancienne Honoré Champion, 1926–1973.

I.Delta — Bernand, André. *Le Delta égyptien d'après les textes grecques, I: Les Confins libyques.* 3 vols. Institut français d'archéologie orientale du Caire, mémoires publiés par les membres 91. Cairo: Institut français d'archéologie orientale du Caire, 1970.

I.DionysosJ — Jaccottet, Anne-Françoise. *Choisir Dionysos: Les associations dionysiaques ou la face cachée du dionysisme.* Zürich: Akanthus, 2003.

IDR — Russu, Ioan I., G. Florescu, C. C. Petolescu, D. M. Pippidi, I. Piso, and C. L. Băluţă, eds. *Inscriptiones Daciae Romanae. Inscripţiile Daciei Romane.* 9 vols. Bucharest: Editura Academiei Republicii Socialiste România, 1975–2001.

I.Eph — Wankel, H., and Helmut Engelmann, eds. *Die Inschriften von Ephesos.* 8 vols. IGSK 11–17. Bonn: Rudolf Habelt, 1979–1984.

IG II^2 — *Inscriptiones Atticae Euclidis anno posteriores. Inscriptiones Graecae II.* 4 vols. Berlin: Walter de Gruyter, 1913–1940.

IG IV — Fränkel, M., ed. *Inscriptiones Graecae Aeginae, Pityonesi, Cecryphaliae, Argolidis.* Berlin: Georg Reimer, 1902.

IG V — Kolbe, W., and F. Hiller von Gaertringen, eds. *Inscriptiones Laconiae, Messeniae, Arcadiae.* 2 vols. Berlin: Georg Reimer, 1913.

IG VII — Dittenberger, Wilhelm, ed. *Inscriptiones Megaridis et Boeotiae.* Berlin: Georg Reimer, 1893.

IG IX/1^2 — Klaffenbach, Günther, ed. *Inscriptiones Graecae IX, 1.* 2nd ed. Berlin: Walter de Gruyter, 1932–1968.

IG X/2 — Edson, Charles, ed. *Inscriptiones Graecae Epiri, Macedoniae, Thraciae, Scythiae. II: Inscriptiones Macedoniae, Fasc. 1: Inscriptiones Thessalonicae et viciniae.* Berlin: Walter de Gruyter, 1972.

IG XI/2–4 — Dürrbach, Félix, F. F. Hiller von Gaertringen, and Pierre Roussel, eds. *Inscriptiones Deli.* Berlin: Georg Reimer, 1912–1927.

IG XII/1–7 — Hiller von Gaertringen, F., W. R. Paton, J. Delamarre, and E. Ziebarth, eds. *Inscriptiones insularum maris Aegaei praeter Delum.* 9 parts (part 6 never published). Berlin: Georg Reimer, 1895–1915.

IG XIV — Kaibel, G., ed. *Inscriptiones Siciliae et Italiae, additis Graecis Galliae, Hispaniae, Britanniae, Germaniae inscriptionibus.* Berlin: Georg Reimer, 1890.

IGBulg — Mikhailov, G., ed. *Inscriptiones Graecae in Bulgaria repertae.* 4 vols. Serdica (Sofia): Academiae Litterarum Bulgaricae, 1956–1966.

IGFayum	Bernand, Étienne, ed. *Recueil des inscriptions grecques du Fayoum*. 3 vols. Leiden: Brill; Paris: Institut français d'archéologie orientale, 1975–1981.
IGLAM	Le Bas, Philippe, and William Henry Waddington, eds. *Voyage archéologique en Grèce et en Asie Mineure, Tome III: Inscriptions grecques et latines recueillies en Asie Mineure*. Paris: Firmin Didot Frères, 1870.
IGLS	Jalabert, Louis, René Mouterde, et al., eds. *Inscriptions grecques et latines de la Syrie*. 21 vols. Paris: Paul Geuthner, 1929–1986.
IGOlbia	Dubois, Laurent, ed. *Inscriptions grecques dialectales d'Olbia du Pont*. Hautes Études du monde gréco-romain, 22. Geneva, 1996.
IGRR	Cagnat, R. L., J. F. Toutain, V. Henry, and G. L. Lafaye, eds. *Inscriptiones graecae ad res romanas pertinentes*. 4 vols. Paris: E. Leroux, 1911–1927.
IGSK	Inschriften griechischer Städte aus Kleinasien. Bonn, Rudolf Habelt, 1972–.
IGUR	Moretti, L., ed. *Inscriptiones graecae urbis Romae*. Rome: [Istituto Italiano per la Storia Antica], 1968–1990.
I.HierapJ	Judeich, Walther, Carl Humann, Conrad Cichorius, and Franz Winter, eds. *Altertümer von Hierapolis*. Jahrbuch des kaiserlich deutschen archäologischen Instituts, Ergänzungsheft 4. Berlin: Georg Reimer, 1898.
I.Iasos	Blümel, W., ed. *Die Inschriften von Iasos*. 2 vols. IGSK 28/1–2. Bonn: Rudolf Habelt, 1985.
IJO	Noy, David, Alexander Panayotov, Hanswulf Bloedhorn, et al., eds. *Inscriptiones Judaicae Orientis*. TSAJ 99, 101, 102. Tübingen: Mohr Siebeck, 2004.
I.Kamiros	Segre, Mario, and Giovanni Pugliese Carratelli. "Tituli Camirenses." ASAA 27–29, n.s. 11–13 (1949–1951): 141–318.
I.KamirosSuppl	Pugliese Carratelli, Giovanni. "Tituli Camirenses, Supplementum." ASAA 30–32, n.s. 14–16 (1952–1954): 211–46.
I.Kibyra	Corsten, Thomas, ed. *Die Inschriften von Kibyra, I: Die Inschriften der Stadt und ihrer näheren Umgebung*. IGSK 60. Bonn: Rudolf Habelt, 2002.

I.KilikiaBM II — Bean, G. E., and T. B. Mitford, eds. *Journeys in Rough Cilicia, 1964–1968*. Tituli Asiae Minoris, Ergänzungsband 3. Vienna: Böhlaus, 1970.

I.KilikiaHW — Heberdey, R., and A. Wilhelm, eds. *Reisen in Kilikien*. Kaiserliche [Österreichische] Akademie der Wissenschaften, Philosophisch-historische Klasse, Denkschriften 44,6. Vienna: Böhlaus, 1896.

I.Knidos — Blümel, Wolfgang, ed. *Die Inschriften von Knidos*. IGSK 41. Bonn: Rudolf Habelt, 1992.

I.Kyme — Engelmann, Helmut, ed. *Die Inschriften von Kyme*. IGSK 5. Bonn: Rudolf Habelt, 1976.

IK Apameia — Corsten, Thomas, ed. *Die Inschriften von Apameia (Bithynien) und Pylai*. IGSK 32. Bonn: Rudolf Habelt, 1987.

IK Byzantion — Lajtar, Adam. *Die Inschriften von Byzantion*. IGSK 58. Bonn: Rudolf Habelt, 2000.

IK Kalchedon — Merkelbach, Reinhold, Karl Dörner Friedrich, and Şahin Sencer. *Die Inschriften von Kalchedon*. IGSK 20. Bonn: Rudolf Habelt, 1980.

IK Klaudiu Polis — Becker-Bertau, Friedrich. *Die Inschriften von Klaudiu Polis*. IGSK 31. Bonn: Rudolf Habelt, 1986.

IK Rhod.Peraia — Blümel, Wolfgang, ed. *Die Inschriften der Rhodischen Peraia*. IGSK 38. Bonn: Rudolf Habelt, 1991.

IK Sinope — French, David H. *The Inscriptions of Sinope*. IGSK 64. Bonn: Rudolf Habelt, 2004.

ILCV — Diehl, Ernst. *Inscriptiones latinae christianae veteres*. 4 vols. Berlin: Weidmann, 1924–1931.

I.Lindos — Blinkenberg, C., ed. *Lindos: fouilles et recherches, 1902–1914. II: Inscriptions*. 2 vols. Berlin: Walter de Gruyter, 1931–1941.

ILLPRON — *Inscriptionum Lapidarium Latinarum Provinciae Norici usque ad annum MCMLXXXIV repertarum indices*. Berlin: Walter de Gruyter, 1986.

ILMN — Camodeca, Giuseppe, ed. *Catalogo delle iscrizioni latine del Museo nazionale di Napoli*. Vol. 1: *Roma e Latium*. Napoli: Loffredo, 2000.

ILS — Dessau, Hermann, ed. *Inscriptiones Latinae Selectae*. 3 vols. Berlin: Weidmann, 1892–1916.

I.MakedD — Demitsas, M. G., ed. Ἡ Μακεδονία ἐν Λίθοις φθεγγομένοις καὶ μνεμείοις σῳζομένοις. 2 vols. Athens: Ek tou Typographeion ton Adelphon Perre, 1896.

I.Miletos — McCabe, Donald F., ed. *Miletos Inscriptions: Texts and List.* Princeton Project on the Inscriptions of Anatolia, Institute for Advanced Study, Princeton (1984). Packard Humanities Institute CD no. 6, 1991.

IMT — Barth, Matthias, and Josef Stauber, eds. *Inschriften Mysia and Troas.* Munich: Leopold Wenger Institut, Universität München, 1993–1996.

I.Parion — Frisch, P., ed. *Die Inschriften von Parion.* IGSK 25. Bonn: Rudolf Habelt, 1983.

I.Perg — Fränkel, M., ed. *Die Inschriften von Pergamon.* 3 vols. Berlin: W. Spemann and Walter de Gruyter, 1890–1969.

I.Perinthos — Sayar, Mustafa Hamdi, ed. *Perinthos-Herakleia (Marmara Ereðlisi) und Umgebung. Geschichte, Testimonien, griechische und lateinische Inschriften.* Österreichische Akademie der Wissenschaften. Philosophisch-historische Klasse. Denkschriften 269. Vienna: Böhlaus, 1998.

I.Priene — Hiller von Gaertringen, F. F., ed. *Inschriften von Priene.* Berlin: Georg Reimer and Walter de Gruyter, 1906.

I.Prose — Bernand, André, ed. *La Prose sur pierre dans l'Égypte hellénistique et romaine.* 2 vols. Paris: Édition du Centre national de la recherche scientifique, 1992.

I.Rhamnous — Petrakos, Vasileios C., ed. Ὁ ΔΗΜΟΣ ΤΟΥ ΡΑΜΝΟΥΝΤΟΣ· Συνοψή τῶν ἀνασκαφῶν καὶ τῶν ἐρευνῶν *(1813–1998)*, II. Οἱ ἐπιγραφές. Βιβλιοθήκη τῆς ἐν Ἀθήναις Ἀρχαιολογικῆς Ἑταιρείας. Vols. 181–82. Athens: Hēen Athēnais Hetaireia, 1999.

I.Sabazios — Vermaseren, Maarten Jozef, and Eugene N. Lane, eds. *Corpus Cultus Iovis Sabazii.* EPRO 100. 3 vols. Leiden: Brill, 1983–1989.

I.ScM I–V — Pippidi, Dionisie M., Iorgu Stoian, Alexandru Avram, Emilia Dorutiu-Boila, eds. *Inscriptiones Daciae et Scythiae Minoris antiquae. Series altera: Inscriptiones Scythiae Minoris graecae et latinae.* 5 vols. Bucharest: Editura Academiei Republicii Socialiste România, 1983–2000.

I.Smyrna	Petzl, Georg, ed. *Die Inschriften von Smyrna.* IGSK 23–24/1–2. Bonn: Rudolf Habelt, 1982–1990.
I.Stratonikeia	Sahin, M. C., ed. *Die Inschriften von Stratonikeia.* 3 vols. IGSK 21–22. Bonn: Rudolf Habelt, 1981–1990.
I.Trall	Poljakov, F. B., ed. *Die Inschriften von Tralleis und Nysa.* IGSK 36/1. Bonn: Rudolf Habelt, 1989.
JIGRE	Horbury, W., and D. Noy, eds. *Jewish Inscriptions of Graeco-Roman Egypt.* Cambridge: Cambridge University Press, 1992.
JIWE	Noy, D., ed. *Jewish Inscriptions of Western Europe.* 2 vols. Cambridge: Cambridge University Press, 1993–1995.
LBW	Le Bas, Philippe, and W. H. Waddington, eds. *Inscriptions grecques et latines recueillies en Asie Mineure.* 2 vols. Paris: Firmin-Didot, 1870.
LSAM	Sokolowski, Franciszek, ed. *Lois sacrées de l'Asie Mineure.* École française d'Athènes. Travaux et mémoires, fasc. 9. Paris: E. de Boccard, 1955.
LSCG	Sokolowski, Franciszek, ed. *Lois sacrées des cités grecques.* École française d'Athènes. Travaux et mémoires, fasc. 18. Paris: E. de Boccard, 1969.
LSCGSup	Sokolowski, Franciszek, ed. *Lois sacrées des cités grecques: supplément.* École française d'Athènes. Travaux et mémoires, fasc. 11. Paris: E. de Boccard, 1962.
MAMA	Calder, William M., E. Herzfeld, S. Guyer, and C. W. M. Cox, eds. *Monumenta Asiae Minoris antiqua.* London: Manchester University Press, 1928–.
OGIS	Dittenberger, Wilhelm, ed. *Orientis Graeci Inscriptiones Selectae. Supplementum Sylloge Inscriptionum Graecarum.* 2 vols. Leipzig: S. Hirzel, 1903–1905.
O.Strass	Viereck, P., ed. *Griechische und griechisch-demotische Ostraka der Universitäts- und Landesbibliothek zu Strassburg im Elsass* I. Nos. 1–812 Berlin: Weidmann, 1923.
O.Thebes	Gardiner, A. H., H. Thompson, and J. G. Milne, eds. *Theban Ostraca.* 4 vols. London: Humphrey Milford and Oxford University Press, 1913.
Pais	Pais, Ettore. *Corporis Inscriptionum Latinarum Supplementa Italica 1. Additamenta ad vol. V. Galliae Cisalpinae.* Rome: Salviucci, 1884.

P.Assoc — De Cenival, Françoise. *Les associations religieuses en Égypte d'après les documents démotiques.* Publications de L'institut français d'archéologie orientale du Caire. Bibliothèque d'étude 46. Cairo: L'Institut français d'archéologie orientale, 1972.

P.Athens — Petropoulos, G. A., ed. *Papyri Societatis Archaeologicae Atheniensis.* Athens: Bibliothēkē tēs Athēnais Philekraideutikēs Hetaireias, 1939.

P.Bagnall — Ast, R., H. Cuvigny, T. M. Hickey, and J. Lougovaya, eds. *Papyrological Texts in Honor of Roger S. Bagnall.* American Studies in Papyrology 53. Durham, N.C.: American Society of Papyrologists, 2013.

P.Berl.Bork — Borkowski, Z., ed. *Une description topographique des immeubles à Panopolis.* Warsaw: PNW-Editions scientifiques de Pologne, 1975.

P.Berl.Spieg — Spiegelberg, Wilhelm, ed. *Demotische Papyrus aus den Königlichen Museen zu Berlin.* Berlin: Giesecke & Devrient, 1902.

P.Cair — Spiegelberg, Wilhelm, ed. *Die demotischen Denkmäler.* 3 vols. Strassburg: W. Drugulin, 1906–1932.

P.Cair.Zen — Edgar, C. C., ed. *Zenon Papyri.* Catalogue général des antiquités égyptiennes du Musée du Caire. 5 vols. Cairo: Institut français d'archéologie orientale, 1925–1940.

P.Corn — Westermannn, William L., et al., eds. *Greek Papyri in the Library of Cornell University.* New York: Columbia University Press, 1926.

P.Dem.Louvre E 7840 — De Cenival, Françoise. "Comptes d'une association religieuse Thébaine datant des années 29 à 33 du roi Amasis (P. Démot. Louvre E 7840 Bis)." *Revue d'Égyptologie* 37 (1986): 13–29.

P.Enteuxis — Guéraud, Octave, ed. ΕΝΤΕΥΞΕΙΣ: *Requêtes et plaintes addressées au Roi d'Egypte au IIIe siècle avant J.-C.* Publications de la Société royale Iegyptienne de payrologie. Textes et documents 1. Cairo: Institut français d'archéologie orientale, 1931.

P.Hamb — Meyer, P. M., et al., eds. *Griechische Papyrusurkunden der Hamburger Staats- und Universitätsbibliothek.* Leipzig: B. G. Teubner, 1911–1984.

P.Hamburg. Bibliothek.dem 1 — Erichsen, Wolja. "Der demotische Papyrus Hamburg." *Acta Orientalia* 26 (1962): 97–107.

Philippi — Pilhofer, Peter. *Philippi. Band II: Katalog der Inschriften von Philippi*. WUNT 119. Tübingen: Mohr Siebeck, 2000.

P.Iand — Kalbfleisch, C., et al., eds. *Papyri Iandanae, cum discipulis*. Leipzig: B. G. Teubner, 1912–1938.

P.Köln — Kramer, B., and R. Hübner, et al., eds. *Kölner Papyri*. Cologne-Opladen: Westdeutscher, 1976–.

P.Lille.dem — Sottas, H., and F. de Cenival., eds. *Papyrus démotiques de Lille*. Paris: Paul Geuthner, 1927–1984.

P.Lond — Kenyon, F. G., W. C. Crum, and T. C. Skeat, eds. *Greek Papyri in the British Museum*. 7 vols. London: British Museum, 1893–1974.

P.Louvre. Eisenlohr — Donker van Heel, Koenraad. *Abnormal Hieratic and Early Demotic Texts*. Leiden: Brill, 1996.

P.Mich — Edgar, C. C., et al., eds. *Michigan Papyri*. Ann Arbor: University of Michigan Press; Amsterdam: J. C. Gieben, 1931–1996.

P.Mich.Zen — Edgar, C. C., ed. *Zenon Papyri*. Ann Arbor: University of Michigan Press, 1931 (= P.Mich I).

P.Mil.Vogl — Vogliano, A., et al., eds. *Papiri della R. Università di Milano*. Milan: Istituto editoriale Cisalpino, 1937–1981.

P.Oxy — *The Oxyrhynchus Papyri*. London: Egypt Exploration Society, 1898–.

P.Petaus — Hagedorn, U., D. Hagedorn, L. C. Youtie, and H. C. Youtie, eds. *Das Archiv des Petaus*. Opladen: Westdeutscher, 1969.

P.Petr — Mahaffy, John P., ed. *The Flinders Petrie Papyri*. 3 vols. Dublin: Academy Press, 1891–1905.

P.PragSatzung — Erichsen, W., ed. *Die Satzungen einer ägyptischen Kultgenossenschaft aus der Ptolemäerzeit nach einem demotischen Papyrus in Prag*. Det Kongelige Danske Videnskabernes Selskab. Historisk–filosofiske Skrifter 4.1. Copenhagen: I kommission hos Munksgaard, 1959.

PSI — *Papiri greci e latini*. Pubblicazioni della Società italiana per la ricerca dei papiri greci e latini in Egitto. Florence: F. Le Monnier, 1912–.

P.StanGreen.dem	Arlt, Carolin, and Andrew Monson. "Rules of an Egyptian Religious Association from the Early Second Century BCE." In *Honi soit qui mal y pense. Studien zum pharaonischen, griechisch-römischen und spätantiken Ägypten zu Ehren von Heinz-Josef Thissen*. Edited by Hermann Knuf, Christian Leitz, and Daniel von Recklinghausen. Orientalia Lovaniensia Analecta 194, 113–22. Leuven: Peeters, 2010.
P.Tebt	Grenfell, B. P., A. S. Hunt, J. G. Smyly, et al., eds. *The Tebtunis Papyri*. 4 vols. London: Egypt Exploration Society, 1902–1938.
P.VindSal	Salomons, R. P., ed. *Einige Wiener Papyri*. Studia Amstelodamensia ad epigraphicam, ius antiquum et papyrologicam pertinentia 4. Amsterdam: A. M. Hakkert, 1976.
P.Würzb.dem	Vittmann, Günther. "Eine Urkunde mit den Satzungen eines Kultvereins (P. dem. Mainz 10)." In *Von Theben nach Giza. Festmiszellen für Stefan Grunert zum 65. Geburtstag*. Edited by F. Feder, L. Morenz, and G. Vittmann. Göttinger Miszellen. Beihefte 10, 169–79. Göttingen: Seminar für Ägyptologie und Koptologie, 2011.
SB	Preisigke, F., F. Bilabel, et al., eds. *Sammelbuch griechischer Urkunden aus Ägypten*. Strassburg: K. J. Trubner; Wiesbaden: Otto Harrasowitz, 1915–.
SEG	Hondius, J. J. E., A. G. Woodhead, G. Pfohl, et al., eds. *Supplementum epigraphicum graecum*. Leiden: Sijthoff and Brill, 1923–.
Sterrett, EJ	Sterrett, John R. S. *An Epigraphical Journey in Asia Minor*. Papers of the American School of Classical Studies at Athens 1883/84. Vol. 2. Boston: Damrell and Upham, 1888.
StudPal	Wessely, C., et al., eds. *Studien zur Palaeographie und Papyruskunde*. 22 vols. Leipzig: E. Avenarius, 1901–1924.
TAM	Österreichische Akademie der Wissenschaften. *Tituli Asiae Minoris*. Vienna: Hoelder-Pichler-Tempsky, 1901–.

Christ's Associations

INTRODUCTION

In the mid-second century of the Common Era about sixty men, probably stonemasons, met in the temple of the Emperor Titus on the Campus Martius in Rome to form an association devoted to the healing god Aesculapius (Greek Asklepios) and Hygia, the goddess of health.[1] They inscribed the bylaws of their club on a large plaque, where they recorded their thanks for a gift of the use of a chapel on the Via Appia in which their meetings and banquets were to take place (fig. 1). The chapel belonged to Salvia Marcellina, the widow of a freed slave who had been in the service of the imperial household. Together with another donor, Publius Aelius Zenon, Salvia Marcellina provided an endowment sufficient to pay for seven meetings of the collegium—four banquets and three other meetings. The association elected two kinds of officers, a president (*quinquennalis*) and several supervisors (*curatores*). Because the bylaws describe its officers and their duties with the clause "those who at that time *happen to be* the president or supervisors" rather than naming specific people, we can conclude that the collegium had a system of periodic elections and rotating leadership. There were, however, some permanent positions—the "mother" (*mater collegi*) and "father" (*pater collegi*), respectively Salvia Marcellina and Aelius Zenon—and several members were designated as *immunes*, exempt from paying dues, probably in recognition of previous services as presidents or supervisors. The bylaws allowed the collegium to elect new members to replace those who had died or resigned, up to a total of sixty members; it collected dues, in part to pay for the funerals of deceased members; and it took great care to ensure that those in charge of finances discharged their responsibilities honestly. Members were required to attend every meeting unless excused by reason of being out of town or "prohibited by some serious condition."

Figure 1. Bylaws of the collegium of Aesculapius and Hygia (CIL 6.10234). Musei Vaticani, Museo Pio Clementino, Cabinetto dell'Apoxyomenos, inv. 1176. (Photo by the author.)

I begin with this example of a small face-to-face association because the inscription tells us a great deal about it: its size, the social level of its members, the location of their meetings, financial details, and even the menu of their banquet. At sixty members it was about twice as large as most cultic associations but a bit smaller than many occupational guilds. Since it seems to be composed of freed slaves, its members were neither the superrich of Roman society nor the very poor but somewhere in the economic middle. The inscription provides information about the location of the meetings and what happened at each of the seven meetings and banquets, even including how much wine each member was to receive. "Banquet" is an exaggeration, since the fare was simple—bread and wine. We also learn about the financial structure of the group—that it paid for its activities through a combination of endowment income and the collection of dues—and we learn about its administrative structure and its principal activities. Even though the majority of the members were freed slaves, the inscription also indicates how this association was connected through patronage to wealthier and more powerful members of Roman society, including some who had been in the service of the emperor.

By contrast, we know almost nothing about the assemblies of Christ followers, called in Greek *ekklēsiai* or less commonly *synagōgai* (both terms meaning "assemblies").[2] Our ignorance is a function of the kinds of data that we have about Christ assemblies. Almost all our primary evidence comes from literary sources—gospels, letters, and tractates from members of those Christ assemblies. These provide scant descriptions of the groups for which they were penned, probably because such information was hardly relevant to the subject matter of these writings. The letters of Paul and other early Christ followers routinely employ the terms *ekklēsiai* and *synagōgai* but are silent about the details of the organization of Christ assemblies.[3] Paul's letters are occasional: they address only the issues with which he was concerned and ignore matters of common knowledge between him and his addressees. Hence, he is unconcerned to address most of the issues that interest us, such as group size, the methods of selecting leaders, and the financing of the group. In all probability these issues were unproblematic. This means that scholars are left to infer or speculate how Christ assemblies came into being, their size, their modes of governance, their finances, the location of their meetings, and the types of people who belonged to them. The problems involved in drawing a picture of the early Christ assemblies are exacerbated by the fact that our documents are written using insider language and rhetorical flourishes that resist easy translations into unambiguous descriptions of the groups' actual sizes, practices, and relationships to others.

The literature of the Jesus movement of the first two centuries fails to provide information on a host of topics. Paul's undisputed letters say nothing directly on the size of any of those Christ assemblies. Paul names various people at Corinth (and its port Cenchreae), Philippi, Rome (or Ephesus), and probably Colossae. Names in Greek and Latin often convey information about the legal status of their bearers, and this makes it possible to infer that some of the members of the Christ assemblies addressed by Paul were slaves or freed slaves. But what proportion of the group were slaves or free? How large was each of these groups? Do the people whom Paul names represent 10 percent or 25 percent or 75 percent of the total group? Since there is no way to answer these questions in the abstract and since Paul typically does not name people with whom he disagrees or whom he criticizes, it is difficult to estimate the group size. Moreover, Paul resorts to such vague phrases as "those from the *oikos* (family/house/workshop) of Aristoboulos" (Rom 16:10), "the brothers with them" (Rom 16:14), and "the assembly at your house" (Phlm 2), which leaves it uncertain whether the groups he addressed numbered only a handful of people, or twenty-five, or one hundred. There are no names at all in 1 Thessalonians, Galatians, James, 1 Peter, 2 Peter, and Jude, and so we are at a loss as to the size of the Christ assemblies represented by these letters.

Paul also says almost nothing about the organization and leadership structures of the groups. He names "supervisors" (*episkopoi*) and "assistants" (*diakonoi*) at Phil 1:1, and in 1 Thess 5:12 he refers to "those who labor among you, your leaders (*hoi proistamenoi*) in the Lord, and those who admonish you." But he provides no indication of their duties or the terms of office or how these leaders were chosen. The author of 1–2 Timothy and Titus writing in Paul's name imagines Titus appointing "elders" (*presbyteroi*) in each city (Titus 1:5). But the Pastoral letters are pseudepigraphical, written decades after the death of Paul, and are scarcely a guide to the practices of Paul's assemblies. It is not even obvious that the author's representation reflects how church officers in the second century were appointed.

Another issue concerns finances. Some scholars think that Christ assemblies were attractive because, in contrast to other associations, they did not charge monthly dues or initiation fees and did not expect contributions to a funeral fund but nevertheless offered frequent meals to members. In this scenario free meals and funerals supposedly gave Christ assemblies a competitive recruitment advantage in the marketplace of ancient cults. This argument concludes from the fact that membership dues and funeral fees are not mentioned, at least in Paul's letters, that none was charged. Yet it is obvious that *someone* provided the food and paid for funerals even if the food offered was rather modest and funerals were basic. James, 1–2 Peter, Jude, the *Didache*, the Letter of Barnabas, the letters of Ignatius of Antioch, *1–2 Clement*, and the Letter of Polycarp are also silent on the financing of the communal meal. The silence of these authors on the topic of funding only suggests that financial practices—whatever they were—did not pose immediate problems and hence did not require comment. Silence cannot be used to argue that membership fees were or were not collected.

COMPARISON AND THE TAIL OF *T. REX*

If our sources do not tell us much about the nature of early Christ assemblies, is there anything more to be said? I suggest in the pages that follow that there is more to be learned through careful *comparison* with other ancient groups with comparable functions. These comprise a broad and diverse set of small face-to-face associations that are extremely well attested throughout Mediterranean antiquity. They include immigrant or diasporic groups, cultic associations, occupational guilds, neighborhood clubs, and *collegia domestica* (associations connected with a large household). In today's world these associations would look less like contemporary churches with hundreds or even thousands of members and more like the Rotary Club, a local branch of the American Legion, a union local, or an association of Italian or German immigrants in a particular town or city, with only a few or perhaps a few dozen members. These analogies are hardly exact, since local Rotary Clubs, the American Legion, and trade unions are now integrated into highly organized translocal networks, while most—but not all—ancient associations were very loosely affiliated with other groups. Nevertheless, ancient associations, like their modern counterparts, were locally organized, relatively small, and provided a variety of benefits to members.

Like the collegium of Aesculapius and Hygia, we have a good deal of data on many ancient associations, including data on all of the topics about which we know little for early Christ assemblies: their typical size, their membership profiles, their patterns of leadership, their finances and financial administration, the frequency and location of their meetings, the menu of their banquets, the ethical rules that governed membership, admission requirements, the conditions under which members could be expelled, and the relationship to the cities in which they lived and the civic elite who controlled those cities. Comparison of Christ assemblies with these associations will help us think about those assemblies.

Comparison is a very particular type of scholarly enterprise. Setting two or more objects side by side and identifying similarities and differences is a *heuristic* tool for creating interpretive possibilities about the lesser known phenomenon. It lets us see possibilities that we otherwise might have missed. Comparison of Christ assemblies with associations, or any other kind of social group for that matter, does not manufacture new data that we hitherto lacked. Nothing short of new discoveries of documents produced by or about those groups will provide additional data. Nor for comparison to be useful is it necessary to assume that Christ assemblies *were* associations, although as will become very clear, the many similarities between Christ assemblies and various associations justifies classifying Christ assemblies among associations, at least for certain analytic purposes. Still less does comparison necessarily assume a genealogical relationship between the items compared—that Christ assemblies were "influenced by" or "borrowed from" or "originated from" this or that Greek or Roman association. Influence and genealogy are in most cases very difficult to demonstrate. My interest in this book is neither genealogical nor taxonomic but heuristic. To claim that comparison is a heuristic practice is to say that it enables us to "discover"—*heuriskein* means "to find or discover"—possible understandings in the lesser known object. Paleontology offers a useful analogy in its use of comparative methods.

In comparative vertebrate anatomy paleontologists compare the pelvic girdles, hind limbs, and tails of living vertebrates, about which we know quite a lot and which we can study in detail, with similar structures in the fossilized remains of dinosaurs, about which we know much less. Comparison of dinosaurs with living species does not, of course, produce any new data about dinosaurs; but it creates interpretive possibilities for the data we do possess, and it rules out other possibilities. Theoretically, one might compare *T. rex* with any vertebrate, although it makes little sense to compare it with a chimpanzee or mouse, since the skeletal structures and morphology of *T. rex* and its size are so different from either of these. Instead, paleontologists compare *T. rex* with living vertebrates whose pelvic structures and legs are of a similar proportion and that have similar load-bearing capacities. Owing to the weight of *T. rex*—between 5 and 8 metric tonnes—the mechanics of the hip, femur, and lower leg structures must have been comparable to large vertebrates such as elephants and rhinoceri. Or *T. rex* can be compared with vertebrates that belong to the "extant phylogenetic bracket"—that is, vertebrates which have skeletal structures that are similar to those of *T. rex*, ranging from birds to crocodiles. For comparison to be useful, it is unnecessary to suppose that *T. rex* was directly related in evolutionary terms to any of these modern vertebrates; *T. rex* is not in fact a direct ancestor of elephants or rhinoceri, and while its skeletal structures have some affinities with birds, its evolutionary relationship with birds is not direct. Comparison, however, is not necessarily about genealogy and establishing family trees; instead, comparison helps us to think about specific features of *T. rex* and to establish some interpretive parameters, for example, about the kinds of locomotion that were possible (and likely) for *T. rex*.

Was the large tail of *T. rex* simply a counterweight for its very large head? Comparison with the femur and the tail structure of living vertebrates, both those with muscular tails (alligators and crocodiles) and those with nonmuscular tails (birds), suggests that it was not. The tail played a role in forward locomotion. As it turns out, the top of the femur and tail vertebrae of *T. rex* have insertion scars—places where a tendon and muscle were connected to the bone. This suggests that, as with the modern alligator, the long tail muscle was attached to the femur. The contraction of the tail muscle pulled the femur backwards, giving it considerable power in the propulsive phase of walking. The gait of *T. rex* likely would have been similar to that of an alligator and unlike the gait of a bird, for whom knee flexion is more important.[4] Hence, even though the muscles and tendons of *T. rex* have not survived, comparative anatomy allows paleontologists first to *notice* the insertion scar on *T. rex*'s femur that might otherwise have been missed, then to realize its significance for locomotion, and finally to suggest something about the kind of movement that might be expected of this long-dead dinosaur. That is, in spite of the fact that *T. rex*'s muscles and nervous system have long since disappeared, comparison of *T. rex* remains with the alligator's femur and tail structure allows researchers to make some plausible suggestions about *T. rex*'s forms of locomotion.

Comparison also helps to rule out certain possibilities as unlikely. How quickly could a *T. rex* move? We know a good deal about how fast large quadrupeds such as elephants and rhinoceri can move and how much muscle mass is required to achieve those speeds. The key difference between an elephant or a rhinoceros and a *T. rex*, however, is that these modern mammals were quadrupeds while *T. rex*, like the modern chicken, was a habitual biped, sharing pelvic girdles and leg structures that allow for bipedal movement. If we know the ratio of the total body mass to the muscle mass in the legs that is needed to achieve certain forward speeds in the chicken, it is possible, by scaling this ratio upward, to estimate the maximum speed for *T. rex*. Recent estimates of the leg muscles of a *T. rex* amount to 14–20 percent of its total body mass. This would rule out the speculation that *T. rex* could move at a speed of 20 meters per second (44 miles per hour): that would have required very much larger leg muscles.[5] Again, the point is that in paleontology comparison is a heuristic tool that allows researchers to ask questions about the dinosaur, to see possibilities that might not otherwise have occurred to them, and to discipline their imaginations about what was possible and what was not possible or at least not very likely. Of course, *T. rex* had unique features; comparative anatomy does not suppose otherwise. It is possible that *T. rex* was able to move in ways that a crocodile or a chicken could not. But that would require structures that would allow such movements, and for this, evidence is needed.

A final note on comparison. Similarities, as Jonathan Z. Smith has pointed out, do not inhere in the phenomena themselves; instead, "it is the scholar's intellectual purpose—whether explanatory or interpretative, whether generic or specific—which highlights the principled postulation of similarity which is the ground of the methodical comparison of difference being interesting."[6] *We* notice elements in two or more objects that *we* see as "similar" and deem those similarities to be of importance because we are interested in shape, or locomotion, or size, or strength, or color, or function, or some other characteristic. That is, the scholar—or in this case, the paleontologist—chooses to compare two or more vertebrates for a specific and limited intellectual outcome. The comparison of *T. rex* with crocodiles or elephants or chickens might at first glance seem absurd, since they differ in many ways: crocodiles and elephants are quadrupeds not bipeds, and chickens are so much smaller than *T. rex*. But comparison is valuable not because an elephant or a chicken is genetically related to *T. rex*, but because a particular feature of *T. rex* can helpfully be compared with these vertebrates. Elephants and rhinoceri are not related to *T. rex* in evolutionary terms, and even the hip structure of modern birds is not directly related to "lizard-hipped" sauropods. What makes the comparison of *T. rex* and the chicken useful is the fact that both are "habitual bipedals": their normal means of locomotion is bipedal, whereas modern lizards are capable of bipedal movement only for short bursts. Focusing on this detail of similarity and the muscle mass that is required to achieve certain forward speeds turns out to be helpful for establishing what speeds a *T. rex* could have achieved. In order to think about a different problem, paleontologists focus upon the structural similarities of tails and femurs in *T. rex* and the modern alligator. In other words, comparisons are determined by the questions that researchers wish to address. Comparisons are not appropriate or inappropriate in themselves but only insofar as they are related to the theoretical interests and purposes of a scholar. To reiterate: Comparisons are *limited*; they are adduced to help us think about specific problems such as the function of a tail, or the maximum forward speed that *T. rex.* could achieve. They do not tell us everything we want to know about *T. rex*. One *comparandum* does not provide the key to everything, but it does assist in our thinking about one feature.

ASSOCIATIONS AND CHRIST ASSEMBLIES

To apply this analogy to our thinking about Christ assemblies: We know much more about the social and organizational practices of Greek and Roman associations than we do about those of early Christ assemblies. Adapting the terminology of comparative vertebrate anatomy, these associations can be treated as the "extant morphological bracket" of Christ assemblies, broadly speaking, a good comparative set of phenomena. We can then canvas data about associations—their typical size, leadership patterns, fiscal practices, activities, and internal and external relations. Setting these results beside the sparse data from Christ assemblies will then allow us better to visualize the nature of those assemblies. This does not mean that Christ assemblies must have been in all ways identical to particular associations or that associations are the only salient comparative examples to invoke. But it does set some parameters for our thinking. In other words, knowing about what was typical in comparable associations will help to discipline our imaginations as to what was both possible and likely for Christ assemblies. Without such controls, our imaginations can run free and turn to baseless speculations, as with a *T. rex* that could run 20 meters per second.

Comparison of Christ assemblies with Greek and Roman associations can do more. It allows us to make connections that would have been obvious to ancient observers, who indeed saw Christ assemblies as examples of associations, but that often seem not to have occurred to modern scholars of early Christianity. Just as in comparative anatomy, which allowed the paleontologist to notice insertion scars in the dinosaur that are also present in a modern vertebrate, knowledge of how other face-to-face groups functioned and the typical problems and challenges that they encountered will help us to see early Christ assemblies in a different light, to understand better the kinds of problems and challenges that they may have faced, and to detect in the writings of Christ assemblies traces of those problems and challenges. As I will show in relation to issues of Paul's collection for the Christ group in Jerusalem (Rom 15:26), knowledge of the fiscal practices of Greek cities and Greek associations helps us better to understand the challenges that Paul faced and to see in his letters the reflection of problems that otherwise have almost completely gone unnoticed. That is, the value of comparison is heuristic: it allows us to notice in the lesser-known data relationships and dynamics that otherwise would be overlooked. To paraphrase the anthropologist Claude Lévi-Strauss, "associations are good to think with."[7]

There are no right or wrong kinds of groups to which Christ assemblies can meaningfully be compared. If we are interested in the size, governance practices, finances, and civic relationships of Christ assemblies—that is, their social organization—Greek and Roman associations are salient *comparanda* simply because these, like Christ assemblies, were forms of social organizations, but social organizations about which we have detailed information. It should be emphasized, however, that there is plenty in the life and history of early Christ assemblies where the study of associations will tell us little or nothing. If, for instance, we were interested in the intellectual culture of early Christ assemblies and how they constructed their respective theologies, Greek and Roman associations probably would be of little help. We might instead turn to philosophical schools and the intellectual traditions of Hellenistic Judaism as the appropriate comparative partners. If our interests were the "bookish" practices of Christ assemblies—that is, the ways in which Christ assemblies instrumentalized the value of knowledge derived from books such as the Septuagint—then the practices of Judean assemblies, the reading practices of Roman elite, and the "textual communities" in the Middle Ages might be useful *comparanda*. And there are undoubtedly some aspects of Christ assemblies for which it is difficult to find any helpful analogy. The scope of comparison is limited by the theoretical interests of researchers and is useful insofar as comparison helps to illuminate the particular (and limited) problems on which they are working. It does not solve all problems, but it illumines some.

ARE THERE ANCIENT RELIGIONS?

It might be noticed that I have not used the word "religion" or "religious" in connection with either Christ assemblies or Greek or Roman associations. I in fact avoid these terms throughout this book, except for quotations and a few points where the term has salience in relation to modern cultural constructions. Instead I use the term "cultic" to refer to practices that are associated with devotion to a deity. The noun "religion" and the adjective "religious," so common nowadays, are anachronistic in three respects when applied to antiquity.

First, Greek, Latin, and Hebrew all lack words that map precisely onto our word "religion," which *we* understand as a collective term that embraces sets of beliefs, doctrines, institutions, and practices and that represents a sector of culture conceptually distinct from "politics," "economics," "science and medicine," "arts and entertainments," etc. For us, "religion" is a more or less unified cultural construct that can be set contrastively against the "secular" realm.[8] Americans, at least in theory, separate church and state.

Such a distinction is a modern one. Modern Hebrew had to reshape the word *dat* to become a collective term that denotes the assemblage of beliefs and practices associated with devotion to God, since biblical and Mishnaic Hebrew lacked such a term and hence a conceptual distinction between the "religious" and "secular" realms. Of course, ancient languages had words for temples, altars, sacrifice, priests, and processions, and they had words for the attitudes and behaviors that we associate with "religion": piety, fear (of the gods), reverence, (im)purity, defilement, prayers, oaths, and so forth. Greek had the words *thrēskeia* and *eusebeia*, sometimes misleadingly rendered into English as "religion," but the terms are better translated as "piety" or "pious practice." The Latin word *religio* and the adjective *religiosus*, etymologically related to the modern word "religion," normally referred, respectively, to "rites" (*religiones*) and to scrupulous people (*religiosi*).[9] According to Cicero the opposite of *religio* was not secularism but "superstition," that is, an obsessive or uninformed performance of certain rites (*De natura deorum* 2.71–72). No ancient word existed that *collectively* represented all the items that we now associate with "religion."[10] Moreover, most of those items that we bundle together under the term "religion" were in antiquity *also* connected to realms that we would now identify as politics, the family, and the economy.

This means that our word "religion" is the wrong shape to fit the ancient world. It is both too broad and too bounded: too broad because it includes many items such as doctrines, creeds, and a package of ethical practices that were not part of *religio;* and too bounded because "religion" is implicitly distinguished from "secular" and "nonreligious" aspects of culture whereas the rites that constituted *religio* were intimately associated with family life, public life, city politics, the army, and market practices. Our word "religion" creates a misleading impression that there were things called the "religion of the Greeks" and the "religion of the Romans" or the "religions of Judeans"[11] that ancient people would identify as discrete portions of their respective cultures.

The second anachronism concerns the way in which religion is now conceived, as a matter of an individual's interior conviction and experience. This reflects developments that began only in the early modern period. The privileging of subjective experience over ritual performance or collective action as essential to being "religious" gained an enormous boost with Friedrich Schleiermacher's famous characterization of piety as a "feeling of absolute dependence."[12] The influence of Schleiermacher's conception of religion as a matter of interior experience and personal transformation should not be underestimated, especially when it was coupled with the development of Freudian psychoanalysis and William James's stress on religious experience at the beginning of the twentieth century and slightly later with theological developments informed by Martin Heidegger's existential analysis. Religion and religiosity have become intensely identified with individuals and their experiences of self-transcendence, personal integration, mindfulness, and a host of other individually focused beliefs and practices.

Earlier scholarship perhaps unconsciously assumed that "religion" as interior experience was a universal phenomenon. Arthur Darby Nock's conception of "conversion" illustrates this individualistic, experience-oriented view of religion. For him, conversion was "the reorientation of the soul of an individual, his deliberate turning from indifference or from an earlier form of piety to another, a turning which implies a consciousness that a great change is involved, that the old was wrong and the new is right."[13]

This treats conversion as a matter of individual choice based on some interior mental state, where the individual decides to embrace one deity and abandon another. But this is hardly the obvious way to think about conversion, especially in contexts in which personal identity was formed collectively, as it was in the ancient Mediterranean. In fact this is also the case for most of the world's non-Western cultures. As Zeba Crook has argued, conversion is better understood as a social phenomenon and has more to do with the realignment of *social* connections than it does with individual psychology. Conversion is not just a matter of the soul or mind but of one's social and affective alignments.[14]

The assumption that religion is essentially about interior experience has had a pernicious effect on the assessment of non-Western and premodern "religious" practices. If one assumes that religion is essentially a matter of individual experiences of transformation, it is tempting to suppose that the civic and imperial rituals of Greek and Roman cities, which prioritized the careful performance of public sacrifices and acclamations of the tutelary deities of a city, would have little or no appeal to ordinary citizens; they would be, in Nock's words, only "an outward sign of loyalty which involved little sentiment."[15] This view of religiosity of course has a certain apologetic convenience, since it implicitly characterizes the "religious" practices of Greek and Romans as hollow and without emotional appeal. It provides a ready explanation for the eventual successes of Christ groups, which supposedly managed to transcend ancient religiosity and provided an emotionally fulfilling religious experience.

The difficulty with this view is that by all accounts, ancient Mediterranean cultic practices were neither in decline nor bankrupt in the late Hellenistic and early imperial periods. The cities of Asia Minor, Greece, and Italy had a lively cultic life; they continued to attract civic patrons who laid out considerable funds to purchase priesthoods; subelite populations actively participated in the cults of a large variety of deities; and the public participated enthusiastically in festivals, processions, and other cultic events. As Simon Price notes, "The problem with emotion as the criterion of the significance of rituals is not just that in practice we do not have the relevant evidence but that it is covertly Christianizing. The criterion of feelings and emotions as the test of authenticity in ritual and religion is in fact an appeal to the Christian virtue of *religio animi*, religion of the soul, that is, the interiorized beliefs and feelings of individuals."[16]

Crook has shrewdly observed that Nock's characterization of conversion makes it a personal choice by a bounded individual governed by his or her own psychological needs.[17] Understandings of personhood, however, are culturally constructed and vary from one culture to another. For most of the world's cultures personhood is constructed in a collectivist context rather than one that imagines society as an aggregate of individuals.[18] As Clifford Geertz famously observed, "The Western conception of the person as a bounded, unique, more or less integrated motivational and cognitive universe; a dynamic center of awareness, emotion, judgment, and action organized into a distinctive whole and set contrastively both against other such wholes and against a social and natural background is, however incorrigible it may seem to us, a rather peculiar idea within the context of the world's cultures."[19]

The collectivism of ancient Mediterranean culture is obvious in many ways. Naming conventions typically identified people by reference to larger identity groups in which they were embedded. Hence freeborn individuals were identified in relation to their fathers and sometimes grandfathers or in relation to their towns or regions of origin. Freed slaves—at least Roman *liberti*—bore the name of their former owners. Genealogies had a critical importance in preserving and articulating identity. Because identifying people by means of their cities or regions of origin was so common, ethnic generalizations were also common and served as caricatures of types of people: "Judeans don't associate with Samaritans" is the Samaritan woman's rejoinder to Jesus in John 4:9; when Nathanael is told of Jesus, he quips dismissively, "Is anything good able to come out of Nazareth?" Epimenides's caricature "all Cretans are liars" was widely quoted in antiquity, including in Titus 1:12. Finally, reverence toward one's ancestors and the funerary practice of being buried with one's family point to the importance of being embedded in a larger collectivity. These are only a few of the features of collectivist cultures that reinforce the privileging of "groupness" over individual identity.

The effect of collectivism on personhood is well illustrated by the American Afghan writer Tamim Ansary, who reflected on his experience growing up in Kabul and then moving to the United States:

> In the compounds [in Kabul] people spent all of their time with the group. As far as I can tell, none of my Afghan relatives was ever alone or ever wanted to be. And that's so different from my life today, here in the West. Because I write for a living, I spend most of my waking hours alone in my basement office. Oh, I jog, do errands, see people I know—but mostly its just a man and his thoughts in a blur of urban landscape. If I'm too much with other people, I need to balance it with some downtime. . . . We need solitude, because when we're alone, we're free from obligations. . . . My Afghan relatives achieved the same state by being with one another. Being at home with the group gave them the satisfactions we associate with solitude—ease, comfort, and the freedom to let down one's guard. The reason for this is hard to convey but I'm going to try. Namely, our group self was just as real as our individual selves, perhaps more so.[20]

Of course, modern Kabul and ancient Rome differ in many ways. The point here is that in collectivist cultures, personhood is constructed in very different ways than it is in the highly individualistic cultures of the modern North Atlantic. When personhood is constructed collectively and where the group and its needs prevail over the individual, we should also expect that collective practices—processions, sacrifices, festivals, communal meals, and other rituals expressing "groupness"—will lie at the center of personhood. This is not a sign of a defective culture but of a collective one.

To conceive of religion as essentially individualistic and a matter of the beliefs and inner dispositions of the subject is, as Talal Asad points out, coherent with Western liberal constructions that separate "religion" from other realms of human activity:

> Any view of religious life that requires the separation of what is observable from what is not observable fits comfortably with the modern liberal separation between the public spaces (where our politically responsible life is openly lived) and the private (where one has the right to do with one's own as one pleases). The idea seems to be that one's beliefs should make no difference to publicly observable life and, conversely, that how one behaves can have no significance for one's "inner" condition.[21]

Yet for Romans, Greeks, and others in antiquity cultic practices were anything but invisible, private, inconsequential. On the contrary, cult was practiced in multiple visible forms, on multiple occasions, and in multiple venues, from the daily reverencing of the *Lares* (household spirits) in one's home, to the dedications and sacrifices to gods and heroes by individuals and groups, to the cultic activities of representatives of the state. It was, in Keith Hopkins's words, "a world full of gods,"[22] and their presence was visibly acknowledged in a wide range of human activities because the gods were considered as interested parties in everything that humans did.

The third problem with the use of the term "religion" is that in the modern era there is a strong tendency to privilege beliefs as constitutive of religion and to treat rituals and other practices as secondary or even as unimportant or empty. This is in part related to the tendency to treat the essence of religion as a matter of individual choice and interior experiences; and it is also the product of historical disputes in the early modern period about doctrines and beliefs, which prioritized the conceptual content of various forms of Christ devotion and debated which doctrines were true and which were false or misguided, and which treated the "rituals," especially of Roman Catholicism and Eastern Christianities, as empty and devoid of real "religious" content.

The focus on "faith" as something with propositional content—whether a doctrine or belief was true or untrue—stands in marked contrast to the conception of *pistis/fides* at least before Augustine in the fifth century. *Pistis* in Greek and *fides* in Latin had the primary connotation of the "loyalty" that was basic to relationships within families, between citizens and their leaders, between the army and the emperor, and between people and the gods. Of course, *pistis/fides* in the discourse of early Christ assemblies had some propositional content; but demonstrating *pistis* is not just a matter of affirming "I believe that *x* is true," but rather of showing faithfulness or loyalty. *Pistis* understood principally as assent to propositions and credal statements would not achieve central importance until several centuries later.[23]

While in modernity, "faith" is a word narrowly associated with religious activities, *pistis/fides* in ancient Mediterranean discourse had an extremely broad application, found in connection to the relationships of husbands and wives, friends, slaves and owners, patrons and clients, and the army and the emperor as well as to political and legal relationships. In these contexts, it meant loyalty and trustworthiness—that is, it was a term of social relations. The gods exemplified *fides* (trustworthiness) in their benevolence toward humans, and humans were expected to be loyal toward the gods. Of course, Greeks and Romans for the most part believed that the gods existed and were interested parties in human affairs and could harm or benefit humans under the right circumstances. To this extent it is true that belief involved certain propositions, and as Teresa Morgan has argued, some ancient authors—mainly those with philosophical interests—argued that erroneous beliefs about the gods undermined the efficacy of rituals. But there was also a pervasive uncertainty as to whether particular beliefs *about* the gods were reliable or not. So the center of gravity of piety lay not with affirming certain propositions as true but in the performance of rituals that attracted the gods' attention and produced favorable conditions for human life.[24]

The Roman prioritizing of the appropriate performance of certain rites helps to make sense of the younger Pliny's encounter with *Christiani*, as he called them, in Bithynia in the early second century CE. As the governor of the province, Pliny had become aware of Christ followers and interrogated some of them. His concern had to do with possible "crimes" (*flagitia*) that they may have committed, although his examination failed to turn up any. Nevertheless, "If they confess, I question them a second time and a third time, adding the threat of punishment. Without hesitation, I ordered led away [that is, executed] those who persist. I have no doubt but that, whatever the nature of the crime they may have confessed, their stubbornness (*pertinacia*) and inflexible obstinacy (*obstinatio*) ought to be chastened" (*Ep.* 10.96.3). Pliny was not particularly worried about the beliefs of these *Christiani*. Doubtless he thought them stupid and misguided. After an examination he determined that their practices were harmless in the sense that there was nothing that threatened Roman interests in Bithynia; they simply had perverse and excessive practices (*superstitio prava et immodica*, 10.96.8). Pliny did execute a few who persisted in maintaining their confession, either because he knew that they would refuse to burn incense to the image of the gods and the emperor—a mark of political disloyalty—or because resistance to a Roman magistrate (*obstinatio*) was a punishable offense.[25] He had warned them to stop, and they did not. His main verdict on the Christ followers, however, was that it was a *superstitio*, Cicero's term in *De natura deorum* 2.71–72 for obsessive practices that failed to demonstrate the care and seriousness that true worship of the gods demanded.

Pliny was aware that *Christiani* extolled Christ as a god, but he surely also knew of many other groups that reverenced non-Roman gods. What they believed about those gods was irrelevant. He was concerned with practices that might be construed as subversive of Roman interests.

The understanding of Roman "religion," in which creeds were practically unknown and rituals took precedence over faith (understood as assent to propositions) stands in stark contrast to a common understanding of "religion" that emerged in the seventeenth century, when religion came to mean a system of ideas. Typically, "religion" was identified with Christianity as the religion par excellence and was set over against the "secular realm."[26] Whether or not this seventeenth-century conception of religion was appropriate for its time, it was clearly inappropriate for understanding "religions" in the premodern period.

The question that remains for us is whether the term "religion," which has so complicated a history and which has often been defined in ways that presuppose developments that are largely or wholly unattested in the ancient world, retains any utility as an analytic category. Edwin Judge urged that the Christ movement should not be considered to be a religion at all. After all, it had no statues, temples, altars, priests, or bloody sacrifices. "It is hard to see," he said, "how anyone could seriously have related the phenomenon of Christianity to the practice of religion in its first-century sense."[27]

One might try to rescue the term religion as it applies to the ancient world by invoking the distinction between *emic* and *etic* terminology, or an almost parallel distinction between description and redescription. Emic language is insider language used by the groups we study—early Christ devotees and those who belonged to guilds and clubs of various sorts. As I have argued above, no ancient term maps onto our term "religion," and hence we cannot translate the emic terms *religio* and *thrēskeia* by our word "religion" without falling into anachronism. "Religion" is both too broad and too bounded a term to represent either the Latin or the Greek term.

Etic language, by contrast, is the language that *we* use to describe or redescribe ancient phenomena. Hence, we might propose the term "religion" as an *etic* term to organize behaviors and practices that *we* identify as "religious." Etic analysis is a matter of reclassifying or redescribing emic language for our analytic purposes and in ways that reflect our organization of culture.

Could we rescue "religion" as a second-order analytic category and apply what we mean by "religion" to the ancient world? It could be pointed out against Judge's comment, for example, that although Christ assemblies did not feature the activities of prominent Greek and Roman cults, they did engage in prayer, ritualized eating, an entrance ritual that involved washing, and communal songs directed at their deity—all activities that we associate with "religion." Pliny reports that the *Christiani* he interrogated admitted that they met before dawn to sing a hymn (*carmen*) "to Christ as to a god," and they took oaths not to engage in crime, theft, or adultery and not to betray a trust or to refuse to repay a loan. Their ritual also included a communal meal (Pliny, *Ep.* 10.96.7).[28] Moreover, early Christ assemblies used cultic vocabulary in a metaphorical sense. Paul describes the Philippian gift to him as a *thysia*, "sacrifice" (Phil 4:18); according to the author of Hebrews, Christ followers "have an altar" (*thysiastērion*, 13:10); and Ignatius of Antioch imitates the processional language of the cult of Dionysos by referring to the Ephesian Christ followers as "god bearers, temple bearers, Christ bearers, (and) bearing of holy things" (*Eph.* 9.2). Considering this imitation of cultic Greek and Roman language by Christ assemblies, might we still use "religion" as an etic term to denominate these practices?

The question that immediately arises is, what is gained and lost by doing so? Jonathan Z. Smith has argued that religion is an etic or redescriptive term: "Religion is solely the creation of the scholar's study. It is created for the scholar's analytic purposes by his imaginative acts of comparison and generalization. Religion has no independent existence apart from the academy."[29] Nevertheless, whether religion *should* be understood as a second-order analytic term for the academic analysis of cultic practices, that is not in fact the only or principal way that the term is used today. Given the long and complex history that has gone into the Western construction of religion, it seems to me that the dangers in using this term with regards to antiquity outweigh its benefits. Religion nowadays stands in sharp contrast to the secular; it is essentially a matter of interior convictions; and it is constituted by assent to certain propositions. None of these applies to antiquity. To use the term runs the risk of slipping into the tendency to think of "religion" as conceptually and practically separated from political, family, military, market, and other practices. Secularism, however, was simply not an option in antiquity; the gods were imagined to be involved and interested in all aspects of human life, from the home, to the state, to the army, to the market, and accordingly cultic practices were found virtually everywhere;[30] and as Pliny's letter makes clear, what one believed was much less important than the practices in which one engaged. For these reasons I avoid the terms "religion" and "religious."

There are two important consequences of the approach enunciated above. First, the principle that "no right or wrong kinds of groups to which Christ assemblies can meaningfully be compared" means that comparison is not predetermined by assumptions about the genealogy or taxonomy of Christ assemblies. While it is common in the study of Christian origins to assume that Judean synagogues are the proximate "source" of the practices of Christ assemblies, the heuristic approach that I have taken means that *any comparandum* can potentially illumine the practices of Christ assemblies. Second, the recognition that there is no such thing as "religion" in the ancient world also implies that there are no grounds for comparing Christ assemblies only or principally to "religious" associations such as Judean assemblies or Greco-Roman cultic groups. These might be helpful in some cases, but insofar as virtually all associations had cultic aspects, it is methodologically problematic to select only a subset of associations that *we* deem to be properly "religious" and privilege these as *comparanda*. Since comparison is always local, particular, and limited, many kinds of associations have the potential to illumine particular aspects of Christ assemblies.

It is also true, alas, that we in fact know very little about Judean synagogues in the first three centuries. We have physical remains of buildings, some dedications and honorific inscriptions, and literary descriptions of activities but no membership lists and very limited indications of financial practices of synagogues, the social catchment of members, and how leaders were chosen.[31] We are as much in the dark about Judean synagogues on a host of topics as we are about Christ assemblies. When Judean assemblies offer useful *comparanda*, as they do especially when it comes to the discussion of the Pauline collection and recruitment practices, I use these data; but on many other topics, Judean assemblies are not as useful *comparanda* as one might suppose.

"ASSOCIATIONS" AS A SECOND-ORDER TERM

What governs comparison is not whether the groups with which I compare Christ assemblies were "religious" or not but instead whether a particular comparison illuminates something about Christ assemblies. It is not feasible to compare Christ assemblies to "associations" *as a whole*, since associations themselves show an extremely wide range of organizational and practical options. Fruitful comparisons are local and limited, focusing on particularities—for example, meal practices, or the vetting of new members, or recruiting practices, or postures toward the city.

It is all too common in the academic study of early Christ assemblies (or Judean *synagōgai*) to find certain kinds of comparisons ignored or even disqualified, usually on the grounds that Christ assemblies were not associations (or philosophical groups) or that they rarely *called* themselves by terms used by associations such as "collegia" or *thiasoi* and therefore should not be compared with these.[32] Such an argument not only misunderstands the point of comparison—that it is a heuristic exercise and not a genealogical one—but it also confuses emic and etic approaches to the study of antiquity.

There is in fact no single word in Greek or Latin for what I call an "association"; rather, there are many terms for these small groups: such as *collegium, corpus, coetus, factio,* and *familia* in Latin, and *thiasos, koinon, synagōgē, synodos,* and dozens more in Greek. We use "association" in English and French and *Verein* in German, but these are *our* terms. It is doubtful that a collegium of carpenters in Ostia would have seen themselves as belonging to the same genus as a *synodos* of devotees of the Egyptian goddess Thermouthis in Upper Egypt. A generic term simply did not exist that was equivalent to our etic term "association." For this reason, it is fatuous to object to classifying the emic terms *ekklēsiai* or *synagōgai* as "associations" on the grounds that they did not think of themselves as "associations."[33] No ancient person could have done so, since the linguistic apparatus that would have allowed such a classification did not exist. This, however, does not prevent *us* from using the term association as a superordinate term for small face-to-face groups that *we* see as similar *in certain specific respects* and to mobilize those similarities in the service of understanding.

A NOTE ON TRANSLATIONS

Unless otherwise noted, all translations are my own. Throughout this book I render Greek and Latin terms that appear in the literature of Christ groups by using translations that attempt to indicate to the English-speaking reader the relation of these words to ordinary Greek and Latin usage, instead of using an English translation that in effect separates the word from ordinary Greek or Latin usage. The Greek term *dikaiosynē* is routinely rendered in biblical translations as "righteousness," a term in English whose semantic range today is restricted to the narrow realm of ecclesial discourse. We do not speak of accountants as "righteous." *Dikaiosynē* in Greek, however, covers a range of meanings, from "justice" to "fairness" to "honesty." When the financial officers of clubs are commended *dikaiosynēs heneka*, it is not their "righteousness" that is being recognized but their honesty: they did not misappropriate club funds, and they gave an honest accounting of the funds under their control at the end of their term. To translate this and other terms consistently with their standard "biblical" renderings when they appear in the writings of early Christ groups has the effect of implying that the ways in which Christ groups talked about themselves somehow distinguished them from all others, since they occupied a separate "churchly" linguistic realm. They did not.

For analogous reasons I translate *ekklēsia* not as "church" or even "community," since both terms subtly separate Christ groups from the many other assemblies that existed in the ancient world. Instead, I render it as "assembly," which is after all the basic meaning of the term. This, commentators routinely point out, is the Septuagint's rendering of the Hebrew *QHL*. But it is also the standard term for the political assembly in a Greek city. To render *ekklēsia* as "church" obscures the semantic context to which the term belongs. The same goes for *synagōgē*. This term was never the exclusive property of diasporic Judean groups. On the contrary, it simply meant "assembly" and occurs as the designation of several kinds of cultic groups—even a "synagogue of barbers." Moreover, *synagōgē* in some contexts simply refers to the "meeting" of any group, however else that group called itself.

I render *episkopos* as "supervisor" instead of "bishop," both to reflect the basic meaning of the Greek term and because other groups had *episkopoi* or *epimelētai*, both evidently having a supervisory or presiding role. Similarly, the translation of *diakonos* as "servant" or "assistant" is preferable to the exclusively ecclesial translation "deacon."

Especially when discussing Christ assemblies and their members in the first and early second century CE, I avoid the terms "Christian" and "Christianity" because these subtly imply that there was already a separate "religion" that we can identify as "Christian," distinct from Judean pieties.[34] The term *Christianos* seems to have been coined in the late first or early second century, probably by outsiders and then adopted by Christ followers.[35] Only when describing developments in the third century CE do I use the terms "Christian" and "Christianity."

Some of these translations are admittedly lumpy and unwieldy in English, but they also avoid creating or feeding the ethnocentric and anachronistic implications of the more usual vocabulary used in the study of the early Jesus movement.

NAMES

This book pays considerable attention to names. Hence it is important for readers to understand the idiosyncrasies of Greek and Latin names.

The standard way in which to refer to a freeborn man or woman was to use a given name and a patronym: Stratōn son of Aristodēmos, or Dionysia daughter of Asklēpiadēs. In locations such as Athens or Alexandria citizens had not only a given name and a patronym, but also the name of a "deme" or precinct organization in which they had membership. Thus, the full name of an Athenian citizen would take the form Stratōn son of Aristodēmos of (the deme) Acharnai. Resident aliens in Athens, called *metics*, lacked the demotic designation but like citizens had a patronym. This sometimes makes it difficult to distinguish a *metic* from an Athenian citizen if the citizen's name was written without a demotic, as is often the case. In some instances, the *metic*'s city of origin appears in the name: the name Mēnis son of Mnēsitheos of Herakleia indicates that Mēnis came from Herakleia Pontika in modern-day Turkey.

Slaves lacked a patronym, since legally a slave had an owner rather than a father. Often, slaves had distinctive names: a name that identified the geographical area from which he or she came (Lydia = the Lydian), or a non-Greek name (Bithys), or a name that focused on a particular physical or character trait (Pyrros = redhead; Onēsimos = useful), or an abstract noun (Elpis = hope), or the name of a god (Hermes, Artemis).[36] Yet slaves might also have Greek names that were also borne by citizens, which means that it is not always easy to know whether someone who lacked a patronym was a slave or freeborn.

The name of a Roman male citizen, called the *tria nomina*, has three main components: the praenomen (equivalent to the English given name); the nomen or family name; and the cognomen, an additional name. There were relatively few *praenomina* and only seventeen that were common.[37] This meant that many men were named Gaius or Marcus, and several males of the same family might have the same praenomen. Since the praenomina were the least distinctive way to refer to males, they tended to be abbreviated simply as M. for Marcus, C. for Gaius (or Caius), D. for Decius, T. for Titus, and so forth. A full Latin name would appear as M. Sedatius C(ai) fil(ius) Severianus, that is, Marcus Sedatius Severianus, son of Gaius (Sedatius). Sometimes the Roman tribe is also added.

A woman did not have a praenomen, and her nomen was feminized. Thus, a woman of the Iulian family was known as Iulia. The daughter of Ancharius Celer was named Ancharia Luperca (CIL 11.2702), taking the nomen of her father and adding a cognomen inflected as a feminine.

Roman slaves, like Greek slaves, had a single name, but freed slaves (*liberti*, *libertae*) took the nomen of their former owner (who now became their patron) and the slave name became their cognomen. Hence, a freedman of Q. Gavius might be named Q. Gavius l(ibertus) Quinti Onesimus, that is, Quintus Gavius Onesimus, freedman of Quintus Gavius. Cicero's full name is Marcus Tullius

Cicero, and his manumitted slave Tiro became, upon manumission, Marcus Tullius l(ibertus) M(arci) Tiro, that is, Marcus Tullius Tiro, freedman of Marcus (Tullius Cicero). A female slave who was manumitted lacked a praenomen and took a feminized form of her patron's nomen: for example, Sextilia M(arci) l(iberta) Modesta, that is, Sextilia Modesta, freedwoman of Marcus (Sextilius).

The names of Roman slaves were often distinctive. In Italy and in Roman colonies, a single Greek name or a freedman with a Greek cognomen often signaled a servile ancestry. Thus, the full name of T. Flavius Epaphroditus might be T. Flavius l. Titi Epaphroditus, that is, T(itus) Flavius Epaphroditus, freedman of Titus Flavius. Epaphroditus is one of the most common (Greek) slave names. Equally, he might have had a freed grandfather and simply retained the Greek cognomen even though he was now freeborn. Other common slave names included the names of gods (Phoebus, Hermes) or heroes (Alexander) or a characteristic (Onesimus = useful; Felix = lucky) or an abstract noun (Eros = love, Elpis = hope, Tyche = fortune; Eutyches = good fortune; or Irene = peace).[38]

1

A World of Associations

Associations in the sense that I use the term in this book were permanent and private: permanent in contrast to temporary ad hoc political coalitions, and private as distinct from such civic organizations as the citizen assembly and precinct associations of citizens in an ancient city.[1] They are sometimes termed "voluntary associations" to distinguish them from kin groups, but the adjective is misleading. Membership in occupational guilds was likely a pragmatic necessity, and since in some locales authorities used guilds as the node for tax extraction, membership was practically obligatory. In some associations membership may have been a hereditary obligation, where children naturally followed a parent.

Life in Greek and Roman cities and towns was organized around two poles, the polis (city) and the family, and it is between these two poles that associations were found. Neither "city" nor "family" in Greek and Latin has precisely the same connotation that the words have in English. For Greeks, a polis was not simply a settlement that had met some population threshold, as is true in many modern states. A polis normally had certain amenities: a public archive, a theater, a central *agora* (marketplace), and a gymnasium where competitive games were held and socialization among citizens took place.[2] But above all, a polis was a political community composed of citizens (*politai, cives*), usually freeborn adult males who exercised various forms of political power. It also included their dependents (women and minor children), *metics* (foreigners resident in the city), and usually slaves.[3] The polis had clear definitions of who qualified as a citizen and who did not; it normally had a god (or gods) as a civic protector. Civic rituals, sacrifices, processions, games, and festivals in which citizens (and sometimes *metics*) participated created a sense of belonging and civic pride. During the period of Athenian democracy, participation in the civic assembly, called the *ekklēsia,* was restricted to the adult male citizens. The political boundaries of Athens, however, were not entirely impenetrable: *metics* and others who had benefited the city might be granted exemptions from certain *metic* taxes and in some cases were even made citizens.

The Greek *oikos* or *oikia* (household) as a unit of production and consumption was constituted, according to Aristotle (*Politics* 1253b1–14), by three relationships, all focused on the dominant male: the owner and his slaves, the husband and his wife, and the father and his children. Many Greek households might also include newlyweds, the children of sons and adopted sons, and other relatives who were under the protection of the household head. The Roman *familia* (household) differed slightly from the Greek *oikos.* From a legal point of view the Roman *familia* included all people subject to the authority (*potestas*) of the principal male (paterfamilias), including sons, daughters (at least until their marriage), adoptive sons, grandchildren, and in some forms of marriage the wife of the paterfamilias. In more popular usage the Roman *familia* included all who were related by blood through males.[4] *Domus* in Latin is even broader and included not only the legal *familia,* but also the wife, slaves, and freedmen/freedwomen attached to a household. There is, however, a good deal of slippage between the terms *familia* and *domus:* for example, funerary inscriptions of slaves and freed slaves associated with the elite Roman family of Sergia Paullina refer to their association not only as the *collegium quod est in domu Sergiae Paullinae* (association which is in the *domus* of Sergia Paullina), but also as the *collegium familiae* (association of the *familia*) of Sergia Paullina, even though none of them was related to Sergia Paullina by blood or adoption.[5] In some contexts *familia* referred only to the slaves belonging with a household.

In spite of differences between Greek and Roman families, each had its own cultic observances in household shrines, each had domestic rituals, and each provided its members with senses of identity, honor, and self-determination. There was thus a kind of symmetry between the polis and the *oikos* or *familia.*

It is between these two poles that "associations" were found. Although there is a wide spectrum of associations with hardly any two being exactly alike, for analytical purposes it is useful to divide them into several partially overlapping subspecies: (1) diasporic or immigrant associations organized around a common ethnic identity, (2) cultic associations devoted to the worship of a deity or hero, (3) occupational or professional guilds organized around a common trade or profession, (4) neighborhood clubs composed of people who lived on the same street or in the same block (called an *insula*), and (5) associations of people associated with large Roman households (*collegia domestica*).[6] These are rough categories, not watertight compartments, and in later chapters I focus primarily on cultic associations and occupational guilds, about which we know the most.

Because in antiquity what we think of as "religion" was not a discrete and separate domain within culture but a component of nearly all aspects of life, most of these associations, like families and cities, engaged in devotions to a deity or hero, and most would have reverenced gods or heroes in their meetings. Some associations named themselves for the deity they reverenced, for example, the *Aphrodiastai*, or the "artists associated with Dionysos." Immigrant and diasporic associations naturally brought with them their ancestral cults, and in that sense diasporic groups were also cultic associations. Occupational guilds, too, often had cultic practices: sailors and warehouse workers and shippers might name themselves for their patronal deity Poseidon and observe festivals that honored that god.

Since trades often clustered in the same neighborhood, some occupational guilds might also be neighborhood associations and include members not by virtue of their trade but because they lived on the same street where the occupational guild had its workshops. Domestic associations comprising the slaves, freed slaves, clients, and trades associated with a large Roman *domus* might also have cultic functions, as is the case with the large association connected with the household of Pompeia Agrippinilla, which was an association devoted to Dionysos and the performance of the mysteries of Dionysos.[7] This fivefold typology should therefore be used rather loosely. Moreover, in many cases we know the name of an association but not all of the activities that might have been related to it. If all we knew of the collegium of Aesculapius and Hygia mentioned in the Introduction derived from CIL 6.10234, we might classify it as a "cultic association." But the inscription AE 1937, 161, discovered on the Via Appia very close to where the collegium had its clubhouse, suggests that they were stonemasons.[8] The *familia Silvani* was evidently a cultic association devoted to Silvanus (AE 1929, 161); but because Silvanus was associated with agriculture and forests and because their shrine was located outdoors in a grove, they might also have been an occupational guild of some type.[9]

DIASPORIC OR IMMIGRANT ASSOCIATIONS

Some of the earliest associations in Greece consisted of immigrants to Athens from Egypt, Syria, Asia Minor, and Thrace, who naturally brought with them their ancestral cults and practices. Excluded from participation in the political structures of Athens, a few of these *metics* successfully petitioned the

Athenian citizen assembly (*dēmos*) to be allowed to purchase land and to build temples to their deities. A decree of the *dēmos* in 333/332 BCE concerned the request of a group of Phoenician merchants from Kition in Cyprus to establish a temple (probably a small shrine) in Athens's port, the Piraeus. The motion was put by Lykourgos son of Lykophron: "Since the Kitian merchants (35) are making a legitimate request in asking the People (*dēmos*) for the right to acquire the land on which they propose to establish a shrine to Aphroditē, be it resolved by the People to grant to the Kitian (40) merchants the right to acquire the land to establish the shrine of Aphroditē, in the same way that the Egyptians also established the shrine of (45) Isis" (IG II^{2} 337 = GRA I 3, lines 33–45; Piraeus).

This inscription nicely illustrates several features of immigrant associations. First, in order to purchase land and to build on it, a foreign association needed the right of *enktēsis*, the permission to own land, and this required approval by the *dēmos*.[10] This was the case even though the Kitians were not asking to build within the walls of Athens but only in the port of Piraeus. To secure such permission, the group had to cultivate good relations with the Athenian assembly. In fact, the Kitians had managed to obtain a powerful Athenian ally, since the motion was proposed by the famed Attic orator Lykourgos, the city treasurer of Athens between 337 and 324 BCE. Since these Kitians were merchants, it is likely that the Athenian decision to grant the merchants' request had to do with the economic benefits that trade would bring to Athens, not because Lykourgos was interested in either Phoenician or Egyptian cults.[11] Second, the inscription illustrates the overlap in the taxonomy of associations between an immigrant association that might also be considered as an occupational or professional guild and an association engaged in the cult of a deity. Third, the Kitians called their deity Aphroditē, but this was not the Aphroditē known from classical myths and representations. It was instead a Hellenized version of the Syrian goddess Astartē, with a different set of founding legends and a different iconography. The Kitians no doubt chose the name Aphroditē because of a tradition at least as old as Herodotus identifying Astartē with Aphroditē and because both deities were associated with fertility and love.[12] Finally, however we might choose to classify these Kitian merchants and the "Egyptians" also mentioned in the inscription—as diasporic, or occupational, or cultic associations—they must have constituted organized groups with sufficient resources to purchase land, build shrines, appoint priests to officiate, and mount the sacrifices and festivals associated with those shrines.

Throughout the Hellenistic and Roman periods, we find a plethora of diasporic associations, usually pursuing their ancestral cults. In her survey of the almost seventy associations attested on the Aegean island of Kos, Stéphanie Maillot has counted at least eleven associations of foreign immigrants, including groups from Thrace, Laodicea, Damascus, and Egypt.[13] Delos, a key node in trans-Mediterranean shipping, was particularly rich in diasporic associations: there we find groups from Egypt, Tyre, Beirut, Syria, Samaria, Judea, Italy, Athens, and Bithynia.[14]

Diaspora associations display a variety of levels of assimilation to their host cities. An inscription (ca. 250 BCE) from the Piraeus records the decree of an association of settlers from Sidon in Phoenicia that commends a certain Shama-Baʿal, also known by the Greek name Diopeithes. As president of the association, Diopeithes had paid for the construction of the forecourt of the temple of Baʿal-Sidon (the Lord of Sidon), whose construction, like the temple of the Kitians, had undoubtedly required the permission of the Athenian assembly.[15] The association voted to "crown" the donor with an expensive golden wreath on the fourth day of their festival, called a *marzeaḥ*. What is remarkable about this inscription is that all but the last line is inscribed in Phoenician, which would of course have been unintelligible to virtually all Athenians. The association evidently made no attempt to assimilate their god to a Greek god such as Zeus. They retained his Semitic name and they brought with them the practice of the *marzeaḥ*, a banquet and drinking festival to which the god fictively invited participants. They did, however, imitate the Greek practice of "crowning" benefactors, and they employed a standard Athenian formula at the end of their decree: "thus the Sidonians will know that the association knows how to recompense those who carry out a public function for the association"—a not very subtle advertisement of the association's willingness to do likewise for any other person who benefited the group.

Other immigrant associations displayed strong assimilation to Greek culture. The immigrant associations on the island of Delos wrote their inscriptions in flawless Greek, using the stereotypical structure of Greek honorific inscriptions, and built their temples using the pattern of Greek rather than Near Eastern temples.[16] An extraordinary inscription celebrates the arrival on Delos of the Ptolemaic deity Sarapis. It relates a tale that the god communicated in a dream to an Egyptian priest, Apollonios, that Sarapis wanted a temple of his own. Sarapis—that is, a cult statue of the god—had been brought to Delos by Apollonios's grandfather and had been kept in Apollonios's rented rooms rather than in a proper shrine. The god now wanted a temple. But the plans to build a shrine provoked fierce opposition among some Delians. This opposition may have been a reaction to the appearance of a foreign cult connected with Egypt. The land proposed as the site of the shrine did not infringe on the rights of others; it had been used only as a garbage dump up to that time. A lawsuit was brought against the Egyptian priest, but according to the story, the god intervened and the suit was decided in the favor of Apollonios.[17]

Remarkably, the entire drama is composed in heroic hexameter, imitating the style of Homeric hymns and replete with phrases borrowed from Homer, Callimachus, and Theocritus. An invention of the Ptolemies, the Macedonian rulers of Egypt, Sarapis was already a hybrid deity, combining the Egyptian Osiris-Apis (a divinized bull) with the iconography of Hades-Pluto. Now the Delian Sarapis not only *looked* like a Greek deity, but the tale of his arrival was constructed to *sound* completely Greek. This strategy was evidently successful, for two additional temples for Sarapis were built there, and the cult of Sarapis spread widely throughout the Mediterranean.[18]

The assemblies (*synagōgai*) of Judeans in the diaspora can also be regarded as another instance of associations with links to a distant homeland and engaged in their ancestral practices of piety. It is sometimes supposed that "synagogues" were quite distinct from either cultic associations or other diasporic groups. Yet the term *synagōgē* overwhelmingly preferred as a moniker by Judean groups in Asia Minor and Italy was scarcely the exclusive property of Judean associations. It was used by several other associations, and the term was an extremely common way to designate the "meeting" of any group.[19] The title *(archi)synagōgos* as a designation for the president of an association is even more common. Of course, the classification of Judean synagogues as a subtype of diasporic associations does not mean that synagogues did not have distinguishing features (as did most other diasporic associations).[20] But it makes little sense to insist, as some have, that in spite of the marked similarities with other diaspora associations, Judean synagogues should be treated as though they were somehow sui generis and incomparable.[21]

An honorific inscription attests the existence of an association of Jewish immigrants to the town of Phokaia in western Asia Minor: "Tation daughter of Straton son of Empedon, having constructed the building (*oikos*) and the enclosure from her own resources, granted (them) to the Judeans. The assembly (*synagōgē*) of the Judeans honored Tation daughter of Straton son of Empedon with a gold crown and (the right to sit on) the front bench (*proedria*)" (IJO II 136 = GRA II 106; Phokaia, III CE).

This inscription is silent about the particular practices of this group, although it is likely that as with other Judean *synagōgai*, the *oikos* was a rectangular hall with benches along at least three of the walls.[22] What it does tell us is that these immigrants used the Greek language, adopted the typical Greek practice of honoring a benefactor with a crown and an inscribed stele, and offered Tation, whose name gives no indication that she was Judean, the honored front seat in the assembly hall.

CULTIC ASSOCIATIONS

Partly overlapping diasporic groups was a second type of association, organized primarily around the cult of a deity or hero and, in Roman times, a divinized emperor or other imperial figure. Known by a dazzling array of names,[23] these had been attested in Athens since the time of Solon (early sixth century BCE), who allowed their existence provided that they did not act against the interests of the city.[24] Cultic associations were extremely popular throughout the Hellenistic and Roman periods, with groups dedicated to a wide range of Greek and Roman deities, well-known heroes like Asklepios and Herakles, and numerous deities imported from Thrace, Anatolia, Syria-Palestine, and Egypt.

In his book on the Piraeus, the port of Athens, Robert Garland provides a snapshot of just how many cultic groups were located there from the fifth to the first centuries BCE. Inscriptions are found attesting the cults of more than fifty deities.[25] Similar arrays on this scale could probably be found in many large cities, especially those with ports or along major trading routes.

Cultic associations, because they were not necessarily linked either to an ethnic identity (like diasporic groups) or to a trade or craft (as with occupational guilds) had the capacity to attract the broadest spectrum of participants: citizens, immigrants, women as well as men, slaves as well as freedmen/freedwomen. This does not mean that all such associations were inclusive; some admitted only a very narrow range of members, but others embraced people of multiple legal and social statuses, genders, and ethnic identities.

In the early fourth century BCE, one of the earliest attested Athenian associations devoted to Herakles seems to have had a membership restricted to Athenian demesmen and therefore males. The free population of Athens was divided into 139 precinct organizations called demes, and in this case all of the members belonged to the deme Kydathenaion, also the location of a shrine to Herakles.[26] Another association, this time devoted to Dionysos, that probably met in the converted house of an Athenian demesman, consisted of fifteen *orgeōnes* (sacrificing associates), all identified by a patronym and their deme affiliation.[27] This narrow membership profile was probably true of the famous Iobakchoi of Athens—an association whose name indicates their devotion to Dionysos.[28] Although the inscription lacks a membership roster, it lists the civic honors that members might typically achieve. Most of these were honors and offices open only to (male) Athenian citizens.

In contrast to the fourth-century citizen-only association of Herakles mentioned above, by the mid-second century, a *synod* of Herakles, also located in Kydathenaion, listed thirteen new members, including four identified by their deme (and hence, citizens) but also two foreigners, one house-bred slave, and six without indications of a deme or other identifications, likely either slaves or freedmen.[29] Slightly later a group of *Sabaziastai*, named for the Thracian-Phrygian deity Sabazios, included several Athenian demesmen, a priest from Antioch, several *metics* (immigrants from Miletos, Macedonia, Laodicea, Apameia, and Maroneia [Thrace]), and probably one slave.[30] Mixed cultic associations became even more common during the Roman period, for example an association devoted to Theos Hypsistos in Beroia, which included two or three Roman citizens, handworkers, several freeborn members, and some slaves.[31]

The large slave population in the Latin West meant that many cultic associations drew their members largely from the ranks of slaves and freed slaves. The famous collegium of *cultores* (devotees) of Diana and Antinoüs from Lanuvium near Rome is a case in point. That slaves and freedmen were members is clear from the bylaws, which include provisions that members who have just been freed from slavery should make a special contribution of wine and that the collegium should observe funerals for slave-members even if their owners unreasonably refused to relinquish the body for burial.[32] The patron of the collegium, however, was not a freedman but Lucius Caesennius Rufus, the patron of the municipality of Lanuvium and a civic magistrate. We should therefore not suppose that because the collegium was composed of freedmen and slaves, it was for the socially marginal. On the contrary, this group was extraordinarily well connected. The collegium demonstrated its loyalty to the city not only by advertising in its bylaws the connection to Caesennius Rufus, but by undertaking to observe his birthday and the birthdays of his wife and brother; and they designated themselves as a *collegium salutare*, that is, a group devoted to the *salus Augusti* (the well-being of the emperor) and to Hadrian's deceased lover, Antinoüs.[33] Although it is sometimes supposed that in the early second century there was a ban on collegia of this sort—and indeed, their bylaws expressly quote the *senatus consultum* limiting associations to meeting only once a month and existing only for the sake of collecting funds for the funerals of members—these *cultores* of Diana and Antinoüs were apparently in no danger of being suppressed, having demonstrated their loyalty to the Roman order, from the emperor all the way down to the municipal patron.[34]

Some associations appealed mainly or exclusively to slaves. In the second century CE Xanthos, a Lycian slave in Laurion on the coast of Attica, founded a temple and cult of Mēn Tyrannos, the Phrygian moon god.[35] The inscriptions—two versions of the same text—state that Mēn "chose" Xanthos for this task, probably in a dream. Since Lycian slaves had been brought to work in the silver mines in the area, the temple was undoubtedly to serve the cultic needs of Xanthos and his fellow Lycian miners. The inscription sets out the rules governing access to the temple, the distribution of sacrificial meat at monthly sacrifices, and the succession of priests after Xanthos's death. It concludes: "Those who wish may convene a club (*eranos*) for Mēn Tyrannos (may do so) for good fortune. . . . And may [the god] be very merciful to those who approach with sincerity" (IG II^2 1366, lines 21–22, 25–26 = GRA I 53).

Even earlier, in second-century BCE Egypt, a papyrus account book attests a small club consisting exclusively of six to ten slaves who met in various locations, including in the Iseion (temple of Isis) in Philadelphia.[36] We know little else about their activities except that they met for a simple meal at least once a month and perhaps more frequently and that they kept careful records of their income and expenditures and the names of those attending each meeting.

Associations in Attica from an early date attest membership by both women and men. An honorific decree from Salamis lists fifteen *thiasōtai*—a term normally used for members of noncitizen associations—of whom three were women.[37] A few decades later a stele erected by another group of *thiasōtai* devoted to Artemis lists those who "have contributed the required money into the 'fund' in accordance with the law [of the *thiasos*]." The list had at least six men and five (or six) women in facing columns (the stone is broken at the top, and hence it is unclear whether there were more names). There is no indication whether this list represented husbands and wives.[38] A few years later the same group of *thiasōtai* honored their president (*archeranistēs*) Sophron and decreed that an honorific decree and membership list be inscribed, listing "names of all of the members, the men and the women separately."[39] The list has fifty-eight names, thirty-seven men in columns 1–2 and twenty-one women in columns 3–4. Seventeen of those names (both male and female) are routinely attested as the names of slaves, freedmen/freedwomen, or foreigners, and ten are borne exclusively by foreigners.[40] A larger cultic association from late second-century BCE Athens, probably devoted to the Syrian goddess Atargatis includes twenty-seven men (including one Athenian demesman) in the first column, thirty-two women in the second, and thirty-five names in a final column, including four demesmen and two women. The list was cut in several phases, and throughout, both women and men were present.[41]

A few associations stated their membership policies explicitly, in almost Pauline language. An early-first-century BCE household-based association in Philadelphia (Lydia) was founded by a certain Dionysios who, following the orders that he had been given in a dream, set up altars in his house to perform "cleansings and mysteries." He was also commanded to open his house "to men and women, free people and household slaves."[42] The purifications and mysteries are not explained in the inscription, but they appear to have been associated either with Zeus Sōtēr (Zeus the Savior) or with Agdistis, a Phrygian manifestation of the Mother of the Gods, or both. Christian polemicists often dismissed Greek mystery cults as orgiastic and characterized by various excesses; however, participation in this household cult required the observance of a strict ethical code and involved the ritual touching of the stone on which the cult group's regulations were inscribed, evidently as a way of certifying one's compliance with that code.

It is not only that immigrants brought with them their deities and introduced them into Greece and Italy. In many cases Greeks and Romans took on these cults themselves. The cult of the Anatolian Great Mother existed in Athens as early as the fourth century BCE, probably brought by immigrants from Phrygia.[43] But by the third century a group of Athenian citizens took over the cult of the Great Mother, substituting a priestess for the priest of the immigrant group and offering sacrifices to the goddess in a temple dedicated to her.[44] This group of citizen-devotees of the Great Mother is attested in many inscriptions that range from the third century to the first century BCE, and the native (immigrant) group appears to have faded away. Much later the Judean cult of Christos would be brought to the Greek East by Jews such as Paul, but it became installed as a *Greek* cultic association in cities like Thessaloniki and Philippi.

OCCUPATIONAL GUILDS

A third type of association is the group formed around an occupation or profession. These did not function like modern trade unions to control labor in certain sectors of the economy or like medieval guilds, which monopolized production in towns and created a system of apprenticeships and masters, passing on the secrets of a trade. There are a few instances of occupational guilds attempting to guard production in their areas against the intrusion of another similar guild. The disruption of the supply of bread at Ephesus due to riots by bakers is sometimes described as a "strike."[45] Even more famously, Luke imagines that Paul's successes in converting people in Ephesus (Acts 19:23–41) provoked a riot of the Ephesian silversmiths. But such events were rare. Such guilds were once thought to have had only social functions, but it now is better to think of them as networks of trust. They certainly had social (and cultic) functions and provided burial for members and occasions for sociality. But

Philip Venticinque has recently argued that at least the *effect* of occupational guilds was also to streamline the processes of the supply of raw materials and the production of finished goods and, from the perspective of the state, to serve as nodes for the extraction of certain taxes and duties.[46] Hence, while perhaps not formed for economic reasons, their sociality likely had economic benefits.

The variety of self-designations used by occupational guilds is impressive: *ergasia, koinon, homotechnon, plateia, plēthos, proedria, symbiosis, synagōgē, synedrion, synergasia, synētheia, synodos, syntechnia, technē*, and *phylē* in Greek, and only a slightly smaller selection in Latin, including *collegium, coetus, corpus, corporati, curia*, and *familia*. Other occupational guilds simply named themselves after the trades in which they engaged, resulting in an equally diverse and highly differentiated set of names. For example, the care and sale of textiles was managed by a plethora of guilds: textile workers, several types of wool weavers, wool cleaners, linen weavers, hemp workers, towel weavers, weavers of Tarsian fabrics, dyers, purple-dyers, white-washers, fullers, felt-hatters, and carpet cleaners.[47] In the Latin West a similar array of collegia can be found in many cities: builders and carpenters, textile dealers, tree-carriers, wool workers, fullers, boatmen and registrars, wine dealers, clothing dealers, bakers, sailors, ship builders, merchants of ivory and citrus wood, and grain measurers, to name only some of the more common.[48] Several hundred different guilds are known from the Latin West.[49] The large Piazzale delle Corporazioni in the Roman port of Ostia has sixty-one stalls with mosaic inscriptions advertising traders (*negotiatores*) of rope, grain, leather, wood, and ivory and numerous guilds of grain shippers (*navicularii*), each identified by their original ports: Alexandria, Carthage, Tunisia, Mauretania, and the Rhône Valley.[50] The number of occupational guilds implies that almost all sectors of the economy beyond primary agricultural production were in the hands of guild members. There is even evidence from Egypt of guilds of landowners and of cattle and sheep breeders.[51]

A telling index to the number of occupational guilds in any given location comes from Egypt. Because of Egypt's dry climate, many administrative documents have been preserved there on papyri that perished in other parts of the Mediterranean. Among these administrative documents are *grapheion* registers—lists of declarations, petitions, registrations, and other documents processed by a village administrator. A *grapheion* register from the village of Tebtynis in the Fayûm for the year 45/46 CE, P.Mich II 123, lists the documents that the administrator, Kronion, filed from Thoth 30 to Kaisareios 30 (that is, September 27, 45—August 23, 46 CE). During those eleven months Kronion processed documents from guilds of *apolysimoi* (those exempt from forced public service), sheep and cattle owners, weavers, dyers, fullers, wool-beaters, wool merchants, shepherds, builders, oil merchants, and three other associations named for various individuals. A survey of all the first-century papyri that mention associations in Tebtynis, a town of four thousand to seventy-five hundred inhabitants, gives evidence of the existence of at least twenty-two different guilds.[52] Adult males, the typical members of occupational guilds, accounted for about one-third of the total population (i.e., thirteen hundred to twenty-five hundred men). Thus if we assume an average guild size of twenty to thirty members, the guilds of Tebtynis would represent a substantial fraction (17.6 to 33 percent) of the adult male population of the town.[53] Similar calculations have been made for the metropolis of Oxyrhynchus in the third century: Alston and Alston, estimating the population at between twelve thousand and twenty-one thousand, calculate the population of tradesmen at about 28 percent of all males.[54] Fellmeth even suggests that the majority of the urban poor in Rome belonged to guilds because of relatively inexpensive membership costs and the benefits they offered to members.[55]

Although occupational guilds were almost exclusively composed of the non-elite, they were often connected via patronage to the civic elite. During the principate of Trajan, a guild (*synergasia*) of fullers—the ancient equivalent of laundry workers and dry cleaners—had a statue made and an inscription cut praising the guild's benefactor, Titius Flavius Montanus.[56] Montanus, a Roman citizen, is known from other sources and was a member of an aristocratic family in Kibyra (Phrygia) with an impressive curriculum vitae. The inscription does not indicate how Montanus became a benefactor to the fullers, but as prefect of the artisans, he would have been responsible for the regulation of the trades. Since fullers often used the pavement in front of their shops to dry clothing, they might have needed permission from the prefect to do so.[57] Or he may have contributed money to their common fund or hosted them for a banquet at his villa.

In another honorific inscription erected by an occupational guild, the benefactions of the patron are explicit. After listing the impressive accomplishments of Ammius Manius Caesonius Nicomachus Anicius Paulinus, senator, consul for the year 334 CE, and prefect of the city, the inscription continues:

> Because of his foresight, service, and integrity in public affairs (*res publica*), and through his attentiveness, he restored and adorned the *insulae* (neighborhood blocks) of the guild of tanners (*corpus coriariorum*) to their former pristine state in accordance with the decrees of previous emperors (10) [Lucius] Septimius Severus, and Marcus Aurelius Antoninus [i.e., Caracalla], both emperors. In glorious memory and in all proper justice, the guild of tanners

set up (this statue) to their worthy patron. (CIL 6.1682, lines 6–14; Rome, 334 CE)

These and other honorific inscriptions are testimony to the way in which occupational guilds are part of the "joined up" nature of social relations in the ancient Mediterranean. In imagining ancient Roman society, we should not think of it as a series of horizontal layers defined by income levels but instead as vertically integrated pyramids with elite at the top, connected through patronage and benefaction to multiple associations of nonelite, including freeborn, freedmen and freedwomen, and slaves, citizens, resident aliens, and foreigners. The tanners of Rome belonged to the "patronage pyramid" of Ammius Manius Caesonius.

Occupational guilds sometimes served the wealthy as the guardians of their tombs, or they kept their memories alive with yearly commemorations. A donor from Hierapolis (Phrygia) provided money for a yearly "grave crowning" and guaranteed that this would happen by naming three guilds as guardians: "(The tomb of) Aurelius Zotikos Epikrates. . . . I leave to the guild of nailsmiths 150 denarii for the grave-crowning every year at the tomb; if they do not do it, it will be the responsibility of the guild of coppersmiths; but if they do not do it, it will be given to the management of the purple-dyers" (I.HierapJ 133.a, b.1–6; after 212 CE).[58] Epikrates obviously had patronage connections with all three guilds, and although he assigned the small endowment and the management of his tomb to the guild of nailsmiths, he had the two other guilds serve as watchmen to ensure that the terms of his endowment were observed.

What were the main activities of occupational guilds? If we had to rely solely on inscriptions from Asia, we might conclude that occupational guilds functioned only to organize their trades and to bury members. Indeed, participation in the burial of members is well attested. For example: "Year 232, (month of) Audnaios 3 [i.e., 147/148 CE]. The *synodos* of (the street of the) leather workers honored Primus son of Mousaios, who lived 57 years" (SEG 29:1183; Saittai, Lydia).[59] Associations of various sorts collected a small monthly funeral fee called a *taphikon* from members so that when they died, enough funds would be held by the association to provide for a funeral. Associations also typically required attendance at the funerals of members.

Communal banquets were perhaps the most common feature of guild life. Three papyrus bylaws from Tebtynis in the principate of Tiberius, P.Mich V 243–45, prescribe monthly banquets and impose rules of conduct upon members, fining them for misconduct. These bylaws also mention periodic excursions from the town (Tebtynis) to the city (Arsinoë-Krokodilopolis) for meals, which members were expected to attend. They required members to celebrate a variety of events, including a member's marriage, birth of a child, or purchase of land. Just as the Iobakchoi celebrated the civic honors bestowed on their citizen members, occupational guilds found ways to mark and celebrate the achievements of their members.

Fortunately, data from Egypt, which has yielded both inscriptions and papyri, present an even fuller picture of the activities of occupational guilds (and cultic associations). Because Egyptian practice required associations to file yearly updates to their bylaws in the town archive, and because we have the monthly account books of several associations, we know the range of their activities in considerable detail. Guilds often functioned as a kind of social safety net, guaranteeing financial and other kinds of support to members who found themselves in distress and even fining members who failed to render assistance. Some undertook to stand surety or to offer bail in the case of members who were arrested or imprisoned; some provided loans; and almost all devised behavioral rules to limit rivalry and other agonistic behavior and any actions that would damage the interests of fellow members.

Occupational guilds also had a public face, not only presenting themselves to the city in the honorific inscriptions that they erected for benefactors, but appearing as a group on various public occasions. The theater at Bostra reserved one row of seats for the bronze smiths, three rows for the leather workers, and three for the goldsmiths. The theater in Miletos has six rows of seats reserved for goldsmiths and some identified as the "emperor-loving" (*philaugustoi*) goldsmiths. The odeon in Gerasa (modern Jerash) had seating reserved for the town council (*boulē*) and for the various "tribes" that comprised the citizenship; but it reserved one of the front rows for the guild of linen workers.[60] This is not only an indication of the economic importance of the linen trade to Gerasa, but also points to the profile that the linen workers' guild enjoyed collectively. Dio Chrysostom (*Or.* 34.21–23) suggests that individually linen workers were not usually wealthy enough to buy citizenship; but when they took their front seats in the odeon at Gerasa, they sat not as isolated and poor individuals but *as a guild* that enjoyed recognition by the polis. Some guilds even adopted exalted if not mildly pretentious titles like "the worldwide and most august *sanhedrin* of linen-weavers," as linen workers called themselves in Miletos (I.Miletos 939).

Occupational guilds, then, were encountered in many aspects of civic life: they were present at funerals, organizing the funeral or at least mourning the deceased; their decrees and rosters were visible outside their clubhouses; they gathered as a group at the theater; their banquet venues were known and in some cases visible from the street; and they conducted some of their activities in public spaces. Whatever title guilds used, membership provided social identity and prestige that as individuals the members would not have; and as a guild they were on display as part of the city, irrespective of whether they were citizens or not.

NEIGHBORHOOD ASSOCIATIONS

I have already noted that membership in some associations was sometimes a function of where one lived rather than one's occupation or ethnic identity group. The dossier of neighborhood associations is smaller than that for cultic associations and occupational guilds: almost all the evidence comes from Macedonia and Asia Minor, and it consists of honorific inscriptions and funerary monuments.[61]

Many funerary inscriptions are found in the town of Saittai in Lydia, attesting the involvement of associations in the burial of members. In addition to the honoring of Primus son of Mousaios, mentioned above, is the tomb of forty-year-old Trophimos son of Apphias, who was buried by a neighborhood association known as "the street of linen workers" (*hē plateia tōn leinourgōn*, SEG 31:1026; 162/163 CE). This association undoubtedly included linen workers but may have included others who lived and worked on the same street. Sometimes an occupational guild might identify itself with a particular street, as is the case with a guild (*synētheia*) of purple-dyers in Thessaloniki, who called themselves the "purple-dyers of the eighteenth street" (IG X/2.1 291 = GRA I 79; late II CE).

In Phrygia a street association honored a Roman as a benefactor to the city and erected a statue and an inscription for him: "Those working (*ergastai*) on Bath Street have set up the statue under the care of Eumenes son of Dionysios and Julius Doubassion and (25) in accordance with the decree of the city" (IGRR IV 791.20–25 = GRA II 115; Apameia Kelainai [Phrygia], ca. 69–81 CE). The inscription tells us nothing about the regular activities of this street association although their self-designation as *ergastai* (workers) suggests that they were engaged in trades, perhaps in workshops located along Bath Street. Harland has pointed out that the city of Apameia Kelainai had several such street associations that erected honorific monuments: "those from Bath Street," "those from the colonnaded street by the bath-house," and "the artisans (*technitai*) from Shoemaker Street."[62]

Because the dossier of neighborhood associations is limited and does not include any membership rosters or bylaws, these associations turn out to be less useful for thinking about Christ groups. Richard Last, however, has recently challenged the common model for imagining the Christ assembly at Corinth, according to which it comprised several "house churches" that occasionally assembled together. He suggests instead that one might also understand the phrase "the entire assembly" (*hē ekklēsia holē*), which occurs in 1 Cor 14:23 and Rom 16:23, to refer to a collection of contiguous houses and workshops located along a street or in a *vicus*, or neighborhood.[63]

COLLEGIA DOMESTICA

Although I initially distinguished between associations and (birth and adoptive) families, associations closely connected to influential Roman families are also attested. For example, there are several instances of an association identified as the *collegium familae NN* (collegium of the family of NN) or the *collegium quod est in domo NN* (collegium that is in the house of NN) or *liberti et familia NN* (the freedmen/freedwomen and family of NN). These collegia are not groups of family members but rather collegia composed of the slaves, freed slaves, and other domestics associated with a wealthy Roman family.

One such collegium is that of Sergia Paullina, who belonged to a wealthy family with extensive holdings around Pisidian Antioch and who was a descendant of Lucius (or Quintus) Sergius Paul(l)us, a governor of Cyprus in the 30s or 40s CE, who is mentioned in Acts 13.[64] Sergia Paullina was doubtless the patronness of the collegium, but the group consisted of the slaves and freedmen/freedwomen attached to her house, who left a series of funerary monuments, for example, CIL 6.10263: "To the divine spirits. (Dedicated to) Lucius Sergius Trophimus, beloved father. Sergia Eutychia his daughter, who belongs to the collegium of the family of Sergia Paullina, made (this monument)."

The Greek cognomina of Trophimos (healthy) and Eutychia (lucky) indicate that both are of servile origin, while the fact that both have Sergius/Sergia in their names indicates that they were freed slaves and had assumed their former owner's (and now patron's) family name. Several other burials of members of this collegium are extant, all slaves or freedmen/freedwomen of Sergia Paullina's family (CIL 6.9148–49, 10260–64). The phrase that Paul employs in Philemon 2, "the *ekklēsia* at your house," may be just this kind of collegium, especially since Philemon was also a slave owner.

We might also consider as a *domestic* collegium the extremely large Dionysiac association of Pompeia Agrippinilla, located southeast of Rome.[65] This group, whose membership roster is inscribed on three faces of a large marble block, consisted of 402 members, both men and women (fig. 2). The association was presided over by Pompeia Agrippinilla, wife of a Roman senator, Marcus

Figure 2. Association of Pompeia Agrippinilla (IGUR 160). Inscribed statue base, front face. Metropolitan Museum of Art, New York, Fletcher Fund 1926 (20.60.70ab). (Photo by the author.)

Gavius Squilla Gallicanus, one of the two consuls for the year 150 CE and later proconsul of Asia. Both sides of the family were from the highest levels of Roman society: they included senators, and both Agrippinilla's father and her son served as consuls. Agrippinilla herself was the priestess of this Dionysiac association, and her daughter, (Cornelia) Cethegilla, was "torchbearer," a key position in a Dionysiac group. Eighty percent (323) of the 402 names listed in the inscription are of Greek origin, slaves or freedmen/freedwomen from the East, all attached to Gallicanus's *familia*.[66] The association, however, evidently included not only slaves and freed slaves, but also a few members of Gallicanus's retinue. The inscription is organized by the offices and functions held by each member—a rather dazzling array of twenty-two categories. All of the torchbearers, priests, and priestesses—the senior roles in a Dionysiac group—bear Latin names and unsurprisingly are either members of Gallicanus's family or his retinue. But the other roles were assumed by a mixture of people, both men and women, with Latin and Greek names and hence include freeborn, freedmen/freedwomen, and slaves. In the relentlessly hierarchical world of Rome, with vast differences in power, status, and wealth between the elite and nonelite, a domestic association in which most roles were open to all may have relativized, at least fictively, social hierarchies. The association created a "make believe" world in which every member had a part to play and an important status in the mysteries of Dionysos; in some limited sense all were "equal." Belonging to such a large "family" patronized by the most powerful in Roman society also connected members, however modest in status, to broad and far-reaching social networks that doubtless conferred status and perhaps certain benefits on individual members.

GENRES

In what ways might these various associations be compared profitably to Christ assemblies? At this point it is important to be aware of the shape of the data that we have, both from associations and from Christ assemblies. We know about associations principally from epigraphic monuments and from *nonliterary* documentary papyri—that is, papyri that record day-to-day transactions set down by Egyptian administrators in their archives. Almost all our knowledge about Christ assemblies derives from *literary* sources, either the literary production of Christ assemblies themselves or the comments of Greek and Roman writers, most belonging to educated and elite social registers, quite unlike the Egyptian scribes who preserved information about Egyptian clubs, guilds, and associations. In other words, our data about associations and Christ assemblies come from very different social registers and are found in different genres.

Several thousand documents from and about associations are extant. In the early 1900s, Jean-Pierre Waltzing published nearly twenty-five hundred inscriptions, mainly in Latin, and in 1909 Franz Poland catalogued well over fourteen hundred Greek inscriptions and papyri.[67] Since that time the dossier has increased substantially, with the publication of many more epigraphic monuments and thousands of papyri unknown at the time that Waltzing and Poland published their collections. Several epigraphic and papyrological genres are represented in the dossier.

BYLAWS

Perhaps most important are the bylaws, called *nomoi* in Greek and *leges* in Latin, mostly from cultic associations. These date from the fourth century BCE to the third century CE and amount to thirty-nine inscriptions and papyri, some complete and others quite fragmentary.[68] While the particulars of these bylaws vary considerably, most give regulations concerning the entrance requirements, the conduct and nature of meetings, behavior expected at common meals, disciplinary practices, and the financing of the association.

Did Christ assemblies have bylaws? James Hanges has suggested that the cryptic phrase in 1 Cor 4:6 *to mē hyper ha gegraptai* ("not going beyond what is written") may refer to the written bylaws of the Corinthian Christ group.[69] Perhaps 1 Cor 14:33b–35, which prohibits women from speaking in the assembly, is a fragment of a bylaw, analogous to a regulation of the Athenian Iobakchoi that restricts speech-making and unauthorized singing.[70] Even if this is so, we no longer have access to the full bylaws. Among documents of Christ assemblies, the *Didache* 6–15 is the closest relative to a *nomos*, and Matthew 5–7 and 18 also have elements of an association's rule insofar as they elaborate behavioral rules for members (Matt 5–7) and disciplinary procedures for exclusion of members (Matt 18). Christ assemblies in the third and fourth centuries developed extensive "church rules" such as the *Didascalia*, the *Apostolic Canons*, the *Apostolic Constitutions* and other rules to govern the life of their groups.

FOUNDATIONS

Closely related to bylaws are foundations, established by a donor and often prescribing a yearly banquet or some other commemoration of the tomb of the donor and his or her family. The best known of these is the Testament of Epikteta (210–195 BCE) from Thera in the Aegean islands, an inscription of almost three hundred lines setting out the regulations for the establishment of a *koinon andreiou tōn syngenōn* (association of relatives) and the conduct of a yearly three-day festival to honor the Muses, Epikteta's husband, and her sons.[71] Lesser-known foundations are SEG 58:1640, establishing a funerary cult to be managed by a guild of coppersmiths, and CIL 10.6483 in the time of Hadrian, which records the donation of a building by a Roman matron so that the devotees of Jupiter Axoranus "might in perpetuity hold a banquet in it in the memory of her husband." Such foundation documents are important not only because they provide a glimpse of the ways in which associations gained resources in order to conduct their meetings and banquets, but also because they offer examples of how groups composed of nonelites were connected via patronage to people of much higher social and economic status.

There are no identifiable examples of foundation documents for early Christ assemblies. At least two explanations of this lacuna are possible. Almost all of the foundation documents we have are epigraphic. But inscriptions from Christ groups before about 200 CE are extremely rare, either because they did not produce them or because we cannot identify the inscriptions *as Christian* in the absence of typically Christian names or the use of paralinguistic marks that are peculiar to Christians.

MEMBERSHIP ROSTERS AND CONTRIBUTION LISTS

Hundreds of membership rosters (*alba*, sing. *album*) and contribution lists, sometimes attached to an association's bylaws, provide invaluable data on the complexion of groups. Analysis of the names often can indicate whether membership was restricted to citizens, or to males alone, or whether these groups include people of multiple legal and social statuses and both genders. Rosters, some of which are complete, also indicate the size of the association. In rare instances where we have *alba* from the same group over several years, it is possible to track membership expansion or decline. Intriguingly, some lists show that names have been erased, which raises the question of why this occurred.

A membership list is the equivalent of a group photograph. Its organization, like a group photograph, indicates internal hierarchies. *Alba* are sometimes divided into subgroups, each headed by a divisional leader, or parsed into categories according to the function of each member. Since virtually all associations had some kind of hierarchy, it is no surprise that their *alba* tend to list patrons first, then officials, followed by other classes of membership. A roster of a guild of builders and carpenters from Aemilia (CIL 11.1355) places the patrons at the top, then the *decuriones* (the name for divisional leaders), then *immunes* (dues-exempt members), then the *matres* (mothers), and then the general membership. The list also singles out certain individuals, such as the "father of the collegium," the scribe, the diviner (*haruspex*), and two physicians. Even when the roles of members are not identified in the inscription, the order and position of names are usually clues to the organization of the group. Members who occupied higher roles within the group tend to appear at the top of the list.

Other *alba* were cut in several stages, with late-joiners added at the end of the last inscribed columns. In a few instances, we possess multiple *alba* that span several decades of the existence of an association or guild. In these cases, it is possible to observe the rise of certain members within the group. People who occupied the position of a new recruit in the first *album* might, by the time of the cutting of the second and later *album*, have moved up the list and even risen to positions of leadership. Hence, these *alba* provide a kind of moving picture of recruitment and the inner dynamics of the group.

Did Christ assemblies have *alba?* Certainly, by the fourth century the church officially enrolled catechumens on a list, and in the early fifth century Augustine refers to the possibility of erasing someone's name from the membership list.[72] But from the first to third centuries we have no membership rosters of Christ assemblies. The idea of membership lists, however, is not foreign to the mental world of early Christ cults. Psalm 69:28 depicts God as having a book of names, blotting out some names and enrolling others. Paul invokes God's book of life in Phil 4:3, as does the Apocalypse of John (Rev 21:27). In the early second century the writer of 1 Timothy speaks of the "enrolling" of widows, using a verb that in the context of associations refers to the inscribing of a name on a list (1 Tim 5:9). Whether the earliest Christ assemblies compiled membership lists, there is no doubt that later Christ assemblies did.

ACCOUNTS

Accounts of the day-to-day operations of associations have been preserved on papyri, including ledgers of monthly contributions and expenses for each of several meetings and lists of members who were present.[73] Some of these include notations of members who are in arrears in their dues or who owe fines for various infractions of the bylaws. Some ledgers distinguish between members and guests, and where multiple banquets are noted, we can observe that guests at one banquet became members at subsequent banquets. Since these accounts frequently list not only the monthly dues, but also the costs of meals, we can gain insight into the economics of the group—how many members and what level of contributions it took to finance the monthly dinners. None of these is extant for early Christ assemblies.

HONORIFIC DECREES

In a culture in which honor was a critical commodity and the recognition of largesse and excellence was expected, associations, like cities, routinely approved decrees honoring members who had provided exemplary service and patrons who had benefited the group in some way. The monarch or emperor might also be the object of honorific decrees. Recognition normally took the form of a proclamation in the group's assembly and the crowning of the honoree with a wreath of olive, ivy, or, in the case of major donors, gold. If the honoree was not present or was deceased, his or her statue could be crowned. The proclamation and crowning might also be accompanied by the erection of a stele that contained the text of the honorific decree.

A typical example of such a decree comes from Athens (138/137 BCE) and concerns one of the yearly supervisors (*epimēletai*), in fact an immigrant from Herakleia in Pontus. It reads in part:

> In order that the *orgeōnes* be seen to be honoring those who benefact the gods and themselves, the *orgeōnes* have decided to commend (*epainēsai*) Sarapion son of Poseidonios of Herakleia and to crown him with an olive wreath and a woolen fillet, which is in accord with ancestral custom, on account of the piety that he has shown to the gods; and further, that the secretary and the (current) supervisor shall announce the crowning along with the other (honors) following the libations in the temple. If they should fail to make the announcement or to crown him, they will be fined 50 drachmae, sacred to Aphroditē. This decree shall be inscribed on a stele and erected in the temple. (AM 66:228 no. 4 = GRA I 39)

This decree conforms closely to the form of the honorific decrees of the Athenian civic assembly. It calls for an erection of a stele, but the main honorific action is the public announcement made in the association's meeting place. Many inscriptions threaten a fine for failing to award the honor. Some are frank in indicating that they act in order "to be seen to be honoring those who benefit the gods and themselves" (lines 12–13). These latter clauses of the decree underscore the importance of visibility: those deserving of honor, whether gods or humans, are to be honored visibly; and for the association, being *seen* to be the kinds of people to recognize and reward piety and meritorious actions is essential. Unseen honor is no honor at all, and failure to recognize virtue is shameful.

Honorific decrees are extremely common and even include one voted for a *prospective* patron. A collegium of builders (*fabri*) voted to honor Ancharia Luperca, daughter of a deceased patron and the wife of a current patron of the collegium. The decree praises Ancharia "because of the chastity of her way of life and the purity of (her) sacred habits" (CIL 11.2702). The builders erected a bronze statue for her in their clubhouse (*schola*) so that "her devotion toward us and our goodwill toward her will be visible for all in the public view," and they also attached a patron's plaque (*tabula patronatus*) to a wall in her house—all this evidently to persuade her to continue the largesse that her father and husband had shown to the collegium. In this way, all who entered the clubhouse would see a permanent reminder of Ancharia's largesse, and those who entered her house—presumably her elite peers—would see a tangible record of her role as a benefactor and know that the collegium *fabri* was among her grateful clients. If, as Monica Trümper has suggested, the honorific plaques set up in temples and guildhalls functioned like business cards, displaying the names of all those who had benefited the group,[74] we might add that the patrons' plaques in Ancharia's house were the business cards of all her grateful clients, advertising her generosity and public-mindedness.

We might smile at such unembarrassed efforts of an association to attract support. But it must be remembered that such honorific decrees were an essential part of the symbolic exchange between the elite and nonelite. Recognition of largesse was essential to the quid pro quo of social exchange. For our purposes, these honorific decrees provide important data about how associations were connected to elite networks in spite of the fact that most of their members were not elite.

The language of honorific decrees is sometimes effusive but almost always stereotyped. It provides a lexicon of typical virtues celebrated by associations—piety (*eusebeia, pietas*) toward the gods, goodwill (*eunoia*) toward the association, honesty (*dikaiosynē*) in relation to financial matters, moral excellence (*aretē, kalokagathia*), zeal (*philotimia*), generosity (*aphilarguria*), and magnanimity (*megalopsychia*), to name only some of the more common virtues.[75] These are also the virtues typically celebrated by the city; hence, the association's adoption of this moral lexicon signaled its allegiance to the values of the city, even though many or most association members were not citizens.

It is sometimes claimed that Christ assemblies refused to participate in the culture of honoring patrons.[76] Of course we do not have honorific decrees that can be identified as coming from Christ assemblies, in part because before about the third century CE we cannot identify *any* inscriptions as Christian.[77] Nevertheless, the vocabulary of honorific decrees has a strong overlap with the moral lexicon of early Christ assemblies, which also celebrated piety (*eusebeia*), justice or honesty (*dikaiosynē*), and virtues (*aretai*). In 1 Cor 11:2, 17, 22 Paul employs the term "commend" (*epainō*), the most common verb used in the construction of honorific decrees. James 2 imagines offering a wealthy patron the best seat in the *synagōgē*, just as Tation had been offered the front seat in a *synagōgē* as an acknowledgment of her largesse (see above). Acts 4:36 reports that a wealthy Levite named Joseph had sold land to give it to the apostles, and in exchange they gave him the honorific name "Barnabas," which means "son of consolation."

Christ assemblies could not isolate themselves from Greek and Roman culture in which the conferring of honors was the critical currency of social exchange. Whether or not they tried to limit or modify or adapt honorific practices, they could not have ignored them completely.

DEDICATIONS

Honoring people of superior station (including divine individuals) was, like the acknowledgment of the excellence of leaders and patrons, a part of the regular activities of associations. A Judean *proseuchē* (prayer house) dedicated its building to the well-being of the Ptolemaic king and queen and their children;[78] two centuries later a guild of sheep breeders dedicated a building to the well-being of Augustus and to Sobek, the crocodile god of Soknopaiou Nesos in the Fayûm.[79] Another two centuries on, a collegium of men and women who worked in the imperial warehouses in Rome dedicated a shrine (with contribution list) to the *numina* (divinity) of the house of Augustus. They called themselves a *collegium salutare*, that is, a collegium dedicated to the well-being (*salus*) of the emperor.[80]

Like honorific inscriptions, dedications provide avenues into the moral world of associations, for they illustrate how associations participated in a more general culture in which expressions of piety and loyalty toward the gods, heroes, and rulers were ways to perform citizenship. Everyone from the emperor on down made such dedications; hence, in imitating these practices, associations replicated common civic values and thus demonstrated their "fit" with the city.

Did Christ followers engage in honorific practices? First Peter 2:17 recommends, "honor everyone, love the brotherhood, fear God, honor the emperor (*basileus*)"—advice that is wholly consonant with the ordinary expectations of piety and loyalty to those of superior station. About the same time the author of 1 Timothy enjoins praying "for kings and all who are in high positions" (2:1–2), and a century later, Tertullian assures his addressees that Christians pray for the emperors (*pro imperatoribus*), for those in authority, and for the state of the world (*pro statu saeculi*).[81] Commentators on 1 Peter, troubled by the implication that early Christ followers honored the emperor, often try to drive a wedge between "honoring" the emperor and "fearing" God, supposing that "honoring the emperor" is equivocal or empty or even ironic, since no Christ follower would ever do such a thing. Yet we shall see that the plain sense of "honor" in

1 Pet 2:17 should lead us to suppose that this author at least saw no problem in honorific practices.

BEQUESTS AND ENDOWMENTS

Associations not only collected dues from members, but also benefited from time to time from endowments, either from members or from patrons; or they raised money for special projects through subscriptions from their members. Salvia Marcellina and P. Aelius Zenon's endowment to the collegium of Aesculapius and Hygia (CIL 6.10234) mentioned in the Introduction was enough to pay for four banquets and three other meetings of the group. Endowments were often of a monetary sort but could also take the form of the use of property: a Roman woman allowed a collegium of Silvanus to use a building on her property as a meeting place (CIL 6.10231); and a donor in Stobi (Macedonia) converted the lower floor of his house for the use of an assembly of Judeans, reserving the upper floors for his own use.[82]

Monetary endowments were usually very modest: a member of a large Ostian collegium bequeathed 4,000 sesterces (1,000 denarii) to his association in support of one of the regular banquets. At normal interest rates, this sum would be enough to purchase only 6 to 8 *amphorae* of wine, scarcely enough for the complete banqueting needs of the more than one hundred members.[83] A freedman in Umbria bequeathed 1,000 sesterces (250 denarii) to a collegium of textile dealers, sufficient perhaps for a yearly graveside banquet but nothing more than that. These rather modest endowments were rather typical. Large endowments were more the exception than the rule.

Paul's letters and James say little about endowments. Acts, however, depicts Barnabas as donating the proceeds of the sale of land to the Jerusalem assembly (4:36). There are reasons to doubt this story as historical,[84] but the important point is that Luke in the second century imagines the Christ assembly as the recipient of endowments. The story in Acts 5:1–11 of the would-be donors, Ananias and Sapphira, offering only a partial endowment and suffering for their deception—a case of benefaction gone wrong, as Richard Ascough terms it[85]—represents a contrasting story and implies that the ideal donor is expected to give all to the assembly. But Luke's story seems to be a matter of wishful thinking. The analysis of the actual endowments shows that donors were almost never as selfless as the Lukan ideal implies. A few donors gave fantastic sums: Marcion of Sinope is reported to have given 200,000 sesterces to the *ekklēsia* of Rome in the second century, a gift that was eventually returned to him when he was deemed to be a heretic.[86] But that was hardly the total of Marcion's fortune, and most donors gave much less.

SUBSCRIPTIONS

Associations not only received funds and other resources from patrons; they sometimes raised funds through subscriptions, a practice in which each member contributed small amounts to fund a particular project. For example, members of an association of *Amphieraistai* (devoted to the healing god Amphieraus) donated "as each was able" to create a fund with which to repair the temple belonging to the group.[87] The members of a Judean synagogue in Cyrenaica likewise raised 208 drachmae for the repair of their building by soliciting donations from their eighteen members.[88] On Rhodes a subscription mounted to provide gold crowns for three of the civic deities included contributions from individuals and from seven associations.[89] In this way associations, which on Rhodes included many foreigners, could signal their commitment to their host city and its projects.

Subscription lists from early Christ assemblies are lacking. This is perhaps for two reasons. First, while some subscription lists were inscribed on stone, others were kept on nondurable materials such as wood or parchment, which of course have not survived the Mediterranean climate. Second, most inscribed lists from associations were connected to the repairs of buildings owned by these groups, but before the fourth century CE it is very difficult to identify any buildings that Christians used.[90]

Nevertheless, by the fifth century we have Christian subscription lists, for example, a fine mosaic inscription on the floor of the ruins of a church underneath the thirteenth-century Cattedrale di Santa Maria del Fiore in Florence, listing fourteen donors and the lengths of mosaic pavement funded by each for the building of the church.[91]

FUNERARY MONUMENTS

Occupational guilds and *collegia domestica* are often known through the funerary monuments that they erected for members, and also for the fact that they were named as guardians of the tomb of a donor, responsible for observing yearly graveside commemorations. Some associations owned their own tombs and inscribed detailed regulations concerning access to the tomb and the disposition of the member's share if he or she left the association. The well-known *cultores* of Diana and Antinoüs collected the modest monthly dues from members to have sufficient funds to contribute to the burial of members at the time of their deaths (CIL 14.2112).

We are less well informed about how the earliest Christ assemblies managed the disposition of their dead, although they presumably took responsibility for the burial of members, at least for those whose families were not available to do so but also for those who might otherwise afford a dignified burial.[92] It is not until the third century CE that epitaphs can be identified as Christian and then usually on the basis of paralinguistic marks (anchors, fish, chi-rho monograms [☧], and depictions of a shepherd) rather than the name of the deceased or any textual indications.

The documents surveyed thus far all derive from associations. But we also have documents from other sources, mainly administrative, that mention associations.

GRAPHEION REGISTERS AND TAX DOCUMENTS

The daily logs of documents registered by a village administrator (*komogrammateus*) or nome administrator (*nomogrammateus*) are also important sources of knowledge about associations. Some list the kinds of association-related documents processed by the village administrator—the registration of bylaws, tax payments, and petitions, for example—which provide an indication of the number and variety of associations in a given location. Other documents from the village archives include such miscellaneous items as a papyrus listing the water bill for Arsinoë-Krokodilopolis in the Fayûm that mentions the payments by the leaders of a *proseuchē* (the typical Egyptian name for a Judean synagogue) and an *eucheion* (perhaps another Judean building).[93] These administrative documents provide useful information about how associations of various types related to the administration of the towns and cities in which they were found, as well as important financial matters.

It is impossible to identify Christ assemblies among these kinds of documents, which does not mean that Christ assemblies never came into contact with village administrators. It only means that neither the name of the group nor the name of its president gives any hint as to the nature of the group. We have, for example, associations identified with a generic title such as "the association (presided over by) NN"; it could well be a Christ group. Unless, however, the names were Ioannes (John) or Athanasios, typical fourth- and fifth-century Christian names, we could not identify the group as Christian.

CIVIC DECREES, DECREES OF PREFECTS, AND IMPERIAL DECREES

I have already mentioned a decree of the Athenian assembly authorizing the Kitian merchants to purchase land for a temple. Associations are also mentioned in the decrees of various imperial figures and in documents of the Roman Senate. Of course we also have Pliny's correspondence with the Emperor Trajan (*Ep.* 10.96–97) in 109–110 CE, which mentions *Christiani* and includes Pliny's inquiry of Trajan as to how they should be treated. This, however, is one of the very few items of imperial correspondence that mentions Christ followers in the second century.[94]

PETITIONS

As we shall see, the bylaws of associations, at least in some contexts, had contractual force, binding members in a legal relationship. Because of this, applications could be made to the civil administrator when there was an allegation that an association had breached its responsibility to a member. There are several examples of petitions to a *stratēgos* (a governor in an Egyptian nome) by the spouse of an association member, complaining that the association had failed to contribute to the funeral costs of the deceased (P.Enteuxis 20–21). Associations might also bring petitions to the relevant authority complaining of perceived wrongs. A guild of weavers wrote to the *stratēgos* of the Arsinoite nome requesting that no more of its members be conscripted for liturgical duties, having already lost four of their twelve members, probably for guard duty on the grain transports that went down the Nile to Alexandria (BGU VII 1572; Philadelphia, 139 CE).

We have no comparable documents from Christ assemblies in the first century. But starting in the second, educated apologists such as Justin Martyr and later Tertullian wrote *apologiae* (literally, defenses) that, while they did not address such specific grievances as those found in papyrus complaints, offered defenses of the practices of Christ groups and pleaded for state recognition of the legitimate place of Christ assemblies in the empire.

LETTERS

Letters to, from, and about associations also supply important data about the kinds of issues that associations experienced. For example, members of a guild of traders from Tyre stationed in Puteoli (Italy) wrote to the civic assembly in Tyre complaining that they had exhausted their resources and required assistance from the Tyrian merchants stationed in Rome (IGRR I 421). In the letter from the Fayûm in Egypt, a young man tells his father and mother that he had been invited to become a member of a cult association devoted to the mysteries of Sarapis, indicating that he could join as the manager (*agoranomos*), which would also net him an honored place at the banquet (P.Mich VIII 511). Documents of these sorts do not provide us with very systematic data about associations, but they do offer occasional glimpses that are otherwise missing in the bylaws of associations or other association documents.

Letters are important documents of the early Christ movement—Paul's letters; those written under Paul's name (Colossians, Ephesians, 2 Thessalonians, 1–2 Timothy, Titus, 3 Corinthians, the letter to the Laodiceans, the letters of Paul and Seneca); the letters written in the names of James, Peter, Jude, John, and Barnabas; and the letters of Clement of Rome, Ignatius of Antioch, and Polycarp of Smyrna. These letters, many of them pseudepigraphic, provide some information, often en passant, about the groups that are addressed. But since their purposes are usually exhortation, correction, or polemic, the information they provide about social organization is almost always fragmentary.

MISCELLANEOUS DOCUMENTS

Finally, numerous miscellaneous documents provide occasional glimpses into the life of associations: a letter of a patron resigning from the association for lack of resources (P.Mich IX 575; 184 CE); the declaration of the election of a patron (CIL 11.970); the account of a trial that involved an association of fullers and dyers (P.Tebt II 287); and a rather pathetic notice posted by the president (*magister*) and treasurers of a collegium of Jupiter Cernenus in Albernus Maior in Dacia, declaring that the membership had declined drastically, the co-president had never attended a meeting, and the association did not possess a single coffin. It concludes: "no member should suppose that, should he die, he belongs to a collegium or that he shall be able to make any request of them for a funeral" (IDR I 31; 167 CE).

THE STRANGE PROFILE OF EVIDENCE

It is worth pausing to ask why there is such a dearth of documents from Christ assemblies in certain categories: bylaws, foundations, *alba*, honorific decrees, dedications, and funerary monuments. And why are letters—Paul's letters and those of other Christ devotees—overrepresented, relatively speaking?

Some of the answers have to do with the chance survival of ancient documents. Although we have a large dossier of documents of many genres and representing thousands of ancient associations, it is rare to have more than a *single* document from any association and almost no instances of multiple genres of documents from the same association.[95] From the Athenian association of Herakles mentioned above, probably only two documents are extant, both membership rosters, but there are no bylaws or dedications. All we have from the *cultores* of Diana and Antinoüs is a single inscription, CIL 14.2112: we have their bylaws but no *alba*, no honorific decrees, and no documents of any other kind. The same is true of almost all occupational guilds in Asia Minor: we have funerary inscriptions and occasional dedications from some of those groups but no membership rosters and no bylaws. Additionally, epigraphic finds are very unevenly distributed both geographically and chronologically. There is a large volume of inscriptions from fourth- and third-century BCE Athens, but very little has been preserved from Corinth, even after its refoundation in 44 BCE. Almost all our data on Macedonian associations come from the imperial period rather than from Hellenistic dates. The reasons for the lack of preservation are diverse: bronze tablets were melted down to make cannons; marble inscriptions were burned to produce lime; some were recut and used for building blocks; and others were so eroded that they cannot be read.

The papyrological profile is just as erratic. Apart from a few papyri in the Dead Sea rift valley, almost all papyri come from a few Egyptian sites. Hundreds of thousands of papyri are extant (perhaps only 5 percent published), but they come mainly from a handful of large finds in Upper Egypt and the Fayûm. The vagaries of preservation, both for inscriptions and for papyri, mean that unless an association recorded its activities in Hellenistic Athens, or Thessaloniki in the Roman era, or the Fayûm or Oxyrhynchus, no record of it would survive.

There is another factor that contributes to the odd profile of preservation. Associations of textile dealers (*collegium centonariorum*) are attested throughout Italy and the Western Provinces. Jinyu Liu collected 234 Latin inscriptions from local guilds of textile dealers, yet not one of them includes the association's bylaws.[96] This cannot be because they lacked bylaws: their clubs were large and relatively well-off; they enjoyed a high profile within the cities in which they were found; and they were exempt from certain taxes. They must have had bylaws governing admission, dues, benefits, meetings, and banquets. Yet not a single inscription records those bylaws.

The absence of bylaws for the *centonarii* cannot simply be ascribed to chance survival of the epigraphic records, since it is not only the textile dealers for whom we lack bylaws, but also several other extremely well-attested Roman occupational guilds: the builder-carpenters, *dendrophors* (tree-carriers), fullers, bakers, sailors, boatmen and registrars, ship builders, and grain measurers. No bylaws for occupational guilds from Asia Minor are extant. It would be incredible if none of these associations had bylaws and equally incredible if *all* the inscribed bylaws of these groups had been accidentally lost. It seems much more likely that their bylaws were kept on such perishable materials as wooden tablets or parchment or papyrus, as they were in Egypt. Most of the bylaws on papyrus that we have come from one village in Egypt, Tebtynis, either from the second century BCE or from a single administrative archive, that of Kronion, the administrator of that town at the time of Tiberius.[97] Several of the bylaws from the Latin West that have survived seem to have done so because they were parts of *other* epigraphic genres, appended, for example, to acknowledgments of the gifts and donations of influential individuals. This is the case with the bylaws of the collegium of Aesculapius and Hygia (CIL 6.10234) and the bylaws of the *cultores* of Diana and Antinoüs (CIL 14.2112). That is, in at least some instances where we have bylaws, the reason they were inscribed may have less to do with the need to inscribe bylaws on stone and more to do with the need to acknowledge a donor's generosity in a durable and highly visible manner.

The lack of preservation of bylaws for Christ assemblies is perhaps not so surprising then, given the fact that we also lack bylaws for much more powerful and better attested associations. The lack of epigraphic and papyrological evidence of bylaws does not, however, necessarily mean that there were no bylaws regulating those associations. In this case absence of evidence is not evidence of absence.

Hence, it is not especially odd that our documentation about Christ assemblies in the first and second centuries is so limited and confined largely to one type of medium, papyrus or parchment, and mainly includes letters and tractates.[98] These were not preserved because of the social and organizational data that they contained but because they were (or were thought to be) the writings of the heroes of the early Christ groups: Paul, James, John, Jude, Peter, Clement, and Hermas. That is, we have data from ancient associations and data from Christ groups for very different reasons: in the former case, we have mainly the original documents produced for honorific purposes or stored in administrative archives and discovered through archaeology; in the latter, they are much later copies of now-lost originals, preserved for didactic, hortatory, and liturgical reasons.

In sum: There are peculiar gaps in our information on ancient associations, in part due to chance survival and the media choices of individual groups for preserving their information. There are also odd profiles of preservation, with one epigraphic genre overrepresented in one geographical region and almost absent in another; or rich data from one time period and absent in another. Yet if there are odd gaps in our data on associations, there are very large holes in our data on early Christ assemblies.

CONCLUSION

The point of this survey of associations is to indicate that associations were numerous, varied, and extremely widespread. They were found both in cities and in the countryside, and their demographic reach ranged from citizens to aliens resident in cities, from the freeborn to freedmen and freedwomen and slaves, from associations of handworkers and artists to cultic groups. Most social registers were represented in associations, the main exception being the ruling elite—the top 1 to 3 percent of ancient society. But the elite frequently served as patrons and patronesses of associations, offering monetary and material resources, access to their network of clients, and a form of legitimacy as clients of the rich and powerful. Tenant farmers, peasants, and day laborers—a large, mostly rural component of ancient society—are the other exceptions, who seem not to have been very well represented in associations, if at all. Yet there were associations of landowners and many rural associations connected with trades such as sheep herding and donkey transport and industries such as weaving, pottery production, fishing, and oil manufacturing. In other words, associations represented the "middle" of Mediterranean society, located between the very narrow slice of the elite and the larger sector of people engaged in primary agriculture, mostly in villages and on farmsteads. This is, of course, the demographic that is thought to be the sector in which the Christ cult first spread. Given the widespread and pervasive nature of associations, it is difficult to imagine that anyone in the Mediterranean would not have come into contact with associations of various sorts, and given the organization of trades into occupational guilds, a significant portion of the population would have been members or would have had family who were members.

Whether or not *we* choose to classify Christ assemblies as a type of association, there is no doubt that groups of subelite people who joined together in the cult of Christos would have come into regular contact with other associations, which naturally would have offered various models for organization. Some recruits to Christ assemblies might have been members of other kinds of Greco-Roman associations. There is little doubt that to the outside observer Christ assemblies would have resembled other associations.

2

Modeling Christ Assemblies

Membership in ancient associations offered *connectivity*: the creation of a social space in which people unrelated by blood could be connected with peers, with people of higher station via patronage, with people of different ethnic identities, with people of differing legal statuses, and even with other locales either within a city or in other cities.

In this chapter I examine six examples of associations, each offering some analogies to the complexion and organization of various Christ groups. Two kinds of evidence allow us to see the various ways in which diverse people were connected to one another. The first is membership rosters, called *alba* in Latin, which provide complete or nearly complete lists of members. *Alba* are especially useful in indicating not only the size of groups, but also the kinds of people who were members and the kinds of relationships that associations created. Although we lack *alba* of Christ assemblies for the first few centuries, it will quickly become clear that these six associations offer a spectrum of associative practices, some of which find some resonances with the fragments of information that we have about Christ assemblies.

The second type of evidence documenting connectivity, available especially from Egypt, are the careful records that many associations kept of their meetings—who attended, who was absent, and the income and expenses for each meeting. In some instances, we even have month-by-month records of the complexion and activities of the group.

Because names often provide some indications of rank and legal status, *alba* can tell us whether elite individuals were present and how they were connected to the association. These *alba* provide a picture of the membership at large, a virtual "group portrait"—how the group as a whole was organized, and how members were connected with each other and with people outside the associations. The inscription and the quality of the engraving afford clues about the social and economic standing of the group.

Associations can be thought of as social networks—arrays of people related to one another by multiple connections. One of the important characteristics of networks is that they have properties—in fact *create* properties—that do not exist in "nodes" or isolated individuals. In network theory this is called emergence. Emergence is a characteristic of many kinds of collectivities in several areas, for instance, in biology (birds flying in a V shape), physics (water molecules arranging themselves into crystalline lattices at freezing temperatures), and social systems (which create hierarchies and other relationships).[1] But emergent properties are not reducible to individual birds, water molecules, or people; they are the product of network dynamics. Each network has its own ecology, creating social space in which individuals are arranged in categories to foster interactions of various sorts. Network structure facilitates the flow of certain properties, most importantly social capital, trust, a sense of belonging and worth, and competences or skills relevant to the nature of the network.

The social capital conveyed through a network is dependent on the prestige associated with that network. The alumni of prestigious universities gain social capital simply by being alumni, independent of their own achievements. Membership can also foster the acquisition or improvement of certain skills: belonging to a prestigious golf club naturally has the tendency to "up one's game," since the network creates certain performance expectations. Belonging to a book club that discusses important literature creates an incentive for members to develop literary expertise and heightened aesthetic sensibilities they might otherwise lack as individuals. But most importantly, the connectivity that is intrinsic to network membership creates trust among members because of shared values and pursuits. The more densely connected the network is, the greater the level of trust that members can have in each other. Ties are also stronger when members are connected to one another in multiple ways—by kinship, common occupation, common educational experience, common places of residence, common cult, common gender, common legal status, common friends or neighbors.

Examples of cooperative behavior fostered by network relationships are many. Popular media are replete with stories of Mafia soldiers refusing to cooperate with police even when offered lower sentences; they are willing to accept prison sentences rather than betray the network. This behavior underscores the "benefit" (from the perspective of the criminal organization) of cooperation and trust. Or one could cite examples of resistance fighters captured by the Gestapo, who refused to give up their compatriots even though they incurred much more serious penalties by their refusal. In these cases, the "glue"—cooperation and trust—that is a property of the network is stronger than self-interest. In trust networks members act cooperatively to further the interests of the collectivity, knowing that in the long run this benefits everyone.

I present six such membership rosters and visualizations of each network because they offer actual models of networks that generate trust and a sense of belonging that can help us imagine how Christ assemblies may have arranged themselves.

THE BOATMEN AND REGISTRARS OF OSTIA

One of the largest known Ostian associations, the guild of boatmen and registrars (*lenuncularii tabularii auxiliarii*), was responsible for meeting cargo ships arriving in the harbor of Ostia outside Rome, towing them to their berths, and registering the cargo before it was placed on barges to be hauled up the Tiber to the city.[2]

Six *alba* of the *lenuncularii* are extant, two of them complete: one from 152 CE and the other from 193 CE.[3] Fragments of a third *album* date to 213 CE.[4] The first, NCE 2594 = CIL 14.250 (fig. 3), is a large, well-engraved tablet with the names of the patrons, the honorary president for life (*quinquennalis perpetuus*), the current president, the past president, and 125 *plebs*, the common Latin term for ordinary members and one that is obviously borrowed from the political organization of the people of Rome. The second roster, elegantly inscribed forty-one years later (NCE 7080 = CIL 14.251, fig. 4), has more names (258 *plebs*); and the fragmentary third *album* is estimated to have had 290 names, along with the names of patrons and several honorary and current presidents. All of the members have *tria nomina*, the three-part name that indicates Roman citizenship. Only four are specifically identified as freed slaves (*liberti*), although as will become clear, many more were probably freedmen or the descendants of freedmen. No slaves are listed, even though Ostian guilds owned slaves, who likely did most of the heavy labor.

Each of the rosters was designed in such a way as to be able to register changes in leadership and the addition of new members. Note the blank spaces below PATRONI and the space above PLEBS in figure 3 in the first column, designed to accommodate the names of new patrons who might be co-opted later and the names of the new presidents (*quinquennales*) as they were elected to five-year terms.[5] The name of the current *quinquennalis*, M. Cornelius Secundus, is placed to the right of a set of five equestrian patrons and engraved in heavier

Figure 3. Album of the guild of boatmen and registrars (*lenuncularii tabularii auxiliarii*) (NCE 2594 = CIL 14.250; Ostia, 152 CE). Rome, Capitoline Museums, Archivio Fotografico dei Musei Capitolini. © Roma, Sovrintendenza Capitolina ai Beni Culturali (used with permission).

Figure 4. Album of the guild of boatmen and registrars (*lenuncularii tabularii auxiliarii*) (NCE 7080 = CIL 14.251; Ostia, 193 CE). Rome, Capitoline Museums, Archivio Fotografico dei Musei Capitolini. © Roma, Sovrintendenza Capitolina ai Beni Culturali (used with permission).

letters, an indication of a later addition. The outgoing *quinquennalis* could then be designated as an honorary president simply by inscribing of QUINQPERP (*perpetuus*) above his name. Note also in figure 4 more blank space below the list of three PATRONI (one name was erased) and below the *quinquennales* in column 1. The fourth column of the first *album* is engraved in smaller, more crowded letters, except for the final six names, which are much larger than the rest (see fig. 3). These variations indicate several different engravers adding names at different times. The seventh and eighth columns of the second *album* are squeezed both horizontally and vertically, with letters of varying heights and styles (see fig. 4). Evidently the *album* originally had been designed for seven columns, but more names and an eighth column were added by later engravers. Once all space in an *album* had been filled, another was started. The members still living at that time were transferred to the next *album*, and space was left to add new recruits.

The last two *alba* of 193 and 213 CE show a large degree of overlap in names despite a twenty-year gap. Names that appeared in the squeezed eighth column of the roster of 193 reappear now in the sixth column of the *album* of 213, which seems to have had as many as ten columns. Undoubtedly, many of those listed in the first few columns of the *album* of 193 had died by 213, and hence those whose names had been inscribed in the last columns in 193 had now "moved up" the list of 213. Thus, *alba* provide a kind of moving picture of the leadership and membership of a group. It is unlikely that the guild was much larger than 100 to 130 members at any given time.[6]

Five features of these lists are striking. First, in both CIL 14.250 and CIL 14.251 the first people named are patrons. All of them are known from other sources to be of the senatorial rank (*ordo*) and were indeed of consular rank.[7] All four patrons of CIL 14.250 are also listed, along with their sons and several others senators, as the patrons of another association, the guild of bargemen (*scapharii*), to which they are said to have contributed funds for the enlargement of a temple (CIL 14.246; Ostia, 140–170 CE). Since senators were often patrons of multiple guilds and since, as I will note presently, none of them had strong familial relations to any of the guild members, they are best treated as "external patrons"—that is, patrons who supplied resources and prestige to the group but who were in no way active members. After all, senators were the cream of imperial society and would not routinely associate socially with people who were far below their station. The relationship of patronage, however, created a connection that benefited both patron and client: the boatmen and registrars derived prestige from their association with the grandees of Roman society. For their part, the senatorial patrons could boast the support of a large guild, since patronage also implied loyalty (*fides*) on the part of the clients. The fact that these senators were patrons of other guilds—

in this case the bargemen and two other guilds—also created an indirect, lateral affiliation between the boatmen and registrars and these other three guilds. Thus, several guilds belonged to the client network of these senators.

The involvement of Roman elite in the guilds of Ostia, as well as those of Portus, is not surprising when one considers that it was through these ports that much of the wealth of the empire—food, wine, oil, and other commodities—flowed to Rome. The control of the movement of goods was essential to the political control of the city, and the senatorial elite had every reason to serve as patrons to the guilds that oversaw the transport of goods up the Tiber. This was not out of a fear of the harbor workers going on strike—strikes were very rare in antiquity; instead, the elite of Rome wanted to be identified publicly with the feeding of the city, and being patrons of some of the essential links in the alimentary chain ensured such visibility.[8]

Second, three of the patrons of boatmen and registrars, M. Sedatius Severianus, his father M. Sedatius Severus, and T. Prifernius Paetus Rosianus Geminus, were patrons not only of the guild of bargemen (CIL 14.246), but also of another unnamed Ostian association whose partial *album* is preserved in CIL 14.247, evidently much smaller than the *lenuncularii*.[9] M. Sedatius Severianus and his son M. Sedatius Gallus were also the patrons of yet another guild whose fragmentary *album* is extant (CIL 14.248).

The Sedatii are an interesting family. Although both father and son were Roman citizens and senatorial in rank, the nomen Sedatius and the son's cognomen Gallus point to the origin of the family in Gaul.[10] The family likely hailed from the region around Limonum Pictonum (Poitiers) in Gaul. In fact, the term *lenuncularii* as the name of a guild is attested epigraphically *only* in Ostia and in Gaul, in Arelate in the Rhône Valley.[11] What these prosopographical data suggest is that the boatmen and registrars of Ostia were connected not only via their patrons to several other Ostian guilds, but also to boatmen and registrars of the Rhône Valley.

Third, the presidents of the guild—called *quinquennales* and identified in the *alba* as the current president, former presidents, and (honorary) presidents for life—are overwhelmingly servile in origin. All bear *tria nomina* and were thus citizens at the time they served as presidents. Their Greek cognomens, however, suggest that slaves were in their family trees. In his analysis of dozens of occupational guilds from Ostia, Royden concluded that of those presidents whose status was identifiable, two-thirds were freedmen and only one-third were born free; but *all* 217 presidents had slave ancestries.[12]

Fourth, most ordinary members were also freed slaves or their children. Many have Greek cognomens, and even those with Latin cognomens might have had slave ancestry if their emancipated parents gave them a Latin cognomen. Nevertheless, the *album* of 152 CE has four equestrians (*equites*) as patrons and an imperial freedman, while the *album* of 193 indicates that in addition to patrons of senatorial rank, the guild had six equestrian patrons. In 152 the guild named a freedman, M. Cornelius Epagathus, and his son, M. Cornelius Secundus, as president for life and current president, respectively.[13] But by the time that the *album* of 193 was cut, Epagathus's grandson M. Cornelius Valerianus was both a patron *and* the president of the guild and had risen to the rank of a local magistrate (*decurion*) of Ostia. One of his two sons achieved equestrian rank (CIL 14.341).[14] Hence, the descendants of Epagathus the freedman had amassed sufficient wealth not only to meet the census requirement of probably 100,000 sesterces to attain a role in the civic government of Ostia with the status of decurion, but eventually of 400,000 sesterces to meet the census requirement of an equestrian.[15]

Finally, as the network visualization of the guild suggests (fig. 5), this guild was not simply a group of individuals connected with each other by only a

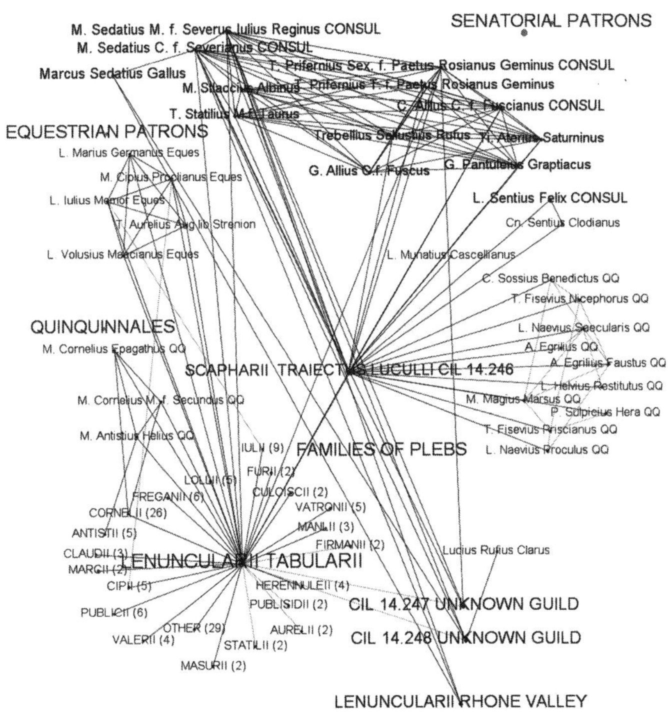

Figure 5. Network visualization of the boatmen and registrars (*lenuncularii*, CIL 14.250). A name followed by a number in parentheses, e.g., "VALERII (4)," indicates that four members of the Valerii *gens* were *plebs* in the guild.

common occupation. The boatmen and registrars were connected in multiple ways, including to at least three other guilds via their patrons. Two of the equestrians and all the presidents (current, past, and honorary) had family ties to other guild members. The current president, M. Cornelius Secundus, was the son of the honorary president M. Cornelius Epagathus; twenty-six of the *plebs* belonged to the Cornelii family as either kin or freedmen; and another fourteen members were either Iulii or Cipii, connected to two of the equestrian patrons, L. Iulius Memor and M. Cipius Proclianus. A further five members belonged to the family of one of the former presidents, M. Antistius Helius; and five members, including two father-son groups, were connected to the first *pleb* named on the list, M. Lollius Marinus. That is, almost half of the members belonged to one of five family groupings.

The *album* of 193 CE shows a similar pattern: more than half of the members were connected to the eight families of the equestrian patrons and the presidents. In short, belonging to the boatmen and registrars of Ostia provided multiplex forms of connectivity: connections based on a common occupation, family ties, and ties with guild members who had achieved decurial or equestrian rank, or who would achieve those ranks shortly.

We should also assume that among the general membership there were connections that were not based on family ties or a common occupation. It is antecedently likely that many were neighbors, living in the same housing blocks, perhaps near the large warehouse Horrea Epagathiana et Epaphroditiana (I,VIII,3) built between 145 and 150 and named for Epagathus and his family. Others would have been connected through marriage or membership in the same cultic associations. The network visualization is thus incomplete but nevertheless underscores the multiple ways in which members were interconnected internally to each other, externally to their patrons, and via their patrons to other occupational networks both in Ostia and in the Rhône Valley.[16]

As a whole, Ostian occupational guilds were large and wealthy. Excavations at Ostia have revealed the existence of several large clubhouses and temples owned by these guilds. The guilds seem to have used the temple in the middle of the Piazzale delle Corporazioni (II,VII,4),[17] and the bargemen (*scapharii et lenuncularii traiectus Luculii*) had a basilica (I,II,3). Buildings are also still visible in Ostia that belonged to the builder-carpenters (*fabri tignuarii;* I,XII,1), the ship builders (*fabri navales;* III,II,1–2), the grain measurers (*mensores frumentarii;* I,XIX,1.3), the Ostian sailors (*navicularii ostienses;* IV,V,15), and the caulkers and rope makers (*stuppatores;* I,X,3)—testimonies to the wealth of these guilds.[18] Wealthy patrons of senatorial rank were prepared to supply funds for the construction of buildings and temples that were to be used by guild members.

The fact that collectively the *lenuncularii* were relatively well-off does not mean that individual *plebs* were. Epagathus's family would eventually rise in prominence and income. Income, however, is not the principal or the most important determinant of social standing. A better index of the relative standing of members is *connectivity*: viewed as a network, the boatmen and registrars connected individuals of varying income and social levels through kinship, occupation, and patronage ties and probably other social and spatial links. What created social standing or social capital were the emergent properties of trust, a sense of belonging, and the prestige of a large and undoubtedly influential guild centrally involved in the feeding of Rome. Patronage by people of superior rank underscored the social capital of the guild. This prestige is reflected in the high quality of the engraving of the *alba* of the *lenuncularii*, undoubtedly set up in a publicly visible space to advertise the importance of the group and the standing of its members.

What might their regular meetings have looked like? M. Cornelius Valerianus, who had achieved decurial status, and his son, who eventually became an equestrian, were nonetheless listed as *plebs* in earlier *alba*. They probably participated in the activities of the group. After all, they had made their fortunes as *lenuncularii* and likely employed many of their relatives as boat pilots or registrars. It is unlikely, however, that the senatorial patrons were members in the ordinary meaning of that term, especially since several of them were the patrons of other guilds as well. In a highly stratified society there were occasions when the elite would engage with those below them in status, normally when the elite wished to demonstrate their largesse in a publicly visible way and when the clients wanted to offer demonstrations of gratitude and loyalty. But for the elite to routinely fraternize with subelite inevitably would have brought criticism from their peers and threatened injury to their social standing. Thus, we might expect the four senators of CIL 14.250 to be present when the plaque was unveiled in their honor and set up in the harbor area of Ostia. Perhaps the guild might have celebrated the birthdays of their patrons, at which there would undoubtedly be additional expressions of gratitude and displays of loyalty.[19] But apart from those occasions, the guild likely met in Ostia without their patrons.

What emergent properties flowed through this network? A painting now in the Musei della biblioteca Apostolica Vaticana usually connected with the bargemen illustrates some of those properties (fig. 6).[20] The painting shows several figures on the deck of a boat, the *Isis Geminiana*; one, labeled *magister*, stands on an elevated deck at the stern holding the rudder, and two others stand amidships inspecting grain that is being poured into a vessel on the deck. A fourth holds counting beads, evidently to record the quantity of the grain. Meanwhile,

Figure 6. Fresco of the boat *Isis Geminiana*. Musei Vaticani cat. 79638. © Vatican Museums (used by permission of the Musei Vaticani). (Photo by the author.)

a fifth figure directs two others, probably slaves, carrying sacks of grain up the gangplank. The painting thus illustrates the varieties of technical competences that *lenuncularii* had to develop and that were available through the network: the supervision of work, the management of slaves, accounting skills and registering cargo, and skills for interacting with those guilds with which the *lenuncularii* had business. Belonging to the network fostered the development of these properties in members.

The network also created a sense of belonging and of having a place in the network, whether as one of the presidents, as dues-exempt members, or as one of the *plebs*. Given the dynamic nature of the network, membership also meant that one could anticipate "moving up" in the network, from a late-joiner listed in the final columns of one *album*, to a higher position on the next *album*, or even to the level of one of the presidents. The fact that the *lenuncularii* were connected with the cream of Roman society and played a critical part in the feeding of Rome also meant that prestige and social capital were network properties in which all members participated.

THE BUILDER-CARPENTERS OF LUNA

Engraved on two tablets, the *album* of the guild of builder-carpenters (*collegium fabrum tignuariorum*) (CIL 11.1355a, b) of the town of Luna two hundred kilometers northwest of Rome provides an example of another occupational guild, but one that differs in important respects from that of the boatmen and registrars (fig. 7). This well-engraved roster has a total of ninety-one names. The

Figure 7. Album of the guild of builder-carpenters (*collegium fabrum tignuariorum*) of Luna (CIL 11.1355a,b). (Photos by Federico Frasson, *Le epigrafi di Luni romana* [Alessandria: Edizioni dell'Orso, 2013], figs. 87 and 89; used with permission.)

first column names fourteen patrons, all identified by full *tria nomina.* At the bottom of this column a fifteenth name appears, Numisius Tacitus, identified as the "father of the guild" (*pater collegii*). Since his name and title are squeezed both vertically and horizontally, he was probably not part of the first stage of engraving but was added at the point he was chosen as *pater.* Moreover, in rather large and crude letters (pointing to a different engraver), he is designated as *bisellarius,* that is, an official entitled to sit in a specially decorated chair. Thus, at least three stages are visible in the first column: the inscribing of the names of the first fourteen patrons, the addition of Tacitus as *pater,* and the subsequent qualification of Tacitus as *bisellarius.*

The second column lists five *decuriones,* divisional leaders. The title *decurio* is common in some of the larger guilds and is borrowed from the political structure of towns, which had several decurions, or town counselors. Four blank lines follow the list of decurions, leaving room for the names of future decurions to be inscribed. In contrast to the *album* of the boatmen and registrars, however, there is no indication that any of the patrons or decurions was of senatorial or equestrian rank; some may have been local magistrates in Luna or other individuals of some social standing.

Column 2 also lists seven officials within the group, including a diviner (*haruspex*), a secretary (*scriba*), and two doctors (*medici*). The general membership, carved on a fragmentary column 3 and two columns on a partly broken second plaque, records forty-seven men (one is erased), two *immunes* (probably former officers granted exemptions from monthly dues), three "mothers" (*matres*), two "daughters" (*filiae*), and finally six men at the end of the list, probably late-joiners. There are thirteen small family groups of two to six people, but no single family dominates the general membership as the Cornelii did in the case of the boatmen and registrars. The list includes mostly freeborn and freedmen/freedwomen, but two imperial slaves were also present. The second plaque was paid for by the *bisellarius* of another association, whose son was listed as one of the *immunes* of the builder-carpenters. This act of benefaction created a link between the builder-carpenters and the *dendrophors* (tree-carriers), an association dedicated to the worship of Cybele or the Magna Mater.[21] The link between the builder-carpenters and other associations was not established by patronage, as it was in the case of the boatmen and registrars, but by the many connections that existed among the membership in general.

The category of "mothers" is of special interest since, as Emily Hemelrijk has shown from an examination of a large dossier of inscriptions that mention *matres,* the mothers are neither external patrons nor obviously wives of the officers of the group. Since in *alba* the names of *matres* typically appear next to either the patrons or the *immunes* (as they do here), it is likely that they were listed there because as members they had benefited the guild in some conspicuous way.[22] In this case, one of the mothers, Iulia Probita, belonged to the same family as one of the daughters and four other members. Hemelrijk suggests that they should be seen as parallel to the *pater collegii*, who appears to have functioned as a president, listed just after the patrons and just before the divisional leaders. This might even suggest some leadership role for the *matres*. Hemelrijk's tabulation of all of the twenty-seven known *matres collegii* shows that they were, with only three exceptions, freedwomen or slaves (like the male members of those collegia).[23]

The members of this guild were connected internally not only through a common trade, but by multiple other connections, including familial bonds. This guild was also connected externally to the town via their patrons and to the *dendrophors* via one of their *immunes*. We might also assume that the diviner (*haruspex*), the secretary (*scriba*), and the two physicians (*medici*) were also connected to their respective professional associations in Luna. Figure 8

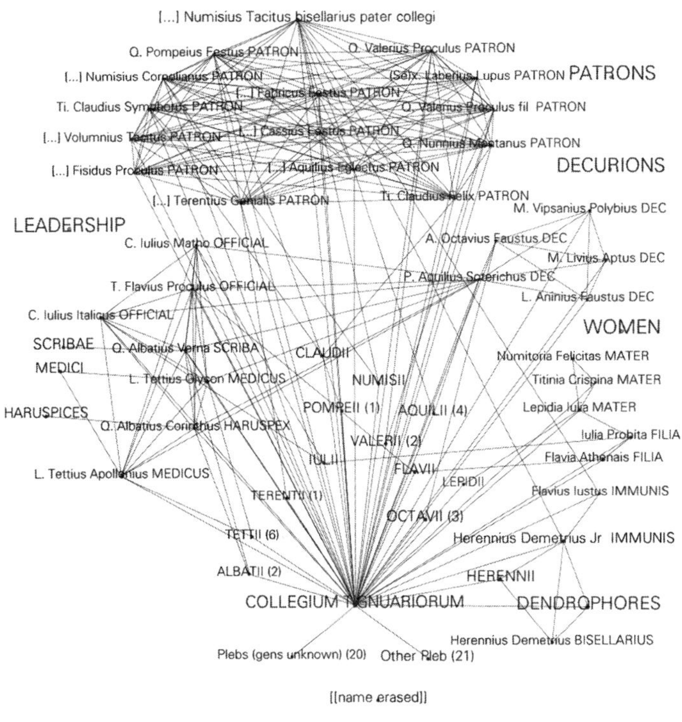

Figure 8. Network visualization of the builder-carpenters (*fabri tignuarii*) of Luna (CIL 11.1355a,b). A name followed by a number in parentheses, e.g., "ALBATII (2)," indicates that two members of the Albatii *gens* were *plebs* in the guild.

provides a network visualization of the guild that underscores the multiple ways in which members were connected.[24]

Again, it is impossible to ascertain the economic level of any member, but that is hardly the primary determinant of status. Visually the two plaques present the guild with its impressive numbers (seventy-five, excluding the patrons), its connections to the town, its internal hierarchies, and its connection to another local guild. The emergent properties of the network undoubtedly included the prestige of being connected to a guild with a large number of municipal patrons and with network connections to the *dendrophors*. Since both the *immunes* and *matres* were likely benefactors of the guild, the guild itself evidently had sufficient social capital to attract both patrons and other donors, which in turn was conveyed to members of the network.

THE "FAMILY OF SILVANUS"

Evidence of a cultic association and one not nearly as wealthy or well connected as the boatmen and registrars was found in a grove near the town of Trebula Mutuesca, near the modern commune of Monteleone Sabino sixty kilometers northeast of Rome. An inscription, probably part of a statue base, was discovered bearing the bylaws (*lex*) of a cult association and its membership roster (fig. 9).[25] The inscription, whose final panel was cut in 60 CE, records the bylaws of a group that styled itself the "family of Silvanus" (*familia Silvani*) and that honored Silvanus, the god of the woodlands.[26] The *album* has seventy-eight names, cut in several stages, with eight names erased (though still partially visible).

Three people named in the group seem to have been especially prominent. The first, Marcus Valerius Dexter, was a freeborn Roman citizen who paid for the statue of Silvanus and supplied one meal for the group consisting of cakes and honied wine. The Valerii were a very large and distinguished family associated with the Sabine area northeast of Rome, but little is known of M. Valerius Dexter. He was not of senatorial or even equestrian rank.[27] Some commentators suppose that he was a president (*magister*) of the group, though the inscription does not indicate this. His name appears only on the top frame of the inscription but not in the membership roster itself (as M. Cornelius Secundus's name did in CIL 14.250). This might suggest that he was also an "external patron," that is, a moderately wealthy commoner who offered benefactions to the group but was not expected to participate actively. The inscription declares Dexter to be an *immunes*, exempt from paying dues, but this does not tell us whether he was a member or not, since it was common (and of course prudent) to declare

Figure 9. Album and bylaws of the *familia Silvani* (AE 1929, 161; 60 CE). Rome, Museo Nazionale Romano, Terme di Diocleziano inv. 108765/108768. (Photo by the author.)

generous patrons as dues-exempt, in case they occasionally attended a meeting. Irrespective of whether he was a functioning member, the *familia* nevertheless reciprocated his generosity by mentioning him prominently it its bylaws.

The second notable member, Marcus Valerius Phoebus, bears a cognomen typically associated with slaves and was likely a freedman of M. Valerius Dexter. He served as the treasurer (*quaestor*) of the group and was responsible for preparing the membership roster. Marcus Valerius Firmus, another relative of M. Valerius Dexter and member of the association, paid for the cutting of the final part of the inscription and its erection in the grove.

The cult of Silvanus is known from many other inscriptions and seems to have appealed especially to slaves and freedmen.[28] Silvanus never belonged to the official pantheon honored by the elite of Rome but was typically associated with those connected with agriculture and the forests.[29] The occupations of members are not mentioned in the inscription, but given the connection with Silvanus and the location of the inscription (in a grove), it is possible that the guild was involved in some kind of agricultural pursuit, forestry, or the sale of wood. As far as the bylaws is concerned, however, the main activities of this group were the conduct of periodic sacred rites and meals, probably in the grove, and the provision of burial for deceased members.

The membership list, created in several stages, provides an important glimpse of the profile of the group: of the seventy-eight members, twenty-five were free-born citizens identified not only by the *tria nomina*, but also by their Roman tribal affiliation. All of the remaining fifty-three members were citizens bearing the *tria nomina*, but at least nineteen have Greek cognomens, usually a sign of servile origins.[30] The other thirty-two with Latin cognomens are probably also former slaves or the children of former slaves.

Like the roster of the boatmen and registrars, the *album* of the *familia Silvani* shows that almost half of the named members belong to one of nine family groupings. The largest of these was the Valerii (eight members) and was clearly the dominant family, contributing the patron and two others Valerii in influential positions. This again illustrates the fact that connectivity was one of the building blocks of associative life, even in a cult association. Associations enhanced connectivity by connecting people of different family groups.

The roster does not identify by name any officers except the treasurer, M. Valerius Phoebus. The bylaws attached to the membership roster, however, indicate that the group elected a president (*magister*) (probably yearly) to conduct sacred rites for the god. Several subleaders called *decumani* (leaders of a tenth part) headed smaller subdivisions of the group and were responsible for maintaining the membership lists of each of the divisions and erasing the names of those who withdrew or were expelled from the group (eight names were erased after the inscription had been cut). The group had a treasury assembled from member contributions, from which the sacred rites were funded. The president was expected to make extra contributions on these occasions. In the event of the death of a member, each was required to contribute 8 sesterces (2 denarii) toward his funeral so that no monies would have to be used from the treasury. The *familia* also insisted that these contributions occur in a timely fashion (within three days), and it required full participation in the member's funeral. Those who failed to attend were fined.

The association was not a secret society. The inscription was cut after the *lex Iulia de collegiis* of 21 BCE and a series of other measures supposedly designed to limit or outlaw associations.[31] Yet there seems to be no anxiety about the legitimacy of the group. The members of this *familia* provided their full legal names, effectively advertising that they were all Roman citizens. While some associations would cite a portion of the *senatus consultum de collegiis*, evidently to signal ostensible compliance with the law restricting the existence of associations,[32] the *familia Silvani* did not even bother to do this. Perhaps because this collegium was not located in Rome or because its members were engaged in trades that were beneficial to the Roman economy or for some other reason, they appear to have been untroubled by concerns about legitimacy.[33]

In sum, the *familia Silvani* was an association consisting largely of "middling" individuals and was patronized not by someone of curial rank but by a commoner. Dexter's patronage was quite modest: he supplied the cult statue and paid for a single meal of simple fare. That was enough to earn him recognition. The members were certainly not wealthy or of noble birth; they may have been connected by a common trade, but they were also connected by both familial and tribal connections, certainly by a common cult, and by the fiction of belonging to the god's *familia*. They collected funds to provide for their own funerals and for the performance of sacred rites and probably for common meals.

As commoners and former slaves, they were unable to aspire to the higher rungs on the Roman ladder of status, but within the association individuals could participate in sacred rites and banquets and periodically serve as one of the subleaders and perhaps even as a yearly president. The emergent properties of the network are, accordingly, connectivity and hierarchy, but a hierarchy in which all members theoretically could participate. Service to the deity was also an emergent property, along with the confidence that upon death, members could rely on the *familia* to provide them with an honorable burial, attended by the full membership of the group (fig. 10).

DEVOTEES OF ATARGATIS FROM ATTICA

A white marble stele dating from after 135 BCE was discovered in a private house just to the northwest of the center of Athens (IG II^2 2358, fig. 11). Unlike the inscription of the *familia Silvani*, this inscription does not contain the bylaws of the cult association, but it does provide a list of members, cut in several stages.[34] Neither the name of the association nor the name of the deity is preserved, but for reasons that will become clear, it was probably an association devoted to the Syrian goddess Atargatis, brought to Athens by Syrian immigrants from Antioch and ultimately Hierapolis. Apart from the identification of the second and third individuals as *archeranistēs* (president) and priest, respectively, no title holders are named. The mention of a priest suggests that this is the roster of a cult association.

Centered and at the head of the inscription is one name, although badly damaged. Eirēnē daughter of Eirēnaios of Antioch had the stele set up.[35] Next come the association president, Eirēnaios of Antioch, probably a relative of

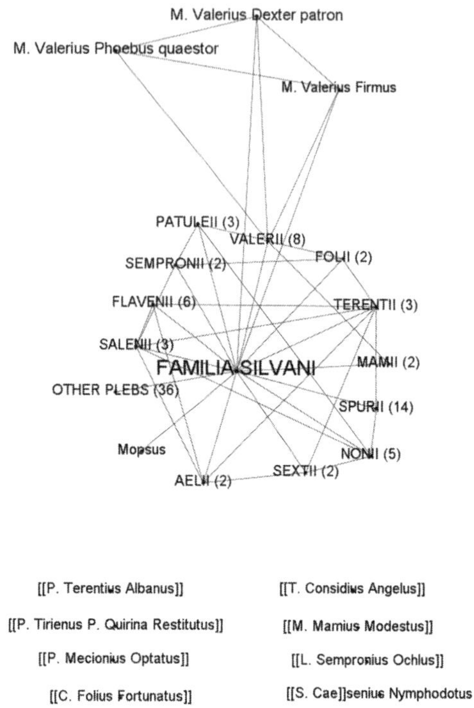

Figure 10. Network visualization of the *familia Silvani* (AE 1929, 161). A name followed by a number in parentheses, e.g., "VALERII (8)," indicates that eight members of the Valerii *gens* were *plebs* in the guild. ⟦. . . .⟧ are erasures.

Eirēnē; and Eirēnaios the younger was the priest, perhaps a son or another relative of Eirēnē. The fact that Eirēnē and Eirēnaios are of Antiochene origin suggests that the deity was Syrian, probably Atargatis, who had arrived in Athens via Delos.[36]

The list reveals an association that was mixed in terms of ethnicity, legal status, and gender, a development in Athenian associations in the second century BCE.[37] Eirēnē and Eirēnaios were from Antioch, and several other members have names that are unusual among Athenians but common elsewhere, including at least three from Thrace.[38] This likely means that they were *metics* (noncitizens, resident in Athens) or slaves from elsewhere. Many of the names are those typically borne by slaves—for example, Bithys, Parnassos, Onēsimos, Strymon, Daos, Eutychis, Arsakes, Botrys, Sardion, Erotis, Persis, Doris, Musta,

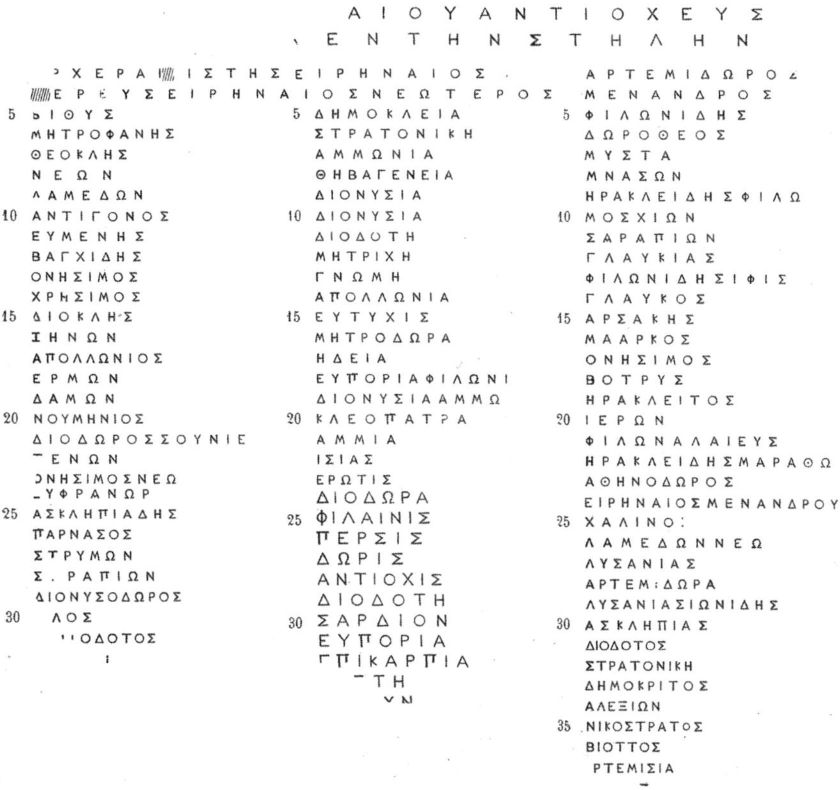

Figure 11. Album of the cult of Atargatis (IG II² 2358).
From a facsimile by Adolf Wilhelm, 1896.

Chrēsimos, and Noumēnios.[39] There are at least two father-son combinations, the son being designated as NN "the younger." Since both the father and son in one of these combinations are named Onēsimos (a common slave name),[40] we might conclude that the elder Onēsimos had been emancipated and accordingly his son could legally acknowledge his father (rather than his owner).[41]

Column 1 has twenty-seven male names, including one Athenian citizen; column 2 has thirty female names; and the final column has thirty-five names, including three citizens and three women. There is no indication of how the men and women were related, whether as husbands and wives, fathers and daughters, or slaves and emancipated slaves belonging to a large family group.

Although the inscription now has three columns, the first stage of the *album* had only fifty-seven names (fifty of which are legible), divided between men (column 1) and women (column 2). Successive cutters added two women (stage 2—note the larger letters in column 2, lines 24–25), then four more (stage 3, lines 26–29), then at least five more women (lines 30–34), completing column 2, and thirteen men (column 3, phase 4, lines 1–15), then six additional men (stage 5, lines 16–21), and finally seventeen names, nine men and eight women (stage 6).[42] Like the *alba* discussed earlier, IG II^2 2358 provides a kind of moving picture of the history of the cultic association as it recruited new members (none is stricken from the list).

An Athenian citizen, Diodoros of Sounion, belonged to the first stage of the list, and three more citizens would be included in its later expansions. At the time that the inscription was cut, Diodoros does not seem to have been especially prominent in the group; his name appears more than halfway down the first column and after the names of several slaves. Other data suggest that he might have become more prominent, and his name provides a clue to the identity of the deity that was reverenced. To judge from the accomplishments of Diodoros's son Theodotos, whom we know from other inscriptions, Diodoros was likely also a person of some wealth and influence.[43] Theodotos became the priest of Atargatis on Delos in 113/112 BCE.[44] In fact, it was sometime between the time IG II^2 2358 was cut and 113/112 BCE that Athenians, who controlled Delos, took over the cult of Atargatis from the Syrians, identified the deity as Aphroditē Hagnē (Aphroditē the Pure), and took responsibility for the yearly appointment of priests.[45] Thus it seems reasonable to suppose that IG II^2 2358 also comes from the cult of Atargatis while Syrians were still in control of the cult in Athens.

The cult of Atargatis, which was based in Hierapolis in Syria, was an exotic and cosmopolitan cult, requiring temporary abstinence from fish, pork, sexual intercourse, and contact with blood but promising health and well-being to its devotees.[46] It attracted people from numerous legal and social status categories—freeborn, emancipated slaves, and slaves, both men and women, and Athenians and immigrants.[47] At the time that IG II^2 2358 was cut, the association was led by Antiochene immigrants, probably well-to-do.

The inscription does not indicate the relationships among the devotees of Atargatis, but since the patron, president, and priest are Antiochene in origin and at least some of the other members are from the East, it is reasonable to suppose that the core of the association consisted of immigrants from Syria who came with their slaves and dependents. Yet the fact that many of the slave names are typically Greek—for example, Onēsimos, Chrēsimos, Noumēnios, Erōtis, and Doris—and others are Thracian means that some may have been the slaves of Greek owners too (or given Greek names by their owners). The connectivity

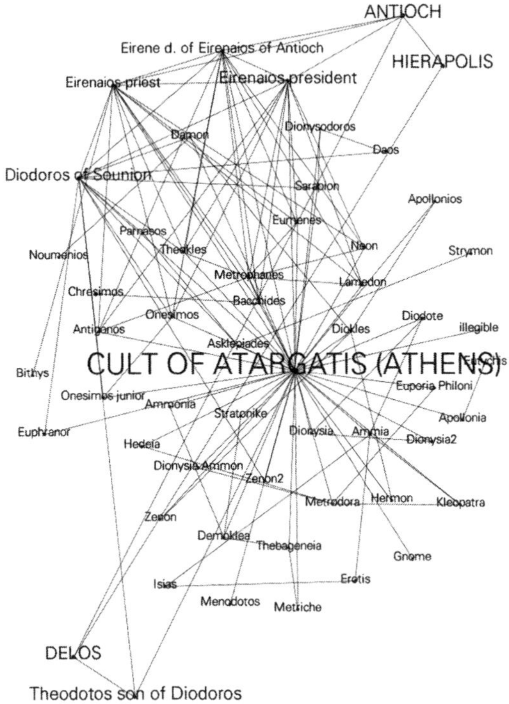

Figure 12. Network visualization of the devotees of Atargatis (IG II² 2358).

characteristic of this cult association rested not only on the networks that existed within a well-to-do Syrian family of *metics*, but also on at least one prominent Athenian family that would later become much more involved in the devotees of Atargatis. Figure 12 offers a hypothetical visualization of the cultic network that notes not only the internal connections of the Athenian cult, but also the external connections to Hierapolis, Antioch, and Delos.[48]

As I note shortly, one of the noteworthy aspects of the cult of Atargatis was its discourse that the god (rather than a human) had convened the association. The property of being the god's choice was a powerful factor, especially in a group that embraced multiple ethnicities and legal statuses. The presence in the group of Athenian demesmen, one whose son would become a priest of Atargatis on Delos, also created social capital for the members, who were now connected not only to Antioch via their priestess, but also to Delos via the son of one of their members.

THE DEVOTEES OF THEOS HYPSISTOS

From Beroia in Macedonia we have another list of names dated sometime before 212 CE. The stele I.Beroia 27 does not name the association or the deity, but the relief of an eagle surrounded by garlands identifies the group as devoted to Theos Hypsistos (highest god).[49] The stele has an inscribed wreath, with six names within the wreath and thirty names surrounding it. At thirty-six members, this group is almost exactly at the mean size of cultic groups. None of the individuals named is identified by a title, but the six people whose names appear within the wreath are either leaders or honorees. These include two bearing *tria nomina* (Q. Furius Valens and M. Opinius Onēsimos) and four handworkers: Akanthos the coppersmith, Bassos the goldsmith, and two stonemasons, Rufus and Metrodoros.

The other thirty names include eleven men identified by their trades (two nailsmiths, a dyer, a felt hat maker, a leather strap cutter, a *rhexos* [breaker?], a gardener, a goldsmith, a wrestler, a fuller, and a builder) and nine free men (identified by a patronym). One bears the name of a Roman family (Ulius Flavius), and four, probably slaves, are without patronyms or designations of trade. Five names are only partially preserved.

Although Q. Furius Valens is the first named within the wreath, the other Roman citizen, M. Opinius Onēsimos, is named only after a coppersmith and a goldsmith and before the two stonemasons. He bears a servile cognomen, indicating that he was a freedman or the descendant of a freedman, and he is not identified by a trade. Because the order of names is usually indexical to status, we are likely not wrong in supposing that Q. Furius Valens was either the patron of the group or its most prominent member, but that the coppersmith and goldsmith also had rank within the association and hence merited naming within the wreath, even before a Roman freedman.

The engraving of the stele is extremely crude, indicating that the group could not afford a finely cut monument from a professional shop. The names of I.Beroia 27 themselves suggest a mixed association, with at least one freedmen, a number of freeborn handworkers, some slaves, and two or perhaps three Roman citizens. Q. Furius Valens was likely the person of the highest status, although he is not known to be of senatorial or equestrian rank. His *gens* (clan) was an old republican Roman family, and during the imperial period several Furii of high rank served in administrative positions on Delos and in Moesia Inferior.[50] It is possible that Valens was a local magistrate in Beroia, or he may simply have been a moderately wealthy commoner who had some reason to be associated with the devotees of Theos Hypsistos, composed mainly of handworkers, perhaps because he was the owner of their shops.

Almost half of the members (fifteen) were tradesmen representing twelve different trades.[51] We might surmise that the two goldsmiths—one appearing within the wreath and the other in the list of members—were relatively well-to-do since they were associated with the production of luxury products. It is impossible to guess the income levels of the others, but it is inherently unlikely that they all occupied a relatively high economic bracket. What united them, however, was neither their trade nor their income level but their connection to a deity and to a patron evidently willing to support this cult group.

The cult of Theos Hypsistos is widely attested from the second century BCE to the fifth century CE in Athens, Sparta, Macedonia, the Thracian areas (Thracia, Dacia, and Moesia Inferior), the Bosphorus region, the Aegean islands, Crete, Asia Minor, Cyprus, Syria, Phoenicia, Palestine, Egypt, and even Italy and Spain.[52] While the epithet *hypsistos* (highest) is associated with a number of deities, it is especially common as Zeus Hypsistos and Theos Hypsistos. The epithet of course is also frequently associated with the Judean deity.[53] This means that in certain areas, for example in Lydia and Phrygia, where settlements of Judeans are known to have existed, dedications to Theos Hypsistos might be dedications by Judeans to their deity.[54] Without any other indication on the inscription—a menorah or lulav for example—it would be impossible to tell whether the dedication was to the Judean Theos Hypsistos or another deity with the same epithet. The cult of Theos Hypsistos was largely aniconic, and according to Mitchell, most dedications were "the humble offerings of humble people." Even those set up by people of higher status (Roman citizens) are rather unassuming—as this monument certainly is.[55]

We have, then, in I.Beroia 27 a cultic association largely composed of craft workers and slaves, probably of varying income levels. The association honored at least one person of higher status. We should not automatically assume that Q. Furius Valens was a member in the sense that he attended meetings and outings of a group of handworkers; he may well have been, but his presence on the stele may also be an indication that he was a patron of the group—that is, he provided resources, however modest. Perhaps he occasionally offered them a banquet. In that sense, like the patrons of the boatmen and registrars or the *familia Silvani*, he may have been an "external patron." But it is impossible to know for sure: he might also have been a devotee of the deity and a functioning member of the group.

Although we know nothing about the relative income levels of Q. Furius Valens or any of these handworkers, we should think instead about the network properties that membership conveyed to members. As an association of handworkers or slaves connected with workshops, the devotees of Theos Hypsistos

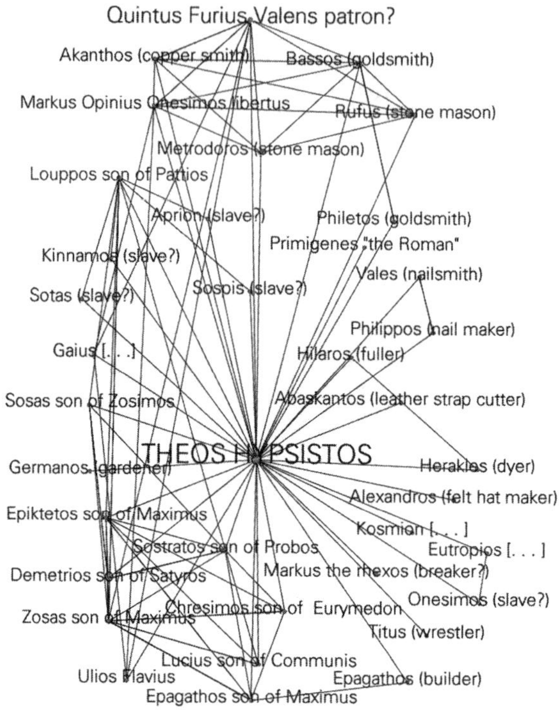

Figure 13. Network visualization of the devotees of Theos Hypsistos (I.Beroea 27).

could not boast the kind of prestige that the boatmen and registrars enjoyed. Yet they participated in honorific practices—the inscribing of the names of honorees within a wreath on their *album*—and benefited from whatever largesse Q. Furius Valens was able to offer. Membership in their association not only created bonds among members and perhaps laterally with the individuals of other occupational guilds related to the various trades represented in the club, by its members, but also connections to individuals of varying social standing. Figure 13 thus visualizes the network as connected via patronage to Q. Furius Valens and each of the craft workers related to other members of their craft as well as to the deity.[56]

A VILLAGE CLUB IN THE FAYÛM

A papyrus from the village of Philadelphia in the Fayûm in the second century BCE (SB 3:7182) offers an instance of a very differently complected association.[57] The papyrus contains the account of several meetings held by a village club, listing the attendance at each of the meetings, the dues collected, and the expenses for each banquet. The club probably consisted of only seven or eight members. Guests were present at some of the meetings, and one of those guests, Thibron, eventually became a member. A second guest failed to attend any more meetings. All of the members are identified by a single name (i.e., without a patronym). Since the members' names are a combination of nicknames that draw attention to physical or other characteristics—Kamax (vine-prop), Thribon (delicate)—or the names of Greek gods (Hermias, Bakchos), it is likely that all were slaves, although one of the two guests was not.[58] The monthly dues for each of the banquets were small, from the equivalent of 0.5 drachmae to 1.6 drachmae. Some of the larger sums may have included arrears from a previous meeting or fines levied for misconduct. The fee structure might also have allowed for a sliding scale of contributions, as was the case in other Egyptian groups.[59] The food that was served at each of the "banquets" was even more modest, with sometimes cheap unfermented grape juice and sometimes wine. This was an itinerant group: the association evidently did not own its own meeting place but met variously in a harness room, a storehouse, once in the dining rooms connected with a temple of Isis (an Iseion), and once in the room (or workshop) of one of its members.

The fact that the club met once in an Iseion does not necessarily mean that this was a cult association devoted to Isis, though it might have been. The most popular deity of the Fayûm was Sobek (or Souchos) the crocodile god, but Isis, Thoeris, and Anoubis are also well attested. One of the club's officers is called a banquet manager (*hieropoios*). This seems to be an instance of "title borrowing"—the appropriation of a title of an Athenian official who organized animal sacrifices. It is unlikely that this club engaged in animal sacrifice, for animal sacrifice played a very minor part in Egyptian cultic practices and this association surely did not have the funds to afford animals to sacrifice.[60] More likely, the group's titles for officers—*hieropoios* and *epimelētēs* (supervisor)—were imitations of Athenian and Macedonian associations that routinely used these titles.[61]

Since the association kept careful records of income, expenditures, and who was present at each banquet, we know that the membership was stable at about seven, almost all of whom attended each meeting. A supervisor or banquet manager was selected to preside at each of the meetings. There are, however, no indications of patrons or well-born individuals, either as members of the group or as external patrons to donate a cult statue or to supply a meal or otherwise to support the group. The dues paid by the members funded the meals that they ate and probably the rental of the meetings spaces that they were able to use.

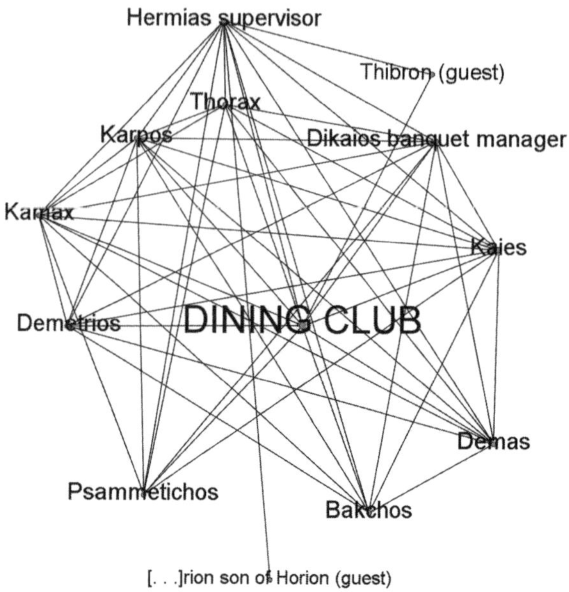

Figure 14. Network visualization of a village dining club (SB 3:7182).

This group met at least monthly. As far as we know the club was not connected to village elite, and its modest meals and itinerant meal practices suggest a relatively poor membership, but connectivity is underscored by the stability of meal attendance. Since the account covers six meetings with attendance records for each, it is easy to see that the supervisor Hermias attended all six meetings, three other members attended five of the six meetings, and three more attended four meetings. The group must have had some attractive features, since in at least one instance they were successful at recruiting a guest to become a regular member. Figure 14 offers a hypothetical visualization of the network of the group.[62]

COMPARING CHRIST ASSEMBLIES AND PRIVATE ASSOCIATIONS

Comparing Christ assemblies with associations, about which we know quite a lot, helps to create imaginative possibilities to get us beyond the various impasses and dead ends that have plagued the interpretation of Christ assemblies.

Even a cursory look at the six associations discussed above makes clear that the size and internal structure of associations varied greatly. Not only are there variations among occupational guilds like the boatmen and registrars of Ostia and the builder-carpenters of Luna and cultic associations like the *familia Silvani,* the devotees of Atargatis in Athens, and the devotees of Theos Hypsistos in Macedonia; there are also significant variations *within* each type of association. Insofar as membership rosters offer a kind of group portrait, the size and organizational complexity decrease dramatically from the boatmen and registrars to the village club, from more than one hundred members related to the city (and to other cities) and to each other in complex ways, to only seven or eight members with a very simple internal structure. Likewise, the degree of connectivity to civic elite varies widely: the boatmen and registrars were extraordinarily well connected, and the builder-carpenters of Luna and the devotees of Atargatis probably had connections to local people with some wealth and influence; but the *familia Silvani* and the devotees of Theos Hypsistos were at best connected to well-to-do commoners, and the village club had no patrons on the horizon.

Some groups are relatively homogeneous in membership. The boatmen and registrars were mostly males engaged in a cluster of occupations related to the transportation of goods through Ostia, and the majority were freedmen and their descendants. The builder-carpenters of Luna were also associated with building trades but included physicians, a diviner, a scribe, and several "mothers" and "daughters." The village club evidently consisted exclusively of slaves, even if a freeborn person attended one of their dinners. In other instances, however, the membership embraced multiple legal and status categories—freeborn, freedmen and freedwomen, slaves, citizens, and foreign residents. Some associations seem to have been gender-exclusive, whereas others incorporated women, both as officers and as ordinary members (the devotees of Atargatis) or as a special category of "mothers" and "daughters" (the builder-carpenters of Luna).

We do not have membership rosters for Christ assemblies that would permit the analysis provided above for these six associations.[63] No names at all are mentioned in Galatians, and the letter to Philemon is so sparse on details of the assembly that little can be surmised apart from the fact that it is connected with Philemon's household; but some inferences about the Christ assemblies at Philippi, Corinth, and Thessaloniki can be drawn. It is an error, however, to suppose that all Christ assemblies in Paul's day exhibited a single and consistent demographic complexion and the same degree of connectivity to a town.

THE PHILIPPIAN CHRIST ASSEMBLY

Philippians names only four people: Epaphroditus, sent by the Philippian assembly to assist Paul; two women (Syntychē and Euodia); and one other man (Clement). Epaphroditus ("lovely") is a very common Greek slave name, which accounts for the large number of Roman freedmen with this as a cognomen. We cannot rule out the possibility that Epaphroditus was freeborn, but since the name is overwhelmingly servile, it is rather likely that he was a slave or a freed slave.[64] That would certainly not be surprising in the Roman colony of Philippi.

The other three names are borne by both freeborn and slaves, and hence the legal status of these individuals cannot be determined, although Syntychē is very likely servile in origin.[65] Paul describes all three as having "struggled" with him "in the gospel," which interpreters plausibly take to mean that they were in positions of some authority in the group.[66] Acts also highlights the role of Lydia,[67] a merchant of luxury items dyed in purple (*porphyropōlis*), who hosted Paul in her house (16:14–15, 40).[68] Whether this is a reliable historical detail or an expression of Luke's tendency to associate Paul with people of influence cannot be determined with any certainty; but it does agree with other data from Philippians to the extent that women are represented as influential in the group and, as I argue, that the assembly had commercial interests.[69]

Julien Ogereau has made a strong case that the commercial language in Philippians ought not be interpreted metaphorically but on the contrary suggests that Paul and the Philippians were involved in some kind of commercial venture.[70] In particular, Ogereau points out that several terms and phrases belong to the technical vocabulary of commercial relationships: "partnership in the gospel" (*koinōnia eis tēn euaggelion*, 1:5); "my partners" (*synkoinōnoi mou*, 1:7); Paul's statement in 4:15 that no assembly of Christ followers had partnered with him "for an account of expenditures and receipts" (*eis logon doseōs kai lēmpseōs*); and *apechō*, meaning "receive what is due" (4:18).[71] As Phil 1:5 makes clear, this relationship was not merely between Paul and one member of the assembly such as Lydia, as Fleury has supposed,[72] but with the entire Philippian assembly. The assembly had supported Paul financially at several points (4:15–18) and in a detail that had puzzled commentators; Paul evidently considered their support not to be a matter of a gift but one of the fulfillment of a financial agreement (4:18): "In pragmatic terms, Paul's language creates the strong impression that an actual business transaction has taken place: he has received all of that which was intended for him (by virtue of some obligation) (*apechō panta*), for he has been paid in full (*peplērōmai*). Epaphroditus has dutifully performed his *leitourgia* by delivering the supplies."[73]

Incidentally, Ogereau's thesis implies that the Philippian assembly as a whole was not composed of people at the bare subsistence level. But for our purposes it also suggests that the *ekklēsia* at Philippi was a group engaged in some kind of commercial venture that included Paul as a partner. Its membership extended to both women and men, and at least some were freedmen or freedwomen, probably investing their slave property (*peculium*).

The builder-carpenters of Luna also present the picture of a group engaged in a commercial activity with a gender-mixed membership and with women in some positions of influence. Like the Philippian assembly, the builder-carpenters included freeborn and freed individuals. CIL 11.1355 does not indicate which deities might have been part of the guild's cultic regime, but their lateral connection to the *dendrophors* suggests that the cult of Silvanus and Cybele were likely part of their repertoire.

I am not suggesting, of course, that the two groups were comparable in all respects. As I insisted in the Introduction, productive comparison is usually a *limited* comparison. The builder-carpenters were a large association, had several civic *patroni*, and had a highly differentiated governance structure, with a "father," "mothers," a *bisellarius*, several decurions, and members who had been declared *immunes*. The Philippian assembly, devoted to an obscure Eastern hero, had only supervisors (*episkopoi*) and assistants (*diakonoi*) and probably lacked the kind of elite civic connections that the builder-carpenters enjoyed. In this latter respect, the Pauline Christ assembly resembled another Philippian association, a second-century group of devotees of Silvanus.[74] This group of *cultores*, with seventy male members, freedmen and freeborn (CIL 3.633.b), contributed to the building of a shrine and a bronze cult statue of Silvanus; however, there is no indication of any connection with civic elite.[75]

The fact that Paul does not address any of the supervisors or assistants by name is seldom remarked upon by commentators but finds an explanation in associative practices. Many—even most—groups elected leaders yearly, or in the case of the *lenuncularii* and other Italian guilds, for terms of three to five years. This explains why in the case of the boatmen and registrars that blank space is left in the album of 193 CE (see fig. 4) to accommodate the names of new *quinquennales* who would be elected in the future, and why in the case of the album of the builder-carpenters of Luna Tacitus's name is tucked into the first column after the other names had been inscribed: he had been elected or appointed as *pater* and *bisellarius* only after the inscription was first cut. The engraver also left space in the second column, knowing that in the future new decurions would be added as previous decurions cycled out of their office. The same electoral practice is attested in the *cultores* of Silvanus at Philippi, since three of the four panels, each inscribed at a different time, name three *different* priests of the association. If the Philippians engaged in the same practice of rotating leadership, Paul might not know at the point of writing who in the Philippian assembly were *episkopoi* and *diakonoi* and so could not address them by name.[76] He did know, however, that Syntychē, Euodia, and Clement were influential figures.

To judge from the contents of Philippians and what Paul appears to assume to be the values shared with the Philippians, we might conclude that the properties that emerge in the network included the cultivation of high moral values (truthfulness, piety, honesty, purity, reputation, praiseworthiness; 4:4) conceived as a quasi-athletic contest for moral excellence and leading to a "prize" (3:14). Paul's praise of the Philippians for their willingness to share (2:17–18, 4:14–15) probably also indicates that the group cultivated an ethos of resource sharing and mutual support.

THE CORINTHIAN CHRIST ASSEMBLY

The Christ assembly at Corinth, about which slightly more is known, is also more complex. Paul's advice to the married and unmarried (1 Cor 7:1–17), his comments on women's activities in the assembly (1 Cor 11:2–16), and the fragmentary list of members of the assembly in Romans (16:1–2, 17–23) all indicate that the Corinthian assembly included both men and women. Paul also names Phoebe, described both as an assistant (*diakonos*) of the Christ assembly in the adjacent town of Cenchreae and as his patron (*prostatis*) and the patron of many others.

Of the seventeen named individuals who appear to have had some connection with the Corinthian Christ assembly, Fortunatus (1 Cor 16:17) was almost certainly a slave or a freedman, and Tertius (Rom 16:22) was likely also of servile origins.[77] Since the situation of slave-members is addressed in 1 Cor 7:21–24, it seems certain that the assembly included at least some slaves and probably freedmen and freedwomen as well.[78] Prisca and Aquila are said in Acts to be curtain or awning makers (*skēnopoioi*) and according to Acts belonged to the same craft as Paul (*homotechnon*, 18:3);[79] there may have been other handworkers too. At the time of the writing of 1 Corinthians Stephanas's household seems to have been the most prominent family in the assembly, since Paul assigns to Stephanas precedence as the first Achaian adherent and recommends that all "submit" to his family (1 Cor 16:15–16). This of course does not tell us much about Stephanas's relative economic standing, but it does imply a high social standing *within* the group.

Did the assembly include Judeans? If Acts is to be credited, an assembly president (*archisynagogos*) named Crispus "believed" along with his entire household and was baptized (Acts 18:8). In that case Crispus would be both

Judean in origin and a person of high social standing and some wealth, since synagogue presidents were usually expected to underwrite some of the costs of synagogue maintenance.[80] Yet Paul's mention of Crispus in 1 Cor 1:14 gives no hint of either his role in a Judean assembly or even that he was Judean.[81]

Despite the puzzles created by Acts, it seems highly likely that the Corinthian assembly was ethnically mixed. First Corinthians 12:2 seems to suggest that all were pagans (*ethnē*), but 1 Cor 10:32 and 12:13 indicate that both Judeans and pagans were part of the Christ assembly. Moreover, in both Corinthian letters Paul routinely cites the Septuagint as proof-texts, which implies that at least part of his addressees were Judean and expected to understand references to Moses and key events in Israelite history.

Not all the group were Judeans, however. First Corinthians 8:7 indicates that some members formerly participated in festivals where animals sacrificed to pagan deities were consumed, and the scenario implied in 1 Cor 10:27 is that of a member of the Christ assembly being invited to a meal at which meat from a temple is offered, which probably means that the member in question is a Greek and not a Judean.

The Corinthian assembly does not seem to have included people of especially high social standing. Although Erastos (Latinized as Erastus) and Gaius are sometimes proposed as being of high status, it is unlikely that either was of the curial class. Paul names both of them far down the list of those sending greetings in Roman 16, which would be very unusual had either been a major benefactor or patron (see further, chapter 6).

The mention of Gaius presents other puzzles. Many commentators treat him as the "host" and patron of the Christ assembly; however, it is now clear from Richard Last's work that this translation of *xenos* is incorrect.[82] As Last has shown, *xenos* in the rest of the New Testament, in first-century documentary papyri, and in other sources normally means "guest" or "stranger," not "host."[83] Accordingly, when Paul is listing those who are sending greetings to the assembly/assemblies in Rome, Rom 16:23 must be rendered "Gaius, my guest (*xenos*) and (the guest) of the entire *ekklēsia* sends greetings." If Gaius is a guest of the Corinthian group, there is no reason to suppose that he was the grand patron of the Corinthian assembly or a person of any special wealth.

Adding to the puzzle is the fact that oddly, Gaius is identified by his praenomen rather than a distinctive cognomen, the more common way to refer to people with Roman names. Paul's greeting is rather like me in Toronto telling a correspondent in London (which I have not yet visited), "Philip sends his greetings." Clearly, my correspondent in London would have to know which of the many Philips in Toronto I had in mind. If Philip were a native

Torontonian and if I had never visited London and if this were my first letter to my friend in London, how could she possibly know this Philip? And why would it be meaningful to say that Philip says hello? In Latin this problem is exacerbated: whereas English has hundreds of given names for males, only seventeen were common for Romans, and one in five men had Gaius as a praenomen. Tens of thousands of men in Rome had Gaius as a praenomen, and thousands of Corinthian males were named Gaius.[84] If Gaius were a native Corinthian, there is no reason to suppose that anyone in Rome would know who Gaius was or which of the thousands of Corinthian Gaii was sending his greetings.[85] Romans 16:23 makes sense only if Gaius was a member of the *Roman* Christ group who had recently come to Corinth. In effect, Rom 16:23 means, "*Your* Gaius, who is my guest and the entire assembly's guest, sends his greetings." In that case, however, there is no reason for thinking that he was a person of especially high social standing; he simply may have been a merchant who traveled to Corinth on business or a handworker who came to Corinth for work.[86]

The Corinthian Christ assembly, then, included both genders and people of a variety of legal statuses, such as slaves, perhaps freedmen and freedwomen, and freeborn. Greeks—perhaps even a few citizens of Corinth—and resident aliens of Judean origin were members. It boasted at least one member who was connected to the civic administration, Erastos the city manager, and had at least one patron, Phoebe of Cenchreae. If we were to visualize this group's network, it might look similar to that of the devotees of Atargatis (see fig. 12), which was also mixed in gender, legal status, and citizenship and had at least one connection to an Athenian demesman whose son would become influential in the Atargatis cult on Delos.

What might be learned from placing the Corinthian Christ assembly beside the devotees of Atargatis? Both were devoted to an Eastern deity or hero; they had similar membership profiles; and as foreign cults in a Greek city they may have faced analogous challenges.

It is in cultic groups that we expect to find the greatest degree of gender, ethnic, and status inclusivity, and this is certainly true of both the Corinthian Christ assembly and the Atargatis devotees.[87] The cult of Atargatis had been imported from Syria to Athens probably via Delos in the second century BCE and evidently appealed to a wider swath of Greek society than some of the older cultic associations. Its language was distinctive in at least one important respect. The founding of most associations in Achaia was usually presented as the initiative of an individual: "NN convened (*synagō*) the association in honor of the god."[88] By contrast, the founding of associations devoted to Atargatis was the *deity's initiative*, and its members were called "the *thiasōtai* whom [the goddess] gathered (*synēgage*)."[89]

The idea that the deity took the initiative in the formation of the group is also part of a number of other foundation documents of associations, often related to the deity giving instruction in a dream that a group be founded.[90] This way of depicting the origin of the group, sometimes coupled with the idea that the god invites participants to the banquet, was especially useful in the case of groups that cut across most of the dividing lines of ancient society: ethnicity, legal status, and gender. The public organizations in Athens were typically the preserve of male citizens and hence excluded women, resident aliens, and slaves. A group that embraced foreigners and citizens, men and women, slaves, and freed and freeborn individuals could well be regarded as deviant or dangerous.[91] Representing the founding of the group as the deity's initiative served as a useful rhetorical strategy to diminish suspicions that might otherwise attach to such a mixed group.

Paul adopted a similar strategy. Although he used the verb *synagō* only once (1 Cor 5:4), he relied heavily on the notion that God has "called" adherents of the Christ cult—using *kaleō* and its cognates. Members are in fact referred to as "the called" (*hoi klētoi;* 1 Cor 1:2, 24). This motif appears elsewhere in Paul's letters,[92] but it appears with special density in 1 Corinthians, where the critical issues of the letter include the reconciliation of tensions within the group created by status and ethnic differences.[93] Of course, the idea of divine calling is not Paul's invention; it is found commonly in the Septuagint with God's call of Israel, the prophets, and others. The point here is that Paul mobilizes the idea of divine calling precisely to account for the fact that Judeans and Greeks, women and men, slaves and free belong to the Corinthian assembly. Moreover, he calls the communal meal *to kyriakon deipnon*, "the emperor's banquet," as though it were Christ's banquet (1 Cor 11:20).[94] There is of course no direct relationship between the cult of Atargatis and the Christ cult, nor are these the only two cults that depict the god as issuing an invitation to a dinner. The idea of deities or heroes gathering cultic groups around them, however, was a powerful metaphorical device to justify the existence of socially mixed groups that might otherwise be thought peculiar or even deviant.

Despite the connectivity that the discourse of divine gathering nurtured, ethnically mixed associations faced potential pressures, especially when their practices deviated significantly from the norms of their host cities. Some of the exotic practices of Eastern associations were remarked upon, but only as curiosities. The nighttime torch race staged by the Thracian devotees of Bendis in Athens attracted the attention of Athenians, including Socrates.[95] Such displays of exotic behavior are probably not unlike the colorful and lively Ratha Yatra processions in many North American cities when Hare Krishna devotees pull a large decorated cart with heavy ropes. They are fun to watch, but like Socrates, few onlookers are inclined to join the group on that account.

Other practices produced more tension. In Syria devotees of Atargatis were forbidden from eating fish, which they deemed to be sacred.[96] The cult of Atargatis in Smyrna forbade the injuring or killing of fish and invoked a curse upon anyone who did.[97] On Delos, however, surrounded as it was by the Aegean and for whose economy fishing was central,[98] the cult of Atargatis adjusted its regulations, requiring only three days' abstinence from the consumption of fish before entry into the temple. It is not difficult to recognize analogous adjustments in the Christ cult, in particular in settings such as Corinth. Not only was circumcision not practiced for new male members of the Christ assembly, but Paul's advice in 1 Corinthians 8–10 indicates that meat sacrificed to idols, which in Judea was sanctioned entirely, was no longer treated as something intrinsically defiling. It was instead problematic only to the extent that eating it would offend or "injure the consciousness" of a weaker member of the assembly.

THE THESSALONIAN CHRIST ASSEMBLY

Because Paul's letter to the Thessalonians names no members of the Thessalonian assembly at all, the onomastic observations that were possible in relation to the Philippian and Corinthian assemblies are impossible here. There are three clues, however, to the demography of the assembly.

First, Paul's statement that the Thessalonians "turned from idols to serve the living and true God" (1 Thess 1:9), coupled with the fact that Paul never cites the Jewish Scriptures as proof-texts, indicates that the Thessalonian assembly was gentile, not partly Judean as Acts 17 implies.

Second, Paul stresses his "labor and toil" and his work while he was in Thessaloniki (1 Thess 2:9) and reminds his addressees to "work with their hands" (4:11). Manual labor and those who made their living through handwork were generally poorly regarded, especially by the elite.[99] Yet Paul appeals to his own labor and that of his addressees to establish common ground. This is strikingly different from the way he invokes manual labor in 1 Corinthians, where he contrasts *his* work and toil with the wisdom, strength, and fine reputation (*endoxoi*) of the Corinthians. That is, in 1 Thessalonians Paul's appeal to manual labor is a way to connect with his addressees; in 1 Corinthians it is a way to underscore the differences in social standing. This rather strongly suggests that the Thessalonian assembly is composed of handworkers.[100]

Third, despite the standard gender-inclusive English renderings of *adelphoi* in 1 Thessalonians as "brothers and sisters," there are no indications of the presence of women in the Thessalonian assembly. Paul's advice in 1 Thess 4:4, "each of you must know how to control his own *skeuos* in purity and honor," uses a term that is best understood either to mean "vessel," that is, one's wife, or as a euphemism for the penis.[101] Again, the contrast with 1 Corinthians is striking. There Paul addresses widows (7:8) and women whose husbands are nonbelievers (7:10–11). In 1 Thessalonians Paul's androcentric language seems to imply that only men are present or at least that Paul thinks only in terms of the male members.

These three observations are consistent with the hypothesis that the assembly addressed is an association of handworkers, perhaps an association of curtain makers or leather cutters. Occupational guilds tended to be either all male or all female, but nothing like the gender-inclusive cultic association of Atargatis or the Corinthian Christ assembly. We need not suppose that all members of the assembly were curtain or awning makers, although that is possible. Equally possible is that the group resembled the all-male devotees of Theos Hypsistos, who were mainly handworkers—goldsmiths, leather cutters, and nailsmiths—united in the cult of Theos Hypsistos and perhaps their neighborhood location.

Paul's letter does not use any leadership titles such as "supervisor" (*episkopos*), nor does it identify anyone in a leadership position. Neither does I.Beroia 27 for that matter, although the design of the inscription suggests that the six men whose names are enclosed in the wreath were singled out for honor, probably by virtue of the leadership that they had shown or in the case of Q. Furius Valens perhaps because he was a patron. That the Thessalonian Christ assembly had some sort of governance is evident, even if Paul also fails to mention titles or refer to specific individuals. He does counsel the Thessalonians to "recognize (i.e., respect) those who preside (*proïstamenoi*) over you" (1 Thess 5:12), using a participle that is widely attested in the governance language of associations.[102]

In striking contrast to the data from 1 Thessalonians, Acts claims that the Christ assembly in Thessaloniki had attracted many of the "leading women" (or "wives of the first citizens," Acts 17:4). But Paul's several allusions to afflictions experienced by the assembly (1 Thess 1:6, 3:3–4) and his comment that his addressees "suffered from your own countrymen" (2:14) make this rather unlikely. It is true that such references are hardly transparent and probably do not refer to violent repression or physical violence. Whatever kind of "affliction" Paul has in mind, a group that had strong connections to the ruling elite of Thessaloniki or even a Roman citizen like Q. Furius Valens probably would have been protected from any such pressures. The Dionysiac group of Pompeia

Agrippinilla or the Iobakchoi of Athens, patronized by Herodes Atticus,[103] a senator and tutor of Marcus Aurelius, had little to fear, since they lived under the protective umbrella of local grandees and powerful patrons. Luke certainly would like his readers to believe that Paul and the Christ groups he founded were warmly regarded by Roman elite. Paul's description of the Thessalonian Christ group suggests, however, that women were not present at all, let alone elite women. And the group could not depend upon protection from local elite. Luke's representations likely reflected the civic relations in his day, probably in the early second century, when some Christ groups had attracted imperial freedmen with some degree of political influence.[104]

This brief survey of the data from three Pauline Christ assemblies has made three key points. First, as with other associations, there is considerable variation *within* Christ assemblies in terms of their membership profiles. The Corinthian group appears to have been the most diverse, including both Greeks and Judeans, men and women, and people of various legal statuses. The Philippian assembly, perhaps connected with a commercial venture in which Paul was involved, also embraced women and men, probably freedmen and freedwomen or slaves. The Thessalonian assembly, by contrast, seems more homogenous, including only men and probably only slaves, free handworkers, and perhaps some freedmen.

Second, the degree of connection to influential people in the city likely varied as well. By the time that Paul wrote Romans, the Corinthian Christ assembly included Erastos, a city manager. Yet the fact that Erastos is named in Romans 16, almost at the end of the list of those greeting the addressees of the letter, should caution us against assuming too quickly that he was a patron or prominent member of the assembly. Like Diodoros of Sounion, who belonged to the devotees of Atargatis but whose position on the membership list does not suggest special prominence, at least at the time that the list was first engraved, Erastos was not the most influential person in the assembly. Paul in fact thinks that Stephanas should be regarded as the most important at Corinth (1 Cor 16:15–16). The Christ assembly in the adjacent town of Cenchreae had a prominent woman as a patron, Phoebe. In the case of the two Macedonian assemblies in Philippi and Thessaloniki, it is more difficult to detect any important connections to people of influence within the city.

Third, although it is impossible to determine the economic standing of any individual named by Paul, it is a priori likely that, as with the urban population as a whole, the members represented a range of economic levels. Membership in an association or a Christ assembly did not obviate disparities among members in their income levels; but focusing on income levels obscures the real benefit that membership provided: the emergent properties of trust, social capital, striving for moral excellence, and in the case of the Thessalonian Christ assembly, the valorization of handwork.

SOCIAL CAPITAL: MEMBERS AND EXTERNAL PATRONS

The preceding discussion has focused on six Greek and Roman associations and three Christ assemblies, pointing out the differing complexions of these groups. It has also stressed that associations created connections for people beyond their families, in some instances people of vastly different social ranks, those of different occupations and ethnicities, and those of various legal statuses and genders. These connections are not trivial; they are what create social capital, and as I suggest in chapter 11, the social capital generated by connectivity was a primary factor in recruitment.

What is social capital? The term was popularized especially by Pierre Bourdieu, who distinguished social capital from other forms of symbolic capital[105]—economic capital and cultural capital, the latter referring to symbolic goods that can be acquired that afford advantages to those who possess them, such as having an education from a "good" university or having certain skills and manners of speech. According to Bourdieu, however, social capital always has to do with belonging to a network or group: "Social capital is the sum of the resources, actual or virtual, that accrue to an individual or group by virtue of possessing a durable network of more or less institutionalized relationships of mutual acquaintance and recognition."[106]

Social capital can also be thought of as "the advantage created by a person's location in a structure of relationships."[107] Social capital can involve access to information that would otherwise be unavailable; access to resources, prestige, and high standing in the eyes of others; and the availability of people whom one can trust and upon whom one can depend for assistance and opportunities for advancement and cooperative action.[108] Social capital was especially critical in a social environment that otherwise did not provide support for individuals facing the vagaries of death, disease, injury, dislocation, and marginal employment as well as the fear of oblivion.

Ancient associations (and Christ assemblies) generated social capital in several forms, each of which flowed from being connected.

EXTERNAL PATRONS

For the boatmen and registrars, membership in the guild afforded a connection with the cream of society and a social register to which individual freedmen could never aspire. Even if the connection was as ephemeral as a senator's name on the guild's *album*, the connection could be mobilized to the benefit of the group and its members. By himself, an individual boatman in Ostia could not claim attention from any member of the aristocracy; hundreds of *lenuncularii* with elite patrons were another story.[109]

Financial gain was not likely the reason for connections with the elite or wealthy commoners. In fact, in most cases the monetary value of benefactions seems to have been quite modest;[110] this was certainly the case with M. Valerius Dexter's benefaction—a cult statue and one meal—to the *familia Silvani*. The patrons of the boatmen and registrars and the builder-carpenters need not have provided much in the way of monetary benefits to individual members; even if they provided funds for the enlarging of a guild's temple, such benefaction did not directly improve the financial standing of individuals. The sheer fact of elite benefaction, however, conferred prestige that could be mobilized to attract new members, to advertise the status of the collegium within the city, and to cement the imaginary bonds of connectivity up the social ladder. A vertical connection to the elite conferred its own kind of benefit.

The patron, of course, got something out of the exchange too. As I have suggested, it is hardly coincidental that senators are listed first as the patrons of the boatmen and registrars since their connection to a large and critically important guild also allowed them to display themselves as instrumental in the feeding of Rome. Patrons might be honored at banquets specially arranged for them at which they would sit in the seats of honor and enjoy double portions of the wine and food; sometimes, a guild might erect a statue of its patron in the clubhouse, and as the inscriptions connected to the boatmen and registrars, the builder-carpenters, and the *familia Silvani* visually illustrate, patrons' names appear prominently on the cornice of the inscription or in large letters in the first column.

There was no doubt a pecking order in associations, at least from the standpoint of potential patrons. Those that were centrally involved in the grain supply and the transport of other foodstuffs offered the most social capital to potential patrons. Smaller associations, including most cultic associations, had less to offer highly ranked patrons, which accounts for Fellmeth's finding (see chapter 6) that in Italy (and probably elsewhere), cultic associations were much less likely to attract patrons of the senatorial or equestrian rank. Cultic associations, however, were also quite unlikely to be the recipients of endowments from the elite. Luke's suggestion in Acts 13:7–12 that a Roman senator, L. Sergius Paulus, was won over to the Christ cult as a result of Paul's activities on Cyprus is more likely a matter of Luke's wishful thinking in the second century than it is a historical reminiscence.

MEMBERS

Social capital was also generated internally by the complex mixture of obligations and ritualized behavior created by a group's charter.[111] Cooperative action by members means that *A* assists *B*, which creates an expectation in *A* for reciprocation and *B*'s obligation to do so. The stable social environment of strong networks means that the "credit slips" that cooperative actions produce will be repaid. Associations typically underscored the value of trust and cooperation by imposing such behavioral obligations on members as assisting other members in need, treating fellow members ethically, and ensuring that all members attended member funerals.

Associations observed various ritualized behaviors such as regular meals (normally governed by rules), periodic processions, and participation in the funerals of fellow members. Such practices are not epiphenomenal to associative life; they are in fact what constitute the group *as a network*, since they create multiple and complex ways in which members are joined to one another. It is just this complex form of connectivity that creates, in Bourdieu's words, "a durable network of more or less institutionalized relationships of mutual acquaintance and recognition."[112]

Christ devotees were not merely united in their devotion to a deity or hero, but also formed a complex web of social and ethical obligations to one another. They participated in ritualized behaviors—baptism, the "emperor's banquet," a kiss of peace—and shared linguistic conventions such as calling each other *adelphos/-ē*, (kin) and imagining themselves as parts of a body or a constituent assembly (*ekklēsia*) or some other collective identity. The high value placed on connectivity is also reflected in the high frequency of *syn-* compounds in Paul's language: Christ devotees as said to be co-buried (*synthaptō*), co-glorified (*syndoxazō*), co-struggled (*synagōnizomai*), co-labored (*synergeō*), co-died (*synapothnēskō*), and even co-crucified (*systrauroō*). Connectivity was a critical value, and accordingly, both ritualized actions and linguistic preferences that promoted a sense of belonging were common in Christ groups.[113] These all function as ways to create social capital.

The results (and benefits) of social capital did not go unnoticed by others. In the fourth century CE the Emperor Julian bemoaned the fact that "none of the Judeans beg and the impious Galileans (i.e., Christ followers) provide not only for themselves, but also for our people."[114] The strong bonds of trust created by the connectivity had tangible benefits for members and, as Julian saw matters, for others as well.

CONCLUSION

How then should we imagine Christ assemblies? Examination of the data from Philippians and especially 1 Corinthians suggests that Christ assemblies embraced people of a wide range of social standings as actual, functioning members. There is little likelihood that those of the curial ranks (*ordines*) had any interest in Christ assemblies, at least in their earliest phases. After all, even in the case of the large and highly organized occupational guilds such as the boatmen and registrars, it is unlikely that their senatorial patrons were members in the ordinary sense of that term. Instead, as we have seen, they were "external patrons." It was only in the early or mid-second century that wealthy freedmen and freedwomen would be enticed to join Christ assemblies, and by the late second and early third centuries, Christ assemblies could boast members of the curial ranks.

Second, as I have hinted throughout, it is inherently likely that Christ assemblies displayed a similar mixture of members who were better and worse off financially. It is fatuous, however, to attempt to sort out the income levels of individuals, either those named in associations' *alba* or those named in Christ assemblies. The data are simply not of the sort to support such a quest.

Third, variation in the size, structure, and complexion of private associations is the rule, just as it is in the case of the three Christ assemblies known from Paul's letters. We could plot the associations analyzed above with respect to at least five different scales:

1. Ethnic diversity versus ethnic uniformity
2. Gender diversity versus gender exclusivity
3. Diversity versus uniformity in the legal status and citizenship of members
4. Connectivity to civic elite
5. Lateral connections to other groups

The boatmen and registrars register high on the scale of connectivity to civic elite, uniform legal status (all were citizens and freedmen), and lateral connections but very low on gender and ethnic diversity. The builder-carpenters of Luna come out higher on the gender scale, but their civic connectivity is not as strong. They may have attracted local gentry but nothing more impressive than that. The Corinthian assembly and the devotees of Atargatis rank high in ethnic and gender diversity and had one or two members who were either citizens or engaged in civic government (Diodoros, Erastos). Paul's Philippian Christ assembly seems to have included various legal statuses and both men and women, but the group probably was not well connected to civic elite. The Thessalonian Christ assembly was probably low on both gender and ethnic diversity scales, and low on civic connectivity—even lower than the devotees of Theos Hypsistos.

Finally, despite diverse membership profiles, each of these groups functioned in the first place as a social space for connectivity and for the generation of social capital. They accomplished this by a variety of strategies, depending on the complexion of the group. For the boatmen and registrars, already connected by membership in several families, periodic banquets and participation in civic festivals made them visible as a group engaged in the critical business of feeding the city. The very naming of members on a plaque exhibited in public space alongside distinguished patrons was also a claim to social capital for both the boatmen and registrars and the builder-carpenters. The use of fictive family language is found in the builder-carpenters, the *familia Silvani*, and of course Christ assemblies. Groups with a high degree of ethnic, gender, and legal diversity such as the devotees of Atargatis and the Corinthian Christ assembly could claim to have been chosen by the god; but such claims are also found in the Thessalonian Christ assembly, who are said to be elected (1 Thess 1:4), "sons of the light" (5:5), and "destined for salvation" (5:9), and the devotees of Theos Hypsistos, whose members claimed to be "adopted brothers" of the god. The provision of funerals for members, the communal celebration of accomplishments, and the corporate commiseration in adversities likewise served as means to reinforce connectivity among members and to confer a sense of belonging and value.

Social capital is an "emergent" feature of social networks. This is a property that does not inhere in individuals but that "emerges" in network relationships. In some cases, associations, conceived of as social networks, encouraged the development of certain technical competences, for example, the skills associated with the transport and registration of cargos of grain. But more importantly, the kinds of interactions typical of associations—common meals, the ritualized acknowledgment of the accomplishments of one's peers, and solidarity with fellow members in life and death—generated trust. Just as the alumni of a prestigious university share in the prestige of that university, associations with elite patrons, or those who claimed special relationships with deities, communicated that prestige to members. Some associations were especially well-known to cultivate strong affective bonds and to communicate that social capital to all members. Social capital is thus the currency of ancient social relationships. Social standing is not indexical to income but is instead a function of the strength and character of connections to one's peers and, in some cases, to the civic elite and to the city.

3

Visualizing Christ Assemblies: Size and Space

Scholars of Christian origins have rarely addressed the membership practices of Christ assemblies in a systematic fashion, but it is precisely here that comparative analysis of Christ assemblies with Greco-Roman associations can be very useful, since much is known about the practices of the latter and this can help to set some parameters for our reconstructions. Comparison with the membership practices of associations puts into focus several features of rarely explored associative life, in particular the likely size of Christ assemblies and the venues that they used for their meetings. Others include the role of naming members in a society in which belonging and connectivity are so important, how members knew that they were members of a Christ assembly, and the premium that was attached to attendance by all members at every meeting. Most of these issues would not even have occurred to us were it not for comparisons with other face-to-face associations in the ancient world. Comparison helps both to make our thinking about Christ assemblies more concrete and to let us see new interpretive possibilities.

Why should we select cultic associations and occupational guilds as the *comparanda* for these questions? The answer is simple. For several cultic associations and occupational guilds, we have membership lists and hence know the group size. In other instances, archaeological remains of guildhalls, association banquet rooms, cemeteries, and Judean assemblies allow some guesses at the size of groups that used such spaces.[1] It would be valuable to have empirical data on the size and demography of other small groups in antiquity—for example, philosophical groups—but unfortunately no such data are available. Philosophical groups evidently did not keep membership lists, and although we know something about their meeting places, these venues seem hardly comparable to any likely meeting place for Christ assemblies.[2]

HOW LARGE WERE EARLY CHRIST ASSEMBLIES?

An important matter that has received only slight attention but where knowledge of ancient associations assists our reconstruction of early Christ assemblies has to do with size. Since many membership *alba* are extant, we do not have to guess at the size of these groups. We can draw quantitative conclusions about the typical ranges of membership numbers and hypothesize about factors affecting the size and complexion of various groups.

Estimating the size of Christ assemblies is beset with methodological problems. Acts offers some estimates of numbers, but those data are utterly unreliable. The other two approaches use data from Paul's letters to arrive at hypothetical group size or draw inferences about the size of Christ assemblies from the space available to them. As will become clear, however, neither of these approaches is very reliable either.

ESTIMATING NUMBERS

Acts routinely notes the numbers of people converted by the apostles and Paul. For example, Luke claims that at Peter's first preaching, three thousand were baptized and became Christ followers (Acts 2:41), and a few days later that number had increased to five thousand (4:4). This pattern repeats throughout Acts, which claims large numbers of converts. When Paul returned to Jerusalem, we are informed that there were already "many tens of thousands of believers" (21:20).[3]

These are palpable exaggerations. To take only the statements about Jerusalem, Luke's numbers in Acts 2–4 would imply that almost 10 percent of the population of, say, sixty thousand became Christ followers overnight. Acts 21:20 suggests that a large fraction of the population of Jerusalem were Christ followers by the 50s.[4] Curiously, we hear nothing more of these supposed tens of thousands: they simply vanish from narrative view. Luke's figures do not even tally with the probable demographic situation of the early second century when the numbers of Christ followers were high enough to be noticed by outsiders such as Pliny the Younger. But even for that time, numbers in the tens of thousands are too high.[5]

Only slightly less unreliable are estimates that are based on the number of people named in Paul's letters. In this approach, names are counted, and the numbers are then increased by a multiplier on the assumption that each named person stands for two or four or ten unnamed people. Murphy-O'Connor, for example, argues that each of the fourteen Corinthian males named in 1 Corinthians and Romans 16 was likely married (hence 14 × 2 = 28) and that the households of Crispus (Acts 18:8) and Stephanas (1 Cor 1:16, 16:15–16) also included children and slaves (thus, hypothetically, 2 × 10). A "realistic figure" for the Corinthian assembly, he suggests, might be around fifty people.[6] De Vos adds that in addition to Crispus and Stephanas bringing dependents with them, Erastos and Gaius could have brought as many as twelve to fifteen members each. Moreover, he speculates that if the Pauline faction numbered "conservatively" forty to fifty, the "anti-Pauline" faction was at least as large, resulting in numbers in the order of one hundred.[7] Welborn thinks that the wealthiest households—those of Gaius, Erastos, and Crispus—might each have brought many dependents so that an estimate of one hundred members is not unreasonable.[8] Even higher estimates have been offered employing the same basic method.[9]

A multiplier, however, is only as good as the assumptions upon which it rests. Murphy-O'Connor assumes that spouses of members were also members, even though as 1 Cor 7:12–13 makes clear, some husbands of female members were not adherents themselves. There are just too many imponderables in this kind of calculus to be reliable: Did Crispus and Stephanas have children and slaves, and if so, how many? And would these automatically have become members? Was Phoebe married, and if so did she have children? Did Stephanas or Crispus remain members of the Corinthian group?—they are not mentioned later in Romans 16 when other Corinthian members are named. What percentage of the entire group do those named in Romans 16 represent? And if, as I have argued earlier, Gaius was not a host but a Roman *visitor*, there is no reason to suppose that he had a retinue at all.

The method of name-counting results in wildly disparate estimates owing to the vagaries involved in positing a reliable multiplier. Richard Last, for example, questions the assumption that most members at Corinth are not named by Paul. While he doubts that the actual size of the assembly can be determined, he sets the bare minimum as low as ten by counting the number of people named and the few additional people whom Paul's statements appear to presuppose.[10] He also makes the important point, often ignored by others, that the size of the group was likely variable: by the time Paul writes Romans, Prisca and Aquila were no longer in Corinth; and Phoebe, the patron and assistant of the assembly at Cenchreae (seven kilometers southeast of Corinth), may not have been a regular member of the Corinthian assembly at all. As I have just noted, some of the names that appear in 1 Corinthians—Chloe, Crispus, Stephanas, Fortunatus, Achaicus—are missing from the greetings at the end of Romans 16, written only a few years after 1 Corinthians. It would be surprising that their absence from the greetings was a matter of Paul's inadvertence, given the fact that in 1 Corinthians Stephanas appears to be a leader in the Corinthian assembly (1 Cor 1:16; 16:15, 17). This might mean either that these people are no longer members of the Corinthian Christ assembly because of death or defection or that Paul no longer treated them as allies.

A final approach factors spatial considerations into estimates of group size. Gaius in Rom 16:23 has almost always been the focus of attention.[11] Since it is common to suppose that the Corinthian Christ group consisted of a number of "house churches," Gaius's house, where the group sometimes gathered, must have been quite large. Famously, Murphy-O'Connor observed that the standard U-shaped *triclinium* of the Anaploga villa in Corinth could not fit more than nine diners, which hardly would have sufficed for a group of forty to fifty. But Murphy-O'Connor observes that elite houses built in the *domus Italica* style typically had an atrium averaging about fifty-five square meters (the atrium in the Anaploga villa was only thirty square meters). Theoretically, an area that size could hold fifty diners, but since atria typically had an *impluvium*, a shallow rain-fed pool that took up floor space, thirty to forty diners would be more reasonable provided that there were no vases or furniture.[12] Of course, there are no grounds for supposing that the Anaploga villa belonged to Gaius; but Murphy-O'Connor treated this as a typical elite house.[13] This led him to devise an explanation of the divisions and tensions at the Corinthian meal (1 Cor 11:17–34): the "first-class believers" reclined on cushions in Gaius's *triclinium*, but everyone else ate seated in the atrium. For his part, de Vos accepted that most Roman houses would not accommodate more than fifty diners, even with the atrium, and because he speculated that the Corinthian group was closer to one hundred in size, he suggests that Gaius might have supplied a purpose-built clubhouse large enough for the entire group.[14] Welborn, who argued that the Corinthian group numbered about one hundred, looked to houses that had multiple reception rooms or multiple atria that could accommodate hundreds of visitors.[15] He identified at least one partially excavated house in Corinth that was likely large enough for one hundred people.[16]

Some have proposed nonelite venues for Christ assemblies in Corinth. Again, taking the size of the Christ group to be about fifty, David Horrell looked to the remains of *insulae* on Corinth's East Theater street. It would not be impossible, Horrell urges, that the "small traders and business folk" who comprised the Christ assembly could have "crammed" into the second floor of adjoining Buildings 1 and 3, which measured in total about ten by five meters.[17] This is not impossible, of course, but it assumes that the second floor space above the butchery shops was a *single* ten-by-five-meter room rather than cut into several smaller apartments. Moreover, while it might be possible to cram fifty people into a fifty-square-meter room, it would be nearly impossible to imagine conducting a meal in so cramped a space. Either fifty is too large a group or the dining space would need to be significantly larger.

Like Horrell, Peter Oakes suggests that "the majority of house churches are unlikely to have included a member of the elite, in which case the group will not have generally met in elite houses."[18] And like Murphy-O'Connor, he assumes that a Christ group in Pompeii might have comprised forty people (thirty in Rome). There is, of course, not much reason to suppose that a Pauline assembly existed in Pompeii before the city's destruction in 79 CE;[19] but the advantage of imagining Pompeii as a venue for a hypothetical Christ assembly is that unlike most archaeological sites where all that remains are the outlines of gross structures, the circumstances of Pompeii's destruction afford the scholar with the opportunity to coordinate house size with the social standing of its occupants. Excavations at Pompeii not only exposed a series of houses, but small finds—jewelry, tools, furniture, domestic items—and house decorations preserved by volcanic ash, and these permit inferences about the social standing of the occupants of those houses.

As a thought experiment Oakes focuses on the housing block in *Regio* I, *Insula* X, in Pompeii, known as the "Insula of the Menander" (fig. 15).[20] This block included a mansion (House 4: 1,700 m^2); a very small workshop (House 6: 40 m^2) cut out of the corner of Houses 4 and 7 to serve as a workshop and house of a stoneworker and his wife; and House 7 (310 m^2), occupied by a handworker. The dimensions and decorations of House 4, "House of the Menander," indicate that it belonged to one of the Pompeian elite, perhaps of senatorial rank. The tiny House 6 contained stonecutting tools and was probably rented by slaves or clients of the owner of the House of the Menander. House 7 had eleven rooms, including an atrium, peristyle garden, and portico. It was found to contain woodworking tools and surgical instruments in addition to domestic items, and hence belonged to a handworker, the kind of person who belonged to a Christ assembly. Oakes christens this handworker Holconius and concludes that the house was large enough for a Christ assembly of forty people.[21]

Although Oakes's approach to membership is speculative, it has the virtue of coordinating the space hypothetically available to a Christ assembly with the

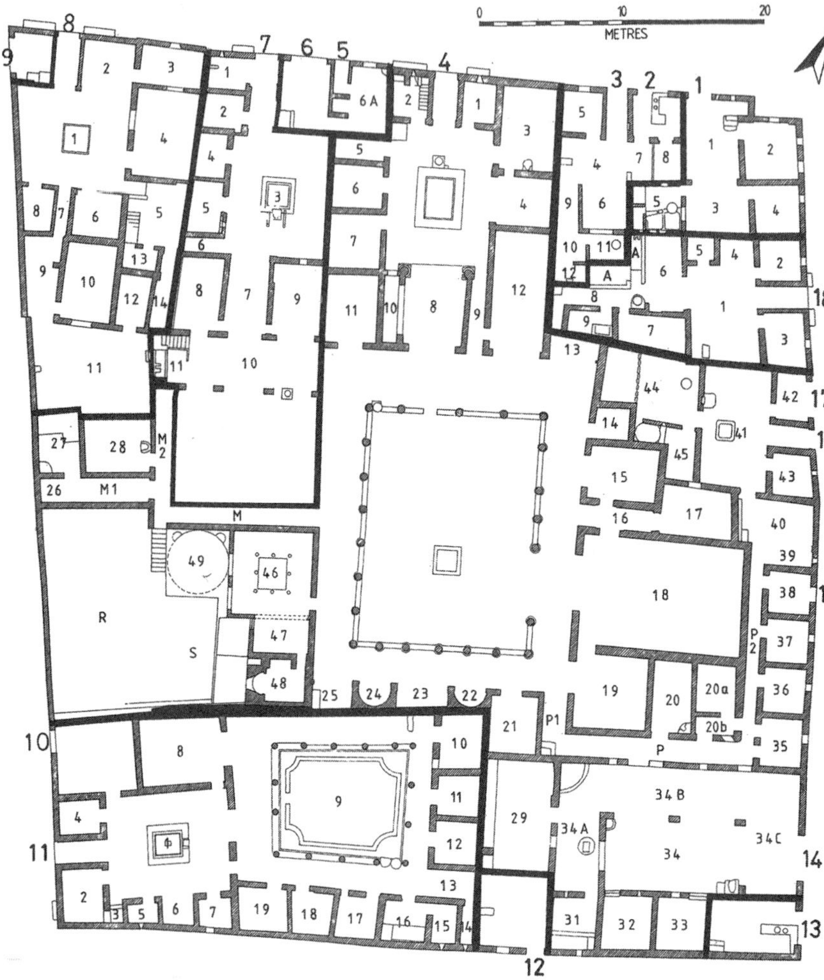

social standing of the host (an artisan with some resources). If one grants the premise that a Christ assembly numbered thirty to forty people, there is indeed no compelling reason to suppose that these numbers could be accommodated only within an elite villa. A building like Holconius's house could have accommodated the assembly. This conclusion is all the more important for Corinth once it is recognized that Gaius is not an elite host with a villa but a *guest* of the Corinthian assembly; hence, speculations about the size of Gaius's house are beside the point.

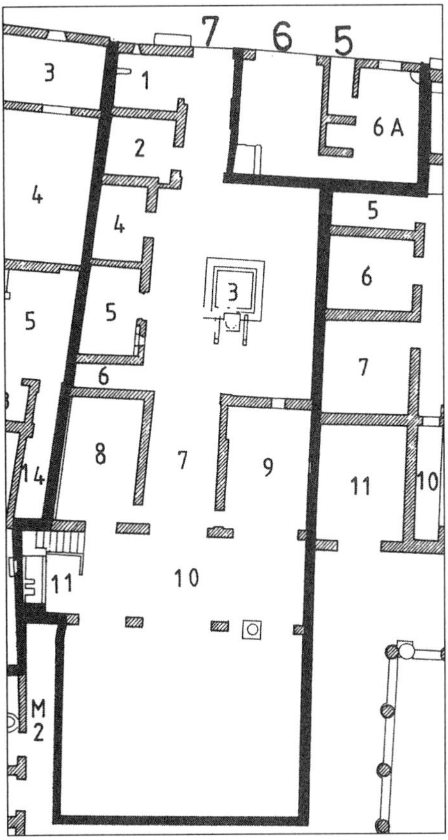

Figure 15. The Insula of the Menander, Pompeii (*Regio* I, *Insula* X), with detail of House 7. Drawn by S. Gibson, J. S. Gregory, R. J. Ling, and D. Murdoch, from Roger Ling, *The Insula of the Menander at Pompeii*, vol. 1: *The Structures* (Oxford: Clarendon, 1997), fig. 24. (Reprinted with permission of Prof. Ling.)

David Balch offers a third response to Murphy-O'Connor that modifies both the assumptions that a group of fifty could be accommodated only in the combination of a *triclinium* plus an atrium and that elite houses were the only available venues for a Christ assembly. In Pompeii some of the houses—the Casa dei Vettii (VI,15,1) for example—had not one but four *triclinia*, three facing the peristyle garden. If Christ groups met in such a house, the invidious differentiation between those who were able to recline in a *triclinium* and those who had to sit in the atrium would disappear: forty to fifty could be accommodated in four *triclinia*. Moreover, Balch argues that peristyle courtyards may have been fitted with benches that could accommodate larger numbers of diners.[22]

Balch's more important intervention is to argue that the assumption that the elite villa was the primary site of dining for Christ groups is problematic. Many other possibilities existed, from inns and taverns where diners would sit rather than recline,[23] to peristyle gardens, some fitted with masonry *triclinia* and others with movable benches that could accommodate many more than nine to seventeen diners.[24] Whether or not Christ assemblies existed in Pompeii, the force of Balch's argument is that, assuming that dining facilities in other locations were as varied and diverse as we know them to be in Pompeii, it is easy to suppose that a group of forty to fifty Christ devotees might be accommodated in some of the larger dining spaces that were available.

The tacit or explicit assumption in all of these approaches—those of Murphy-O'Connor, Horrell, Oakes, and Balch—is that Christ assemblies typically included forty to fifty people. Hence, these approaches begin with an assumption about size and draw inferences about space. Dennis Smith inverts this approach. On one hand he agrees with Oakes against Murphy-O'Connor that "it is highly unlikely that early Christians gathered in the kinds of elite houses that one finds typically at Pompeii and Ephesus."[25] On the other hand, Smith rejects Oakes's supposition that the "assembly hall" (i.e., Oakes's atrium, garden, and portico) was the main venue for Christ groups. On the contrary, Smith insists, "whatever the social class, if guests were entertained they would have been entertained according to the protocols of the culture, namely at a reclining banquet."[26] The descriptions of Jesus's final meal with his disciples, Luke's discourse of table etiquette, and even John's description of the wedding in Cana all imagine the Greek practice of reclining at a banquet. In Smith's view Paul's advice in 1 Cor 14:30 to defer to one who receives a revelation "while sitting" presupposes the situation typical of a *triclinium*, where some recline and people with lower status sit.[27] According to Smith, all of these data point to the use of a *triclinium* or *stibadium* as the normal practice of Christ assemblies, and this automatically limits participation, since it would have been impossible to put more than twenty people, reclining or seated, into a *triclinium*. Were a Christ group to grow beyond these numbers, the normal strategy would not be to seek larger facilities but instead to split into two smaller dining groups.[28]

Smith's view that the assemblies and meals of Christ groups were conducted exclusively in houses has in turn faced a major challenge from Edward Adams.[29] Adams points out that the phrase *hē kat' oikon ekklēsia* (the assembly at the home of . . .) occurs only four times in Pauline and deutero-Pauline letters, twice in conjunction with Prisca and Aquila (1 Cor 16:19, Rom 16:5) and once in Philemon (2) and a fourth time in Col 4:15. Crucially, two of these occurrences indicate that *oikos* should not automatically be rendered in English as "house"; on the contrary, *oikos* can refer to a wide variety of structures. The *oikos* of the artisans Prisca and Aquila was likely their workshop (*taberna*) where they also lived. As a workshop, it could not have accommodated more than about ten people.[30] Only the occurrences in Philemon and Colossians refer to Christ assemblies located in someone's house, hardly an indication of the exclusive or even normal use of houses by Christ assemblies.

The phrase *hē kat' oikon ekklēsia* (the household assembly), moreover, presupposes a *conceptual* distinction between "house" and "assembly"; that is, the "assembly" is *not* a house. To illustrate with a modern example: when a newly founded congregation meets in a school gymnasium, storefront, or warehouse, that space *becomes* a synagogue or church and ceases to be just a gymnasium, storefront, or warehouse. If usage is persistent, the architecture might eventually be transformed. But even without such a transformation, the space is transformed conceptually. In the language of critical spatial theory, space is a *product* of the social practices that occur in that space.[31]

Paul of course knew nothing of critical spatial theory. Yet he implicitly distinguishes in 1 Cor 11:20–22 between the *ekklēsia* when "all come together" and the houses of members: each space has a distinct set of behaviors appropriate to it. So too the post-Pauline interpolation in 1 Cor 14:33–35 distinguishes between conduct appropriate for women *en tais ekklēsiais* (in the assemblies) and that appropriate *en oikō* (at home), even if Christ assemblies happened to occur in household space. The pseudo-Pauline Pastoral letters invoke the metaphor of the "household of God" (*oikos theou*) as a description of the *ekklēsia* (1 Tim 3:15) and yet distinguish between what occurs in houses and what ought to occur in the assembly. Like the Pauline Christ group at Philippi, the Pastoral writer names as officials for the assembly supervisors (*episkopoi*) and assistants (*diakonoi*)—terms that do not belong at all to the semantic field of the management of houses. Hence, while it is possible to imagine *ekklēsiai* meeting in houses, the "assembly" is conceptually distinct from the house and in no way necessarily dependent upon the house.

Although both the canonical book of Acts and noncanonical acts imagine much activity in houses, there are good reasons to think that the house was not the exclusive setting for Christ assemblies. As will be noted below, *triclinia* were also found in purpose-built dining rooms that could be rented.[32] *First Clement*, Hermas, and Ignatius are either silent on the use of houses as meeting spaces[33] or refer to nondomestic venues. The Martyrdom of Justin reports that Justin's group met at the baths of Myrtinus in Rome;[34] Celsus dismissively describes Christ followers as frequenting the *oikoi* of wool workers, leather cutters, and fullers, which can only refer to their workshops.[35] Adams also devotes a full chapter to comparative data, indicating that while some associations met in houses, others met in a wide variety of venues, from purpose-built clubhouses to temples, inns, restaurants, and baths.[36] To this list we could add warehouses (*horrea*).[37] Each of these venues become *ekklēsia* space when they are used as such.

Two important points can be gleaned from the discussion of archaeology and space. First, Adams is surely correct that Christ groups probably used nondomestic venues, especially workshops. And second, the insistence that Christ followers employed only *triclinia* and that they always reclined (which would have required more space than sitting) is problematic, especially since workshops and inns were not always outfitted as *triclinia*, and open gardens and peristyle gardens where dining occurred may or may not have had *triclinia* at all.

THE SIZE OF GREEK AND ROMAN ASSOCIATIONS

The logical problem with the foregoing discussion of group size and space is that it begins either with assumptions about group size (Murphy-O'Connor, Horrell, Oakes, and Adams) or with restrictive assumptions about the only possible venues for dining (Smith). I have already argued that the assumptions that go into estimating group size are exceedingly dubious. And as Adams (and Balch) has pointed out against Smith, we need not assume that the *triclinium* was the exclusive site of dining.

Where does that leave us regarding the question of the size of Christ assemblies? At least for the first and second centuries, we have neither membership rosters nor archaeological sites that were incontestably used by Christ assemblies and can be measured.[38] For the third century (ca. 240 CE) a house church at Dura-Europos is attested. An assembly hall measuring 12.9 by 5.15 meters (65 m^2) was created in a house by removing a wall, destroying an earlier *triclinium*, and installing a small raised platform (*bēma*) at one end of the hall.[39] Kraeling, the excavator, thought that the hall could hold sixty-five to seventy-five people,[40] but without a membership roster to confirm this, it is impossible to know. Likewise, new excavations at Kfar Otnai (Legio) in the Jezreel Valley exposed a third-century assembly hall of five by ten meters, with three mosaic inscriptions, including a dedication by a centurion, who paid for the pavement.[41] Presumably this hall could accommodate a maximum of fifty to sixty people, but again, without a membership list we are left without any reliable measure. We can, however, think about the size of Christ assemblies in relation to the size of other cultic associations whose *alba* are known.

Table 1 at the end of this chapter lists 141 associations from the late fourth century BCE to the fourth century CE, divided into occupational guilds (n = 47), cultic associations (n = 92), and two *collegia domestica*. As the table shows, the size of associations varied widely, from just four to more than thirteen hundred, from a tiny cultic association of the *orgeōnes* of the gods (IG VII 33) to an enormous guild of carpenters in Rome (CIL 6.1060, 1030). There are no extant *alba* from neighborhood associations or from Judean assemblies.

The division into occupational guilds, cultic associations, and *collegia domestica* is artificial from some perspectives insofar as most associations had cultic dimensions. Nevertheless, I have divided the list into groups that appear to be organized primarily around an occupation or profession and those organized around the cult of a deity. For analytic purposes I have set the final category aside, because we have only two such collegia for which *alba* are available: one with a current membership of 31 and the other with 402 members. The disparity is so large and the sample group so small that statistical inferences are unreliable.[42]

The two remaining categories, occupational guilds and cultic associations, reflect the different patterns of membership. Occupational guilds were mostly gender-exclusive and tied to an occupation, and they tended to recruit individuals of a narrow range of legal statuses (often freedmen). Cultic associations—at least some—exhibited greater diversity in ethnic and gender composition and in the legal status of members. But there are also significant differences in size. The occupational guilds for which we have preserved *alba* ranged from 5 to 1,330 members, more than one-third having memberships of more than 100. The mean is 164.89 and the median is 60. Naturally, the largest of these guilds would have required significant space for meals and other common events.

Statistical generalizations can be misleading, especially when the data are "lumpy." We have better data about the size of Italian guilds than about Greek, Macedonian, and Asian guilds because many *alba* are preserved from Italy. The largest guilds by far were Italian, with a mean size of 272.42 members, a median of 125, and the mode (the most frequently occurring number) of 60. There are good grounds for suspecting that other Italian guilds for which we have no *alba* were also large. The Roman and Ostian guilds of the boatmen and registrars (*lenuncularii*), bargemen (*scapharii*), builders (*fabri*), carpenters (*tignuarii*), textile dealers (*centonarii*), and tree-carriers (*dendrophoroi*) all left *alba* with large memberships. The very same guilds are attested in other Italian towns but without *alba*. Yet where *alba* from these towns are available, the membership was similarly large. For example, the guild of carpenters at

Ravenna at 560 members (CIL 11.126) was even larger than the carpenters of Ostia, which had 350 members.

Asia Minor and Egypt offer a different picture. Hundreds of inscriptions and papyri attest the presence of guilds involved with food production, metal working, textile manufacture and cleaning, transportation and cartage, building, and many other trades. But hardly any membership rosters are preserved.[43] One might surmise from the report in Acts 19:24–25 that the artisans (*technitai*) connected with the silver trade in Ephesus numbered at least several dozen if they created a civic disturbance that would attract the attention of the magistrates. The same conclusion is suggested by the later report of a work stoppage of the bakers in Ephesus.[44] But in neither case is it possible to arrive at reliable numbers. In Egypt, price declarations from early-fourth-century Oxyrhynchus name dozens of occupational guilds of goldsmiths, iron workers, coppersmiths, bread bakers, tavern keepers, beer merchants, wine merchants, oil workers, and many others. No membership rosters are available, and so we are at a loss as to whether such guilds had a dozen members or fifty or one hundred. Guilds are also known to have been involved in some of the large agricultural estates in Egypt. An account from the Heroninus estate in the Fayûm lists payments to four *synodoi*, apparently groups of cowherds and donkey drivers, which were likely not much larger than twenty workers;[45] and a later account from the Apion estate near Oxyrhynchus lists nineteen different associations (*koina*) of cowherds, vinedressers, and others.[46] Ruffini has suggested that each of these guilds had only ten members, although without membership lists this is guesswork.[47] What is clear statistically for occupational guilds is that these guilds included both extremely large and powerful guilds associated with the grain and building trades and with textile manufacture, and also quite modest agricultural guilds.

The contrast with the ninety-two cultic groups is striking: in the first place, the size range is more restricted—all are less than 100—the mean is 29.29, the median 24, and the mode only 15. Thus cultic associations tended on average to be smaller than occupational guilds and certainly very much smaller than those involved in the grain trade, shipping, building, and textiles. It is in occupational guilds that one could expect to find patrons of senatorial and equestrian ranks, while cultic associations appear to have been able to attract patrons from among only local magistrates and well-to-do commoners.[48] Large occupational guilds simply had more symbolic capital to offer their patrons, and they required significant space in which to meet. Smaller cultic associations likely needed smaller spaces for their meetings but also attracted less highly placed patrons and benefactors.[49]

There is another problem with statistics. Most *alba* offer a snapshot of membership at the time the inscription was cut; we should not assume that membership was stable. The list of the devotees of Atargatis has a total of ninety-seven legible names.[50] At least six cutters had been active in engraving the list while it was in use, the first responsible for the first fifty names and perhaps as many as fifty-seven. Additional names were added, but it is impossible to know how many years elapsed between the initial cutting and the final additions.[51] It is unlikely, however, that this picture is one of simple growth from fifty to more than one hundred members. More likely, deaths and defections required the replacement of members, with the result that the association was never as large as the inscription might first imply.

An even clearer example of the growth and decline of membership is offered by the *album* of a Mithraic association in Noricum. A bronze plaque records the names of ninety-eight Mithraists who lived in Virunum (modern Klagenfurt, Austria) between 183 and 201 CE (fig. 16).[52] The occasion of the inscription was twofold: the rededication of a temple that had collapsed and had been rebuilt by the members; and a convocation "for the sake of mortality" (*mortalitatis causa*), probably to commemorate five of the initial members who had died. Their deaths seem to have been the result of the Antonine plague, which returning military troops had brought from the East.[53] The names of the deceased Mithraists are marked in the *album* with the Greek letter *theta* (*th*[*anōn*], "died"). The list, however, was clearly devised in several stages, since the lettering on its four columns changes abruptly at several points. The first column and a half provide a snapshot of the thirty-four original members in 183, including the five who are marked as newly deceased. Eighteen additional groups of names were then added to the originally blank parts of column 2. Then eight names in 184 were added, evidently to replace the five deceased, and then between one and eight names were added in each of the following years from 185 to 201, with the final name squeezed at the bottom below a dedication.[54]

Over the next eighteen years (184–201 CE) there must have been additional deaths, though none is marked with a *theta*. The yearly intake of new members was at least in part to compensate for deaths and defections. The first new member inducted in 184 CE is designated *pater* (father, column 2.10), the highest grade in the Mithraic hierarchy, probably introduced to replace one of the two fathers who had died as a result of the plague.[55] Piccottini's prosopographical analysis of the names suggests that there are numerous sibling and father-son relationships within the group. Hence, the sons and brothers of the original thirty-four members followed their fathers or brothers in joining the group at

Figure 16. Mithraic album, Virunum (183–201 CE). *Detail:* Deceased members with names marked with a *theta* on the left. Landesmuseum Kärnten, Klagenfurt, Austria. (Photo by the author.)

dates after 183.[56] The "steady-state" size of the group was probably never more than forty.

What tentative conclusions can be drawn from these comparative data? First, it seems much more likely that Pauline Christ assemblies initially numbered in the 15–30 range—that is, between the mode of 15 and the mean of 29.29—rather than the inflated numbers proposed by some. A Christ assembly of one hundred members would make it the largest attested cultic group in the entire Mediterranean! Only when Christ groups could attract elite patrons, as they would do in the fourth century, can one imagine larger groups. On the other hand, I see no reason to argue with Smith that the Corinthian Christ assembly was limited to those who could fit into a *triclinium*, since Adams and Balch are surely right that single *triclinia* were not the only venues available for the meetings of associations.

Second, I have already suggested that the disparities between Paul's list of Corinthians who send greetings in Romans 16 and those he names in 1 Corinthians might indicate either deaths or defections after the writing of 1 Corinthians. The Mithraic *album* from Virunum points unquestionably to the ebb and flow of membership, starting at thirty-four members and followed by recruiting to compensate for deaths. That defections from Christ assemblies occurred is attested by Pliny in Bithynia in the early second century when he reports to Trajan that upon examination of those named as Christ followers, some admitted to having been members three years ago, some many years ago, and others even twenty years ago—but they were no longer members.[57]

Third, as Oakes and Adams have insisted, it is unnecessary to tie the meetings of Christ assemblies exclusively to the space made available by elite Romans. Commoners such as Oakes's "Holconius" had sufficient space for thirty devotees. In fact, a group of fifteen to thirty could have been accommodated in many venues.

DINING SPACES OF GREEK AND ROMAN ASSOCIATIONS

Adams's insights can be made more concrete by examining a few representative cases where we know both the size of the association from an extant membership roster and the space used by that association. Most associations had banquets and for these purposes either owned or rented dining space. These ranged from large, purpose-built structures that could accommodate large numbers to much smaller owned or rented dining spaces to spaces adapted to dining on an ad hoc basis.[58]

Occupational Guilds

The expansion of the harbor at Ostia by Trajan in the years between 100 and 112 CE also resulted in the growth of collegia there and the expansion of some of their clubhouses and temples. Large guilds such as the ship builders (*fabri navales*) of Ostia owned a temple complex (III,II,1–2)[59] with two large halls (16 × 25 m and 16.0 × 14.5 m) at the front and rear of the temple that were likely used for assemblies and dining, with ample space for its ninety-four members.[60] An even larger Ostian occupational guild, the builder-carpenters (*fabri tignuarii*), owned a large building, the Caseggiato dei Triclini (I,XII,1), built about 120 CE with a central courtyard (13.5 × 21.5 m) and nine rooms facing the courtyard. Four of these along the eastern side of the courtyard, each measuring about five by seven meters, were fitted with masonry *triclinia* later in the second century (fig. 17).[61] The *album* of the guild, discovered in the central hall, indicates a membership of 352,[62] clearly much too large to be accommodated in the four *triclinia* on the ground floor. Two internal staircases still visible led to the four upper floors, some of which might have had other dining rooms.[63] An additional twelve to twenty standard *triclinia* on the upper floors might have been adequate for such numbers. Van der Meer suggests that banquets must have been staggered at different times.[64] As Bollmann points out, however, even before the construction of the masonry *triclinia* in the four side rooms (totaling 140 m^2), these rooms and the large courtyard (292.25 m^2) could have been used for the banquets.[65] The use of portable couches, widely

Figure 17. *Triclinium*, Ostia Antica, Caseggiatto dei Triclini (I,XII,1). (Photo by the author.)

evidenced by frescoes and mosaics, easily could have accommodated the diners in the hall and side rooms.[66]

The association of the Berytian *Poseidoniastai*—merchants, sailors, and warehousemen on Delos—was at once a guild of immigrants to Delos (mostly) from Beirut, who had shrines to Poseidon as their patron deity, and an occupational guild engaged in the shipping of goods to and from Delos. Excavations on Delos have identified an elegant peristyle building forty-five by thirty-five meters containing a sanctuary with four shrines, and a large hall (15.80 × 13.37 m) with a red band on the floor one and one-half meters from the wall, indicating the placement of couches (*klinai*) for dining.[67] Trümper estimates that the room accommodated nineteen to twenty couches, making it suitable for thirty-eight to forty diners. A second hall (13.0 × 10.5 m), luxuriously decorated, could have held fifteen to seventeen couches (thirty to thirty-four diners), and a third, smaller room (8.0 × 7.4 m) is more poorly preserved and might have served either as a dining room with ten to eleven couches or as a service room. Trümper concludes that "if the two or three banquet rooms were used simultaneously, they would have provided space for at least 68 to a maximum of 96 members on 34 to 48 couches."[68]

The size of the membership is a little more difficult to determine, since the habit on Delos was usually to inscribe only the names of magistrates, not the general membership. For example, ID 1751 is a bilingual dedication of the magistrates of the *Poseidoniastai* (ca. 125 BCE), giving the names of four *magistri* in both Greek and Latin. This probably implies an association of perhaps forty to sixty people in total, assuming that one magistrate represented ten to fifteen members. Fortunately, we have two other lists from the group. ID 2611 (late II BCE) is a subscription list of forty-eight *Poseidoniastai* who were donors to a building project. The second is a membership list (ID 2629; late II BCE) inscribed on a statue base. The base has two inscribed faces, and although both surfaces are fragmentary and damaged, the legible portions imply a minimum of twenty-eight members. The list was probably longer, since the top parts of both faces are broken off so that we have only the bottom portions of both.[69] The space available in the first two halls of the clubhouse easily could accommodate a membership of thirty to forty-eight people, as Trümper has shown.

Cultic Associations

Cultic associations tended to be on average significantly smaller than occupational guilds; for that reason, it is a priori likely that they required less space for their banquets.

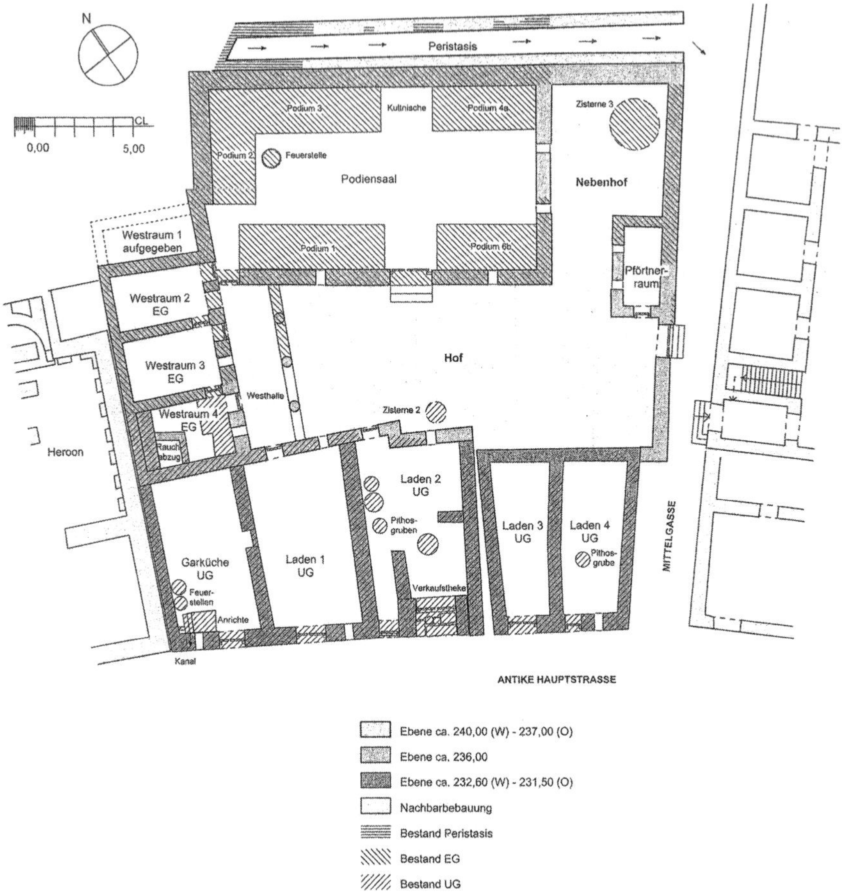

Abb. 16. Kaiserzeitliches Hofhaus. Grundriß Bauphase 4, Rekonstruktionsvorschlag. M. 1 : 250

Figure 18. House of the Cowherds, Pergamon. Fourth building phase (II CE). From Holger Schwarzer, *Das Gebäude mit dem Podiensaal in der Stadtgrabung von Pergamon* (Berlin: Deutsches Archäologisches Institut, 2008), Abb. 16, p. 62. (Used with permission of Prof. Schwarzer.)

The clubhouse for the Dionysiac cow herders (*boukoloi*) in Pergamon began as a Hellenistic peristyle house, perhaps built in the second century BCE, with an atrium and three rooms along the north side, including a small dining room that could have held thirteen small couches.[70] Two dedications by the chief cowherd (*archiboukolos*) in the late first century BCE found in the dining room indicate that it was already in use as a cultic banquet room.[71] During the first half of the first century CE (third building phase), two of the north rooms were enlarged by moving the walls at the expense of the atrium, producing a room of 9.0 by 7.7 meters,[72] and early in the second century the two rooms were amalgamated (fourth building phase, fig. 18), resulting in a *triclinium* of 16 by 9 meters, with masonry couches 2 meters deep, interrupted on the long axes by the entrance (between couches 1, 6b) and a cultic niche (between couches 3, 4a) and on the short axes by a narrow entrance, resulting in about 26 linear meters of dining space.[73] Assuming about 1 meter per diner, the *triclinium* could accommodate twenty-six to forty-three diners.[74]

This accords remarkably well with the available epigraphic data. I.Perg 485 from the first century is a membership list of the *boukoloi* that lists twenty-four members in all.[75] A slightly later fragmentary inscription, I.DionysosJ 98 (109/110 CE), had at least seventeen names on it.[76] Thus the archaeological data and the physical dimensions of the dining space accord well with the epigraphic indications of the size of the membership during the third and fourth building phases (I to early II CE).

A similar correlation can be seen with a dining space for an association devoted to the Egyptian deity Harpokrates from Tebtynis in 43–49 CE. P.Mich V 246 names the fifteen association members and the contributions of each member for the banquet. The papyrus indicates the seating arrangement, allocating to each member a specific place on the three couches and designating a couch master (*kleitarchēs*) for the second and third couches.[77] The papyrus does not indicate the location of the *triclinium*, but excavations near the temple of Soknebtynis in Tebtynis reveal three *deipnētēria*, dining halls fitted with standard masonry couches, located on the processional way in front of the temple; they are between 9 and 10 meters long and 7.5 and 8.5 meters wide, and each could easily accommodate the fifteen diners of the association.[78] In fact one of these three *deipnētēria* bears the building inscription with the text "(Dedicated) when Onnophris son of Potamon was the president (*prostatēs*) of the association (*synodos*) of Dorophoros," indicating that at least one of the three dining rooms was used by an association for its banquets.[79]

Finally, we turn to the monthly income and expense account for a very small association from Philadelphia in Egypt with only six to ten members (SB 3:7182, II/I BCE). This papyrus not only indicates the monthly contributions of members toward the dinner expenses and records the attendance at each of the dinners, but also records the location of each dinner. The club met in various places: twice in a storeroom (*thēsauron*), in the house or workshop of one of the members, in the Iseion (temple of Isis), presumably in one of the *deipnētēria* connected with the temple, and twice in the harness room of a stable.[80] None of these banquet locales could have been very large, and only the meeting in the Iseion was likely in a venue specifically intended for formal dining.[81] Yet this itinerant arrangement was apparently adequate for the members of the association, which never recorded more than ten diners at one meeting, and at most meetings only six or seven were present.

None of this is to deny that houses also provided the venues for the banquets of cultic associations. A Zeus cult in Philadelphia (Lydia) was evidently hosted by a certain Dionysios, to whom the god gave commandments to open his house to "men and women, free and slaves."[82] Presumably, the size of the cult group was limited by the size of Dionysios's house, probably accommodating not more than a dozen or two people. At the other extreme, the Dionysiac association of Pompeia Agrippinilla, which met on her estate at Torre Nova in the Italian Campania, boasted 402 members.[83] Whether this group ever met for banquets is unknown, but since Dionysiac performances typically occurred outdoors, space was not as critical a constraint as it was for associations that relied on dining spaces in temples, workshops, houses, and *deipnētēria*.

SIZE AND SPACE: HOUSES, WORKSHOPS, AND CEMETERIES

The data from early Christ assemblies are not of the sort that permit direct inferences concerning the size of those groups. The best that we can do is think comparatively. The cultic associations whose rosters we have ranged from a handful of members to almost 100, with a mean of 29.29, median of 24, and mode of 15. Unless one were prepared to believe that the Corinthian Christ assembly was among the largest cultic groups attested in the entire Mediterranean, it seems best to consider a modest size as the more plausible. A group of fifteen to thirty members would be a safer estimate. Interestingly, the statistical mode of 15 is exactly the number that a *triclinium* or *stibadium* could accommodate. It is important, however, to keep in mind that membership size likely varied from one month to another, owing to mortality, defection, and recruitment.

The physical constraints of space represented an obvious limitation on the size of groups that met to dine. Nevertheless, it is clear from the foregoing discussion and from Adams's work that a large variety of spaces were available to associations and, in theory at least, to Christ assemblies. A small Christ assembly consisting of perhaps a dozen or two members—as the handworker group represented by 1 Thessalonians might have been—could have met in a workshop or a storeroom (*horrea*) or a private house. A small Thessalonian group of thirteen male "table companions" (*synklitai*) devoted to the Egyptian god

Anoubis honored a freedman for establishing their "house" (*oikos*) (IG X/2.1 58).[84] Presumably this "house" was domestic space or a workshop; even a small shrine was sufficient to provide space for thirteen diners whether or not it was outfitted as a *triclinium* or *andrōn* (an all-male dining room in a Greek house). The even smaller association of slaves from the Fayûm (SB 3:7182) met variously in storerooms, harness rooms, and a house or workshop.

For a slightly larger group of two dozen, a number of venues were possible. The *orgeōnes* devoted to the hero Egretēs (IG II^2 2499 = GRA I 7) owned a shrine that they leased out but retained the right to use the kitchen, shed, and two *triclinia*. This implies a rather small association, since two *triclinia* could not accommodate many more than thirty members.[85] We do not have a plan of the shrine and so do not know whether the two dining rooms faced each other across a courtyard or were adjacent. In either case, however, we would not have to imagine Murphy-O'Connor's scenario, according to which some of the members were relegated to sit in the atrium while the more privileged dined reclining.

To meet in a precinct associated with a temple likely would have violated the sensibilities of a Christ assembly such as the Corinthian group; nevertheless, many other options were available. I have already mentioned the house of the Dionysiac "Dancing Cowherds" in Pergamon, which was not associated with any temple but whose *triclinium* could seat at least twenty-four diners.[86] The Mithraic association whose *album* was mentioned above had in addition to a temple, a building in a bath complex in Virunum that included an eight-by-twelve-meter dining room apparently sufficient for its thirty-four members and perhaps a few more if new recruitment outstripped the effects of the Antonine plague.[87]

Dining facilities were also available for rental. In a letter from the early second century the manager of a complex containing some dining rooms (*symposia*) complains to the owner of the complex that he had been unable to rent them out, either as living space or for banquets, and so asked to be relieved of his managerial responsibilities.[88] The letter gives no further details of the space available, but it at least indicates that dining spaces unconnected with temples were available for those who needed them.

References to space in the earliest writings of Christ assemblies are both infrequent and vague; such phrases as "Prisca and Aquila . . . and the assembly that is at their *oikos* (house/workshop)" (Rom 16:3, 5) and "the assembly at your house (*kat' oikon sou ekklēsia*)" (Phlm 2) do not reveal very much about the physical space that is in view. I have suggested that because Prisca and Aquila were handworkers, their *oikos* was probably a workshop (*taberna*) that doubled as living quarters and meeting space. Philemon's *oikos* (Phlm 2) was likely his residence: he apparently had quarters large enough to include a guest room (*xenia*, Phlm 22). Beyond this it is impossible to ascertain Philemon's social standing. He might have owned (or rented) a modest house such as the craftsman Holconius imagined by Oakes, or perhaps he had something on a grander scale.[89]

Given the variety of meeting spaces available and the variety of spaces employed by cultic groups whose locations we know, it is best not to suppose that early Christ groups adopted only a single venue (the private house). A variety of venues were available for meals, including private houses, rented *hestiatoria* (dining rooms), workshops, warehouses, and cemeteries. Nor should we assume that any Christ assembly always met in the same venue for each meeting. Itineracy was not uncommon.

Two texts offer the opportunity to visualize the spaces used by some Christ assemblies. James 2 proposes a scene of two strangers entering a Christ assembly (*synagōgē*). The wealthier of the two is shown to a seat of honor, while the poor man is asked to stand or to sit "under my stool," that is, in the serving area (2:3). Scholars have debated what kind of physical space James has in mind, but both Daniel Streett and Ben-Peter Smit, apparently quite independently of one another, have suggested that James here imagines the communal meal.[90] The fact that both need to be directed to appropriate seats suggests that James is not thinking of regular members, who would know their seats, but imagines invited guests or even uninvited visitors, neither of whom would know where to sit.[91]

Even though the author objects to this practice, James appears to imagine a *triclinium* or *stibadium* as a typical venue for the meal of a Christ assembly where, following common practices, the assignment of seats is indexical to status. This scenario is consistent with dining in a private house, in a dining space belonging to the group with fixed couches, or in a rented *deipnētērion*.

In 1 Cor 14:23 Paul imagines a "nonbeliever" (*apistos*) entering the assembly and hearing people speaking in tongues and supposing that they are mad. Several venues are consistent with this scenario.

Elite houses: At least two versions are possible. In order to observe the proceedings that took place in an elite *domus Italica*–type house, the outsider could have entered through the vestibule and entrance passage (*fauces*) and then proceeded into the atrium, the *tablinum*, and to the back of the house, where the *triclinium*/*triclinia* and peristyle were located.

The front portions of a Roman house (*fauces, atrium, tablinum*) were assumed to be open to the public, but the *triclinium*, bedrooms, and bathrooms were, according to Vitruvius, considered private.[92] Hence, one would have to imagine the visitor in 1 Corinthians viewing what was occurring in the *triclinium*, having penetrated far into the back of the house. Such a scenario is not impossible given that elite houses were designed to accommodate guests, invited and not.[93] Yet if visitors were invited, they might also be prepared in advance for what they were to witness, thus diminishing Paul's worry that they might think the Corinthians mad. The alternative—that a visitor was not invited—implies a rather bold visitor who would penetrate the private sections of the house uninvited.

A second version of this scenario has been sketched by Joel Weaver, who points out rightly that according to census records from Egypt, many houses had multiple owners, such that one owner (or occupant) of a house might own one-half or one-third of a house, sharing it with one or more co-owners.[94] Hence, a house in which an assembly met might be accessible to co-occupants who were not themselves members of the assembly and who would witness what was occurring in the *triclinium*.

Insulae: Horrell's suggestion affords a second possibility: that meetings occurred not in an elite house but in a second or higher story apartment in an *insula* complex. The excavations at Ostia show that access to the upper floors of the apartment blocks was by means of open stairways, located between the *tabernae* on the first floor. Moreover, these stairways were open to the streets directly adjacent to the *insulae*. Thus, we might imagine an uninvited guest—a neighbor or a passerby who heard singing or chanting—climbing the steps to enter the apartment.

Tabernae: A third scenario is even easier to imagine. *Tabernae* (workshops) were typically located along main streets or just off central courtyards accessible from a public street (fig. 19). Excavations at Ostia show *tabernae* located along the main north-south street (*cardo*) and the main east-west street (*decumanus*) and around the forum—the town center. In Pompeii many *tabernae* are located along the (approximately) east-west Via dell' Abbondanzza and the north-south Via Stabiana or around the forum. Several *tabernae* surveyed by Bollmann show architectural adaptations suggesting use as small cultic sites by associations.[95] If Christ assemblies were hosted by handworkers such as Prisca and Aquila, we might visualize them meeting in workshops located on public thoroughfares and therefore easily accessible from the street.

Rented triclinia and deipnētēria: Purpose-built dining spaces were sometimes located near the street. Three small dining rooms with *triclinia* excavated in

Figure 19. (*Top*): *Taberna*, Ostia Antica, Casa di Diana (I,III,3). (*Bottom*): *Taberna*, Pompeii (VII,IX,9), beside a *domus Italica* (VII,IX,8). (Photos by the author.)

Tebtynis were located on the main processional way that led to a temple although the dining rooms were not attached to the temple complex. One of these is known to have been used by an association.[96] At Pergamon the large *triclinium* of the Dionysiac Dancing Cowherds was in a complex of shops and workshops only a few steps from a main street.[97] Each of these venues was easily accessible from a public street and so would have afforded a passerby attracted by singing or chanting the possibility of entering an assembly.

Cemeteries: Finally, *triclinia* (or *biclinia*, with two benches) were built in cemeteries to facilitate regular funerary commemorations. Many of the tombs in the Isola Sacra (the Necropolis of Portus) are outfitted with banqueting spaces. *Biclinia* were typically positioned just inside the atrium of the tomb complex and in front of the burial chamber itself and were large enough to accommodate ten to twelve diners (e.g., Tomb 15, fig. 20, top).[98] Another set of dining benches was uncovered in another complex, this time arranged in an L-shape (E43, fig. 20, bottom). The fact that tomb complex 86 had a purpose-built oven for the preparation of meals indicates that these *biclinia* were used for regular graveside dining. All of these tombs, moreover, are located within a few meters of the Via Severiana, which leads from Ostia to Terracina. Any passerby on the road could easily see and hear the banquet. The archaeological remains of cemeteries indicate that their associated dining facilities were not designed to accommodate hundreds of people but at most one or two dozen.

Whether or not Christ assemblies used the Isola Sacra of Ostia, there is no doubt that they used cemeteries as meeting spaces, as Ramsay MacMullen has shown.[99] He notes Tertullian's report of a pagan complaint against Christians in North Africa, "no *areae*—no burial-grounds for the Christians" (*Scap.* 3), which makes sense only if they were known to frequent cemeteries. The fourth-century *Acta purgationis Felicis episcopi Autumnitani* has a local magistrate refer to cemeteries as the place that Christians make their prayers (§5).[100] To this we can add Dunbabin's description of the frescos in Christian catacombs, dated to the third and fourth centuries, which indicate that Christ followers met in tomb complexes, some of which were outfitted with *triclinia* or *stibadia*.[101] But perhaps the clearest evidence of all that Christ followers continued to use cemeteries as venues for meeting and banquets at least until the late fourth century is Augustine's lament in *Ep.* 22 (392 CE), where he decries what he describes as sumptuous banquets in cemeteries where, evidently following Roman funerary practice, money was distributed to those present.[102]

The data from cultic associations whose membership size, profile, and meeting places are known can serve as useful guides for thinking about the likely size

Figure 20. (*Top*): Isola Sacra, Tomb 15, with a *biclinium* within an atrium. (*Bottom*): Isola Sacra, Tomb E43. Remains of L-shaped masonry dining benches inside tombs E43–44. (Photos by the author.)

and venues of Christ assemblies. These data suggest that we should imagine relatively small Christ assemblies, at least at first, employing a range of dining and meeting spaces comparable to those that we know were used by cultic associations. This does not settle either the size or the meeting spaces used by Christ assemblies, but it does provide some known analogies.

Table 1. Membership statistics

Name	*Type*	*Location*	*Size*
OCCUPATIONAL GUILDS			
ITALY			
CIL 6.1060, 10300	*Fabri tignuarii* (builder-carpenters)	Regio I, Rome, 198 CE	1,330
CIL 5.5612	*Fabri et centonarii* (builders and textile dealers)	Regio XI, Sibrium, III CE	1,200
CIL 5.5888	Unknown	Regio XI, Mediolanum, date?	600
CIL 11.126	*Fabri tigunarii* (builder-carpenters)	Regio VIII, Ravenna, III CE	560
CIL 11.125	*Centonarii* (textile dealers)	Regio VIII, Ravenna, 161–166 or 198–211 CE	400
CIL 14.4569	*Fabri tignuarii* (builder-carpenters)	Regio I, Ostia, 198 CE	350
CIL 14.256	*Fabri navales* (ship builders)	Regio I, Portus, III CE	349
CIL 6.9404	*Fabri soliarii baxiarii* (shoe makers)	Regio I, Rome, date?	300
CIL 5.5701	*Fabri et centonarii* (builders and textile dealers)	Regio XI, Casatenovo, III CE	300
NSA (1953) 278–82 (no. 42)	*Lenuncularii* (boatmen)	Regio I, Ostia, 213 CE	290
CIL 6.9405	*Fabri tignuarii* (builder-carpenters)	Regio I, Rome, II CE	220
CIL 14.246add	*Scapharii et lenuncularii* (bargemen and boatmen)	Regio I, Ostia, 140–172 CE	181
CIL 14.251	*Lenuncularii* (boatmen and registrars)	Regio I, Ostia, 192 CE	130
CIL 14.250	*Lenuncularii* (boatmen and registrars)	Regio I, Ostia, 152 CE	120
NSA (1953) 282–85 (no. 43)	*Fabri navales* (ship builders)	Regio I, Ostia, late II/III CE	94
CIL 11.1355a, b	*Fabri tignuarii* (builder-carpenters)	Regio VIII, Luna, II CE?	91
CIL 10.3699	*Dendrophors* (tree-carriers)	Regio I, Cumae, 251 CE	88
CIL 14.255	Public slaves	Regio I, Ostia, II CE	81

Name	Type	Location	Size
AE 1977, 265b	*Fabri* (builders)	Regio VIII, Ravenna, 287–304 CE	80
CIL 14.2408	Actors	Regio I, Bovillae, 169 CE	60
CIL 14.4573	Fullers	Regio I, Ostia, 232 CE	60
CIL 6.10234	Stonemasons	Regio I, Rome, 153 CE	60
CIL 6.30983	Salus Augusta	Regio I, Rome, first half II CE	59
CIL 14.252	*Lenuncularii* (boatmen and registrars)	Regio I, Ostia, 200 CE	34
CIL 6.1052	*Paedagogi puerum* (teachers)	Regio I, Rome, 198 CE	24
CIL 9.3188	*Scabillarii* (musicians)	Regio IV, Corfinium, date?	22
ASIA AND THE WESTERN PROVINCES			
Pliny, *Ep.* 10.33	*Fabri* (builders)	Nicomedia, early II CE	150
ILLPRON 1450–57	*Centonarii* (textile dealers)	Noricum, second half II CE	93
ILLPRON 610	*Subaediani* (builders)	Noricum, second half II CE	57
CIRB 1134	*Naukleroi* (sailors)	Gorgippia, 173–211 CE	44
I.Parion 6	Fishermen	Parion, Mysia, I CE	16
I.Parion 5	Fishermen	Parion, Mysia, II CE	14
TAM Suppl III 201	Stonemasons	Western Rough Cilicia, mid-I CE	10
Egypt			
P.Corn 23	Weavers	Philadelphia, I CE	88
BGU VII 1615	Weavers	Philadelphia, 84 CE	30
I.Prose 40	Farmers	Psenamosis, 67–63 BCE	29
P.Mich V 244	*Apolysimoi* (those exempt from forced public service)	Tebtynis, 43 CE	24
P.Athens 41	Donkey drivers	Unknown, I CE	19
P.Berl.Spieg 3115	Funerary workers	Memnoneia, 109–108 BCE	18

(*continued*)

Table 1. *(continued)*

Name	*Type*	*Location*	*Size*
P.Mich V 243	Sheep and cattle owners	Tebtynis, time of Tiberius	16
PSI VIII 901	Fishermen	Tebtynis, 46 CE	14
SEG 41:1612–15	Ironworkers	Hermonthis, 324–357 CE	13
BGU VII 1572	Weavers	Philadelphia, 139 CE	12
P.Mich II 121r IV.6.9–12	Weavers	Tebtynis, 42 CE	5
StudPal IV 58–83.410–16	Rug beaters	Ptolemais Euergetis, 73 CE	5
StudPal IV 58–83.418–24	Potters	Ptolemais Euergetis, 73 CE	5
P.Oxy VII 1029	Hieroglyphic carvers	Oxyrhynchus, 107 CE	5
COLLEGIA DOMESTICA			
CIL 6.9102	*Collegium domesticum*	Rome, *Libertorum et familiae* NN, I CE	31
IGUR 160	Dionysos	Terre Nova, ca. 150 CE	402
CULTIC ASSOCIATIONS			
CIL 6.647	Silvanus	Regio I, Rome, III CE	99
SEG 54:235	Herakles	Epano Liosia, mid-I BCE–late I CE	99
IG II^2 2360	Zeus, Antha	Athens, mid-I BCE	84
CIL 3.633 II	Silvanus	Philippi, II CE	69
IG XII,5 186	Unknown	Paros, III BCE	65
IG II^2 1292	Sarapis	Athens? Piraeus? 215/214 BCE	65
IG II^2 1343	*Soteriastai*	Athens, 37/36 or 36/35 BCE	60
CIL 6.30983	Aesculapius	Rome, time of Hadrian	59
IGBulg III/1 1517	Dionysos	Philippopolis, Thrace, 241–244 CE	59
AE 1929, 161	Silvanus	Trebula Mutuesca, 60 CE	58
IG II^2 1297	Artemis Kallistē	Athens, 236/235 BCE	58

Name	Type	Location	Size
IDR I 31	Jupiter Cernenus	Albernus Maior, Dacia, 167 CE	54
IG V/1 210–12	*Tainaristai* (sanctuary of Tainaron)	Sparta, 30–20 BCE	52
CIRB 1282	Theos Hypsistos	Tanais, 228 CE	52
CIRB 1279	Theos Hypsistos	Tanais, 225 CE	51
IG II[2] 2358	Atargatis	Athens, ca. 135 BCE?	50
CIRB 1280	Theos Hypsistos	Tanais, 225 CE	47
SEG 46:1520	Apollo Pleurnos	Sardis, 90s BCE	44
IG II[2] 2361	Belela	Piraeus, 200–211 CE	43
I.Kyme 37 = GRA II 105	Mandros Kaion	Kyme, late I BCE/early I CE	43
IG X/2.1 68	Zeus Hypsistos	Thessalonike?, late I CE	38
I.Perg 374	*Hymnodoi* of the god Augustus	Pergamon, 129–138 CE	38
CIRB 1277	Theos Hypsistos	Tanais, ca. 173–211 CE	37
I.Beroia 27	Theos Hypsistos	Beroea, before 212 CE	37
CIL 11.6310	*Cultores* Iovi Latii	Regio VI, Pisaurum, I/II CE	35
CIL 11.5737	Mithras	Regio VI, Sentium, III CE	35
CIL 6.631	Silvanus	Regio I, Rome, 177 CE	34
AE 1994, 1334	Mithras	Virunum, Noricum, 184–201 CE	34
SEG 46:800	Zeus Hypsistos	Pydna, 250 CE	34
SEG 39:737	Samothracian deities, Herakles	Rhodes, 185 BCE	33
I.ScM III 35	Dionysos	Kallatis, Sythia Minor, III BCE	33
CIL 6.7459	Unknown cult	Regio I, Rome, II CE	33
P.Lond VII 2193	Zeus Hypsistos	Philadelphia 69–58 BCE	32
CCID 373	Jupiter Dolichenus	Rome, early III CE	32
P.Cair 30605	Sobek	Tebtynis, 145 BCE	31
SEG 46:864	Unknown cult	Pautalia, 150–200 CE	31
OGIS I 130	Various gods	Satis Island, 143–142 BCE	30
SB 3:6184	Thriphis	Ptolemaïs Hermiou, 138/137 BCE	29

(*continued*)

Table 1. (*continued*)

Name	*Type*	*Location*	*Size*
CIRB 1262	Unknown cult	Tanais, II CE	29
SEG 49:814	Dionysos	Thessalonike?, III CE	28
P.PragSatzung	Unknown cult	Tebtynis, 137 BCE	27
I.Smyrna 765	Anoubis	Smyrna, early III BCE	27
IG XII,3 330	Muses, heroes	Thera, 210–195 BCE	25
IG II^2 1322	Amphieros	Rhamnous, III/II BCE	25
CIL 3.633 III	Silvanus	Philippi, II CE	25
IG II^2 2499	Egretēs	Athens, 306/305 BCE	24
I.Perg 485	Dionysos	Pergamon, I CE	24
CIL 6.1052	Unknown cult	Regio I, Rome, 198 CE	24
IG II^2 2354	Unknown cult	Athens, end of III BCE	23
IG VII 2463	Athena	Boeotia, late IV BCE	22
CIRB 1283	Theos Hypsistos	Tanais, ca. 228 CE	21
IG VII 3224	Friends of the gods	Orchomenos, I BCE	21
I.Miletos 798	Sanctuary association	Miletos, 79/78, 43/42, or 41/40 BCE	20
P.Cair 30618 A–B	Unknown cult	Tebtynis, II BCE	20
P.Cair 31179	Sobek	Tebtynis, 147 BCE	19
IG II^2 4817	Unknown cult	Athens, II/III CE	19
SEG 41:1329	Meter Oreia	Karain, Asia Minor, late II CE	18
CIRB 1260	Theos Hypsistos	Tanais, 155 CE	18
IG X/2.1 259	Zeus Dionysos Gongylos	Thessalonike?, I CE	17
CIRB 1259	Unknown cult	Tanais, 104 CE	17
I.DionysosJ 94	Dionysos	Pergamon, II CE	17
P.Cair 30606	Sobek	Tebtynis, 158/157 BCE	17
Dura-Europas 871	Atargatis	Dura-Europas, 153 CE	17
IG II^2 2355	Asklepios	Athens, III BCE	16
IG II^2 2343	Herakles	Athens, ca. 400 BCE	16
P.Mich V 247	Unknown cult	Tebtynis, early I CE	16
Agora 16:161	Unknown cult	Athens, early III BCE	15
IG II^2 2347	Unknown cult	Salamis, ca. 300 BCE	15
IG XI/4 1223	Sarapis	Delos, 196 BCE	15

Name	*Type*	*Location*	*Size*
IG II^2 1325	Dionysos	Piraeus, 185/184 BCE	15
IGOlbia 11	Zeus Soter	Olbia, late IV BCE	15
P.Petr III 136	Unknown cult	Arsinoites, 231 BCE	15
P.Mich V 246	Harpokrates	Tebtynis, 43–49 CE	15
I.Miletos 796	Agathe, Tyche, Apollo, and Hermes	Miletos, 190–189 BCE	13
SEG 46:744	Zeus Hypsistos	Edessa, 51 CE	13
IG X/2.1 58	Synklitai	Thessalonike?, early II CE	13
ID 1758	Hermes, Poseidon, Apollo	Delos, 74 BCE	13
IG II^2 1335	Sabazios	Piraeus, 101/100 BCE	12
IGBulg III/2 1626	Asklepios	Augusta Traiana, III CE	12
P.Lille.dem. 31	Souchos	Arsinoites, III BCE	11
IG II^2 2353	Asklepios	Athens, mid-III BCE	11
SEG 43:59	Unknown cult	Rhamnous	11
P.Assoc pp. 45–51	Sobek	Tebtynis, 151 BCE	10
ID 1760	Lares Competales	Delos, 100–98 BCE	10
P.Mich V 248	Unknown cult	Tebtynis, early I CE	9
Dura-Europas 904–5	Gadde	Dura-Europas, III CE	8
Dura-Europas 871	Atargatis	Dura-Europas, 153 CE	17
SB 3:7182	Unknown cult	Philadelphia, II–I BCE	8
IG II^2 2348	Unknown cult	Athens, end of IV BCE	6
ID 1768	Lares Competales	Delos, ca. 100 BCE	5
SB 5:8805	Stonemasons	Ptolemais Hermiou (Egypt)	5
IG VII 33 + A2	*Orgēones* of the gods	Megara, late I BCE	4
TOTAL			141
Mean			77.15
Median			29
Mode			15
Maximum			1,330
Minimum			4

(*continued*)

Table 1. (*continued*)

Name	*Type*	*Location*	*Size*
TOTAL OCCUPATIONAL			47
Mean			164.89
Median			60
Mode			5
ITALY ONLY			25
Mean			272.42
Median			125
Mode			60
TOTAL CULTIC			92
Mean			29.29
Median			24
Mode			15
Maximum			99
Minimum			4

4

BELONGING

In the second half of the second century CE in the town of Virunum, a builders' guild erected a marble plaque with their membership roster bearing fifty-seven names—thirty-five men and twenty-two women.[1] The men are listed in columns 1 and 2, with three spaces left blank at the bottom of column 2, presumably to accommodate the names of newer male members. The women occupy columns 3 and 4. At fifty-seven members, the collegium was of modest size for an association that was involved in a building trade, where membership was often double or triple that size, at least in large Italian cities. Analysis of the names suggests that most of the women listed (engraved in slightly smaller letters) were the daughters, sisters, or wives of the men.

Five of the names, two men from column 2 and three women in columns 3 and 4, had been erased so efficiently that no trace remains. The erasure of names from monuments is a well-known phenomenon associated with the practice of *damnatio memoriae*, or memory sanction, famously visited upon the names of the elite, including disgraced emperors, senators, and imperial women.[2] It is less widely known that the names of ordinary people were also gouged out of lists that were on display in the group's meeting space, yet such memory sanctions in private associations are well attested.[3]

The intent was not simply to shame but to obliterate. Often, the erasure is so complete that the offending name cannot be recovered. We should assume, however, that many of those who belonged to the guild and others too knew whose names had been erased, making the erasure even more pungent. In a culture where immortality was as much a matter of the survival of one's name in posterity as it was a matter of individual postmortem survival, *damnatio memoriae* struck at the very heart of identity.

The premium that Romans placed on *memoria*—commemoration by family, descendants, grateful clients, and friends—is amply attested in the wealth of funerary monuments erected not only by the superrich, but by people of very modest means. Being named responded to the fear of oblivion, of disappearing without a trace, whether one's name was on an elaborate and costly monument, or on one erected by a freedman proudly displaying the tools with which he earned a living, or on a simple columbarium plaque. Tacitus concludes the biography of his father-in-law Gnaeus Julius Agricola, by evoking this fear: "For indeed oblivion buries many of the men of old, as the inglorious and ignoble; Agricola will survive for posterity, his story told and handed on" (*Agricola* 46).

In the case of senators and emperors, memory sanctions were related to the efforts of emperors to suppress the memory of predecessors, rivals, and opponents and the resolve of the Roman Senate to erase the memory of disgraced emperors.[4] It is difficult to imagine how in the modern world such a practice could be implemented. To erase the name of a disgraced U.S. president or Canadian prime minister from public memory would be unimaginable, requiring not only the removal of official portraits from government buildings, but the redacting of tens of millions of documents, public and private, print and electronic, to remove the offending name.[5] In the imperial period, where proportionately fewer records and images of any individual existed, it is nonetheless an impressive testimony to the sheer determination to suppress the memory of disgraced emperors that strenuous efforts were made to erase names and images not only on public display, but also from private records—in both Rome and the provinces.

What would have prompted the erasure of names of the members of private guilds and associations? At least three possibilities could be considered. The first is that erasure might have been the collateral damage of a senatorial *damnatio*. In a first-century *album* of a *collegium domesticum* consisting of the freedmen and slaves associated with a large household, the name of the patron had been erased from the heading at the top of the *album*. All that remains in the heading is LIBERTORUM ET FAMIL⟦——————⟧ (CIL 6.9102; Rome, I CE). The third partial word can easily be restored as *famil[iae]*, meaning the enslaved and freed members of the household. But the owner's name is gone. The offending name that was chipped out was likely that of a Roman citizen, probably one of the elite, who had fallen into disfavor. The erasure of his name is an instance of a political memory sanction. But what is just as interesting is that part of the names of ten of the first eleven *plebs* in the *album* were also erased.

D	Fe[————]	l(ibertus)
D	⟦————⟧ochus	l(ibertus)
⟦D	————⟧icius	l(ibertus)
⟦D	————⟧us	l(ibertus)
⟦D	—————⟧	l(ibertus)
D	⟦—————⟧mus	
D	Co⟦——————⟧	
D	Iul(ius) Philonicus	
	⟦——————⟧	
D	⟦——————⟧s	
D	⟦———————⟧	
D	Lucanus	
⟦D⟧	Sex(tus) Pil⟦————⟧us	

The first five names are specifically designated as *liberti* and the other five were likely freedmen as well. Although fragments of their cognomina are still visible, each nomen (family name) was carefully removed. The significance of these erasures is clear: upon manumission a freedman assumed the nomen of his former owner and took his slave name as a cognomen. Accordingly, we should suspect that the name in the heading belonged to an elite Roman citizen, perhaps a senator, and that the intent of the memory sanction was not only to obliterate from memory his name, but also any person who bore his family name. The names of the ten freedmen were casualties of association.

This cannot be a complete explanation, however, even for CIL 6.9102. There is another erasure in this *album*, at the bottom of column 2 (line 82). The erased name was a single name, not the tripartite name of a freedman. Since it appears surrounded by other slave names, it was probably that of a slave (who did not bear a nomen). Accordingly, one might suggest a second explanation for erasure: that names were erased as members died.

This possibility, however, can be dismissed. Deceased members are in fact marked as such in this *album*; even the first ten whose nomina were erased were also marked as deceased and their cognomina remained visible. Forty-nine names in the first three columns (including the first ten) are marked with "D," for *decessit* (he has died).[6] The last four members (lines 84–87), added later to the *album* by a different cutter, are marked with a *theta*, Θ (*thanōn*, deceased), also a common way in Latin *alba* to marked deceased individuals.

Since one of the key roles of *collegia domestica* was to provide burial for deceased members, it would be highly incongruous to erase the names of the deceased who had just been honored by the group through the provision of a funeral. "D" indicates that the member was deceased *and* that a funeral had been provided for him or her. This implies that the name in CIL 6.9102 column 2 line 82 that was erased was eliminated for another reason.

A third explanation of erasure is suggested by an *album* of the *familia Silvani* dating to 60 CE (see chapter 2). There, erasure of a name is the penalty for failing to comply with the bylaws of the association. The inscription prescribes:

> *ex cuius decuria deliquerit* | *eorum cura erit tollere. si ita non fecerit d(are) d(ebeat)* HS X
>
> From which *decuria* (one) is absent, it will be their (the officers responsible for the *decuria*) responsibility to erase (the name). If one does not do so, he will owe (a fine) of 10 sesterces.[7]

Since the immediate context concerns a member failing to participate in, or contribute to, the funeral of a member, *delinquo* probably means "to fail" or "to offend" against the bylaws by not attending and contributing to the funeral of a member.

The bylaws of a collegium of ivory and citrus wood dealers from the time of Hadrian (CIL 6.33885) suggests something similar. This was a relatively unusual group that was utterly exclusive, barring from membership anyone who did not deal in ivory or citrus wood. Its bylaws included the provision, "It has been decided that if someone other than a merchant of ivory or citrus wood is admitted to this collegium by the fraudulent action of the *curatores* (officers), for that reason will the (names of the) *curatores* be scraped (*raderentur*) from the list (*ordo*) and erased from the *album*." Presumably, the person who was fraudulently admitted would also be removed from the *album*.

Compliance with the disciplinary practices of the group was paramount since those practices underwrote the solidarity of the association. The secretary of an association would arrange the erasure of any member who had failed to comply with the bylaws of the group in a manner so egregious that the imposition of fines and other disciplinary sanctions were not deemed sufficient. Or perhaps fines and other disciplinary measures had been ignored. In the case of the ivory and citrus wood dealers even the officers who had been complicit in the induction of unqualified members would suffer similar obliteration.

MATERIALIZING BELONGING IN ASSOCIATIONS

I begin with the phenomenon of memory sanctions because it underscores the critical importance of being named, being there, being visible—that is, belonging. Memory sanctions were effective precisely because in Mediterranean antiquity identity was intimately linked to being part of a collective. Individuals were routinely identified with a larger group—a family, a guild, a precinct organization, a neighborhood, or one of the elite social configurations.[8] It is perhaps difficult for the modern reader to appreciate the importance of *being seen* to belong to a group until one considers its opposite. Imagine what it would mean to be Photoshopped out of the picture of one's graduation class or from the photograph of a wedding party, leaving a blank space where a figure had once been.

The materialization of belonging to an occupational guild or cultic association by the construction of lists must be seen in the broader context of civic practices. Public space of Greek and Roman cities was a place of lists. Athens displayed the names of archons, youths in military training (*ephebes*), public benefactors, public debtors, traitors, deserters, people granted citizenship, people tried for homicide, war casualties, magistrates, landholders, Panathenaic victors, and so on. Roman towns displayed consular *fasti* (lists of the yearly consuls), lists of augurs and senators, and lists of civic events. Lists of civic officials, benefactors, and other notables were found almost everywhere. These served to locate individuals within the complex space of a city or town.[9] We should think of these lists not simply as administrative archives. They were the ancient equivalent of group portraits: they not only indicated who belonged, but also articulated hierarchies. Although in many cases there is no archaeological record of where an *album* of an association was discovered, it is likely that it was posted on the walls of the group's assembly hall so that all could see it. Just as in a group photograph the spatial arrangement of figures is indexical to status, the order of names in an *album* indicated who were the patrons, the honorary members, and the leaders and other functionaries, and who were the *plebs*. In instances where we have multiple rosters from the same association—as is the case with the boatmen and registrars (see chapter 2)—comparison of the location of the names on each of the rosters shows how certain individuals have "moved up in the world" by having their names inscribed progressively higher on succeeding rosters, sometimes beginning as *plebs*, and eventually achieving the position of president or even patron.

The *alba* of antiquity no longer have exact counterparts in the modern world and hence it is easy for us not even to think about the functions of ancient rosters. We do not live in cities where organizations obsessively display lists in public spaces. Some civic buildings have lists of former mayors or prime ministers, and we can see the photographs of graduates in the halls of high schools and colleges and read the names of deceased soldiers in city spaces. But we don't publicly list current members of our fire departments or electricians' guild or expect to see membership lists of synagogues or churches. Our public lists are mainly commemorative and archival. Ancient lists, by contrast, were essential media for communicating the critical "commodities" of honor and shame, the recording of social obligation, and above all, belonging.

There is another reason why the use of membership lists in "religious" groups might strike us as otiose. Since the beginning of the early modern period a significant shift has occurred in the conception of membership, especially in "religious" groups. The center of gravity has shifted from the larger collectives—the church or the synagogue—as the locus of stable religious identities to the individuals who elect to affiliate with a collective with which they agree or feel at home. The rhetoric of identity has shifted from group membership to individual experience and choice.[10] Because of the overwhelming focus on interior experience and personal choice, merely being on a membership list would now seem superfluous.

How different it was in Mediterranean antiquity! Lists played several critical functions: to honor members, to undergird their various mutual obligations, and to make them "visible."

HONORIFIC FUNCTIONS

Membership rosters were as common in Greek and Roman associations as they were in other aspects of civic life. The *album* was not simply an archive; it served an honorific function, certainly by featuring the names of patrons and leaders but also by displaying the names of all members. As such, rosters functioned as tangible expressions of one's connectivity and belonging. They were artifacts to which one could point as evidence of belonging to a group, and thus they functioned as vehicles to communicate and materialize social capital.

The materiality of lists aided in this function. Lists, as Rosalind Thomas has observed, were deliberately designed to be maximally legible, even to those with marginal literacy. Literary texts and the texts of many inscriptions were written *scripta continua*, with no word breaks or punctuation. This format made reading extremely difficult except for the tiny few who were formally trained. By contrast, lists arranged each name (occasionally two names) on a line of its own and often inserted spaces or medial dots between the nomen and the cognomen (e.g., see fig. 3) or between the name and the patronym, making it a simple matter for even the marginally literate to identify their names on the list. The list is literally a monumental waste of space insofar as its verbal contents could be compassed in many fewer lines and in a much smaller inscription, if it had been engraved in a continuous stream of characters. But that was the point. A list is intended to be seen and read by all. Thomas, commenting on lists of debtors and malefactors, remarks on the "punitive power of the list," the power of the list to shame individuals and to compel compliance with civic values through the fear of public exposure.[11] Membership lists, however, also participated in the power to honor by rendering permanently visible the names of patrons, leaders, and ordinary members of an association. This is a powerful antidote to the fear of oblivion that infected everyone.

The *alba* of associations served a double function. On one hand, they monumentalized membership by identifying members and making their names permanently visible. Being named was a way to signal that members shared in the social capital of the group. On the other, the arrangement of names on the *alba* underscored hierarchy and thus provided a kind of visually stylized picture of the organization of the group. It mattered where one was on this list, just as in photographs of modern sports teams one expects to see the captain, coach, and other key players in the front row and other players at the back. The location of a name in an *album* indicated status. The *album* also signaled that the members collectively adhered to the codes and values of the group.[12]

The honorific function of a list is illustrated by a mid-third-century fragmentary inscription from Athens, which is a decree authorizing the erection of a stele to honor the officials of the members (*thiasōtai*) of an Artemis cult association. This inscription (IG II^2 1298 = GRA I 20) not only inscribes those who are honored, but also the names of all of the *thiasōtai*:

----	----
Mene--	----
Doriōn	Kallistion
Noumenios	Dorkion
Pheidias	Kompsē
Sosigenēs	Simalē
Diēs	Mēlis

For good fortune! In the year that Diomedon was archon, month of Skirophorion, at the regular meeting: Dionysios son of T [. . .] made the (following) motion: be it resolved by the association of *thiasōtai*: Whereas (those listed below) have acted honorably (10) and piously in all matters and in regard to the gods, let (the members) set up a stele in the temple of Artemis and inscribe the names of all of the *thiasōtai* on it and also inscribe (the names) of the priests who happened to serve in the year that (15) Diomedon was archon, if it is agreed by the association that they properly administered the things pertaining to the gods. And (be it resolved) also to inscribe the names of the associates (*synthiasōtai*) who join, once they have contributed the (share) of the money that is their due in the "fund" (*eranos*), in accordance with the law. Each shall register himself and his dues with the treasurer and the secretary.

(The members honor)

the treasurer	the secretary
Dionysios	Theopropos
—	—

Since both the top and bottom of the inscription are broken off, many details are missing. The top evidently contained a full membership list, divided into men (column 1) and women (column 2) and parsed into the membership categories of full members (*thiasōtai*) and associate (or perhaps probationary) members (*synthiasōtai*). These are all listed in the nominative case where they function as the logical subject for the honorific action itself, "(these honored) the treasurer Dionysios and the secretary Theopropos."[13] Since the inscription is also broken at the bottom, we have only the names of the treasurer and secretary (in the accusative) but lack the names of the priests who had been chosen for that year.

The significance of the construction of this decree and membership list should not be missed. On one hand, virtue in ancient society—having served the gods "honorably and piously"—deserved to be recognized, whether such recognition was inscribed on a stele and set up in front of a temple so that passersby could view it or was simply announced at the next assembly so that all could hear. The twenty-first-century custom that identifies some donors to a symphony orchestra or a university as "anonymous" would have struck ancient Mediterranean people as not only quaint, but idiotic. Anonymous virtue is no virtue at all.

On the other hand, associations such as the *thiasōtai* of Artemis *also* created a full membership list, arranged by various membership categories. Because a list is a kind of snapshot of the group, it is a tangible expression of the kinds of connectivity available in the association, some being listed as full members, others as associates, some as priests, others as treasurers. Modern symphony orchestras single out benefactors in their programs, parsing them into such categories as "Platinum Donors," "Gold Benefactors," or "the Conductor's Circle" on the basis of the amounts of money donated. But they would hardly list everyone who had subscribed to the symphony season. This is because, apart from the extra paper that a full list of subscribers would require, we assume that most of the subscribers to a symphony are probably members of many other identity groups: families, workplaces, churches, tennis clubs, volunteer organizations, or trade unions. Patronage of symphony orchestras is epiphenomenal to the main constituents of social identity. In the ancient context, by contrast, most nonelite individuals likely belonged to only one or two nonfamilial groups. It was correspondingly more important to signal belonging in that group and to be *seen* to belong.

The rosters of associations thus served at least two important functions: the very act of naming people in legible ways served an honorific function, warding off the fear of oblivion; and they represented identities relationally, by defining people in relation to others.[14]

LEGAL AND FINANCIAL FUNCTIONS

The inscription cited above, IG II[2] 1298, illustrates another more pragmatic function of lists. There, the list of names records contributors who donated to a common fund; hence the roster provides a public record of those who are entitled to benefit by way of receiving loans. The legal function of membership lists is best illustrated by the bylaws of associations from Ptolemaic and early Roman Egypt where each member approved the bylaws by signing the document or having the scribe sign for them. Although they were not inscribed on stone but rather recorded on papyrus, the recording of names played an important function by indicating rights and responsibilities. P.Mich V 243 (Tebtynis, time of Tiberius) records the bylaws of a guild of sheep and cattle owners. It not only lists the monthly contributions expected of each member, but imposes on each certain behavioral rules. The papyrus concludes with a list of members, each of whom signaled approval by indicating *eudokō*, "I approve." That the document was legally binding is clear from its closing formula, *kyrios estō ho nomos*, "this law shall be valid":

> If a member ignores someone (i.e., another member) who is in distress and does not assist in helping him out of his trouble, he shall pay 8 drachmae. Whoever at the banquet, when taking his seat, shoves in front of another shall pay an extra 3 obols to sit in his own place. If a member prosecutes or calumniates another (member), he shall be fined 8 drachmae. If a member commits intrigue against, or corrupts the home of another (member), he shall pay 60 drachmae. If a member has been arrested for a private debt, they (the other members) shall stand surety for him for up to 100 silver drachmae for 30 days, during which time he shall release the men (from their pledge). May health prevail! If one of the members (*synoditai*) should die, all the members shall be shaved and shall hold a banquet for one day, each member contributing immediately 1 drachma and two loaves. In the case of other deaths (i.e.,

> the death of family members), they shall hold a banquet for one day. Whoever does not shave his head shall be fined 4 drachmae. Whoever does not defile himself (by participating in the funeral) or has not put a wreath at the tomb shall be fined 4 drachmae. Other matters shall be as the association decides. This law shall be valid when signed by the majority of members. When validated, it shall be returned to the president.

These undertakings are not trivial. Violations of etiquette, failure to contribute dues, or failure to attend the funeral of a member led to fines. The undertakings could be enforced not only by the association itself, but by the courts. That breaches of association bylaws were actionable in law is demonstrated by the complaint to the *stratēgos* (governor) by a woman whose deceased brother was allegedly mistreated by his association. P.Enteuxis 20 (Magdôla, Arsinoites, 215 BCE) is the petition of Krateia, the sister of a deceased member of an association. She claims that when her brother died, the association members failed to attend the funeral or to hand over the funeral fee (*taphikon*) to her, to assist with expenses. In a second hand, the *stratēgos* orders an assistant to examine the bylaws of the association in question and to "compel the parties to come to a fair resolution."

The papyrus indicates what we know from other associations as well, that members contributed a small monthly fee to build up a fund, called a *taphikon* in Greek and *funeraticium* in Latin, to pay for the funerals of members. As in P.Mich V 243, members were expected to participate in the funerals of their fellows. Krateia claims that her brother's association failed to observe its own regulations when it came to the disbursement of the *taphikon* to which, presumably, her brother had dutifully contributed. The *stratēgos*' command to an assistant to "examine the association's bylaws" presupposes that copies of the bylaws *and* the appended membership list were available in the village archives. If the name of the plaintiff's brother was indeed inscribed and if he was in good standing, the association could be compelled to hand over the funeral fee.

The function of membership lists, then, clearly goes far beyond merely recording for posterity the names of members. These lists served to render real the relationships among the members, to recognize their place in the association, and to underscore the rights and privileges that pertained to membership. Whether the rosters of associations were inscribed on stone and affixed to the clubhouse wall or written on papyrus (as they were in Egypt) or on wooden tablets, the recording of the names of members materialized the relations among members, conferred on them a place within the group, and underscored the rights and obligations of members. *Lists made visible the connections that existed among people.* This is also why the erasure of a name from an *album* was so potent a sanction. Erasure evoked the anxiety of oblivion, of never having been there at all.

THE TECHNOLOGIES OF BELONGING

Belonging and connectivity, or we might say "groupness," were performed in other ways too, including processions, baptism, rosters, meals, rules, sanctions, and mandatory attendance.

PROCESSIONS

Public processions afforded occupational guilds and cultic associations the opportunity to display themselves, both to themselves as a group and publicly to others. In Athens the Panathenaic Procession, held every four years, included citizens and foreign residents and served to demonstrate loyalty to Athena and the city. There is no reason to doubt that cultic associations also joined in this procession. Plato, moreover, channeling Socrates, mentions the civic spectacle of the nighttime torch race and procession from the city center (*asty*) to the Piraeus that featured both Athenian and Thracian devotees of the Thracian deity Bendis marching together.[15]

There is relatively scant direct testimony to the participation of guilds in processions but little reason to suppose that this was unusual. From a late date, the biographies of Gallienus and Aurelian record the emperors' triumphal processions, which featured guilds marching with their banners.[16] Earlier, the *dendrophors*, mostly freedmen associated with the cult of Cybele, staged yearly processions memorialized on numerous reliefs.[17] A relief from Le Musée d'Aquitaine from the late second century depicts four men carrying a large decorated tree trunk through the city, probably a representation of the procession of *dendrophors*.[18] In the Latin West, in Asia Minor, and in Egypt, associations also participated in publicly honoring the emperor and other civic benefactors.[19]

Although the data on the processions of occupational guilds and cultic associations are sparse, the ethnography of contemporary groups that conduct processions through civic space might help us to understand what "work" a procession did for an association. Religious sodalities in Spain and Italy and in ethnic neighborhoods of North American cities frequently conduct such processions, with members of the group carrying sacred objects, wearing distinctive clothing, or holding banners or flags. Processions are scripted and marshaled performances. Each participant plays a distinct role in the whole, as one who carries an object, leads or follows those who do, or performs certain gestures, and so on. The procession is a communal performance. Like communal meals, processions function to make the group visible to itself, and they materialize bonds between the individual and the group through the sheer physicality of movement of bodies through civic space.[20]

Did Christ groups organize processions in the pre-Constantinian period? As Philip Harland has rightly observed, Ignatius of Antioch imitates the processional language of the cult of Dionysos, which featured "god bearers," "basket bearers," and "phallus bearers."[21] Ignatius says of to the Ephesian Christ followers: you are "all associations, god bearers, temple bearers, Christ bearers, (and) bearers of holy objects" (*synodoi pantes theophoroi, naophoroi, Christophoroi,* and *hagiophoroi, Eph.* 9.2). In *Eph.* 12.2 Ignatius imagines that the Ephesians are the *parodos* of those who are taken up to God, Paul's fellow *mystai.* There he uses *parodos,* a term that refers to the first entry of a chorus onto a stage, and *summystai,* a standard term for a participant in a Dionysiac procession. Whether or not Christ followers engaged in actual processions, Ignatius's language at least implies a social imaginary in which they paraded through the city, displaying their holy objects and themselves to each other and to the city.

Earlier still, 2 Cor 2:14 invokes the image of God leading a triumphal procession (*thriambeuō*) at which the "fragrance of his knowledge is spread around." This plays on the common practice in processions of using incense, scented oil, or other aromatic substances to signal the approach of the god or goddess[22] and the use of roses in the festival of the *rosalia.*[23] Because rituals of belonging that involved processions were so much a part of the life of the ancient city, it is hardly surprising that at least the *idea* of processing together was part of the social imaginary of Christ assemblies.

The procession fictively levels status inequalities within the group by the act of having all members, rich and poor, male and female, participate in the ritual, moving together as a single body. At the same time, processions express internal hierarchies, manifest in who leads the procession, what clothing is worn, and the roles assigned to various participants. Like the creation of rosters and the staging of meals, processions are not simply activities in which a group also happens to engage; they are activities that constitute the group as a group and that articulate structures within the group. Belonging is both performed and displayed.

BAPTISM

In Christ assemblies baptism eventually became a marker of membership. Although there is no reference to baptism in 1 Thessalonians, the earliest of the Pauline letters, by 1 Corinthians baptism seems to have become a norm.

Despite some misgivings about baptism expressed in 1 Cor 1:13–17, Paul treats it as the instrument that communicates the spirit and marks entry into a corporate and mixed body: "For by means of one spirit all of us were baptized into one body (*sōma*), either Judeans or Greeks, whether slaves or free people, and all drank one spirit" (1 Cor 12:13).

By the time of the writing of the letter to the Romans in the late 50s, baptism is presupposed as a universal identity marker in Pauline assemblies, since Rom 6:3–11 theorizes water baptism as carrying key theological significance: "as many of us who are baptized into Christ Jesus have been baptized into his death" (6:3).

In neither 1 Corinthians nor Romans is baptism treated as a ritual that one undergoes simply as a personal experience. Rather, it marks the individual's *entry into a corporate identity.* Paul speaks of being baptized *into one body,* which creates a new identity. By the time of the *Didache* in the early second century, baptism was the sine qua non for admission to the communal banquet: "Let no one eat or drink from your thanksgiving (meal) except those who have been baptized in the name of the Lord, for it is also about this that the Lord has said, 'Do not give what is holy to dogs'" (9.5).

In behavioral terms, baptism was a form of "signaling"—indicating one's compliance with group norms by submitting to a water ritual. This was not an especially costly signaling practice, requiring the same level of commitment as circumcision of males or scarification or shaving one's head. Nor was it an ordeal, as is attested in Mithraic initiation.[24] Baptism, nevertheless, signaled entry into the group, since it was conducted in the presence of the group and with a naked initiate. In later practice it culminated a complex initiatory process that began with catechetical instruction.

Initiation into the Eleusinian and the Korybantic mysteries included washings, dancing, and sacrifices.[25] As far as we know, however, water rituals were not practiced by occupational guilds or by most cultic associations. The most obvious analogy is provided by Judean associations, for which water rituals were critical both as a purificatory practice and for the initiation of proselytes. This might be the origin of the practice of Christ assemblies.[26]

Irrespective of the form, many associations maintained some type of entrance ritual—an ordeal, a test, or a water ritual. Entry into cultic associations was frequently marked by a "vetting" called the *dokimasia.* For example, a late-fourth-century BCE association devoted to the Thracian goddess Bendis stipulated that new members should undergo a scrutiny: "(20) So that there may be as many associates (*orgeōnes*) of the sanctuary as possible, it is permitted for anyone who so wishes to contribute [. . .] drachmae to become a member of the sanctuary and to be inscribed on the stele. Let the members vet (*dokimazō*) those who are to be inscribed on the stele, and hand over the names of those approved to the secretary in the month of (25) Thargelion" (IG II² 1361.20–25 = GRA I 4; Athens, 330–324/323 BCE).

The use of the verb *dokimazō* (vet) clearly mimics the practice of the Athenian assembly for examining candidates for office.[27] It was designed to assess probity of life and to expose moral failings.[28] By the imperial period, the *dokimasia* included a moral examination: "It is not permitted for anyone to enter this most holy assembly of *eranistai* without being first vetted (*dokimazetō*) as to whether he is pure and pious and good. Let the president, the *archeranistēs*, the secretary, the treasurers, and the syndics examine (the candidate)" (IG II² 1369.32–33, 34 = GRA I 49; Liopesi [Attica], II CE).

Although the bylaws of the group do not indicate its main activities, the reference to *hagnos* (pure) as a requirement of new members might suggest that some kind of cultic activity was part of the group's practice, since the term is typically associated with the prerequisites for entry into a shrine and participation in sacrifice.[29] In the late Hellenistic and early Roman periods, *hagnos* came to be used metaphorically and applied to the condition of the soul. The fact that *hagnos* is set alongside *eusebēs* (pious) and *agathos* (good) points in the same direction.[30]

Examination of members was also current in Christ groups, although not specifically connected with initiation. The verb *dokimazō* appears several times: in 1 Cor 11:28–29 and 2 Cor 13:5–7, Paul advises self-examination before the communal meal and insinuates that some might be "unapproved" (*adokimoi*). The Pastoral writer prescribes the scrutinizing of assistants before their being allowed to function in that capacity (1 Tim 3:10). And in the late first or early second century, *1 Clement* claims that the apostles "appointed the first fruits of their ministry as supervisors and assistants, testing them through the spirit" (*dokimasantes tō pneumati*, 42.4).

Thus, whether a group used baptism, a *dokimasia*, some other initiatory rite, or some combination of these, entry into the group needed to be marked. In this sense, Christ assemblies were no different from many other associations.

MEMBERSHIP ROSTERS

Entrance rituals, as important as they undoubtedly were, functioned alongside continuing markers of membership and belonging such as the communal meal and processions. Entrance into groups, however, had to be not only regulated but also recorded. The Iobakchoi of Athens solved this problem by having the priest record the names of those who had been vetted and had paid fees (IG II^2 1368.62–63). Guilds that produced membership rosters, such as those already discussed, were in effect recording all those who had been duly admitted.

What of Christ assemblies? By the fourth century catechumens were enrolled on a list, and in the early fifth century Augustine refers to the possibility of striking someone's name from the membership list.[31] Did Christ groups at the time of Paul keep such records? We cannot answer this question. The possibility that they did should not be too quickly dismissed, however, given how common it was for other associations to keep such records. It would be easy to think that if the group were small, as I assume the Corinthian Christ assembly was, it would perhaps not be difficult to have informal knowledge of who was and who was not a member. Yet even a very small cultic association in the Fayûm (Egypt) with only six to ten members nevertheless kept careful records of those who had attended each of its meetings.[32] In fact many associations with fewer than fifteen members still thought it important to have a roster of members, a fact that undoubtedly points to the importance of *being named* that was fundamental to ancient Mediterranean culture.

At least by the second century the Pastoral writer speaks of "enrolling" widows who met the requirements for support (1 Tim 5:9), using the same verb, *katalegō*, that is routinely used for the official enrolling of individuals in various groups.[33] About the same time Lucian's satire *De morte Peregrini* 11 claims that Peregrinus had endeared himself to a group of Christ followers who "supposed him to be a god, used him as a lawgiver, and inscribed (*epegraphanto*) him as their president." Lucian here assumes that part of the group's recordkeeping would include the inscribing of the names of officials and, probably, of members.

The idea of membership lists is certainly not foreign to the mental world of early Christ assemblies. As early as Exodus, one sees the notion of God having a book from which names of Israelites could be blotted out (Exod 32:33), and Psalm 69:28 likewise imagines God having a book of names, blotting out some and enrolling others.[34] The Lukan Jesus assures his followers that their names are "written in heaven" (Luke 10:20). Paul invokes God's book of life in Phil 4:3, which in this imaginary is the membership list of the commonwealth (*politeuma*) of heaven (Phil 3:20). No doubt drawing on this motif, the Apocalypse of John describes a "book of life" in which only the "clean" are enrolled (*gegrammenoi*, Rev 21:27). Failure to find one's name there means being "thrown into the lake of fire" (Rev 20:15).[35] Hermas refers on several occasions to enrollment in the Book of Life.[36] Given the legal as well as honorific functions of lists, being enrolled in the "book of life" imaginatively encodes one as a "citizen" of a new commonwealth with certain rights and privileges that pertain to this fictive citizenship.

Second Corinthians 8:6 and 8:10–11 might be interpreted in the context of list maintenance. Paul here writes to the Corinthians from Macedonia, obviously concerned with the state of the collection that was begun the previous year. Paul was worried that when he arrived in Corinth the collection would be incomplete and hence at a level that would leave him embarrassed. He therefore mentions the arrival of Titus, whom he sent to Corinth to complete the collection (8:6). He continues, "and I give my opinion in this matter; for it would be advantageous for you, who began already last year, not only to do (this) but also desire to do (it), and now also to complete it (*epitelesate*), so just as you were eager to desire (it), so also you will complete (*epitelesai*) it from the resources you have" (8:10–11). Richard Ascough notes the formal use of *epiteleō* in 8:6 and 8:10–11, which he points out has the nuance of the completion of a cultic duty.[37] We might then ask: How would the Corinthians know when their duty was completed?

The simplest way to know that the collection was completed is to produce a contributor list with the contribution of each member recorded. Employed for fund-raising both by Greek cities and by various associations, subscriptions, called *epidoseis*, aimed at full participation of the citizen or association membership. For this reason, the contributor list likely corresponded very closely to the full membership list. It is not unreasonable, then, to imagine that the Corinthians had a list of contributors—or at least Paul expected them to have one—that could be presented to Titus upon his arrival.

Early Christ groups functioned in a context where membership lists were routinely employed and where membership was monitored. Christ groups invoked as meaningful the notion that their deity kept membership lists. Thus, we could well suppose that there was a Corinthian "group portrait." Such a group portrait would have had the same functions as the *alba* of other associations: to render members visible to each other, to record all those who had submitted to the group's initiation, to record their names and thereby to honor them, and to document the mutual moral obligations that membership in the association created.

MEALS

Communal meals are perhaps the most commonly attested practices of associations, including Christ assemblies. Evidence of dining practices in Judean assemblies is provided by the archaeological remains of *triclinia* at a few Judean assemblies and literary references to communal dining.[38] Evidence of communal dining in Greek and Roman cultic associations is plentiful.

As performances of belonging, these meals can be regarded as instances of what Claude Grignon, discussing meals in early modern French society, has called segregative commensality (see more in chapter 7). Segregative commensality serves to reinforce the "We" by rejecting the "not We"—strangers, rivals, enemies. According to Grignon it is "a group technique and sometimes a group therapy, a way for the group to make itself visible and concrete to itself, and, first of all, to number its members, to register recruitments and defections, comers and goers."[39]

Paul in 1 Cor 5:11 treats the communal meal as a site to register who is a member and who is not. Those who fall below the ethical standards of the group should be excluded from the communal meal: "But now I am writing to you not to associate with anyone who bears the name of brother who is immoral (*pornos*) or greedy or is an idolater, reviler, drunkard, or robber. Do not even eat with such a one." Participation in the communal meal thus signified that those who were present had subscribed to the group's ethical regime. They were reliable and trustworthy. This also meant that exclusionary practices were needed to police the borders of the group.

John Donahue recognized that association meals are excellent examples of segregative commensality: membership gave members visibility to themselves and visibility within the polis. It created the space for conviviality. And because associations tended to mimic the political and social hierarchies of the city, their meals allowed members to participate in a polity from which, outside the association, they were excluded. According to Donahue, these meals "provided a setting not only for social interaction but also for creating hierarchies that could not be found outside of the collegium. Only in this context, for example, could a common cult worshiper become a leader and confirm his status through his access to the largest amount of food and drink."[40]

Because segregative commensality functions to create social interaction, enhance group identity, and mimic external hierarchies, the menu of a banquet is of less importance than the performance of the banquet itself. Indeed, a survey of the menus of Roman collegia confirms that in most cases the menu was simple: bread and wine (*pane et vino*), with occasional additions of figs or sardines. The point of the meal was not to dine sumptuously but to *see oneself* as dining with the group and to *let others see it*.

Associations also practiced a form of transgressive commensality—a form of eating that invoked social borders and temporarily suspended these borders "in the neutralized and ritual parenthesis of a meal."[41] This occurred when they invited their patrons to dine, as they might have done to celebrate patrons' birthdays or otherwise to honor them and recognize their largesse.[42] The invitation to dine did not permanently efface status differences, but in the ritual space of the dining room where all reclined together and ate portions defined by the association's bylaws, status differences were temporarily leveled. Even if patrons received double portions of food and drink and were shown the best seats in the dining room, these occurred *on the association's terms.* Once the meal was over, the status quo returned: patrons were superior, and association members were in their debt. But during the meal what really mattered was the fact of eating together. The collegium displayed itself as a group to patrons, and patrons basked in their commendations and toasts. Both gained social capital.[43]

The simplicity of the menu of association banquets underscores that something other than sustenance was at stake. Two features of the association meals are important to observe, both related to "belonging."

First, regulation and orchestration were critical features of the meals of cultic groups. Some associations stipulated the menu and regulated the amount of bread and wine (sometimes other foodstuffs) to be provided to each of the diners, even indicating the quantity of the wine to be consumed.[44] This was very different from elite dining, where food and drink were apportioned differentially, resulting in complaints from those who felt they had not been provided a dinner commensurate with their social standing. What made the rules of associations distinctive is that types and quantities of food and wine were expressly prescribed. In some instances, the bylaws mandated double portions of food, wine, and *sportulae* (after-dinner presents)[45] for leaders and those honored by the group as a material way of recognizing hierarchy and status. In other instance, bylaws insisted that all have precisely the same menu as a way to underscore a notion of equality (in spite of whatever status differentials existed among members in society at large). That is, like processions, where movements, order, clothing, and roles were prescribed and scripted, the meals of associations were scripted and orchestrated. The food that was consumed was less important than the fact that eating followed prescribed rules.[46]

Orchestration of dining draws attention to its character as a performance, converting the ordinary human activity of eating into an activity that, in the words of Catherine Bell, defines or reaffirms "the full extent of the human and cosmic community."[47] It matters less which elements of dining were orchestrated and scripted—whether the amount of food and wine provided to each diner, or the type of food used, or seating arrangements, or some other feature of the meal such as the distribution of *sportulae* or formalized prayers and hymns performed at the meal. Associations and Christ assemblies formalized their meal practices in a variety of ways. What mattered is that everyone knew that there were prescribed ways to enact dining.[48] The effect of ritualization is to draw attention to the performance itself, a performance in which all participate and everyone has a role to play. Eating becomes an orchestrated *communal* practice that recasts an ordinary human activity as a ritual of belonging.

Segregative commensality was especially important for groups that brought together around a common table people of varying social statuses, genders, and ethnicities—people who otherwise would not dine together. Not all associations (or probably Christ groups for that matter) were heterogeneous in social status, gender, and ethnicity. But some were. Segregative commensality served to construct the diverse members *as a group*.

Second, dining together, despite its constructive intent, was also the occasion for conflict. The centripetal dynamics of the communal meal could and did come into conflict with centrifugal tendencies inherent in ancient status and ethnic structures. Irrespective of the fact that a meal might be intent on leveling status differences, the fact remained that seating arrangements necessarily articulated a hierarchy, and other practices, such as mandating larger shares of the food and drink for certain people, displayed status differences. Associations (and Christ groups) had to manage the tensions between centripetal and centrifugal forces.

Most association bylaws contained provisions to outlaw conflicts at the meal, ranging from verbal insults to "seat stealing" (taking the seat of another as a competitive display) to physical assault. If conflict was inherent in relatively homogenous groups such as the Iobakchoi of Athens,[49] it was all the more likely in groups that embraced members of different ethnic identities or different social statuses. In Christ groups well-known conflicts were recorded in Gal 2:11–14 and 1 Cor 11:17–34, in the first case prompted by the ethnic complexion of the Antiochene Christ assembly as including both Judeans and pagans. In the second case it appears to have been status divisions in the Corinthian group that occasioned conflict.

The communal meal, which displayed "belonging," also materialized hierarchies. This was an almost inevitable consequence of the dining venues typical of the ancient world—a *triclinium*, *stibadium*, or other banqueting hall. If someone reclined on the "first seat," then someone else had to recline on the lowest couch or had to sit. Even if a group inclined toward an egalitarian meal practice, the physical constraints of dining facilities implied spatial hierarchies.

A variety of strategies are attested either to enhance some of the hierarchical aspects of dining or to mitigate differences in status among members. Some associations recognized internal status differentials by mandating differing quantities of wine and *sportulae* to members. The collegium of Aesculapius and Hygia allocated differing amounts to the president (*quinquennalis*), *pater collegii* (father of the collegium), dues-exempt members, and supervisors (*curatores*), with some receiving two or three times what ordinary members received. Hierarchical differences, however, were mitigated by the fact that the president and supervisors were not permanent officers but rotated either yearly or every three to five years.[50] This meant that while they may have enjoyed the larger distributions in the year(s) they served in office, another contingent of officers would replace them and enjoy those benefits.

The *cultores* of Diana and Antinoüs (CIL 14.2112; Lanuvium, 136 CE) prescribed that each member receive bread costing 2 asses, four sardines, a table setting, and wine. Quantities of wine were left unspecified, but since 4 *amphorae* of wine (about 104 liters) were required for each meal and assuming forty-eight members, each member would receive 3 sextarii (1.6 liters), which is exactly the amount of wine allotted to each of the ordinary members of the collegium of Aesculapius and Hygia.[51] The president, and perhaps past presidents, however, were given half again as much, in recognition of their service.

Somewhat more unusually, a collegium of ivory and citrus wood dealers in Rome adopted a practice that aimed at leveling the dining space by insisting that each diner receive exactly the same amount of relatively modest food at each meal: bread and wine at most banquets, and on the special New Year's feast, cake and dates and Carian figs and pears (CIL 6.33885; Rome, time of Hadrian). This combination of modest food and the insistence on equal portions, even for the president and four supervisors, seems to have been an effort to reduce the appearance of inequality of members at the meal.

In some cases, it was not the food and wine that indicated status differences but seating. A papyrus from the Fayûm in the first half of the first century CE indicates that a cultic group devoted to the Egyptian deity Harpokrates assigned the president the seat of honor at the banquet. The president was responsible for providing food, including two spice dishes and a vetchy (legume) dish for each member—hence, an equal allocation of food. But the other members were arranged on each of three couches, each position corresponding to a different level of contribution.[52] The codicil of the group's bylaws records the agreement of each member to this arrangement, with the formula "I NN voted," presumably as a way to record members' consent to the hierarchical seating arrangement, probably to obviate any later disagreements. Other associations anticipated conflict over seating and were sufficiently concerned about it that they prescribed fines for "seat-stealing."[53]

The point, to reiterate, is that it mattered less which elements of the meal were scripted or whether different quantities of food and drink were allotted to diners or whether all ate from the same menu. What mattered was the fact that eating was orchestrated by the common consent of group members and that dining thus materialized the relationships within the group and made belonging visible.

We are less well informed about the menu of the meals of Christ assemblies. The descriptions of the meal in 1 Cor 11:23–26 and the *Didache* 9.2–4 feature bread and wine, and Pliny's comments about *Christiani* in Bithynia indicate that their meal was of "harmless" food (*cibum promiscuum tamen et innoxium*).[54]

Paul says nothing about seating arrangements, yet some groups were concerned about seating. Both Jas 2:1–13 and Luke 14:7–14 were keenly aware of the fact that seating was related to status. James's sharp critique of the scenario of the rich man and the beggar entering the *synagōgē* and being seated very differently appears to reflect a concern, hardly unique to Christ assemblies, to reduce competitive displays at the table and to create a fictive equality among members. He characterizes those who practice differential seating arrangements as "judges with evil thoughts" (2:4) and suggests that such a display of partiality gainsays any claim to live in accord with the Torah. For his part, Luke offers two bits of advice: first, to take the lowest seat on the couch on the calculation that one might be asked to "move up"; and second, to invite only those who could not return an invitation, presumably in order to avoid participating in the competitive game of inviting one's peers to a display of conspicuous consumption, knowing that one then would be invited by a peer to a similar display. Neither of Luke's bits of advice would have been simple to instrumentalize in an actual meal setting of a Christ assembly. They are, rather, examples of discourse that is intended to problematize competitive tendencies in Christ assemblies rather than to mandate actual prescriptions.

Hence, communal meals functioned as performances of belonging, making the group visible to itself, articulating who belonged and who did not. Through rule-based practices the group indicated that all belonged, and *how* they belonged, taking steps to mitigate and neutralize tensions that could fracture and compromise "groupness."

RULES

The materialization of belonging by participation in processions, by the creation of lists, and by dining practices thus was common in Greco-Roman associations and in Christ groups. These technologies of belonging were particularly important with groups composed of people of diverse social statuses, genders, and ethnicities, for these could not rely on other kinds of connectivity such as kinship or tribal loyalties to underwrite solidarity with the group.

Yet there were also countervailing pressures. The importance of showing and receiving honor, so critical in the moral world of antiquity, meant that some group members would be recognized, or expect to be recognized, in ways that distinguished them from others. This, coupled with the very materiality of group practices—that lists always have higher and lower entries and that dining venues always had better and worse seats—accounts for the fact that technologies of belonging were also accompanied by expressions of hierarchies of status.

A wide variety of strategies was available to associations and to Christ assemblies both to create "groupness" and to mitigate competitive tendencies that might undermine the sense of belonging beyond the communal meal. The strategies Christ assemblies implemented to create a sense of belonging and the challenges that they faced in mitigating competition do not seem to be qualitatively or quantitatively different from those that are visible in the practices of a variety of associations. Christ assemblies and associations approached the benefits of membership and the challenges to group solidarity in much the same way.

We are far from having a complete picture of the behavioral standards for all associations, owing to the relative dearth of association bylaws, but where bylaws exist they invariably impose behavioral norms on members. In many cases the bylaws include provisions that apply to behavior outside the narrow confines of the meeting itself, requiring members to assist others in distress. A Demotic bylaw from the mid-second century BCE requires, "If one of our members finds another member on the road to the dock (?) a similar place and he says, 'can you give me some money [. . . ,]' and he does not give (it), his fine is [. . . *deben*, except if he swears] an oath before the god, saying, 'I [cannot give] him (anything)'" (P.Cair 30606.21; Tebtynis, 158/157 BCE). A similar provision is found two centuries later in another rule from Tebtynis, as we have seen: "If a member ignores someone (i.e., another member) who is in distress and does not assist in helping him out of his trouble, he shall pay 8 drachmae" (P.Mich V 243.6; Tebtynis, time of Tiberius).

A century before the Common Era, a household cult dedicated to Zeus and other gods outlined a complex set of norms for its participants. Each was required to swear

> by all the gods neither to know nor make use knowingly of any deceit against a man or a woman, neither poison harmful to men nor harmful spells. They

> are not themselves to make use of a (20) love potion, abortifacient, contraceptive, or any other thing fatal to children; nor are they to recommend it to, nor connive at it with, another. They are not to refrain in any respect from being well-minded toward this *oikos*. If anyone performs or plots any of these things, they are neither to put up with it nor (25) keep silent but expose it and defend themselves. Apart from his own wife, a man is not to have relations with another married woman, whether free or slave, nor with a boy nor a virgin girl; nor shall he recommend it to another. Should he connive at it with someone, they shall expose such a person, both (30) the man and the woman, and not conceal it or keep silent about it. Woman and man, whoever does any of the things written above, let them not enter this *oikos*. For great are the gods set up in it: they watch over these things, and will not tolerate those who transgress the ordinances. (35) A free woman is to be chaste and shall not know the bed of, nor have intercourse with, another man except her own husband. But if she does have such "knowledge," such a woman is not chaste but defiled and full of endemic pollution, and unworthy to reverence this god whose holy things these are that have been set up. (40) She is not to be present at the sacrifices, not to strike against (?) the purifications and cleansings (?), nor to see the mysteries being performed. But if she does any of these things from the time the ordinances have come on to this inscription, she shall have evil curses from the gods for disregarding these ordinances. For the god does (45) not desire these things to happen at all, nor does he wish it but he wants obedience. The gods will be gracious to those who obey, and always give them all good things, whatever gods give to men whom they love. But should any transgress, (50) they shall hate such people and inflict upon them great punishments. (TAM V 1539.17–50 = GRA II 117; Philadelphia (Lydia), ca. 100 BCE; trans. AGRW 121)

These rules applied not only to etiquette at the communal meal, but to the general conduct expected of members.

Members were expected to conform to certain norms, but given the nature of ancient society, it could be taken for granted that *others* would take note of such behavior and understand it to be a marker of belonging to a particular association. Indeed, a fragmentary Attic inscription from the late fourth or early third century BCE, after outlining a series of bylaws, states, "And if a member should be wronged, they and all the friends shall come to his assistance, *so that everyone might know that we show piety* (10) *to the gods and to our friends*" (IG II^2 1275.7–10 = GRA I 8; Piraeus, 325–275 BCE; emphasis added).

Rule-based behavior was expected to be noticed and understood as such. Second-century opponents of the Christ movement certainly noticed that

Christ followers aspired to high ethical standards. Celsus sneered at their meeting in "women's apartments, or leather shops, or fullers' shops to learn about perfection (*to teleion*),"[55] but in spite of this snobbery he understood that they valued the pursuit of knowledge, even if in his view they lacked the means to engage in a pursuit of true philosophical knowledge. Galen was more generous, commenting on Christ followers' contempt of death, their self-control in matters of food and drink, and their "keen pursuit of justice."[56] Christ devotees themselves, however, promoted a robust set of behaviors and seemed confident of how their ethical standards would be noticed and appreciated by others:[57]

> 1 Thess 4:9, 11–12: For you yourselves are "God-taught" to love one another. . . . (and) aspire to live quietly, to mind your own affairs, and to work with your hands . . . so that you might act decently toward outsiders.
>
> 1 Pet 2:12: Hold to an honorable standard of behavior (*anastrophē*) among the gentiles, so that even though they malign you as evildoers, from continuing to observe your honorable deeds they may glorify God on a day of visitation.
>
> John 13:35: In this fact everyone will know that you are my disciples, if you love one another.

It is not that the ethical standards of Christ followers were dramatically different from those of many other elective groups.[58] In the second century Diognetus admitted that Christ followers were in fact very much like others: they were not distinguished by their territory, language, or customs, and they followed the customs of their host lands in clothing, food, and other matters of life; they were different only in their refusal to expose infants and in their practice of nonretaliation toward those who persecuted them (Diognetus 5.1–15).[59] Later we hear of their refusal to attend the gladiatorial games and their criticism of the homosexual practices evidenced especially among the elite. Perhaps most dramatically, Eusebius reports that during the plague of Cyprian that struck Alexandria in the 260s, Christians there did not flee the city as many others did but instead remained to take care of the sick, including their pagan neighbors.[60] Of course, many of these contracted the plague and died; but the care they had offered to others was undoubtedly noted as a distinctive mark of ethical conduct and contributed to a positive reputation, just as the author of 1 Peter had hoped.[61]

SANCTIONS

Associations and Christ assemblies alike developed strategies for controlling and sanctioning misbehavior of members who violated the ethical code of the group. I have already noted that in the Latin West, the dramatic sanction of a *damnatio memoriae* might be imposed, erasing the name of an offender from the association's *album*. Less dramatically, other associations levied fines, as P.Cair 30606 above. Although it is sometimes supposed that private associations were moral free-for-alls, this is in fact a dramatic misrepresentation: Egyptian, Athenian, and Italian associations sanctioned misbehavior at meetings and interference with the operation of the group, usually by imposing fines. Misbehavior at meetings included verbal abuse of a member, physical abuse of a member, fighting, raucous talk about members' families and genealogies, accusations against members, taking another member's seat, drunkenness, interrupting the convivial atmosphere, or more generally, sordid behavior.[62] Obstructing the workings of the association included interfering with the duties of the president, violation of the association's laws,[63] and refusal to attend meetings.[64]

Many of these violations brought relatively minor fines and reprimands; however, other infractions were treated much more seriously. Bringing a lawsuit or indictment against another member could attract a substantial fine.[65] Especially serious was a refusal to attend the funeral of a member (or one of a member's family).[66] The most serious sanctions were applied against those who "committed intrigue" (i.e., adultery) with people from a member's family.[67] Because trust and a sense of belonging were so important to the dynamics of associative life, the acts, such as these, that most threatened solidarity attracted the heaviest sanctions. Members also assumed positive obligations, most notably to assist another member in distress, either by directly helping him or her or standing surety if the member had been arrested.[68]

To those who know the literature of the early Jesus movement, much of this will look familiar. Paul was aware of sexual misconduct within the Corinthian group. He was also aware of lawsuits among members, which he counseled should be settled within the group and not taken to the civic courts.[69] The sanctioning of misbehavior in Christ assemblies is most clearly seen in 1 Cor 5:1–8 where Paul addresses the case of a man who has had an incestuous relationship, declaring that he should have been "removed from your midst" (5:2) and later lists others who should be excluded from the communal meal (5:11). The details of this sanction on the man guilty of incest are particularly interesting since, while Paul was not in Corinth at the time, he claims to be present "in spirit" (*en pneumati*) and to have already judged the offender as though he had been present. He then orders that when the assembly gathers, Paul being present "in spirit," they should deliver (*paradidōmi*) the offender to Satan "for the destruction of the flesh" so that the *pneuma*—the unifying *pneuma* of the group—might be preserved uncontaminated (5:3–5).

First Corinthians 5:1–5 suggests that Paul and the Corinthians engaged in spirit practices by cursing the offender in order to do him harm.[70] Since *paradidōmi* has juridical overtones,[71] 1 Cor 5:5 conveys the sense of the assembly collectively rendering its judgment upon the man. Moreover, as Papathomas observes, the grammar of 1 Cor 5:5 suggests that "to deliver such a person" (*ton toiouton*) articulates a general rule (rather than an ad hoc judgment applicable only in this case). Such a rule would be analogous to the disciplinary rules of Greco-Egyptian associations, which also frame rules with the demonstrative pronoun *ho toioutos*.[72]

I have paused on 1 Cor 5:5 as a practice that sanctions behavior via special powers claimed by the group so as to point to an analogous practice from more than a century before. The participants in the domestic Zeus cult in Philadelphia mentioned above not only swore an oath to maintain the ethical code of the group, but signaled their adherence to the group by ritually touching the stele on which the association's rules were inscribed. This act seems to have been construed as a means of detecting those who were not complying with the cult's regulations. Unworthy touching of the god's stele would result in "great punishments": "At the sacrifices, both the monthly and annual ones, may they—as many men and women who have confidence in themselves—touch this inscription in which the ordinances of the god have been written, so that those who obey these ordinances and those who disobey them may be evident" (TAM V 1539.54–59 = GRA II 117).

Paul also claims that violations of principles of equity at the communal meal have resulted in the illnesses and even the deaths of some members (1 Cor 11:27–30). Like the Philadelphia association that invoked a material practice infused with divine power, the Christ assembly in Corinth used ritual eating as a way to mark belonging and compliance with the group's ethical codes. It is for this reason that 1 Cor 5:11 counsels excluding from the communal meal those who do not comply with the ethical rules of the group. In the Philadelphia group the assembly space is depicted as a site of divine power such that unworthy touching of the group's stele can have dangerous, even lethal consequences. For Paul, the presence of a person who has egregiously violated the group's rules is a threat to the *pneuma* that inhabits group space and is shared by members (1 Cor 5:5), and unworthy actions of members can result in the illness or death of members. Whether the bylaws and ethical codes were enforced by divine sanction or by threatening fines, as in the case of Egyptian, Athenian, and Italian associations noted above, the net result was that members could be held to certain ethical standards.[73] This also meant that members could rely on their fellows to conform to certain ethical standards. This is the essence of a network of trust.

MANDATORY ATTENDANCE

One of the striking features of ancient associations is that, unlike modern churches and synagogues, where casual, even promiscuous patterns of attendance are common, regular and consistent attendance at meetings and banquets was expected. Indeed, absences were routinely penalized.[74] This is undoubtedly because in a culture marked by collectivism and permeated by the quest for honor—that is, recognition of achievements *by others*—absence from communal events was potentially an aggressive act.

The penalizing of members who did not attend meetings is one of the most consistent features of associations. One of the earliest instances is from the fourth century BCE: "Whoever is at home in Athens and in good health but does not contribute, owes 2 drachmae, sacred to the goddess" (IG II^2 1361, lines 19–20 = GRA I 4; 330–324/323 BCE).[75] Similar regulations are found in bylaws from Attica well into the second century CE: "If one of the Iobakchoi, knowing that a meeting ought to be convened for this purpose, does not attend, he shall pay a fine of 50 light drachmae to the treasury (*koinon*)" (IG II^2 1368, lines 96–99 = GRA I 51; 164/165 CE).

From the early imperial period we encounter differential fines for absenteeism, depending on whether the meeting was in the village (of Tebtynis) or in the city (of Arsinoë-Krokodilopolis): "If a member is sent an announcement of the meeting and does not attend, he shall be fined 1 drachma (if the meeting is) in the village and 4 drachmae if it is in the city" (P.Mich V 243; Tebtynis, time of Tiberius).

What was at stake in enforcing attendance? In some cases the insistence on attendance had a financial purpose. Ptolemaic papyri show that associations kept careful accounts of income and expenses, recording not only the dues paid by each member, but also the amounts still owed along with the expenses for a banquet.[76] P.Tebt I 118 (Tebtynis, 112/111 BCE) is such an account, registering the attendance and expenses at each of three banquets. The account indicates that the cost of mounting each banquet was about 2,200 Ptolemaic (bronze) drachmae, which meant that twenty-two members had to be present, each paying 100 drachmae.[77] At two of these banquets not all members appeared, and so paying guests had to be recruited. This suggests that at least one of the motivations for insisting on attendance (and fining those who were absent) had to do with the economics of the banquet. Beer or wine, the single largest cost, was purchased by the *amphora* (approximately 26 liters) or by the "jar" (*keramion*, 9.72–12.96 liters) rather than by smaller amounts. The dues collected had to reach the threshold cost of wine if there were to be a banquet at all. Given late-second-century BCE wine prices in the Fayûm, 2,200 bronze drachmae would buy one *keramion* of wine, or about a half liter per person. Beer was cheaper, but there was undoubtedly a threshold cost for jars of beer.

Broekaert has suggested that associations that were involved in commercial enterprises had a stake in compelling attendance of all members, since meetings and banquets were venues at which internal disputes might be solved.[78] We should not, however, limit the rule to the resolution of conflicts in the commercial sector. The *Didache* enjoins members to resolve conflict before participation in the communal meal "lest your sacrifice be profaned" (14.2). This of course presupposes that members are in attendance if conflicts are to be resolved.[79]

In the case of P.Mich V 243 cited above, the differing levels of fines for nonattendance at a banquet in the village and one in the city may have been due to higher costs associated with the rental of dining space in the city. But we might also consider another factor. Since dining venues were often semipublic, the association had a stake in ensuring that every couch in the dining room was full; a partially empty table not only put a strain on the association's coffers, but it made the association look weak and unappealing.

The enforcement of attendance was also related to the honorific activities of associations. Honorific decrees often conclude with a provision that should those charged with enacting the decree (by announcing the crowning at the next meeting and eventually inscribing the decree on a stele) fail to do so, they would incur a fine.[80] Both the failure to enact the group's honorific act and deliberate absence from meetings where such honors were accorded amount to snubs of the honoree. Staying away from a meeting where a fellow member is to be honored is in effect a refusal of honor.

It is perhaps surprising to the modern reader that such care should have been taken to record for each meeting who was present, who contributed, and who did not and to penalize those not in attendance. These practices underscore the degree to which associations attempted to create stable and consistent social relationships, to mitigate agonistic behavior represented by absenteeism, and to insist on high standards of participation by all.

When we turn to Christ assemblies we find very little direct evidence of measures taken to require attendance. The *Didache* encouraged attendance, not by threatening a fine but by promising a benefit—the presence of the deity: "My child, remember the one who is speaking to you the word of God day and night, and fear him as the Lord; for where authority (*kyriotēs*) is, there is the Lord (*kyrios*). And you shall seek daily the face of the holy ones so that you might rest in their words" (4.1–2).

The problem of nonattendance, however, did not go unnoticed. Hebrews 10:24–25 complains, "let us consider how to provoke one another to love and good deeds, *not neglecting to meet together, as is the habit of some*, but encouraging one another, and all the more as you see the Day approaching" (NRSV, emphasis added). The strategy in Hebrews is to associate absenteeism immediately with sin and enmity: "For if we willfully persist in sin after having received the knowledge of the truth, there no longer remains a sacrifice for sins, but a fearful prospect of judgment, and a fury of fire that will consume the adversaries" (10:26–27, NRSV).

Although there are few data on how other Christ assemblies managed issues of attendance, it seems unlikely that they could have been untouched by the factors that affected other small groups: the pragmatic needs to negotiate conflicts, many of which would have required regular face-to-face contact; financial needs arising from activities that the group undertook that required regular attendance and support; the importance of honoring members after their deaths; and the cultural imperative to be *seen* to be a group at a table with no empty seats. This is a point where the methodological approach enunciated in the Introduction is important to recall: comparison establishes an interpretive framework that helps us think about Christ assemblies and to pose the question, How did Christ assemblies manage the issue of attendance, which was evidently such a pressing one for other associations? Fines might have been too blunt a tool to use. We might, however, see in the discourse of early Christ assemblies another kind of currency—implied promises of benefits that presence in the assembly brought (*Didache*), the development of a language of sin and its removal through presence in the assembly (*Didache*), threats of divine sanction, and the specter of a fiery judgment visited on those who fail to attend (Hebrews).

THEORIZING RULES

Why would one join a group that imposes high ethical demands and threatens fines or divine sanctions for misbehavior? Studies in evolutionary anthropology and behavioral economics have helped to theorize the functions of rules and sanctions. Groups that have high behavioral expectations of their members and conduct rituals that are "costly-to-fake" have the double effect of enhancing intragroup cooperation and commitment and of discouraging "free riders"—those who wish to belong to the group for its benefits but with little or no commitment to the practices or values of the group. In effect, compliance with the rules—contributing dues, attending meetings and funerals, observing appropriate etiquette—are easily observed by others and serve as heuristics for the less empirically obvious values that are at the heart of the life of the group: trust and solidarity. And it is easy to spot those who try to free-ride by avoiding such costs.

Richard Sosis analyzed two hundred U.S. communes, parsed into socialist, anarchist, and other secular groups on one hand and Shaker or other religious groups on the other. In general, "religious" communes survived four times as long as secular ones, and Shaker groups lasted eighteen times as long as utopian socialist groups in spite of the fact that they did not allow marriage and hence could not avail themselves of intergenerational recruitment.[81] In addition, Sosis and Bressler showed that communes (usually religious communes) with strict behavioral rules ("costly requirements") such as the prohibition of the consumption of alcohol, coffee, tobacco, and meat or the control of jewelry, clothing, hairstyles, and communication with the outside also had greater longevity than secular communes and were much less likely to dissolve as a result of internal disputes. These findings presumably reflect a high level of intragroup commitment and suggest that costly requirements have the effect of enhancing solidarity. Sosis and Bressler do not claim that costly requirements are the only factor that account for longevity, but they argue that they are a necessary condition of long-term survival.[82]

Can costly signaling theory be applied to groups in antiquity? Since virtually all ancient associations had a "religious" component and none was "secular" in the modern sense, it is problematic to apply one aspect of Sosis's analysis directly to antiquity. All groups had a cultic life and (one presumes) supposed that the gods were in some way interested in what they did. The other aspect of Sosis's analysis, however, is applicable: rule-based groups create and maintain intragroup solidarity, and those groups that have a more robust sets of requirements have some advantage over those that have fewer behavioral regulations.

Looking at a time closer to the imperial period, Sheilagh Ogilivie discussed medieval merchant guilds between 1000 and 1500 CE and the ways in which they generated social capital for their members.[83] To recall Bourdieu's definition of social capital, it is "the aggregate of the actual or potential resources which are linked to possession of a durable network of more or less institutionalized relationships of mutual acquaintance and recognition . . . which provides each of its members with the backing of the collectivity-owned capital, a 'credential' that entitles them to credit, in the various senses of the word."[84] In this context, social capital results from resource pooling and reputational pooling, which in turn results in a shared stock of knowledge, norms, sanctions, and collective action, created by closed and multiplex social networks. "Multiplex connections" generate social capital because members interact and are linked with one another in multiple ways—through work, economic activities, cultic commitments, politics, neighborhood locations, demographics, and culture—and it is these connections that facilitate the sharing of knowledge and the creation of shared norms and sanctions.[85]

The combination of multiplex relationships and a strong sense of belonging created a social zone of intense interactions and the generation of social capital. Members—at least in associations that were successful in establishing and enforcing behavioral norms—could rely on other members to treat them in civil ways not only in the communal banquet, but in other realms of activity; to conduct themselves in moral ways in relation to families; to support them during times of adversity; and in the end honor them in death. Of course, sanctions could be, and were, mobilized on occasion to penalize or even expel those who violated the norms of conduct, as they were in the case of the incestuous man of 1 Cor 5:1–5. The sanctions that were typical of association bylaws and of Christ assemblies are not evidence that there were widespread violations of these norms; instead, they signal the association's resolve to create a social space in which members could gain connectivity and social capital. The positive effect of sanctions was to produce a network of trust.

5

Christ Assemblies in the Urban Economy

Where on the social ladder of Mediterranean antiquity should we envision members of early Christ assemblies, and how should they be placed in relation to those who belonged to associations? How should we imagine the social ladder itself? Up to now the answers to these questions have been framed almost exclusively in economic terms: in the popular imagination it is virtually a truism that members of early Christ assemblies were overwhelmingly poor, eking out a living at the subsistence level. A few scholars include a sprinkling of the very wealthy among a poor majority. Others place the economic center of gravity higher, with a socially pretentious "middling group."

The purpose of the following two chapters is twofold: first, to discuss recent models of the structure of the Roman economy, whether we should imagine a binary division between a small number of superrich and the remainder of the population at the subsistence level, or an economy that included a larger middling group, positioned between the very poor and the very wealthy. If the economy was divided unevenly between the 1–3 percent superrich and the remainder with only subsistence level incomes, then it is a priori likely that most Christ followers were also very poor. As will become clear, however, the second model is the more plausible one, and this means that it is likely, in theory at least, that some Christ followers belonged to the economic middle.

It is mistaken, however, to conceive of status in economic terms. Moreover, the effort to specify the economic level of early Christ followers is problematic for two reasons: On one hand, the data that we have about them are not of the sort that discloses reliable information about economic level. And on the other—and much more importantly—income is not the sole or even primary measure of social standing. Instead, *connectivity* is a far better measure of standing, that is, the degree to which individuals were connected with others via patronage, elective formations, and family groups.

If a modern sociologist were to be asked how to construct a sociological profile of a particular group of Christians, she or he would want to know about the median family income of churchgoers, the size of each churchgoing family, employment and educational profiles of members, the percentage of income contributed to the church, the average weekly attendance, the number of other organizations to which family members belonged, their attitudes about politics, and various contemporary data on the relative importance that each member attached to the Bible, church dogma, apocalyptic beliefs, the afterlife, female clergy, same-sex marriage, and so forth. Almost all these data are unavailable to historians of the earliest Christ assemblies. The sum of information we have consists in the proper names of people associated with those assemblies, a handful of comments about the occupations or other characteristics of a few of these people, and references, generally sympathetic, to "the poor" and less so to "the rich." It is perhaps because of the discourse on wealth and poverty and because economic models of social standing have become so central to the conception of the nature of modern societies that most scholarly literature on early Christ assemblies has conceived social standing in terms of economic scales. Yet "rich" and "poor" are both relative and slippery terms. Without more reliable metrics, it is precarious to equate "poor" with "subsistence level" or "rich" with the top 3 percent of Roman society.

It is not that early Christ assemblies did not include people at the bottom of imperial society: no doubt they did. The point, instead, is that the data we have do not provide us with such economic information, and the attempts to squeeze detailed economic conclusions from sparse data seem more a matter of a priori assumptions about early Christ assemblies than a matter of historically defensible conclusions. Even more importantly, it is anachronistic to base an understanding of imperial society on the model of industrial societies, layered by income levels—the "working class," the "lower middle class," the "upper middle class," the "upper class" and so forth—or to think of income as the primary independent variable of social standing. Such a model distorts our imagination of imperial society and, with it, the nature of Christ assemblies. There was no ancient middle class, at least in the sense that "middle class" is a meaningful socioeconomic category in modern Western economies and refers to a sector of the population that can be said to have common interests and common identity markers.[1] There was an "economic middle"—meaning a sector of the population that was poised between bare subsistence and the superrich; but there is little evidence to support the contention that this middling sector ever developed a consciousness or common identity comparable to those of "white-collar workers" or "blue-collar workers" in modern industrial societies. More critically, the factor that determined social standing was not income but *connectivity*—the individuals and groups with which one was connected and the social capital that such connections generated.

THE "OLD CONSENSUS"

Scholarly discussion often refers to an "old consensus" and a "new consensus" concerning early Christ assemblies. The former, usually associated with Adolf Deissmann (1866–1937), who taught at Heidelberg and Berlin, took the view that the early Jesus movement was primarily a movement of the "lower strata" of ancient society. The latter (and supposedly more recent consensus) holds that Christ assemblies attracted all but peasants and the highest reaches of imperial society and otherwise represented a range of social levels, from the urban poor to those who were relatively well-off.

Deissmann's views were prompted by the work of Karl Kautsky, a leading theoretician of the German Social Democratic Party. According to Kautsky, the Jesus movement exemplified a struggle of the poor against the rich. Its earliest forms, which Kautsky saw in Luke and James, were characterized by "class hatred" of the rich. Matthew, a revisionist, found the "the audacious and revolutionary character of enthusiasm and Socialism" dangerous and so conveniently omitted from his gospel as many sayings as he could that inclined in that direction. When he could not get rid of such popular sayings as the beatitudes of the Sermon on the Plain, Matthew rewrote them, substituting the banal "blessed are the poor in spirit" for the more radical "blessed are the poor" (Luke 6:20). Matthew's neutering of the original message reflected a "ecclesiastical opportunism" that suppressed any elements that would endanger the existence of the Christ assemblies as they tried to make peace with imperial society.[2]

Deissmann's famous *Licht vom Osten* (translated as *Light from the Ancient East*), published in 1908, and his *Primitive Christianity and the Lower Classes*, published later the same year,[3] took issue with Kautsky, rejecting the notion that the Jesus movement began as a political movement. He agreed, however, that the earliest Christ assemblies belonged to the "lower strata." He based this conclusion on the unsophisticated level of Greek that could be seen in newly discovered Greco-Egyptian papyri and the unsophisticated level of Greek found in Paul's letters. Supposing that the hundreds of papyrus letters, petitions, and lease and loan documents that had been discovered by that time reflected the Greek of the lower social strata, he concluded that these early documents, including the letters of Paul, came from the "illiterate lower strata" of ancient society. Of the writings in the New Testament, only the letter to the Hebrews rose to the level of literary art.[4]

This view of the earliest Christ assemblies is remembered as the "old consensus." Yet Deissmann soon altered his views. In his 1912 book on Paul, he repeatedly associated Paul with the "*middle* and lower strata,"[5] revised his earlier judgments of Paul's literary abilities upward, and argued that Christ assemblies had some members who were well-to-do, such as those who hosted "house churches," including Gaius of Corinth and Erastos the city manager (Rom 16:23). Deissmann even entertained the possibility that some elite were present, in particular the high-status women of Macedonia mentioned in Acts 17:4. In order to reconcile Acts with Paul's reference in 2 Cor 8:2 to the "deep poverty" of the Macedonians, however, Deissmann conjectured that these wealthy women joined but soon defected from the group.[6]

Hence, while Deissmann is still remembered as emphasizing the poverty of the earliest Christ assemblies, he in fact eventually came to a view that is little different from the "new consensus." Adolf von Harnack arrived at a similar conclusion: the bulk of members of Christ assemblies came from the urban poor, something that pagan opponents were quick to point out and that apologists such as Justin Martyr and Origen did not deny. But there was also relatively early evidence of the presence of the wealthy, the educated, and even individuals of high rank. Harnack pointed not only to the wealthy women of Acts 17:4, but also to the governor Sergius Paulus (Acts 13:7–12), Dionysios the Areopagite (Acts 17:34), and Erastos (Rom 16:23), whom Deissmann had earlier treated as "middle strata."[7]

Deissmann's attempt to coordinate the unliterary character of Greco-Egyptian papyri with the supposedly unliterary nature of documents produced in early Christ assemblies and his conclusion that both came from the "illiterate lower strata" of ancient society are exceedingly problematic. As should be obvious, those who produced Greco-Egyptian papyri and the documents of Christ assemblies were not illiterate: they were literate scribes. There were indeed many levels of ancient scribalism, from the barely literate, to low-level scribes who produced administrative and legal documents to the scribes of professional scriptoria responsible for elegant book rolls, to those who crafted literary works, and several levels in between.[8]

As Deissmann came to recognize, Paul's Greek, and even that of James or Hebrews, was far from classical, but it was not the product of unskilled writers either. Arthur Darby Nock once observed that to one who knows classical (Attic) Greek, the differences between it and New Testament Greek will be obvious, and one might be tempted to exaggerate the similarities between the New Testament and the Greek of Greco-Egyptian papyri. However,

> any[one] who knows the papyri first and then turns to Paul is astonished at the differences. . . . Nothing could be less like the Pauline letters than the majority of the documents in Deissmann's *Light from the Ancient East.* Paul is not writing peasant Greek or soldier Greek; he is writing the Greek of a man who has the Septuagint in his blood and has a supreme self-confidence in using words which allows him to play tricks with a sentence, to make his queer explosive transitions in the middle of a phrase.[9]

Deissmann eventually acknowledged that the terms "lower strata" and "upper stratum" were notoriously ill-defined. It makes little sense to speak of the urban "lower strata" as a meaningful category because these included an unwieldy collection of status groups: freeborn workers; domestic slaves; freedmen of elite houses; shop owners; artisans in a wide range of workshops and industries; merchants; small manufacturers, some of whom owned or rented houses; and the indigent, handicapped, widows, and chronically ill. Greeks and Romans had classifications of identity, but rarely as blunt as simply classifying people into upper and lower strata.[10]

There is a yet deeper problem. The use of "stratum" or, worse, "class" to speak of Greco-Roman antiquity is misleading and anachronistic.[11] In the wake of the Industrial Revolution, societies came to be imagined as divided horizontally into "strata" defined either by income or, for Marxist analysis, in terms of their relationship to the means of economic production. But that model of society is foreign to antiquity.

As Géza Alföldy has insisted, the modern notion of "class," which is dependent on ownership of productive means (land, workshops), the allocation of labor, and, inevitably, income level, is inappropriate for the description of ancient society.[12] Instead of the horizontally layered picture with which we are familiar, the fault lines of ancient society ran vertically, in particular in the subelite sectors.

The curial ranks—senators, equestrians, and civic magistrates—were finely and minutely stratified, with each rank having a different minimum wealth requirement and strong consciousness of who belonged to each of these ranks. The picture is very different for those below the curial ranks. In the subelite sector of ancient society there is little or no evidence of "class consciousness." Nothing suggests that the very large slave populations, freeborn urban subelite, or freedmen and freedwomen ever thought of themselves as constituting distinct classes, each with common characteristics and interests.

The subelite population is best conceived as the base of a pyramid with divisions running vertically. Alföldy comments:

> At best we can describe [the nonelite sector] as various strata, *without implying that these social groups were stratified in a hierarchy*. . . . There were no clear social divisions running horizontally through the lower strata, whereas within the upper strata there were clear distinctions within the positions of the various strata. . . . In the determination of social realities in the Roman world it was by no means *only* the fixed positions within a social hierarchy that matter, but also the *personal relations between individuals placed higher and lower*, which were always of greatest importance—for example, within the *familia*, between a slave and his master, in a civic community, between a plebeian client and his *patronus* of the local elite, or on an estate, between the labour force and the estate-owner.[13]

The last sentence is critical. Social standing was not so much a matter of one's position on a ladder of status defined by income but rather on a ladder of *connectivity*. This does not minimize or deny that vast differences in status, power, honor, and wealth existed between the elite and the rest of the population. It does, however, mean that social standing depended on connectivity to sites of social power. The slave who belonged to a wealthy and powerful family was much better off, and had a much higher real social standing, than a freeborn worker or shop owner who was poorly connected. Cicero's freedman Tiro was much better off than a freeborn artisan. An artisan who belonged to a guild patronized by the emperor or a senator might not have had a larger income than an unattached artisan, but his connections placed him higher in social standing. This does not mean that individual guild members would have direct access to the emperor or senator; but merely belonging to a guild that had imperial patronage conferred a higher status on each member. And unlike the experience of slaves in the United States, emancipated slaves in the Roman Empire were eager to advertise and maintain their relationship to their former owners, because the connection conferred status. Connectivity mattered.

Instead of imagining ancient society as a series of horizontal layers, we should visualize a complex web of relationships of dependence and social obligation in the shape of a pyramid. At the top are the curial ranks and connected downward are imperial freedmen and freedwomen; well-to-do commoners; veterans; the owners of shops, workshops, and farms; administrators within the complex provincial administration; lessees of shops and farms; tenant farmers and handworkers; free laborers; domestic slaves; slaves in workshops; and agricultural slaves. People who lacked any durable or productive connections were at the bottom.

While in general the freeborn ranked higher than slaves or freed slaves, well-connected slaves or freed slaves probably had a higher effective social standing. Similarly, guild members connected with people of rank were better off than those who lacked patronage connections, or who were connected only to commoners. Connectivity was as much vertical as it was horizontal, or more so.

SOCIAL STANDING IN THE ROMAN EMPIRE

The ancient Mediterranean was finely attuned to rank, social standing, and legal status. I use "rank" to refer to formally defined status groups, for example, those designated by inclusion on lists of people eligible to serve high political office or lists of citizens or lists of those belonging to the curial ranks (that is, those who met certain property requirements and who possessed a Greek education). "Legal status" refers to whether one was freeborn, a slave, or an emancipated slave (freedman/freedwoman) and whether one was a citizen of a city or a resident alien. "Social status" or social standing has more to do with achievement and the kinds of influence and power (including wealth) that one could mobilize. While those of high rank normally had wealth and power, some achieved high standing without the formal markers of rank, although in the long run, high social standing might eventually be converted into rank.

In the Greek East citizenship was a common way to mark identity. Thus, populations of a city could be parsed into several groups: citizens (*politai*) with full legal rights and their wives (*politides*), emancipated slaves (*apeleutheroi*), slaves (*douloi*), resident aliens (*paroikoi, metics*), and foreigners or visitors (*xenoi, parepidēmoi*). Romans in the early imperial period also distinguished people on the basis of citizenship—citizens of Rome (*cives*) and free citizens of any other city (*perigrini*)—and on the basis of legal status, whether people were freeborn (*ingenui*), emancipated slaves (*liberti/-ae*), or slaves (*servi/-ae, verna*). During the first three centuries of the Common Era, Roman citizenship was gradually made available, first to freeborn residents of Italy and later to non-Italians, including members of provincial elite and those who had the resources and influence to purchase citizenship.

The freed slaves (both men and women) of a Roman citizen gained upon their manumission the *tria nomina*, the three names that marked a Roman citizen. Thus, when emancipated, Cicero's slave Tiro became Marcus Tullius *libertus* Marci Tiro, that is, Marcus Tullius Tiro, a freedman (*libertus*) of Marcus (Tullius Cicero). Tiro's former slave name became his cognomen, a permanent reminder of his servile origin; but he was also now a member of the Tullii, Cicero's family. Although freedmen generally could not serve in public office, their sons could;[14] hence, manumission was a potential road for slave families to achieve a higher social standing and in some cases, high rank. A centurion upon his discharge from the legion might become a magistrate of a provincial town, and the veterans of the Roman auxiliary forces became citizens upon their discharge from service (legionaries were already citizens). In 212 CE through the *Constitutio Antoniniana* promulgated by Caracalla, citizenship was extended to all residents of the empire (except slaves).

Romans had other classification systems. Within the aristocratic rank (*ordo*) there were distinctions between senators and equestrians (*equites*), the former limited to six hundred families, each having a census requirement (i.e., landed wealth) of not less than 1 million sesterces and the latter with a census requirement of 400,000 sesterces. Families that fell below these census requirements were removed from the rolls and replacements recruited, often from the provincial elite. Within the senatorial and equestrian ranks there were gradations of status. Senatorial families that had former consuls among their ancestors could boast of that fact. Equestrians who had served in public office came to be described as a kind of equestrian nobility.[15] Local magistrates called *decuriones* had variable census requirements; they and the councilors (*bouletai*) who served in towns and cities throughout the empire were known as the "first men" (*prōtoi, primores viri*).[16]

The aristocratic construction of the ladder of status gave pride of place to noble birth (*eugeneia*), distinguished ancestry, landownership, certain occupations, the reception of honors, success in public office, and physical prowess. This meant that most people were by definition relegated to the lower rungs of this ladder. Since landownership and farming were deemed the noblest of sources of wealth, the senatorial aristocracy, which owned vast tracts of land, had an advantage over the equestrians, who engaged in various forms of large-scale business. The monopolization of land by the senatorial elite had the effect of excluding most of the population from ever achieving high rank. Professions that depended upon skill and learning such as the pursuit of the law, medicine, teaching, or architecture were honorable ones; manual labor, handwork, and any pursuits that required only physical labor, or that provoked the ill-will of others or that appealed to sensual pleasures, were mean and base occupations, at least in the eyes of the elite.[17] Since public office was open only to freeborn citizens and in the case of Rome was dominated by the curial class, the ability of others to acquire status and high honors through public service was limited.

Owing to the stubbornly hierarchical construction of society, examples of commoners achieving high rank were rare. Advancement happened, however, as the example of the grandson of M. Cornelius Epagathus attests (see chapter 2). One important avenue for upward mobility was manumission. The freedmen of Roman citizens became citizens themselves. Some acquired fantastic fortunes, as did the fictional character Trimalchio in Petronius's *Satyricon.* Such men achieved much higher social standing and were no doubt the envy of many freeborn citizens and probably even aristocrats. In most cases their servile origins blocked them from achieving the rank of an equestrian or a senator or a even a local magistrate, except for a few provincial towns, including Corinth. Their male children could achieve those ranks, however. The slaves, freedmen, and freedwomen of the emperor, known as the *familia Caesaris* (family of Caesar), constituted a special category. Some of these achieved wealth that was unimaginable for most Romans and because of their connection with the imperial house enjoyed considerable political influence and power.[18]

The curial rank—senators, equestrians, and the magistrates of the cities and towns of the empire—likely comprised only 1 percent of the total population of 60 million, perhaps 350,000–500,000 (including their family members), with another 100,000 veterans of the legions, some of whom would become local magistrates in the towns in which they settled and thus entered the rank of local magistrate.[19] What about the remaining 99 percent?

ECONOMIC SCALES AMONG THE SUBELITE

In addressing the issue of the social standing of Christ followers, the tendency in recent scholarship has been to frame the discussion in economic terms rather than other metrics of social standing. Justin Meggitt has urged that the social level of Pauline churches mirrored that of the general situation of nonelite in the empire.[20] According to Meggitt, the great majority of the nonelite in Greek and Roman cities lived at or near the bare subsistence level, and the demography of Christ cults simply mirrored this general pattern: "The Pauline Christians *en masse* shared fully the bleak material existence which was the lot of more than 99% of the inhabitants of the Empire, and also . . . of Paul himself. . . . To believe otherwise, without clear evidence of the contrary, given the near universal prevalence of poverty in the first-century world, is to believe in the improbable."[21] Yet even if we were to take the view that income was the primary independent variable of social standing, there are several quantitative reasons to reject this binary view of the economy.

SUBSISTENCE OR MORE?

It has been common to suppose that for preindustrial economies like that of the Roman Empire, subsistence-level incomes were the norm for the overwhelming majority of the population and that the elite corralled most or all of the other disposable wealth.[22] This assumption, however, is not borne out by the study of other preindustrial economies, where, as Allen, Bengtsson, and Dribe have shown, real wages were quite volatile over long periods, with some periods during which the average nonelite income was depressed and others when such incomes were several times subsistence level.[23]

Data from the Mediterranean suggest that the first century CE saw an overall growth in gross domestic product (GDP), as evidenced by several metrics: an increase in the length of the human femur, normally taken as a symptom of improved nutrition; an increase in lead and copper pollution, pointing to an increase in metal smelting; and an increase in the number of fish-salting vats, indicating a greater availability of marine protein.[24] Of course the benefits of increased GDP were not spread evenly throughout the population, but the increase in the length of human femurs suggests that nutrition was generally enhanced because the elite cannot have been solely responsible for the increased consumption of fish. According to Kehoe, the increase in commerce and manufacturing during the early imperial period would have had as its chief beneficiaries people of more modest status, "from wealthy freedmen to independent artisans."[25]

That Egypt in the first to third centuries CE might have been better off than is often supposed is argued by Dominic Rathbone, who noticed that in the approximately twenty thousand papyri from that period, the term *penēs* (poor) appears only four times and *ptōchos* (beggar) only three times, all in metaphorical contexts. Moreover, in complaints about theft and assault the accused are never identified as beggars or tramps but as neighbors or craftsmen or simply as "men I do not know."[26] In literary sources (Philo and Clement of Alexandria) *ptōchos* (beggar) appears, but always in the context of comment on biblical texts or in moralizing discourse. This invites three possibilities: the usual view, that poverty is rarely remarked upon because the elite, from whom most of our literature derives, ignored it; that poverty was in fact not as widespread as usually assumed; or, with Peter Brown, that poverty and the moral requirement of charity were in a sense "invented" by Christian bishops as a strategy to undergird their own legitimacy.[27]

Rathbone begins with the case of widows who appeal to the prefect for assistance on the grounds that they are "helpless and alone." Yet as Hanson has documented, these widows, when they are reported in census documents, were living with adult sons or other male relations or in predominantly female households.[28] This suggests that the plea "helpless and alone" is rhetorical rather than representative of the actual helpless situation of a widow.

Even more striking is Rathbone's finding concerning taxation. Examination of tax records in the Fayûm indicates almost universal compliance with the poll tax. The poll tax, which applied to nonelite Egyptians, in the Fayûm amounted (along with several other taxes) to the equivalent of the average pay for around forty-five days of agricultural labor. Even in the wake of an excessive Nile inundation in 45 CE that disrupted agricultural production, more than half of poll-tax payers in Philadelphia had paid their poll tax by the end of the 46/47 year, some had made partial payments, and 30 percent were in arrears. But by 50/51 CE normal payments had resumed. In 57 the tax collector in another village requested that twenty-eight of approximately nine hundred eligible taxpayers—much less than 10 percent of the population—be written off because they were unable to pay. Rathbone's view is that "few villagers in Roman Egypt were chronically unable to pay the poll-tax," which in turn implies a very low level of real poverty.[29]

THE STRUCTURE OF THE ROMAN ECONOMY

While the elite no doubt profited from GDP growth, it must have had some effect on subelite as well.[30] Walter Scheidel and Steven Friesen offer a broadly representative approach to the issue of the size and distribution of the Roman economy that suggests the existence of an economic middle.[31] Beginning with the likely GDP of the Roman Empire in the early first century, and factoring in the average tax rate of 5 percent[32] and the census requirements of various classes of elite that account for about 3 percent of the population,[33] Scheidel and Friesen calculate that the remaining 97 percent must have had an average per capita income of the equivalent of 425–540 kilograms of wheat.[34] This is between one-fifth and one-half higher than minimum subsistence levels of 335–390 kilograms.[35] The logical inferences from these data are either that everyone enjoyed a level of income 20–50 percent above subsistence with no one at the subsistence level or that income levels of the subelite were scaled from the subsistence level (or below) to up to ten times subsistence.[36]

In order to account for the difference between bare subsistence requirements (390 kg wheat) and the actual mean income of subelite people (425–540 kg wheat), Scheidel and Friesen propose a hypothetical model that parses subelite income levels into eight brackets. These brackets range from 8.4 to 10 times subsistence (3,275–3,930 kg grain equivalent) down to less than 300 kilograms of grain yearly and even less than 164 kilograms, which would indicate starvation. They then distribute income levels according to two scenarios, one "optimistic," with an overall mean per capita income of about 575 kilograms of wheat equivalent, and the other "pessimistic," with a mean of about 460 kilograms (but each scenario accounting for the quantitative data) (Table 2).[37]

Table 2. Wealth distribution in the Roman Empire

Level	*Wheat (kg)*	*Percent of population* Pessimistic	*Percent of population* Optimistic	*Mean per capita income*	*Aggregate (millions kg)* Pessimistic	*Aggregate (millions kg)* Optimistic
5	3,275–3,930	0.4	0.8	3,602.5	978	1,957
4	2,620–3,275	0.6	1.2	2,947.5	1,201	2,402
3	1,965–2,620	1	1.8	2,292.5	1,557	2,802
2	1,310–1,965	1.5	2.7	1637.5	1,668	3,002
1	655–1,310	3.5	6.5	982.5	2,335	4,336
0.75–0.99	491–655	8	19	573	3,113	7,392
0.50–0.74	327–491	60	55	409	16,663	15,274
0.25–0.49	164–327	22	10	245.5	3,667	1,667
Total		97	97	459	31,182	38,832

Scheidel and Friesen still assume that subsistence-level households accounted for between 84 percent ("optimistic") and 90 percent ("pessimistic") of the population. Nevertheless, between 7 percent ("pessimistic") and 13 percent ("optimistic") of the population represented "middling" incomes. This model has at least two noteworthy implications. First, the aggregate income and expenditures of this middling sector rivaled that of the numerically very much smaller elite sector. Even using the pessimistic estimate, the middling sector, at 4.8 million people, vastly outnumbered the aristocrats by more than a factor of ten, and this meant in turn that they collectively represented a major economic block. Second, this middling sector was likely distributed unevenly: assuming that only 10–15 percent of the population was urban,[38] middling incomes were likely more common in cities than in rural areas, with the result that anywhere from one-eighth to one-quarter of the urban population fell into the middling category.[39]

If we were to follow the logic of Meggitt's argument that the demography of Christ assemblies mirrored that of urban society in general, we would have to suppose that while many members of urban Christ assemblies were quite low in economic level, 12–25 percent belonged to the middling sectors of the Roman urban economy and had incomes ranging from 1.7 to 10 times subsistence level. Yet it hardly follows that the income profile of particular groups necessarily mirrored the income profile of the city as a whole: a guild of shoemakers would not necessarily have wealthier and less wealthy members. Nor would a Christ group *necessarily* have members with a range of income levels. An inference from the profile of the city as a whole to a particular civic group is scarcely legitimate.

The Scheidel-Friesen model is predicated on many insecure assumptions, including estimate of GDP, the size of the subsistence population, and the way that the middling incomes are distributed above what subsistence requires. Peter Temin, for example, estimates the GDP of the empire at 50 percent higher than Scheidel and Friesen,[40] which would inevitably raise the mean per capita income and the numbers in the middling group. Nevertheless, the basic thesis that the overall GDP of the empire implied an average income of more than subsistence level means that some version of the Scheidel-Friesen model would offer a working account of income distribution.

THE DISTRIBUTION OF LAND

While Scheidel and Friesen begin at the macro-scale of the Roman economy as a whole and the likely distribution of wealth, another approach begins locally and examines the distribution of wealth in specific regions.[41]

For modern economists, inequities in the distribution of wealth can be measured by the Gini coefficient, a statistical tool that indicates the degree of deviation from full equality in a given society or economic group. This index plots how the overall wealth or income of a society is distributed among each decile of the population. The resulting Gini coefficient is a fraction between 0 and 1 indicating, respectively, full equality and complete inequality in the distribution of wealth (fig. 21).[42]

Gini analysis has been used in classical studies to analyze the distribution of land (and as we will see, the size of houses). This is not a full measurement of the distribution of wealth, since it captures only those people who owned land, not those who derived income in other ways. Nevertheless, since the ownership of land was one of the principal status markers, the distribution of land provides a partial picture of the scale of social status. For antiquity, Gini analysis indicates several important points: (1) that unsurprisingly, a good deal of landed wealth was concentrated in the hands of a relatively small elite, but (2) that in contrast to what the binary model of the Roman economy predicts, the elite did not control the overwhelming majority of land; instead, (3) wealth was distributed unevenly from one locale to another, with some areas evidencing very unequal patterns of landownership and others tending to a much more equitable pattern of ownership.

Richard Duncan-Jones was one of the first scholars of Roman antiquity to apply Gini analysis to land registers that recorded area measurements, valuation, tax liability, or water requirements in six locations, three from Italy, one from Numidia, one from Asia (Magnesia), and one from Roman Egypt

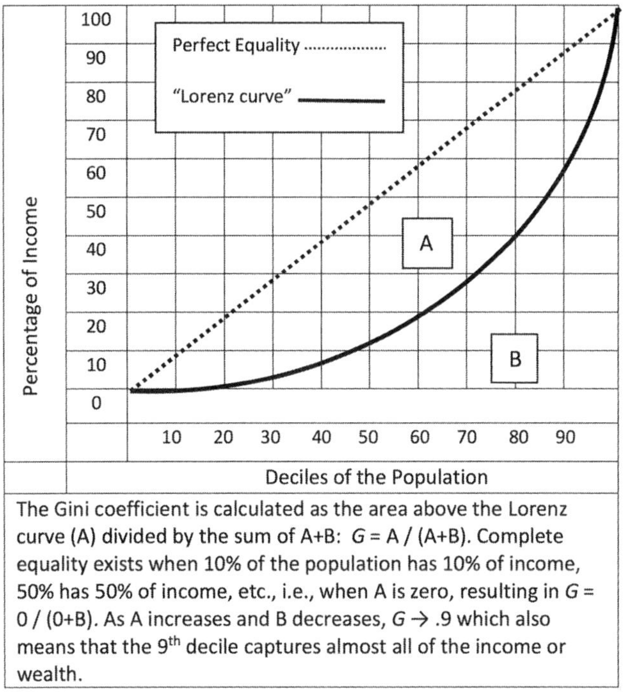

Figure 21. Gini coefficients.

(Hermopolis).[43] In each case Duncan-Jones plotted the number and size of plots of land against the roster of owners. For example, a register from Ligures Baebiani (southern Italy, 101 CE) shows that two individuals owned 21.3 percent of the land and the poorest eight had only 3.6 percent; but the distribution of the remaining 75 percent of plots was weighed toward smaller sized plots (valued at 25,000–100,000 sesterces). This resulted in a Gini coefficient of 0.435. Analyses of other registers produced varying Gini coefficients: 0.526 for forty-seven estates in the northern Italian town of Veleia; 0.394 for the thirty-six farms in Volcei in the south of Italy; 0.679 for Magnesia on the Maeander (early IV CE: eighty-one farms, sixty-seven owners), where the richest 7.5 percent owned almost half of the total; and 0.815 for Hermopolis in Upper Egypt, where 3.5 percent of the 198 owners controlled 53 percent of the land.

Alan Bowman reexamined the mid-fourth-century CE land registers from the Hermopolite nome in Upper Egypt, which contained nearly complete records of holdings by the inhabitants of two towns, Hermopolis and Antinoopolis, which faced each other across the Nile. Both had a high degree of inequality in the distribution of land, with Antinoopolis at 0.622, only slightly lower than Duncan-Jones's figures for Hermopolis (0.815) across the river. In both towns, however, land was not exclusively in the hands of the elite (bishops, magistrates, ex-magistrates, and veterans); it also existed in smaller allotments to various artisans (wool workers, donkey drivers, coppersmiths).[44] Yet as the Gini coefficients indicate, the distribution of land was more unequal than equal.

The findings for the fourth-century Hermopolite nome contrast with those for the village of Kerkeosiris in the Fayûm to the north, where complete records are available for the village in 116/115 BCE. There the Gini coefficient is 0.374, indicating a relatively high degree of equality in landownership.[45] Plot sizes fall within a narrower bracket, which Bowman suggests may have been the result of efforts of the Ptolemaic administration to respond to grievances of the underprivileged that had earlier led to political unrest. Bagnall surveyed several Fayumic towns, confirming the findings of Bowman and others.[46] The list of landholdings from these towns of course does not give a complete picture of the economy of the Fayûm, since there is no way to measure the relative wealth of those who owned no land at all.

To repeat: These data do not give a complete picture of the distribution of wealth, since they do not consider that some villagers might have owned land outside the nome, nor can it factor in the entire holdings of metropolitans, who probably owned other land. Nor is there any way from these data to estimate the income of artisans who did not own land at all or those who worked in workshops *and* owned small plots of land (as was the case in Hermopolis). That is, the data on landownership cannot be translated simply into a picture of the distribution of income within a village. What these data show, however, is that (1) predictably, wealth in the form of land was unevenly distributed, with greater concentrations in the hands of the elite and city residents; (2) the way in which land was distributed varied widely from one region to another, with some regions having more equitable distributions of land; and, most importantly, (3) the distribution of land was not confined to elite sectors but is attested, with significant variations, in nonelite sectors. This is not what the binary approach to the economy would predict; in that view, the Gini coefficients should always be 0.9 or higher.[47]

HOUSING

Instead of using landownership as a proxy for wealth, another approach to the problem of the distribution of wealth focuses on housing, which generally ranks as the most significant expenditure after food (except in the wealthiest sectors of society). The two towns of Pompeii and Herculaneum, destroyed in the eruption of Vesuvius in 79 CE, offer important data for Roman-era housing because their houses and fixtures were preserved in layers of ash and because the size of the two towns can be estimated fairly accurately from modern excavations. Moreover, although Pompeii and Herculaneum are in some respects unique in the level of preservation, they turn out to be typical in the average size of house. Houses in several sample areas of the two towns, which range from 241 to 289 square meters (average, 271 m^2), fall in the middle of the range of other houses from Greece, Asia, and Syria: Priene (207 m^2), Abdera (212 m^2), Piraeus (242 m^2), Miletos (259 m^2), Olynthos (294 m^2), and Dura-Europos (311 m^2).[48]

Andrew Wallace-Hadrill studied housing at Pompeii, selecting three sample groups totaling 234 houses. Using thirteen ranges from 0–99 square meters to very large houses of 2,000–2,999 square meters, he tabulated the size of each of the 234 houses (Table 3).[49] It is not surprising that some houses in the sample, undoubtedly belonging to the elite, are larger than 1,000 square meters. Nor should it surprise that the largest single group of houses includes those smaller than 100 square meters. In fact, more than 56 percent of the houses have areas of 200 square meters or less, with only two to six rooms.

At the time of the eruption of Vesuvius the population of Pompeii is usually set at about ten thousand within the walls. For estimating how that population was distributed, Wallace-Hadrill cites ethno-archaeological and historical

Table 3. Distribution of the size of houses (Pompeii)

Size (m^2)	*No. of houses*	*Average size (m^2)*	*Average open space (m^2)*	*No. of rooms*	*Total rooms*
0–99	82 (35.04%)	38	0	2	164
100–199	50 (21.37%)	145	2	6	300
200–299	31 (13.25%)	240	22	9	279
300–399	19 (8.12%)	337	73	9	171
400–499	19 (8.12%)	435	87	12	228
500–599	11 (4.70%)	527	85	13	143
600–699	7 (3.00%)	665	103	17	119
700–799	2 (0.85%)	775	134	18	36
800–899	2 (0.85%)	825	165	21	40
900–999	0	—	—	—	0
1,000–1,099	6 (2.56%)	1,152	179	20	120
1,100–1,199	3 (1.28%)	1,677	215	32	96
2,000–2,999	2 (0.85%)	2,658	692	33	66
Total	234				1,762

data indicating that the average density in houses that are not considered to be overcrowded is about one person per room.[50] He notes further that although the houses smaller than 100 square meters are the most numerous, they also account for a relatively small proportion of the population. The next two bands (100–199 and 200–299 m^2) turn out to have a greater share of the population, because houses in these bands tend to have an average of six to nine rooms each and thus presumably have more inhabitants per house. Since the total number of rooms in the sample is 1,762, the houses in the second and third bands represent 32.8 percent of the population of the sample.[51]

Estimates of the excavated and unexcavated areas of Pompeii imply that the town had a total of 1,200–1,300 houses. Thus Wallace-Hadrill's sample of 234 houses accounts for about 18.7 percent of the total population, or about 1,870 people. The average number of people per house would then be eight. Since it is usual to assume that a Roman family included about four people,[52] and since first-century Italy was a slave-owning society with many households having at least one slave, a model has to take into account this population. I propose a model that accounts for the total population of Wallace-Hadrill's sample of 234 houses by assuming that the lowest band (0–99 m^2, two rooms) housed families that did not own slaves and that the remaining bands, with larger space and more rooms per house, housed families with two slaves per house for houses of 100–199 square meters (six rooms), rising to twenty-eight to twenty-nine slaves per household for the houses of larger than 1,100 square meters with more than thirty-two rooms. This model posits a total population of 1,928, only slightly larger than the projected population of 1,870. Slight reductions in the number of slaves in some of the houses larger than 600 square meters would still keep the average occupancy at less than 1.0 person per room and bring the model into conformity with the projected population of 1,870 (Table 4).

These figures are all hypothetical but are reasonable given standard assumptions about family size, occupation levels, and the number of slaves (and freedmen) in Roman society. What is noteworthy for our purposes is that the model also suggests that the houses in the range of 100–400 square meters account for almost two-fifths (38.9 percent) of the entire Pompeian population and about 43 percent of the houses. These are houses of relatively modest scale; as Wallace-Hadrill's tables indicate, they are not the smallest or the poorest. If there is a correlation between house size and wealth, these data suggest that a significant proportion of the population lived well above subsistence level and some had modest wealth. There are still inequities *within* this two-fifths of the population, but the distribution of housing is more equitable than in Pompeii considered as a whole.

Table 4. Hypothetical distribution of population (Pompeii)

Size of houses (m^2)	*No. of houses*	*Assuming four people per family*	*Total slaves*	*Total occupants*	*Percent of population*
0–99	82	328	0	328	17.01
100–199	50	200	100	300	15.56
200–299	31	124	155	279	14.47
300–399	19	76	95	171	8.87
400–499	19	76	152	228	11.83
500–599	11	44	99	143	7.42
600–699	7	28	91	119	6.17
700–799	2	8	28	36	1.87
800–899	2	8	34	42	2.18
900–999	0	0	0	0	0.00
1,000–1,099	6	24	96	120	6.22
1,100–1,199	3	12	84	96	4.98
2,000–2,999	2	8	58	66	3.42
Total	234	936	992	1,928	100.00

Geoffrey Kron arrived at a similar conclusion. He began with Pompeii and compared Pompeian houses with published data on English houses in the nineteenth and early twentieth centuries. Wallace-Hadrill's second smallest quartile of Pompeian houses ranges from 50 to 170 square meters, with an average size of 108 square meters, that is, more than twice as large as the typical English lower-middle-class terrace house of the early twentieth century.[53]

Moreover, Wallace-Hadrill's data indicate that more than one-half (59 percent) of the houses in the sample with walls that could be assessed had at least one decorated room—probably an understatement of the evidence, since very few second stories are preserved. In fact *all* of the houses in Herculaneum that had second-story rooms that survived had decorated walls, and all five of the Pompeian houses for which second-story rooms are preserved were decorated. In houses smaller than 100 square meters, decoration was rare though not unattested (17 percent).[54] In the middle two quartiles of houses—that is, in houses still well smaller than the dimensions of elite houses—the likelihood of decoration increased with the size of the house. These data led Kron to conclude that the middling group in Greco-Roman society was larger and more affluent than has generally been conceded and that the binary description of society is probably wrong. He argues that

> Roman Italy, like Classical, Hellenistic and Roman Greece, was a far less polarized society than is generally assumed, and the social importance of a

> substantial and affluent middle-income group ensured that mean and median incomes remained well above subsistence. Unlike poor agrarian societies dominated by very small, although often wealthy, elites, such as 18th century England, or 19th century Southern Italy, India, China, or New Spain . . . , Greco-Roman society, like that of Renaissance Holland or Italy, seems to have been very much a prosperous middle-class society, more reminiscent of Western European society following the dramatic democratic social changes of the 1870s and the 1940s and 1950s, than the grim inegalitarian society of the ancien régime.[55]

Finally, a survey of Roman Corinth likewise suggests that housing was not simply divided between magnificent houses and poor slums, but that a significant "middle" register existed. Dirk Jongkind observes: "The variety of housing in Corinth shows us a society which cannot be simply divided into an elite and a very poor non-elite. The non-elite were not all extremely poor nor did all lead a life just above abject poverty. Such generalizations are not supported by the archaeological evidence."[56]

Returning to Scheidel and Friesen, a rough estimate of the Gini coefficient can be proposed for the Roman Empire as a whole: "Our two scenarios [optimistic and pessimistic] yield almost identical measures of 0.42 and 0.44. . . . This indicates that Roman inequality fell right in the middle of a broad historical range. More importantly, our results are markedly lower than Gini coefficients of 0.52 and 0.59 for Britain in 1759 and 1801, respectively, and of 0.59 for late eighteenth-century France."[57]

There is no doubt that the early Roman Empire was marked by significant social inequality. Not only did the dominant classification systems favor the citizen, the freeborn, the wealthy, those of noble lineages, and those with the resources to achieve public office, but small numbers of elite controlled a disproportionate percentage of the wealth. Nevertheless, the binary view of the economy—with the elite controlling almost all of the wealth and everyone else hovering at subsistence level—does not match the quantitative model produced by Scheidel and Friesen; the data adduced by Rathbone, Duncan-Jones, Bowman, and Bagnall; or the data concerning Roman-era housing. All of these findings point to a subelite population that exhibited multiple levels of income and wealth from subsistence upward to a reasonably comfortable existence.

THE "NEW CONSENSUS"

If Greek and Roman urban economies admitted of significant scaling in wealth between bare subsistence and elite wealth, how might we imagine the members of Christ assemblies? Critical to this discussion are two questions: Can the wealth levels of nonelites be known as it can be for members of the curial ranks? and Is income the major determinant of status for nonelites? I argue that both questions should be answered in the negative. But first some context to this discussion.

Since the 1970s it has been usual to argue with the "new consensus" that all economic and social strata of imperial society were represented in early Christ assemblies with the exception of the rural poor and civic elite. Wayne Meeks summarizes the new consensus well:

> The extreme top and bottom of the Greco-Roman social scale are missing from the picture. It is hardly surprising that we meet no landed aristocrats, no senators, *equites*, nor (unless Erastus might qualify) decurions. But there is also no specific evidence of people who are destitute—such as the hired menials and dependent handworkers; the poorest of the poor, peasants, agricultural slaves, and hired agricultural day laborers are absent because of the urban setting of the Pauline groups. There may have been members of the Pauline communities who lived at the subsistence level, but we hear nothing of them.[58]

There is almost no disagreement with the second part of Meeks' statement—that Christ assemblies or a least the assemblies we know did not include the rural poor. There is less consensus on how far up the social ladder to place other members—which will occupy us in the next chapter.

One might well ask, Why does this debate matter? Why is it consequential whether Christ assemblies were composed exclusively of people on the lower and middle rungs of Roman society or also had a few members of elite orders? Or, to frame the question not in terms of income levels, Why does it matter whether the early Christ followers in the cities of the empire were connected to the sites of social power—the curial ranks—or only to the local gentry, or were completely unconnected? These questions are important for several reasons, some having to do with understanding the internal dynamics of Christ assemblies, and others having to do with their place in the ancient city.

In the first place, the presence of Roman elite or at least people of high social standing with some of the trappings of high status might help to account for some of the dynamics evident in Christ assemblies. The presence of higher status people in the Corinthian assembly is essential to Theissen's explanation of the conflict between the "Strong" and the "Weak" about eating food that had been sacrificed to pagan deities (1 Cor 8–10). And it is essential to his explanation of conflicts around the communal meal between the "haves" and the "have-nots" (1 Cor 11:17–34). In both cases Theissen saw these conflicts as primarily between the social practices and cultural expectations of members of higher rank, who wanted to preserve their social ties with other elite or semi-elite Corinthians outside the Christ assembly and their sense of privilege on one hand and the egalitarian expectations of poorer members on the other.[59]

Second, the growth of Christ assemblies and their recruitment possibilities will look different depending on whether they were composed mainly of the poor and disenfranchised or whether they included affluent members with multiple social connections. Thomas Schleich, who characterized early Christ assemblies as a "religion of the civic middle-strata" (*Mittelschichten*), argued that Christ assemblies were composed of, and appealed to, the "economically dynamic strata, merchants, handworkers, and business people."[60] These were people who had financial means, wide-ranging social contacts through which the message of Christ assemblies could spread, and houses in which their meetings could take place. The presence in Christ assemblies of household slaves, who otherwise played insignificant roles in the first century, is explicable for Schleich if householders brought their slaves with them. Thus, in spite of what opponents like Celsus would later say, early Christ assemblies were not dominated by slaves and the destitute;[61] on the contrary, they were primarily "middle-strata" groups. According to Schleich, this construction makes sense of another datum: "for only in this context are the issues intelligible of money and possessions, the social obligations of the wealthy, the duty of care that is emphasized, and discourse about table fellowship, and the responsibility to accommodate, which occupy so much space in the New Testament writings."[62]

The presence of members with at least modest wealth is also central to Wayne Meeks's model for Christ assemblies. In *The First Urban Christians* he argued that the most prominent of Paul's circle, including Paul himself, displayed "high status inconsistency": their "achieved status is higher than their attributed status."[63] Pauline assemblies were populated by freed slaves, artisans, merchants, and wealthy women who in society at large could not achieve a high rank according to the formal metrics of Roman society. Yet they had abilities, aspirations, achievements, and resources in many ways comparable to those who fulfilled the qualifications of a noble birth, public service, and wealth. Without necessarily suggesting a causal relationship between status inconsistency and the willingness to embrace the Christ cult, Meeks wondered whether there was some relationship between the presence of status-inconsistent people and a belief system that traded in symbols of personal and communal transformation and that expected an evil world to be "encompassed by God's judgment and grace."[64]

Third, the complexion of Christ assemblies may be related to the kinds of activities in which members engaged. Edwin Judge contended that the presence of the middling strata is essential to understanding Christ assemblies as "scholastic communities": "Far from being a socially depressed group, then, if the Corinthians are at all typical, the Christians were dominated by a socially pretentious section of the population of the big cities. Beyond that they seem to have drawn on a broad constituency, probably representing the household dependents of the leading members."[65]

Judge described Paul as a "sophist," that is, as a traveling intellectual relying on hospitality, an expert talker and persuader, dedicated to his mission, and intolerant of criticism. The groups to which he appealed were unlike cult associations: Christ assemblies did not use temples or conduct sacrifices. Instead, they engaged in ethical and philosophical debate: "While the ultimate objective [of the Christ followers] may be communion with God, the means to this end are distinctly intellectual: the correct interpretation of the law and the prophets, or the comprehension of the message of the gospel—such are the immediate objects."[66]

If the activities of Christ assemblies centered on intellectual pursuits, Judge's assumption seems reasonable that the *social* center of gravity lay with the "socially pretentious"—people with some education and wealth and at least modest social standing. He noted that many of those named in Paul's letters and in Acts—Aquila, Prisca, Rufus, Julia, Justus, Crispus, Gaius, Quartus, Fortunatus—have Latin names and thus are probably Roman citizens; others such as Erastos had high status by virtue of their office.[67] Although Christ assemblies probably included poorer people (because householders brought their retinues of slaves, artisans, and clients with them), the dynamics of these groups was the inverse of Deissmann's: the Jesus movement was not a movement of poorer people with a smattering of wealthy; instead, the culture of Christ assemblies was the creation of "highly articulate people with social influence," who exported that culture downward to poorer Christ devotees.[68]

Fourth, understanding the social complexion of Christ assemblies helps to address the issue of how Christ assemblies could position themselves vis-à-vis others, both competitors and allies. Groups that had members with higher social status or influential patrons would naturally have access to greater and better resources than those without influential patrons. In certain areas of the empire and at certain times, there were efforts to suppress associations for fear of the subversive activities in which they might engage. As we shall see, having a wealthy and influential patron likely served as insulation against such action. On the other hand, not having high-status members and having to rely exclusively on the internal resources of a group might have created strong ties of solidarity and led to the development of social strategies to compensate for the lack of external resources.

Finally, the issue of the complexion of Christ assemblies is related to the degree to which they "fit in" or failed to "fit in" with civic society in general. The writings of early Christ devotees provide occasional glimpses at conflict over the degree to which Christ followers should fit in or not, as for example, the issues Paul addressed in 1 Corinthians 8–10 where some of the members participated in meals at pagan temples or in the houses of people outside the Christ assembly (8:10, 10:27–28). Theissen has argued that it was likely the wealthier and higher statused people who would normally be invited to dine at a pagan temple or to accept dinner invitations where food that had been sacrificed to pagan deities was served.[69] If so, the questions arise: To what extent did wealthier Christ followers regard belonging to a Christ assembly as compatible with other kinds of social attachments? To what degree could (and should) they participate in Corinthian society at large? The author of the Apocalypse of John had a clear answer to these questions: he was bitterly critical of the Christ assembly at Thyatira for its participation in pagan banquets, rejecting the practice entirely (Rev 2:20–24). Likewise, the author or editor of the *Didache* (6.3) forbids the consumption of meat that had been sacrificed to pagan deities. These differences in behavior are probably in part a function of differences in the social registers of the members of the assemblies at Corinth and Thyatira on one hand and those of the authors of the Apocalypse and the *Didache* on the other.

The results of this chapter are threefold. In the first place it is clear from recent analyses of the Roman economy that there was a significant middling group, particularly in cities, where Christ followers were initially located and eventually flourished. This at least raises the theoretical possibility that some of the earliest Christ followers might have been located in those middling levels. Yet, second, the fact that there were people of middling economic level hardly necessitates the conclusion that any or all the members of Christ assemblies belonged to those middling levels. There is no reason in the abstract to conclude that Christ assemblies mirrored the general structure of Roman society. Members may have been all very poor, as the caricature of the "old consensus" held, or have displayed a range of poorer and middling people, as the "new consensus" suggests, or even had a center of gravity that lay with the middling groups (as Judge and Schleich have argued). But nothing can be decided in the abstract. The issue of how to locate Christ followers comes down to names: Does evidence exist of the presence of wealthier people in Christ assemblies?

This will be the concern of chapter 6, which will also discuss other indices of social status.

Finally, I have suggested that despite uncertainties, the issue of the social register of Christ believers is consequential. It matters to a host of topics—group dynamics, governance, and recruitment, for example—how we imagine the social register of the members of Christ assemblies since decisions of this nature have a profound bearing on how we read the texts produced by those assemblies and their members.

6

THE SOCIAL LEVEL OF CHRIST ASSEMBLIES

If the Roman economy showed a significant portion of the population poised between the superrich and those at the subsistence level, it does not necessarily follow that Christ followers mirrored that distribution, with many at the subsistence level and perhaps 25 percent much better off. Can one move from the general model of the economy to a defensible model of economic patterns in Christ assemblies? In this chapter I argue that the quest for an economic model for Christ assemblies is in fact futile, because we have almost no reliable data for determining wealth levels of most people. Yet we are not left without answers, because the more important measures of status are the connections of people to the sites of social power, the sources of prestige and honor, or, more generally, social capital.

Gauging the economic level for Christ assemblies presents an immediate problem: no direct data are available from Paul's letters about the relative economic standing of his addressees apart from Paul's vague and highly rhetorical statements about the "extreme poverty" of some and "wealth" of others. The same is true of the individual guild members such as the boatmen and registrars of Ostia. While collectively the boatmen and registrars were well connected to the sources of social power, it is impossible to know the economic standing of individual members, apart from some guesses about M. Cornelius Epagathus and his immediate family. It turns out to be impossible to move from general models of the distribution of wealth, landownership, and the size of houses or from the likely economic standing of collectivities like the boatmen and registrars to the income level of any individual.[1] It is only in the case of the elite that one can arrive at some estimate of wealth, and that is only because the census requirements for senators, equestrians, and decurions are generally known. That is where our investigation begins.

CHRIST FOLLOWERS OF HIGH RANK?

During the second and third centuries some people of high rank—more women than men—became associated with Christ assemblies: a handful of imperial freedmen (and freedwomen?) and maybe even an equestrian or two in the early to mid-second century; a few individuals of senatorial rank during the period of the Severan emperors (193–235 CE); and more still in the latter part of the third century, in spite of persecutions in 250–251 and 257 during the principates of Decius and Valerian. But even in the third century, the number of elite individuals connected with Christ assemblies was not in the thousands but more likely was less than one hundred.[2] If the numbers of high-born individuals in the second century were small, we should probably not expect very high numbers in the first century either.

Efforts to detect Christ followers of high social and economic standing in the first century CE take two different approaches. On one hand, attention has been focused on three references in Acts and Paul's letters to people who, if the reports are reliable and if their titles are interpreted accurately, were of high social standing—one belonging to the senatorial rank and two others in the curial ranks of Athens and Corinth. These are Sergius Paul(l)us, named in Acts 13:7–12; Dionysios of the council of the Areio Pagus (Acts 17:34); and Erastos, the city manager named in Rom 16:23. The second approach is to posit proxies of wealth such as the ability to travel or to host a Christ assembly and then to identify people in whom those proxies are present. The first approach aims at identifying people of rank who, because of prevailing census requirements, would have had significant wealth; the second tries to identify individuals who had personal resources that exceeded the level of basic subsistence but without assuming anything about rank.

SERGIUS PAULUS (ACTS 13:7–12)

There is no doubt that the Sergii Paulli were a senatorial family in the first century CE associated with the area around Pisidian Antioch.[3] At least one first-century inscription attests a member of this family as the governor of Cyprus, the ostensible location of Paul's encounter with Sergius Paulus in Acts 13:7–12.[4] Hence, there is good evidence that Luke, writing at the end of the first century or in the early second, knew of either L. Sergius Pau(l)us Pau(l)lus on Cyprus and placed Paul and Sergius Paulus there. Whether the chronology implied by Luke's account and whether the story of Paul's encounter with a Roman procurator have any historical substance are different issues entirely.

There are several puzzling aspects of the report in Acts 13:12. Luke connects the encounter with Sergius Paulus with a tale of Paul's encounter with a magician named Bar-Jesus or Elymas in which Paul blinds the magician. The story ends with Sergius Paulus expressing astonishment "at the teaching of the Lord" and "believing" (*episteusen*). Curiously, Sergius Paulus is not subsequently baptized, as occurs routinely in other conversion stories in Acts, and the "conversion" of this high-ranking Roman is narrated as if it were of no consequence. Indeed, it *has* no consequences, since there is no story of the ensuing conversion of the household of Sergius Paulus (contrast, Acts 11:14; 16:15, 31; 18:8) or of the formation of a Christ assembly on Cyprus.[5] These peculiarities lead one to suspect that Luke has assembled the story from bits of local knowledge of Cyprus to advance the impression that Paul was given a sympathetic hearing by a person of high rank, a literary device that he routinely uses elsewhere.[6]

Whatever historical detail exists in the Acts 13 account, it falls far short of evidence of a Roman senator becoming a member of a nonelite cult. The story in Acts leaves no impression that a Christ assembly was formed in Paphos under Sergius Paulus. After all, as proconsul Paulus was in Cyprus for only a single year; and since he was likely aiming at higher appointments, it is difficult to imagine any reason for him to patronize an assembly of Christ followers that had no conceivable potential to advance his political fortunes. A Christ assembly was hardly comparable to the guilds of Ostia or Portus or Rome, which attracted senators as patrons because these guilds were uniquely engaged in the feeding of Rome and thus gave to senators and other elite public visibility as benefactors. Thus, in spite of appearances, Acts 13 is not evidence of a senator being a member or even patron of a Christ assembly. Writing at the beginning of the second century CE, Luke may have imagined that people of high rank might be attracted to Christ groups—he addresses Theophilos as *krasiste*, "excellency," as though he were writing to someone of rank. But even he is not so rash as to suggest that Paul baptized a Roman senator.

DIONYSIOS OF THE AREIO PAGUS

Luke's story in Acts 17:34 can be treated in the same way. There Luke reports that after Paul's speech in Athens on the Areio Pagus, which was met with some skepticism by the philosophers there, some were attracted and "believed" (*episteusan*). These included a woman, Damaris, and Dionysios, a member of the council of five hundred, officially called the "council of the Areio Pagos."[7] Again, Luke does not claim that any of these "believers" was baptized. His description implies that Dionysios belonged to the decurial rank under Roman rule. Yet like the account of Sergius Paulus, the story raises suspicions. According to 1 Thess 3:1, Paul had been in Athens before his visit to Corinth; yet in 1 Cor 1:14 he admits having baptized only two people, both from Corinth, as the "first converts" (first fruits) of the province of Achaia (16:15). In other words, Paul's own account of converts in Achaia casts serious doubt on the claim in Acts that Dionysios and Damaris in Athens were converts before Corinth.[8]

The best interpretation that can be put on the stories in Acts 13 and 16 is that Luke, like James and *1 Clement*, wished to represent the Christ cult as something to which a person of rank might be attracted or at least ought to take seriously. Luke's *episteusen/-an* ("he/they believed") only amounts to a claim that these elite were favorably disposed to Paul. Yet as optimistic as Luke might be about the prospects of the Christ movement, he does not go as far as suggesting that people of senatorial or decurial rank were baptized.

ERASTUS/ERASTOS OF CORINTH

While the two previous candidates for individuals of high rank come from Luke's tales about Paul, the final candidate and undoubtedly the most controversial comes from Paul's own hand. In Rom 16:23, in a list of people greeting the Roman assembly, Paul refers to Erastus as *oikonomos tēs poleōs*, the city manager. The Greek name Erastos (Latinized as Erastus) means "beloved." (In what follows I use the Greek spelling Erastos when discussing Greek texts and inscriptions and the Latinized spelling Erastus when discussing Latin inscriptions.) Since the name occurs in Corinth, a Roman colony, one might assume that Erastos was either a slave or a freedman who took his former slave name as a cognomen. The name, however, is attested of citizens in Athens, including the eponymous archon from 163/162 BCE and four other citizens in the time of Claudius.[9] During Hadrian's principate, the emperor wrote to the council of Ephesus asking that they elect a certain Erastus—surely a Roman citizen—to the municipal senate.[10] In Latin inscriptions the name Erastus is borne equally by slaves, freedmen, and freeborn people, with at least seventeen clear instances of freedmen, whose names take the form (for example) M. Ulpius Aug(usti) l(ibertus) Erastus (CIL 6.8875).[11] Hence, the onomastic profile does not afford a clear basis for deciding whether Erastos was a slave name, the servile cognomen of a *libertus*, or the cognomen of a Roman *ingenuus* (freeborn person).

The interpretation of this figure became controversial largely because of the discovery in 1928–1929 of a donative inscription in the agora of Corinth: *E*] *rastus pro aedilit*[*at*]*e* | *s*(*ua*) *p*(*ecunia*) *stravit*, "E]rastus, in return for his aedileship, laid (the pavement) at his own expense."[12] In the wake of Gerd Theissen's discussion of the inscription it has been common to assume that the Erastus of the inscription and the Erastos of Rom 16:23 are the same person.[13] If this equation could be sustained, the Erastos of Rom 16:23 was in high public office, since in the political structure of Corinth as a Roman colony, the two aediles elected yearly were responsible for the maintenance of public streets and buildings and were junior only to the two *duoviri* who administered the colony. This would not settle the issue of whether Erastus was freeborn or a freedman, since in Roman colonies, including Corinth, freedmen could serve as magistrates.[14] But it would make Erastus a man of considerable wealth, able to shoulder the responsibilities and costs of aedileship.

Three considerations weigh against this identification, however. First, the initial dating of the inscription to the first century was made not on the basis of any stratigraphic or paleographic data but solely on the basis of the *assumed* identity of the Erastos of Rom 16:23 and the Erastus of I.Corinth.Kent 232. Subsequent excavations, however, have shown that the slab on which Erastus's name is inscribed had been moved from its original location to serve as part of the foundation for a Byzantine wall. The original location of the slab was, according to the excavator, Charles Williams, a plaza that now covers a latrine that was in use into the Hadrianic period. This implies that the plaza and the Erastus inscription date from late in Hadrian's principate *at the earliest* and that the Erastus of I.Corinth.Kent 232 cannot be the Erastos of Rom 16:23.[15]

Second, while Kent, who originally published I.Corinth.Kent 232, suggested that the name Erastus was uncommon and that this favored the identity of two Erasti,[16] Meggitt has shown that there were at least seventy-five instances of the cognomen Erastus or its Greek form, Erastos.[17] In fact the majority of the Greek occurrences are from Attica and the Peloponnese; the name was not at all uncommon, a finding that undermines the easy identification of Erastus with Erastos.

The third issue concerns the term "*oikonomos* of the city." Is *oikonomos* an appropriate rendering of aedile? Some have argued that it is, but there is now broad consensus that aedile was usually rendered in Greek not as *oikonomos* but as *agoranomos*, literally the market manager.[18] Aware of this difficulty, Theissen conjectured that the Erastos of Rom 16:23 had been a lesser official, a *quaestor*, at the time that Paul wrote Romans and was only later elected as aedile.[19] But this effort to harmonize the two Erasti involves positing an otherwise unknown stage in Erastos's career; it is not evidence of their identity but rather a speculation that *presupposes* their identity.[20]

Paul, nevertheless, does identify Erastos as city manager, and this suggests a relatively important role in the administration of Corinth. To what does this term refer? While the terms aedile and *agoranomos* appear several times in Corinthian inscriptions and a catalogue of known aediles has been assembled by Kent, *oikonomos* occurs but once in a funerary monument and from the late Roman period.[21] The term *oikonomos tēs poleōs*, however, is attested in many other Greek cities, especially in Asia Minor. This means that *oikonomos tēs poleōs* might be *Paul's term*, not a term indigenous to Corinth, although it presumably had some Corinthian equivalent.[22]

Inscriptions from other cities indicate that *oikonomos tēs poleōs* is used of both freeborn civic magistrates and of slaves (and perhaps freedmen). Weiß claims that before the second century the term usually designated freeborn people, not slaves.[23] But his argument requires excluding inscriptions from the first or early second century that are imprecisely dated "imperial period" in which the *oikonomos* is clearly a slave.[24] In fact the overwhelming majority of inscriptions from the early imperial period that use the term use it in relation to a slave.

The statistical distribution of freeborn versus servile *oikonomoi*, of course, does not settle the issues of the rank and social standing of Erastos. A critical question is why Paul chose to identify him as "city manager" when he has identified other people in Romans 16 only in relation to himself ("my fellow worker[s]," "my guest and guest of the entire *ekklesia*"). Jewett conjectures that Paul did so because, in an effort to impress the Roman recipients of the letter, he wanted to underscore that his plans to conduct a potentially subversive mission to Spain came with the endorsement of a high-ranking Roman official in Corinth.[25] Weiß doubts that sufficient personal connections existed between the Roman colony of Corinth and the Judean expatriate community in Rome in the mid-50s CE for Erastos's name to carry any weight. Instead, he thinks that Paul mentioned the title of Erastos (whom he assumes to be an aedile) because he used him as a model of someone of influence who had *renounced* his position within Roman society to become a Christ follower.[26] But to suppose that Erastos had renounced his aedileship is entirely gratuitous and is, in fact, even more implausible than Jewett's suggestion. If Erastos had been a former aedile, one would expect Paul to call Erastos *ho pote oikonomos tēs poleōs*, or *ho oikonomēsas*, "who was *formerly oikonomos*," both perfectly ordinary ways of designating a former officeholder. Instead, Erastos is presented as a current officeholder.

Attention to the ways in which the title "city manager" appears in public inscriptions provides a clue to Paul's usage. It is found in two main contexts: first, in civic decrees, where the *oikonomos* is enjoined by the assembly or council to set up and pay for a statue or a stele for an honoree. In that context the use of the title is administrative, to identify the official charged with a particular task, whether it is a *tamias* (city treasurer), *stratēgos* (governor), *grammateus* (secretary), or *oikonomos tēs poleōs* (city manager). In such cases, *oikonomos tēs poleōs* is often simply abbreviated as *oikonomos*, it being self-evident in a civic inscription that the term refers to the city's *oikonomos* and not some other *oikonomos*.[27] The full title, however, typically appears in funerary monuments and in private dedications, where the use of the title is designed not only to identify the deceased or the dedicator, but also to emphasize his status. For example, a slave's epitaph from Cos reads: "(Tomb) of Philētos, manager of the city of the Coans, who served blamelessly as manager in the 23rd year" (I.CosED EF 6; Cos, imperial period). Another slave made a dedication to Sarapis: "Apollonidēs, the manager of the city, dedicated this offering cup to Sarapis" (SEG 39:1316; Kyme, I/early II CE).

The point is that in spite of the fact that the *oikonomos* might be a public slave, a freedman, or a freeborn citizen, the title *was* a status of pride and it advertised the holder's record of service to the city.[28] Hence, when Paul uses the full title, it is to draw attention to Erastos's status and his service to the city.

Whatever his role in the city of Corinth was, Erastos is not likely to have been a particularly influential member of the Corinthian Christ assembly, however. In the list of those greeting the recipients of the letter in Roman 16, Erastos is not named first, as one would expect were he one of its most influential members; he comes after Paul's immediate co-workers and relatives, Timothy, Lucius, Jason, and Sosipater (16:21); after Tertius, the scribe (16:22); and after Gaius, the guest of the entire *ekklēsia*.[29] Since the order in which names are cited usually indexical to status, it is unlikely that Erastos had the highest status *within* the Christ assembly. He is unlikely to have been a patron like Phoebe. Yet Paul's naming of him along with his title draws attention to a connection between the Corinthian assembly and a figure of at least modest status within the city.

OTHER CHRIST FOLLOWERS OF RANK?

The results of this survey confirm Meeks's intuition that in the first century, there were likely no Christ followers of senatorial or equestrian rank. Only toward the end of the second century is it possible to detect some people of rank, and even then, they were still very few in number. In this context it is worth considering the findings of Ulrich Fellmeth, who surveyed the membership of numerous Italian professional associations and Roman cultic groups. He found that while people at the ranks of senator and equestrian were attested in professional associations, often as patrons, it was very uncommon for cultic groups to include such people. In his investigation of twenty-three hundred names of those who appear in twenty-nine rosters of Italian associations, senators were found in occupational guilds such as the boatmen and registrars (*lenuncularii tabularii auxiliarii*) (see chapter 2), the ship builders (*fabri navales*), or the grain measurers (*mensores frumentarii*), but *none* is attested as either a patron or a member of a cultic group. He reported the same profile for equestrians: in occupational guilds equestrians were found among the members or patrons, but none was attested in a cultic group. It is only when one looks for local magistrates that one can find evidence of their presence in both occupational guilds and cultic groups.[30]

This pattern also accords well with the famous *cultores* of Diana and Antinoüs (CIL 14.2112), a cultic association of slaves and freedmen devoted to Diana and Antinoüs, the emperor Hadrian's deceased lover. The collegium's patron was Lucius Caesennius Rufus, a local magistrate but not of senatorial or even equestrian rank. Likewise, the collegium of Aesculapius and Hygia found patron/members in the wife of Gaius Salvius, who was an assistant to a minor imperial procurator in charge of the imperial picture gallery, and two other imperial freedmen, Marcus Ulpius Capito and Publius Aelius Zenon.[31] None of these belonged to the curial rank, and Publius Aelius Zenon was likely a freedman.

It is unlikely that members of the senatorial and equestrian aristocracies were opposed in principle to associating with cultic groups. It certainly has nothing to do with the "religious" nature of those groups, for there is a strong record of aristocrats building public temples.[32] By the third century CE a handful of aristocrats eventually did come to be associated with Christ groups. What was at stake in their choice to do so?

The exchange of symbolic capital was a critical factor in the practice of patronage. That is, a senator or equestrian gained symbolic capital by being named as the patron of a group; and the more prominent the group and greater its visibility within the city, the greater the symbolic capital. In the case of the large transport and grain-measuring guilds of Ostia, it is clear what such guilds had to offer their patrons, since they were important to the economy of Ostia and to the feeding of Rome. The many small cultic associations of Ostia, devoted to Silvanus, Isis, Sarapis, Mithras, the Magna Mater, and other deities, could not offer as much to the grandees of Roman society.

There are only a few exceptions. A handful of cultic associations did manage to attract people of senatorial rank, all outside of Rome and Ostia and most of them from the second century CE. Some of these associations were composed of well-to-do citizens, and in two instances citizens who were members were also eligible to be elected to civic offices—that is, citizens of relatively high social standing. These exceptions to the pattern described by Fellmeth help us to think further about the dynamics of patronage.

Of the many cultic associations in the Greco-Roman world, Dionysiac groups seem to have attracted the most highly placed patrons. In the second century CE, three had patrons of consular rank: the "Dancing Cowherds" of Pergamon, the Iobakchoi of Athens, and the cult association of Pompeia Agrippinilla.[33] The first two of these had an important factor in common: their membership consisted of freeborn people of relatively high social status. The Dancing Cowherds of Pergamon in the early second century, patronized by C. Antius Aulus Iulius Quadratus, consisted of one woman and sixteen men, either Roman citizens or freeborn Greeks (a first-century inscription, I.Perg. 485, listed twenty-four members). The group was sufficiently well-off to own a very large clubhouse located along a main thoroughfare in the city. Although the association was small, Harland points out that one of the Cowherds was also a member of another association of "hymn-singers" who honored the Emperor Hadrian and that others members had links to other groups.[34] Given the size and location of the Dancing Cowherds' clubhouse, they can hardly be thought to have been a poor or marginal group. Quadratus's patronage of this group afforded him a connection with well-to-do citizens, some associated with the imperial cult; for their part, the Dancing Cowherds gained a connection with an influential civic patron.

The situation is analogous with the Iobakchoi, patronized by Herodes Atticus, one of the wealthiest men of the Antonine period and *consul ordinarius* for 143 CE.[35] Although we lack a membership list for the Iobakchoi, their members were undoubtedly drawn from the privileged ranks of Athenian society. They were citizens who were eligible to be named to civic magistracies, hence people of high social standing. They also owned a building with a hall of eleven by eighteen meters between the Pnyx and the Areio Pagus near the western slope of the Acropolis. This was not a club of poor artisans but of citizens close to the government of Athens—the kinds of people who could give symbolic capital to Herodes Atticus and people who could benefit from patronage by a senator and one of the empire's wealthiest citizens.

The extraordinarily large mid-second-century Dionysiac association patronized by Pompeia Agrippinilla, also of senatorial rank, offers a different situation.[36] This was a group consisting of a few members of Agrippinilla's immediate family and many of her slaves brought from Asia Minor, where she had strong political connections. The association was located on the estate of her husband, M. Gavius Squilla Gallicanus (PIR^2 G114), a few kilometers southeast of Rome and was organized to enact Dionysiac mysteries, assigning roles in the performance to each member. One might surmise that Agrippinilla's engagement with the association was a means to exert social control on her domestics, who, owing to their rural location, could not easily join another association.[37]

But the sheer size of the club—by far the largest cultic association we know—also gave Agrippinilla social capital.

There are a few other instances of cultic associations patronized by those of high rank.[38] A Dionysiac association in Ephesus (I.Eph 1267) was patronized and presided over by C. Flavius Furius Aptus, whose house was modified to accommodate the association.[39] Since no membership list is extant, it is impossible to know the social standing of the members of this association. But it is known that the family of Furius Aptus had gained Roman citizenship, and although he was not of senatorial rank, he was an equestrian, and his son, T. Fl. Lollianus Aristobulus, was admitted to the senatorial order. Even before the elevation of his son as a senator, members of the family had enjoyed prestigious civic positions in Ephesus.[40]

Two Judean assemblies (*synagōgai*) also received the patronage by people of senatorial rank, two women, both of senatorial rank (*clarissimae*). The first assembly, attested in an inscription dated late in the first century CE (IJO II 168), had benefited from the patronage of Julia Severa, priestess of the imperial cult. Her husband, L. Servenius Capito, was not a senator, but her son L. Servenius Cornutus became a senator under Nero. The family was very well-to-do and influential in Phrygia.[41] Since we have no membership list, it is impossible to know the social status of the synagogue members, except that the honorary assembly president, Publius Tyrronios Klados, was evidently a Roman citizen. The second, a mid-third-century Judean assembly in Tralleis (IJO II 27), was patronized by Claudia Capitolina, daughter or sister of the proconsul of Asia and married to a senator and priest of Zeus Larasios.[42] Again, nothing is known of the social (or legal) status of the members of this assembly, and hence it is impossible to surmise the nature of the social exchange that occurred between patron and client.

It might be noticed that I have spoken of senators as patrons rather than as members of associations. This is because it seems extraordinarily unlikely that a senator would deign to be a member of a guild, especially a cultic association, whose members were significantly below his station. A senator such as Herodes Atticus was indeed elected chief priest of the Iobakchoi, but this was likely an honorific role rather than a functional one. Edwin Judge's point about the Eastern Mediterranean is likely applicable more generally:

> In the eastern Mediterranean it was self-evident that members of the Roman aristocracy would not belong to a local cult association. Their needs were very amply gratified by the exclusiveness of the circles to which they were admitted. . . . The only Roman aristocrats likely to be found in the east were the provincial governors themselves and a few members of their

> staffs; distinguished local politicians who had been elevated for their services in order that outstanding talent for leadership should have a vested interest in the Roman loyalty; and millionaires on business from the capital, together with local magnates who attracted official attention by public benefactions. It might occasionally happen that Christians met such persons, but plainly not on their own ground.[43]

The outcome of this survey suggests, perhaps unsurprisingly, that during the first century, Christ assemblies attracted no one of senatorial rank. Patrons of this rank were rare for any cultic association in the first century CE. There is not even good evidence of patrons of equestrian rank, although James in the early second century CE was prepared to imagine the possibility of an equestrian visiting a Christ assembly (Jas 2:1–3).

THE NONELITE IN CHRIST ASSEMBLIES

What about the majority of members of Christ assemblies? The challenge in gauging the relative status of the nonelite is that there are practically no reliable data with which to work. In assessing the relative standing of individuals named in Greek and Latin literature, it is common to rely on onomastic data—the name, which in Greek and Latin often allows us to distinguish between the freeborn and slaves.[44] A name by itself sometimes allows us to conclude that the person is a slave (or freed) or freeborn but usually nothing about his or her social standing or, still less, about income level. Since onomastic data are unhelpful, interpreters often turn to other proxies for wealth and social standing.

Paul's comment in 1 Cor 11:22 is often read selectively to draw the conclusion that most of the Corinthian Christ followers were very poor. There, Paul accuses his addressees, who evidently allocated food at the communal meal differentially, of shaming "those who do not have (food? houses?)" (*tous mē echontas*). Many commentators fix on this clause as proof that a significant part of the Corinthian assembly was extremely poor.[45] Yet Paul's comment must be seen in the context of his rhetorical intervention, which is filled with hyperbole. He begins by stating that when the assembly gathers as a whole (*epi to auto*), there are not only factions but "each person takes preferentially his (her) own meal while eating,[46] (and) that one is hungry and the other drunk" (11:21). These are plainly exaggerations, for it makes no sense literally to suppose that *everyone* took his or her own meal by preference. Moreover, it is unclear whether the clause in 11:21 means that some have *come* hungry or drunk or whether that is the outcome of the dinner. Paul's rhetorical question in the very same verse, "Surely you have houses for eating and drinking, don't you?," suggests the former. When one weeds out the rhetorical excess of Paul's intervention, his real objection is that he did not perceive the Corinthians' meal as a genuinely communal dinner, for he characterizes their banquet as though it were a series of individual dinners (*idia deipna*)—everyone eating separately even if they did so at the same table.[47] There surely were better-off and poorer people in the group, but 1 Cor 11:21–22 hardly justifies the conclusion that some of the Corinthians have fallen *below* the subsistence level.

Another strategy is to focus either on the occupation or on the legal status of the person named. Thus Friesen suggests that Onēsimos, possibly a runaway slave, would have been "near the bottom of the [economic] profile" and that Paul, as a handworker, fluctuated from below subsistence level when working as an artisan to moderately well-off when he stayed as a house guest of people with moderate surpluses.[48] The problematic nature of these assumptions is obvious: it is by no means self-evident that Onēsimos was a runaway. In any event, Paul's declaration that while he was in prison Onēsimos had become "useful" to him—a pun on his name, which means "useful"—can hardly imply that Onēsimos is without resources, since assisting Paul in prison would require some resources.

Likewise, the assumption that handworkers were normally destitute is simply wrong.[49] Numerous inscriptions are extant in which guilds of tent or curtain makers—Paul's occupation[50]—erected funerary monuments for their members, honorific inscriptions for their various benefactors, and, in the case of a guild called "the most sacred guild (*synergasia*) of leather workers" in mid-second-century CE Lycia, an inscription honoring a civic official and Asiarch. They did so at the behest of the city council.[51] Honorific decrees were normally elaborate and therefore costly. The last-mentioned inscription shows that the leather worker guild was not a group of marginalized workers but had connections to civic hierarchies. Of course, one cannot conclude that all handworkers were well-off or that all occupational guilds in Macedonia enjoyed the same level of prosperity and status evidenced by some guilds in Asia Minor and Italy.[52] But by the same token, it is fatuous to suppose that all Thessalonian leather workers were living at or below the subsistence level.

Some use Paul's comments in 2 Corinthians 8–9 to index the economic level of the Christ assemblies in Macedonia. There Paul reports that the Macedonian assemblies had been involved in collecting funds for Jerusalem. Writing to the Corinthians, whose collection efforts had evidently stalled and who seem to have developed some distrust of Paul's motives, Paul boasts that the Macedonians "out of their deep poverty" (*hē bathous ptōcheia autōn*) had nonetheless "overflowed in a wealth of generosity" (8:2). Commentators who emphasize the extreme poverty of the Macedonian assemblies routinely focus on the first part of Paul's sentence and ignore both the second and the rhetoric of Paul's intervention. Plainly, this is an exaggeration of the Macedonians' situation designed to shame the better-off Corinthian assembly into being even more generous.[53] Paul threatens that the Macedonian delegation will arrive with Paul at Corinth bearing their collection and that both Paul and the Corinthians would be shamed if the Macedonians realize that the Corinthians have not produced anything at all, or much less than what might be expected of them (9:4). In another part of the Corinthian correspondence, Paul recalls to the Corinthians that the Macedonians had supported him when he was in need in Corinth (11:9). Hence, despite Paul's exaggerations, the Macedonian Christ assemblies cannot have been destitute or barely eking out a subsistence existence.

A final strategy for estimating social standing and wealth and perhaps the most dubious of all has been to use as proxies references to officeholders, the ownership of slaves, the control of houses, evidence of hospitality or services rendered to Christ assemblies, and the ability to travel.[54] Theissen and Meeks use these proxies, and Friesen and Longenecker employ them to populate a seven-level model of the Roman economy, which Friesen called a Poverty Scale (PS) and Longenecker an Economy Scale (ES).[55] These scales are adaptations of the general model for the Roman economy discussed above (chapter 5, Table 2) but attempt to convert this abstract model into a grid on which to place named people in Pauline letters. There are some differences between Friesen and Longenecker's models, in particular in the size of the population that is supposed to belong to the middling groups, but for our purposes the differences are not especially important.[56] Table 5 summarizes the results of Theissen, Meeks, Friesen, and Longenecker regarding social standing in Pauline Christ groups.

These models have the great virtue of bringing a degree of concreteness to our imagination of Pauline groups despite the tentativeness with which they have been advanced. Yet apart from the inclusion on this list of Gaius, who should be treated as a guest rather than as the host of the Corinthian group, the difficulty with all such proxies for wealth is that they simply do not reliably produce economic conclusions. The ownership of slaves is not an unambiguous sign of wealth because many subelite families of modest means might own a slave or two.[57] The ability to travel, a proxy used by Theissen and Meeks, is not necessarily a mark of wealth or high(er) social standing: the wealthy might travel, but so did merchants and some artisans (such as Paul). Others probably traveled as a result of displacement. And unless we know the size of housing *and* the size of a Christ assembly that used a house, it is impossible to judge

Table 5. Social standing in Pauline Christ groups

Poverty scale (PS)	*Theissen 1979/1982*	*Meeks 1983*	*Friesen 2004*	*Longenecker 2011*
PS1–3: "Upper strata" SF: 2.8% (BL: 3%)	Erastos (*quaestor*) Stephanas, Phoebe?			ES1–3: "Upper strata"
PS4: Moderate surplus (or "people of wealth") SF: 7% (BL: 15%)	Prisca, Aquila, Sosthenes, Crispus, Gaius, Titius Justus and "the great majority of the Corinthians known to us by name"	Gaius, Crispus, Prisca, Aquila, Ampliatus, Andronicus, Junia, Epaenetus, Silvanus, Stephanas	(Chloe), Gaius Erastos? Philemon? Phoebe? Prisca? Aquila?	Gaius, Phoebe, Erastos Crispus? Stephanas? Philemon? (Chloe?)
PS5: Stable near subsistence SF: 22% (BL: 27%)			Erastos? Philemon? Phoebe? Prisca? Aquila? Stephanas? Chloe's people? Many Corinthians?	Crispus? Stephanas? Philemon? (Chloe?) Prisca? Aquila? Some Christ groups
PS6: Subsistence SF: 40% (BL: 30%)	Achaicus, Fortunatus, Tertius, Chloe's people		Stephanas? Chloe's people? Many Corinthians? Macedonians Paul (sometimes) Onesimos? "Those who have nothing" at Corinth?	Prisca? Aquila? Some Christ groups
PS7: Below subsistence: SF: 28% (BL: 25%)			Onesimos? "Those who have nothing" at Corinth? Paul (sometimes)	

Note: The percentages in column 1 are those of Friesen (SF), with those of Longenecker (BL) in parentheses. This I have guessed from the general descriptions of Meeks and Theissen as to how to place people, and I have collapsed Friesen and Longenecker's equivocal categories (PS 4/5, PS 5/6, and PS 6/7) into single categories and placed questionable individuals in two categories when they might be found in either.

the economic level of the owner. We would also have to know whether the host was an owner or a tenant. A house or apartment (or *taberna*) that could accommodate a group of ten to thirty people is very different from one that could accommodate sixty to one hundred.[58]

Even though Longenecker is more generous in estimating the size of the "middling" category (15 percent)—people with moderate surpluses, including merchants, traders, some freedmen and freedwomen, and artisans—he generally follows Friesen in estimating the majority of Pauline Christ followers at the subsistence and near-subsistence levels. He added Phoebe and Erastos to Gaius in the "moderate surplus" category but demotes Prisca and Aquila to "near or at subsistence," leaving only Stephanas, Philemon, and Crispus straddling the moderate surplus/near subsistence categories (see Table 5).[59] The insistence of the extremely low economic level of the majority of Christ followers is striking, especially given the fact that Scheidel and Friesen, Friesen, and Longenecker all appeal to models that imply broadly stratified economies. They nevertheless seem committed to locating Christ assemblies at the bottom of those strata, relying on Paul's rhetorical flourishes and on highly ambiguous markers of wealth.

Longenecker is also keen to distinguish Christ assemblies from the many associations that are found in the ancient Mediterranean.[60] He does so by citing two studies of Roman associations in Italy and Roman professional associations in the East: "there is a difference between the economic profile of *collegia* in general and urban Jesus-groups. While there were *collegia* whose membership included 'poorer' sectors of society (i.e., funerary associations of the second century CE and beyond), *collegia* members generally were drawn from the upper echelons of the urban *plebs* and can best be characterized as 'employers' rather than 'employees.'"[61]

It is a mistake, however, to assume any uniformity in Greek and Roman associations and especially to conflate cultic associations with the occupational guilds connected to critical economic activities such as the grain supply.[62] Generalizations of this sort are either false or unfounded, since there is both wide variation among associations and because in most cases we have no reliable way to determine the economic level of individual members in any of them.[63] To take only two of the associations discussed in chapter 2: In guilds like the boatmen and registrars of Ostia, which collectively were undoubtedly wealthy, it is unlikely that all members were wealthy or that all were at the same economic level. To judge from the poor quality of their membership *album*, the devotees of Theos Hypsistos, mainly composed of artisans, were not especially well-off collectively. But that hardly means that they all shared the same social standing or income level. Longenecker sagely observes that Pauline rhetoric in 2 Corinthians 8–9 depicts the Macedonians as uniformly poor and the Corinthians as being better off; but he recognizes that this masks the income disparities of both groups, shifting the likely standing of the Corinthians upward and the Macedonians downward.[64] Accordingly, it is important not to take Paul's rhetorical construction of the groups at face value, as it is Paul's construction of the situation to serve his own aims. The same, incidentally, is the case with 1 Corinthians 11, where Paul appears to parse the group into the privileged and the very poor—also a rhetorical construction rather than an economic description.

The effort to assign named people in Pauline groups to specific economic registers, however appealing this might be, founders on the nature of the data. It is only within the *ordo*—senators, equestrians, and decurions—that we can guess economic standing, because of the census requirements that were attached to those ranks. With all others it is impossible to know much about economic standing without pertinent data. Unfortunately, no such data exist for Pauline Christ followers.

SOCIAL STANDING AND CONNECTIVITY

The insistence on the depressed social and economic levels of the earliest Christ assemblies elicited the following comment from Edwin Judge long ago:

> Modern Christians, uneasy about the respectability of a faith that is supposed to have revolutionary implications, like to cultivate the idea that it first flourished among the depressed sections of society. Others again have an ideological interest in identifying its impetus as that of social discontent. Given a belief in class struggle, it is easy to take a group of Galilean peasants, add the community of goods, Paul's "working with his hands," and the "not many wise . . . not many mighty, not many noble" at Corinth, and thus discover a movement of protest among the working classes; or alternatively an internal proletariat breaking down the old civilization in favour of the emergent new one, given that one has been initiated into the rhythms of civilisations.[65]

Judge's comment underscores the fact that a common belief about the social level of Christ followers is less a function of reliable data, still less of the use of *comparanda*, than of theological assumptions. But is it possible to do better?

If we focus only on the question of the economic level of early Christ assemblies, probably not. The absence of usable onomastic information on the members of Christ assemblies makes impossible the kind of assessment that is possible in the case of Roman senators and equestrians. The proxies for wealth and social standing that have been invoked cannot in most instances bear the weight that is expected of them. However, there is another way to think about the complexion of Christ assemblies.

It is more productive to inquire into the social standing of collectives, in this case associations. The foregoing discussion has suggested that while individual members of associations might be better or worse off in relation to income, as collectivities some associations could wield considerable symbolic capital and confer this upon members. Several factors contribute to the social standing of a group, one of them we might imagine as "vertical," that is, connections to people of higher status, and two as "horizontal," connecting guild members to people and associations of comparable status.

Vertical connectivity: The quality and nature of a group's external connections undoubtedly contributed to the social standing of its members. The boatmen and registrars of Ostia enjoyed the patronage of the cream of Roman society. This did not necessarily translate into the economic advancement of individual members even if the occasional member might advance in rank and standing. Patronage of the collegium by senators, however, lent prestige and influence to the group as a whole. Lower down the status ladder, patronage of the *cultores* of Diana and Antinoüs by a local magistrate (CIL 14.2112) or the connection of the builder-carpenters of Luna (CIL 11.1355ab) with local magistrates undoubtedly gave prestige to these groups in their local contexts.

Horizontal connectivity with other groups likely also conferred status. The most prominent of the interconnected guilds were the "artists associated with Dionysos" and the "the *synodos* of traveling athletes associated with Herakles."[66] Both were networks of local associations whose members could move from one city to another, carrying diplomas that allowed them free movement. These guilds, already the recipients of the patronage of various Hellenistic monarchs, could also claim imperial patronage from the time of Claudius onward and could refer to themselves with such grandiose titles as, for example, "the world-wide association of wreath-crowned victorious artists associated with Dionysos and the Emperor Caesar Titus Aelius Hadrianus Antoninus Caesar Pius" (i.e., Antoninus Pius) or the "the sacred athletic *synodos* of traveling athletes associated with Herakles of (Emperor) Hadrianus Antoninus Septimius" (i.e., Septimius Severus).[67] Other forms of external linkages among guilds existed. The boatmen and registrars were laterally connected via patronage to several other guilds involved in the feeding of Rome and to similar guilds in the Rhône Valley. The builder-carpenters of Luna not only had connections with members of the local gentry through their patrons, but also with the *dendrophors* via the family connections of one of their *immunes* and probably a former leader. An epitaph from early-second-century Rome records that a certain L. Calpurnius Chius, a wealthy freedman, had been president of the grain measurers guild and of the collegium of Silvanus Augustus Major (which supervised weights and measures) in Ostia and curator of the barge operators' guild; but he was also a member of the association of *dendrophors* associated with the cult of Silvanus and Cybele (CIL 14.309). And the devotees of Atargatis of Athens were connected with an evidently important group of immigrants to Athens from Antioch but also had lateral connections with the Atargatis temple on Delos via the family connections of one of its citizen-members. Multiplex connectivity did not necessarily translate into a higher economic standing for any particular member, but belonging to one of these interlocked networks—the more connected the better—almost certainly conferred a higher social standing on every member.

For the first century CE it seems unlikely that Christ assemblies could have benefited from the kinds of patronage evidenced by the artists associated with Dionysos, the athletes, or the boatmen and registrars. The only person of any status named in Pauline letters is Erastos of Corinth, and he appears so far down the list in Romans 16 that he is not likely to be a principal benefactor or a benefactor at all. Phoebe, named as a patron, is not clearly a woman with senatorial or equestrian connections, or even one of the local gentry. It would not be until the Severan period that Christ assemblies would attract patrons of senatorial rank, and even then, probably not patrons of consular rank. Christ assemblies, however, seemed to have established interlinked networks, hardly on the scale of the Dionysiac artists, but connecting a few nodes together through exchange of traveling figures such as Paul or Prisca and Aquila and by the exchange of letters. By the time Paul wrote Romans, his network consisted perhaps only of Corinth, Cenchreae, a few Macedonian sites, probably Ephesus, and, he hoped, Rome, the Galatian assemblies already having defected.[68] In the early second century the letters of Ignatius of Antioch attest a network that connected a few Christ assemblies in Asia and Rome, and a little later in that century a network of assemblies at Sparta, Athens, Nicomedia, Gortyna, Amastris, Knossos, and Rome is evidenced in the correspondence of Dionysios of Corinth.[69]

Internal connectivity: Internal relationships represent another form of horizontal connectivity that confers status. Social capital was not only generated in the exchange between external patrons and members, but also among members themselves. In order to grasp the mechanisms by which social capital or esteem was created, it is useful to look at a model from behavioral economics.

Geoffrey Brennan and Philip Pettit's influential book *The Economy of Esteem* argues that the quest for esteem is a significant factor in social organization and even in economic production. Because humans are evaluative beings and thus constantly evaluate each other, esteem—or as ancient Mediterraneans would call it, honor—is a "commodity" that is sought, given, withdrawn, and withheld.[70] According to Brennan and Pettit esteem or honor is allocated in society on the basis of systematic determinants that include performances of status and how those performances are made known to others. Although esteem or honor cannot be bought or exchanged like another commodity, Brennan and Pettit describe the possibility of "esteem services": providing another with the opportunity to increase esteem by creating a social space in which one can "shine" and accomplishments or "performances" can be recognized by others.[71] In musical circles this is known as "giving a musician a break," that is, providing an opportunity to perform and to have her or his excellence be recognized by others; in academic circles, it is creating the opportunity for a brilliant student to offer a paper at a major scholarly conference. And so on.

Brennan and Pettit treat modern "voluntary associations" (as they call them) as social spaces that offer "esteem services."[72] While in the general population the abilities and achievements of an individual might well go unnoticed, small face-to-face associations offer attention and testimony to individual members' merits and performances. Because associations are inherently competitive, they create a space in which achievement is prioritized and individual members can excel at the relevant activities. Not only does membership allow an individual to shine, but the recruiting of an accomplished new member can have a multiplier effect on the association. When a stellar tennis player joins a club, not only does she or he gain esteem, but the average performance of all members will also increase—the effect of reputational pooling. Conversely, because voluntary associations are organized around particular activities, they are also characterized by a high degree of what Brennan and Pettit call "behavioral loyalty." This means that "free riders"—those who fail to promote group activities or who attract the disesteem of fellow members—represent a threat to the group and may be expelled.

Although Brennan and Pettit focus on contemporary associations, their model of "esteem services" is useful for thinking about ancient associations. The associations that were patronized by the cream of ancient society conveyed the greatest sense of honor to their members (through the vertical axis of status acquisition). But all associations adopted strategies that lifted members out of the anonymity of imperial society in general, making them visible to each other and creating a social space in which honor and social capital could be achieved. They did this in various ways.

First, many associations employed familial language to describe internal relationships even though members were not necessarily related by birth or by adoption. This is most obvious in the case of the *familia Silvani* (chapter 2), which fictively constructed the group as the god's family. Even with occupational guilds, the construction of a fictive family was possible, as is the case with the builder-carpenters of Luna (chapter 2), which designated certain members as *pater collegii* and *mater collegii*. While patrons were often external to the group, the evidence suggests that "fathers" and "mothers" took part in the day-to-day life of the group.[73] As Riet van Bremen and Philip Harland have shown, fictive parental language is well attested not only in the West, but also in the Greek East, both in civic titles and in associations, designating citizens (for cities) and members (for associations) who have distinguished themselves in some way and thus gained the title *patēr* (father) or *matēr* (mother).[74]

Harland, moreover, has collected numerous instances of associations, mainly in the Greek East, that used the term *adelphoi* (brothers) to refer to fellow members.[75] Such fictive family language is found in both occupational guilds and cultic associations. The funerary regulations of a first-century association of stonemasons near Lamos in Rough Cilicia, near Paul's hometown of Tarsus, refer to members as "brothers."[76] The term *adelphos* seems to have been especially common in connection with associations devoted to Theos Hypsistos in Macedonia, Pontus, and the Bosphorus region. Two "brothers" set up a dedication to Theos Hypsistos in Pontus in Asia Minor in the first or second century CE,[77] and in the early third century a series of inscriptions from the Bosphorus region from associations devoted to Theos Hypsistos name members as "adopted brothers."[78] The sense of the latter usage seems to be that the god has adopted members as his children, thus constituting members as siblings.

The analogy with the language of Christ assemblies is obvious: Paul's letters, James, *1 Clement*, and *2 Clement* show that the members are routinely addressed with the vocative *adelphoi*,[79] and Paul even refers to himself as a "father" of the Thessalonian and Corinthian assemblies (1 Thess 2:11, 1 Cor 4:15). Both are clearly used to imply a quasi-familial relationship among Christ followers. Scholars in the past who have noted the heavy usage of fictive family language in Christ assemblies have sometimes considered it as a feature that distinguished Christ assemblies from most other groups[80] or have argued that such language derived not from associations, where its use was restricted to Roman influence, but rather from Hellenistic synagogues.[81] Harland has in fact shown that family language was much more common in the East than is usually thought, but he is careful not to frame the issue of fictive family language in Paul as a matter of "borrowing" or "influence," especially since "influence" or "noninfluence" is so difficult to prove.[82] My point here is only to underscore that Christ assemblies and many Greek associations employed similar strategies for building esteem and social capital: individuals gained a(nother) family through membership in an association.

Second, associations created social spaces in which the achievements of other members could be recognized. The Iobakchoi of Athens mandated that members who had received various civic honors, had married, or had children born to them should offer a libation to the other members.[83] A guild of sheep and cattle owners in first-century Tebtynis similarly decreed that members who married, to whom children had been born, or who had purchased land or livestock should contribute (extra) funds to the guild for the monthly banquet.[84] While it might appear to the modern reader that the member was being taxed for achievement, the logic is in fact quite different. In the ancient Mediterranean, honor and reputation were the most valuable commodities; money was an instrument used to achieve honor. By providing funds or offering libations, members became visible to their fellows, advertising their achievements to them. And on the logic that a rising tide floats all boats, the increased honor of one member had a positive effect upon the honor of all members.

Third, many associations, adopting the practice of "flat" or rotating hierarchies, afforded members—all members, at least in theory—the opportunity to assume leadership, usually for one year.[85] This was perhaps a mimicry of the political structure of Athens, whose eponymous *archon* served only a single year, allowing all (male) citizens the potential to assume the presidency of the assembly once. Associations routinely honored their leaders, sometimes by setting up honorific inscriptions, by simply recognizing the leader's status by banquet seating, by according the leader double portions of food and drink, or by some other honorific practice. The practice of "flat hierarchy" meant that while hierarchy was still a structuring feature of the group, the rotation of leaders meant that honors in the long run were distributed throughout the group.

Fourth, recognition of the achievement of members is also seen in the very common practice of honoring them, usually outgoing officers, for their service. For example, an association of *Soteriastai* in Athens honored their founder Diodoros son of Sokrates for serving as president (*archeranistēs*), then treasurer during four different years and then priest for one year. Part of the degree reads:

> For good fortune, it was resolved by the *koinon* of the *Soteriastai*, whose *archeranistēs* is Diodoros son of Sokrates of (the deme) Aphidna, ‹to commend Diodoros son of Sokrates of Aphidna› and to crown him with an olive wreath on account of the zeal that he has continually shown for the *synodos*. He is to be crowned yearly by whoever happens to be the treasurer in the same way as the priests and the president (*archeranistēs*). There shall be a proclamation, that "the *koinon* of the *Soteriastai* crowns Diodoros in accordance with this decision (*dogma*)." (IG II^2 1343.32–39 = GRA I 48; 37/36 or 36/35 BCE)

As this inscription makes clear, it was expected that the treasurer changed frequently—hence the clause, "whoever happens to be the treasurer"—and that it was customary to "crown" the yearly priests and the president. Thus "esteem services" were offered routinely to those who acted in accordance with the group's rules, and they could bask in the honors during the year they served.

Two other features of associations underscore the fact that belonging and the esteem that it conferred figured importantly into the calculus about one's social standing. Onno van Nijf has pointed out that although associations commonly provided burial for members, not everyone joined an association because they could not otherwise afford a funeral. Other options for burial existed, and indeed cheaper ones, especially outside of Rome. This means that burial by an association was a *choice* and not always a necessity.[86] Burial by one's association conferred prestige and status that individual burial did not. Second, the practice of erasing names of former members from the rosters of associations suggests that being *named* on an association's roster conveyed social capital and that, contrariwise, the erasing of a name was the association's way of erasing that social capital.

Does this allow us to see the practices of Christ assemblies as "esteem services"? It seems clear that mutual recognition was alive and well in the Thessalonian assembly: "Now concerning fraternal affection (*philadelphia*), you do not need to have anyone write to you, for you yourselves are 'God-taught' to love one another" (1 Thess 4:9). Paul here mobilizes the notion of *philadelphia*, proverbially the strongest and most enduring form of affection among people, and congratulates the Thessalonian assembly for evincing this virtue.[87] At the end of 1 Thessalonians he returns to the topic of mutual encouragement and recognition (5:11), enjoining group recognition of those who served as leaders (5:12).

Christ assemblies also created a social space in which members' needs and achievements could be recognized. James 5:13–15 encourages members to call on the assembly for support in times of distress and to advertise felicitous occasions by contributing songs. In 1 Cor 14:26 Paul recommends that in communal gatherings each member should contribute a hymn or teaching or revelation. This is not simply a matter of everyone "pitching in," but instead a matter of each member contributing and being recognized for that contribution. Paul's advice in Phil 4:8 is replete with vocabulary that is conventional in associative practices of the communal commendation of excellence: "Finally, brothers (*adelphoi*), whatever things are true, whatever are honorable, whatever are just, whatever are pure, whatever is pleasing, whatever is commendable (*euphēma*), if there is any excellence (*aretē*) and if there is anything worthy of praise (*epainos*), consider these things."

In Rom 12:10 Paul advises that the addressees "take the lead" (*proēgoumenoi*) in honoring one another, and in 1 Cor 12:26 he reminds the readers that when one member is honored, "all rejoice together with him/her." Christ assemblies, no less than other associations, were sites where communal values and achievements could be recognized and commended and social capital generated for their members. As Harrison points out, Paul even urges that Christ assemblies honor those who are *lesser (hysteroumenoi)* in the group to prevent divisions in a unified "body of Christ" (1 Cor 12:23–25).[88] This advice would seem to be a strategy not unlike the practice of associations that engaged in rotating hierarchies.

It is often pointed out that Christ assemblies did not erect honorific plaques for their members, and this sometimes leads to the inference that they, different from occupational guilds and cultic associations, refused honors to their members.[89] This conclusion, of course, does not accord with the various Pauline and Jacobean texts just cited, which suggest that excellence and achievement were recognized and celebrated. Moreover, the presence or absence of honorific inscriptions is a function of the "epigraphic habit,"[90] which varied widely from locale to locale and from one period to another. Athens from the fourth to the second century BCE produced hundreds of inscriptions, and Rome had the greatest density of honorific inscriptions during the Antonine and Severan periods. Other areas and other times produced fewer monuments. Some honorific decrees might have been recorded only on nondurable media such as papyrus, as they were in Egypt.[91] This means of course that any honorific decree recorded on papyrus or wood outside of Egypt has not survived. But the most important element in the recognition of excellence was the commendation of members during the assembly itself, and not the cutting of an inscription. This required no large outlay of cash, but it also left behind no durable record.

In sum, both associations and Christ assemblies were sites for the generation of social capital and its conferral on members. They did this by a combination of strategies: some groups attracted and co-opted patrons of high rank in order to boost the profile of the entire group; others formed lateral connections with comparable guilds and associations. Internally, a variety of practices were designed to confer status on individual members, by recognizing and rewarding the performance of the ethical codes that lay at the heart of each association. As individuals, many, perhaps most, members of occupational guilds and cultic associations could not claim an especially high social standing. But as members of a collectivity that traded in social capital and offered esteem services, such people, by virtue of their connections through the group, could achieve a higher social standing, at least within the confines of the group. In a few instances, they may have been able to mobilize their standing and gain a higher social position within the ancient city.

7

MEALS

Communal meals were among the most consistent practices of associations and guilds in the ancient Mediterranean. Of course, they required financing. As with many other topics treated in this book, we are poorly informed about the meal practices of Christ assemblies, at least in the first century of their existence.

The dearth of direct information about the meals of Christ assemblies has created much room for speculation. Some have supposed that Christ groups offered their meals gratis and that this gave them a competitive advantage in the recruitment of members over groups that charged membership dues.[1] This advantage would be even greater if free meals were provided not only monthly but weekly, or so the theory goes. Yet someone had to provide food and finance the meal. As it turns out, 1 Cor 11:17–34 is almost always the focus of efforts to think about who provided the meals of Christ assemblies. Commentators are nearly unanimous in espousing one of two models: either a few wealthy patron-members of the Christ group provided the meal;[2] or all of the members were expected to contribute food, with the wealthy providing more and better food than the poor, who might bring little or nothing at all.[3] I refer to the first model as the "elite patronage" and the second as an "eranistic" model. These will be juxtaposed with two other models we know from Greco-Roman associations: "peer benefaction"—the support of the communal meal by members based on a rotating roster—and member contributions.

ELITE PATRONAGE

For Theissen the Christ assembly at Corinth had adopted a patronage model, and this, combined with the internal social and economic stratification of the group, was at the root of the conflict to which Paul adverts in 1 Cor 11:17–34. Theissen begins with Paul's assertion "for when eating each one takes a meal of his own (*to idion deipnon*) and one is hungry and another is drunk" (11:21). This, he argues, indicates that the Corinthian practice was for the wealthier members to supply food for all: "If some Christians have no *idion deipnon*, that suggests that not all contributed to the Lord's Supper but that the wealthier Christians provided for all *ek tōn idiōn* [at their own expense]."[4]

The problem at Corinth in Theissen's view was twofold. First, the wealthier members who supplied the food ate it as a private meal (*idion deipnon*) rather than as part of a communal meal; and they began eating early, before the communal meal, apparently consuming much or all of what they had brought.[5] This model assumes that association meals followed the practice—or at least the caricature—of elite Roman dining where the host allocated food differentially, providing better or more food to guests of higher status and poorer food to guests of lower status.[6] Theissen even suggests that the wealthy justified this practice by appealing to the tradition of the Lord's Supper, arguing that this tradition applied only to bread and wine and not to any other foodstuffs that were consumed.[7]

This raised a second problem: the wealthier members were behaving not (in my terms) as peer benefactors but as patrons, using the meal to display their status. Theissen appeals to the bylaws of the *cultores* of Diana and Antinoüs (CIL 14.2112) in support of the practice of allotting portions of the meal differentially to officers of the group and to the ordinary members. Taking this to be a norm for all associations, he concludes that the wealthy "not only ate by themselves and began before the regular Lord's Supper but also had more to eat."[8] Hence in Theissen's view, Paul's intervention addressed the two aspects of dining that he found problematic. On one hand, Paul was critical of the individualistic aspects of Corinthian dining that he caricatured as having a "private meal" (*to idion deipnon*) and instead stressed the communal nature of the "emperor's banquet" (*to kyriakon deipnon*), as he calls it.[9] On the other, Paul was critical of the wealthy assuming the role of patrons, allocating varying qualities and quantities of food to Christ believers and thereby underscoring the social differences between rich and poor; that is, a model of "peer benefaction," where wealthier members should have shared food with poorer members, had slid into a model of patronage and its attendant demeaning consequences.

Theissen's argument that Paul wishes to elevate communal interests over individual interests is, I think, consistent with the drift of Paul's general approach throughout 1 Corinthians where he stresses corporate values and the metaphor of the "body of Christ" over the individual, edification over self-assertion, and deference to the sensibilities of others over the exercise of one's freedom. More problematic is Theissen's misunderstanding of the Lanuvium inscription and as a result the confusion of two distinct forms of banqueting—the banquets offered by the elite as performances of their social status on one hand, and the meals of associations on the other, which were in fact performances of equality. Association meals inevitably had hierarchical dimensions, because organized groups must have leaders and because seating arrangements necessarily imply a hierarchy. But these meals were not in general the kinds of meals about which Martial, Pliny, and Juvenal complained, where food was allocated differentially such that some dined on luxuries and drank the best wine while others ate much poorer quality food.[10]

The patron of the *cultores* was Caesennius Rufus, the sole magistrate of the municipality of Lanuvium and the patron of that town. Three years after the *cultores* had been founded (by whom we do not know) Caesennius promised to give the group the interest on 15,000 sesterces, which amounted to 800 sesterces, or 5.3 percent. The *cultores* reciprocated by undertaking to hold events that honored the birthdays of Caesennius and several members of his family. There is nothing in CIL 14.2112, however, to suggest that Caesennius was ever present at any of the meals or that he supplied or allocated any of the food. On the contrary, the interest was distributed to the members in two allotments of 400 sesterces as "presents," called *sportulae*, on August 13, the birthday of the goddess Diana, and on November 27, the birthday of Antinoüs. The sum each member received was likely about 8 sesterces (i.e., 2 denarii), twice yearly.[11] It was not Caesennius who provided the food for the group's six banquets but four of the association's magistrates (*magistri*) appointed annually for this purpose:

> (48) Masters (*magistri*) of the dinners made in the order of the membership list (*album*) [. ? .], four at a time will be required to supply an *amphora* of good wine each, and bread to the value of 2 asses for however many members the collegium has, four sardines, (50) the preparation of the couches, and hot water together with the service. Likewise, it was agreed that any member who had been made president (*quinquennalis*) in this collegium, he shall have to be exempt from contributions for the time when he is *quinquennalis* and that to him a double share from all the distributions be given. Likewise, it was agreed that to the secretary (*scriba*) and the messenger (*viator*), who are to be exempt from contributions, a share and a half in every distribution be given. (55) Likewise, it was agreed that whoever has performed the function of *quinquennalis* honestly, to him because of this honor a share and a half of everything be given, so that the rest will hope for the same through rightful conduct. (CIL 14.2112.48–56)[12]

It is conceivable that Caesennius was present in November and August when his *sportulae* were distributed or on one of the birthdays that the association celebrated. Yet it is curious that the bylaws make no provision for him being given a double portion of the food and drink, something that would be expected were he to attend. This suggests that he was not anticipated to be present at any of the six banquets. There is even less reason to suppose that he attended any of the business meetings (*conventus*) that were held separately.

Since the bylaws indicate the menu of each of the banquets, it is possible to calculate the cost of each banquet and the contribution of each of the four banquet *magistri*. Even using relatively high estimates of the cost of wine, the cost comes out to about 21 denarii per meal for each *magister*,[13] not an insignificant amount and an indication of the economic standing of each member. In the following year, four would retire as *magistri* and four others would replace them. As far as the bylaws are concerned, then, the banquet was not the responsibility of the patron; members were responsible—hence a model of peer benefaction. In fact, the patron's financial inputs (800 sesterces/200 denarii yearly) were less than the aggregate inputs of the yearly *magistri* (about 500 denarii), or 126 denarii for each *magister*.

Despite uncertainties in relation to banquet costs, the meal practice of the *cultores* does not support Theissen's views that the patron either supplied the food or arrogated to himself a larger or better portion of the food and drink. On the contrary, the bylaws instrumentalized a notion of member equality by regulating the meal and its menu and by implementing a practice of having members take turns at providing the meal in accordance with a rota.

The bylaws of the Roman collegium of Aesculapius and Hygia (CIL 6.10234), probably a guild of stonemasons, offer a somewhat more complicated but illuminating example of the financing of communal dining.[14] Salvia Marcellina established the collegium, allowing it the use of a chapel on the Via Appia just outside the city that could serve as their clubhouse (*schola*). She provided an endowment for the group but limited the maximum size of the group to sixty members. The inscription records two endowments, hers and that of another freedman, Publius Aelius Zenon, totaling 60,000 sesterces, the interest on which (750 denarii = 3,000 sesterces) was to fund six events. At one event only *sportulae* were distributed, but there were also to be five banquets at which *sportulae*, bread, and wine were on offer. A seventh banquet was separately funded by the president but on the same terms as the five dinners provided for by the endowment.

The bylaws assume that the two patrons, designated "mother" and "father" of the collegium, would be present at each of the meetings and banquets, although Salvia evidently did not take part in the drinking. At the first yearly meeting celebrating the birthday of the emperor, the collegium distributed *sportulae* to all members (including the patrons) in amounts ranging from 1 denarius (4 sesterces) for each of the *plebs* to 3 denarii (12 sesterces) for the patrons and other distinguished members. At the five banquets *sportulae*, bread, and wine were offered. The *plebs* received bread instead of money, but all who were present received wine in varying amounts, from 9 sextarii (4.86 liters!) for the most distinguished members to 3 (1.62 liters) for the *plebs*. The bylaws stipulate in detail how much is to be given to each member on each occasion in the following form (I list only the first meeting of September 19 and the first banquet of November 4, the anniversary of the founding of the association, since all the other banquets are identical):

> On the 13th of the Kalends of October (September 19) (which is) the birthday of our emperor Antoninus Pius, father of the country, they shall distribute the *sportulae* (10) in the Temple of the Deified (Caesars) in the shrine of the Deified Titus. Gaius Ofilius Hermes, *quinquennalis* for life or whoever (the *quinquennalis*) might be at that time shall receive 3 denarii; Aelius Zenon father of the association (*pater collegi*), 3 denarii; Salvia Marcellina mother of the association (*mater collegi*), 3 denarii; dues-exempt members (*immunes*), (11) 2 denarii each; the supervisors (*curatores*), 2 denarii each; members, 1 denarius each.
>
> It was also agreed (that) on the 4th of November, the anniversary of the association, they shall distribute from the above-mentioned interest in our clubhouse near the (temple of) Mars: to the president, 6 denarii; to the father of the association, 6 denarii; (12) to the mother of the association, 6 denarii; to dues-exempt members, 4 denarii each; to the supervisors, 4 denarii and ‹to all members› bread (worth) 3 asses each. Measures of wine: for the president, 9 sextarii; for the father of the college, 9 sextarii; for dues-exempt members, 6 sextarii each; for the supervisors, 6 sextarii each; for individual members, 3 sextarii each. (CIL 6.10234.9–12).

The economics of the bylaws are worth exploring. The endowment of 60,000 sesterces would generate 750 denarii yearly at a typical 5 percent rate of return. The first meeting at which only *sportulae* were distributed represented a cost of 72 denarii, but each of the five banquets would have cost more: 42 denarii for *sportulae*, because the *plebs* received bread instead of money; 7.5 denarii of bread; and 86 denarii of wine (approximately 6 *amphorae* for each banquet).[15] Thus the cost of each banquet including *sportulae* would be 135.5 denarii, and the total cost of the six events would be 750 denarii (i.e., 5 × 135.5 + 42), exactly the size of the income from the interest.[16]

Three important observations deserve to be underscored. First, this is a rare instance in which the endowment, unusually large in this case, appears to have been able to underwrite the costs of six of the association's events.[17] As will become clear, in most other cases endowments were much smaller, as indeed was the case with the *cultores* of Diana and Antinoüs. This meant that for most association meals, other sources of income had to be sought. Second, CIL 6.10234 is an example in which endowment income not only supplied *sportulae,* but also paid for six of the banquets. The seventh banquet, it should be remembered, was due to the individual generosity of the current president, who agreed to host a banquet once yearly—hence, a matter of peer benefaction. Third and rather unusually, the two patrons were imagined to be present regularly at meetings. Yet the value of the *sportulae* and the quantities of food and drink were not at the whim of the patrons (or anyone else) but were regulated strictly by the bylaws. The two patrons themselves would of course receive larger distributions of *sportulae* and food, as would the president and the *curatores.* But since the leaders of this group rotated, the result was that many members could look forward to receiving more during the period that they served as *quinquennalis* or *curator.* Both CIL 14.2112 and CIL 6.10234 offer examples of "flat" or rotating hierarchies, which seem to have been designed both to meet the practical needs of governance but also as strategies to underscore the fundamental equality of all members.

The meals of most associations were not especially sumptuous, contrary to the polemical interventions of Varro, Philo, or Tertullian.[18] On the contrary, the food for each of the *cultores* consisted of bread worth 2 asses, four sardines, and wine. The members of the collegium of Aesculapius and Hygia received only bread and wine. While for a few association banquets meat was on offer, a survey of the menu available at other association meals indicates that bread and wine (*pane et vino*) and sometimes oil (*oleo*) were the normal fare. Meat was the exception rather than the rule.[19]

The simplicity of the fare suggests that something important was at stake. If sumptuous dining or even better-than-normal dining was not what association meals offered, what did they offer? Dining venues, especially those typically used by associations, were easily within public view.[20] They were held in dining rooms attached to temples, in rented *hestiatoria* (dining rooms), in *triclinia* located near main thoroughfares, on funerary couches in cemeteries along main roads, and in *tabernae* and *horrea* near the street. Their function thus was demonstrative or *performative:* the point was to dine together and to be *seen* to be dining together.[21] This is also the reason that the Egyptian guild of sheep and cattle owners and the association of *apolysimoi* (those exempt from forced public service) imposed higher fines on those who failed to attend a meeting in the city (Arsinoë-Krokodilopolis) than on those who failed to attend a meeting in the village of Tebtynis.[22] More was at stake in being seen as a group in the city: empty places at the banquet would have been taken as visual evidence of the inability of the group to muster sufficient social capital to retain its members, and hence a great shame.

The function of various types of meals is clarified by a typology proposed by Claude Grignon for early modern French society. The meals of Roman elites are in Grignon's terms instances of "institutional commensality," which serve to maintain and extend networks of allies and protégés, to "keep up one's position," and to reinforce hierarchical relationships.[23] Dining with the elite male's peers and with his clients served to cement his position in institutional hierarchies. The meals of associations, by contrast, were instances of "segregative commensality," which displayed the group to itself *as a group* and thus reinforced a sense of belonging and achievement. The semipublic nature of dining also meant that the association meal displayed the group to others and advertised its "groupness." Because collegia belonged in a culture in which achievement through public service was a badge of honor that deserved recognition, in John Donahue's assessment, they "provided a setting not only for social interaction but also for creating hierarchies that could not be found outside of the collegium. Only in this context, for example, could a common cult worshiper become a leader and confirm his status through his access to the largest amount of food and drink."[24]

Thus, both the meals of patrons for their peers and clients and the semipublic banquets of associations performed social identities. But they functioned differently: one to maintain strategic networks and to exhibit the host's superior status, and the other—the collegial banquet—to create a group identity for people who were normally excluded from civic hierarchies and to mimic the hierarchical and honorific practices in those cities.[25] While both the *cultores* of Diana and Antinoüs and the collegium of Aesculapius and Hygia benefited from patronage, the role of patrons—even if they were present—was submerged by the rules governing the meal. Undoubtedly members expressed gratitude to patrons for their generosity, but nothing suggests that patrons could act in the way that Theissen imagines. On the contrary, the rules of the meal had the effect of reinforcing the *equality* of diners even if they also recognized the service that the group's leaders—the *quinquennales*, secretaries (*scribae*), and other officials—played in the life of the group.

With a relatively large endowment, enough to pay for *sportulae* and five of the six dinners, the collegium of Aesculapius and Hygia was unusual. More commonly patronage took a much more modest form, either underwriting the cost of a single meal (or less often several meals) for one year or paying for one yearly meal. Inscriptions from Greece and the Aegean islands likewise attest the generosity of patrons who supplied one or two banquets, but there is little or no evidence of a continuing obligation to fund the banquets or sacrifices. For the Latin West John Donahue has collected other examples of one-time banquets offered by patrons.[26] It is obvious that in such instances the other meals of these groups had to have alternate funding mechanisms.

Many inscriptions attest continuing, usually annual, banquets, most often connected with funerary commemorations or the birthdays of donors. The foundation of Epikteta on Thera about 200 BCE is one of the best-known examples of a continuing endowment.[27] The donor Epikteta built a Mouseion for her deceased husband and sons and established by her testament a funerary association of twenty-five male "relatives" with a gift of 3,000 drachmae. The interest from this endowment, 210 drachmae (7 percent), was to fund a yearly three-day set of sacrifices and banquets dedicated to the Muses, Epikteta, her husband, and her deceased sons, now part of a hero cult. The decree also established monthly officers (*epimēnioi*) selected by rota on the basis of age who were to perform sacrifices and distribute part of the offerings to the members present.

The Mouseion and its enclosure remained the property of Epikteta's daughter Epiteleia, as did the properties generating the 210 drachmae. Accordingly, there were provisions to ensure that if Epikteta's heirs failed to deliver the money to the *koinon*, the association could recover the sum from the produce of Epikteta's estate (lines 69–75).

Although Epikteta's estate contributed funds to support the three-day sacrifice, the monthly officers from the group were also expected to provide at their own expense good wine sufficient for three toasts, a crown, music, and perfumed oil (lines 139–42). The inscription even imagines the possibility of the exhausting of the rota of monthly officers (*epimēnioi*), who served at their own expense, and mandates the selection of other members by rota, who would receive 50 drachmae each to perform their service (*leitourgia*) at the festival (lines 155–60). This probably means that these officers were expected to spend about 50 drachmae in the normal execution of their responsibilities. But it also implies that it could be expected that a member would serve once a year as a monthly officer, with the financial obligations attached to that role, but that the member should not have to foot the bill for additional liturgies in a given year. Such a provision was probably enacted to take into account that in a small association of twenty-five members, some members on the rota might decline to serve—something that other bylaws also anticipated—and hence one might move through the entire membership list quickly. Hence, even when endowments were available, *leitourgiae* in the form of member contributions might be expected to cover all of the expenses of banquets and sacrifices.

Other funerary bequests were even more modest. A grain measurer from Ephesus contributed 500 denarii to the "workers in the gateway near Poseidon's statue," evidently a neighborhood association, requiring them to care for his grave and that of his wife.[28] The bequest stipulated that once a year, wine, candles, and garlands worth 10 denarii be purchased and the remainder be used for a "feast." Given prevailing interest rates, the income on 500 denarii would be 25–30 denarii. After discounting the cost of the garlands and candles, the "feast" would probably be quite modest. And if the "workers" were to have any other meetings or meals during the year, they would have to fund them in other ways.

The Latin West offers many examples of funerary bequests. In Ravenna, for example, Lucius Publicius Italicus, a member of the carpenters' guild (*collegium fabrum*) donated 30,000 sesterces (7,500 denarii) so that on the festival of Neptune the decurions of the guild could distribute *sportulae* of 2 denarii (8 sesterces) to each member.[29] The interest on the endowment is unknown, but in Italy it would have ranged between 375 and 900 denarii (i.e., 5–12 percent).[30] Since the carpenters' guild was very large—the donor belonged to the twenty-eighth division, or *decuria*, each *decuria* having a minimum of twenty-two members[31]—the distribution of *sportulae* likely would have consumed a large fraction of the interest. The terms of the bequest, moreover, stipulated that his own *decuria*, the twenty-eighth, should receive 150 denarii from the interest to decorate with roses his wife's grave and those of his two sons, to perform a sacrifice, and to hold a banquet at the graveside with the remaining money. Since the cost of roses is stipulated as 25 denarii and the sacrifice as 12 denarii, the *decuria* had 112 denarii available for its meal. To put this into context, each of the banquets of the *cultores* of Diana and Antinoüs more than a century earlier cost 84 denarii for forty-eight diners. If the *decuria* had twenty-two to twenty-four members, and taking into account that by the mid-third century inflation had increased the costs of commodities two to three times from their mid-second-century levels, the banquets for the *decuria* would have been comparable to those of the *cultores*.[32] But their banquets occurred only once a year. If the carpenters' guild as a whole or other *decuriae* within the guild had meals, as they surely did, they would have to fund them in other ways.

For the funerary endowments discussed above, the donor was not present. In the case of other endowments, a patron might attend, although inscriptions rarely provide any indication of this. A large inscription from Lavinium records the gift of C. Servilius Diodorus, an equestrian who had served in multiple military and civilian offices throughout the Severan empire and was also a priest at Lavinium.[33] He had set up a statue to his deceased wife Egnatia Salviana and at a later date established an endowment of 20,000 sesterces for the *dendrophors* of Lavinium. The interest, 1,000 sesterces (5 percent), was to be distributed as *sportulae* to the *dendrophors* and fund a yearly banquet on his birthday in the public square. It is possible that on some occasions Diodorus was present. No details of the banquet are provided, but the distribution of *sportulae* and the food, whether in equal amounts given to every *dendrophor* or differing amounts corresponding to the rank of members within the group, would have been a rule-based practice presumably set out in the bylaws of the association.

If Diodorus were present, such events performed status in two ways. Diodorus's status was marked by his distribution of *sportulae* and his provision of a public meal for the entire association. On Grignon's model of commensality, this was a matter of transgressive commensality—a person of superior rank eating with his social inferiors.[34] This act constitutes a temporary dissolution of social boundaries—like the chief executive officer of a company eating with factory workers—but in fact *underscores* social boundaries. For the *dendrophors*, however, the distributions and the meal were performances of segregative commensality, underscoring their "groupness" and equality, however that equality was articulated.[35]

In the mid-first century CIL 6.9254 (Rome, I CE) attests an endowment by a decurion of the textile dealers (*collegium centonariorum*) of 5,000 denarii bearing interest of 600 denarii (12 percent) to be paid out only as *sportulae* to the members on the birthday of Augustus (September 23). Like the carpenters, the textile dealers formed large and well-endowed guilds with several hundred members each, so that 600 denarii yearly would imply a distribution of 1–3 denarii, depending on the membership size. This level of distribution is well within the expected range for *sportulae*.

Table 6 offers a list of one hundred associations in both the Greek East and the Latin West and the endowment that each received. These include sixteen that received a one-time gift, usually a banquet or distribution of *sportulae*. Since these were nonrepeating gifts, no endowment sum is recorded. The remaining eighty-four associations include fifty-nine occupational guilds, twenty cultic associations, one *collegium domesticum*, and four associations of youths (*iuvenes*).

The large and socially muscular guilds—the sailors (*nautae*), builders (*fabri*), textile dealers (*centonarii*), and *dendrophors*—attracted the largest sums. Yet, only ten of the eighty-four associations enjoyed endowments of more than 30,000 sesterces. The mean is just over 11,000 sesterces, the median is 3,450 sesterces, and the mode is 2,000 sesterces. At 5 percent interest, a bequest of 3,400 sesterces would yield only about 43 denarii, enough for a very modest banquet once a year for a group of thirty to fifty members.

This finding is consistent with Jinyu Liu's study of a smaller set of endowments in the Latin West. She observed that fewer than one-third of endowments were greater than 20,000 sesterces.[36] (Table 6, with a larger sample, has only fourteen of eighty-four in this range.) The vast majority ranged from 1,000 to 8,000 sesterces. At the usual interest rates of 5–12 percent, these endowments would yield enough for one meal yearly but not more than that.[37]

There are several important observations to make. The first concerns the rank of the donors. In general, patrons of senatorial or equestrian rank are missing. Only two senators (nos. 1 and 21 in Table 6) and two equestrians (nos. 2 and 24) are listed, and they patronized occupational guilds rather than cultic associations. This pattern is consistent with the findings of Ulrich Fellmeth, who observed that the involvement of senators and equestrians in associations was limited to occupational guilds, and indeed large guilds such as the *fabri*, *dendrophors*, *centonarii*, and *lenuncularii*.[38] The more usual patrons of associations, both cultic and occupational, were local magistrates (decurions), Augustales,[39] and well-to-do commoners (*plebs* or freedmen).

A broader survey of endowments by Jean Andreau reinforces this finding. He tabulated 147 endowments, not only for associations, but for cities and smaller towns (*pagi*). His data indicated that senators (four or five) and equestrians (eleven) were in the minority. Town magistrates accounted for more than one-sixth (twenty-five) of the endowments, Augustales another eighteen, and commoners slightly less than one-quarter (thirty-six). Although the mean for the endowments established by senators and equestrians was high—more than 1 million sesterces for senators and almost 400,000 sesterces for equestrians—these figures fell precipitously when it came to local magistrates (98,000 sesterces), Augustales (30,383 sesterces), and commoners (19,719 sesterces). Interestingly, Andreau identified eleven women as donors, who as a group were responsible for a *higher* mean (158,900 sesterces) and median (30,000 sesterces). This perhaps puts into perspective Salvia Marcellina's rather high endowment for the collegium of Aesculapius and Hygia in Rome (CIL 6.10234).[40] Andreau's tabulation also confirms that senators and equestrians typically gave funds to cities and towns rather than to occupational guilds (only one or two instances). He records no instance of senators and equestrians providing funds for cultic associations.[41]

Table 6. Endowments for occupational guilds and cultic associations

	Name			Endowment (HS)	Yield (HS)
	ONE-TIME BENEFACTIONS				
1	CIL 14.4557	Unknown		?	?
2	CIL 11.7805	*Centonarii*	Textile dealers	30,000	?
3	CIL 11.4395	*Iuvenes*	Youths	?	?
4	CIL 11.6358	*Fabri*	Builders	?	?
5	CIL 11.1027	*Centonarii*	Textile dealers	?	?
6	CIL 11.5792	*Fabri*	Builders	?	?
7	CIL 6.630	*Silvanio sodalium*	Association of Silvanus	?	?
8	CIL 6.253	*Cultores domus divinae Augustae*	Devotees of the household of the divine Augustus	?	?
9	CIL 6.4421	*Domus Marcellae*	Household of Marcella	?	?
10	CIL 6.9044	*Domus Augustae*	Household of Augustus	10,000	?
11	CIL 3.1971	Unknown		?	?
12	CIL 10.3699	*Dendrophors*	Tree-carriers	?	?
13	CIL 10.5968	*Dendrophors*	Tree-carriers	?	?
14	CIL 11.6310	*Cultores Iovis Latii*	Devotees of Jupiter Latius	?	?
15	CIL 14.119	*Canephores*	Basket bearers	?	?
16	CIL 10.6483	*Cultores Iovis Axorani*	Devotees of Jupiter Axoranus	?	?
	OCCUPATIONAL GUILDS				
17	AE 1977, 298	*Nautae*	Sailors	150,000	7,500
18	CIL 5.5272	*Centonarii*	Textile dealers	80,000	4,800
19	CIL 5.4990	*Nautae*	Sailors	60,000	3,000
20	CIL 6.10234	*Collegium Aesculapi et Hygiae*	Collegium of Aesculapius and Hygia	60,000	3,000
21	CIL 11.7872	Scabillares	Musicians	30,000	1,500
22	CIL 5.5272	*Fabri centonarii*	Builders and textile dealers	30,000	2,000
23	CIL 11.126	*Fabri*	Builders	30,000	1,500
24	AE 1998, 282	*Dendrophors*	Tree-carriers	20,000	1,000
25	CIL 5.1978	Unknown		20,000	2,400
26	CIL 6.9254	*Centonarii*	Textile dealers	20,000	2,400
27	CIL 12.4393	*Fabri*	Builders	16,000	960
28	CIL 5.4016	*Nautae*	Sailors	12,000	600
29	CIL 6.29700	*Piscatores urinatorii*	Fishermen and boatmen	12,000	600
30	CIL 5.4489	*Fabri*	Builders	10,000	?
31	AE 1951, 94	*Centonarii*	Textile dealers	10,000	?
32	CIL 6.1925	*Dendrophors*	Tree-carriers	10,000	500
33	CIL 9.5568	*Fabri tignuarii*	Builder-carpenters	10,000	600
34	CIL 10.451	*Dendrophors*	Tree-carriers	8,000	400

Interest	Benefactor	Distribution	Location
	Senator, freedman	Banquet + *sportulae*	Ostia (Regio I)
?	Equestrian	Banquet + *sportulae*	Ocriculum (Regio VI)
?	Decurion	*Sportulae* (of HS30) + banquet	Ameria (Regio VI)
?	Augustalis	Bread + wine + *sportulae* (HS50)	Pisaurum (Regio VI)
?	Augustalis, freedman	Banquet	Brixellum (Regio VIII)
?	Augustalis	Banquet	Tuficum (Regio VI)
?	Imperial freedman	Banquet	Rome (Regio I)
?	Two freedmen	Bread, wine, *sportulae*	Rome (Regio I)
?	Freedman	Banquet	Rome (Regio I)
?	Freedman	Money for dinner	Rome (Regio I)
?	*Pleb*	Banquet	Salona (Dalmatia)
?	*Pleb*	Bread + wine + *sportulae* (HS32)	Cumae (Regio I)
?	*Pleb*	Banquet + *sportulae*	Signia (Latium and Campania)
?	*Plebs*	Bread + wine + *sportulae* (HS2)	Pisaurum (Regio VI)
?	*Pleb*	Bread + wine + *sportulae* (1 denarius)	Ostia (Regio I)
?	Two women	Banquet	Ulubrae (Regio I)
5.0%	*Pleb*	?	Brixia (Regio X)
6.0%	*Pleb*	*Sportulae*	Comum (Regio XI)
	Freedwoman?	?	Brixia (Regio X)
5.0%	Freedwoman, freedman	Six distributions of *sportulae* + bread + wine	Rome (Regio I)
5.0%	Senator	?	Spoletium (Regio VI)
6.7%	Decurions	*Sportulae* + oil	Comum (Regio XI)
5.0%	Decurion	*Sportulae* + banquet	Ravenna (Regio VIII)
5.0%	Equestrian	*Sportulae* + banquet	Lavinium
12.0%	Decurion	*Sportulae*	Opitergium (Regio X)
12.0%	*Pleb*	*Sportulae*	Rome (Regio I)
6.0%	*Pleb*	Banquet	Narbo (Gallia Narbonensis)
5.0%	*Pleb*	?	Arilica (Regio X)
5.0%	*Pleb*	*Sportulae*	Rome (Regio I)
?	Freedwoman?	*Sportulae*	Brixia (Regio X)
?	Freedwoman?	?	Comum (Regio XI)
5.0%	*Pleb*	*Parentalia*	Rome (Regio I)
6.0%	*Pleb*	Banquet	Tolentinum (Regio V)
5.0%	Decurions	*Sportulae* + banquet	Eburum (Regio III)

(continued)

Table 6. (*continued*)

Name				Endowment (HS)	Yield (HS)
35	AE 1965, 144	*Centonarii, utricularii, dendrophors*	Textile dealers, bladder boat operators, tree-carriers	6,400	800
36	CIL 11.6520	*Dendrophors, fabri, centonarii*	Tree-carriers, builders, textile dealers	6,000	?
37	AE 1987,198	*Dendrophors*	Tree-carriers	6,000	300
38	CIL 14.326	*Dendrophors*	Tree-carriers	6,000	720
39	CIL 14.326	*Dendrophors*	Tree-carriers	6,000	720
40	CIL 14.326	*Dendrophors*	Tree-carriers	6,000	720
41	CIL 11.4391	*Centonarii*	Textile dealers	5,000	250
42	CIL 14.246	*Scapharii*	Barge operators	4,000	200
43	CIL 5.4017	*Nautae*	Sailors	4,000	200
44	CIL 11.1436	*Fabri navalium*	Ship builders	4,000	200
45	Pais 181	*Fabri*	Builders	3,500	210
46	CIL 6.9626	*Corpus mensorum*	Association of measurers	3,400	?
47	CIL 14.326	*Dendrophors*	Tree-carriers	3,000	360
48	CIL 5.2864	*Centonarii*	Textile dealers	2,000	242
49	CIL 5.5287	*Fabri*	Builders	2,000	?
50	CIL 5.5658	*Centonarii*	Textile dealers	2,000	?
51	CIL 5.4449	Unknown		2,000	100
52	CIL 5.4015	*Nautae*	Sailors	2,000	?
53	CIL 5.4488	*Fabri, centonarii*	Builders, textile dealers	2,000	?
54	CIL 5.4015	*Navicularii*	Pilots	2,000	100
55	CIL 14.326	*Dendrophors*	Tree-carriers	2,000	240
56	CIL 14.326	*Dendrophors*	Tree-carriers	2,000	240
57	CIL 14.326	*Dendrophors*	Tree-carriers	2,000	240
58	CIL 14.326	*Dendrophors*	Tree-carriers	2,000	240
59	CIL 14.326	*Dendrophors*	Tree-carriers	2,000	240
60	CIL 14.326	*Dendrophors*	Tree-carriers	2,000	240
61	CIL 14.326	*Dendrophors*	Tree-carriers	2,000	240
62	CIL 5.2046	*Fabri*	Builders	2,000	100
63	I.Eph 3216	*Prometres*	Grain measurers	2,000	100
64	CIL 5.4418	*Dendrophors*	Tree-carriers	1,000	?
65	CIL 5.5447	*Centonarii*	Textile dealers	1,000	?
66	CIL 11.5047	*Centonarii*	Textile dealers	1,000	?
67	CIL 5.6363	*Fabri*	Builders	1,000	?
68	CIL 6.1872	*Piscatores urinatorii*	Fishermen and boatmen	1,000	?
69	CIL 11.6371	*Fabri*	Builders	1,000	50
70	CIL 11.132	*Fabri*	Builders	1,000	50
71	AE 1991, 823	*Aeneatores*	Trumpeters	1,000	50
72	CIL 12.731	*Nautae*	Sailors	800	40
73	CIL 5.4416	*Fabri*	Builders	500	?
74	CIL 5.4294	*Lumentarii*	Carriage drivers?	400	?
75	CIL 5.2315	*Nautae*	Sailors	400	?

Interest	*Benefactor*	*Distribution*	*Location*
12.5%	*Pleb*	*Sportulae*	Alba Augusta (Gallia Narbonensis)
?	Augustalis	Oil	Sassina (Regio VI)
5.0%	*Pleb*	*Sportulae* + banquet	Ostia Antica (Regio I)
12.0%	*Pleb*	?	Ostia Antica (Regio I)
12.0%	*Pleb*	?	Ostia Antica (Regio I)
12.0%	*Pleb*	?	Ostia Antica (Regio I)
5.0%	Decurions	Banquet	Amelia (Regio VI)
5.0%	Augustalis	Banquet	Ostia Antica (Regio I)
5.0%	*Pleb*	Banquet + roses	Arilica (Regio X)
5.0%	*Pleb*	Roses	Pisa (Regio VII)
6.0%	*Pleb*	*Parentalia* + wine +	Aquileia (Regio X)
?	*Pleb*	*Sportulae?*	Rome (Regio I)
12.0%	*Pleb*	?	Ostia Antica (Regio I)
12.1%	Decurions	?	Patavium (Regio X)
?	Augustalis	?	Comum (Regio XI)
?	Augustalis	?	Tavernerio (Regio XI)
5.0%	Augustalis	Sacrifices	
?	*Pleb*	Banquet + roses	Arilica (Regio X)
?	*Pleb*	?	Arilica (Regio X)
5.0%	*Pleb*	Banquet + roses	Arilica (Regio X)
12.0%	*Pleb*	?	Ostia Antica (Regio I)
12.0%	*Pleb*	?	Ostia Antica (Regio I)
12.0%	*Pleb*	?	Ostia Antica (Regio I)
12.0%	*Pleb*	?	Ostia Antica (Regio I)
12.0%	*Pleb*	?	Ostia Antica (Regio I)
12.0%	*Pleb*	?	Ostia Antica (Regio I)
12.0%	*Pleb*	?	Ostia Antica (Regio I)
5.0%	*Pleb*	Wine?	Bellunum (Regio X)
5.0%	*Pleb*	Banquet	Ephesus
?	Augustalis	?	Brixia (Regio X)
?	Augustalis	?	Clivio (Regio XI)
?	Augustalis	Funerary banquet	Mevania (Regio VI)
?	*Pleb*	Flowers,	
?	*Pleb*	*Sportulae*	Rome (Regio I)
5.0%	*Pleb*	*Sportulae*	Pisaurum (Regio VI)
5.0%	*Pleb*	Banquet + roses	Ravenna (Regio VIII)
5.0%	*Pleb*	*Sportulae*	Brixia (Regio X)
5.0%	*Pleb*	Annual sacrifice	Arelate (Gallia Narbonensis)
?	Augustalis	?	Brixia (Regio X)
?	Augustalis	*Sportulae*	Brixia (Regio X)
?	*Pleb*	Roses	Atria (Regio X)

(*continued*)

Table 6. (*continued*)

Name				Endowment (HS)	Yield (HS)
76	CIL 5.7906	*Centonarii*	Textile dealers	?	?
	CULTIC ASSOCIATIONS				
77	CIL 10.444	Silvanus		50,000	2,500
78	OGIS 326	Attalists		42,000	2,100
79	CIL 11.2596	Mithras		32,000	1,600
80	CIL 14.2112	*Cultores* of Diana and Antinoüs		15,000	800
81	IG II^2 1326	Dionysos		6,000	720
82	CIL 6.10297	Unknown		5,000	50
83	ILS 7215	*Cultores* of Hercules		4,000	200
84	CIL 10.5654	*Cultores* of the goddess Ceres		4,000	480
85	CIL 6.10297	Unknown		4,000	40
86	IG IX,2 1107b	*Hypostoloi*		4,000	?
87	CIL 5.8654	*Cultores* of the goddess Ceres		2,000	240
88	CIL 5.8655	*Cultores* of the goddess Ceres		2,000	240
89	CIL 5.4440	Collegium of the *lares*		2,000	?
90	CIL 6.10297	Unknown		2,000	20
91	IG XII,3 329	Unknown		2,000	?
92	CIL 5.2072	Heraclenses		1,600	80
93	Philippi II 133/ G441.13–16	Sourgethes		600	?
94	CIL 5.2072	Ciarnenses		400	20
95	CIL 5.2072	Association of women		400	?
	Family associations				
96	IG XII,3 330	*Collegium domesticum*	Household collegium	12,000	840
	Iuvenes (youths)				
97	CIL 10.5657	*Iuvenes*		2,000	240
98	CIL 5.5907	*Iuvenes*		1,600	80
99	CIL 5.5907	*Iuvenes*		1,600	80
100	CIL 5.5134	*Iuvenes*		80	12
	STATISTICS				
	Total			100	
	Mean (HS)			11,185	
	Median (HS)			3,450	
	Mode (HS)			2,000	

Interest	*Benefactor*	*Distribution*	*Location*
?	*Pleb*	Banquet + roses	
5.0%	*Pleb*	Five yearly banquets	Caposele (Regio I)
5.0%	Local elite	Sacrifices + meetings	Teos, Ionia
5.0%	*Pleb*	Oil and ?	Montalcino (Regio VII)
5.3%	Decurion	*Sportulae*	
12.0%	Athenian demesman	Sacrifices	Piraeus (Attica)
1.0%	?	Banquet	Rome (Regio I)
5.0%	Freedwoman	Banquet	Castrum Truentinum (Regio V)
12.0%	Decurion	*Sportulae* (and one-time dinner)	Fabrateria Vetus (Regio I)
1.0%	?	Banquet	Rome (Regio I)
?	?	Yearly meeting	Demetrias (Magnesia)
12.0%	Augustales	?	Concordia (Regio X)
12.0%	Augustales	?	Concordia (Regio X)
?	?	Roses	Brixia (Regio X)
1.0%	?	Banquet	Rome (Regio I)
?	?	Meeting + banquet?	Thera
5.0%	*Pleb*	?	Feltria (Regio X)
?	?	Funerary banquet	Philippi (Macedonia)
5.0%	*Pleb*	?	Feltria (Regio X)
?	?	?	Feltria (Regio X)
7.0%	Local elite	Sacrifice + meal	Thera
12.0%	?	*Sportulae*	Fabrateria Vetus (Regio I)
5.0%	?	Roses	Mediolanum (Regio XI)
5.0%	*Pleb*	Roses	Mediolanum (Regio XI)
15.0%	*Pleb*	Funerary observance?	Bergomum (Regio XI)

(*continued*)

Table 6. (*continued*)

Name	*Endowment (HS)*	*Yield (HS)*
One-time benefactions	16	
Occupational guilds	60	
Mean (HS)	11,753	
Median (HS)	3,400	
Mode (HS)	2,000	
Cultic associations	19	
Mean (HS)	9,421	
Median (HS)	4,000	
Mode (HS)	2,000	
Family associations	1	
Associations of youths	4	

Note: HS indicates sesterces.

Second, it is important to observe that a patron who we might suppose to have been very wealthy typically gave relatively modest amounts and mainly as endowments for funerary commemorations or to celebrate birthdays—that is, either as one-time-only banquets or as banquets or distributions that occurred once yearly. Of those we have surveyed, *none* was prepared to fund all the yearly activities of their client associations. The most generous were Salvia Marcellina, who funded six banquets of stonemasons, and a first-century freedman, L. Domitius Phaon, who contributed funds to an association devoted to Silvanus to support five of the association's banquets and sacrifices.[42] Most patrons were content to fund a single yearly event. Moreover, as Table 6 shows, donors like the donor of CIL 14.2112 funded the distribution of rather modest *sportulae* in the range of 1–2 denarii, or they provided funds for the association to buy roses to decorate the tomb of a deceased family member.

The implications of these data for Christ groups should be obvious. First, unless the Corinthian Christ assembly had attracted a benefactor far more generous than Salvia Marcellina of CIL 6.10234 or L. Domitius Phaon of CIL 10.444, it could not have funded its weekly or even monthly meals from endowment income alone. The assembly could not have done so even at half the size of the

Interest	*Benefactor*	*Distribution*	*Location*

sixty members of the collegium of Aesculapius and Hygia and serving, like that collegium, only bread and wine. As a small cultic association composed of non-elite Corinthians, immigrant Judeans, and a few slaves devoted to an obscure Eastern hero, it is extremely unlikely that the Corinthian Christ assembly was in a position to attract a donor of high rank or even a combination of donors. This is not to deny that a patron of a Christ assembly might have provided a meal for the group from time to time, perhaps even a yearly meal. To have donors prepared to give large sums, however, Christ assemblies would have had to possess far more social capital than we can reasonably expect of them, at least in the first century of their existence.

A second observation is also pertinent. The known examples of elite patronage of associations give us no reason to suspect that patrons engaged in the kind of behavior that Theissen imagined at the communal meal of the Corinthians, consuming most or all of the food before others arrived. On the contrary, patrons were probably not present at all and in any event in no position to control the distribution of food. All of the data we have suggest that association meals were regulated by bylaws that prescribed the amounts of food and the size of *sportulae* to be given to each member. Those bylaws aimed at some version of equality, whether equality was measured arithmetically (every member receiving the same amount) or geometrically (where the value of *sportulae* and the amount of food were proportional to the position and role the recipient had within the group).[43] And even in the latter case, it is critical to note that the differential in food and *sportulae* between the *plebs* and honored members seldom exceeded the ratio of one to two or three. Association meals thus constructed members as equal, irrespective of whether a patron was present or not.

ERANISTIC BANQUETS

The alternate to the model of elite benefaction proposes that all members were expected to bring foodstuffs to the banquet.[44] In this view, the better endowed brought more and better food, and poorer members brought little or no food. In theory this practice would not have presented a problem except that it is also assumed, as with the model of elite patronage, that the wealthier members either began to eat before others arrived or simply appropriated more food, leaving the poor with little or none.[45] This model was worked out in detail by Hans-Joseph Klauck and Peter Lampe and is a version of the Homeric *eranos*.

Klauck adduces a meal associated with the cult of Sarapis as a strong analogy to the practice of the Corinthian Christ group. In this meal, described by Aelius Aristides, the god was regarded as "both their chief guest (*daitymōn*) and host (*hestiatōr*)," and so "he offers the libations and also receives the libations, joining in the reveling and inviting the revelers himself" (*Oratio* 45.28 Dindorf; my translation).[46]

Since such banquets often occurred in temples, Höfler had reasoned that the idea that the god could be both host and guest meant concretely that participants offered foodstuffs to the god, which in turn became the gifts of the god to the diners.[47] The problem at Corinth, Klauck argues, was that instead of treating all of the food as "the Lord's," the wealthy treated the food as their own and ate accordingly. The wealthy also began to eat before the poor arrived, thus leaving the poor with little or nothing.[48]

Meals to which diners brought food are often called *eranous*.[49] Although the term is more commonly used to designate a common fund to which members of a club contributed and out of which loans were made, or as a term for the association itself (semantically equivalent to *thiasos*),[50] an *eranos* meal is attested since Homer and Hesiod and was one in which participants brought their own food.[51] This practice is imagined in Aristophanes's *Wasps*,[52] and something similar is described by Xenophon where Socrates complains of differential allocations of food:

> Whenever some of those who gathered together for a dinner brought only a little fish and others brought more, Socrates ordered the serving boy either to put the small contributions into the common pot or to divide it out equally among the diners. So those who had brought more felt ashamed not to share in what has been contributed to the common pot and not to contribute what they had brought. Therefore, they also put their own food into the common pot, and since they did not get any more than those who had brought a little, so they stopped buying so much fish. (Xenophon, *Mem.* 3.14.1; trans. LCL, adapted slightly)

Lucian's *Lexiphanes* and Athenaeus also describe lavish banquets to which participants were to bring foodstuffs.[53]

Is there any evidence that such contributors' meals were common in other Greco-Roman associations? Coutsoumpos confidently asserts that "Greco-Roman clubs of all types often had potluck dinners" and claims that literary and epigraphic sources "often describe rules for their *eranos* meals."[54] Unfortunately, as the subsequent discussion shows, this is not the case.

In the second century CE Athenaeus knew of two kinds of contemporary dinners funded on the basis of member contributions, even though he does not attach the term *eranos* to either. One he called "the basket dinner" (*to apo spuridos deipnon*), to which the invitees brought their own food.[55] In the same section he discusses another form of the meal, a "contribution dinner," which was supported by monetary contributions (*to deipnon apo symbolōn*).[56] Athenaeus does not connect either of these two meals with the practices of contemporary cultic associations or occupational guilds.

Peter Lampe prefers the model of the basket dinner to the contribution dinner for imagining the practice of the Corinthian Christ group. This preference seems to hang on two assumptions: that food was differentially allotted, with the rich taking more than the poor, and that the rich arrived earlier and began to eat before others arrived. On the further assumption that monetary contributions would have been brought to the dinner itself, only the basket dinner makes sense. If money had been brought to the dinner, it would be cumbersome to imagine two trips to the market to secure food, one for the early-arriving wealthy and a second for the tardy poor.[57] Yet as we shall see, this latter assumption is false: it is not necessarily the case that monetary contributions were collected only at the time of the meal. And if contributions were collected at other times—say, monthly or in advance of the meal and then food and drink were purchased by the treasurer or some other agent—it is just as possible that latecomers could be disadvantaged because the food purchased for the meal had already been consumed. This means that the assumption that is essential to Lampe's scenario is that the problems at the Lord's Supper had to do with late arrivals. Without it, the whole scenario collapses. As we shall see below, this assumption is also dubious.

Just as problematic is Lampe's argument from analogy. After citing the text of Aelius Aristides noted above, to the effect that Sarapis is both host and guest at his banquet, Lampe concludes that the meal that Aristides associated with the cult of Sarapis was an *eranos*, that is, one to which participants brought foodstuffs.[58] Yet this is a misreading of *Oratio* 45.27, where Aristides asserts:

> Humankind exceptionally makes this god (Sarapis) alone a full partner in their sacrifices, summoning him to the feast and making him both their chief guest (*daitymōn*) and host (*hestiatōr*), so that *while different (gods) contribute to different banquets* (*eranous*), he is the universal treasurer (*plērōtēs*) for all banquets and has the rank of symposiarch for those who assemble at times for his sake. Just as Homer said that Athena herself both offered libations and effected each prayer, so he is a participant in the libations and is the one who receives the libations, and he goes as a guest to the revel and issues the invitations to the revelers, who under his guidance perform a dance secure from the consequences of evil and who bring home along with their crowns high spirits and respond with a return invitation. . . . To such an extent he is involved in human affairs.[59]

As the citation makes clear, there is nothing here to suggest that the *Sarapiastai* practiced an *eranos* meal. Aristides's point is to contrast Sarapis with the other gods, and he employs the image of the *gods* contributing to a banquet as a metaphor for their presence at the banquet. It tells us nothing about how the *Sarapiastai* funded their meals.

Epigraphic evidence from groups of *Sarapiastai* from Attica, Lesbos, and Cos indicates that *Sarapiastai* operated in much the same way as other *thiasoi*, collecting funds for their sacrifices and banquets—and therefore having a treasurer (*tamias*) as one of their prominent officials—commending benefactors, and paying for honorific steles.[60] There is no epigraphic evidence to suggest a version of the basket dinner in use by *Sarapiastai*.[61] No other associations of the early Roman period are known to have engaged in the eranistic practice that Lampe imagines for the Corinthians. It is true that some groups imposed liturgies on leaders to supply meals; but in these cases, the liturgical requirement existed only as long as the person or people in question were in office (normally one year), at which point another member assumed that responsibility. This model presumes that most or all members were able to assume a liturgical role by rota.

PEER BENEFACTION: LITURGIES AND MEMBER CONTRIBUTIONS

If it is unlikely that early Christ groups could fund their meals by relying solely on elite patrons or wealthy members and if there is no evidence that the Homeric *eranos* was adopted as a model for providing meals for associations contemporary with Christ groups, what is left?

Elsewhere I have surveyed how associations financed their meals.[62] Some sources of income—fines levied on members for infractions of the rules, legacies, and the occasional gifts of benefactors—were occasional and too highly variable to be a stable basis for the funding of regular activities. Some groups expected members who had received civic honors, who had celebrated births or marriages, or who had received legacies to give special gifts to the club. Some took up special collections, but these were usually to bail out the association when the common fund had failed or to fund special projects.[63]

Initiation fees were another source of income but probably sufficiently unpredictable to be the sole source or funding for meals. The recruiting of new members also would have had the effect of increasing the aggregate cost of meals, unless there was a corresponding loss of members through deaths and defections. In cases in which an association owned property, rents were available, but these normally were not used to fund meals but instead to make repairs on buildings or to distribute as *sportulae* at meetings. We are left with two credible funding models: peer benefaction (or the model of rotating liturgies) and member contributions.

Peer benefaction and rotating liturgies are amply attested in Greek and Roman associations. I have already noted the system of rotating liturgical expectations for the *magistri* of the *cultores* of Diana and Antinoüs and the expectations that the monthly officers established by the testament of Epikteta would take turns at presiding at the festival, providing wine, crowns, and perfumed oil at their own expense. An inscription from Ionia lists the goods promised and delivered to a Dionysiac association by various members (the first two names are missing *in lacuna*): "[. . .] pro|vided sufficient wine; | previously . . . he had | promised [. .] *metrētai* . . . | (5) | [. . .]goras son of Protamachos | provided sufficient wine; | he had promised 100 *metrētai*; | Dionysios son of Dionysios provided | sufficient wine and cooks || and musicians | for banquet and [. . .] *choinikes* of bread. | . . ." (SEG 31:983, lines 1–11; near Magnesia ad Maeander, Ionia).

The quantity of wine in line 7 (100 *metrētai,* or 3,900 liters) is obviously far too great for a single banquet. It is likely that the individual in line 5 had agreed to supply wine for a number of banquets, perhaps a year's worth of dinners, and had provided (*parechō*) the appropriate amount for the banquet in question.

Even clearer is the role of officers in a Dionysiac association in Pergamon, whose rule prescribed that three officials—the *eukosmos* (the officer in charge of order), the priest, and the secretary—provide the bread, wine, and table settings for each of four banquets and that the *eukosmos* provide wreaths for each of the thirty-six members at the monthly celebrations of Augustus's birthday.[64] The formula that prefaces each of these prescriptions, "which things NN shall provide in the year of his office," indicates that these officials served for a year at a time, so that with a membership of thirty-six, each could expect a liturgical obligation only once in twelve years.

Although the Dionysiac association of Pergamon included mostly Roman citizens, some probably quite wealthy, liturgical obligations existed much lower down the economic ladder too, in associations that likely could not rely on any endowment income from wealthy benefactors. An association in Tebtynis in Ptolemaic Egypt left a detailed account of the financing of several months of banquets.[65] The account is very fragmentary, but two important features are evident. First, the association employed a system of "flat hierarchy," rotating offices through the membership. Second the "normal" monthly contributions by members were very modest: 100 copper (AE) drachmae per diner, in the devalued currency of the late second century, the equivalent of 0.21 silver (AR) drachma.[66] However, Frag. 2.r.2 (lines 22–38) indicates that the "magistrates for the month of Pauni" contributed an additional 815 AE drachmae (= 1.7 AR drachmae) and that the five "banquet managers" added another 1,000 AE drachmae (= 2.08 AR drachmae). These extra funds brought the monthly account to a level where monthly dinners could be afforded.[67] Another account from the same period, SB 3:7182, probably from an association of slaves,[68] indicates the use of a flat hierarchy, as evidenced by the repetitive use of the formula "in the month that NN was the supervisor (or sacrifice-maker)." This perhaps also explains the variability of dues contributed, since leaders were often expected to make increased contributions in recognition of their offices.

Finally, the bylaws of a group of devotees of Zeus Hypsistos stipulated: "[the president] should make for all the contributors (*syneisphoroi*) one banquet a month, the first day, in the sanctuary of Zeus, at which in a common dining room (*androon*) they should pour libations, pray, and perform the other (10) customary rites on behalf of the god and lord, the king" (P.Lond VII 2193, lines 7–10; trans. AGRW 295).

The yearly president here is tasked with arranging twelve banquets. At least some of the expenses likely came from the thirty-two contributions that are listed on the fragmentary verso of the papyrus and which range from the equivalent of 1.6 to 2.5 drachmae. Owing to the fragmentary state of the papyrus, it is unclear whether the contributions would cover the full cost of the banquet. But it is inherently likely that the president was expected to provide some of the food or wine.

A document that is clearer in this respect is P.Mich V 246 (Tebtynis, 43–49 CE), where the yearly president of an association devoted to Harpokrates was expected to provide monthly to each of the members various spices, cakes, and other dishes. The other members contributed monetary sums, presumably for the wine or beer. Their seat at the *triclinium* was related to the size of the monthly payment.[69]

The two Ptolemaic accounts, P.Tebt III/2 894 and SB 3:7182, also illustrate what was by far the most common mechanism for funding the meals of associations: monthly fees, called *phora*, *symbola*, or *stips menstrua* and levied to maintain the solvency of the association's treasury and from which loans were made, funeral costs were paid, and items for the banquets were purchased. The account book of a small association (P.Tebt I 118; Tebtynis, 112/111 BCE) reveals an association that charged a very modest monthly membership fee of 100 AE drachmae to fund its banquet. If fewer than the needed twenty-two members came, the group invited (paying) guests so that it could achieve the threshold of 2,200 AE drachmae (equivalent to 4.5 AR drachmae) to be able to afford one jar (*keramion*) of wine and some bread.

Membership dues are mentioned in most of the extant association rules, and it seems obvious that this was the usual method for funding associations' activities.[70] A remarkable account book of an association in the Fayûm from 231 BCE, dated to November 8, lists the expected income from association members following the monthly dinner on the previous day:

> Thoth 19, year 17 (November 8, 231 BCE)
> Ktēsippos, monthly officer: 3 (drachmae?)
>   Dues (*symbolē*): 1 (drachmae) 1/4 (obol)
>   He owes 2 3/4 (obols)

and on account: 1/4 (obol), making 4 (drachmae) 3 1/4 (obols)[71]
Kleainetos, monthly officer: 3 (drachmae)
  Dues: 1 (drachma) 1/4 (obol)
  he owes: 2 (drachmae) 3 (obols), making 6 (drachmae) 3 1/4 (obols)
Pythion api(. . .) dues: 3 obols
he owes: 2 (drachmae) 4 1/2 (obols), making 3 (drachmae) 1 1/2 (obols)
Dorion, priest: 2 (drachmae) 4 (obols)
Nikias the younger, a priest: 3 (drachmae)
Eurylochos, dues: 1 (drachma) 1/4 (obol)
  he owes as a loan: 1 (obol)
and on account: 1 1/2 (obols), making 1 (drachma) 2 1/2 (obols)
Sokratēs, dues: 1 (drachma) 1/4 (obol)
  he owes on account: 1 1/2 (obols), making 1 (drachma) 1 3/4 obols
Artemidoros, dues: 1 (drachma) 1/4 (obol) (P.Petr III 136.i.1–18)

The dues payable are constant at 1 drachma 1/4 obol or 1 1/24 drachmae. But the two officers, Ktēsippos and Kleainetos, paid an additional 3 drachmae, probably as a liturgical obligation of their offices. No dues are registered beside the names of the two priests, which might suggest that they are both dues-exempt (*asymbolos*); but this status did not excuse them from contributing to the banquet. Only the last three names paid only dues, although two of them are listed as being in arrears.

It may perhaps surprise the modern reader to see the care with which associations kept accounts of their income and expenses—this account later lists the cost for the meal that was held on a previous day and included bread, eggs, nuts, dried figs, chickpeas, and one crown, perhaps for one of the officers or priests. Given the date of the account and the date of the dinner, it appears that on the day following the dinner the treasurer of the association tallied the cost of the dinner and the amounts owed by each member—some of whom were already in arrears, perhaps from a previous banquet. The account does not indicate when the members were expected to settle their accounts, but it was apparently not at the banquet itself. The mention of the account (*logos*) points to a reserve fund from which the association purchased items for each dinner and then charged members for their dues and liturgical obligations after the dinner. This account, like that of P.Tebt III/2 894 and several other Egyptian associations, shows that the meals were funded through a combination of member dues and extraordinary liturgical payments that were expected of the officers in the year they served.

That dues were routine in associations is indicated by two features of the bylaws and other documents of associations. First, both bylaws and account books regularly designate people as dues-exempt, which is meaningful only if dues collection was the norm.[72] Second, many bylaws include clauses that prescribe fines and other penalties should a member fail to pay in a timely fashion. For example, the bylaws of the Iobakchoi state: "Each (member) shall speak and act and be zealous (for the association), contributing to the fixed monthly dues (*phora*) for wine. If he does not fulfill (these obligations), he shall be shut out of the gathering and those named in the decree shall be empowered (to enforce this), except (in the cases of people who are) out of town, in mourning, or ill" (IG II^2 1368.45–51 = GRA I 51; Athens, 164/165 CE).

There is no direct evidence from Pauline letters of the existence of rotating liturgies or monthly contributions, nor is any other mechanism for funding the communal meal mentioned. Paul's letters are not the kind of media in which one would expect such practices to be mentioned unless there were abuses. Analogously, there is strong evidence of the practice of the collection of monthly dues in associations in Italy, Attica, and Egypt but no mention at all of this practice in Asian associations. This is not because associations in Asia Minor did not collect dues or because they did not have banquets. Instead, it is due to the genre of the monuments that are preserved: we have only two examples of bylaws from Asian groups, I.Perg II 374 and TAM V 1539, the first mentioning both initiation fees and rotating liturgies and the second, a family association, saying nothing at all about its finances. We would not know anything of the practices of Christ groups unless we were to have a copy of their bylaws, or an account book. Of course, we have neither.[73]

The data from associations provide a framework for possible funding practices. It is theoretically possible that, extraordinarily, Christ assemblies had attracted donors of sufficient wealth and motivation to be able to fund all of their meals. It is possible that Christ assemblies engaged in eranistic practices even when no other comparable associations did. But to assume either of these is to resort to an atypical scenario, not one that is known. The first case is dramatically atypical. None of the associations surveyed above could rely on a patron to fund more than six meals yearly, and in most instances the patron provided only one. To imagine that Christ assemblies adopted either of these two unusual practices also inevitably raises the question: Why did no ancient contemporary notice and comment on such practices?

This leaves two possible models, rotating liturgies and member contributions, both of which are well attested in ancient associations, individually or operating in tandem with one another. The usual objection to either of these suggestions is normally that some of the Corinthian Christ followers were extremely poor, and so it would have been impossible for them to assume a liturgy or to contribute dues.[74] This assumption, however, is problematic on two grounds. First, the data that we have simply do not allow us reliably to assess the income levels of early Christ followers. The metrics invoked to establish the economic level of early Christ followers are in fact not reliable indicators. And second, associations, especially those lower on socioeconomic scales, devised ways for members with meager resources nonetheless to participate in this moral economy. So important was the value of belonging and connectivity that associations with poorer members found ways to accommodate them. The association of slaves in SB 3:7182 evidently had a sliding scale of contributions, from 270 to 365 AE drachmae (i.e., 0.56–0.76 AR drachma), and P.Tebt III/2 894 records contributions of 100, 200, and 300 but also 160 and 215 in debased copper drachmae. Those with very modest resources could be accommodated and still receive the recognition and symbolic capital that support for the association produced.[75]

Several scholars treat the supposed lack of membership dues as a *reason* for the growth of Christ believers among the poorer sectors of the population.[76] The appeal of Christ groups, Pilhofer claims, lay in the fact that "no other group in the Roman Empire offered these people the possibility to be able to have a full meal at least once each week."[77] He contrasts Christ groups with the meal practices of the *cultores* of Diana and Antinoüs, who offered only "six *free* meals per year":[78]

> This offer (of food) loses its attraction when one compares it with that of the Christian community: instead of the six meals provided here [i.e., in CIL 14.2112], the [Christian] community offered more than fifty. From the point of view of the poor, this was a comparative paradise. From the economic perspective alone conversion to Christianity was without question worth it for the poor. The days of the *cultores Dianae et Antinoi* were thus numbered: they could not compete on economic grounds with the Christian offer.[79]

In addition to the fact that this is a serious misreading of CIL 14.2112, there are other problems with Pilhofer's argument. First, his account leaves unexplained the source of the funds for the fifty meals a year. Ebel conjectures that the funding for the meals came from "voluntary payments in accord with the financial capabilities of individual members."[80] Yet that would not distinguish Christ groups from other cultic associations, which also relied on member contributions, in some instances adjusted to the members' capacity to pay. The question that Ebel does not address is whether purely ad hoc contributions—if that is what she has in mind—are sufficiently predictable as a basis for the operation of a group with twelve to fifty-two communal dinners yearly.

A second problem concerns the more fundamental assumption of the Pilhofer-Ebel model. Why join the *cultores* of Diana and Antinoüs when, as one of the yearly *magistri*, one would have to contribute from one's own resources to the six yearly banquets? Why agree to join the association of Epikteta when, as a monthly officer, one would be responsible for paying 50 drachmae for one of the sacred meals every few years? The fact that people did this, and did it routinely, should alert us to the fact that financial expenditures had very different social and symbolic valences than they have for modern people. As we have seen, the principal values of antiquity were honor, connectivity, and social standing. Money was a means to achieve these, not an end in itself. Financial support for one's collegium was a way to realize those values and to materialize one's membership.

The twenty-first-century North Atlantic individual might regard "getting something for nothing" as an incentive to join a group. There are good reasons, however, to think that free riders would not have contributed to group cohesion and solidarity and would not have contributed to group growth or longevity. Contributions (whether monetary or nonmonetary) serve to signal and to materialize belonging and to share in the social capital offered by the group. This is precisely the reason that donation lists, donative inscriptions, and even registers of funds paid for a meal, with the name of the contributor clearly marked, had such critical importance in antiquity. This was not simply an exercise in financial accountability but in *moral accounting*.[81]

Contributions play important roles in group life. Michael Lambek has shown how contributions, even small ones, function in the formation of a social imaginary. He observes in relation to the (contemporary) Sakalava, a group in Madagascar: "It is here that ordinary people most directly experience their own participation (their will, intentionality, and agency) and identification with the ancestral system, which can thrive only through their commitment to service." Each act of giving is formally *received* with thanks, clapping, speeches, and the like, and the reception constitutes a form of recognition. Acts of giving take place in a sociable context, with music, drink, and warm fellowship. Everyone appears to have a stake in the maintenance and reproduction of the politico-religious system; they are proud to have the honor to participate.[82]

What Lambek describes in a contemporary African group is equally applicable to the moral economy of antiquity, in which acts of giving, even modest monthly dues, were recorded and service to the group was celebrated and rewarded with recognition. Memberships costs, always scaled to the means of the members, serve as ways to demonstrate and perform membership and to weed out free riders, those who wished to benefit from membership without shouldering any of the costs, whether monetary or performance-based costs. On Richard Sosis's showing, it is not groups that impose membership costs whose "days are numbered"; on the contrary—and perhaps ironically—membership costs as a form of "costly signaling" in fact enhance and undergird group solidarity and contribute to the longevity of the group. Clubs with low membership costs are the ones that are likely to fail.[83]

The foregoing does not mean that Christ groups did not sometimes welcome those with few resources or that some of a group's attraction had to do with a reputation that it embraced members of a wide variety of economic registers. But the early Christ groups such as those represented by the *Didache* (11–12) were conscious of the problem posed by free riders, both traveling prophets and others who wished to settle with the group, and devised means to exclude people who were not prepared to contribute. Richard Last has recently mounted an argument, using data from associations, to show that the author of 2 Thessalonians invokes the behavior of Paul, who points out that he did not eat for free (*dōrean*) but worked with his own hands, even though he might have claimed an exemption from dues based on his role (*exousia*, 2 Thess 3:9). The writer seems to have been concerned about those who were "disorderly" and who did not work and so counsels the group to keep a list (*sēmeiousthai*) of those who do not pay and have nothing to do with them—not to expel them, but to put them to shame (3:14).[84]

This understanding of 2 Thess 3:6–15 accords remarkably well with the disciplinary practices of other associations, which expected and monitored dues payments and had graduated strategies for dealing with free riders: an initial disciplinary action intended to put the offender on notice, probably followed by expulsion.[85] We should not automatically assume—and Paul does not—that those who did not contribute were too poor to do so. The author of 2 Thessalonians indeed assumes that they can work. Nonpayment of dues was an issue addressed in a number of association bylaws by means of adding fines, or disciplinary exclusion or even expulsion. What 2 Thess 3:6–15 reveals is that this Christ assembly, like other associations, had an interest in its own solvency and so devised means to ensure that its costs—meals, funerals, and other expenses—could be met by regular contribution of dues. Later, the author of Hermas would articulate a system of moral accounting according to which the wealthy with material resources should contribute to the poor, and the poor should reciprocate with prayer for the wealthier members in a system of quid pro quo exchange.[86]

To summarize what can be concluded of cultic associations and occupational guilds: These groups met often monthly, sometimes more frequently, and for simple food. They collected modest dues and in some cases accommodated members who could not pay as much as others. Contributions and service to the group were both expected and rewarded, since these were the ways to materialize belonging and commitment and to receive recognition. Contributions and/or rotating liturgies are both viable and plausible ways to imagine the funding of the meals of Christ groups.[87]

ARRIVING LATE FOR DINNER?

A common explanation of the problems at Corinth involves the scenario that some arrived at the banquet early and began to eat while others arrived late. The almost automatic assumption is that it must have been the poor who arrived late, and they did so because they had to work long hours, or as slaves they were not in control of their own time.[88]

These assumptions are curious, reflecting anachronistic views of Roman slavery, views of labor based on the organization of labor in post–Industrial Revolution societies, and modern conceptions of the "working poor" and the "idle rich." There is no a priori reason to suppose that the wealthier members of an ancient group would necessarily arrive earlier than poorer members.[89] Late arrival at a dinner is a literary trope and has little to do with distinctions between the poor and the rich. In Plato's *Symposium* Socrates arrives late for Agathon's dinner and is still given a seat (175C). In Lucian's *Symposium* 12–13 Alcidamas the Cynic arrives uninvited at a symposium, and since all the places at the *triclinium* are occupied, he is offered a place to sit rather than a bench on which to recline. Offended at the affront to his social status, he declares that he will take his dinner standing, "and if I get tired I'll lie on the floor, leaning on my elbow, with my cloak under me, like Herakles in the pictures they paint of him." The scenario that Luke paints in Luke 14:7–11 assumes that people of higher status sometimes arrived late and could displace others from their places.[90]

All these examples, however, concern occasional banquets, usually of the elite, not the routine meetings of associations comparable to the Christ group at Corinth. *None* of the association bylaws we know thought to comment on late arrival as an issue of concern. Associations often penalized absenteeism, probably because a "full table" was a way for a group to mark its importance, just as any elite householder aspired to having a well-visited house (*domus frequentata*).[91] While the twenty-first-century reader is aware of many excuses for late arrivals, as the result of being busy at the office or of slow traffic, subway delays, or childcare responsibilities, the ancient reader, attuned to the metrics of group honor, seems to have been more worried about absenteeism, since this endangered the honor of the group. Late arrival was evidently not an issue.

What of the assumption that long working hours would have prevented some members from arriving on time? This reflects a misconception of both the realities of labor among artisans and the organization of Roman domestic slavery. An important feature of the ancient economy was the reality of structural *underemployment*. This stands in contrast to post–Industrial Revolution tendencies toward the maximization of labor inputs and vertical integration of economic sectors. Structural features of both the ancient crafts from which, presumably, many of the Christ followers were drawn and the organization of the Roman household contributed not to full employment but to underemployment.

Underemployment is a basic feature of agrarian economies. In cities where many crafts were located, the combination of a high degree of specialization in crafts and the lack of vertical integration of industries led to structural underemployment. Harris observes that the building trades, for example, were highly specialized, with masons, sculptors, wax modelers, woodcarvers, carpenters, sawyers, joiners, lathe workers, painters, gilders, and other laborers all working under the direction of architects.[92] This naturally led to partial employment for many workers, since not all these workers could be active simultaneously. At the same time there was little vertical integration, meaning that those who produced raw materials (clay, wool, leather, etc.) were not directly involved in the industries that used these materials to produce ceramics, bricks, amphorae, shoes, textiles, and so forth.[93] Moreover, manufacture was often "bespoke," or made-to-order. This meant that just as in early modern Europe, artisans did not keep inventories of unsold goods but worked at the whim of the consumer—a system that produces periods of underemployment or even unemployment, punctuated by periods of frenetic activity.[94] The calendar of religious festivals also led to fluctuating demands for certain items (e.g., wreaths).

Even more important were seasonal alterations that affected many industries. Here one thinks of any trade dependent on maritime shipping, which was halted during the winter months. Industries connected with viticulture and textile production were dependent on the vintage, the flax harvest, and shearing seasons. The net result was that while at certain times some workers might have had little time to participate in club activities, at other times they would be able to banquet with their peers. Indeed, the fact that occupational guilds were extremely common suggests that onerous working conditions were not a major factor affecting workers' participation in guilds.

Nor is there any good reason to suppose that all domestic staff had to work long hours and were therefore obliged to arrive late at communal dinners. Slaves belonging to the household of a Christ follower would presumably arrive at the meal as part of the retinue of their owners; slaves serving as doorkeepers of an elite house might not arrive at all. Moreover, the high degree of differentiation within categories of labor in the Roman household inevitably led to underemployment. Treggiari notes that the domestic staff of Augustus's wife Livia had forty-six distinct posts and other imperial households had comparable numbers of jobs for slaves, freedmen, freedwomen, and freeborn artisans. Treggiari comments: "To us most of this will seem to mean conspicuous waste of the master's money and the slave's time. Many of the staff were under-employed. But the purpose of a large household was not to achieve economy or a fulfilling career for slaves; it was to keep the owner from an undignified reliance on outside plumbers, perfumers and cobblers and, most important for the ruler, to make a display."[95]

Treggiari's point is underscored by the jurists' distinction between slaves "who work" and "those who do not work" (*qui opus non facerent*),[96] that is, between those involved in rural work (*opus rusticum*) and those whose duties were to attend to their master or mistress. Saller, in agreement with Treggiari, but focusing on the work of female slaves, concludes "and if male slaves [in the household] were underemployed, the female slaves in their households were even probably more so."[97]

There is little reason to think that the pattern of underemployment of slaves in nonelite households was much different from that in elite households. Hence, the general point should be clear. In distinction to the function of domestic slaves in some early modern slave-owning societies, the Roman household did not aim at the rationalization or maximization of labor inputs by requiring slaves to work long hours. And as noted above, the proliferation of workers' guilds in the ancient world is testimony *against* the assumption that work was so onerous that attendance at the meetings of occupational guilds was impeded because of work. Were artisans systematically encumbered by long hours of work, there would have been no occupational guilds at all.

This produces a very different picture from what is imagined by exegetes of 1 Cor 11:17–34—of the poor, slaves, or handworkers delayed or prevented from attending a banquet of a Christ group because of their long hours of work. Some might have been impeded from time to time; but given the structure of labor, it is hardly likely that slaves or artisans were systemically impeded by reason of excessive labor. The slaves of SB 3:7182 evidently had no difficulty in attending their banquets.

READING THE CORINTHIAN MEAL

Communal meals were performances of fictive equality. They were also sites of intense competition, as is clear from association bylaws that routinely inveighed against stealing other members' seats, fighting, or calumniating another member and otherwise asserting privilege over another.[98] As John Donahue wryly notes, control of food is among the most effective means by which to underscore the difference between one person and another.[99] Fighting over food, moreover—even when the food is simple bread and wine—was a typical way of asserting individual privilege.

In order to account for 1 Cor 11:17–34 one does not need to imagine Theissen's scenario of elite patronage or Lampe's model of an *eranos* meal, neither of which has much evidence to commend it. Nor it is necessary to imagine the poor appearing late at the dinner, especially because Paul's scenario begins with a threefold assertion that the assembly has *already* come together (vv. 17, 18, 20). Whether the food for the "emperor's banquet" (*kyriakon deipnon*) was funded by member contributions or by rotating liturgies or both, the distribution of food and drink had become an issue—or at least Paul *thought* that it had become an issue.[100]

Food for the banquet would have been procured either by those whose liturgical responsibility it was to supply it (as in CIL 14.2112) or by those designated by the president to purchase and prepare it. At this point Paul's hyperbole and sarcasm obscure the situation. His assertion in 11:21 that "*each preferentially receives* his own dinner"[101] is a caricature, since it is logically impossible for everyone to receive preferentially. His point is to underscore the threat to collective values posed by individual performances of status. Continuing in the same sarcastic register, he describes the attendees of the banquet: "one (comes/is) hungry, another (comes/is) drunk."[102] The characterization of the meal as a "private meal" (*idion deipnon*) is likewise sarcastic.

Behind Paul's exaggerations and sarcasm one can glimpse what was occurring, however. Because the practice of differential allotment of food (and *sportulae*) to functionaries was widely known and, evidently, unproblematic, it is unlikely either that this was unknown to Paul or that it was particularly objectionable.[103] Moreover, if the Corinthian groups adopted the practice of a rotating "flat hierarchy," the net result would be the equal distribution of honors over time. Nor was the issue a debate over arithmetic rather than geometrical equality.[104] Instead, the issue that most commonly affected associative life was the problem, voiced by Plutarch's character Lamprias, of people at banquets "seizing the portions of another, and unjust greed in regard to what (should be) in common" (*Quaest. conv.* 244C). Seen in the context of the rule-based dining practices of associations, Paul in effect caricatures the problem at Corinth as the consequence of not adhering to the group's own rules. Depending on how one reads 11:21, either some "come" to the meal hungry or drunk, or hunger and drunkenness are the result of the meal. On the first reading some, through a lack of attention to the rules, claim hunger and eat more than they should with the result that their greed shames those who otherwise would receive their portion. Some come drunk and misbehave, a problem that was routinely addressed in association rules. On the second scenario, the overconsumption (greed) of some left others without their portion, while others consumed more wine than rules allowed. It is impossible to decide between these two scenarios, and perhaps pointless, since Paul is caricaturing and exaggerating the problem in order to underscore what he sees as a ritual failure: the communal meal has dissolved into a series of private meals.

This is not, as some suggest, because the Corinthian group was still in its infancy and had not yet established a stable discipline.[105] Rather, this was simply a common and nearly ubiquitous feature of association meals, which were, as indicated above, simultaneously sites of the performance of equality and sites of intense competition. The allotment of food and drink was ideally rule-based, whether it authorized certain people to receive more during their periods of service or whether it insisted on absolute arithmetic equality.[106] But the fact that association bylaws typically had to devise ways to manage conflict indicates that competition over status was also common.

Paul's point is that the common interests (*ta koina*) or "the body" (*to sōma*), as he puts it, should prevail over individual assertion and competition. For to do otherwise is not to "discern the body." As elsewhere in 1 Corinthians, collective values are to prevail over individual assertion.

It is unfortunate that we do not have a "1 Corinthians" for a few Greek or Roman cultic associations in which writers complain that their banquets are not always sites of the harmony and solidarity that the rule intended but were infected with destructive competition. Plutarch's *Quaestiones conviviales* perhaps provides something of a glimpse, although he is describing elite banquets, not the meals of associations. We also do not have for Pauline groups what association charters and account books provide—a detailed way in which banquets were funded and managed, details on how much meals cost, and prescriptions about how food and drink were distributed or at least how distributions were supposed to occur. Yet the things we do possess—literary texts from Christ assemblies and epigraphic and papyrological evidence from multiple associations—tell similar stories, but from different perspectives and in different genres. The banquets of Christ groups and cultic associations were communal meals where members dined with, or at the invitation of, their deities and where they materialized a sense of belonging and "groupness." Ideally, they were sites for the performance of equality among members who were excluded from participation in elite culture. They did not always succeed in materializing a sense of equality among members, but they functioned in this way sometimes. That was much of their attraction.

8

The Collection

A second example of fiscal management about which we have useful comparative data concerns the "collection for the poor of the saints of Jerusalem" mentioned at several points in Paul's letters.[1] With a few exceptions the analysis of Paul's collection has been conducted without attention to the financial practices known from the Greek and Roman world.[2] If any analogies are adduced at all, it is usually the didrachma tax imposed on Judean males or collections for the poor mentioned in later rabbinic literature.[3] Yet the collection, maintenance, and distribution of communal funds were extremely common throughout the ancient Mediterranean world, and many of the practical issues that Paul's groups had to face find close parallels in other small groups and in the administration of Hellenistic poleis.

I do not intend to suggest that Hellenistic practices "influenced" the collection for the poor. It would be impossible to demonstrate such a genealogical relationship in any case, short of Paul indicating that he was imitating the financial practices of Corinth or Thessaloniki or the temple tax, which of course, he does not do. Nevertheless, the practices current in Greek cities will alert us to the issues that were at stake in collections and the problems that they generated. Knowledge of those practices and problems will help us to see the Pauline collection in a different light, to understand better his statements about the collection, and in fact to raise questions about it that would have occurred to most ancient Greeks but have not occurred to exegetes of Pauline literature. As always, my interests are heuristic not genealogical, and I do not want to fall into the apologetic trap of deciding where Paul's primary "influences" lay.

It is uncontroversial that the Corinthians had written to Paul inquiring about the collection and that 1 Cor 16:1–4 is his responses to their questions.[4] But oddly, it has been common to suppose that the Corinthians were unpracticed in collecting funds and accordingly inquired as to how to organize the collection. Thus Conzelmann concludes that "there is obviously as yet no organized system of finance. Not even a collection at the service or worship is envisaged, if each is to 'lay by him in store' his own contributions."[5] Downs argues similarly: "In fact, Paul's instructions regarding the organization of the contribution for Jerusalem in 1 Cor 16:1–4 seem to imply that the congregation of his mission in Galatia and Corinth did not regularly administer funds."[6]

Yet it infantalizes the Corinthians to suppose that they were somehow so naive that they needed instructions on how to collect funds. As will become clear, we have epigraphic evidence from Achaia, the Isthmus, and the Peloponnese that groups of handworkers and resident aliens in those areas—that is, precisely the kinds of people who made up the majority of Pauline groups—had been engaged in collecting funds for at least four hundred years before Paul arrived in Corinth and that special collections of the sort in which Paul was engaged are particularly well known. Besides, the idea of collecting money for a common project is hardly a conceptually challenging notion. We scarcely need to suppose that Christ groups who wanted to assemble special collections needed either outside models or detailed instructions from Paul.

The issues for the Corinthians and about which they expressed concern in their letter to Paul were not how to collect funds but instead flowed from the basic dynamics of fiscal management and from the fact that these funds were being collected for a nonlocal group, the *ekklēsia* in Jerusalem. These factors naturally raised the questions of how to ensure that such funds collected for that purpose would be delivered to their intended recipients and how an accounting of the full amount would be guaranteed. That is, the concern that the Corinthians expressed derived not from not knowing how to collect money, but from the anomalous nature of the collection and the peculiar fiscal problems that such a collection presented.

Three features common to collective fiscal practices will help us to gain some insight into Pauline collection: the management of common funds with special interest in security, the according of due recognition for largesse, and the ideology at work in such collections.

COLLECTIONS FOR COMMON PURPOSES

The Pauline collection, insofar as it was a collection assembled from multiple individual contributors, from contributors located in multiple cities, to be delivered to people in yet another city, has several potential points of contact with various financial practices known in the Greek world. Since Paul's collection involved funds raised from many cities and delivered to what those in Jerusalem might have regarded as the central or dominant Christ assembly, the most obvious analogies are the Greek federal states called *koina*, in which individual poleis paid taxes to a common fund at their *koinon* headquarters.

During the Hellenistic period, federated cites were common. On mainland Greece and the Peloponnese about 40 percent of poleis belonged to a *koinon*.[7] In Asia, thirty-six cities of Lycia were likewise organized into a *koinon* that acted as a federal state issuing decrees and making alliances on behalf of member poleis, with a central *koinon* sanctuary at Letoön and an oracle of Apollo at Patara.[8] In some *koina* the member cities paid taxes to support common military needs, and some contributed funds in support of a central sanctuary.

Despite the possible analogy between the financial practices of Greek *koina* and Paul's collection, however, there are very significant differences. In the first place, *koina* were normally constructed on the basis of cities in contiguous regions where it made sense to foster interregional trade and to have common military interests. Some *koina* looked to a common eponymous ancestor and maintained a common central sanctuary. Both factors make it difficult to argue that the *koinon* model has much salience in our case, since the Greek cities in Macedonia and Achaea were scarcely contiguous with Judea either geographically or culturally. Although one might argue that the common acceptance of the Christ cult by the assemblies in Judea, Macedonia, and Achaia was analogous to cities in a *koinon* having a common founding mythology, it is hardly the case that Jerusalem or the Christ assembly there functioned like a common central sanctuary. It is conceivable that those in Jerusalem might have *thought* of their Christ group as preeminent and as the founding site of the Christ cult and therefore deserving of recognition; but that is not how Paul regarded the matter, even though in Romans 15 (writing to those who had not been involved in the collection at all) he cast the collection as a kind of exchange between gentile assemblies with material resources and Jerusalem and its "spirit resources" (15:27). In his correspondence with the contributing assemblies he framed the collection not as an exchange but rather as relief for the poor (Gal 2:10) and as a matter of euergetism (2 Cor 8–9). Nowhere does Paul treat the collection as a one-sided payment of gentile *ekklēsia* to a central or founding group.

The practice of Judean diasporic assemblies collecting funds for the support of the temple in Jerusalem could be seen as a variation on the *koinon* model.[9] Since it involved the collection and transportation of funds from throughout the Roman Empire to Jerusalem, it can be seen as a partial analogy to Paul's collection. We know relatively little about how this collection was organized, apart from the facts that collections seem to have been organized at the level of cities and that imperial edicts tried to protect their transport to Jerusalem.[10]

There is no way to know whether either Paul or the Jerusalem group (or both) had the synagogue collections in mind in conceiving the collection for the poor. In any event, the gentile groups that participated in Paul's project likely would know nothing of the practices of Hellenistic synagogues, and Paul never presented the collection to them in those terms. Moreover, the Pauline collection was presented as support, not for a central sanctuary or for the provision of sacrifices but for the "poor" in the Jerusalem group.[11]

EPIDOSEIS (SUBSCRIPTIONS)

A better analogy to the Pauline collection is the *epidosis* (plural: *epidoseis*), or subscription, a fiscal practice widely attested in the Greek East in both cities and private associations.[12] This rarely had a translocal aspect to it, but like the Pauline collection an *epidosis* was assembled from multiple individual contributors in support of a common project.

Public subscriptions are known from Athens, other parts of Greece, the Aegean islands, Asia Minor, Cyrenaica, Sicily, and Egypt and from the fourth century BCE to well into the imperial period.[13] They were used for a variety of purposes: for the construction or repair of city walls, sanctuaries, and public buildings; for the support of sacrifices, religious festivals, or games; for the purchase of grain in times of shortage; for ransom to pay for the return of prisoners and victims of piracy; and for the purchase of oil for the gymnasium. These normally were not ongoing collections but were raised for special needs. As Chaniotis observes, Greek cities had relatively sophisticated fiscal systems in place to take care of routine expenses, but for less predictable expenses they turned either to external assistance (loans from foreign benefactors) or to contributions from citizens and foreign residents in the form of "organized contributions (*epidoseis*), and voluntary donations (*dōreai, euergesiai*)."[14] The (yearly?) collections undertaken by Hellenistic synagogues thus resembled in some respects the *epidoseis* of Greek cities but were imagined as ongoing projects.

An inscription from Cos (III BCE) concerning funds for the repair of a temple is unusually helpful for illuminating the mechanism for the collection of funds:

> (*front face*) When Philotas was *monarchos* . . . Theugenes son of Hekatodoros proposed (the following motion).
>
> Four men shall be elected in order that, when the money has been secured, the work that remains on the temple of Apollo may be carried out quickly and

> the complete work on the roof and the door may not be in danger of being spoiled through further delay; and in order that not only the city may be seen to have been actively involved in construction of the temple but also the god from the funds that he has, and individuals willing to make pledges for this purpose, the rites in the shrine may be conducted with more magnificence on completion of the temple; for good fortune, let it be decided that the *neōpoiai* (temple managers) shall pay 2000 drachmae to the men elected (to administer) the funds of the god and that individuals from among members of the deme and the other citizens and resident aliens who are willing shall pledge (*epaggeilasthai*) no less than 30 drachmae for the construction of the temple; they should make the pledge within a year at the meetings which occur in the deme, beginning with the month of Dalios in the term of Philotas and they should make the payments of the money to the men elected in three installments, paying the first straightaway after the making of the pledge, the next within six months, and the remaining one in the same way. And in order that there may be a record [. . .]
>
> (*back face*) [. .] until the sums pledged are paid and the decree is passed by the city. When the works have been completed, if any money remains from the payments, it shall be handed over by the men in whose term they are paid to the *napoiai* [i.e., *neōpoiai*] who are in office. (SEG 50:1050; Cos, III BCE)[15]

The repair of the temple needed extraordinary funds, and rather than solicit these funds from a wealthy patron, the polis decided that a public subscription was useful. Not only citizens but *metics* were invited to participate. The process was clear: prospective contributors would "promise" (*epaggeilasthai*) amounts in their regular deme meetings and then pay that amount in three installments over the course of a year. The minimum contribution was set at 30 drachmae, with no maximum. Parker and Obbink note that this amount was the price on the island of Cos of a full-grown sheep and thus not beyond the means of anyone with at least a modest income.[16] At the conclusion of the process, a record could be drawn up and the total amount could be handed over to those charged with the repair of the temple. Like many other subscriptions, this *epidosis* was structured in such a way as to obtain maximal participation by citizens of Cos and other residents there.

Without a maximum allowable donation, a donor's promise of a contribution could be occasion for theatricality, affording wealthier donors the opportunity to display their largesse (and for the miserly to be publicly heckled).[17] This type of *epidosis* allowed individual donors to gain considerable symbolic capital, especially when donations were coupled with such epigraphic practices as highlighting the name of the first to contribute,[18] arranging the contributions in descending order by the amount contributed, or flushing the amounts to the right margin of the inscription, making it easy to compare one donor with another.[19]

Yet other practices are attested that had the effect of rendering status less visible. Some *epidoseis* set a minimum *and* a maximum contribution, thus preventing the superrich from outshining those with more modest resources.[20] The arranging of the list simply in the order in which the contributions arrived[21] or listing of names in alphabetical order[22] also had a leveling effect. A few *epidoseis* had contributors all give the same—usually quite small—amount.[23] An *epidosis* from Tanagra (Boeotia) raised in order to relocate the sanctuary of Demeter and Kore has ninety-five donors—all women—with all but the last six contributing 5 drachmae.[24] Eleven of the eighteen contributors to the renovation of a Judean assembly building in Berenikē (Cyrenaica) in 56 CE contributed 10 drachmae, and a further four (including two women) gave 5.[25] In contrast to the practice of variable contributions, which made visible status differences, these more communitarian practices, as Ellis-Evans observes, rendered less visible "the vast disparities of wealth and power that characterized *polis* life . . . and the succession of similar sounding sums suggested to the audience that the act of giving, rather than the amount given, was what mattered."[26]

Contributions were elicited not only from citizens, but from resident aliens and even foreigners. An *epidosis* inscription from Cos calls on contributions from all: "It was resolved: those who wish to promise (to contribute), citizens, women citizens, bastards, resident aliens, and foreigners (should do so)" (I.CosPH 10; 202/201 BCE).[27] In the early second century CE, a project to beautify Erythrai (or perhaps Smyrna) attracted contributions from citizens as well as from a group called "those formerly of Judea" (*hoi pote Ioudaioi*), evidently not citizens, who had collectively raised 1,000 drachmae.[28]

As noted in connection with SEG 50:1050 cited above, the use of the verb *epaggellesthai* is noteworthy since it points to the practice of the contributor "announcing" or "promising" the value of his or her contribution and then at some point in the future delivering it. The gap between promise and fulfillment—the latter marked with such verbs as *syntelō* (complete) or *apodidonai* (pay)—accounts for the repeated phrases such as one finds in an *epidosis* inscription from Lindos: "They promised (*epaggeilanto*) to give freely of their money . . . and they kept their promise (*synetelesan*) according to what they had promised" (I.Lindos II 252.3, 6). Those who reneged on their promises were remembered, and as a speech in Isaeus shows, their names might be inscribed on a list of defaulters.[29] Both the public display of contributor lists and the display of defaulters underscores the social capital that was generated (or lost) through *epidoseis*.

Although many of the known *epidoseis* were used in order to fund building projects or in times of military need, there is good evidence that they were also collected for the purchase of grain in times of shortage, which is presumably what was intended in Paul's collection for the "poor."[30] An interesting example comes from Iasos, a fragmentary *epidosis* that shows one larger contribution and then a series of smaller ones, with the intent of creating a permanent endowment to supply grain in times of shortage:

> These, wishing from their own free will to reinforce democracy from their own resources, have contributed funds for the purchase of grain so that the *demos* will always live happily, having an abundance of grain, with all the citizens having a supply of grain from the common fund, in accordance with decree. Menesthenes son of Klean, from his own resources and for his son Kleanax gave 600 drachmae; Phanyllos . . . from his own resources and for his son . . . 200 drachmae; . . . son of Nemertes. . . . (I.Iasos 244; Iasos, mid-II BCE)[31]

Klean and Kleanax, who contributed 600 drachmae, were probably afforded the first position on the donor list, but after them the contributions decline in size. Since it is impossible to know the original dimensions of the stone, we cannot know how many contributors were listed and whether this Iasean *epidosis* achieved its goal of an endowment whose interest could supply grain to the city. What is noteworthy—and a topic to which I shall return—is the connection that the inscription makes between citizen and noncitizen contributions and the support of democracy.

Associations also organized *epidoseis* for special projects such as the building of a temple or the purchase or repair of a necropolis.[32] Since one of the advantages that an association offered to its members was burial, it is unsurprising to find on Rhodes an *epidosis* inscription that records the contributions of members toward the purchase of land for a communal necropolis. The association bears the rather grandiose title of the Samothracian *Aristobouliastai Hermaistai Panathenaistai:* "In the year that Nikasagoras was priest, the following members (*eranistai*) agreed to enhance the association (*eranos*) by promising (*epaggeilanto*) to contribute freely money to purchase this place (cemetery) and they (in fact) paid (*apedōkan*)" (SEG 39:737; Rhodes, 172/170 BCE).[33] What follows is a complete list of thirty-six donors, the first three contributing 105, 205, and 280 drachmae; five more giving 20–50 drachmae; and the remaining twenty-five each giving 5 drachmae. The two critical stages in the *epidosis*, "promise" (*epaggeilanto*) and "payment" (*apedōkan*), are marked in the inscription. In this case the association was able to report full participation in the subscription.

Given the frequency with which *epidoseis* occurred not only in Greek cities, but in small cultic and diasporic associations and the ways in which they were publicly advertised, it would be difficult to suppose that the Corinthian Christ assembly was unaware of how to take up a collection. Although one need not suppose that the Pauline collection directly borrowed the practice of subscriptions, it is clear that the subscriptions of Greek cities and associations were similar to the Pauline collection in several respects. First, the advice Paul gives in 1 Cor 16:1–4 suggests that he imagines the collection to involve most or all of the Corinthians. His advice is addressed to "each of you" to set money aside (16:2) and in that sense is aimed at the same full level of participation that *epidoseis* also hoped to achieve and that some did achieve. Second, like the Coan *epidosis* cited above, the collection would take at least a year to accumulate, which also seems to presume that many donors could not afford to give the entire amount pledged on the spot. Hence, Paul's advice that "every first of the week each of you should set aside whatever is to the good" (16:2). And third, in 1 Corinthians 16 but especially in 2 Corinthians 8 and 9 Paul was acutely aware of the gap between initiating the collection and bringing it to completion, something that is clearly underscored also in the stereotypical language of "promise" and "completion" in the *epidosis* inscriptions. These marked similarities of Paul's collection with *epidoseis* will assist us in thinking about other aspects of Paul's collection, where it can be shown that several of the problems he encountered were also fundamental to the voluntary collections of Greek cities and associations.

MANAGEMENT, SECURITY, AND AUDIT

One of the most commonly recurring elements in private association inscriptions pertaining to the management of funds is the insistence on adequate audit procedures. A single example will suffice. In early-second-century CE Attica, an association of *Herakleiastai* whose activities included sacrifices and banquets was funded through an endowment, the purchase of priesthoods, entrance fees, and member contributions.[34] The treasurer was enjoined not to expend more than 300 drachmae on dinners;[35] if he did, he would incur a fine of three times the sum in excess of 300 drachmae (lines 13–15). A former treasurer, if he were discovered though audit to have purloined funds for his own use, would be subject to a similar fine (lines 15–16). Those deputed to purchase wine and meat for the banquets who did not deliver the goods were to be fined twice the value of what they were to supply. The treasurer was required to provide an account of his income and expenses, and auditors were appointed to scrutinize this:

> Likewise, when the treasurer provides an accounting, after a meeting (30) has been called, they shall appoint three auditors and the auditors shall swear by Herakles and Demeter and Korē . . . (40). And let the account be closed when the auditors, having taken an oath, return the accounts to the *archeranistēs*, and indicate whether the treasurer owes anything. (SEG 31:122, lines 29–30, 40 = GRA I 50; trans. AGRW 9)

Each of these regulations points to a deep concern that an association's funds would be secured against theft and misuse. That careful auditing of the work of the treasurers and secretaries and scrutiny of their accounts were normal practices in associations is indicated by the frequency with which former treasurers and secretaries are commended "on account of their honesty (*dikaiosynē*)."[36] Concern about the disposition and integrity of common funds was simply a standard part of associative life.

Very few data are available on just how private associations assembled members' contributions. Our ignorance of associations is perhaps due to the fact that because the procedure for receiving contributions was self-evident to them and entirely unproblematic, the available inscriptions and papyri tell us nothing. Contributions might have been presented in some ritualized form or simply delivered to the secretary or treasurer at each meeting or at some specified time during the month. What is abundantly clear is that associations kept careful records of contributions, endowments, extraordinary gifts, fines, and other income, as the following two inscriptions illustrate:

> The dues (*phora*) must be brought to the treasurer (so that) loans can be made. Whoever does not pay shall be fined a double amount. Whoever does not pay at all shall be expelled from the association (*exeranos*). (SEG 31:122 = GRA I 50: a synod of *Herakleiastai*)

> None of the Iobakchoi who has not paid (the contributions) for either the meetings on the ninth (of the month) or the annual festival is permitted to enter into the gathering, until it has been decided by the priests whether he should pay the fee or be allowed to enter (anyway). (IG II^2 1368 = GRA I 51: the Iobakchoi of Athens)

Although the exact procedure for the payment of dues is not described, the two-stage penal procedure of SEG 31:122 suggests that there was a point at which payment was expected and that after some period of grace, free riders were expelled.[37] IG II^2 1368 suggests that in this case dues were expected before the monthly meetings and yearly festival and that records were kept so that free riders could be identified and prohibited from participation.[38] Egyptian club accounts—P.Petr III 136, SB 3:7182, P.Tebt III/2 894, P.Tebt I 118, P.Tebt I 177, and P.Tebt I 224, for example—illustrate the careful bookkeeping practices of various associations, documenting income from dues, members who had paid in full, members who were in arrears, members who were dues-exempt (*asymbolos*), and the expenses incurred for each banquet.

There is no reason to suppose that the Corinthians were any less invested in the solvency of their group or the management and security of funds that they collected. In the case of the funds used for normal operations—the providing of monthly or weekly banquets—procedures presumably were in place analogous to what are widely reported in other associations.

As soon as the collection from each of the Pauline assemblies had been completed and assembled into a larger fund, a special problem presented itself: how to ensure that the funds intended for the assembly in Jerusalem would reach their destination. This is not an issue that naturally arose from *epidoseis* since the monies collected in one city or association were spent locally. The typical concerns of associations about financial propriety, however, help us to see what was at stake in 1 Cor 16:1–4.

Paul's comments concern the securing of the collection against theft and misappropriation, the delivery instructions, and the issue of due acknowledgment. Paul addresses two critical topics in 16:3: first, he assures the Corinthians that the collection will be delivered by *hous ean dokimasēte*, "those whom you approve"; then he indicates that they will travel with a letter from him, presumably explaining the collection, its sources, and its intended recipients.

As is obvious in the case of funds that are being transported to a different locale from where they are raised, there was a danger of loss and misappropriation. For this reason, envoys *approved* by the Corinthian group would assume responsibility for the honest conveyance of the collection. The term Paul uses, *dokimazō*, is well attested in both civic and association contexts, signifying the vetting of prospective citizens, candidates for office, and candidates for membership in an association to ensure that they are worthy and reliable.[39] The point for Paul is that honorable and reliable envoys *of the Corinthians' choosing* will deliver the collection. Hence, Holmberg's comment apropos of the description of the entourage in Acts 20:6, which included representatives from Beroia, Thessaloniki, Derbe, and Asia, that "Paul's churches, represented by an (*unnecessarily*) large delegation of Gentile Christians" fundamentally misses the point of such a delegation.[40] Each Christ group that had contributed had a stake in guaranteeing that *their* funds would be secure from theft and fraud and would be delivered to the intended recipients.[41]

An additional indication that the security of the collection was at stake, both for the Corinthians and for Paul, is Paul's phrasing in Rom 15:28: "having completed this [the collection] and having certified (or authenticated) this 'fruit' for them [i.e., the Corinthians]." The use of *sphragizō* underscores the importance of a formal authentication or "sealing" of the gift that Jerusalem is to receive. The verb, found often in connection with the delivery of letters or the production of copies of documents, carried with it a nuance that care has been taken to guard against fraud and deception.[42]

This also implies that *all* the funds collected would have to be accounted for at some point. Commenting on Acts 20:4, Munck assumes that part of the collection would have been used to defray traveling expenses.[43] This may be so, but if we were to assume that the fiscal procedures employed here were the same as those employed in the case of the movement of other envoys, a strict limit would be placed on how much of the collection, if any, could be expended for travel. More likely, if we take seriously analogous situations where envoys of one group or city traveled to make a petition or otherwise interacted with authorities elsewhere, they would have traveled "at their own expense" (*ek tōn idiōn*).[44] In this way the full amount of the collection would reach Jerusalem and receive a proper accounting when the envoys returned.

The second issue raised in 1 Cor 16:1–4 concerns Paul's own role in the collection. Paul, at least at the time of 1 Corinthians, underscores that he is diffident as to whether he will even go to Jerusalem. For this reason, a letter of introduction would be essential to ensure the delivery of the collection, for if Paul were to accompany it, no such letter would be needed. But his conditional statement, "but if it should be suitable for me also to go [to Jerusalem], they [the envoys] will travel with me" (16:4) and the diffidence he expresses are ways to signal that he would not be in a position to misappropriate the collection, either because he might not be going to Jerusalem at all or because in any case he would be accompanied by those whose task it was to guarantee the proper delivery of the collection.

Hence, Paul's comments in 1 Cor 16:1–4 have nothing to do with the Corinthians' inexperience in collecting money, either for themselves or for some other purpose. Instead, their questions reflect the typical concerns that arose in virtually all associations concerning financial propriety. Paul's statements are intended to assure the Corinthians that their contributions will not fail to arrive in Jerusalem and that Paul himself, even though he had initiated the collection, does not stand to benefit financially from this enterprise.

RECOGNITION OF LARGESSE

A consistent feature of Greek donative inscriptions is that due recognition of the benefactor or patron was essential. This was simply part of the nature of exchange, whereby a patron or group of benefactors provided a benefit to the polis or to an association and the polis or association in turn recognized this largesse in some kind of public form. This type of exchange provided benefits to the polis or association and symbolic capital to the donor or donors.[45]

There is plenty of evidence that the recognition of largesse was critical. A standard provision in an honorific decree was the requirement that the supervisor or secretary of the association arrange for the crowning of those who had demonstrated largesse and that crowning be announced, usually at the next meeting. This was not simply a matter of acknowledging benefactors but also of acknowledging *piety* toward the gods. For example, an inscription from Athens:

> In order that the *orgeōnes* be seen to be honoring those who benefact the gods and themselves, the *orgeōnes* have agreed to commend Sarapion son of Poseidonios of Herakleia, and to crown him with an olive wreath and a woolen fillet, which is in accord with ancestral custom, on account of the piety (*eusebeia*) that he has shown to the gods; and further, that the secretary and the supervisor shall announce the crowning along with the other (honors) following the libations in the temple. If they should fail to make the announcement or to crown him, they will be fined 50 drachmae, sacred to Aphroditē. This decree shall be inscribed on a stele and erected in the temple. (AM 66:228 no. 4 = GRA I 39; Athens 138/137 BCE)[46]

A Roman benefactor of a group of *Poseidoniastai* on Delos in the mid-second century BCE was likewise honored and allowed to set up a bust with the honorific inscription in the compound, "or in whatever other place he may decide, except for the *naos* or the *pronaos*" (ID 1520.24–26). The decree then threatened with a large fine anyone who attempted to remove the bust or alter the decree (lines 56–66).

The need for such proscriptions points both to the critical importance that public recognition of benefactors played in the economy of benefaction and to the agonistic culture of antiquity, where honors for one person might be imagined as coming at the expense of a competitor. Even in the case of *epidoseis*, where the names of those who contributed very small sums to a common project were recorded, it was important that all donors be named and thus receive credit for their contributions. The idea that collections taken up for a temple or for some public good or contributions to an association for the building of their clubhouse or the repairs to their cemetery would come without the names of the contributors, even if they had given only a few denarii, would have struck everyone as odd and even ungrateful.[47] Hence we find *epidoseis* like IG II^{2} 2332 with its more than four hundred names, each person contributing 5 or 10 drachmae, or smaller *epidoseis* for the purchase of a Rhodian necropolis (see above) with the names of its thirty-three donors. Largesse recorded was largesse recognized; unrecorded largesse was not only pointless but bordered on impiety.

Given the normal expectations of some form of reciprocity in acts of benefaction, I suggest that the point of Paul's undertaking in 1 Cor 16:3, that he would send approved Corinthians to convey *their* gift, not be missed. The critical part of this sentence is *tēn charin hymōn*, "your gift"—for from the point of view of the Corinthian donors, it was as essential as it was for Ephesian, Athenian, or Coan contributors that the source of their gift be acknowledged. The presence of envoys from each Christ group would guarantee that due credit for the gift would be recorded.

We therefore should imagine that when the envoys arrived in Jerusalem, they carried not only coin, but a parchment list of the names of those who had contributed or at the very least the names of each of the gentile groups involved, and perhaps even the amounts each contributed.[48] Paul, as it would turn out, was also positioned to gain significant social capital from *hē diakonia mou* (my service), as he calls it in Rom 15:31, since he was acting as a broker of a benefit and, at least as far as the Jerusalem group was concerned, as a partner fulfilling his part of an agreement.[49] But that should not obscure the likelihood that each of the Christ groups represented by the collection would expect to be credited as well.

THE IDEOLOGY OF PUBLIC SUBSCRIPTIONS

Epidoseis were powerful tools of social formation because they called not just upon the wealthy but upon all residents—citizens, *metics*, and even foreigners—to contribute to a common project and thus to "perform" their membership in the polis.

Civic identity in Greek cities was constructed in a variety of ways, such as through participation in festivals, dramatic performances, and processions. In the Hellenistic and Roman periods acts that benefited the city became conspicuous ways to perform citizenship. It is not difficult to see how the value of cooperation built into polis ideology could be mobilized in support of collective actions on behalf of the polis, in particular in the practice of the *epidosis* as a performance of citizenship. Hence, I.Iasos 244 (see above) could claim that participation in an *epidosis* amounts to a support of democracy. Insofar as *metics* and foreigners were also called upon to support the city, the *epidosis* was also a performance of those virtues intimately connected to civic identity. Ellis-Evans puts it this way:

> Public subscriptions sought to encourage members of the *polis* community to reproduce civic values by publicly acting them out. Through the serialization of communitarian acts of generosity, both the initial performance and the subsequent epigraphic monumentalization promoted a specific set of values as normative for the inhabitants of a *polis*. Since, in the political imaginary of the *polis* of Tanagra, the women of Tanagra should be particularly concerned for the temple of Demeter and Kore, the *polis* makes them act out this ideal when it holds a public subscription. Because *polis* ideology imagines that all parts of the population, citizen or otherwise, would want to defend their home, at the Koan war subscription we witness otherwise politically disfranchised individuals, who would usually be passive observers or altogether absent from a subscription, making contributions alongside citizens. The reverential place allotted to the man who promises first romantically imagines the surge of emotion a wealthy patriot feels when a subscription is announced.[50]

Epidoseis, insofar as they frequently received contributions from noncitizens and in a few instances solicited contributions *exclusively* from noncitizens,[51] served as ways for *metics* and foreigners to demonstrate their commitment to the polis. Such service brought with it the reasonable expectation that the polis would reciprocate, sometimes with the conferral of the title *euergetēs* (benefactor) or with exemption from *metic* taxes, and more rarely, a grant of citizenship.[52]

Public subscriptions, then, simultaneously mobilized the value of cooperation and civic pride that was part of Greek society and the competitive instinct for honor. An example of cooperation and competition functioning together is provided by an Athenian *epidosis* inscription that commends a certain Apollas son of Tharrhymon, a noncitizen from Sikyon in the northern Peloponnese, for having contributed to an Athenian *epidosis* "without having been asked" and for having contributed *first*. He also gave the *most* that was allowed by the terms of the *epidosis*. Thus Apollas is said to have "*competed* with the citizens."[53] The function of the inscription is obvious: to commend a foreigner for exemplary behavior but also to stir Athenians to action, provoked by civic pride and competition for honor.[54]

Public subscriptions thus served multiple functions: they afforded those without sufficient financial resources to be individual benefactors the opportunity to participate collectively in acts of benefaction. *Epidoseis* allowed contributors, whether citizens or *metics*, to perform their loyalty to the polis, and in the case of nonresidents, to achieve through reciprocity closer affiliation with the polis. These subscriptions simultaneously engaged cooperation and competition and allowed for a spectrum of practices, from those that blatantly encouraged agonistic competition among the wealthy and powerful to other forms that intentionally masked status differences and created a model in which communal ideals took precedence over competition for honors. Yet even in the latter form, competition resided not in *how much* one contributed but in *whether* one contributed, since it was immediately known who did and who did not contribute. Extraordinary contributions by *metics* and foreigners stood out in particular.

Epidoseis mounted by private associations functioned analogously, to allow members, irrespective of their resources, to materialize their membership in the group by supporting a common project. Given the record-keeping propensities of associations, contributors would know that their contributions would be noted, whether through the erection of a stele that recorded their names, a record within the group's archives, or simply an announcement at the next meeting.

THE PAULINE COLLECTION AND THE FISCAL PRACTICES OF GREEK POLEIS

What have these fiscal practices to do with the Pauline collection, and how might the model of *epidosis* cast some light on Paul's situation?

First, the *epidosis* offers an analogy for a community-based fund-raising project rather than a model based on the largesse of the elite. While some *epidoseis* imposed no upper limit on contributions and thus allowed for theatrical offers by the elite—thus making these *epidoseis* a site of the performance of status—others limited the contributions and even restricted them to a given, usually very modest, sum, thus taking the focus from status display and placing it on communal benefaction. Since Paul evidently could not rely on elite benefactors to contribute large sums, a more "democratic" practice like that of the *epidosis* commended itself as a viable model. Moreover, the *epidosis* of SEG 50:1050 allowed for amortized contributions, dividing even the relatively modest sum of 30 drachmae into three installments spread over a year (see above). Paul clearly has something like this in mind in 1 Cor 16:2.

Second, I have suggested above that envoys mentioned in 1 Cor 16:3 had the role not only of guaranteeing the delivery of the collection against theft and misappropriation, but also, in keeping with the dynamics of an *epidosis*, of ensuring that credit was given to those who had contributed. This would be entirely in accord with donative practices in the Greek world, as anonymous donations had not yet become a cultural practice. Whether credit took the form of a list of the names of individual contributors, comparable to many of the *epidosis* lists that we have, or a list of the assemblies that had contributed is a matter of speculation; both forms of lists are attested.[55]

Third, the gap between promise and delivery troubled Paul, as it did the organizers of public subscriptions. Nothing in the tone of Paul's letter in 1 Cor 16:1–4 suggests that the Corinthians rejected the proposal for a collection out of hand; instead, they were concerned with the details of its security and delivery. Whether they had already "promised" certain sums before the writing of 1 Corinthians is unknowable. But by the time of 2 Corinthians 8, Paul seems to have feared that the collection had broken down; hence, his rhetoric in this letter is to encourage the collection, which was also the point of sending Titus and "the brother" to Corinth to complete it.[56] Even later, in 2 Corinthians 9,[57] Paul says that he has boasted that the Corinthian collection was complete "since last year," although it is clear from his anxiety that he is unsure that this was the case.

Given the fact that *epidoseis* employed peer pressure and the possibility of the public shaming of those who refused to contribute as motivations for action,[58] Paul's statement in 2 Cor 9:4 is unexceptional: he threatens in a not-too-subtle way that the imminent arrival of Macedonians in Corinth who have contributed will put to shame Corinthians who have not. Paul here is relying on the agonistic instincts of his addressees and an appeal to civic pride.[59] He did not have the option of a threat of the public shaming of noncontributors by placing the names of deadbeats on a public list. Instead, he conjures a scenario of the humiliation of himself and the Corinthian noncontributors upon the Macedonians' arrival in Corinth. No public inscription would be cut, but in the small face-to-face world of associations and *ekklēsiai* all would know who had contributed and who had not.

While there are obvious similarities between the *epidoseis* of Greek cities and Greek associations on one hand and the Pauline collection on the other, there are at least three important differences. First, we have no evidence of any *epidosis* organized for the benefit of residents of a city or members of an association other than that of the donors themselves. There is of course evidence that noncitizens might support the collection of a city, as in the case of the "former residents of Judea" contributing to a civic project in Erythrai or Apollas of Sikyon contributing to an Athenian *epidosis* (see above). But the beneficiaries of an *epidosis* were normally the residents of the city who had contributed, not some distant city or its residents.

Second, it is also true that *epidoseis* were not normally framed as relief for "the poor" (*ptōchoi*). It is widely acknowledged that support for the poor qua poor is likely the result of transformations that occurred in late antiquity.[60] The idea of a special collection for the *ptōchoi* probably would have struck many Greeks as a curiously counterintuitive undertaking.[61] Funds raised by *epidoseis* were not typically for individuals or groups of individuals but rather for the building of temples or the repair of property, although a few inscriptions expressly name the entire *dēmos* as the recipient of the funds when those funds were being used for the purchase of grain.[62] The "poor" as such were rarely the object of such undertakings, even if the *dēmos* in times of need was.

The letter of Pliny to Trajan (*Ep.* 10.92–93) might seem an exception. In that correspondence, Pliny informs the emperor of the desire of the Amiseni, a free city federated to Rome and therefore not directly under Roman control, to form an *eranos*, a term often denoting an association that collected funds to be re-lent out to members, like a credit union. Trajan agreed but on the condition that "these contributions are employed, not for the purpose of riot and faction but for the support of commoners" (*sed ad sustinendam tenuiorum inopiam utuntur*). Although *tenuiores* is sometimes rendered as "poor" or "indigent," the term is in fact a designation of social standing, not income. It is not equivalent to *egeni* (poor, indigent).[63] Hence, Trajan's concession is not a gesture to relieve urban poverty but is intended to allow for the orderly burial of the dead who might otherwise have no easy access to burial. A few years after Pliny's time, a *cultores* of Diana and Antinoüs formed a club, citing in their bylaws a *senatus consultum* that permitted groups to meet (only) monthly and only for the purpose of collecting funds for the burial of the dead.[64] The bylaws make it clear that it was the collegium's members who were the beneficiaries of these funds and not the poor more generally.[65] It is unlikely that Greek or Roman clubs ever collected money to be disbursed to the poor in general. This is probably true of Christ groups as well. Longenecker admits that care for the poor in Pauline groups was mainly for their poor, even though Paul sometimes speaks as if he has others in mind too.[66] The Pauline collection was expressly aimed at the impoverished people within the Jerusalem assembly.

Third, Paul's collection was framed not only as a collection for the "poor," but as a collection for members of a *different* ethnic group. Welborn has aptly observed that "it must be emphasized how anomalous Paul's appeal to the principle of 'equality' between Jews and Greeks would have seemed. A careful examination of edicts and petitions, together with the relevant passages in Philo and Josephus, provides no grounds for thinking that Jews enjoyed equal rights identified with citizens in any of the Greek cities of the Roman east."[67]

In 2 Corinthians 8 and 9, Paul grounds the appeal for the collection in the notion of *isotēs*, "equality." The larger political context is supplied by attempts at the articulation of equality, in particular the failed struggle only a decade before for equal civic rights (*isopoliteia*) between Judeans and Greeks in Alexandria and the periodic eruptions of conflict between Judeans and gentiles in Caesarea over the same issue that would become one of the events leading to the First Revolt.[68] Paul's notion of equality in 2 Cor 8:14 is not one of equal civic rights but the rather extraordinary specter of Greeks sharing economic resources with Judeans.

Although the Pauline collection for the poor in Jerusalem is anomalous in the context of Greek *epidoseis* in the sense that it was a collection for a group in a locale far removed from that of the contributors, a similar ideology undergirds both kinds of projects. In a culture in which honor was a key and critical value, euergetism was a powerful tool in the construction of personal and corporate self-esteem. The providing of benefits to the polis or to the group was, to be sure, an important way to address real hardships and challenges that faced the polis and to demonstrate the loyalty of citizens (and noncitizens) to it. But the quid pro quo in this exchange was the public recognition of largesse, demonstrated by lists of donors that could be inscribed in public space and read out in an assembly and made known to all. It was a performance of citizenship. This is true whether the contribution was large or a mere 5 drachmae. Participation in an *epidosis* did not constitute donors as patrons, but it did constitute them as true citizens.

Paul's appeal employs an analogous logic. He begins in 2 Corinthians 8 by citing the Macedonians' insistence on their participation in this collective event, thus appealing to competitive urges among the Corinthians: if "poor" Macedonians were eager to demonstrate their largesse, then better-off Corinthians should do even more. He then swiftly turns to praising the Corinthians for an array of virtues—*pistis, logos, gnōsis, spoudē*, and *agapē* (loyalty, reason, knowledge, zeal, and love)—expressing the hope that they will add *charis* (goodwill, kindness) to their accomplishments (8:7). This is plainly an appeal to something analogous to the civic virtues that were celebrated in public decrees and to competitive outlay characteristic of polis ideology.[69] So too is Paul's mention of his "boasting" about the eagerness of the Corinthians in 2 Cor 9:2 an appeal to civic pride. In these instances, it is not to the needs of the polis of Corinth to which the Corinthians were expected to contribute but the need (*hysterēma*) of the Jerusalem assembly (8:14). In making this contribution, they would constitute themselves *as a group* that existed within a larger political network or fictive translocal polity.

We should not end without commenting on other novel aspects of Paul's project. As I have noted above, his collection was for a nonlocal cause; it was for the poor—not the poor generally but for a specific group of poor in Judea; and it was taken up in Greek cities for people who in the first century (and even much later) did not enjoy *isopoliteia* in most Greek cities. That is, Paul's collection crossed ethnic and political boundaries that were in the first century well guarded and fraught with tensions. As a performance of citizenship in a fictive translocal polity, his *epidosis* constructed a polity that bridged a conspicuous ethnic and political chasm—the chasm between the free Greek cities of Asia, Macedonia, and Achaia and the non-Greek ("Eastern") inhabitants of Roman Palestine. In the wake of disturbances in Alexandria, Caesarea, and Antioch about civic rights for Judeans in 41 CE, and Claudius's famous letter (P.Lond VI 1912) that put an end to the infiltration of Judeans into the citizens' rolls of Alexandria, Paul's collection crossed ethnic boundaries by expressing gentile solidarity with Judeans, or at least Judean Christ followers.

It is an exaggeration to label Paul's project as subversive of patronage, as some have done.[70] Subversion was simply beyond Paul's reach because he lacked the political power and influence to offer an effective challenge to prevailing forms of power and domination. He was not in a position to offer either lampoon or satire that was sufficiently effective to destabilize the power of the elite or to mobilize a critical mass of people to engage in a counterpractice that would offer an alternative to civic patronage. Besides, the *epidosis* was already a counterbalance to patronage, though hardly a subversion of it. It is doubtful that Paul's collection would be noticed by those outside the narrow circle of Christ followers. If it were, it is hard to imagine that a Roman prefect would consider it as anything other than a quaint and benighted practice by an insignificant artisan[71]—certainly nothing to worry or threaten the status quo, since it challenged no one's power or interests.

A better characterization of Paul's project is "transgressive."[72] His rationale for the collection transgressed the boundaries of several cultural practices current in the Greek world, in particular the promotion of an *epidosis*-like collection for an extralocal, non-Greek group. At the same time, the project was deeply committed to the same mechanisms and ideology visible in Greek *epidoseis*: the broad appeal to gentile groups to maximize participation operated by the same logic as Greek *epidoseis*. Paul's collection, at least as he presented it, functioned as a way for individuals and individual groups to perform membership in a broader identity. This is hardly subversion, since it threatened no one, and all the more so if the results of the collection were paltry, as Paul seems to have feared in his comments about the prospects that the collection would be "acceptable" in Jerusalem. Only two or three centuries later, when ecclesiastical powers took control of almsgiving and directed it toward the urban poor can one begin to imagine a practice that subverted the earlier practices of civic patronage by the elite.[73] But such was far beyond Paul's means to effect or, likely, even to imagine.

9

FUNERALS

Before Tertullian, almost nothing is said in the documents of Christ followers about how the dead are to be treated. First Thessalonians, Paul's earliest letter, indicates that he may originally have given this group of gentile Christ followers the impression that none would die, Christ being expected to intervene before the "wrath that is coming" (1:10).[1] As 1 Thess 4:13–18 shows, however, Paul had to invent the idea of the rescue of those believers who had died before the parousia by drawing on the hope of a bodily resurrection, well documented in Second Temple Judaism.

By the time that Paul wrote 1 Corinthians the terrain had shifted. The confidence that all would live to see the parousia had waned, although Paul himself still harbored the belief that he would be alive then. The issue was no longer now whether Christ followers would die but instead the nature of postmortem existence. In Philippians Paul expressed diffidence as to whether he would be alive or not at the parousia, and by 2 Corinthians (4:11–12, 5:1–6) a few years later he had embraced the likelihood of his own death. In Romans no trace remains of the eschatological confidence that Paul had voiced in 1 Thess 4:15 or 1 Cor 15:51, at least about his personal survival.

Christ followers died. How were their bodies treated? The lack of evidence of burials is not because they had dismissed death as inconsequential in light of their eschatological hopes, still less because they were unconcerned with the burial of their dead. It was probably for a much simpler reason: burials of Christ followers before the end of the second century are epigraphically invisible.[2]

An inscription can be identified as Christian by the use of a name that is identifiably Christian or the presence of formulae, terminology, or paralinguistic signs that point to the identity of the deceased as a Christ follower.

Typically Christian names such as Petrus, Matthaeus, Iōannes, Georgios, and Anastasia/-us did not come into widespread use until the third or fourth century CE.[3] Before that time Christ followers had pagan or Judean names. Distinctively Christian formulae such as *in pace* (in peace) begin to appear in the third century and eventually displaced the more usual pagan formula *dis manibus* (to the divine spirits), although for a time the two appeared together on Christian funerary inscriptions.[4] Paralinguistic marks such as anchors, fish, doves, and chi-rho monograms (and eventually crosses) make their appearance in the late second and early third centuries.[5] In rare instances the content of the inscription points to the deceased as Christian.[6]

Before the late second century and probably even the third, most of the funerary monuments of Christ followers were indistinguishable from pagan or Judean monuments. A grave marker from Thessaloniki identifies the deceased as "Apollonios son of Apollonios, *presbyteros*."[7] This might be the grave of a Christ follower, but it might also be a pagan or a Judean grave. The name Apollonios is a common pagan name, and the term *presbyteros* (elder) could be that of an official within a Christ group, but it is also widely attested in Judean assemblies and occupational guilds. The inscription bears a palm branch, but that is not identifiably Christian either. Without any less ambiguous verbal or paralinguistic markers, Apollonios is left invisible as a Christ follower.

In contrast to Judean epitaphs, which often identify the deceased as *Ioudaios*,[8] it is striking that neither *Christianos/-us* nor the term *ekklēsia* occurs in the second or early third century CE. Markus Öhler, however, has recently adduced IK Klaudiu Polis 44, a third-century CE funerary monument of Markus Aurelius Demetrianos, who is described as the first archon of Claudioupolis and one who held "all political offices" as well as the office of president of the games (*agonothetēs*). This elite male and his family are described as *hagnotatoi kai theō pisteusantes*, "the purest ones and believers in God." Since *pisteuō* (believe, be loyal) is mainly attested in Christian inscriptions, Öhler plausibly interprets Demetrianos as a Christ follower. Yet he notes that the inscription does not use the term "Christian" but instead a phrase, "believers in god," that we identify as Christian but that might not have been regarded in that way by all ancient readers. Öhler suggests that the "inconspicuousness" of this and other inscriptions might point to an effort to conceal the identity of Christians during the Severan period. But, he points out, "it is also possible that the religious identity of some Christians was not as straightforward as one might expect. Hence there was no need to develop new dictions, but only small adaptations of traditional forms."[9]

Throughout the Hellenistic and imperial periods, burial was normally a duty of the family of the deceased, so we might presume that families of Christ followers took care of their dead. But at least since the fourth century BCE associations also took some part in the burial of members. Indeed, burial and funerary activities are among the most common activities of associations. This at least raises the possibility that Christ assemblies also might have taken part in the funerals of their own.

ATTENDANCE AT FUNERALS

The clearest indication of involvement of associations in funerals is the common obligation imposed on members of an association to attend the funeral or funerary banquet of those members who had died. Thus, the bylaws of the *familia Silvani* stipulate, "whoever does not participate in the funeral (*exequor*) (of a member) without a (15) good excuse will owe a fine of 20 sesterces" (AE 1929, 161.13–15; Trebula Mutuesca, 60 CE).

This kind of requirement is consistently attested in the bylaws of associations from the early Hellenistic period to the imperial era and throughout the Mediterranean.[10] The requirement of attendance at a funeral probably should be seen in conjunction with the proscription of absenteeism (see chapter 4), as both regulations served to reinforce group solidarity and to advertise to onlookers the extent to which *collegiati* could be depended upon for support, in life and in death.

BURIAL OF ASSOCIATION MEMBERS

Inscriptions attest a wide range of financial practices associated with burial. Some associations assembled a fund called a *taphikon* in Greek and a *funeraticium* in Latin either to pay for the funeral or to be given to the member's family to defray their costs. The *cultores* of Diana and Antinoüs collected a monthly funeral fee (*funeraticium*) of 5 asses (1 1/4 sesterces) from each member. The level of the contribution (i.e., 15 sesterces yearly) was evidently fixed on the calculus that a member would contribute for an average of twenty years and during that time accumulate 300 sesterces. Upon the member's death the collegium contributed 250 sesterces toward his or her funeral (perhaps paid to the family or heirs), the remaining 50 sesterces to be distributed as *sportulae* to those members who attended the funeral. If a member died more than thirty-two kilometers from Lanuvium and the collegium was informed of the death, three members would be deputed to arrange the funeral with use of the funeral fund and were also able to claim 20 sesterces for travel expenses. If a member died and the collegium was not informed, whoever arranged the funeral could claim the *funeraticium* upon presentation of proof of those expenses.[11]

It is not clear whether the *cultores* actually organized the funeral or owned a communal tomb or part of the columbarium in which members could be buried or merely participated in the funeral or subvented some of the expenses. The provision in their bylaws—"whoever from this collegium has died a slave and his body unreasonably has not been released for burial by his master or mistress and he has left no documents, a *funus* with an image will be held for him" (CIL 14.2112, lines 37–39; trans. A. Bendlin)—might suggest that the *cultores* would normally be expected to conduct the funeral, and if a body were not available, they would conduct a mock funeral with an image of the deceased. Yet no other portion of the bylaws provides any hint that the *cultores* did anything more than to contribute a funeral fee (to the family?) and accompany the body to the funeral pyre (lines 25–26).[12]

FUNERALS ORGANIZED BY ASSOCIATIONS

Whether the *cultores* organized the funeral or not, some associations did.[13] This is probably what is implied in an epitaph from Asia Minor in the mid-second century: "Year 232, (month of) Audnaios 3. The *synodos* of leather workers honored Primus son of Mousaios, who lived 57 years" (SEG 29:1183; Saittai, Lydia, 147/148 CE).[14]

It is a common form in Greek funerary dedications to name the association responsible for the burial in the nominative and the deceased in the accusative along with a verb such as "buried" or "honored." In Latin inscriptions the deceased's name is often in the genitive ("[the tomb] of NN") or dative ("[dedicated] to NN"), and the association's name appears in the nominative, presupposing a verb such as *fecit/fecerunt* (it/they made it). For example:

Greek epitaphs

Year 230, 6th of the month of Panemos. The guild (*homotechnon*) of wool-workers honored (*et{e}imēsen*) Octavius Polykleitos, who lived 57 years (TAM V/1 85; Saittai, Lydia, 145/146 CE)[15]

Latin epitaphs

To the divine spirits. (Tomb of) M. Cornelius Proculus son of Marcus. The collegium of textile dealers (*centonarii*) (made this) for M. Cornelius Aequs his father, and Quinta his mother. (CIL 5.4415; Brixia [Venetia et Histria/ *Regio* X])

> To the memory of C. Cassius Agathemerus. The collegium of builders (*fabri*) and . . . (made this). (CIL 5.5761, Mediolanum, Transpadana [*Regio* XI], mid-I–II CE)[16]

The public declaration made by the co-*magister* and treasurers (*quaestores*) of the collegium of Jupiter Cernenus that was noted briefly in chapter 4 makes clear the involvement of the group in burials. It reads in part:

> of the fifty-four members that used to constitute the above-named collegium, there now remain in Alburnus no more than seventeen; that even Julius son of Julius, the co-president (*commagister*), has not come to Alburnus or to (a meeting of) the collegium since the day of his election as (co-)president; that (Artemidorus the co-president) has rendered an account to those who were present of what he had of theirs and was returning and (what he had collected) for funerals; that he had recovered the security he had posted for these sums; that now there were not sufficient funds for any funeral funds (*funeraticia*) nor did he have a single coffin (*loculum*); that no one had been willing to attend meetings on the days required by the by-laws (of the collegium) or to contribute *funeraticia* or money; and that they (the remaining officers) accordingly publicly attest by this notice that no member should suppose that, should he die, he belongs to a collegium or that he shall be able to make any request of them for a funeral. (IDR I 31; Albernus Maior, Dacia, 167 CE)

Not only did this collegium collect money for funerals, but it also evidently had a supply of coffins or burial spaces that it controlled, which had now virtually run out.

CONTRIBUTIONS FOR A FUNERAL

Associations were also involved in burial in less direct ways. As has already been noted, they might simply contribute to the *taphikon* or *funeraticium* accrued by a member whose burial was organized by his or her family.[17] The letter of Krateia cited in chapter 4 offers an example. In that letter the sister of a deceased member of an association complained to the local governor because the association allegedly had failed to pay her the *taphikon* upon her brother's death (P.Enteuxis 20). The payment of the *funeraticium* is recorded in a second-century inscription from Dacia: "For Q. Ianuarius Zosimus who lived 35 years and Ianuaria Candida who lived 30 years. Q. Ianuarius Agathangelus made (this monument) for his dearest children. The collegium of builders (*fabri*) contributed to the *funus* of Zosimus 400 denarii" (CIL 3.1504; Sarmizegetusa [Dacia]).

Zosimus was probably a member of the *fabri* and had accumulated funerary funds managed by the collegium.

In some cases, people buried by their families were identified on the epitaph as guild members. This leaves open the question of whether a *funeraticium* was paid. We might assume that members of the guild at least participated in the funeral in order to honor the deceased even if they did not contribute financially.[18] A sarcophagus now in the Musei Vaticani records the burial of two guild members, a *magister* and president of the guild of builders and his wife, a priestess of the Great Mother.[19] The inscription provides no clue as to who was responsible for the burial or who paid for the sarcophagus; but given the status of the two within their respective associations, it can at least be assumed that association members participated.

OWNERSHIP OF OR ACCESS TO FUNERAL SPACES

Associations that collected dues for a *funeraticium* did not necessarily own graveyards or sections of columbaria where members or people connected with those members might be buried. Some clearly did.[20] Burial grounds could be acquired in at least two ways. Some associations purchased burial grounds or portions of columbaria. For example, an inscription from a columbarium with at least 360 *loculi* (niches for funerary urns) records: "M. Aemilius Crestus, M. Fabius Felix, *curatores* of this monument, the *aedificium* of 36 associates in this monument who contributed money for its construction, shares were accepted. They agreed to have equal portions (*rationes pares*) of the *aedificium.* Enacted September 30 in the year that D. Laelius and G. Antistius were consuls" (CIL 6.11034; Rome, 6 BCE).[21] Similarly, the members of a Judean assembly (*synagoga*) in Ostia purchased a burial area:

> [The assembly of Judeans in the] col(ony) of Ostia, who acquired the place (*locus*) from a collection (?), gave it to the gerusiarch Gaius Julius Justus to build a monument. It was on the motion of Livius Dionysios the *pater* (father) and . . . nus the gerusiarch and Antonius . . . (officer) for life, in the year (of their office), with the agreement of the gerusia. Gaius Julius Justus the gerusiarch made (the monument) for himself and his wife and his freedmen and freedwomen and their descendants, (measuring) 18 feet wide, 17 feet deep.[22]

At other times associations also benefited from the donation of burial space from patrons and members. In the second century a woman, Ulpia Cynegis, donated a part of the Catacomb of Pretestatus on the Via Appia to the "collegium of Aesculapius and Hygia who are stonemasons," reserving twelve funerary urns for herself and her family.[23] Ulpia identified herself as *immunis* (dues-exempt), which implies that she was either a member of the collegium or a benefactor who had been declared to be *immunis* as a result of prior benefaction. Similarly, in the town of Pola a priest of the Mother of the Gods donated a sepulcher to the *dendrophors* of Pola.[24]

Patrons or association members might also allow fellow members access to their family tombs. The tomb of the Octavianii on the Via Salaria in Rome, dating to the first half of the first century CE, contains the remains of at least thirty-one deceased, mostly freedmen and freedwomen. These included the remains of six members of the textile dealers (*centonarii*), including three presidents (*quinquennales*), two decurions, and several women likely to have been the spouses or daughters, and in one case the house slave, of members.[25] It seems likely that these textile dealers had access to these burial spots by virtue of their connections to the Octavianii family, either because the Octavianii were patrons of the group, or perhaps owned some of their workshops, or occupied space that was contiguous with the shops of the *centonarii*. Since one of the Octavianii is listed as a *curator* of another textile guild that produced cloaks for the army, the involvement of that family in textile production seems assured. It was by virtue of that involvement that the *centonarii* had access to a burial place.[26]

The ownership, or at least control, of a cemetery by an association is also signaled by inscriptions that indicate that burial in a tomb was only by the permission of the association officers.[27] Hence it is common to see an inscription with the formula: "(The grave) of Bedasia Iusta daughter of Quintus (Iustus). The collegia of builders and (that of) textiles dealers (*collegia fabrorum et centonariorum*) (and) Gaius Lucretius Ammianus her husband (buried her), having accepted the honor (of burial). The place was given by the decree of the decurions (of the collegium)" (CIL 5.4396; Brixia [*Regio* X]).

Quintus Iustus, Bedasia Iusta's father, was a member of either the *fabri* or the *centonarii* who jointly controlled a burial ground, and it was by virtue of Quintus's membership that Bedasia could be given a burial spot in the cemetery belonging to the two collegia. Whether or not one collegium paid for anything more than the inscribed plaque, the permission of the collegium's officers (here the decurions) was needed.

ASSOCIATIONS AS TOMB GUARDIANS

Associations frequently acted as guardians of tombs, probably those of their patrons or perhaps wealthier members. As chapter 7 documented, this role often came with a bequest and the obligation to engage in "grave crowning" or a commemorative banquet. In some instances donors tried to ensure that their requests would be honored not only by making the guarding of the tomb the responsibility of the guild but by assigning another guild to ensure that the original recipients of the endowment honored the terms of the bequest: "(The tomb of) Aurelius Zotikos Epikrates. . . . I leave to the guild (*syntechnia*) of nailsmiths 150 denarii for the grave-crowning every year at the tomb; if they do not do it, it will be the responsibility of the guild (*syntechnia*) of coppersmiths; but if they do not do it, it will be given to the management of the purple-dyers" (I.HierapJ 133.a, b.1–6; after 212 CE).[28] Here it is likely that the deceased was associated with all three guilds, perhaps as a benefactor or owner of the workshops that they used.

The participation of associations in the funerals of their members thus existed along a spectrum. Some took responsibility for the conduct of the funeral itself, others contributed to the expenses of the funeral, and others allowed the deceased access to the cemetery owned or managed by the association. In other cases guild members evidently had access to family tombs and in a few instances had been given a family tomb to use as their burial location. As John Patterson has concluded:

> The clubs therefore provided a double form of insurance. If a member died without leaving a family, he would be buried by the club and saved from the ignominy and anonymity of a pauper's burial. If on the other hand an heir did exist at the time of his death, the club would provide a sum of money for the heir to pay for the funeral (which would otherwise be the first charge on the estate) or perhaps in some cases a niche in the club's *columbarium*. The clubs provided an institution which could in normal circumstances be relied upon to provide a cash sum to pay for a funeral without (much) danger of misappropriation or loss.[29]

Irrespective of the association's particular financial involvement, attendance at the funeral of the deceased was the norm.

FUNERAL COSTS AND THE PRESTIGE OF BURIAL BY A GUILD

All of this required money. How much is more difficult to estimate because the real costs of funerals varied widely. Reports about the funerals of the elite sometimes refer to extraordinarily large sums spent on the funeral, tombstone, and *sportulae* at the funeral.[30] Of course most of those who belonged to occupational guilds and cultic associations did not come from this sector of ancient society. Their costs were undoubtedly much more modest.

The Emperor Nerva reportedly gave a grant of 250 sesterces to the *plebs* of Rome as *funeraticium.*[31] This is from a chronicle whose reliability is questionable, but at least the sum mentioned sets a benchmark identical with the *funeraticium* offered by the *cultores* of Diana and Antinoüs thirty years later. The most plentiful evidence concerning costs comes from Lambaesis in Numidia, where burial costs ranged upward from 96 sesterces (24 denarii).[32] Richard Saller and Brent Shaw conclude that the cost of funerals was not prohibitively high for "working Romans" and that even the more expensive tombs erected by soldiers "represented a cost of about 2% of their nominal annual income."[33] In the most recent detailed study of burial costs, Schrumpf concludes that a "normal burial," which would cost between 100 and 1,000 sesterces (i.e., 25–250 denarii), could be afforded "without undue burden."[34] Burials in simple funerary urns set in the ground, as is attested at the Isola Sacra, would be even less costly.[35]

The fact that a "basic burial" was relatively inexpensive underscores the point made by Onno van Nijf. Since burial by a collegium was in relative terms more expensive than a simple burial, membership in associations was not likely a function of the inability of members otherwise to pay for funerals. The theory that associations came into being to assist the indigent to obtain a funeral was mooted long ago by Mommsen and others. They were misled by the statements of jurists to the effect that membership in associations was permitted only to *tenuiores* (understood to mean "poor"), who needed assistance to be able to afford even a simple funeral[36]—hence the birth of the notions of a *collegium funeraticium* and a *collegium tenuiorum,* that is, associations organized principally around the burial of poor members. Such a view is now rejected since it is eminently clear that while many, perhaps most, associations were concerned with the burial of members, burial was neither their only function nor their raison d'être.[37] Moreover, since the membership of associations was not restricted to the indigent but included individuals of at least modest income, it cannot be argued that membership in guilds and associations had to do with members' inability otherwise to afford a funeral. In fact, van Nijf contends that "being buried by a collegium was less a necessity than a conscious choice. If we want to be able to explain why people chose to be buried by a collegium, and why they emphasized their membership of collegia at death, we must open up the discussion"[38]

As I have maintained throughout, membership in associations provided connectivity and a sense of belonging. This was materialized in multiple nonfunerary ways, including having communal banquets and assemblies, electing or choosing officers, creating membership lists, making contributions, and performing common cultic practices. But funerary practices were also forms of real and imagined sociability: members of an association participated in the funeral of a fellow member and often in the accompanying meal and distribution of *sportulae*. For the member's part, he or she could imagine being accompanied to the grave, feted at the banquet, and buried along with his or her mates. The connectivity that had been part of association life was imagined to continue after death. The jurists, however, supposed that associations served only the very limited and pragmatic end of providing burial for nonelite individuals. Associative life, however, provided much more than that.[39]

BURIAL AND CHRIST FOLLOWERS

We know practically nothing about the burial practices of Christ followers until the appearance of the occasional epitaph that almost accidentally identifies the deceased as such. The few epitaphs of Christ followers that can be dated to a period before Constantine display a morphology very similar to that of pagan epitaphs and seem to reflect the same spectrum of burial practices as those of guilds and associations: (1) burial of a member by an association, (2) burial in a family tomb, (3) burial of someone identified by his or her trade, (4) burial in a tomb for which an association served as a tomb guardian, and (5) burial in graveyards owned and managed by the associations themselves. For example:

1. "Iulius Iulianus, the most [-----] ☧: the brothers (*adelphoi*) (buried him)." (IG X/2,1 607; Thessaloniki, ca. 200 CE)
2. "Marcus Antoninus Restutus made this *hypogeum* for himself and for those of his *familia* who were faithful in the Lord." (ICUR 3.6555 = ILCV 1597; Rome, Catacomb of Domitilla, 276–300 CE)
3. "✠ Sarcophagus of Zacharia, fuller and papyrus weaver." (MAMA III 361; Korykos, Cilicia, after 350 CE?)

4a. "[Au]r(elius) Philokyris ☧ son of Dion established for himself this tomb from his own resources. I exhort the brothers (*adelphoi*) to take care of it." (I.Perinthos 168; Perinthos, Thrace, after 212 CE)

4b. "I, Aur(elius) Philippianos ☧, made this for myself and my wife Aur(elia) Deknianē ☧ and for my father Aur(elius) Neophytus ☧. If someone should dare to put another (corpse) here, he will have to pay (a fine) to the brothers (*adelphoi*) of 500 denarii." (I.Perinthos 167; Perinthos, Thrace, after 212 CE)

5. "✠ Grave (*thēkē*) belonging to the guild (*systēma*) of linen dealers of the harbor of the city of the Korykaians ✠" (MAMA III 770; Korykos, Cilicia, V–VII CE).[40]

These illustrate how lightly the epitaphs were Christianized. Without the chi-rho monograms (☧) in nos. 1, 4a, and 4b or the crosses (✠) in nos. 3 and 5, these graves could not be identified as Christian at all.

Christian funerary inscriptions are little different from the range of funerary practices attested for associations. The epigraph of Iulius (no. 1) has the same morphology as the epitaph of Primus (chapter 1), buried by his fellow leather workers. It is reasonable to conclude that the "brothers" who buried Iulius assumed financial responsibility for that burial, whether or not they had collected a *funeraticium* like the *cultores* of Diana and Antinoüs. The term "brothers" was not the exclusive property of Christians; guild members sometimes identified themselves as brothers of the deceased.[41] But as nos. 1, 4a, and 4b indicate, the term seems to have been adopted by Christ followers.

The family tomb of Marcus Antoninus Restutus (no. 2) is little different from the tomb of Ulpia Cynegis (see above), who allowed guild members to use her tomb. Christ followers also acted as tomb guardians, as the tombs of Philokyris and Philippianos (nos. 4a and 4b) indicate. As the Philippianos inscription shows, Christ groups functioned in the same way as pagan associations (see above), ensuring the integrity of the tomb, and prepared to prosecute anyone who attempted to place an unauthorized burial there. This is not simply because burial spaces were at a premium but also because in the ecology of burial, it was important that the deceased remain as a part of the imagined community of which he or she was a part in life.[42] These two (nos. 4a and 4b) are obvious examples of this model. Finally, no. 5 offers an example of a guild-owned burial site presumably to which all guild members had access and for which they had contributed funds.

Christ followers also continued to be buried by their occupational guilds. This is something that irritated Cyprian, who complained in the early third century that a Spanish bishop, Martialis, was a member of a collegium and had his sons buried by the same collegium.[43] Cyprian decried this practice as inappropriate for members of Christ assemblies, probably because of the pagan burial rites associated with funerals.[44] Cyprian's views, however, were hardly normative.[45] In fact no compelling archaeological evidence suggests that segregated burial sites were the norm, still less that bishops were in a position to control burials in cemeteries they did not own.[46]

The burials of Christ followers had to be financed. Very late in the second century Tertullian admits that North African Christ followers collected money in their treasury (*arca*), though he was keen to distance their practices from other pagan practices. The contributions, he assures his readers, were not assembled from the obligatory payments of the sort that magistrates paid upon their appointment to an office (*summa honoraria*), dismissing this practice as an example of a "commercial rite" (*redemptae religio*). Instead, "each member adds a contribution monthly (*stips menstrua*), or whenever he is willing, and only if he is willing and if he is able; for no one is forced but each contributes freely. These are the deposits, as it were, of piety. For this money is disbursed not on banquets (*epula*) nor drinking bouts nor unwillingly on eating-houses but to support and bury the poor (*egenis alendis humandisque*)" (*Apol.* 39.5–6).

Despite the clearly defensive and perhaps evasive tone of Tertullian's prose, he uses the same term, *stips menstrua*, that is found in the bylaws of the *cultores* of Diana and Antinoüs to describe the small monthly fee that financed the collegium's funeral fund. Tertullian's apologetic interests are plain in distancing the practices of North African churches from Roman society as far as he could. His apologetic interests likely disguise the actual practices of those churches, which were probably more similar to those of collegia than he would have liked to admit. At the very least, churches would have had to have predictable sources of income to provide burials and the regular banquets (*coena*) that he describes, the cost of which he eulogizes as "expenditures made in the name of piety" (*pietatis nomine facere sumptum*) (*Apol.* 39.16).

We should not assume that Tertullian's model for funding funerals was the only one that Christ groups used. If Christ followers were buried, as surely they were, we must imagine an array of practices. These would have included burial by an occupational guild, whether or not that guild was "Christianized"; burial by the deceased's family but in which assembly members took some part and perhaps contributed funds; burial in a section of a catacomb or columbarium or cemetery that was owned or controlled by the Christ assembly—what Cyprian apparently imagines as ideal; or burial in a tomb complex that included Christ followers along with others. Such burials would have to have been funded by some of the same mechanisms as those used by collegia.

CONCLUSION

Comparison of the banqueting, fiscal, and burial practices of occupational guilds and cultic associations with the sparse data from Christ assemblies suggests that in general Christ groups adopted the same range of practices that are widely attested in pagan groups. In relation to Christian burials, there seems to have been little that is particularly distinctive, apart from the eventual use of special paralinguistic marks on graves and the displacement of *dis manibus* by *in pace* as a funerary formula. Like many of the other practices of Christ groups, their burial practices were designed to cultivate a social imaginary that reinforced members' sense of belonging during their lifetimes and that extended beyond the grave. Death did not sever the connection to the group or one's membership in that group. The construction of the funerary marker served to underscore the abiding importance of belonging and connectivity.

10

Living in the City: Imitation and Ambivalence

In the fourth or fifth century CE an occupational guild of fullers in Flaviopolis in Cilicia commissioned an expensive mosaic inscription to be placed on the floor of a room, probably a church.[1] This was a guild of Christ followers. Not only does the inscription use the self-deprecating term "the lowly guild of fullers" in place of the more usual superlatives *semnotatos* (most august) or *hierōtatos* (most sacred) expected in the self-referential language of pagan occupational guilds,[2] but the inscription specifically invokes Luke 17:10: "For the well-being (*sōtēria*) of the lowly (*eutelēs*) occupational guild (*synergion*) of fullers, receive O Lord, this measure of our fruitfulness from your 'unprofitable (*archeios*) slaves' and grant us forgiveness of sins for our souls and a good defense."

The inscription is of interest in several respects. First, these laborers called themselves a *synergion* (literally, "common work"), a common designation for a guild. The formula "for the well-being of" is typical of other honorific inscriptions. The inscription displays some notable idiosyncrasies of Christ groups: the self-deprecating designation, the call for forgiveness, the notion of a good defense,[3] and the appeal to the Scriptures.[4] Second, in the moral vernacular of fourth-century Christ groups the words *eutelēs* and *archeios* had been relexicalized as honorific terms, as they would continue to be in succeeding centuries.[5] Had these fullers been as self-effacing and lowly and unprofitable as the inscription says, there would have been no inscription at all. Third, by dedicating an inscription in a church, these handworkers redefined themselves not merely as a collection of fullers, who were often the butt of derogatory depictions,[6] but as a public-minded collegium that demonstrated its liberality by contributing to a building project. That is, the dedication transported the fullers within the imagined space of the city from the base social location of manual labor to the honored locale of public benefaction. Finally, the materiality of the inscription—a well-executed mosaic inscription—points to an association that was willing to use its resources not only to engage in the usual activities of an association—communal dining and the burial of its members—but also the euergetic practices of contributing a mosaic inscription to a church.

This example of the fullers' euergetism illustrates the ambiguities of the relationship of Christ assemblies to their cities. On one hand, Christ assemblies adopted language that seems to differentiate and indeed to alienate them from the life of the city, referring to themselves as strangers, visitors, and "most unworthy." These terms, ironically, are claims to exceptionalism. But on the other hand, these groups engaged in activities that can be seen as performances of citizenship, adopting civic practices and contributing to the beautification of public buildings and showing themselves to be well-minded and beneficent people.

ASSOCIATIONS AND THE POLIS

It is a truism that associations mimicked the organizational structures, language, and activities of the cities in which they were found.[7] What Arnaoutoglou says of Athenian associations is generally true of all: "The close connection between the organization of the city and that of an association reveals that the pattern of political activities and organization in Athens influenced decisively that of cult associations. The conceptual horizon of the Athenians, which was reproduced on every occasion, was that of the *polis*."[8]

Virtually all of the available data point to a general practice of associations imitating the language and practices of the city. Several aspects of the records of associations corroborate this conclusion.

EPIGRAPHIC REPRESENTATIONS AND RITUAL TRANSFER

From the earliest periods of Athenian democracy most of the rosters of associations contained only the names of citizens and males.[9] At the beginning of the third century BCE, however, rosters of other associations begin to appear that included women as well as men, *metics* as well as demesmen, and slaves as well as free.[10] It is not that immigrant groups did not exist before that period. Rather, at the beginning of the third century these associations embraced "epigraphic culture" in order to advertise themselves as part of the life of the polis.[11]

Baslez has offered a plausible explanation of this shift toward public self-promotion. She argues that the appearance of *alba* of mixed associations was a strategy that responded to the political environment of the fourth century BCE, when clubs came under attack by Athenian orators for their alleged antisocial behavior and antidemocratic postures. Associations that included non-Athenians, women, and slaves would have been special targets for suspicion. Yet by the end of the fourth century and the beginning of the third, associations acted to dispel suspicion about their potentially subversive nature. Not only did they represent themselves publicly with exactly the same epigraphic genres as those used by citizens—honorific decrees and rosters—but they also stressed their cultic and convivial dimensions (ignoring any potentially political aspects). As pointed out above, the epigraphic genres associations used reproduced the moral lexicon of the city, stressing their compliance with civic values.[12] The production and display of *alba* by diasporic and cultic associations in Athens—and later occupational guilds—are instances of mimicry of polis practices and part of a concerted effort to *look* Athenian and thus to deflect suspicion of subversion.

Mimicry was widespread. The epigraphic genres associations used simply replicated those in use in their host cities. The general morphology of civic decrees was copied; inscriptions were dated by reference to civic archons or emperors; and the key vocabulary of civic discourse was imitated. In Greek, the titles of associations' officers were usually borrowed from civic contexts: *agoranomos* (market supervisor), *archon* (president), *epistatēs* (superintendent), *episkopos* (supervisor), *oikonomos* (manager), *proedros* (presider), *proestōs* (presider), *prostatēs* (president), *stratēgos* (commander), and *phrontistēs* (manager). Roman associations had *aediles*, *curatores*, *decurions*, *quaestors*, and *quinquennales*.[13] The general membership of Latin collegia were called *plebs* or *populi*, and larger collegia sometimes divided their members into *decuriae*, mimicking the structure of Roman towns.[14] This cloning of civic terms sometimes produced striking anomalies. Egyptian associations sometimes boasted an *agoranomos* as one of their presiders, and as I noted in chapter 2 a village association in the Fayûm borrowed the Athenian title *hieropoios* (banquet manager) for one of its officials, in Athens referring to an official who was in charge of animal sacrifice, despite the fact that it hardly could have engaged in animal sacrifice.[15]

Associations not only replicated civic formulae. Athenian cult associations also celebrated standard civic virtues: *aretē* (virtue), *philotimia* (public mindedness), *eunoia* (goodwill), *dikaiosynē* (honesty), *kalokagathia (nobility)*, *eusebeia* (piety), and the like. This alignment of the associations' moral lexicon with that of the city had two effects: it produced subjects compliant to the city, and it advertised to the city that association members, most of whom were ineligible to become citizens, were nonetheless prepared to support the interests of the city.

The imitation of civic practices by associations can be seen as an instance of "ritual transfer"—the use of a ritual from one domain in another domain. The ritual transfer of civic rituals to the association allowed association members, ineligible to receive civic honors, to perform their own honorific rites. Ritual transfer can also be seen in their adoption of the practice of electing presiders yearly and then awarding them honors at the conclusion of their service. This mimicked the structure of the Athenian polis, where the tribes and demes participated in leadership by a prearranged pattern, allowing each to have the honor of leadership. In associations, as we have seen, this produced a "flat hierarchy"—that is, a hierarchical structure but one that was theoretically accessible to all members, in some instances, even slave members.

Alongside officers elected yearly there were also people designated officers as *dia biou* or *perpetuus* (for life). These are probably honorary designations recognizing distinguished service or conspicuous benefaction. The practice of recognizing lifetime officers also mimicked civic practices, where civic patrons were acknowledged prominently in inscriptions but were distinct from the *duoviri* elected yearly to manage the municipality.[16]

As Gordon suggests apropos of Mithraic groups, honorific rituals had another effect. Initiation and honorific practices "simultaneously confirmed the necessity and propriety of the unequal distribution of power and wealth in such a society, and, because it was a temporary, and within an order often reversible, relation, gave the impression that the distribution of those social goods was subject to the intervention of rational good-will. It has thus an important masking effect."[17] Ironically, perhaps, honorific rituals that seem at first glance to distribute honors evenly over the long run nevertheless reinscribed status hierarchies as necessary and "natural" parts of ancient society.

DISPUTE SETTLEMENT

Many associations also assumed a judicial role in dispute settlement among members, insisting that disputes be settled in-house and even fining members for resorting to public courts. Even worse was to go to the courts after the association had adjudicated the matter.[18] Such regulations might be regarded as purely pragmatic, to mediate disputes among members before they became conflicts that might fragment the association. Or perhaps they were an effort to keep the "dirty laundry" within the group and so to protect its reputation among others. Yet it is also worth considering that they functioned symbolically, to mark out the association as a space where a kind of quasi-civic autonomy was claimed and practiced, even within those associations that were not legally constituted as *politeumata*, formally empowered to adjudicate their own affairs, as some Judean diasporic groups were.[19]

INTERPRETING IMITATION

How might such mimicry be understood? Three possible—though not mutually exclusive—accounts might be given: compensation for a declining polis, imitation of civic democracy, and a strategy for the integration of the subelite into the city.

A DECLINING POLIS?

A common explanation for the rise of associations begins from the supposition that the city declined as an institution, either with Macedonian hegemony in Greece after Alexander the Great or with the rise of Rome in the wake of the Second Punic War.[20] In this view, the gradual disintegration of democracy and autonomy and the decline of civic life left a vacuum in Greek cultic experience.[21] Associations—first cult associations and then presumably others—stepped into this breach in order to revitalize religious practices.[22] Ziebarth has put the matter this way:

> The continuing disintegration of bourgeois life and the slackening of family bonds naturally resulted in the situation in which the individual felt alienated from the religious associations which formerly had unified deme and state relationships. In Greece people generally began to feel the need for a personal religion. Private cultic associations accommodated this in the most felicitous fashion. Whoever did not respond to the type of cult of the ancestral divinities joined with like-minded persons in a private cult of the same gods with their own bylaws. For those who experienced tedium with the Greek gods, because they had not been able to stop the disintegration of all old things, small cult associations of foreign gods first founded by foreigners . . . welcomed them in their modest *hieron* (cult center).[23]

This narrative requires some adjustment. The cultic system that Ziebarth imagines being replaced is now called polis religion—arrays of deities and cultic practices tethered to individual cities.[24] In polis religion the social and political identity of the city was coextensive with its "religious" practices. In this sense "religion" was not a discrete and separable feature of civic identity since it permeated and undergirded all aspects of civic life. From at least one perspective, polis religion was essentially a discourse of the elite, who controlled the priesthoods, sustained civic cults through euergetism, and were able to define which practices fell within the purview of the acceptable and which should be rejected—magic, *superstitio*, and other ignoble or depraved practices. Thus the "religion" of a city was essentially embedded in, and homologous with, the social and political structures of the city.[25]

A corollary of the notion of polis religion is that only citizens were able to participate fully in the cult of civic deities; foreigners and noncitizens participated only through the mediation of citizens.[26] The cultic practices of Athens, for example, had to do with Athena Polias ("the city Athena") and Athenian deities and hence it was Athenian citizens who appropriately reverenced Athena, not people of other political communities. In both Rome and Athens various Eastern and foreign cults were also present, at times dismissed and even expelled but also later integrated into the structure of civic religion, as occurred with the Thracian cult of the Bendis in Athens and the Anatolian cult of the Great Mother (Cybele) in Rome.[27] But the majority of foreign cults were never integrated into polis religion.

The assumption that polis religion during the Hellenistic period was increasingly bankrupt and unappealing finds little empirical support, however. As MacMullen and others have shown, civic cults remained vital, priesthoods continued to be in demand, and festivals attracted a wide swath of the ancient population.[28] Cultic associations cannot be viewed simply as compensation for bankrupt civic cults. If anything, they capitalized on the strength and vitality of civic cults by imitating them.

Nevertheless, the paradigm of polis religion affords too little importance to the various elective cults that developed during the Hellenistic period and early empire.[29] While for the curial classes the model of polis religion would remain dominant at least throughout the period before Constantine, Greek cities had substantial populations of resident aliens who adhered to non-Greek cults. The Roman practice of extending Roman citizenship to peoples of very diverse origins also meant that Roman cities included many non-Roman cults. These developments had the effect, probably unintended, of relativizing the dominance of polis and civic religion.[30] Other cultic choices were increasingly available during this period.

In the logic of polis religion, the appropriate reverencing of civic deities was expected to lead to prosperity and the thriving of all the members of the polis. Keeping civic gods happy through sacrifices, processions, and the like was imagined to keep citizens happy. Hence, one might suppose that in the second and third centuries, when plagues killed a significant fraction of the population, and when in the third century the borders of the empire were more seriously compromised by hostile neighbors and civil order was threatened, polis religion might have come under pressure. Indeed, John Scheid suggests that civic ideology began to be chipped away by disease, invasions, and internal strife: "the old religion underwent a transformation and little by little was abandoned for another which seemed to offer more guarantees."[31]

Yet it is one thing to suggest that polis religion might have been compromised but quite another to explain why an alternate elective cult might be embraced as more appealing. It is not at all clear from the available data that cultic groups, including Christ assemblies, experienced dramatic growth during the second and third centuries, the supposed result of disaffected participants in civic cults now migrating to elective cults. There is simply no way to assess the "spiritual needs" supplied by the new cults that were not met by polis religion.[32]

PLAYING WITH DEMOCRACY

A more defensible variant of the "declining city" theory focuses not on the allegedly bankrupt nature of the civic cults but instead on gradual changes in democratic practices and public life. Writing about associations in Athens, Nicholas Jones argued that citizen associations—demes, *phylai*, phratries, "clubs," philosophical schools, *orgeōnes*, and other groups—as far back as the third century BCE were already responses to the failures of Athenian democracy. The characteristics of Greek democracy—equal legal and political rights, direct rule, the right of minority citizen participation, and exclusivity (i.e., participation by citizens alone)—had the effect of excluding many citizens from actual participation.[33] This was in part simply a matter of space: the meeting space for the civic assembly held only six thousand out of a population of thirty thousand citizens, and the distance between the rural demes and the city of Athens made participation by rural citizens difficult. These factors prevented "men of ability" from exercising their talents in the arena of central government, and this, in Jones's view, led to the formation of "neighborhood democracies."[34] Although the focus of Jones's work is on the function and eventual decline of citizen associations, he suggests that the immigrant associations that began to form in Athens during the fourth and third centuries BCE were imitations of Athenian democracy: "Like their classical predecessors, these cultic *orgeōnes*, by rising to the occasion to meet the needs of their members, provide our final example of an association's response to the Athenian democracy."[35]

Just as the deme and phratry associations compensated for de facto exclusion from Greek democracy, immigrant associations—embracing non-Athenians as well as Athenians, including women and slaves as well as men, and reverencing non-Athenian deities—mimicked the roles of the deme associations. As deme associations declined during the Hellenistic period, private associations began to assume the roles of those deme associations in relation to burial and the social relief of poorer members.

It is not that democratic practices disappeared entirely in the Hellenistic period; that would not happen until the medieval period. If the radical form of Athenian democracy did not last, democratic institutions in Athens and other Greek cities survived and still mattered to citizens.[36] Civic politics was marked by increased oligarchization, with local gentry in practice controlling more and more of the political process and more of the prestigious priesthoods and civic positions.[37] The citizen assembly, however, remained an important feature of the political process. There was a subtle shift from the spirit of *isonomia* (equality among all citizens) and *isēgoria* (the right of all citizens to speak to the assembly) to an emphasis on hierarchy, and an accompanying shift from the role of the powerful as protectors of the citizen body to that of being benefactors (*euergetai*) of the city.[38] But citizen participation in the making of laws remained a value. Accordingly, one might see the rise of private associations in Greek cities as part of the effort to maintain and promote the values of *isonomia* and *isēgoria* outside the civic assembly, and among people who were never part of the citizen assemblies.

Without adopting Jones's view of associations as a compensation for the failures of Athenian democracy, Vlassopoulos has stressed the importance of "free spaces" in Hellenistic Athens in nurturing new forms of identity. Free spaces "brought together citizens, metics, slaves and women, created common experiences and interactions, and shaped new forms of identity. We can define a number of such spaces: the agora, the workplace, the tavern, the house, the trireme, and the cemetery."[39]

Vlassopoulos does not discuss in this context the mixed cultic associations that became numerous in Athens from the late fourth century BCE onward. Associations, however, provide even better examples of free spaces than the agora, tavern, and cemetery, since the latter created only temporary and fleeting contact between various status categories. As groups with fixed membership and regular meeting times, these mixed cultic associations facilitated the development of networks among people of varying legal statuses: citizens, *metics*, and both male and female slaves.

The existence of such free spaces and the new forms of sociality that they created do not automatically lead to the compensatory view of Jones. Yet Jones himself notes occasional gestures that some Athenians were willing to imagine alternate forms of democratic practice. Aristophanes's *Ekklesiazousai* entertains the possibility of a government managed by women, and Plato's *Republic* and *Laws* discuss alternate polities, even though Plato's own preferences were less than democratic. These data, Jones argues, point to a general politicization of the population of Athens: "It would be wrongheaded to suppose that the matter of nonparticipation was not a live issue on the grounds, say, that such ideas had never occurred to anyone or still lay centuries in the future."[40]

When citizens and *metics*, women and slaves were found together in the free spaces of associations, a new kind of sociality was formed, mimicking civic practices but creating identities that extended and expanded the classical imagination of the city. It seems plausible to interpret the democratic practices of mixed associations as a matter of "playing with democracy"—not creating an alternate polity that aimed at displacing the civic assembly, but adopting and adapting practices within these small groups that enacted the democratic values of the right of members to have a voice, to be governed by the same rules of conduct, to vote honors, to elect leaders, and to decide matters that pertained to the group.

Roman associations can be seen in a similar light.[41] As the ideals of republican government gave way to a political system that progressively removed most vestiges of self-determination on the part of the (free) populace, associations maintained practices that were in contrast to the increasingly oligarchic practices of the city. The creation of a free space in Vlassopoulos's sense also meant that a member, irrespective of his (and sometimes her) legal status or ethnicity, could serve as supervisor (*epimelētēs, episkopos*), president (*magister, quinquennalis*) or "father/mother" (*pater/mater*). All could participate in elections, have a voice in the governance of the association, and approve motions and decrees.[42] Andreas Gutsfeld has suggested in relation to the "democratic" practices of associations that "one can therefore speak of the associations in social perspective as a countermodel to the highly hierarchically organized urban society."[43] This is not to characterize associations as subversive of civic practices or to suggest that they were set up in opposition to cities; but it does suggest that they represented an alternate space in which older democratic values and practices could be enacted.

INTEGRATION INTO THE POLIS

The notion of associations as free spaces leads to another commonly posited function for associations: the integration of the subelite into the polis. Starting in the late fourth century BCE associations created social spaces that brought together not only demesmen, but men and women, *metics* and slaves, and hence offered vehicles to bridge differences in legal status and ethnic identity in the context of common cultic observances. Since the administrative terminology, the lexicon of virtues and vices, and the practices of these associations mimicked those of the polis, the effect was to orient the kinds of sociality offered by associations toward the polis rather than away from it. The association reproduced civic values and practices in a space that was conceptually distinct from the polis but that looked very much like a mini-polis, with democratic practices, honorific decrees, membership rosters, and common banquets. Associations became "cities writ small."

The sociality of associations, though it cut across social boundaries, did not erase legal distinctions or social hierarchies or create an unambiguously "egalitarian" space.[44] What it did create was a form of connectivity that bridged social barriers of ancient society that were particularly sturdy and enduring, between citizen and foreigner, between elite and commoner, and even between free, freedman/freedwoman, and slave.[45]

Patronage by the elite was a strong instrument of connectivity with the polis, especially in the Latin West, where it is common to find large occupational guilds populated mostly by freedmen and patronized by Roman nobility. Patronage bound the subelite population tightly to the interests of the civic elite. It is impressive just how far the system of patronage reached "downward": the senatorial and equestrian elite patronized some groups, especially those occupational and professional guilds involved in activities necessary to the feeding and supply of the city such as the boatmen and registrars (*lenuncularii*) and the grain measurers (*frumentarii*). But there were many links between patrons of lesser status—town magistrates, minor imperial officials, imperial freedmen, and well-off commoners—who patronized smaller occupational guilds and sometimes cultic associations. Since many of these lesser patrons were themselves connected up the ladder to the civic elite, the integration of even the smaller cultic associations into structures of patronage can be imagined as creating a large web of patronage connections that reached downward from the nobility and compassed a significant fraction of the urban population.

The Greek East displayed an allergy to the notion of personal patronage, probably because it was a visible affront to the strongly held value of the personal autonomy of the citizen. Yet euergetism by the elite was common, imagined as disinterested benefaction rather than as a relationship that tied client and patron together. Moreover, connections between individuals and groups of unequal status could be masked by such terms as *philia* (friendship), even when the relationship in question was purely instrumental.[46] Nevertheless, associations benefited from the connections with highly placed citizens. When a group of *Sarapiastai* in Rhamnous wished to build a temple to Sarapis and Isis, they petitioned a wealthy Athenian demesman, Apollodoros son of Sogenes, for the right to purchase land he owned. Apollodoros refused to take any money for the land, instead donating it to the association. The *Sarapiastai* did not refer to Apollodoros as a patron or even benefactor (*euergetēs*), but his "friendship" with the group nonetheless earned him an honorific decree. Interestingly, the decree does not extol his benefactions to the *Sarapiastai* but rather "the piety that he has expressed towards the gods and the good will and zeal that he has shown to his own citizens (*politas*)."[47] Largesse to a cultic association devoted to Egyptian deities is thus marked as a *civic* virtue, and the interests of the *metic* association are merged with those of the city.

For their part, associations also performed their loyalty to cities. A remarkable Athenian inscription honors an immigrant from Herakleia in Pontus who served as supervisor of the *orgeōnes* of Aphroditē. It states that he "obtained good omens on behalf of the association of *orgeōnes* and the children and women and the *dēmos* of the Athenians," thus signaling not only his service to the group, but their loyalty to Athens.[48] This message of loyalty is reinforced visually by the relief on the monument, which depicts Aphroditē standing with the honoree and Athena in the background holding a spear in her left hand and a phiale or a crown in her right. While the kinds of patronage surveyed in chapter 2 concerned elite citizens engaging in the patronage of occupational guilds, this Athenian association created the means for a wealthy *noncitizen* to appear as a benefactor of the city. This served as a way to integrate subelite and noncitizen populations into the city.

Some associations staged processions and other events that attracted interest in the city at large and that reinforced connectivity with the city. Speaking through Plato, Socrates mentions the civic spectacle of the nighttime torch race and procession from Athens to the Piraeus that featured Athenian and Thracian devotees of Bendis marching together.[49] The point of the spectacle was to show that "the entire (Thracian) *ethnos* lives in concord, the sacrifices and other rites shall be made to the gods, in accordance with both the ancestral customs of the Thracians and the laws of the city (i.e., Athens) and so that it will go well and piously for the entire *ethnos* in matters concerning the gods" (IG II^2 1283, lines 22–27 = GRA I 23).

A third-century BCE plaque, now in the British Museum, depicts Bendis facing two elderly members of the Bendis association, probably supervisors, with eight youths behind them, stripped and ready to run in the race (fig. 22).[50] Such demonstrations of loyalty reinforced the function of associations as instruments of the integration of subaltern populations into the city.

Figure 22. Bendis and the racers. British Museum, BM inv. GR 1895, 1028, 1. (Photo by the author.)

ASSOCIATIONS IN THE POLIS

Although the "declining polis" thesis is problematic as an explanation of the role that associations played in the city, both of the other explanations have something to commend them. Whether there was a perceived failure of Greek democracy, it is clear that associations in the Greek-speaking world imitated the democratic practices of the polis and thus asserted a form of autonomy over their affairs, creating themselves as fictive democracies. Associations both in Hellenistic Athens and in the early Roman Empire, as subelite "micro-societies," reproduced democratic values and elite forms of sociality, stressing equality and autonomy, in political contexts that were increasingly characterized by neither equality nor autonomy.

Mimicry also contributed to the integration of subelite populations into the city insofar as it reproduced civic practices and values in people who were not citizens. For subelite populations that consisted of a heterogeneous mixture of foreign residents from many locales, artisans, slaves, and freed slaves, associations and their mimicry of the civic practice of creating lists offered a material and visual marker of belonging, and in the case of associations that embraced citizen members or patrons, a tangible record of connectivity to the city itself. The mimicry of the honorific practices typical of the civic elite on one hand created internal hierarchies of honor on the other and asserted a place for the association in the fabric of the city. Even a modest association of Christian fullers could represent itself as a publicly minded benefactor. They did not have the resources available to those of the curial classes, but by pooling resources they could still have an effect on the face of the city. They *became visible* to themselves and to others as benefactors, however modest their resources.

CHRIST GROUPS IN THE CITY

I commented earlier on the mismatch of the data that we have for occupational guilds and cultic associations on one hand and Christ assemblies on the other. For Christ assemblies we lack the bylaws, membership rosters, and decrees that would allow us to see the way such groups formally represented themselves. What we have are the ad hoc interventions of Paul and others, who address various local issues, often concerning conflicts. While it remains unclear how many of these strategies were effective, at least we can obtain a glimpse of the social imaginary that writers such as Paul were attempting to advance, whether they were ultimately successful.

In what follows, I first attend to the linguistic choices Christ groups made and the practices that they appear to have adopted, comparing these to the linguistic choices and practices evidenced by private associations. These comparisons suggest that Christ groups to a large measure also engaged in a mimicry of the polis. Then I turn to the overt ways in which (some) Christ groups characterized themselves, as "resident aliens" and as belonging to a different polity, which stands in some tension to their mimicry of the polis.

THE CHRIST GROUPS AS *EKKLĒSIAI*

The most obvious imitation of the polis by early Christ groups is in the use of the word *ekklēsia* to refer to the local assembly in each city. Scholarship has been divided between those who believe that the term in Pauline usage originated with the Septuagint[51] or with Judean usage[52] and those who regard it as borrowed from the standard term for a civic assembly.[53] The issue of the origin of Pauline usage is, however, less important than how the term *ekklēsia* functioned in the contexts in which it was used: in Greek cities *ekklēsia* meant the *political assembly*, a central element in a city's claim to autonomy and a space where civic membership was performed. Even if by the first century CE democratic institutions had suffered some decline, they were still vital in many Greek cities, as Grieb has shown for Athens, Cos, Miletos, and Rhodes.[54] Even more to the point, civic *ekklēsia* are attested in several Macedonian cities, including Thessaloniki and Philippi, and in Corinth, the location of Paul's earliest Christ groups.[55]

Private associations did not commonly adopt the term *ekklēsia* as a designation for their meetings, even though their meetings frequently had deliberative and legislative functions. *Ekklēsia* is attested in only a few private associations, notably a *synodos* of Tyrian Herakleists on Delos, a gymnastic association on Samos, and a family association in Sinuri in Caria.[56] In Athens cultic associations routinely employed the term *agora kyria* (regular meeting) to designate their assemblies,[57] mimicking the older Attic term for the legislative assembly. But in the Hellenistic period, the civic assembly had replaced *agora kyria* with the more common *ekklēsia kyria*. This means that the use of *ekklēsia* by Christ groups is an even more direct invocation of the civic assembly of Greek cities than the practice current in Athenian private associations.

The civic *ekklēsia* was a space in which (male) citizens of varying social levels were brought together. Despite a decline in the sense of *isonomia* and the increasing hierarchicalization of the assembly, the *ekklēsia* still leveled some of the power and status differences within the citizen population. Both private associations that included a mixed membership and the Christ groups at Corinth, Philippi, and Rome greatly expanded the notion of participation, providing "free spaces" in which "playing with democracy" was possible for citizens as well as *metics*, foreigners, women, and slaves.

Paul's use of *ekklēsia* can easily be seen as a mimicry of civic discourse. He tends to use the term to mean an assembly of Christ devotees in a city (analogous to the use of *ekklēsia* more generally); but he also refers collectively to the *ekklēsiai* of provinces,[58] a locution that finds a parallel in the development during the Hellenistic period of *koina*—confederacies of cities in the same regions—a form of political organization that the Romans exploited in provincial administration.[59] Van Kooten in fact concludes, "This way of referring to the *ekklēsiai* . . . at the provincial or . . . sub-provincial level, seems to hint at a conscious paralleling of the Roman provinces which points to an alternative structure of the Roman Empire."[60] Thus, Paul's imagination of the Christ groups in the Roman Empire was easily mapped onto the imperial organization of cities.

Van Kooten also points out a series of functional parallels between Greek assemblies and the *ekklēsiai* of Christ groups: both were places of instruction; both were known for factionalism; both were spaces in which *mania* was restrained;[61] and although Greek civic assemblies were ostensibly closed to noncitizens, in practice strangers could attend the assembly, just as Paul imagines strangers entering the assembly of a Christ group.[62]

Although the *ekklēsiai* of Christ groups also display some idiosyncrasies when compared with the civic assemblies of Greek cities, it is difficult not to view them as representing a counterpart to civic assemblies, even as the practices of civic assemblies were transformed. The *ekklēsiai* of Christ groups, no less than private associations, provided a space in which the values of self-determination and autonomy could be displayed and in which connectivity and network formation mimicking elite networks could be achieved.[63]

CIVIC PRACTICES

The autonomous and self-determining functions of the assembly can be seen in several Pauline and other writings. First, Pauline groups adopted judicial practices that imitated the polis. In 2 Cor 2:5–11 Paul assumes that the disciplining of wrongdoers will be effected by "the majority."[64] Likewise in 1 Cor 5:1–13 Paul, apropos of the incestuous man, prescribes that the Corinthians convoke an assembly at which the matter is considered with Paul "virtually present" and offering his judgment. The result will be the execration of the wrongdoer. There are allusions to banning (5:11) and expulsions, paralleling the practices of many associations and, in fact, the civic assembly. There may even be an allusion to fines. In 1 Cor 3:10–17 Paul alludes to the various "builders" active among the Corinthians and warns that those whose work does not survive the test will "suffer damage" (RSV). The translation of *zēmiousthai* has troubled commentators, who rightly note that the rendering "he will be punished" does not go well with the next, contrasting statement, "but he himself will be saved, though only as one passing through fire" (3:15). The verb *zēmiousthai*, however, appears often in connection with the disciplinary fining of association members who misconduct themselves. Such fines, or fines of officials who fail to enact the association's decrees, do not amount to exclusion from the society; instead, they serve as *disciplinary* punishments. Whether or not Paul has in mind an actual fine, or, more likely, he is invoking fines as a metaphor, the practices of citizen assemblies and associations seem to be on the horizon.[65]

The autonomy of the *ekklēsia* is also expressed in its arrogation of dispute settlement and sanctioning of those who resort to external courts. In 1 Cor 6:1–7 Paul expresses dismay at the report of members taking fellow members to court, insisting that disputes be settled in an internal forum. While this practice can be seen as a way to limit internal conflict and avoid the public shaming of one member by another,[66] it is also an insistence on the right of the group to function as a judicial and legislative body, thus mimicking civic functions. This can be seen in a wide variety of private associations, which likewise forbade members to resort to public courts for the settlement of disputes; and in the case of an Egyptian association from the early imperial period, it was simply stated that "in all other matters [i.e., not specifically named in the bylaws], it will be as the association decides."[67]

Second, as I have argued above, the Pauline "collection for the poor of the saints of Jerusalem" is usefully understood as an instance of a subscription, or *epidosis*, a common practice in Hellenistic and Roman cities and private associations for raising funds for extraordinary purposes. Subscriptions, unlike patronage, relied not on one or two large donors, but on as many small donors as possible, in many instances hundreds of people, each contributing small sums (5–50 drachmae). *Epidoseis* functioned as "performances of citizenship," and as was noted in chapter 8, contributions to *epidoseis* and the support of democracy were expressly linked.[68] Unlike competitive outlays like patronage where "size mattered," subscriptions capitalized on the value of *philotimia* (zeal) for public good in a different way. Since *epidoseis* often set a maximum contribution, large-scale donors were blocked from turning their contributions into theatrical performances. This meant that subscriptions had a leveling effect on participation for the good of the polis. Seen through the lens of civic and association *epidoseis*, Paul's collection aimed at maximizing the number of small contributors and thus engaging the entire assembly in each town in the performance of citizenship even if, as I argued in chapter 8, it was a performance of citizenship in a fictive translocal polity.

Third, early Christ groups appear to have observed a version of democratic practice in choosing leaders by election. Although Bible translations and commentaries routinely translate *cheirotonō* as "appoint," this rendering is justified only in Acts 14:23, "appointing (*cheirotonēsantes*) for them elders in every city," where the grammatical antecedents are Paul and Barnabas. Elsewhere, unless the context demands some other rendering, *cheirotonō* should be translated as "elect," consistent with the basic meaning of "stretch out one's hand" (vote). This translation is required in the case of the three occurrences of *cheirotonēsai* in Ignatius (*Phld.* 10.1, *Smyrn.* 11.2, *Pol.* 7.2), since the verb is connected with *presbeia*/*presbeutēs* (embassy/ambassador), which in Greek usage was always chosen by election.[69] The *Didache* (15.1) also advises that supervisors (*episkopoi*) and assistants (*diakonoi*) be elected (*cheirotonēsate*) after having been vetted (*dedokimasmenous*), using the standard verb *dokimazō* used in Athenian democratic practice in relation to the vetting of candidates for citizenship or public office.[70]

In private associations it was also common both to elect and to vet (*dokimazō*) leaders and envoys who were to have special roles.[71] Hence it is unexceptional that 2 Cor 8:19 indicates that the "brother" was elected by the *ekklēsiai* (presumably in Macedonia) to accompany Titus to Corinth to assist in the collection. The brother is called a *synekdēmos*, a term used to designate approved people accompanying a delegation to another city.[72] On the basis of several first- and second-century CE papyri, Peter Arzt-Grabner argues that the term *cheirotonō* means "elect": "Against this background, the designation of the 'brother' who accompanied (Titus) [8:18] as *cheirotonētheis* (having been elected) sheds light on its importance: chosen by the communities in accordance with a more or less democratic principle (compare the original meaning of *cheiro-toneō*, 'to stretch the hand'), he is now charged to accompany Titus."[73]

Richard Last has made a strong case for rendering 1 Cor 11:19 as, "There also need to be *elections* (*haireseis*) among you in order that the approved ones (*hoi dokimoi*) become persons of distinction."[74] He points out on one hand that *haireseis* is an ordinary term for "election" and on the other that the standard rendering of *haireseis* as "divisions" leads to the counterintuitive result that Paul, who has objected to *schismata* (factions) earlier in 1 Corinthians and in 1 Cor 11:17–34 is troubled by *schismata* at the communal meal (11:19), now either acquiesces to divisions or is speaking ironically.[75] The alternative is to take *haireseis* to mean "elections." In that case, at least part of the issue in 1 Cor 11:17–34 has to do with models of governance in the Christ assembly at Corinth and the presence of *schismata* (11:18), to which Paul offers elections as a solution so that those who are approved will be known to all.

Whether Last is right in regard to 1 Cor 11:19, it remains that the election of leaders and envoys of Christ groups appears to have been a common practice and that in this respect Christ groups mimicked the practices of cities (and private associations). This does not mean that election was the only means of selecting leaders. The presence of wealthy and influential individuals meant that the "democratic" process in both cities and private associations was sometimes adjusted to accommodate the desires of such members. An example of such accommodation is presented by IG II^2 1328 (Piraeus, 183/182 BCE; 175/174 BCE), which contains two decrees of the *orgeōnes* of the Mother of the Gods, the first stating that no woman could be appointed twice as attendant (*zakaros*) until all of the women in the association had taken their turn at this honor. The second, inscribed eight years later, decided that a certain Metrodora should be appointed as attendant for life. It does not take too much imagination to guess why the association agreed to a change in its earlier democratic and "egalitarian" policy and what the stakes would have been should they have decided to maintain that policy. Democratic principles were always in tension with the need to satisfy benefactors and patrons. The custom of yearly rotating leaders practiced by most Greek associations[76] and probably by Christ groups eventually gave way to permanent officeholders.[77]

Finally, we might ask whether Christ groups mimicked civic honorific practices, as many associations did. The frequent answer of scholars is that a distinctive feature of Christ groups is that they refused honors to those who provided them with services.[78]

From the earliest period we indeed have no honorific or dedicatory inscriptions comparable to those of the associations mentioned above. Or at least, if such inscriptions exist, their "Christian" character would be invisible to us without the paralinguistic marks (e.g., chi-rho monograms and crosses) and onomastic indicators that help us to identify Christian papyri and inscriptions from the third century CE onward. But the erection of steles was not the only means of honoring achievement, even for groups that had the resources to have inscriptions cut. The principle honorific acts are the association's decision to honor, the offer of a crown, and the public announcement of the honor, normally in the next meeting. In some instances, the honorific decree was not inscribed but was written on perishable material such as papyrus.[79] Obviously, none of these has survived. These absences of evidence have sometimes led to the conclusion that Christ groups did not engage in honorific practices; but is absence of evidence, evidence of absence?

Harrison has pointed to 1 Cor 12:26, "if one member suffers, all suffer together with it; if one member is honored (*doxazetai*), all rejoice together with it," and Rom 12:10b, "love one another with fraternal affection (*philadelphia*); outdo one another in showing honor (*timē*)," as evidence that Paul "endorsed the appropriateness of honoring fellow Christians"[80]—although there is no indication of how this honoring was imagined to occur.

As I have already indicated, honorific practices were in some tension with the need to limit competition. Hence it is not surprising to see warnings like "Let us not become conceited, competing against one another, envying one another" (Gal 5:26) or the claim that one ought not seek praise (1 Thess 2:6; 2 Cor 10:1–3, 12–18). The seemingly contradictory vectors of the quest for honor and the eschewing of that quest can be reconciled, however, once it is recognized that in the dynamics of honorific cultures, it was critical for benefactors to appear disinterested. Van Nijf puts it this way:

> There was, of course, a widely recognized relationship between generosity and public honor, but this knowledge had to be repressed so that patrons and clients could make the most out of the exchange relationship. It was important (because more prestigious) for patrons that they should not be perceived

> as having bought the honors awarded to them. By the same reckoning, it was important to any self-respecting city (or other body) that its freedom to award (or withhold) public honors, and to decide what shape such honors were going to take, should be recognized.[81]

Van Nijf speaks of the "make-believe" of the honorific culture: patrons presented themselves as disinterested benefactors, and cities (or other honoring groups) as autonomous. The apparent tension between Paul's advice to honor others and at the same time not to seek honor is part and parcel of this make-believe.[82]

What Paul suggests does not distinguish Christ assemblies qualitatively from the honorific practices of other groups, ancient and modern. Although there is an inevitable competitive aspect to honors, analysis of small group practices by behavioral economists suggests that contemporary face-to-face associations offer attention and testimony to individual members' merits and performances—which Paul clearly endorses in Rom 12:10. Associations create a space in which achievement is prioritized and individual members can excel at the relevant activities. The effect of reputational pooling is a benefit to all members of the group.[83] These groups balance the competitive aspect of honoring individuals with strategies to contain and limit the potential for destructive rivalry. Similarly, in Athens associations often advertised their willingness to honor benefactors with the formula "in order that there might be a rivalry (*ephamillon*) among those who wish to be benefactors to the *koinon* and that they might know that they shall receive thanks."[84] The cultivation of "rivalry" might lead to conflict, however. Hence, the behavioral rules described in chapter 4 served to mitigate and suppress destructive conflict. In the delicate ballet of honorific cultures, "rivalry" had to be disguised as a disinterested quest for the good of others.

In sum, Christ groups display significant elements of normative integration into the polis—that is, the degree to which group conduct can be mapped onto more general cultural standards and values.[85] These include, first, the use of the term *ekklēsia* to name their periodic assembly, a term that invoked the values of autonomy and self-determination so prized in Greek civic culture. That Christ groups embraced population groups not normally a part of the polis merely reflects other contemporary responses to the polis, hardly resistance and still less subversion. Instead, the practices of Christ groups represented the extension of the idea of the self-governing polis to groups formally excluded from the polis. In this sense, we might think of the practice of Christ groups as cultivating a "fictive citizenship." At the same time, the *ekklēsiai* of Christ groups did what civic assemblies did: create a space for connectivity and network formation beyond the family.

Second, expression of autonomy was instantiated in several practices that mimicked civic practices: the exercise of judicial functions and dispute settlement; participation in an *epidosis* that had the practical aim of raising funds for the good of distant Christ groups but the symbolic result of a performance of fictive citizenship in a new polity; the use of voting and other democratic practices ("playing with democracy"); and honorific practices that imitated civic practices and served to reproduce general values of generosity, piety, service, and goodwill and to cement the relationship between those with resources to offer and the group that benefited from those resources, which reciprocated with praise.

AMBIVALENCE TOWARD THE POLIS

The relation of Christ groups with the polis was not all mimicry, however; it was characterized by ambivalence too. There are also examples of unvarnished hostility to the polis and its institutions, for example in the Apocalypse of John. Yet outright hostility does not seem to have been the usual posture.

One of the common tropes that appears in the literature of Christ followers of the second and following centuries is that of the "self-as-other,"[86] or perhaps better, the "group as other." That is, many Christ assemblies adopted language that constructed themselves as *not* part of the city, as belonging to an alien polity. This trope is epitomized in the terms *paroikoi* (resident noncitizens), *parepidēmoi* (visitors), and *xenoi* (strangers), which appear widely in the literature of early Christ groups.[87]

From a literary perspective, the notion of "alienness" is probably indebted to Abraham's self-description as a resident noncitizen and a visitor (Gen 23:4; cf. Ps 38[39]:13) and the frequent representation of the heroes of Israel's history as resident aliens in Canaan, Egypt, and Babylonia.[88] Whatever the literary source of these terms, they had widespread appeal in the construction of the identity of Christ followers in the late first and early second centuries. Eventually, *paroikoi* and *paroikia* became stereotyped terms used to describe churches in various locations where they appear to have neither legal nor metaphorical meaning. "The *ekklēsia* that 'sojourns' in Gortyn" seems to mean nothing more than "the *ekklēsia* that happens to be located in Gortyn."[89]

How do we understand the earlier usage of these terms? Do these terms denote legal status vis-à-vis the city and signal the fact that few if any Christ followers had citizen status in Greek cities? Or do they function metaphorically to signal that Christ followers, irrespective of their civic status, represented themselves as transient in the world, by virtue of either their apocalyptic expectations or their baptism and now belonged to a different polity? And what forms of political behavior were entailed in these terms?

FIRST PETER

First Peter famously describes his addressees with the almost oxymoronic term "chosen visitors" (*eklektoi parepidēmoi*, 1:1), and later as "resident aliens and visitors" (*paroikoi kai parepidēmoi*, 2:11). John Elliott urged that at least for 1 Peter the terms are not metaphorical but connote the actual civic statuses of people who are not citizens but resident noncitizens in one of the cities of Roman Asia, or visitors to those cities.[90] He characterizes the position of such people as marginal, "vulnerable," and "tenuous." Such an understanding maximizes the degree of estrangement of Christ followers—at least 1 Peter's addressees—from the city.

Although Elliott is correct that the terms have to do with legal status vis-à-vis the polis, they are not as negatively marked as he makes out.[91] Of course, "resident aliens and visitors" probably would have sought the status of *politai* (citizens) and the various benefits and obligations that accompanied citizenship. Philo reports the injury suffered by Alexandrian Jews who were demoted from being *politai* to the status of "foreigners and aliens."[92] There is plenty of evidence, however, that *paroikoi kai parepidēmoi* was used in the more positive sense of people whose legal status fell short of citizenship but who were nonetheless expected to contribute to the life of the city.

Elliott claims that the largest number of *paroikoi* were found among the rural populace and accordingly supposes that the addressees of 1 Peter are mainly rural folk.[93] Thus for Elliott, *paroikoi* tends to slide from being a designation of legal status to one of ethnic dislocation and displacement.[94] Indeed, according to Stephen Mitchell the rural population of Anatolia was "often described as *perioikoi*, *paroikoi*, *katoikoi*, noncitizen *komētai*, or simply as the common people, the *laos*."[95] This, however, hardly means that people who were called *paroikoi* were necessarily rural. Greek cities had significant populations of noncitizen traders, artisans, and others. The more important feature of the term *paroikos* is its legal significance: whether in reference to a person in the countryside or in a city, *paroikos* indicated someone who did not enjoy the status of a citizen.[96] A critical characteristic of *paroikoi* was that they were either freeborn, or freed, *not slaves*. This point can be illustrated by numerous inscriptions that distinguish between citizens, visitors, *paroikoi,* and slaves as separate and distinct categories. For example, I.AphrodArchive 2.b.1–5 = SEG 32:1097 (Aphrodisias, 88 BCE):[97]

> Whereas Quintus Oppius son of Quintus (Oppius), Roman praetor with proconsul power, has sent (a message) that Laodicea and he himself are under siege, and since the People decided that they should help him in force and that the *paroikoi* and slaves should march out with them and has also chosen in the assembly a man for their leader and it is necessary to dispatch ambassadors too, to inform the proconsul of the policy of our People towards the Romans who are saviors and benefactors, and, if the governor gives any other instruction for the city, to arrange that it is passed on clearly and carried out.[98]

This inscription illustrates three important points: First, *paroikoi* in some cities, while not citizens, were intentionally included in certain aspects of civic life and were expected to contribute to civic life.[99] Second, it is not at all obvious that the term *paroikoi* connoted estrangement, a tenuous existence, or disapprobation; on the contrary, there is good reason to think that Hellenistic and early imperial cities were interested in integrating noncitizen residents into the life of the city.[100] And third, and more important for an understanding of 1 Peter, is the fact that *paroikoi* and *douloi* (slaves) are distinct categories. Since 1 Pet 2:11 addresses the letter's recipients as *paroikoi kai parepidēmoi* and only seven verses later addresses house slaves (*oiketai*), the interpreter would be faced with two options: either to suppose with Elliott that while most of the letter is addressed to freeborn (or freed) noncitizen residents, 2:18–25 turns to slaves who fell outside this category; or to suppose that the words *paroikoi kai parepidēmoi* are being used metaphorically in order to construct an identity as "other." The latter is clearly the less awkward solution.

First Peter surrounds the identity of the *paroikoi kai parepidēmoi* with multiple weighty metaphors: they are chosen through divine foreknowledge and are sanctified by the spirit (1:2); they have been given a new birth (1:3, 23) and inheritance (1:4); they are holy (1:15); and they constitute an elect stock, a royal residence, a priesthood, and a holy company (2:9).[101] All of these metaphors contribute to the construction of the addressees as special, privileged, and distinct.

Even more important is the fact that 1 Pet 2:12 imagines that onlookers who may have been hostile to Christ followers will "watch" (*epopteuontes*) the honorable deeds of Christ followers and will praise God on that account. That is, like the *paroikoi* of the inscription from Laodicea cited above, these *paroikoi* were expected to make a contribution to the city and they will be commended for their honorable deeds. First Peter even imagines that civic leaders will also engage in the commendation of benefactors (*epainon de agathopoiōn*, 2:14), declaring that God's intention is that being benefactors (*agathopoiountes*) will serve to silence critics of the Christ group (2:15).[102] In short, 1 Peter imagines and encourages an open mimicry of the civic practice of benefaction and maintains that this is a means by which Christ followers will secure their place in the city.

Another aspect of the ambivalence of 1 Peter toward civic identity is seen in the tension between assertions of "differentness" and the embrace of rather conventional household ethics. This embrace has been stressed by David Balch, who argued that 1 Peter's use of conventional domestic codes for the management of the household was apologetic, "to reduce the social-political tension between society and the churches."[103] The strategy has sometimes been cast as a matter of assimilation and acculturation,[104] but such a characterization is in contrast to the language of alienness that pervades the letter. Rather than posing a binary choice between resistance and alienness on one hand and assimilation on the other, 1 Peter calls for a more complicated model of mimicry and ambivalence.

A final noteworthy aspect of 1 Peter is the injunction to honor the emperor (2:17). It is usual for exegetes not to take this imperative at face value and instead seek to mitigate the force of the injunction, usually by arguing that 2:17 subtly relativizes the role of the emperor.[105] Nevertheless, we should ask, What would honoring the emperor look like? Whatever equivocations the author had in mind, honoring the emperor, like virtually all other honorific activities, had a *visual*, empirical aspect, as is made clear in the immediate context with the reference to "watching" the honorable deeds of Christ followers (2:12). Honoring was not a private mental act, that is, thinking nice thoughts with one's fingers crossed; honoring people in the ancient world was always a visual and public performance.

Philip Harland has detailed the range of participation in "honoring the emperor" in Greco-Roman associations—from direct participation in celebrations of the emperor by *hymnodoi* and the performing of sacrifices, to less direct forms of participation, including attendance at processions or games, the dedication of buildings to the emperor, decrees of a club that mention the imperial house, or even the naming of the club as a *collegium salutare*.[106] Whatever constituted the "honoring" of the emperor for 1 Peter, it was undoubtedly a visible practice. And the author of 1 Peter does not seem to treat this as a violation of their confession as Christ followers.

HERMAS

The author of Hermas does not employ the term *paroikos* but instead expresses the "group-as-other" notion by claiming that Christ followers belong elsewhere:

> You know, he said, that as slaves of God you are dwelling in a foreign land (*epi xenēs katoikeite*); for your city is far from this city. Therefore, if you know, he said, the city in which you are going to dwell, why are you preparing fields here, and making expensive arrangements, and buildings, and pointless rooms? For whoever prepares these for this city is not able to return to his own city. Foolish and double-minded and miserable one! Do you not know that all of these things are foreign and under someone else's control? For the ruler of this city will say, "I do not wish you to dwell in my city; go away from this city, because you are not living by my laws." Therefore, you who have fields and houses and many other possessions, when he throws you out, what will you do with the field and house and the other things that you have prepared for yourself? . . . So take care: you are dwelling as in a foreign land; do not prepare much except what gives you adequate self-sufficiency, and be prepared so that when the ruler of this city expels you because you have set yourself against his law, you might come out of his city and depart to your city and observe your law, joyfully and suffering no abuse. (Herm. Sim. 1.1–3, 6; trans. LCL)

As Dibelius pointed out, there are affinities with Philo's sentiments in *Cher.* 120 where under Platonic influences he describes the sage as a stranger and resident noncitizen on earth.[107] Yet Hermas's characterization of the Christ follower seems also to imply a social posture. Osiek comments that the "emphasis of [Hermas's] argument is not on the evil of this city but on the contingency of Christians' existence in it and the greater allegiance they owe to another city."[108] For Hermas this allegiance is not only a matter of imagining oneself as part of an alien polity but of adopting certain concrete practices:

> Instead of fields, therefore, purchase souls that are afflicted, as each is able, and look after widows and orphans and do not overlook them; and expend your wealth and all your arrangements on those "fields" and "houses," which you have received from God. . . . This is extravagance, honorable and gracious. Do not be grieved or fearful but have joy. Do not practice the extravagance of the pagans for these are unprofitable for you as slaves of God; but practice your own kind of extravagance by which you are able to be happy. . . . Do your own work, and you will be saved. (Herm. Sim. 1.8, 10).

Osiek argues convincingly that Hermas's addressees include members of a wealthy, social-climbing class of Roman freedmen.[109] Nonparticipation in the life of the city for Hermas amounts to eschewing the acquisitiveness that characterized freedmen, who could use their *peculia* to acquire land. Instead, what Hermas counsels amounts to a mimicry of the euergetic practices of the civic elite, who thereby gain visibility within the city as honorable men (*kaloi kai agathoi andres*). This mimicry is underscored by the parable of the vine and the elm tree in *Similitude* 2 where the "Shepherd" explains that when the rich (Christ follower) assists the poor, "the poor, being provided for by the rich person, appeals to God, giving thanks to him for the one who gave to him" (Herm. Sim. 2.1.6).

> Therefore, both complete a work: Now the poor works by the intercession in which he is rich, which he received from the Lord; this he repays to the Lord who helps him. And the rich man, similarly, unhesitatingly offers the wealth that he received from the Lord to the poor. And this is a great work, and acceptable before God, because he knows about his wealth and has given to the poor from the gifts of the Lord, and rightly completed his service (*diakonia*) to him (Herm. Sim. 2.1.7)

Here the use of *diakonia* is equivalent to the *officium* of the rich. As Greg Woolf explains: "The good citizen's *officium* was to use his good fortune for the benefit of communities to which he had responsibilities. But the relationship was one of reciprocity, not of altruism: in return for his *beneficia* the benefactor wins status and *gratia*."[110]

Hermas's advice can be seen as a transformation of the notion of the *officium* of the rich. Wealthy Christ followers are not obliged to support the urban poor in general—that would be an innovation of later Christian bishops.[111] Hermas did, however, expect them to direct their "extravagance" (*polyteleia* = *prodigi*) to widows and orphans and to "purchase souls that are afflicted." This is a local version of what, in the public sphere, was embraced as a normal form of euergetism. As Hermas's *Similitude* 2 makes clear, the extravagance shown to widows and orphans is not meant to include those outside the group but is directed inward, to members of the group, eligible, presumably, by virtue of their baptism. In exchange, these would give thanks to God for the wealthy benefactor, and the piety of the poor recipient would benefit the wealthy (2.1.6).

As in the case of elite benefaction, Hermas also imagines a reciprocal exchange in which the wealthy donor's largesse is recognized. The poor Christ follower receives support from the rich, and in turn the poor "gives thanks to God" for that gift (Herm. Sim. 2.1.6). It is important to understand the dynamics of this exchange: "giving thanks" is not a private mental act on the part of the poor; it is a public declaration. One need not assume that in Hermas's group the wealthy donor was crowned or that a formal decree was issued; but Hermas imagines a dynamic whereby the identity of the donor is made known by the thankful recipient, and even though Hermas conceives the reciprocal exchange as indirect—the recipient thanks God for the gift that God has supplied through the rich and the rich man makes use of the resources with which God has furnished him—there is hardly any doubt that the donor's reputation as a *kalos kai agathos anēr* (a noble man) would be recognized by all.[112]

Hence, notwithstanding Hermas's declarations that membership in a Christ group entails belonging to an alien polity that observes different "laws" than those of the host city, the *practices* that Hermas encourages, at least in this respect, mimic those of civic society.

BECOMING (IN)VISIBLE IN THE CITY

The foregoing has focused especially on the visual practices of Christ groups: support of poorer Christ followers by wealthier members and the commendation of those practices that were expected by Hermas; 1 Peter's encouragement of "honorable deeds" that are to be seen and commended by others; and some form of participation in imperial honors.

If one approaches "alienness" only as a matter of theological discourse, one is left with a contradiction between assertions of alienness and practices that appear to be "assimilationist." But this is too simplistic an approach. Current anthropology has faced such seeming contradictions between mimicry and alterity and seen in them several cultural strategies.

Mimicry in the groups that are represented by 1 Peter and Hermas can be seen in the imitation of dominant moral and practical forms—euergetism and honorific practices. Mimicry of dominant moral forms can be seen as instances of "passing"—a term that was developed in the context of racialized politics in the nineteenth-century United States, where some blacks were able to "pass" as white, and more recently in the sexualized politics of North America, where men "pass" as women and vice versa.[113] "Passing" on one hand presupposes sharply articulated identity categories of "black" and "white," "male" and "female," and on the other undermines such sharp distinctions by transgressing their boundaries. Andrew Jacobs observes that "passing both undermines and necessitates the recognition of stable, mutually exclusive categories of personhood (categories of race, gender, sexuality, and so on). Passing emerges in social settings that rely on what Amy Robinson and others have called 'specular identification': the interior qualities of a person must be, in some way, legible on the body's surface, conveying deeper, more ingrained and essential aspects of identity."[114]

The social practices of Christ groups had the effect of rendering them simultaneously "visible" and "invisible" in the civic landscape: visible in the sense that their euergetic and honorific practices, as 1 Peter hopes, might attract praise and commendation as the behavior expected of citizens. By mimicking the moral codes (munificence) and practices (benefaction) of the dominant culture, Christ assemblies also were engaging in a form of "costly signaling," that is, requiring of members the expenditure of resources for the benefit of the group, which in turn generated social capital and enhanced group solidarity. Simultaneously such behavior rendered Christ assemblies invisible in the sense that they would become indistinguishable from others who engaged in similar euergetic and honorific practices.

There is, no doubt, an ambivalence at the heart of "passing," since at some level the subjects know that they are not white, or female, or citizens. This ambivalence is manifest in the persistent declarations of Christ groups of their alienness, although empirically they seem not to have looked much different from many other subaltern groups in the city.

Thus mimicry served several broader aims: it underscored the distinctive and special nature of the group, thus strengthening the group's internal cohesion; it advertised to the host polis—in a virtually apologetic way—the group's adherence to broader norms and hence declared their willingness to cooperate with structures of governance and benefaction; and it constructed a set of practices that functioned metonymically in the post-Augustan setting of a "worldwide" empire. To continue with the model of mimicry, we need not suppose that Christ groups offered a perfect mimesis of either Greek or Roman culture. Clearly they did not, and their discourse claimed that they were different. To the outside observer, however, they were in many ways like other subaltern groups that dotted the urban landscape, "fitting in," becoming invisible as subaltern and visible in a kind of fictive citizenship.

CONCLUSION

This chapter has explored tensions between the discourse of early Christ groups and their practices, with special attention to the question of how Christ groups located themselves in civic space. Several data point to the unselfconscious adoption of civic terms and values, analogous to the ways that other subelite groups mimicked civic structures to create a kind of "fictive citizenship," a space in which a sense of autonomy could be achieved and that nurtured connectivity among people from various identity groups. The discourse of Christ groups sometimes promoted the trope of alienness, even though ironically the key terms employed in this strategy, *paroikoi kai parepidēmoi*, belonged to civic vocabulary denoting groups on the outskirts of the city that nonetheless had responsibilities to the polis. Moreover, the practices of these groups connected them with the culture of euergetism and civic responsibility. Perhaps ironically, the very claim of alienness placed them alongside a host of other subaltern groups that claimed the exemplary status and excellence that were fundamental to identity in the ancient world.

11

Getting In, Falling Away

The sense of belonging that was fundamental to associative life involved participating in meals and other communal activities on one hand and experiencing the support and solidarity that flows from close relationships on the other. The cultural value placed on belonging helps to account for a variety of practices of occupational guilds, cultic associations, and Christ assemblies that created and reinforced connectivity. In this final chapter, I address the questions of recruitment, disaffiliation, and expansion of Christ assemblies—in short, how and why recruits were attracted and why some left or were expelled.

In 313 CE the Edict of Toleration granted to Christians and all others "liberty to follow the rite (*religio*) that each one wishes."[1] This did not amount to the adoption of Christianity as a state cult—that would come later—but it relieved the pressure on the assets of Christ assemblies and ended the persecution that had occurred under Constantine's predecessor Diocletian. Before Constantine, Christ followers remained a minority of the population, but in the years that followed the edict Christian numbers grew exponentially, in part because of the edict and favors that Constantine extended to them.

Neither the population of the Roman Empire about 300 CE nor the proportion that were Christian at that time is known with any certainty. The empire at the death of Augustus in 14 CE is estimated at 45–54 million, rising perhaps to 55–65 million on the eve of the Antonine plague (165/166–ca. 180 CE), with the population of the Greek East higher than that of the Latin West.[2] The demographic effects of the Antonine plague are unknown, but conservative estimates suggest 7–10 million deaths above normal mortality.[3] Thus it would seem unlikely that the empire had ever been able to recover fully by the time of Constantine, especially since the so-called Plague of Cyprian struck a century later

(250–270 CE).[4] The numbers often mooted for the empire at 300 CE repeat the estimates of 50–60 million, which is probably too high, given reports of chronic labor shortages, disease, and attacks from barbarian groups at the borders of the empire.[5]

Estimating Christian numbers before 300 is particularly fraught with difficulty. Harnack, following an extensive survey of all of the sites where Christians were reported, estimated that the Christian population was 7–10 percent of the overall population, unevenly distributed, with some areas in Asia Minor being dominantly Christian and others with no significant Christian population at all.[6] If one takes 50 million as the population of the empire, this would imply 3.5–5.0 million Christians about the year 300. Since Harnack's time, however, doubts have been raised concerning the Christian percentage of the population in 300, with guesses ranging between 5 and 10 percent.[7] A few have argued that on the eve of the Edict of Toleration there were entire Christian villages, especially in Palestine and Phrygia, and that most cities in the East had substantial Christian populations.[8] In spite of many uncertainties, Christian numbers must have grown significantly before 300; otherwise, it is difficult to imagine why Diocletian would have expended such effort at suppression and why Constantine would have taken Christians seriously.

In order to account for the growth of Christianity before Constantine, Rodney Stark famously posited that there were one thousand Christians in 40 CE.[9] If, as he supposed, the total Christian population was about 6 million (i.e., 10 percent of 60 million) by the year 300, one would have to assume a growth rate of 40 percent per decade (3.42 percent yearly).[10] While this calculation has been widely appealing, it must be said that neither the initial estimate nor the final figure nor the presumed growth rate is anything more than a guess. The growth rate of 40 percent was based on Stark's observation of growth rates among Mormons.[11] But the growth rate among Mormons is much more variable, depending on the country in which the missionaries are active, and much higher growth rates have been reported among some modern groups. This inevitably leads to the question, Why should Mormon growth rates be taken as normative?[12] Even more importantly, recent analysis of the growth rates of contemporary Christian conversionist denominations shows very wide variations, depending on whether the targeted societies are at the low end of economic development (which show a low rate of conversion), are undergoing development (higher rates of conversion), or are at the high end of economic development (again, lower rates of conversion).[13] This implies that not only is 40 percent growth per decade not a reliable figure but that other factors are involved in rates of conversion. If indeed conclusions from twentieth-century societies could be exported to antiquity—which is highly dubious—conversion rates are likely to have varied widely from one region to another and from one decade or century to another and to have depended on other assumptions we might make about the kinds of social and economic changes that occurred throughout the first three centuries of the Common Era.

Given the mortality spikes that doubtless affected Christ followers during the Antonine and Cyprianic plagues, a smooth geometric growth curve is unlikely. If political and military disruptions are an index of the levels of economic and social stability in the empire, the period from Trajan to the beginning of the Severan dynasty was more stable than the third century that followed. These variations surely would have affected the rates of conversion to nontraditional cults, but it is difficult to know what that effect was. Local harassments of Christians occurred under Nero (ca. 64 CE), Domitian (probably in the 90s), Trajan (about 114–115), Marcus Aurelius (161–180), and Septimius Severus (193–211). More serious empirewide persecutions occurred under Decius (249–251), Valerian (253–260), and Diocletian (at the beginning of the 300s). These doubtless also had effects on recruitment, but it is difficult to know what they might have been. A linear expansion of Christ assemblies is in any case unlikely. As Cavan Concannon has documented, some networks of Christ assemblies in the second century formed, flourished, and then collapsed, which undoubtedly affected their ability to propagate.[14] All of these data render it impossible to plot linear developments in Christian numbers. Most of the data that would be needed for such calculations are simply missing.

In spite of uncertainties about the trajectories of growth, the conclusion seems unavoidable that the number of Christians had increased from a few hundred at the time of Paul to some significant fraction of the empire's population by 300 CE. What was the mechanism for recruitment to Christ assemblies, and why might people have been attracted to them?

RECRUITMENT AND SOCIAL NETWORKS

In popular imagination the main mode of recruitment to Christ groups was via public preaching in the marketplace or open air. This is perhaps based on the fact that Acts has its heroes delivering public speeches on several occasions, some with spectacular results.[15] This impression is reinforced by accounts depicting Jesus's activities in the Synoptic gospels and in John, where Jesus speaks to "crowds."[16] The fact that many of the latter are editorial constructions—for example, Matthew's recasting of Q's inaugural speech, originally addressed to disciples, as a speech to the crowds who hear the entire Sermon on the Mount

(5:1–7:28)—should inspire a degree of skepticism about just how "original" the notion of Jesus or his principal followers recruiting in public may have been.

The idea that the central marketplace of a Greek town (*agora*) was a venue for preaching and recruitment is nevertheless widespread in scholarship. To take only two prominent scholars: C. K. Barrett, commenting on Paul's use of the form of a diatribe, suggests that "it is by no means impossible that some of the arguments in Romans first took shape in this way, in the course of debates in synagogue or marketplace."[17] Helmut Koester argued that by the early imperial period, "the real life of 'philosophy' . . . had left the schools and had gone into the marketplace and onto the streets of the big cities," and it was there that the "army of the wandering missionaries and philosophers" competed with one another.[18]

There are reasons to doubt this picture. It is true that Dio Chrysostom's typology of philosophy elaborated in his "Alexandrian Discourse" devotes considerable space to the Cynics, whom he describes as infesting the marketplaces, begging and "deceiving the young" with scraps of knowledge (32.8–9).[19] There is little reason, however, to think that Christ followers adopted this recruitment pattern, notwithstanding Luke's representation of occasional preaching in public spaces. As Nock observed long ago, according to Pliny, Christ followers met before dawn—which was in fact one of the problems that Pliny had with them. Celsus's complaint about Christ followers is not that they cluttered the city street corners and harassed passersby, but that they met in the houses of various declassé handworkers.[20] Even were we to suppose that Christ followers occasionally preached in the *agora*, Dio's comments on the Cynic philosophers who offered their wares in that venue does not inspire any confidence that Christ followers would have been at all effective in recruitment: "Accordingly, they [the Cynics in the marketplace] achieve no good at all, but rather the worst possible harm, for they accustom the ignorant to deride philosophers, just as one might accustom youths to despise their teachers, and, when they ought to be knocking out their insolence, they actually merely increase it" (32.9–10).

Dio's comments accord with the findings of contemporary sociological analysis of conversion. According to Stark and Bainbridge, Mormon missionaries are successful in effecting a conversion in only 0.1 percent of cases when they knock on the doors of strangers, but this rises to 50 percent when the encounter occurs in the house of a Mormon friend or relative.[21] The same low recruitment rate applies to the activities of, for instance, Hare Krishna devotees and the many other preachers who occupy street corners. According to Stark "the basis for successful conversionist movements is growth through social networks."[22] This finding, moreover, applies not only to so-called new religious movements but to more conventional religious affiliations as well.[23]

It is here that data about associations can again help to supply some models for recruitment. Recruitment was essential to associations, if only to replenish their numbers in response to the deaths or defection of members. Dramatic needs for membership renewal occurred with the Antonine and Cyprianic plagues, when some associations were faced with the prospect of extinction if they were unable to recruit replacements for members who had died. It seems clear that the standard mechanisms for renewal (i.e., recruitment) rested on the existence of social networks through which potential recruits could be identified and persuaded to join.

A NEW RECRUIT FOR SARAPIS

In the early third century CE a certain Ptolemaios, living either in Arsinoë-Krokodilopolis in the Fayûm or in Memphis, wrote to his parents in Karanis, a village on the northern edge of the Fayûm. He told them that he had been invited to join an association devoted to the Greco-Egyptian deity Sarapis and to participate in their banquets.[24] The fee for a new initiate was 24 drachmae, and a seat at the banquet cost an additional 22. He opted, however, to accept the role of *agoranomos*, literally, the "market supervisor," evidently a kind of maître d' for the club. This role exempted him from both fees, but it obliged him to supply five donkey-loads of firewood. He reports that as *agoranomos* he would be entitled to have a seat at the banquet and to receive double portions of the food and drink in recognition of his status. The letter was to request assistance in supplying the wood, for which he promised to reimburse the freight charges. He punctuated the letter with the statement, "for it is not possible for a person to refuse the Lord Sarapis."

The papyrus provides a rare glimpse into recruitment to the cult of Sarapis. The new initiate's fee plus the contribution for a seat at the banquet might seem high by first-century standards at 46 drachmae, but given inflation in the early third century, this amounted to slightly more than one-quarter of the yearly cost of subsistence for one person.[25] This sum was probably beyond the means of most day laborers but within the means of a worker who was paid monthly.[26] Ptolemaios was doubtless somewhat better off than a laborer but still not especially privileged.[27] His letter does not indicate either the cost of the wood and freight or other expenses he might incur as *agoranomos*, and hence it would be premature to suppose that he was choosing the less expensive option. The letter does show, however, that there were several ways to participate in the group.

The wood was for roasting the sacrifices.[28] A few years before Ptolemaios's letter, Tertullian would quip sarcastically, "at the smoke of Sarapis's banquet the firefighters will have to get up."[29] Tertullian may not have been far wrong. Another papyrus from the previous century, P.Petaus 40, probably from Ptolemais Hormou in the Arsinoite nome, lists the contributions for a yearly (?) festival of Sarapis that brought together people from throughout the eastern Fayûm: ten calves and twenty porkers—quite a barbeque![30]

To view recruitment to Sarapis's *klinē* (literally, dining couch) as a transaction, it seems clear what the *Sarapiastai* gained in the exchange. Recruitment of new initiates replaced deceased or absent members; the initiation and banquet fees helped to fund the sacrifices and the meal and to keep the group solvent; and dedicated members enhanced the symbolic capital of the *Sarapiastai* and their influence in the life of the Fayûm. P.Petaus 40 indicates the pull that a strong reputation produces, since the *Sarapiastai* were able to recruit material resources from twenty villages throughout the eastern Fayûm to stage their festival.[31] Moreover, in the logic of ancient cults, the greater the membership of the group, the more prominent its members, and the greater its resources, the greater the reputation for their god Sarapis. The cultural logic at work is "happy gods make for happy humans,"[32] just as unhappy or offended gods can make life miserable.

What did Ptolemaios get in return for his loads of wood? Membership in the *Sarapiastai* was likely an asset, especially for a young man living twenty-five to fifty kilometers away from his home village. His ability to supply the wood for the banquet and presumably his skills as an organizer also netted him the role of *agoranomos*. That role probably included being the liaison between the *Sarapiastai* and those who controlled banquet venues, whether a local dining room or a dining space in the Sarapeion, the temple of Sarapis.[33] This role in turn entitled him to an honored place at the table, double portions, and evidently the recognition of his status as an *asymbolos*, a term designating a person honored by being exempt from having to pay the ordinary dues, yet another indication of the social capital that Ptolemaios achieved.

Since the *klinē* of Sarapis typically occurred in rooms in a Sarapeion (or other temple) or in a room in a private house, there was a natural limit to the number of diners—perhaps as few as nine or as many as twenty. Moreover, Ptolemaios depicts the invitation as coming directly from the god. A seat at Sarapis's *klinē* conveyed with it a sense of exclusivity and privilege. And if the *Sarapiastai* were like other cultic associations we have surveyed, membership also afforded Ptolemaios a social safety net, providing for him should he be arrested or in distress, guaranteeing him a network of support, and in the end ensuring that he was buried honorably. He gained social capital and personal security.

Ptolemaios's recruitment to the *Sarapiastai* was hardly random. He evidently had enough familiarity with the group to know that he could enter either as an initiate or as the *agoranomos*. That he would be offered the supervisory role suggests that members of the group already knew him and knew that he was able, both financially and otherwise, to assume it. That is, we should not assume that the group indiscriminately invited new members or *agoranomoi*; Ptolemaios was already part of a network that connected him ultimately to the *Sarapiastai*.

We do not know the network to which Ptolemaios belonged that enabled connection with the *Sarapiastai*. It was probably not his family network, since the letter to his father does not mention anyone known to his father, which he probably would have done had there been a family network in Arsinoë or Memphis. Ptolemais does, however, appear to know people with donkeys who could bring the wood from Karanis to Arsinoë (or Memphis), which suggests that he belonged to an agricultural or commercial network. As I suggest below, and as the Leonides archive (below) also illustrates, members of networks were often bound together by multiplex relationships—not only by a common occupation, but by cultic or neighborhood connections. Ptolemaios might have accessed a Sarapis network by virtue of where he lived in Arsinoë or because there were *Sarapiastai* in his occupational network.

NETWORK STRUCTURES

It seems likely, both comparatively and taking into account the empirical findings of Stark and Bainbridge, that social networks provided the framework within which recruitment to elective cults, including Christ groups, could occur. Several kinds of networks were available in the ancient city: networks created by diasporic associations (which were sometimes also commercial networks); family networks, consisting only of people related by blood or adoption and various dependents associated with prominent families; occupational and commercial networks; neighborhood networks; and military networks. These networks, moreover, were not hermetically isolated from each other but sometimes overlapped. Such overlaps or network intersections allowed the flow of ideas, cultic commitments, and influence throughout and across networks.

There is considerable evidence that recruitment to associations occurred through family networks. The results of family-based recruitment can be seen in association *alba*, such as that of the collegium of boatmen and registrars from Ostia, where the majority of the members belonged to one of five families through which recruitment of new members presumably occurred. Even the small *synodos* of Harpokrates in Tebtynis with only fifteen members had two sets of brothers from two different families.[34] It is likely that their fathers had been members of the group.

Some associations, such as that of Epikteta (IG XIII/3 330), seem to have been mainly family-based associations. Others gave preferential access to the families of members. The Iobakchoi of Athens offered lower entrance fees to the sons of members, reducing it by one-half (IG II^2 1368.37–41 = GRA I 51). The Iobakchoi, however, had multiple pathways to recruitment and could recruit anyone, most likely Athenian citizens, who were able to meet the entrance fee (of 50 denarii) and pass the society's vetting procedure.

Household networks offered another platform for recruitment. The mid-second-century Mitreo del Caseggiato di Diana (I,III,3–4) in Ostia was located in two small rooms in a private house. Eleven names from the mithraeum can be recovered from several inscriptions and graffiti.[35] These include a patron, M. Caerellius Hieronimus (probably a freedman),[36] another family member, M. Caerellius O[—], and M. Lollianus Callinicus—both likely Roman freedmen. Eight additional names are listed, all without cognomina, including Vlas (= Hylas), (H)ermes, Fortunatus, and Maximus, likely slaves belonging to one of the two families. Given the location of the mithraeum (in a private house) and the onomastic complexion of the names, it is likely that this is a mithraeum composed of the male members of a small *domus* consisting of freedmen and several slaves.

For occupations guilds, the workshop was the probable venue for recruitment although we can only guess at how this occurred.[37] In a few cases, recruitment was very strictly regulated. As we saw in chapter 4, a collegium of ivory and citrus wood dealers in Rome in the early second century imagined the possibility of recruitment of new members but decreed that only ivory and citrus wood dealers could be admitted: "if someone other than a merchant of ivory or citrus wood is admitted to this collegium by the fraudulent action of the *curatores*, for that reason will the (names of the) *curatores* be scraped from the list (*ordo*) and erased from the *album*."[38]

Citrus wood and ivory were imported luxury products, which might explain both why this collegium so jealously guarded its membership list and why others might wish to join.[39] Recruitment doubtless normally occurred only through a network of ivory and citrus wood dealers. The fact that the *curatores* are singled out by the bylaws suggests that recruitment of new members occurred through sponsorship or nomination by a *curator*. But it also seems to presuppose that these officials had network connections with other people, perhaps merchants or artisans, who might see the social advantage of membership in an elite guild.

Other occupational guilds had much more open policies. The builder-carpenters of Luna, for example, were presumably mainly involved in building trades, but their *album* lists two physicians, a scribe, three "mothers," two "daughters," and at least one member who had connections with the *dendrophors* of Luna. Although we have no specifics of their recruitment practices, it is reasonable to suppose that these latter members were recruited through family networks or through connections with other associations or guilds. Thus, while in general we are probably not far wrong to assume that recruitment to occupational guilds was through existing labor and family networks (sons following their fathers), we should also allow for recruitment through lateral connections that a guild might have had with other associations, by virtue of family connections or simply by occupying continuous space in the city.

NETWORK INTERSECTIONS

Overlaps between networks, or what I call "network intersections," allowed for influence and ideas to "jump" from one network to another. Occupational networks and family networks sometimes intersected. Since families were often engaged in the same trades, occupational guilds could include multiple members of the same family. Jinyu Liu has observed that of the ninety-three members of a collegium of textile dealers (*centonarii*) from Flavia Solva in Noricum, a number share the same nomen and therefore were likely related.[40] In a guild of sheep and cattle owners from Tebtynis, twelve of the sixteen members were from four different families,[41] and of the twenty-four members of a guild of *apolysimoi* (those exempt from forced public service) on an imperial estate belonging to the Emperor Claudius near Tebtynis, thirteen were members of six different families.[42] We might assume, accordingly, that family connections were pathways through which new members were recruited.

Network intersection existed not only because of overlaps between occupational and family networks; spatial factors could also create intersections through which cultic knowledge could travel. A fragmentary Ostian *album*, probably for the caulkers and rope makers (CIL 14.257), names a certain [—] rius Fructosus as an ordinary member of the collegium (well down the second column, Frag. a.ii.14), along with his son. A later inscription, however, names him as *patron*(*us*) *corp*(*oris*) *stup*(*patorum*), patron of the guild of the caulkers and rope makers (*stuppatores*), and reports that he was responsible for the building of a mithraeum (I,X,4) within the precincts of their workshop.[43] By the time the second inscription was cut, he had evidently acquired sufficient wealth to undertake the renovation of the precinct of the *stuppatores* and to install a mithraeum there.

The fact that Fructosus built a mithraeum within the precinct of the *stuppatores* naturally made it more likely that some of the *stuppatores* (or members of guilds related to them) would also become Mithraists. This is especially likely in the case of Fructosus's son, a member of the guild and probably also a Mithraist.

The spatial connections of the *stuppatores* did not stop there. They owned a workshop (*officina stuppatoria*, I,X,3) where presumably they plied their trade.[44] In the large central plaza of Ostia, the Piazzale delle Corporazioni, they had a stall (II,VII,4 *statio* 58) that they shared with the rope makers (*restiones*) and where they could advertise their services.[45] The neighbors of their stall included the barge operators on the Tiber (*codicarii*), maritime shippers (*navicularii*), and grain measurers (*mensores frumentarii*), whose stalls were immediately adjacent to their stall.[46] We might therefore visualize the network of which the *stuppatores* were part to consist of a nexus of professional connections that existed by virtue of their physical proximity to other guilds in stalls in the Piazzale delle Corporazioni. Some of these network connections were formed by the fact of associations having stalls immediately adjacent to the stalls of other associations. Other connections existed because of the nature of their trade: the *stuppatores* were closely connected to the *restiones* (rope sellers), the *codicarii* (who operated barges), and the *pelliones* (sail makers). And since the *stuppatores* also had a connection with the cult of Mithras, one can imagine recruitment to that cult as operating through the larger network of occupational guilds centered on the Piazzale delle Corporazioni.

The Caseggiato dei Molini (I,III,1) in Ostia offers a second example of multiplex relationships based on occupation, physical space, and cultic features. This complex of buildings housed a large industrial bakery and presumably the home of the guild of bakers (*corpus pistorum*). It also housed the Saeculo del Silvano (I,III,2), a cultic site that featured a fresco of Silvanus and images of Augustus, Isis, and other deities.[47] The presence of a small shrine devoted to Silvanus might have inclined those bakers who wished to join a cult association to join one devoted to Silvanus. Marlis Arnhold adds that the cult of Silvanus was not likely conducted solely by the bakers but also by other people working nearby.[48] A graffito indicates the presence of a guild of night watchmen (*sebaciarii*) at the shrine.[49] Hence, the conjunction of the workplace of the bakers and a cult site devoted to Silvanus allowed for the intersection of three networks, two occupational guilds and a cultic association, and crossover among the three.

The Tosephta provides a dramatic example of the intersection of a cultic group (or diasporic association) and occupational guilds. *T. Sukk.* 4.6 describes an extremely large synagogue in Alexandria:

> Said R. Judah: Whoever has never seen the double colonnade of Alexandria in Egypt has never seen the glory of Israel in his entire life. It was a kind of large basilica, one colonnade inside another. Sometimes there were twice as many people there as those who went forth from Egypt. Now there were seventy-one golden thrones set up there, one for each of the seventy-one elders, each one worth twenty-five talents of gold, with a wooden platform in the middle. The minister of the synagogue stands on it, flags in his hand. When one began to read, the other would wave the flags so the people would answer "Amen" for each and every blessing. Then that one would wave the flags, and they would answer "Amen." They did not sit in a jumble but the goldsmiths sat by themselves, the silversmiths by themselves, the weavers by themselves, the bronze-workers by themselves, and the blacksmiths by themselves. All this why? So that when a traveler came along, he could find his own fellow craftsmen and on that basis he could gain a living.

The Tosephta takes for granted that occupational groups would be part of a diasporic network and even imagines a way that the building space assisted traveling artisans to connect with the appropriate guild.

Funerary practices and patronage also might create network intersections. In a funerary inscription from second- or third-century Hierapolis (Phrygia) the dedicator and owner of the burial site, Publius Aelius Glykon, established the tomb for himself, his wife, and their children. He also established an endowment so that the "most august *proedria* (assembly?) of the purple-dyers (*porphyrabapheis*)" could observe the Feast of Unleavened Bread and another for the association (*synedrion*) of carpet weavers, so that they might receive distributions (*sportulae?*), half on the Roman New Year[50] and the other half during Pentecost.[51] The fact that Glykon directed funds to be distributed on two Judean festivals probably indicates that he too was a diasporic Judean—almost two dozen inscriptions attest Judeans in Hierapolis.[52] Glykon also had connections with two textile guilds, the purple-dyers and the carpet weavers. Perhaps he was a member or a former president of one or both guilds or a patron of the two. The inscription does not provide any further details. What it does illustrate, however, is the intersection between a cultic association (an assembly of Judeans) and two occupational guilds. It is precisely these kinds of network intersections that might account for the flow of ideas within networks, the creation of trust among the three networks, and perhaps the possibility of recruitment to a Judean assembly, in particular for Jewish purple-dyers or carpet weavers who immigrated to the area of Hierapolis.

Patronage created other network intersections. Philip Harland has shown that an elite Julian family had patronage connections with a synagogue of Judeans in

Akmoneia (MAMA VI 264) through a priestess of the imperial cult, Julia Severa, who was also patron to an association of elders (MAMA VI 263). Her relative, C. Antius Aulus Julius Quadratus, patronized a synod of youths (I.Perg 440) and an association of Dionysiac cow herders (*boukoloi*, IGRR IV 386), while another relative, Julius Amynianus, was a priest of Isis and Sarapis and patron of a group of devotees (I.Trall 86).[53] Here, at least five seemingly disparate associations were integrated into a civic network via the family of their patrons. We are not in a position to know whether information flowed between these network members, owing to the paucity of epigraphic evidence. But these data make clear that we should think of occupational guilds and cultic associations not as isolated groups dotted around the city, but instead as part of complex webs of relations created by the structures of patronage and the topography of the city and its network of streets. Whether recruitment occurred across network intersections is unknown, but at the very least these intersections knitted the subelite population together, created platforms for the transmission of knowledge and influence, and bound groups of artisans to the civic elite.

Finally, interregional travel by people who could utilize commercial networks can go far in accounting for how a cult moved from one city to another. A recently published inscription from Thrace helps show how the cult of Theos Hypsistos was introduced from Asia:

> For good fortune! For the victory and eternal permanence of Emperor Trajan Hadrian Caesar Augustus, (5) Sabina Augusta, and their entire house, and of the sacred Senate and the people of Rome, of Cavarius Fronto, *legatus Augusti pro praetore* of the province of Thrace, and of the council (*boule*) and assembly (*dēmos*) of Ulpia Nikopolis ad Istrum: (10) Iason son of Apphus from Prusias ad Hypium built the shrine (*naos*) of Theos Hypsistos at his own expense.[54]

Iason's inscription is securely dated no later than mid-136 CE (the death of Sabina Augusta) and probably to 135 when Cavarius Fronto was the legate in Thrace.[55] Other Hypsistos inscriptions are extant in Thrace,[56] but this is the first from Nikopolis ad Istrum (modern Nikyup in northern Bulgaria). More important for our purposes is the fact that the dedicator, Iason son of Apphus, hails from Prusias on the Hypios River in Bithynia, near the modern Turkish city of Düzce. Other immigrants from Prusias are known to have been in Thrace, and many other Bithynians, especially from Nikomedia, are attested in Thrace. Two Prusians, both merchants (*emporoi*), are known to have been in Thrace.[57] Although the reasons that Iason went to Nikopolis ad Istrum are unknown, the fact that he built a shrine there indicates that he was a person of at least modest means and may well have been a merchant like the other two Prusians attested in Thrace.[58] Whatever the case, we must assume that a commercial or other network took him—and Theos Hypsistos—to Nikopolis and once he was there, connected him with other Bithynians or Thracians who were or became devotees of the god.

NETWORK RECRUITMENT IN CHRIST ASSEMBLIES

A plausible case might be made for the intersection of occupational guilds, spatial connections, and the flow of information about Christ assemblies. Since trades tended to cluster in the same area of a city or on the same estate, a ready-made network was available for recruitment of new members, should certain cultic practices be adopted by some of the network members. Both Ronald Hock and, more recently, Edward Adams have emphasized the role in Paul's activities played by the workshop,[59] which was, no less than the gymnasium, a venue for philosophical discussion.[60] Celsus sneered at Christ followers in the second century for "going to the women's apartments, or the cobbler's workshop (*skuteion*) or the fuller's shop (*knapheion*) to learn perfection."[61] Indirectly Celsus provides testimony to the formation of Christ assemblies in conjunction with precisely the same sector of society in which occupational guilds functioned. Acts provides some evidence of activities in a workshop: the story in Acts 16:14–15 of the recruitment of Lydia, who was a merchant of purple cloth, suggests that Paul had contact with a network of artisans; and the reference in Acts 18:3 to Paul staying with Prisca and Aquila "because they were of the same trade (*homotechnon*)" and the mention in Acts 19:12 of Paul's "aprons" (*simikinthia*) are other details that point to Paul working in a workshop.

A model for imagining recruitment, at least at Thessaloniki, might begin with Paul arriving in a city such as Thessaloniki and making contact with artisans who shared the same trade, not unlike Iason son of Apphus arriving in Thrace as part of a commercial network. While the Tosephta text cited above pictures the Alexandrian synagogue as a node where artisans with similar trades could find each other, the clustering of trades in certain neighborhoods also made it easy for traveling artisans to connect with members of their trade. Once Paul was connected with an occupational guild as a worker, as he insists he was in 1 Thess 2:9, multiple recruitment paths were opened to him: connections with fellow guild members, lateral connections with other guilds created through physical proximity of his workspace to the workshops of other people, connections created by patronage, or connections that depended on family networks.

The Leonides archive from Oxyrhynchus from the early fourth century provides another case of the intersectionality of occupational and cultic groups.[62] Aurelius Leonides was a member of an occupational guild and undoubtedly Christian. He was a flax farmer and flax merchant but was also an officer in a guild of tow merchants, thus indicating a network intersection between two occupational guilds, or three, if the merchants were distinguishable from the farmers. Found in his archive is a poorly written copy of part of Paul's letter to the Romans (P.Oxy II 209 = 𝔓[10]).[63] The Leonides archive itself allows for the reconstruction of Leonides's network of connections, which also included another flax farmer, Ammonius son of Kopres. But we know from the archive that Ammonius was also a "lector of the former assembly (*tēs pote ekklēsias*) of the village of Chysis"—former because the property of the Christ assembly seems to have been confiscated during the Diocletianic persecution.[64] Hence, we have two men associated with flax production and sales, both evidently Christian and one of them also a member and officer of an occupational guild of tow merchants. A network map that places Leonides at the center would have lines connecting him to the flax merchants, tow merchants, and Christ assemblies; and there would be at least a line from Ammonius directly to the flax merchants and probably lines to connect the flax merchants and the Christ assembly, independently of either Leonides or Ammonius.

The archive is silent about the matter of how Christianized these guilds of tow merchants or flax farmers were. We can see, however, that multiplex connections held Leonides and Ammonius together: they were both flax farmers and merchants, and they were Christian. We might also surmise that others in their professional networks were also Christian.

The available data do not permit the detailed reconstruction of the networks and network intersections that allowed for the flow of knowledge about Christ assemblies and the recruitment of new members. Some preliminary models are possible, however. In the two cases sketched above—Paul's connections with handworkers and the Leonides archive—the presence of Christ followers within a commercial or handworker network presumably allowed for the diffusion of the cult laterally within Thessaloniki and Oxyrhynchus. We might also imagine that as in the case of the boatmen and registrars of Ostia, recruitment to Christ groups occurred through familial networks; and as in the case of the bakers of Ostia, physical contiguity of the meeting place of a Christ assembly with that of another association might have created a network intersection that allowed for attraction and recruitment.

The fact that Paul and other Christ followers traveled and the likelihood that they moved within networks of handworkers or diasporic Judean assemblies might help us to imagine the mechanism for the geographical diffusion of the Christ cult. It has already been observed that the boatmen and registrars (*lenuncularii*) of Ostia had commercial relationships with the *lenuncularii* of Gaul, undoubtedly facilitated by the trading networks that brought wine and other foodstuffs to Rome via Ostia. It is perhaps no coincidence that Christ assemblies were also established in the Rhône Valley at least by the mid-second century, probably facilitated by travel along the same commercial networks. Irenaeus in Lyons had contacts with Christ followers in Phrygia in Asia, which suggests a network that connected the two regions, again probably facilitated by commercial links.[65] We know, for example, of a late-first-century or early-second-century merchant, Titus Flavius Zeuxis of Hierapolis, who claims to have rounded Cape Maleas seventy-two times, presumably on his way to Italy from Phrygia, perhaps engaged in the shipping of textiles produced in his home city.[66] Travelers of this sort, if they were Christ followers, might account for the diffusion of the Christ cult from Asia to Italy and beyond, just as Iason of Prusias ad Hypium introduced the cult of Theos Hypsistos to Thrace from Asia.

If from a structural perspective recruitment operated via handworker, commercial, and trade networks and through network intersections, how might we imagine *why* it occurred?

NETWORKS, THE MARKETPLACE, AND "BOUNDED CHOICE"

The late Hellenistic and early imperial periods saw the growth of elective cults alongside what has been called polis religion in Greek cities and civic religion in the West. While the growth of elective cults cannot be directly attributed to the alleged bankruptcy of civic cults (see chapter 10), it is true that many elective cults became available during this period. John North put the matter this way: "the basic story . . . is one of development from religion as embedded in the city-state to religion as choice of differentiated groups offering different qualities of religious doctrine, different experiences, insights, or just different myths and stories to make sense of the absurdity of human experience."[67]

The introduction of new non-Greek and non-Roman cults did not displace polis religion, but some nontraditional cults thrived among Greek and Roman populations, and some of the traditional civic cults did not, with the result that a few traditional temples fell into disuse. Choice was exercised by devotees, quite apart from what civic magistrates might have thought desirable. Hence, Andreas Bendlin has suggested the metaphor of a "marketplace" of cults:

> This decentralised system of cultic and possibly financial as well as administrative responsibilities created a "market" of small religio-economic entities semi-detached from, rather than conceptually embedded in, the civic system. The market-place metaphor referred to here has been used with regard to the differentiation of religious choices from the early second century and the alleged evolution from a state monopoly on religious identities to their fragmentation in the late republic; it has been employed to label the religious atmosphere of the Roman empire, where different cults and religions were in competition for adherents to their respective cause. Whether the metaphor of the market-place is applicable to the religious realities of later antiquity, however, remains to be seen and whether the metaphor should at all be used within the context of the a priori dualism of embeddedness and differentiation is doubtful. My employing the market-place model does not intend to postulate any dualism of that kind. I wish to describe the scenario outlined before in terms of a religious economy where there existed a market of customers and a range of cults and temples to serve that market. . . . In short, I envisage a deregulated religious pluralism where worshipers with variable commitments and heterogeneous needs instrumentalise a plurality of decentralised and nonexclusive providers of material as well as immaterial commodities.[68]

Bendlin is rightly cautious of a "supply-side" notion of the market—that cults competed with one another for "consumers."[69] Instead he stresses the demand side: the market model allows us to theorize "both the competition between different religious *choices*, cults and gods and the disappearance of some of these choices as natural processes in a self-regulating system."[70] How then might we conceive these choices to have been instrumentalized?

The demand for both material and immaterial goods in the ancient city was constant. The elite had their own means of securing those needs through networks of "friends" and clients.[71] For the subelite, however, given the miserable living conditions of the preindustrial city; pervasive uncertainties about health, nutrition, and personal protection; and the need for the assurance of a decent and dignified burial, it was imperative to establish and maintain social networks in order to survive and thrive.[72] Associations and guilds provided just these kinds of social networks that could deliver material benefits and a sense of belonging both to a human community and to one in which the gods were especially engaged.

The networking of associations created the possibility for the movement of cults from one social domain to another. The basic insight of network theory is that human agency and choice are actualized in a social nexus that makes available or salient certain options but that also makes unavailable or difficult other options. Depending on the structure of the network, some information (or commodities or influence) may be easily available or impossible to obtain.

If we adopt Bendlin's model of the marketplace of cults, it is also important to recognize that choice was not unlimited. On the contrary, choice was "bounded" by the networks to which one belonged. Whereas we live in a consumer society with at least the illusion of unlimited choices, choices within the ancient city were conditioned by a variety of social constraints, conventional practices, and ethnic preferences and by the physical and social opportunities to materialize choices. Presumably, Ptolemaios (see above) did not have the real option of joining an unlimited number of cultic associations: it is doubtful that he could have joined a Mithraic association or the cult of Jupiter Dolichenus, both of which were rare in Egypt. The *Sarapiastai* offered an actual option because his network intersected with theirs and perhaps one or two other cultic networks. He may have had network access to the cult of Theos Hypsistos, which is attested in Egypt,[73] or to the cults of Isis and Sobek, which were widely available in the Fayûm. Even in Ostia, where many cults are attested, bakers or caulkers and rope makers probably did not have an unrestricted choice of cults but would naturally elect to become members of groups that were represented in their respective networks.

The availability of an elective cult in one's network is only one factor. Another has to do with the particular characteristics and ecology of an elective cult. Unfortunately it is often difficult to know much about the particular appeal that an elective cult had, because in some instances we know almost nothing about the practices and mythologies of the group, and in most cases we have no independent access to demographic data on the devotees of those groups. For example, little is known about the mythology of the cult of Mithras. Even the meaning of the ubiquitous statues of Mithras killing a bull with the help of a dog, a snake, and a scorpion is uncertain, because Mithraists left no writings. The cult, which featured small, gender-exclusive, and hierarchically defined cells, evidently appealed to centurions and higher ranks in the military, and for this reason the legions were instrumental in its diffusion.[74] The majority of Mithraists were not military, some military areas were apparently untouched by Mithraism, and Mithraism was extremely popular in towns like Ostia where no legions were stationed.[75] Hence, one must wonder whether it was the hierarchical dimensions of Mithraism that appealed to nonmilitary devotees, or some other aspects of the cult. We also know little of the cult of Jupiter Dolichenus, except that it appealed to women as well as men but also to auxiliary troops from the East.[76] In the absence of information about the mythology and structure of the cult, it is impossible to surmise what its appeal might have been.

In some cases, however, more is known about both the structure and practices of the cults, and their demographic aspects. Some associations, like the cult of Sarapis and the Christ movement, included both genders and people with multiple legal statuses. And from literary and other sources, more is known about their ritual practices and beliefs.

"IT IS NOT POSSIBLE FOR A PERSON TO REFUSE THE LORD SARAPIS": THEORIZING RECRUITMENT

With these words Ptolemaios summarized his decision to join the *Sarapiastai*. An analogous declaration might have been made by a recruit to a Christ assembly. Ptolemaios's statement is both retrospective and perspectival: retrospective in the sense that he had *already* decided to join the *Sarapiastai*, and perspectival because another inhabitant of the Fayûm no doubt would not have chosen as Ptolemaios did. This raises the question: Why did Ptolemaios so choose? We can ask the same question of those who were attracted to Christ assemblies: Why did they join?

The question cannot be answered in full, of course, since we cannot interrogate Ptolemaios or the earliest Christ followers about their decisions. Nor do we have the kinds of demographic data, such as age, income, education, and other attachments, that ideally could contribute to profiles of those likely to embrace a new cult. Nevertheless, some models are available for thinking about Ptolemaios and his recruitment.

Stark and Bainbridge observed that in relation to recruitment to modern new religious movements, whether the potential recruit shared the beliefs of the recruiting group was not the decisive factor. Instead, affective bonds had been established between the potential recruit and the group: "A close watch on recruitment as it occurred revealed the essential role played by interpersonal bonds between cult members and potential recruits. When such bonds did not exist and failed to develop, newcomers failed to join. When such bonds did exist or develop (and when they were stronger than bonds to others who opposed the individual's recruitment), people did join."[77]

Stark and Bainbridge were discussing recruitment to "cults and sects" in contemporary society. Obviously, they had access to various demographic data and the personal histories of recruits that are inaccessible to historians of antiquity. They noted, for example, that those who were recruited were likely to have something bothering them. New recruits had to have some sort of "ideological preparation" for or "predisposition" to the recruiting cult.[78] Of perhaps more relevance is Stark's observation that while recruits to new religious movements retrospectively placed a good deal of stress on the beliefs of the recruiting group—for example, the "irresistible appeal of the Divine Principles" (the doctrines of the Unification Church)[79]—in the preconversion state, recruits were more likely to regard those beliefs as odd but stress the warm and friendly nature of the recruiters. At that stage affective relationships were decisive rather than the beliefs of the group (although beliefs are not wholly irrelevant).[80]

Seen in this light, it is likely that Ptolemaios's declaration about the irresistible attraction of Lord Sarapis was a condensation of the several affective bonds that connected Ptolemaios with the *Sarapiastai*. His declaration also masks a more complex array of social, economic, and emotional benefits that he could receive as a member of the *Sarapiastai*. For a young man who had moved from Karanis to Arsinoë-Krokodilopolis some twenty-five to fifty kilometers distant, being a member of the *Sarapiastai* would provide him with a sense of belonging; social capital as the *agoranomos* of a prestigious group; and, assuming that the *Sarapiastai* were governed by rules that were common in other Egyptian cultic groups, forms of security against arrest, personal hardship, and anxieties about death and burial.

Andrew Monson's model of "trust networks" helps us to think about the benefits that come with membership in a small face-to-face association and hence the attraction that it might have.[81] The behavioral rules of many associations, including Christ assemblies, might seem onerous, and the idea of threatening a fine or expulsion for misbehavior might strike the modern reader as a good excuse not to belong to the group. Yet as Monson argues, the ethical expectations of the group create a framework in which social and other kinds of interactions can occur and afford a level of trust and assurance that one's fellow members will abide by certain ethical standards. It is natural to think that a plumber or lawyer or physician who belongs to one's synagogue or church might be a more reliable and honest person to call in the case of need. This is because we all have an expectation that the behavior required by group membership will also apply to behavior between individual members.

Modern empirical studies of group behavior indicate that membership costs, whether they are monetary, behavioral, or performative, serve on one hand to cement the relationship among those who are willing to pay the costs and on the other to weed out free riders—those who want the benefits of the group but who are unwilling to foot the costs of membership.[82] Ptolemaios was willing to pay the costs of membership—whatever was entailed in serving as the *agoranomos* along with the donkey-loads of wood. Christ assemblies likewise imposed behavioral costs on members, framed, for example, as maintaining holiness (1 Thess 4:4), manifesting fraternal affection (*philadelphia*, 1 Thess 4:9), and avoiding retaliation against fellows (1 Thess 5:15), immorality (1 Thess 4:3), and strong passions (1 Thess 4:5). The deity who called members was imagined as able to effect these behaviors and to preserve members in a blameless state (1 Thess 5:23–24), not entirely unlike the Zeus cult in Philadelphia, where the goddess Agdistis was said to be able to "create good thoughts in men and women, free people and house-slaves," so that they would be able to comply with the rules of the group.[83] Membership in the Christ assembly offered a suite of benefits, including forms of intense interaction, communal dining, funerary benefits, and other goods, all under the auspices of the deity who "called" people to participation. How were such benefits advertised throughout networks?

Living conditions in the ancient city were cramped; everyone lived in each other's front rooms, as it were. The sheer density of the urban population and the nature of nonelite residential construction would make it difficult for any group to keep its activities secret for long. In fact, associations of almost every type deliberately made their activities and benefits known, for this was a strategy for materializing belonging (see chapter 4). They publicly lauded their patrons and benefactors, they advertised their benefactions, and they broadcast their piety toward the gods. As early as the late fourth or early third century BCE, an Athenian association stated in its inscription, "And if a member should be wronged, they and all the friends shall come to his assistance, *so that everyone might know that we show piety* (10) *to the gods and to our friends*" (IG II^2 1275.7–10 = GRA I 8; Piraeus, 325–275 BCE, emphasis added). This is advertising. It was designed to attract potential members who valued both piety toward the gods and wanted the support of their fellows.

Were the practices of Christ assemblies known publicly? In 1 Thess 4:12 Paul assumed they were: outsiders (*hoi exō*) will notice how Christ followers behave and so he enjoins them to behave "decently" or "becomingly" (*euschēmōs*). Moreover, in 1 Thess 1:7–9 Paul claims, not without an element of hyperbole, that everyone in Macedonia and Achaia had heard of the Thessalonian Christ assembly and how they had turned to the "living and true god" and no longer served idols.

This is sometimes taken to mean that the Thessalonian Christ followers took to public preaching. That suggestion is extraordinarily unlikely, given Paul's later admonishment that they should engage in handwork, mind their own affairs, and strive to live a quiet life (1 Thess 4:11). If, as Richard Ascough and

I have argued, the Thessalonian Christ assembly began as an association of handworkers, it would be incredible to suppose that they had put down their tools to become itinerant preachers. Instead, Ascough argues that the Christ assembly did what other associations did: they had made known their devotion to the newly arrived hero and deity, Christ and the god of Israel. They broadcast the story of the arrival of the cult in Macedonia. This would be precisely what the *Sarapiastai* would have done when they advertised the arrival of Sarapis to Delos and Thessaloniki.[84] It was natural—indeed, a necessary expression of piety and loyalty—to advertise the benefits provided by a deity. Thus, it is natural to suppose that neighbors of the Thessalonian Christ assembly knew quickly what deity was being worshipped, the benefits that membership provided, and the kinds of behaviors that could be expected of Christ followers.

Much of the recruitment to associations, including Christ groups, probably belonged to the category of "passive recruitment."[85] John 13:35, momentarily adopting the perspective of the outsider, claims, "By this everyone will know that you are my disciples, if you have love for one another" (NRSV). First Peter 2:12–15 assumes that pagans will observe the behavior of Christ followers and will commend them as "those who do good" (*agathopoioi*). In fact 1 Peter holds that the entire suite of behaviors, of men and women, slaves and free, will be observed by others as illustrative of what one can expect in a Christ assembly. Given the high premium that was placed on belonging to a trust network that mediated strong and direct relationships with others and with a deity, publicly available knowledge about the conduct and benefits of a Christ assembly was a powerful recruitment tool. There were signaling costs—adherence to a strong moral code and no doubt some financial costs; but if we assume that Paul's rejection of circumcision prevailed, it did not impose bodily practices that would have been a disincentive to some.

Stark has suggested that the dramatic ethical commitments of devotees was a factor in recruitment.[86] Christian conduct during the plague of Cyprian, which struck Alexandria in the 260s, was particularly remarkable (and noticed). According to Dionysios of Alexandria, Christians did not flee the city as many others did, but remained to take care of the sick, including their pagan neighbors. Those pagans who had been aided and survived not only would have had a strong demonstration of "costly signaling" but would have been morally indebted to Christians.[87] This likely produced a number of recruits, even though some of the caregivers would have perished in the plague. The Emperor Julian complained that during a food shortage, "it is disgraceful that, when no Jew ever has to beg and the impious Galileans (i.e., Christ followers) support not only their own poor but ours as well, all men see that our people lack aid from us."[88] Observation of the behavior of Christ devotees was likely an incentive to recruitment, at least for some.

Some of the appeal of Christ assemblies can be surmised: they cultivated strong affective ties, participated in communal dining and other rituals of belonging, adopted fictive family language to describe their members, and operated under the auspices of a deity that "called" them and was imagined to have agency in transforming humans. The ethics promoted both in Paul of loving one another and outdoing each other in showing honor (Rom 12:10) and in John of mutual love (John 13:35) aimed at producing a strong network of trust that could have had a strong appeal only for subelite city dwellers.

CIVIC ELITES

Neither senators nor equestrians had any association with Christ assemblies during the first century and probably for most of the second. Christ assemblies simply lacked the social capital to command any attention from such people. With a few exceptions this was also true of most cultic groups. Yet in the second and third centuries, there is modest evidence for the participation of some higher statused people in Christ assemblies—first wealthy freedmen and freedwomen, perhaps some equestrians, and a handful of senators—and more elite women than men. For the elite and semi-elite, the appeal of Christ assemblies was probably not the same as it was for the nonelite.

The evidence for senators associated with Christ assemblies remains very restricted before 312 CE. Werner Eck scoured literary and epigraphic sources for certain evidence of named Christians of senatorial rank before the Edict of Milan and found only seven, four women and three men. This number might expand very slightly if one includes some funerary monuments that are dated vaguely as "late third or early fourth century."[89] Peter Lampe concluded, "before Constantine, not even forty individual persons of the senatorial rank [are known to be] Christians; two-thirds of these are women."[90] T. D. Barnes, however, noted that one of Eck's "certain" Christians was not of senatorial rank but added four more women of rank, to a total of ten.[91] To put this in perspective: In the nearly three hundred years between the mid-first century and the Edict of Milan, there were more than six thousand senators and more than twice that number of women of senatorial rank.[92] Ten *clarissimi* amounts to a tiny fraction of the senatorial elite, with most of these appearing in the third century. The evidence for the participation of wealthy freedmen/freedwomen and equestrians before Constantine is slightly more plentiful, although some of the claims must be weighed carefully.

THE SECOND CENTURY

In the early second century Pliny the Younger claimed that the *Christiani* of Bithynia included "many of every age, all ranks, and even both sexes" (*multi . . . omnis aetatis, omnis ordinis, utriusque sexus etiam*; *Ep.* 10.96.9). Since Pliny refers to ranks (*ordines*), a term that ordinarily refers to those belonging to the highest census ranks, a naive reading suggests that he reports at least equestrians to be present and perhaps senators. Theissen, however, urges caution and argues that Pliny's comments mean at best that some town councilors were members of Christ assemblies by the end of the first century CE. That equestrians and senators were among the ranks of *Christiani* that early would have been incredible.[93]

It is indeed prudent to take Pliny's comments with caution. His letter to Trajan shows heavy dependence on Livy's account of the Bacchanalia conspiracy (*Ab urbe condita* 39.9–19), where he described the early-second-century BCE arrival of Bacchic cults in Rome as a "contagion." These depraved rites (*religio prava*) included nocturnal drinking and orgies, murders and other crimes (*flagitia*), strange prayers (*carmina*) dictated by Bacchic priests, and the imposition of oaths (*sacramentum*) on devotees.[94] It is important to note that Pliny's letter employs the same vocabulary to describe the practices of *Christiani*, which he characterizes as *supersitio prava, immodica*, a "depraved and excessive rite." But in his letter he systematically disarms the suspicion that Christians were like those earlier conspirators: the nighttime meetings were stopped at his order; they did not commit any crimes; the oaths they took were merely to repay debts; their prayer or hymn (*carmen*) was "to Christ as god"; and their meal was of "harmless food." That is, Pliny's letter invokes the Bacchanalia only to show that what had occurred in Bithynia was *not* a similar conspiracy and that his swift action had nipped any problems in the bud.[95]

Hence, when Pliny also claims that the *Christiani* included "many of every age, all ranks (*ordines*) and even both sexes" and reports that his examination had begun with the interrogation of two female slaves (*ancillae*), one must suspect that these features too are likewise shaped by Livy. Livy reported that Roman matrons, Roman citizens, young and old, freedmen, freedwomen, and slaves had been involved—that as many as seven thousand had been implicated. The consul's address to the Senate had warned the senators of the danger that some of their own numbers may have joined the conspiracy. The key testimony against the conspiracy had been provided by a former slave (*ancilla*), Hispala Faecenia, and Livy's account indicates that lists of those suspected of membership had been compiled to assist in their arrest.

There are several other symmetries between Livy's report and Pliny's account. Both involve the production of lists with the names of alleged members. According to Livy those who were only initiated in the cult by repeating a set prayer but who had not committed any crimes were merely imprisoned rather than executed (*Ab urbe condita* 39.18.1). Similarly, Pliny explains that he executed those who refused to sacrifice to the emperor, but those who admitted to having been Christians in the past but were no longer were released without punishment.

The point is not that Pliny has invented his account of the Christians in Bithynia from whole cloth. It seems nevertheless obvious that many of the details deliberately evoke Livy's account of the Bacchanalia conspiracy and do so in order to assure Trajan that the *Christiani* do not pose a real threat. It is unwise, therefore, to take his letter at face value, either his estimates of the numbers of *Christiani* in Bithynia in the early second century or the implication of his use of the word *ordines* that senators or equestrians were involved.

In spite of the doubts that can be cast on Pliny's letter, literary sources from the early second century began to imagine the possibility of people of rank present in Christ groups. The letter of James, composed probably in Rome during the principate of either Trajan or Hadrian,[96] imagines a scenario of a rich man entering an assembly (*synagōgē*) at the same time that a poor man enters (2:1–4). James's description not only underscores the wealth of the man but his rank, the symbols of which are distinguished dress (*esthēs lampra*) and a gold finger ring (*chrysodaktylios*). It is frequently suggested that James has in mind an equestrian, entitled to wear a toga with a narrow purple band and a gold ring on his left hand.[97] The deferential behavior that James describes is precisely the way a group might react to the presence of a potential patron. The scene is fictional, of course; it is not evidence that there were equestrians in Christ assemblies. It is significant, however, that by the time that James was composed, one could *imagine* an equestrian as a possible patron.[98]

There are a few traces of the presence of elite in Christ assemblies in the early second century. Clement of Rome, writing to the Corinthian Christ assembly, implies that in his assembly there were members who were sufficiently wealthy to support the poorer members.[99] This does not of itself imply the presence of people of high rank; but at *1 Clem.* 54.1–4, when addressing what he sees as an insurrection among the leaders at Corinth, Clement suggests to the offenders that a noble person (*gennaios*) would go into exile rather than damage the fabric of the community. The appeal here is to a practice that is well attested in the politics of the Greek and Roman ruling elite—of people of high status going into a self-imposed exile for the well-being of the city.[100] Clement's advice presupposes that the offenders are sufficiently affluent to be able to relocate, and he assumes that the self-exiles will be "welcomed everywhere" (*1 Clem.* 54.3), presumably by other Christ assemblies. This is not compelling evidence of the presence of the well-born in the Christ assemblies of Rome or Corinth any more than James's fictional scenario; but the author of *1 Clement* appeals to values of civic responsibility and the preservation of personal honor that are at home in the ruling elite, and he at least presumes that the Corinthian offenders could be persuaded to emulate such values.

By the mid-second century there may have been wealthy freedmen in the Roman Christ group. Carolyn Osiek has made a plausible argument that Hermas's counsel that wealthy members not invest in their city but instead serve as benefactors of the poor (Herm. Sim. 1.8, 10) appears to address those who might otherwise engage in city-oriented munificence and can be persuaded to redirect their largesse. The quid pro quo, as the similitude of the vine and the elm tree (Herm. Sim. 2) explains, is that the largesse of the wealthy will be recognized and rewarded within the assembly by the prayers and expressions of thanks from the poor who benefited (2.1.6).

During the principate of Commodus (180–192 CE) Irenaeus referred to *qui in regali aula sunt fideles*, "faithful who are in the imperial palace"—probably imperial freedmen associated with the emperor.[101] Eusebius also claims that by that time the situation of Christ followers had improved and that in Rome many distinguished and wealthy families had embraced the cult.[102] Although he stops short of mentioning equestrians or senators specifically, Eusebius's description of them as "conspicuous (*diaphanes*) in wealth and birth" would appear to imply Christians of rank.

For the first half of the second century, the letter of James and *1 Clement* provide only scant evidence of the presence of well-born patrons in Christ assemblies although both documents appear to imagine their presence as distinct possibilities. It is only after the middle of the century—Hermas and Irenaeus—that it is likely that wealthier freedmen/freedwomen and perhaps an equestrian or two might be found in Christ assemblies. During the period of the Severan emperors, however, the situation began to change.

THE SEVERANS AND LATER

In 217 CE a member of the imperial house died and was buried in an enormous and beautifully inscribed sarcophagus. Marcus Aurelius Prosenes had been manumitted either between 161 and 169 or more likely between 176 and 180 under Marcus Aurelius and Commodus and was in charge of the imperial bedchamber (*a cubiculo*). He also held a long list of prestigious procuratorships. His sarcophagus lacks explicitly Christian images but uses the unusual phrase *Prosenes receptus ad deum* (Prosenes, received by God).[103] If, as seems likely, Prosenes was Christian, his affiliation with a Christ assembly cannot have been hidden from the Antonines or the Severans. The fact that he enjoyed such a string of high offices also means that he was unmolested by his imperial patrons.[104] This seems consistent with other data from the Severan period, during which time Christ assemblies appear not to have been harassed and may have attracted a few wealthy benefactors.

The *Acts of Peter*, composed probably during the last decades of the second century, imagines Paul and Peter in Rome, Paul in the company of two equestrians, Dionysios and Balbus, and a senator named Demetrius. The *Acts* features a contest between Peter and Simon Magus, the house guest of another senator, Marcellus, whom Peter eventually wins over. After Peter raised yet another senator from the dead, the *Acts* imagines Peter preaching to a collection of senators, equestrians, and wealthy women and matrons, whom he "strengthened in the faith" (*confortabantur in fide*, 30).

This is an entirely fanciful representation of Peter's activities in the 60s and probably even too optimistic for the Severan period. The picture of Peter in the *Acts* preaching to an assembly of senators, equestrians, and Roman matrons is wishful thinking. Yet as Lampe has observed, the author of the *Acts* must have thought it at least credible that senators *might* be attracted to Christ groups, which implies that at the end of the second century, there must have been at least "one or two equestrians among the Christians of Rome"; otherwise, the story would have been embarrassing and impossible.[105]

During the principate of Septimius Severus (193–211 CE), Tertullian boasted that Christians could be found everywhere except in temples, probably also an exaggeration.[106] Elsewhere, however, he recalls that the emperor protected from the mobs some well-born women and men (*clarissimas feminas et clarissimos viros*) who were Christian.[107] The fact that Tertullian mentions women first perhaps indicates that the preponderance of well-born Christians were women. Only slightly later Hippolytus complained that Callistus, bishop of Rome (217–222 CE), had permitted women of rank—probably meaning women of senatorial families—to cohabit with men of significantly inferior legal status, even slaves, "without a legal marriage." Hippolytus is critical of this practice, but its logic is clear: under Roman law a woman's rank followed that of her father, then her husband, so that a *clarissima* (woman of senatorial rank) who married a commoner or a slave lost her status as senatorial.[108] The evidence of Tertullian and Hippolytus suggests that it was women of high rank, not men, who were first attracted to Christ groups.

This matches epigraphic and other evidence. The first secure evidence of women of rank appears in the third century: a funerary monument records a certain Luria Ianuaria, a Roman woman of senatorial rank who married an equestrian;[109] Tertullian mentions the wife of Lucius Claudius Herminianus, governor of Cappadocia, certainly of senatorial rank;[110] and Hippolytus names the wife of a governor of Syria.[111]

In the mid-third century, Cyprian cites a rescript of Valerian that imposed punishment on bishops, presbyters, and deacons and that threatened senators, men of rank, and Roman equestrians with the loss of rank and property and even execution, adding that Roman matrons should lose property and be exiled and that imperial freedmen who were Christian should be re-enslaved.[112] While this rescript does not permit any estimate of the numbers of senators and matrons of high rank that had become Christians, the plain sense of it is that Valerian was aware that the Christ cult had achieved some foothold among the elite by the mid-third century.

For third-century Rome we have, in addition to Luria Ianuaria, six other funerary monuments for senatorial women and one senatorial male.[113] Since two of the deceased are identified as *clarissimae puellae*, that is, young girls of senatorial families, we should assume that the parents also had that rank. Yet by the eve of Constantine's triumph over Maxentius in 312 CE, the numbers of Christians of senatorial rank were still few.

THE ATTRACTION OF THE ELITE TO CHRIST ASSEMBLIES

What might have been the attraction of Christ assemblies to those of high rank—senators, equestrians, and imperial freedmen? And why would elite women more than elite men seem to have adhered to Christ assemblies? The elite of both genders presumably had resources that insulated them from economic hardships, modes of sociality that provided a sense of belonging, means to ensure appropriate burials, and commitments to civic cults and deities. They did not need the kinds of support that Christ assemblies might have to offer people of more modest status. Two possibilities present themselves: opportunities for patronage and engagement with a "textual community."

ELITE PATRONAGE

Patronage was a common, virtually essential technology of self-representation for the elite. It gave social capital to the donor, enhanced her or his standing within peer groups, and represented the donor as public minded and a person of moral worth. The donor gained social capital by attracting grateful clients, who in turn formed part of the patron's retinue. Clients might erect a statue in the patron's honor or affix a *tabula patronatus* to his or her house for all to see.[114] An inscription from Etruria offers an example of the latter: a builders' guild (*collegium fabrum*) co-opted Ancharia Luperca, the widow of their patron, as patron herself and decreed: "we should erect a bronze statue of her in the clubhouse (*schola*) of our collegium beside that of her husband, Laberius Gallus, so that her goodwill, her devotion toward us, and our goodwill toward her will be visible for all in the public view, and also that a patron's plaque (*tabula patronatus*) be attached to a wall in her house" (CIL 11.2702; Volsinii, 224 CE).

As Monica Trümper has suggested, the honorary inscriptions erected in temples or clubhouses functioned like the business cards of patrons, displaying the names of all those who had benefited the group.[115] In a patron's house they were also the "business cards" of all the patron's grateful clients, advertising his or her generosity and public-mindedness to anyone who came to the house.

Benefaction was intensely individual: commendations of euergetism by the city or an association focused on the individual and his or her public-mindedness (*eunoia*), excellence (*aretē*), piety (*eusebeia*), and disinterested generosity (*aphilarguria*). Such declarations were, in Zuiderhoek's words, a way "to prove that [the recipient] was sufficiently virtuous to justify his position among the ruling elite of the city."[116] Patronage, however, was not simply an opportunity for advancement; it was an obligation. Magistrates and other elite were expected to engage in benefaction as a mark of their own social superiority. Local populations expressed their annoyance when patronage was withheld or offered in forms that did not meet with public approval.[117]

Demographic shifts during the Antonine and Severan periods created new opportunities and expectations for patronage. Civic hierarchies were fragile and volatile. Garnsey and Saller note that the consular families failed to reproduce at a rate of 75 percent per generation.[118] The Augustan marriage laws had already tried to address the dramatic failure of the curial classes to marry and produce children.[119] Males who did not marry were forbidden from making or taking legacies. These laws may have had some effect on maintaining the numbers of the ruling elite, but in the long run the curial class declined. Unpredictable mortality meant that some families failed to produce any heirs that could follow fathers through the *cursus honorum*. The survival of too many children meant that family property was divided, with the result that a family's wealth was diluted and diminished.[120] The result was the gradual decline of the curial ranks so that during the Antonine and Severan periods replacements were recruited, mainly from the provinces. The number of "new men" entering the Senate increased significantly, the consequence of older families dropping below the census requirements of their rank.[121] Analogous shifts likely occurred among the equestrian and decurial ranks as well. Elevation in status, however, also brought with it the expectation of patronage.

Elite benefaction had a distinctive profile.[122] Male senators and equestrians were not among the significant patrons of Christ assemblies or even of other cultic groups, with perhaps the exception of the large associations of *dendrophors* devoted to the Magna Mater/Cybele and a few Dionysiac groups.[123] Women were a different matter. Emily Hemelrijk has collected instances of women of rank attested as patrons of associations: in Italy three of senatorial rank, all patrons of occupational guilds (to which we can add two women who were patrons of Judean assemblies in Asia);[124] five women of equestrian rank, all patrons of occupational guilds; and six not identified by rank, including one who was the patron of the devotees of Jupiter Latium (*cultores Iovi Latii*).[125] To this we should also add Salvia Marcellina, the wife of an imperial freedman, who is also listed as a *mater collegi* of the collegium of Aesculapius and Hygia, and Ulpia Cynegis, who donated a burial place to the same association.[126]

In a much larger study of female benefaction in general, Hemelrijk tabulated 363 female patrons (including civic patrons). Her analysis revealed several noteworthy patterns: First, although there were fewer benefactions by women than by men, the average size of those benefactions was higher. Second, women built bathhouses but not curiae; they did not build fortifications or walls or circuses, but they did build amphitheaters and theaters; and most of all, they built, rebuilt, and decorated temples. And finally, Hemelrijk suggests that subelite female patrons also competed with one another for public visibility as patrons. While about 40 percent of female patrons were from senatorial, equestrian, or decurial families, 60 percent were *libertae* (11 percent) or not specifically identified as people of rank (49 percent).[127]

Thus, while people of rank were more likely to patronize occupational guilds than cultic associations, a few elite are known to have patronized cultic groups, more women than men, and more wealthy freedmen/freedwomen and commoners than senators or equestrians. This also aligns with the survey above of elite and subelite connected with Christ assemblies: there were a few imperial freedmen in the second century, perhaps an equestrian or two, including an equestrian woman. Women of higher rank are attested only in the early third century.

The case of Callistus cited above in all likelihood involved female *patrons* of senatorial rank. Callistus had permitted these women, either unmarried or widowed, to cohabit with men of inferior station. If the fathers of these women were dead—and age tables indicate that a woman older than thirty years was unlikely to have a surviving father[128]—and if there were no other surviving male agnates, the women would have been *sui iuris*, controlling their own property. As indicated above, however, a *clarissima* who contracted an illegal marriage would have lost her rank and control of her property and hence her ability to function as a patron to a Christ assembly. Callistus's concession to these women of rank was likely a function of the benefit that they could offer to the Christ assembly in Rome.

The connections between Christ groups and people of rank were a result of both the needs of the elite and especially the nouveau riche to represent themselves as agents of their wealth and social power and the needs of Christ assemblies to gain resources. Some of these patrons were likely "external patrons"—that is, benefactors, but patrons whose connection with their clients was mainly in name. Julia Severa, for example, as an imperial priestess and a woman of senatorial rank, was a patron of a Judean assembly but hardly a member of the assembly in any real sense of the word. Salvia Marcellina, one of the two patrons of the collegium of Aesculapius and Hygia, was at least minimally involved in her collegium since she was imagined to attend at least some of its banquets. Many other patrons, male and female, probably did not. Nevertheless, a Christ assembly that had received patronage from a person of rank had gained considerable social capital as well as protection from hostile forces in the city.

BOOK CULTURE

If patronage and its benefits provided one basis for a relationship between the elite (or wealthy commoner) and a Christ assembly, were there other attractions for people of higher status? At least one salient possibility concerns the intellectual practices of Christ groups.

One of the markers of elite culture was the ability to read fluently and to engage the content of texts. Lucian of Samosata's satire *The Ignorant Book Collector* lampoons someone who wanted to affect high culture. The ignoramus buys expensive books but without being able to assess their value independently; he has no training and hence has no idea what a book is about; he presents himself in public as a reader but mispronounces words; and although he owns deluxe copies of books, he "maims and murders the content with his accent" (7, trans. LCL).

This lampoon indicates the value that literacy had among the elite. As William Johnson has documented, elite culture adopted a range of literary practices, including group reading, the reading of difficult texts, and the use of texts as an occasion for further discussion and as a "springboard to a mutually understood set of group behaviors that serve to build the sense of an intellectual community."[129] The practice of reading and recitation was not simply a matter of entertainment but served as a basic component in the construction and reinforcement of elite intellectual culture and its shared values and commitments. He summarizes:

> "Reading" in this society is tightly bound up in the construction of the community. Group reading and serious conversation devolving from reading are twin axes around which much of the elite man's community turns. The reading here described—of literary prose—is sharply distinct from pragmatic reading of documents and the like. Reading of literary prose, often difficult and inaccessible to the less educated, is part of that which fences off the elite group from the rest of society. Habits like use of servants to help with the lection, or group reading and discussion, are particular to the social group, and mesh together with other, related customs (such as routinely inviting friends to dinners with performance entertainment). Reading functions as group entertainment, intellectual fodder, and aesthetic delight, but sociologically plays a role beyond the sum of its functional components.[130]

The role of reading in elite self-representation is seen on tombstones. Perhaps best known is the famous "Sappho of Pompeii," depicting a woman with a gold hairnet and earrings, holding a codex and a stylus and looking thoughtful.[131] A sarcophagus relief from Ostia Antica depicts two women, both holding scrolls, the older, seated woman reading to the younger (fig. 23). The modern viewer is likely to miss the importance of the scene. In a culture in which literacy levels were not much more than 10 percent and the ability to read fluently and to comment on the content of a text very much lower than that, the relief is a claim to status. Both women are able to read and to transmit the knowledge that comes from books, and this sets them apart from the overwhelming majority of the population.

Early Christ groups likely could not compete with the resources that were available to Greek and Roman elite—slaves trained to read, extensive libraries, and access to deluxe book rolls. Nevertheless, they created a book culture, privileging reading, discussion, commentary, and discourse that flowed from books. Despite widespread illiteracy, both literary and material evidence suggests that Christ followers valorized literacy and literate culture : the principal agents of the Jesus movement came to be represented as skilled literate communicators; the book, perhaps even a codex, became a special symbol of a Christian confes-

Figure 23. Sarcophagus from Ostia Antica. (Photo by the author.)

sion; and what Brian Stock has called textual communities formed around the reading, study, and preservation of books.[132]

From a very early point in the cultural production of early Christ groups, allusions to books and book culture were recursively embedded in the documents of Christ followers. Most of the texts that we have draw attention to the importance of book culture by "footnoting" other books: Matthew almost obsessively cites the Septuagint in his account of the life of Jesus, anchoring all that Jesus does in the textualized history of Israel. The other gospel writers do the same, constructing the history of Jesus and, in the case of Acts, the history of the Christ group by anchoring them in the history of Israel. Luke, in 4:16–30, represents Jesus as a reader of texts, able to find his way through a codex[133] and to perform a text in public and offer comments on it. Luke's Paul not only can use the Hebrew Scriptures but can quote from Epimenides and Aratus's *Phenomona* (Acts 17:28).

Stock argues in relation to the twelfth-century Waldensians that their adoption of book culture allowed them to create a history for themselves, grounding their practices and beliefs in other more ancient writings.[134] The Waldensians formed themselves around the performance of oral texts, then an educative process, leading to the study, memorization, and preaching of vernacular texts and the historicizing of the community though intertextuality. They associated their community with earlier antecedents by linking themselves to the *Life of St. Alexis* and the *Life of Anthony*.[135] It is not difficult to see that Christ assemblies did something analogous, embedding their history in the history of Israel.

By the second century Justin provides a picture of a meeting of a Christ assembly in which textual practices are at the center:

> And on the day called for the sun, there is a common gathering of all who live in cities or in the country, and the memoirs of the apostles (*ta apomnēmoneumata tōn apostolōn*) or the writings of the prophets are read, as long as time allows. Next, after the reader has stopped, the presider (*ho proestōs*) admonishes and encourages with a speech to imitate these good things. Then we all rise together and pray and, as we before said, after we have finished praying, bread and wine and water are brought, and the president in like manner offers prayers and thanksgivings, according to his ability, and the people assent, saying Amen; and there is a distribution to each and a participation of the food over which thanks have been said, and for those who are not present some is sent through the "servants" (*diakonoi*). (*1 Apol.* 67.3–5)

About the same time, Justin reports the case, mentioned above, of the wife of a highly placed Roman, probably an equestrian, who after learning of the "teachings of Christ" (*ta tou Christou didagmata*) tried unsuccessfully to persuade her intemperate husband to reform. He did not but turned his anger against her teacher Ptolemaios, who was eventually executed (2 *Apol.* 2.9). Lampe wonders whether this Ptolemaios is in fact the author of the Letter to Flora cited by Epiphanius (*Haer.* 33.3–7).[136] If so, we not only have the name of the equestrian woman but also the content of Ptolemaios's teaching, which shows a heavy focus on the interpretation of texts of the Hebrew Bible.

It is not that Christ groups in general rose much above the general level of illiteracy typical of the Roman world. But they privileged the reading of literature, discussion, and commentary on texts; the transmission of knowledge in literature media; and the storage and production of texts. These practices instantiated the value of reading and text-oriented discussion, even amid predominantly illiterate audiences.

This is evident both in the volume of literary material that Christ followers produced and in the contents of those writings. Larry Hurtado draws attention to the fact that more than two hundred writings by Christ followers are known from the first three centuries of the Common Era.[137] This is in sharp contrast to the literary output of other cultic groups such as the cult of Mithras or Jupiter Dolichenus and is very significantly larger than literary texts about the cult of Isis.

Participation in book culture is amply attested papyrologically, not only by the large number of papyrus copies of canonical and noncanonical writings, but also by numerous other data. The appearance of a copy of Irenaeus's *Adversus haereses* in Upper Egypt among the Oxyrhynchus papyri (P.Oxy III 405) only two decades after it was written points to a system of "interlibrary loan" that took literary texts from Gaul to another part of the empire.[138] Copies of Hermas, penned in Rome during the mid-second century, are already attested in Egypt in the latter part of that century or the early third.[139] The Leonides archive mentioned above offers an example of a flax farmer, flax dealer, and officer of an occupational guild also having a copy of Romans (P.Oxy II 209) and a business associate who was a lector in an Oxyrhynchite church. All of these data point to a robust book culture and the value that was attached to knowledge that came from books.

Given the high value that elite Roman culture placed on literacy and literate technologies, and the ability of the elite to read and to comment on texts, it is likely that the literate practices of Christ assemblies held out appeal to the elite—perhaps not to many of the senatorial elite but probably those somewhat lower down the social ladder. As textual communities, Christ assemblies could supply some of the symbolic capital that was so important to those with aspirations to elite culture. And by the end of the second century, Christ groups would begin to develop their own highly literate and educated members—such as Clement of Alexandria, Tertullian, and Origen.

FALLING AWAY

In the early second century Pliny reported to Trajan that some of those who had been denounced to him admitted to having been *Christiani* but had stopped practicing, some three years before and some as many as twenty years before.[140] Pliny was uninterested in how or why such defections occurred, but from what is known about associative behavior in general, several hypotheses are possible.

The simplest scenario relates to a member who is no longer able to make the required contributions to the guild and so voluntarily resigns. P.Mich IX 575 (Karanis, 184 CE), the letter of a certain Epiodoros to the supervisor (*epimelētēs*) of a guild, is one such example. Epiodoros states that he is impoverished (*asthenos*) and no longer able to pay the association's fee. Obviously, dues and other financial inputs were critical in order to preserve the financial solvency of the group. Failure of members to contribute to common banquets would mean the loss of the sociality that was part of the dynamics of associations and Christ assemblies. Without contributions to the *taphikon*, the payments mandated by an association's bylaws to support funerals would be impossible. Without funds for banquets, burials, loans, and other activities, the group would collapse.

There was a considerable range in expectation concerning dues, including some evidence of sliding scales of contributions pegged to the capabilities and resources of each member. The common practice of exempting some members from dues as a result of prior distinguished service, or in the case of 1 Timothy, "true widows" who were to be supported from common funds,[141] also meant that the aggregate contributions from dues-paying members had to be sufficient to cover the entire costs of banquets, funerals, and other expenses. Associations that were unable to maintain the income threshold needed to meet monthly costs would not survive. It seems unlikely that free riders could be supported unconditionally, since they represented a drag on the group. Some, like Epiodoros, resigned.

CIL 6.9102 and the *familia Silvani* offer another scenario: exclusion, rather than resignation, as the result of the failure to pay the appropriate dues or egregious violations of the association's bylaws. Exclusionary rules were essential to the kinds of connectivity nurtured by associations, since they established behavioral thresholds. Rules were in fact positive forces in constructing membership because they could be instrumentalized for creating and maintaining solidarity and trust within the group. The *cultores* of Diana and Antinoüs were explicit in connecting membership with rules, insisting that new members read and agree with the group's regulations: "You who desire to enter this society as a new member must first read the bylaws carefully before entering so as not to find cause for complaint later."[142]

The regulations of a group of *Herakleiastai* from just outside of Athens in the early second century CE included a two-stage provision for dealing with noncompliance with the group's bylaws: one who had failed to pay his membership dues on time should be fined, and if he did not pay the fine, he would be expelled. For this purpose, the group apparently invented the term *exeranos*—that is, ex-member.[143] Since the group kept careful records of income and expenditures and monitored member contributions, it is likely that becoming an *exeranos* also meant having one's name erased from a membership list.

Noncompliance in matters of financial contributions was only one challenge, and probably not the most serious. The rule of the Iobakchoi stipulated that failure to contribute dues could lead to exclusion (IG II^2 1368, lines 65–73), as well as persistent disorderly conduct at banquets. The Iobakchoi also had a multistage disciplinary procedure, first banning a disorderly member from meetings for some period and imposing a fine (lines 84–89) and in some cases requiring an officer bearing Dionysos's staff (*thyrsos*) to "lay it on" the offender. If he refused to leave, he would be expelled by the bouncers (called *hippoi*, "horses") (lines 135–145). Failure to comply with the group's behavioral code was also the subject of several Egyptian bylaws that required members to render assistance to fellow members in distress. In the event of noncompliance, a fine was levied, but it seems likely that persistent failure to assist would lead to expulsion.

Expulsion is a common theme in both the Pauline and the Johannine corpus. Paul's admonition concerning the man in an incestuous relationship to "hand over" the man's flesh to Satan presumably implies an expulsion from the group (1 Cor 5:5) and, as I suggested above (chapter 4), much more than that. From the opposite vantage point, the fourth gospel reflects the exclusion or expulsion of Christ followers from Judean assemblies. Three times the author employs the neologism *aposynagogos* (literally, ex-assembly member) to characterize the Christ followers he addresses (John 9:22, 12:42, 16:2). There is considerable debate about whether there was, as John 9:22 asserts, a formal decision to expel Christ followers from Judean assemblies and, if so, where was this effected, by whom, at what time, and for what purpose.[144] Whatever the case, given the widespread practice of striking names from rosters and the premium that was placed upon belonging, we should think of exclusion from a Judean assembly as involving a material act as well as other sanctions. Since membership in an association involved reciprocal obligations of members to the group and of the group to its members, the elimination of a nonparticipating person from the roster had legal and financial implications as well as representing a moral sanction.

The exclusionary practices of Christ assemblies are often cloaked in metaphor. Matthew imagines offenders against the communal rules being thrown into "outer darkness" where there is a "gnashing of teeth" (Matt 8:12; 13:42, 50; 22:13; 24:51; 25:30). Elsewhere he orders that a recalcitrant offender be treated as a "gentile and a tax gatherer" (18:17). While Matthew dresses up these references to exclusion in highly figurative language, we might well wonder what material practice is in view. Were names ritually blotted out of the parchment containing the list of members?[145]

Falling away at times undoubtedly had to do with the inability of an individual to meet the financial obligations of membership or to comply with the behavioral rules of a group. But in other instances, the loss of members was probably due to external factors and even network collapse. A Mithraic association that had been decimated by the Antonine plague had managed to renew itself by the late second century CE by recruiting new members to replace those who had died.[146] It is easily imaginable, however, that other associations struck by the plague or some other adversity were not able to do this, especially if the family, occupational, or neighborhood networks upon which they relied for recruitment had been compromised. The *cultores* of Jupiter Cernenus had begun with fifty-four members.[147] By 167 CE, however, the membership had fallen to seventeen, with the result that dues were not paid and the collegium found itself unable to pay for any further funerals. The legal notice set up by the remaining officers of the collegium does not state the cause of the collapse, but the date of inscription and its location in Dacia is consistent with the supposition that the cause was the Antonine plague rather than the indifference of its members.[148]

Similar failures affected Christ groups. Cavan Concannon has pointed out that the network of interconnected Christ assemblies associated with Dionysios of Corinth had by the time of Eusebius fallen apart. In the late second century, the letters of Dionysios show that he had a network, probably built upon commercial networks, which connected him not only to Sparta and Athens, but also to Knossos and Gortyna in Crete and Nicomedia and Amastris on the Black Sea.[149] Yet by the time of Eusebius, a century and a half later, Eusebius knew nothing of Dionysios or his network beyond the letters that he found preserved in Caesarea. Whether the failure of the network was due to the plague of Cyprian in the mid-third century, the barbarian invasions that had begun, or simply changes in the patterns of commercial trade is unknown. But fail it did. For Concannon Dionysios's network and its fate illustrates the tenuous and fragile nature of networks, how they can fall apart, be disrupted, and in the end collapse.[150]

I have argued in this chapter that the recruitment of new members should be seen as a matter of both the choices exercised by prospective recruits and the benefits and social capital that membership in associations and Christ assemblies offered. Choice, however, was limited by the networks and connections that individuals had. This also means that falling away from a group was not only a matter of individual choosing not to continue membership, because of the monetary and nonmonetary costs involved, or even exclusion or disaffiliation by the association; it could also have structural causes. The collapse of a network that supported an association and a Christ assembly might be due to disease, adversity, or the disbanding of commercial relationships upon which a cultic network depended. In spite of the benefits of sociality, support, and the prestige that an association like the *cultores* of Jupiter Cernenus in Alburnus Maior might have to offer, the Antonine plague or some other catastrophe evidently decimated the group. It could not mobilize local or interregional networks to recover from those losses. The second-century network of Dionysios of Corinth may have failed for other reasons, such as the defection or deaths of members or the collapse of commercial connections between Corinth, Crete, and the Black Sea. But some networks persisted and were responsible for the diffusion of the Christ cult. The commercial links between, for example, the Rhône Valley, Rome, and Egypt allowed copies of Irenaeus's *Adversus haereses* and Hermas to find their way to Oxyrhynchus in relatively short order. The functioning and structure of networks help us to imagine how associations and Christ assemblies thrived and how some failed to persist.

Conclusion

When I was in graduate school I sat in on an introductory class on the Synoptic problem taught by my mentor. A student, troubled by the implications of source theories and the conclusion that the gospel writers were creative editors who sometimes invented details, proposed a speculative scenario—"Isn't it possible that . . . ?"—which would allow him to rest easily and not have to face the challenge of understanding the gospels and their production in their historical contexts. My advisor simply replied: "Yes, many things are possible. But we have to decide which of the possible solutions are plausible."

This book has privileged comparison as a means of setting the investigation of early Christ assemblies on a more controlled and defensible footing—to move from the possible and speculative to the plausible. As I have argued throughout, knowing about ancient cultic associations and occupational guilds does not create any new data about Christ assemblies. But it does create some new questions with which to interrogate our data and sets some realistic parameters for our reconstructions of a variety of aspects of those assemblies.

To have compared occupational guilds and cultic associations with the very sparse data from Christ assemblies has raised questions that had rarely been entertained up to now. How would we know whether a Christ assembly of thirty or fifty or one hundred was a realistic size? And where would such groups meet? Were other associations that embraced people of multiple ethnic identities, legal statuses, and genders usual or unusual? And would the Corinthian assembly, which clearly included people of a variety of legal statuses and both genders, have struck observers as unexceptional or as odd? What options for funding communal meals were available, and which were the most usual? Would it be usual or unusual for patrons to pay for all of the activities of a Christ assembly?

Did patrons typically give large endowments to the associations they patronized? And what kind of patron should we imagine as a benefactor of a Christ group?—a senator? an equestrian? a wealthy commoner? a woman? a man? Who took care of burials? How were new members recruited?

The point of pursuing these questions and comparisons has not been to arrive at definitive answers but rather to suggest a spectrum of probabilities that match the data from a large number of associations and guilds. To imagine a Christ assembly in the first century with thirty members seems more probable than one with one hundred members. It seems very unlikely that Christ assemblies, at least before Constantine, were patronized by the cream of Roman society and just as unlikely that members of aristocratic ranks, at least in the first and second centuries, would have been involved at all, despite Luke's stories. It is unlikely that the activities of Christ assemblies, if they resembled those of other cultic associations, could be sustained by the endowments of one or two wealthy benefactors. Most benefactors simply were not that generous. Given the unlikelihood that benefactors were in a position to fund all of the meals and burials of Christ assemblies, it is necessary to imagine other funding mechanisms, most probably member contributions or rotating liturgical obligations.

The most important, though perhaps obvious, feature of associations and Christ assemblies is that they fostered *connectivity* among members, sometimes between members and the elite of society, and often lateral connections between one association and another. In the twenty-first century, it is perhaps difficult to appreciate the importance of connectivity, in part because contemporary identity formation is as much based on individual achievements and aspirations as it is on corporate and collective identity. In antiquity, however, identity was largely associated with the group or groups to which one belonged. Social capital flowed from those groups to individuals, and groups profited (or suffered) from the deeds (or misdeeds) of members.

The value of connectivity is exemplified in a number of practices, from keeping and displaying lists; to holding common meals; to collecting funds, both for the group's activities and, in some instances, for other groups in an imagined fictive polity; to participating in the burial of members. These should not be treated simply as activities that the association decided to engage; they were instead the activities that constituted the group as a group. Eating together, participating in a subscription, engaging in processions, and attending the funeral of a colleague were ways of materializing connectivity and displaying the group to itself. These activities were not epiphenomenal but constitutive.

Likewise, the use of bylaws to regulate the group was not simply a pragmatic necessity; rules were fundamental to the construction of the association as a network of trust and were essential for group survival and the generation of social capital. The behavioral rules to which members agreed formed the basis not only for the conduct that one could expect within the association's banquet; they also meant that one could depend on fellow members in other realms as well. The association's rules often extended well beyond the banqueting hall, requiring members to assist fellows in distress or to stand surety should one be arrested. Given the vicissitudes of life in the ancient world, membership in an association or guild provided a kind of social safety net, and this was surely one of the attractions of membership.

The inner dynamics of associations are particularly noteworthy. Beginning in the third century BCE, Athens's associations, especially cultic associations, created "free spaces" that allowed the interaction of people who in the normal course of life would not associate with one another. Resident aliens and citizens, freeborn and slaves, women and men could be found together as members. Undoubtedly, these spaces did not translate into fully egalitarian social spaces, which surely would have elicited some sneers from oligarchic elements in society. But these free spaces were gestures in the direction of less segmented and hierarchicalized social imaginaries. The widespread mimicry of civic institutions and terminology by associations has also invited the conclusions that not only were associations "cities writ small," but they imitated the democratic governance practices of their host cities, voting honors, passing bylaws, and deciding legal cases on their own. This is what I have called "playing with democracy."

The investigation of meal practices also concluded that typically the communal meal instantiated the value of equality, irrespective of whatever social standing a member had outside the group. The combination of rule-based dining, where each member's portion or distribution was regulated, and the practice of systems of rotating governance combined to reinforce the notion of the equality of members, also one of the fundamental values of Athenian democracy. We should not exaggerate this feature of associative life, since there are also plenty of dynamics in the practice of patronage that pushed against the democratic dynamics of associations. When Herodes Atticus, one of the wealthiest men in the Roman Empire, became the chief priest of the Iobakchoi in 164/165 CE, displacing the former chief priest of twenty-three years, this was hardly an expression of democratic practice or values (IG II^2 1368). Other associations seem to have maintained more consistently democratic practices, and even the Iobakchoi had regulations that aimed at member equality.

Understood as social networks, associations afforded members multiplex connections with each other, some stronger, some weaker. Associations viewed as networks sometimes connected members with the elite of society and in other cases created lateral connections with other associations. Thus membership in an occupational guild in one Roman town might bring members into a network that included cultic groups (through which recruitment could occur) and even connections with other associations in remote parts of the empire. The boatmen and registrars of Ostia had connections with the senatorial elite of Rome but, via patronage, also with the boatmen and registrars of the Rhône Valley. Analogous connections are probably at the heart of links between Christ groups in Smyrna and Hierapolis and Christ groups in Lyon in the Rhône Valley, and between the Rhône Valley and the Upper Egyptian town of Oxyrhynchus, where a copy of Irenaeus's *Adversus haereses* turned up only twenty or so years after it had been written.

In this book I contend that certain aspects of Christ assemblies can usefully be compared with aspects of cultic associations and occupational guilds. Although connectivity and the strategies of materializing belonging differed from one group to another, Christ assemblies no less than associations adopted discursive means and engaged in ritualized behavior that cemented a sense of belonging. The devotees of Atargatis in Athens and Sarapis groups developed the language of the god inviting members to participate, not at all unlike Paul's language of being "called" by the deity. This strategy was particularly useful with groups like the Corinthian Christ assembly, which was mixed in terms of members' ethnicity, gender, and legal status, since it added another level of "glue" to hold the group together. Ritualized behavior such as eating together—in spite of the difficulties that Paul perceived at Corinth—was a powerful instrument of group formation since as an instance of "segregative commensality" it displayed the group to itself and through the regulation of food and other distributions it created a fiction of equality.

The Pauline collection can usefully be viewed alongside the practice of *epidosis*, a subscription that collected funds for a project. The problems and challenges typically experienced in *epidoseis* turn out to precisely mirror the challenges that Paul faced in bringing the collection to completion. As a ritual action, *epidoseis* were ways for contributors to perform citizenship, irrespective of their levels of wealth. The Pauline collection was likewise a performance of citizenship, but in his case a performance of citizenship in a translocal polity and, strikingly, a polity that embraced identity groups—Greeks and Judeans—that normally had little to do with one another. This is an instance where comparison reveals not only the similarities between Paul's collection and those of Greek cities, but also the ways in which the ideology of the *epidosis* was transformed to meet the particular needs of Christ groups.

These and other conclusions illustrate the fruitfulness of local and limited comparison of Christ groups with ancient cultic associations and occupational guilds. Comparison does not solve every problem, but it does offer useful heuristic models for thinking about the social complexion of Christ groups, the challenges they faced, and the benefits that they offered to their members.

Glossary

(G) = Greek; (R) = Roman

agora (G)	The central marketplace of a Greek city. Since the *agora* was also a meeting space, the term is sometimes used to denote a meeting of an association and is equivalent to *ekklēsia* (meeting, assembly).
agoranomos (G)	In a civic context, an elected market supervisor. The title, however, was borrowed by some guilds and associations and used for an official, probably responsible for supervising the association's banquet.
album/-a (R)	Membership roster.
amphora	A liquid measure of approximately 26 liters.
as, asses (R)	A small bronze coin worth 1/4 sestersius or 1/16 denarius.
atrium/-a (R)	Interior courtyard in a Roman house, usually located just inside the entrance and serving as a reception space to welcome guests; typically, a square room, partly open to the sky (the *conpluvium*) with a shallow pool (*impluvium*) to catch rainwater. The atrium was also the location of the household shrine (*lararium*).
clarissimus/-i, -a/-ae (R)	Men having the rank of senator, and their daughters, their wives, or their widows. Senatorial families had to meet a census (property) requirement of 1 million sesterces.
collegium (R)	One of the most common Latin terms for "association."
columbarium (R)	A burial site, built partly or completely underground, in which the cremated remains of the deceased are placed in small niches or in small funerary urns. Niches are often marked with a short inscription indicating the name and sometimes the occupation of the deceased.
curator/-es (R)	Supervisor of an association, typically chosen or elected yearly.

decuria/-ae (R) Nominally a division of ten, but in collegia, a *decuria* might be as large as twenty-two (CIL 14.4569).

decurion (R) In the context of a town, a decurion is a town counselor or magistrate. The term was borrowed by Roman associations and used for divisional leaders in charge of a *decuria* (q.v.).

deipnētērion/-a (G) A dining room. Some were attached to a temple or located on the processional way leading to a temple. Others were unconnected to temples.

deme (G) From the late fifth century BCE the population of Attica was divided into ten "tribes" and further into 139 "demes." The division aimed at making each of the tribes equal in population. Each of the tribes included demes that were located physically in the city, the inland area of Attica, and the coast.

dēmos (G) "The People," or the Athenian citizen assembly.

denarius/-i Roman coin, equivalent to 4 sesterces, or 16 asses. One denarius is roughly equivalent to a Greek drachma.

drachma/-ae In the imperial era, a drachma was roughly equivalent to a (Roman) denarius. In Ptolemaic Egypt after 220 BCE one distinguishes between copper or bronze (AE) drachmae and silver (AR) drachmae. After 220 BCE the value of the copper drachma fell in relation to a silver drachma first to 1/60, then 1/120, then 1/240, and finally to 1/480. The value recovered under Roman rule.

epidosis/-eis (G) A collection raised from the population of a city or members of an association for special purposes such as the rebuilding of a temple, repair of walls, famine relief, or purchase of a cemetery.

eques/-ites (R) An equestrian (knight) ranked below a senator but nevertheless had to meet a census (property) requirement of 400,000 sesterces.

eranos (G) An association, originally probably a group whose member contributions created a fund from which loans could be made. The term sometimes refers to the common fund.

freedman/freedwoman A slave who had been manumitted (freed); called *libertus/-i* (male) or *liberta/-ae* (female).

grapheion (G) An administrative archive located in a village or town and containing copies of legal documents, often including the bylaws of associations, letters of complaint, contracts, bills of sale, leases, loans, etc.

hestiatorion/-a (G) A dining room (restaurant).

horreum/-a (R) A granary or warehouses used for storing grain and other products, typically found in port cities such as Ostia. These were sometimes used as meeting spaces.

insula/-ae (R) Housing blocks in Roman cities, usually multistory, containing multiple dwelling units and often with workshops (*tabernae*) on the ground floor and apartments above. Augustus limited the height of such buildings to 70 Roman feet (20.7 m), and after the Great Fire Nero reduced this to 60 Roman feet (17.75 m).

klinē/-ai (G) Dining couches or benches. Some were permanent masonry couches, others were movable wooden couches.

koinon/-a (G) Literally "common," the term can denote a group of cities in a federation, or a term for an association, or the common fund belonging to an association.

libertus/-a (R) A freedman or freedwoman.

magister (R) Supervisor of an association, typically chosen or elected yearly.

metic(s) (G) A noncitizen, resident alien in a Greek city.

nome (G) An administrative division in Ptolemaic and Roman Egypt, governed by a *nomarchēs* (nome governor) and *nomogrammateus* (nome secretary).

obol A copper or bronze coin, usually valued at one-sixth of a drachma, in some instances at one-seventh of a drachma.

oikonomos (G) Manager of a city or an estate.

ordo (R) In the context of Roman society, the *ordo* was a list of those having the rank of senator or equestrian (and perhaps decurion). Some Latin associations used the term for the group of their elected officers.

orgeōnes (G) A term (always in the plural) appearing in the late fifth century BCE in Athens and denoting a group organized around the cult of a deity or hero.

quinquennalis/-es (R) Literally a "five-year" president, though the actual term of these presidents ranged from three to five years.

senatus consultum (R) Legal enactments of the Roman Senate (as contrasted with law [*leges*] of the citizen assembly).

sesterce/-es (sestersius/-ii) 1 sesterce = 1/4 denarius = 4 asses.

sextarius/-i (R) A liquid measure of 0.54 liters.

sportula/-ae (R) Literally "little baskets" are attested only in the Latin West (North Africa, Italy, and the Western Provinces) and refer to small gifts of food (or later, money) given to clients by patrons. Many associations adopted the practice of distributing *sportulae* as part of their meal practices.

stibadium (R) A semicircular dining table (sometimes called a *sigma*).

taberna/-ae (R) A workshop or tavern usually found on the ground level of a housing block (*insula*).

taphikon (G) A funeral fee, assembled from monthly contributions by members of an association and either used for a member's funeral or paid to the deceased's family to assist in the costs of burial. In Latin, a *funeraticium*.

thiasōtēs/-ai (G) — Sometimes spelled *thiasitēs/-ai*, a member or members of an association or *thiasos*, usually a cultic association rather than an occupational guild.

tria nomina (R) — The three-part name of a Roman citizen (including freedmen), consisting of a praenomen, nomen, or *nomen gentilicium* (family name) and a cognomen—for example, Marcus Tullius Cicero, Gaius Iulius Caesar. Women's names lacked a praenomen.

triclinium — A dining room with either masonry or movable wooden couches arranged in a U-shape (two long arms and one short arm). Diners reclined on the couches on their left arms, with their bodies at an angle from the wall. A standard *triclinium* could accommodate nine to seventeen diners.

Notes

INTRODUCTION

1. CIL 6.10234 (Rome, 153 CE); trans. AGRW 322. This is probably the same association as that named in an inscription found reused in the Catacombe di Pretestato, Via Appia Pignatelli (Josi, "Cimitero di Pretestato," 211; Rome, II CE): "To the divine spirits. Ulpia Cynegis, an *immunis* made this (funerary monument) and gave it to the collegium of Aesculapius and Hygiae who are also stonemasons (who work for) our Caesar, but reserved twelve funerary urns (*ollae*) and two sarcophagi for herself and for her own (freedmen)." According to CIL 6.10234 the location of the clubhouse of the collegium was between the first and second milestone on the Via Appia on the left as one left Rome. The find site of AE 1937, 161, was in the Catacombe di Pretestato where it was in secondary usage (Spera, *Il paesaggio suburbano,* 53).
2. On the translation of *ekklēsia* as "assembly," see "A Note on Translations," below.
3. The term *ekklēsia* occurs in the undisputed Pauline letters forty-three times; in Ephesians, Colossians, and 2 Thessalonians, fifteen times; in the pseudo-Pauline Pastoral letters three times; in Acts twenty-three times; in Hebrews three times; in James once; in 3 John three times; in Revelation nineteen times; and in the Apostolic Fathers seventy-two times. *Synagōgē* in reference to an assembly of Christ followers occurs in Jas 2:2; Ignatius, *Pol.* 4.2.
4. Persons and Currie, "Tail of Tyrannosaurus."
5. Hutchinson and Garcia, "Tyrannosaurus"; Benton, "Studying Function and Behavior."
6. J. Smith, *Drudgery Divine,* 53.
7. Lévi-Strauss, *Totemism,* 89.
8. See in general, Dubuisson, *Western Construction of Religion,* 4–5.
9. Cicero, *De natura deorum* 3.3.5, concludes, *harum ego religionum nullam umquam contemnendam putavi,* "Well, I hold that none of these *religiones* should ever be neglected." Cicero uses *religiones* (plural) to mean "observances" or "rites," not "religion" in a modern sense.

10. See Nongbri, *Before Religion*, chap. 2; Fitzgerald, *Discourse on Civility*; and Barton and Boyarin, *Imagine No Religion*.
11. Although the term *Ioudaismos* appears in Gal 1:13, it is erroneous to translate this as "Judaism" in the sense that the term is now used to refer to the religion of Jews. Instead, it refers to the way of life characteristic of Judeans, which included various cultic practices but also other aspects of life. Hence, it is also misleading to take Paul's statement in Galatians as meaning that he "converted" from "Judaism" to "Christianity" (a term that he does not use).
12. Schleiermacher, *Die christliche Glaube*, §4.2: "*schlechthinniges Abhängigkeitsgefühl.*"
13. Nock, *Conversion*, 7.
14. Crook, *Reconceptualising Conversion*; Crook, "Loyalty," 175, later says, "In other words, conversion in the ancient world was measured not by recourse to emotional and introspective experiences, but rather by actions of loyalty or disloyalty extended to a philosophical or divine patron."
15. Nock, *Conversion*, 229. See also Cumont, *Oriental Religions*, 28–29: "Perhaps there never was a religion so cold and prosaic as the Roman. Being subordinated to politics, it sought, above all, to secure the protection of the gods for the state . . . by the strict execution of appropriate practices."
16. Price, *Rituals and Power*, 10; similarly Rives, "Graeco-Roman Religion," 251.
17. Crook, *Reconceptualising Conversion*, 26.
18. Mauss, "Category of the Human Mind."
19. Geertz, "From the Native's Point of View," 31.
20. Ansary, *West of Kabul*, 17.
21. Asad, "Reading a Modern Classic," 214.
22. Hopkins, *World Full of Gods*.
23. Morgan, *Roman Faith*, 30.
24. Morgan, *Roman Faith*, 37–122; Morgan, "Belief and Practice." As Chaniotis, "Emotional Community," 266, observes: Rituals are "institutionalized attempts by humans to communicate with the gods"; "most Greek rituals . . . were meant to attract a god's attention through visual and textual signals and other media of sensual attraction (for instance the burning of incense and of meat and wine on the altar) and to remove any deterrents (for instance impure individuals, unpleasant words etc.) that might prevent the deity from coming."
25. Pliny, *Ep.* 10.96.5. See Sherwin-White, "Why Were the Early Christians Persecuted?" For a different view, see de Ste. Croix, "Rejoinder."
26. On this development, see Fitzgerald, *Discourse on Civility*.
27. Judge, *Social Distinctives*, 130. Similarly, Ebner, *Die Stadt als Lebensraum*, 130.
28. Similarly, Ebner, *Die Stadt als Lebensraum*, 130, who, recognizing the problems involved in applying the term "religion" to early Christ assemblies, nevertheless points out that they engaged in many practices that are comparable to the cults of antiquity: common meals in which Christ was acclaimed as exalted by God; and the use of quasi-sacrificial language (1 Cor 10:16–17) and language of sin-forgiveness (Matt 26:28) comparable to the purpose of sacrificial practices in the Herodian temple. Cultic lan-

guage is also used metaphorically, for example, in the emphasis in Hebrews (13:15–16) on a heavenly temple and cult with Jesus as a high priest offering *thysia* (sacrifice). Similarly, see the claim of Rom 12:1 and 1 Peter that all are now priests, using cultic terms metaphorically.

29. J. Smith, *Imagining Religion*, xi. See also J. Smith, "Religion, Religions, Religious," who points to the expansion of the understanding of the term "religion" beginning in the sixteenth century, which anticipates some of the continuing issues in the study of religion: "(1) 'Religion' is not a native category. It is not a first-person term of self-characterization. It is a category imposed from the outside on some aspect of native culture. . . . (2) Even in these early [sixteenth-century] formulations, there is an implicit universality. 'Religion' is thought to be a ubiquitous human phenomenon. . . . (3) In constructing the second-order, generic category 'religion,' its characteristics are those that appear natural to the other . . . 'knowledge of God' and 'religion' . . . as we understand it. (4) 'Religion' is an anthropological not a theological category. . . . It describes human thought and action, most frequently in terms of belief and norms of behavior" (269–70).
30. See Nongbri, "Dislodging 'Embedded' Religion," who objects to the term "embedded religion" on the same grounds—that although it is perhaps true that religion was "embedded" in other ancient cultural domains, "it facilitates and masks slippage between descriptive and redescriptive uses of the concept religion" (442–43).
31. See the masterful collection of data in Runesson, Binder, and Olsson, *Ancient Synagogue*.
32. Eckhardt, "Who Thought?"
33. See, for example, Gruen, "Synagogues and Voluntary Associations," and his objection to classifying Judean synagogues as associations on the grounds that this "says little about how the Jews *conceived* their own communal assemblages or governed their own communities, let alone about the purposes of their gatherings" (128, emphasis added). See now the responses by Ascough, "Paul, Synagogues, and Associations" and "Methodological Reflections," which make the same point against Gruen: "association" is *our etic term* for small face-to-face groups in antiquity, not *their* term for themselves and hence it is otiose to claim that Jews did not conceive their assemblies as associations. Moreover, Philo, *Prob.* 85, says of the Essenes that they organized themselves *kata thiasous*, "association-wise." Scheid ("Community," 375) points out that there is little in the internal organization of Judean *synagōgai* to distinguish them from other *thiasoi* and *collegia*. Similarly, Bremmer, "Social and Religious Capital," 270.
34. See Mason and Esler, "Judaean and Christ-Follower Identities."
35. The earliest reference is perhaps Josephus, *Ant.* 18.64. See also Acts 26:28; 1 Pet 4:16; Pliny, *Ep.* 10.96; Tacitus, *Ann.* 15.44; and Suetonius, *Nero* 16.2.
36. Reilly, *Slaves*; Fragiadakis, "Sklavennamen"; and the discussion by Vlassopoulos, "Athenian Slave Names."
37. Salway, "What's in a Name?" 125.
38. Solin, *Die griechischen Personennamen*, 1559–1622.

1. A WORLD OF ASSOCIATIONS

1. On the difficulties of a definition of associations, see Arnaoutoglou, *Thusias heneka kai sunousias*, 22–24, the title of whose book recalls Aristotle, *Eth. nic.* 8.9.5 (1160A): "Some associations seem to exist for the sake of pleasure, *thiasōtai* and *eranistai*; for these are for the purpose of sacrifice or social intercourse (*thusias heneka kai sunousias*)."
2. Zuiderhoek, *Ancient City*, 7. There are a few exceptions. Pausanius (10.4.1) says of Panopeus in Phocis (central Greece) that it was a city, "if one can give the name of city to those who possess no government institutions (*archeia*), no gymnasium, no theater, no *agora*, no water descending to a fountain, but live in bare shelters just like mountain cabins, right on a ravine." Thucydides (1.10.2) observed that Sparta did not look like a polis.
3. Hansen, *Polis*, 56–57, offers two definitions: (1) "*polis* is used (a) synonymously with *akropolis*, a small, usually fortified settlement on an eminence . . . ; and (b) synonymously with *asty*, just meaning a town; or (c) synonymously with *gē* or *chora*, meaning a territory" (*polis* plus hinterland). (2) "In the meaning of 'community' *polis* is used (a) synonymously with *politai*, the adult male citizens; (b) synonymously with *ekklesia* or *demos*, as the city's assembly or some other of its political institutions; or (c) synonymously with *koinonia*, the political community in a more abstract sense."
4. Saller, "*Familia, Domus* and the Roman Family." That is, the *familia* included brothers and sisters, even after the death of the father, and cousins, but not their mother's siblings or their children.
5. CIL 6.10260–64 (Rome, early II CE).
6. This is the typology developed by Harland, *Associations, Synagogues and Congregations*, expanding on Kloppenborg, "Collegia and *Thiasoi*." Arnaoutoglou, "Were There Craftsmen Associations?," distinguishes between "occupational groups" and "occupational associations," the latter bearing a distinctive name, owning property, having an organizational structure, and a maintaining a division of labor among its members, while occupational groups display fewer of these characteristics. He distinguishes further between craft associations, engaged in primary manufacturing, and professional associations, such as merchants, shippers, and warehouse workers.
7. IGUR 160 (Torre Nova [Campania], ca. 150 CE).
8. For the identification of the guild of AE 1937, 161, with CIL 6.10234, see above, Introduction n. 1.
9. Dorcey (*Cult of Silvanus*, 89–90), however, points out that a large number of occupational guilds were associated with Silvanus, and the cult was very popular in cities, although with devotees who had some connection to the countryside.
10. On the right to acquire land (*enktēsis*), see Pečírka, *Formula for the Grant of Enktesis*.
11. On this, see Simms, "Isis in Classical Athens."
12. Herodotus 1.105.2–3. On Aphroditē-Astartē syncretism, see Budin, "Reconsideration."
13. Maillot, "Les associations à Cos," 209, 222–26.
14. Trümper, "Where the Non-Delians Met"; Baslez, "Les associations à Délos."

15. Teixidor, "L'assemblée législative"; Ameling, "Κοινὸν των Ϲιδωνίων."
16. Trümper, "Negotiating Religious and Ethnic Identity."
17. IG XI/4 1299 = Bricault, *RICIS*, 202/0101 (ph. 3:pl. xxxix).
18. See further Moyer, *Egypt and the Limits of Hellenism*, chap. 3.
19. Judean groups in Egypt and the Bosphorus region adopted the term *proseuchē* (prayer house) for their associations, but Judean groups elsewhere overwhelmingly called their assemblies *synagōgai*. For the use of the term *synagōgē* by non-Judean groups, see I.Perinthos 49 = GRA I 86 (Perinthos-Herakleia [Thrace], I CE?); I.Perinthos 59.3–5 (Perinthos-Herakleia [Thrace], I/II CE); I.ApamBith 35.7 = GRA II 99 (Apameia, 119 or 104 BCE); and OGIS 326.12 = GRA II 141 (Teos, 146–133 BCE).
20. The heuristic utility in treating Judean synagogues as associations has been recognized widely: Weinfeld, *Organizational Pattern*; Gillihan, *Civic Ideology* (apropos of the Yahad at Qumran); White, *Building God's House*, 82–83; Baumgarten, "Graeco-Roman Voluntary Associations"; and Runesson, *Origin of the Synagogue*.
21. See Ascough, "Paul, Synagogues, and Associations."
22. See Kraabel, "Diaspora Synagogue"; Levine, *Ancient Synagogue*, chap. 8.
23. The Greek terms used for cultic associations (and their members) are numerous, the most common being *koinon, thiasos (thiasōtai), orgeōnes, eranos (eranistai)*, and *synodos;* less common, but still well attested, are *doumos, familia, mystai, hoi peri* NN, *xystos, philoi, plēthos, speira, stemma, synagōgē, synedrion, synklitai, systēma*, and *therapeutai*. Other names are formed from the name of the deities reverenced (e.g., *Sarapiastai, Dionyiastai*). In Latin the most common terms are *collegium, coetus, corpus, cultores, curia, familia, synagoga*, and *sodalis*.
24. Gaius, D 47.22.4 (On the Law of the Twelve Tables): "Members (*sodales*) are those who belong to the same association which the Greeks call *hetaireia*. They are legally authorized to make whatever contracts they may desire with one another, provided they do nothing in violation of the public law."
25. Garland, *Piraeus*, 228–41. In addition to more common Greek deities, the Piraeus had shrines dedicated to Thracian, Syrian, Egyptian, Phrygian, and other Anatolian deities.
26. See IG II^2 2343 = GRA I 1 (Athens, ca. 400 BCE) and the commentary in GRA I 17–21.
27. IG II^2 1325 = GRA I 33 (Piraeus, 185/184 BCE).
28. IG II^2 1368 = GRA I 51 (Athens, 164/165 CE).
29. SEG 36:228 = GRA I 38 (Attica, 159/158 BCE).
30. IG II^2 1335 = GRA I 43 (Piraeus, 101/100 BCE). The cult of Sabazios had arrived in Attica at least by the fifth century BCE since it is mentioned by Aristophanes (*Vesp.* 9–10; *Horae*, Frag. 566; *Av.* 876; *Lys.* 387–90) and Demosthenes (*Cor.* 259–60).
31. I.Beroia 27 = SEG 46:737.
32. CIL 14.2112 (Lanuvium [*Regio* I], 136 CE). The inscription has been republished many times (e.g., ILS 7212, FIRA III 35), but the most recent edition and translations and best analysis is Bendlin, "Associations, Funerals, Sociality."
33. On the meaning of *collegium salutare*, see Bendlin, "Associations, Funerals, Sociality," 220–21.

34. On the scope and implementation of the *senatus consultum de collegiis*, see Camodeca and Buongiorno, "I senatus consulta," and Buongiorno, "Senatus consulta." The *senatus consultum* applied only to cities (*civitates*) and Italian citizens (*cives*) and not to the Roman provinces (*provinciae*). Theoretically, the *senatus consulta* also applied to *coloniae* such as Corinth and Philippi, but much depended on how the *senatus consulta* were implemented outside of Rome.
35. IG II^2 1365, 1366 = GRA I 53; see the commentary in GRA I 53.
36. SB 3:7182 (Philadelphia [Arsinoites], II–I BCE); Scholl, *Corpus der ptolemäischen Sklaventexte*, 1:333–42 (no. 91).
37. IG II^2 2347 = GRA I 12 (Salamis, ca. 300 BCE).
38. IG II^2 1298 = GRA I 20 (Athens, 248/247 BCE).
39. IG II^2 1297 = GRA I 24 (Athens, 236/235 BCE).
40. Arnaoutoglou, "'Ils étaient dans la ville,'" 37–38.
41. IG II^2 2358 = GRA I 40 (Athens, ca. 135 BCE).
42. TAM V 1539 = GRA II 117 (Philadelphia [Lydia], ca. 100 BCE). An English translation is given both in AGRW 121 and in Barton and Horsley, "Hellenistic Cult Group."
43. Garland, *Introducing New Gods*, 45.
44. IG II^2 1316 = GRA I 16 (Piraeus, 272/271 BCE). See the commentary in GRA I 89–96.
45. I.Eph 215 (Ephesus, ca. 200 CE). This has been called a "bakers' strike" (Buckler, "Labour Disputes"), but Arnaoutoglou ("Roman Law and *Collegia*," 39–42) and Zimmermann (*Handwerkervereine*, 84–85) have doubted whether the bakers in Ephesus constituted a guild. In any event, the prefect's decision was not to ban the association (if there was one) but instead to prohibit their gathering as *if* they were a political faction (*synerchesthai . . . kat' hetairian*). See Perry, "'L'État intervint peu à peu.'"
46. On networks of trust, see Monson, "Ethics and Economics," and chap. 4 below. On the economic benefits of such networks, see Venticinque, *Honor Among Thieves*.
47. Zimmermann, *Handwerkervereine*; Dittmann-Schöne, *Berufsvereine*; Sommer, *Rom und die Vereinigungen*, 224–28.
48. See Waltzing, *Étude historique*; Ausbüttel, *Untersuchungen zu den Vereinen*; and Mennella and Apicella, *Le corporazioni professionali nell' Italia romana*.
49. Petrikovits, "Die Spezialisierung," offers a catalogue of trades attested in Latin inscriptions of several hundred designations.
50. Becatti, *Mosaici e pavimenti marmorei*.
51. I.Prose 40 (Psenamosis, 67–64 BCE): "fellow-farmers" (*syngeorgoi*); I.Prose 49 (Psenemphaia, 5 BCE): landowners (*geouchoi*); P.Mich V 243 (Tebtynis, 14–37 CE): guild of *probatoktēnotrophoi* (sheep and cattle breeders); P.Hamb I 34 (Euheremia, 160 CE): guild of *probatoktēnotrophoi* (sheep and cattle breeders).
52. Estimates of the population of Tebtynis vary: Rowlandson, "Agricultural Tenancy," 147, has four thousand to five thousand; and Connor, "Temples as Economic Agents," 25–27, has seventy-five hundred (twenty-five hundred males).
53. I owe this calculation to my doctoral student, Ryan Olfert.
54. Alston and Alston, "Urbanism and the Urban Community," 205. Van Minnen, "Urban Craftsmen," 37–38, extrapolating from Byzantine figures, suggests that "a consid-

erable part of the population (30–50%) did not live on agriculture, but were engaged one way or the other in a particular craft."

55. Fellmeth, "Politische Bewußtsein," 52. Similarly, Gutsfeld, "Das Vereinigungswesen," 18, argues that a large portion of the subelite population were guild members. In 79 CE there were about forty-five associations in Pompeii (Ausbüttel, *Untersuchungen zu den Vereinen*, 33), representing a population of fifteen thousand to twenty thousand. With a mean size of occupational guilds at about one hundred members, this would imply that between 22.5 and 30 percent of the total population belonged to occupational guilds, or 45 to 60 percent of the male population.
56. MAMA VI List 164 = GRA II 114 (Akmoneia, 98–117 CE). See also AE 1977, 802 = SEG 6:167 (Temenothyrai, Phrygia, late I CE): a guild (*synergasia*) of fullers honored L. Egnatius Quartus, prefect of the second Claudia cohort and tribune of Legio VIII Augusta; I.Kibyra 63 (Kibyra, ca. 150 CE): the "most august guild of leather workers" (*he semnotatē synergasia tōn skutobyrseis*) honored their patron, T. Claudius Polemon, Asiarch and twice high priest of the imperial cult.
57. See Flohr, *World of the Fullo*, 319.
58. Other inscriptions that name guilds as guardians of a patron's tomb include IMT 1342, 1346: the *hierē technē* of marble masons (*leukourgoi*); IMT 1937: a *synedrion* of porters (*sakkophoroi*); IMT 1801: the *most holy (hierōtatē) synedrion* of the fullers; IMT 1826: the *most holy (hierōtatē) synedrion* of fishermen; IJO II 132 = I.Eph 1677: Judeans in charge of the tomb of a physician and his wife; and I.Eph 2304: the *synedrion* of physicians.
59. The construction *hē synodos tē‹s› skutikēs* is an abbreviation of *hē synodos tēs plateias tōn skuteōn* (the association of Leather Worker Street). The more usual phrase in inscriptions from Saittai is *hē plateia tōn skuteōn:* TAM V/1 79, 80, 81, 146. This formula reflects the fact that trades tended to cluster together in many ancient cities, with streets named "leather," "silver," "bronze," etc., to indicate the trade practiced there (see MacMullen, *Roman Social Relations*, 132–35).
60. See Van Nijf, *Civic World of Professional Associations*, 257–58. The theater in Miletos is also, famously, the location of the seat inscription for the *Ioudaioi*, who are also called *theosebeis* (pious). See GRA II 135. On the odeon in Gerasa, see SEG 54:1691 (Gerasa, after 165/166 CE). SEG 40:1063 (Saittai, ca. 150–300 CE) offers an interesting parallel to SEG 54:1691, as a list of reserved seats in the stadium at Saittai. There, linen workers also had reserved seats along with the civic tribes of Saittai, with at least six rows of assigned seats.
61. See GRA II index, s.v. "neighborhood or street associations." A few other associations might be added. See the index in GRA III (forthcoming).
62. GRA II 162.
63. Last, "Neighborhood," 414 citing Choat, "City in Roman Egypt," who notes the assemblage of buildings in fourth-century CE Panopolis, Egypt (P.Berl.Bork, 315–330 CE), which records an assembly of Christ followers (Frag. 3.103) located in a house and the buildings that surround it, which include flour mills (3.105), a workshop (*ergastērion*, 4.114), a network of potters (3.106–7), and many other houses. Last concludes: "It is conceivable that this *ekklēsia* primarily attracted workers and residents who lived on

nearby streets. There is nothing uniquely Egyptian about this picture or anything to link it specifically to the fourth century" (414).

64. On the various L. Sergii Paulli attested in the first and second century CE, see chap. 6.
65. IGUR 160; translated and edited in McLean, "Agrippinilla Inscription."
66. See McLean, "Agrippinilla Inscription." The family of Squilla Gallicanus was originally form Mytilene on the island of Lesbos, and Squilla Gallicanus had served as proconsul in Asia.
67. Waltzing, *Étude historique*; Poland, *Geschichte des griechischen Vereinswesens*.
68. *IV BCE:* Paris, Bibliothèque Nationale 241 (ed. de Cenival, "Papyrus Seymour de Ricci") (IV BCE) [TM 46326]; IG II^2 1361 = GRA I 4 (Piraeus, 330–324/323 BCE); *III BCE:* IG II^2 1275 = GRA I 8 (Piraeus, 325–275 BCE) (fragmentary); Agora 16:161 = GRA I 14 (Athens, early III BCE); IG II^2 1283 = GRA I 23 (Piraeus, 240/239 BCE); IG II^2 1328 = GRA I 34 (Piraeus, 183/182, 175/174 BCE); *II BCE:* five Demotic regulations from the same association of the god Sobek, extending over thirty-three years: P.Mil.Vogl.dem. inv. 77–78 (178 BCE) [TM 47204–5]; P.Cair 30606 = P.Assoc pp. 45–51, 218–19 (Tebtynis, 158/157 BCE) [TM 2775]; P.Hamburg.Bibliothek.dem 1 = P.Assoc pp. 59–61, 219–20 (Tebtynis, 151 BCE) [TM 3057]; P.Cair 31179 = P.Assoc pp. 63–68, 221–22 (Tebtynis, 147 BCE) [TM 3025]; P.Cair 30605 = P.Assoc pp. 73–78, 222–25 (Tebtynis, 145 BCE) [TM 2774]. Other Demotic associations: P.Bagnall 42 (Tebtynis, 250–210 BCE) [TM 175279]; P.Würzb.dem 10 (Arsinoites, 245–243 BCE) [TM 133259]; P.Lille.dem 29 = P.Assoc pp. 3–10 (Pisais [Arsinoites], 223 BCE) [TM 2784]; P.StanGreen.dem 21 (Bakchias?, 190–170 BCE); P.Cair 31178 = P.Assoc pp. 39–40, 215–18 (Tebtynis, 179 BCE) [TM 3055]; P.Cair 30619 = P.Assoc pp. 93–97, 227–29 (Tebtynis, 137 BCE) [TM 2776]; P.PragSatzung = P.Assoc pp. 83–91, 225–27 (Tebtynis, 137 BCE) [TM 2928]; P.Berl.Spieg 3115 = P.Assoc pp. 103–31 (Memnoneia, Thebes west, 109–108 BCE) [TM 3058]; P.Cair 30618 A–B = P.Assoc pp. 229–36 (Tebtynis, II BCE) [TM 43286]; *II/I BCE:* TAM V 1539 = GRA II 117 (Philadelphia, Lydia, II/I BCE); *I BCE:* IG II^2 1339 = GRA I 46 (Athens, 57/56 BCE); P.Lond VII 2193 (Philadelphia, Fayûm, 69–58 BCE) [TM 2462]; *I CE:* LSAM 80 = GRA II 152 (Elaioussa Sebaste, Cilicia, 27 BCE–14 CE); P.Mich V 243 (Tebtynis, 14–37 CE) [TM 12084]; P.Mich V 244 (Tebtynis, 43 CE) [TM 12085]; P.Mich V 245 (Tebtynis, 47 CE) [TM 12086]; AE 1929, 161 (Trebula Mutuesca, 60 CE); BGU XIV 2371 (I CE) [TM 3991]; *II CE:* IG II^2 1369 = GRA I 49 (Liopesi, Attica, II CE); SEG 31:122 = GRA I 50 (Liopesi, Attica, ca. 90 CE); CIL 6.33885 (Rome, 117–138 CE); CIL 14.2112 (Lanuvium, 136 CE); AE 2012, 312 (Ostia, II CE); CIL 6.10234 (Rome, 153 CE); IG II^2 1368 = GRA I 51 (Athens, 164/165 CE); IG IX/1^2 670 = GRA I 61 (Physkos, Locris, mid-II CE); *II/III CE:* IG II^2 1365–66 = GRA I 53 (Laurion, late II/early III CE); CIL 8.14683 [EDCS 25601020] (Africa proconsularis, II/III CE?).

    Two charters fall outside our chronological range: a fifth-century BCE Demotic charter of a guild of funerary workers (P.Dem.Louvre E 7840 bis = P.Louvre.Eisenlohr 6 [ed. de Cenival, "Comptes"] [TM 46137]), and a sixth-century CE set of bylaws of a guild of hunters (SB 3:6704); Aphrodito, Upper Egypt, VI CE).

69. Hanges, "1 Corinthians 4:6." Papathomas, *Juristische Begriffe*, 65–66, observes that "to deliver such a person (*ton toiouton*)" in 1 Cor 5:5 is phrased in the same way as disciplinary rules of Greco-Egyptian associations. This might suggest that it is either drawn from a disciplinary rule of the Corinthians or that Paul frames his instruction imitating the style of a disciplinary rule.
70. 1 Cor 14:33b–35 is best thought of as a later interpolation into 1 Corinthians from the perspective of the Pastoral writer, since it so obviously collides with Paul's discussion of prophetic speech in 1 Cor 11:3–16, where women are clearly speaking. See Walker, *Interpolations*. For the Iobakchoi, see IG II^2 1368 = GRA I 51.
71. IG XII,3 330 = AGRW 243 (English translation only).
72. Augustine, *Ep.* 78.4.
73. For example, P.Petr III 136 (Arsinoites, 231 BCE); SB 3:7182 (Philadelphia, Arsinoites, II–I BCE); P.Tebt I 177 (Tebtynis, 112/111 or 76/75 BCE); P.Tebt I 224 (Tebtynis, 109/108 BCE); P.Tebt II 573 (Tebtynis, 26–18 BCE); P.Tebt II 401.23 (Tebtynis, early I CE); P.Tebt II 484v.1–2 (Tebtynis, 14 CE); O.Strass I 791 (Hermonthis [Upper Egypt], II CE); O.Thebes 142 (Thebes, II CE); BGU VII 1648 (Philadelphia, II–III CE).
74. Trümper, "Negotiating Religious and Ethnic Identity," 119.
75. Batten, "Moral World"; Whitehead, "Cardinal Virtues."
76. Countryman, *Rich Christian*, chap. 5.
77. On the methodological problem in identifying inscriptions as Christian, see below, chap. 9.
78. JIGRE 117; Arsinoë-Krokodilopolis, 245–222 BCE.
79. IGFayum I 73.
80. CIL 6.30983 (Rome, Praedia Galbana, first half of II CE).
81. Tertullian, *Apol.* 39.2.
82. IJO I Mac 1 = GRA I 73 (II–III CE).
83. CIL 14.246.50–53 (Ostia, 140–172 CE). Duncan-Jones, *Economy of the Roman Empire*, 364–65, calculates the price of wine in the mid-second century at between 61 and 88 sesterces.
84. The story in Acts of the donation, the depiction of Joseph Barnabas as a Levite and from Jerusalem, and the explanation of how he came to be known as Barnabas are all suspect as Lukan inventions. See Pervo, *Acts*, 128–29.
85. Ascough, "Benefaction Gone Wrong."
86. Tertullian, *Praescr.* 30.2, treats Marcion and Valentinus together, claiming that they had been expelled from the *ekklēsia* in Rome for having corrupted members with their teaching and that Marcion was eventually reconciled with the bishop but died before the reconciliation could be effected. Nothing more is said of his endowment.
87. IG II^2 1322 (Rhamnous, III/II BCE). See also Migeotte, "Les souscriptions dans les associations."
88. CJZC 72 (Bernikē, 54/55 CE).
89. I.Lindos II 252 (115 BCE). See also similar lists from Rhodes that combine individual donors and associations (*koina*): I.Kamiros 159a and I.KamirosSuppl 157b.

90. The most important exceptions are the remains of a church at Dura-Europos dated to the mid-third century CE and a newly discovered building at Kfar Otnai, discussed in chap. 3.
91. Caillet, *L'évergétisme monumental chrétien*, 27.
92. Rebillard, *Care of the Dead*, chap. 3. See below, chap. 9.
93. P.Lond III 1177.57–62; after October, 113 CE.
94. For a discussion of legislation against Christians before Decius, see Barnes, "Legislation."
95. There are a few exceptions. About forty-five inscriptions are related to the carpenters (*tignuarii*) of Ostia Antica, and six *alba* and one funerary inscription are known from the boatmen and registrars (*lenuncularii*) of Ostia.
96. Liu, *Collegia Centonariorum*.
97. Schnöckel, *Ägyptische Vereine*.
98. SEG 51:1437 is a rare second-century funerary inscription dedicated to Flavia Sophe from the Via Latina, which leaves little doubt that the deceased was a Christ follower. See Snyder, "Discovery and Interpretation." The same is true of another inscription, NCE 156, discovered on the Via Latina dating to the second century (ca. 138–192). See Guarducci, "Iscrizione cristiana"; and Snyder, "Second-Century Christian Inscription."

2. MODELING CHRIST ASSEMBLIES

1. "Emergence" has to do with properties of groups or networks that are not reducible to the properties of individual components of those systems. See Clayton, "Conceptual Foundations"; and Sawyer, "Durkheim's Dilemma."
2. The membership of several of the Ostian guilds comprised the owners and managers of the trade and probably excluded the slave laborers. The actual labor of offloading the ships was likely done by slaves owned by the guild. This is even clearer in the case of the *lenuncularii pleromarii auxiliares* (boatmen and auxiliary sailors) who transferred the cargo to barges to carry it up the Tiber. CIL 14.252 lists only twenty-two members but might have had as many as thirty-four. This, however, cannot represent the full contingent of laborers, most of whom were likely slaves. The *album* of the Ostian guild of fullers (CIL 14.4573; 232 CE) lists only thirty-two members (although two columns are missing). Verboven, "Guilds," 182 n. 54, suggests that the guild likely had sixty members. Nevertheless, this cannot represent the total of those who worked in the many fulleries (*fullonicae*) in Ostia; at least six *fullonicae* have been excavated there, and each of them would have had at least a dozen workers.
3. CIL 14.250 (152 CE); CIL 14.251 (193 CE); CIL 14.4567 and 14.4568 (from shortly after 152 CE); NSA 1953, 280 (no. 42) (Ostia, 213 CE); and AE 2001, 622 (Ostia, 217 CE?).
4. CIL 14.250 (Ostia, 152 CE); CIL 14.251 (Ostia, 193 CE); NSA 1953, 278–81 (no. 42) (Ostia, 213 CE).
5. The name *quinquennalis*, literally, a "five-year" person, implies a five-year term, but analysis of the *alba* of associations indicates that the actual term of a *quinquennalis* varied from three to five years. See Royden, "Tenure of Office."

6. Royden, *Magistrates*, 47. In calculating the average size of occupational guilds, I have used 120 for CIL 14.250 and 130 for CIL 14.251.
7. For CIL 14.250: M. Sedatius C(ai) fil(ius) Severianus (PIR[1] S231, PIR[2] 7:306); T. Prefernius Sex(ti) f(ilius) Paetus Rosianus Geminus (PIR[1] 3:691, PIR[2] 6:395); M. Sedatius M(arci) f(ilius) Severus Iulius Reginus (PIR[1] 3:232, PIR[2] 7:307); and C. Al‹l›ius C(ai) fil(ius) Fuscianus (PIR[1] 1:399).
8. On the role of elites in the supply of food, see Erdkamp, "Grain Funds," and Zuiderhoek, "Feeding the Citizens."
9. CIL 14.247 lists only two *patroni*, three *quinquennales*, and seventeen members, called *corporati* rather than *plebs*, the term for general membership in CIL 14.250 and 251.
10. The nomen is derived from the Celtic deity Sedatus, attested in several dedications in Raetia, Pannonia Superior, and Germania Inferior. Since Sedatius was a Roman citizen inscribed in the Quirinal tribe, it is likely that his father or grandfather was made a citizen under Claudius or one of the Flavians. See Halfmann, *Die Senatoren*, 79; and Picard, "Ostie et la Gaule de l'Ouest," 888.
11. Christol and Fruyt, "Neptune." *Lenuncularii* are attested only in Ostia and Portus (AE 1987, 195, 196; CIL 14.250, 251, 252, 254, 341, 352, 409, 451, 4414, 5320; NSA 1953, 280) and in Arelate (AE 2009, 822 and 823).
12. Royden, *Magistrates*, 230.
13. Another son of either Epagathus or Secundus, M. Cornelius Epagathio, appears at the bottom of the list in CIL 14.250, suggesting the he joined the guild late.
14. See the discussion of this family by Tran, "Les affranchis."
15. It is tempting to identify Epagathus as the co-owner of the Horrea Epagathiana et Epaphroditiana (I,VIII,3), dated to 145–150 CE, one of the large grain storage depots in Ostia. In addition to rooms for grain storage the building has a well-executed mosaic of a panther and niches for cult statues.
16. The visualization assumes (1) that the senatorial patrons are themselves connected with one another, just as they are also multiply connected with the *lenuncularii*, the *scapharii*, and several of them with the unnamed guilds of CIL 14.247, 248, and those of the Rhône Valley; (2) that the *equites* of CIL 14.250 are also connected with one another outside the guild itself; (3) that the presidents and former presidents are connected with one another (one is a father-son pair) and with the Cornelii and Antistii; (4) and that many of the *plebs* are connected with one another via their family groupings.
17. For locations in Ostia, see the Preface.
18. Hermansen, *Ostia*, 63–66, 115–20; Meiggs, *Roman Ostia*, 325; Bollmann, *Römische Vereinshäuser*, 170.
19. For a discussion of the *cultores* of Diana and Antinoüs (CIL 14.2112; Lanuvium, 136 CE), see chap. 7. There are many other examples of "external patrons," including CIL 14.409 (Ostia, early II CE), where Cn. Sentius Felix is the patron of sixteen collegia; IJO II 168 (Akmoneia, I CE) records a donation to a Judean synagogue by an imperial priestess, Julia Severa, who is honored as a patron with a golden shield but presumably did not frequent the synagogue except on special occasions.

20. The *Isis Geminiana* fresco comes from the Ostiense Necropolis along the Via Laurentina, columbarium 31 (first half of III CE). It is now in the Musei della biblioteca Apostolica Vaticana, cat. no. 79638.
21. The *fabri tignuarii* and *dendrophors* often appear together in inscriptions but were not formally connected. On the *dendrophors* as both a professional and a cultic association, see Salamito, "Les dendrophores."
22. Hemelrijk, "Patronesses," 127.
23. Hemelrijk, "Patronesses," 138–39.
24. In designing the visualization, I have made the following assumptions: (1) that the patrons, all Roman citizens, have connections with one another independent of the guild; (2) that the divisional leaders (*decuriones*), also all Roman citizens, are closely related to one another; (3) that the diviner (*haruspex*), scribe (*scriba*), and physicians (*medici*) have professional connections outside the guild; and (4) that the *immunes*, probably as former presidents, have connections with the current president.
25. AE 1929, 161 (Tebula Mutuesca, 60 CE). The inscription is now in the Museo Nazionale Romano alle Terme di Diocleziano, Sala IX, inv. 108765/108768; Friggeri, *Terme di Diocleziano*, 173–74; published by Buonocore, "L'album e la lex"; Buonocore and Diliberto, "Approfondimenti sull'album." See the discussion in Dorcey, *Cult of Silvanus*, 84–86.
26. Evans, *Cults of the Sabine Territory*, 61.
27. The name M. Valerius Dexter appears in a funerary monument, CIL 10.3647, where he is identified as a *manipularis* (soldier) on the naval bireme *Neptune*. According to Tuck, "Nasty, Brutish, and Short?," naval recruits served twenty-six years in order to receive full benefits. The average age at death was forty (mean, mode, and median). Since the funerary epitaph is undated, it is impossible to know how old M. Valerius Dexter was in 60 CE. The deceased in CIL 10.3647 might be a cousin, father, son, or uncle of the patron of the *familia Silvani*.
28. Bömer, *Untersuchungen über die Religion*, 1:458–61; Dorcey, *Cult of Silvanus*.
29. Vetter, "Die familia Silvani"; Dorcey, *Cult of Silvanus*, 89–90.
30. Tran, *Les membres*, 124.
31. See Liu, "Local Governments." The texts of the *lex* and *senatus consultum* are not extant, but a series of inscriptions beginning in the first century refer to permission granted by the Senate to meet and form a collegium: for example, CIL 6.2193, lines 4–7 (Rome, I CE): *quibus* || *senatus c(oire) c(onvocari) c(ogi) permisit e* | *lege Iulia ex auctoritate* | *Aug(usti) ludorum causa*, "whom the Senate has given permission to hold meetings, to assemble, and to gather in accord with the *Lex Iulia* by the authority of Augustus for the sake of the games."
32. For example, CIL 6.2193, lines 4–7 (Rome, I CE) (previous note), CIL 6.85 (Rome), CIL 6.1872 (Rome, late II CE), CIL 14.2112, lines 11–12 (Lanuvium, 136 CE).
33. Liu ("Local Governments," 304) has persuasively argued the combination of inefficient enforcement of laws; the lack of competence of local magistrates to interpret laws; the lack of accessibility to legal sources such as imperial constitutions, senatorial decrees, and provincial edicts; and the willingness of magistrates to enforce law ac-

counts for the widely divergent judicial treatment of associations. Similarly, Arnaoutoglou, "Roman Law and *Collegia*."

34. IG II^2 2358 = GRA I 40.
35. GRA I 40 reconstructed the first two lines [----*Eirēnaios*] | [*Eirē*]*naiou Antiocheus*, "Eirēnaios son of Eirēnaios of Antioch," but it is probably better reconstructed as [----*Eirēnē*] | [*Eirē*]*naiou Antiocheus*, "Eirēnē daughter of Eirēnaios of Antioch." A grave inscription from a woman was found, IG II^2 8166 = Agora 17:420 (I BCE): "[E]irēnē daughter of Eirēnaios of Antioch." Athens had a large population of citizens of Antioch. See Osborne and Byrne, *Foreign Residents*, 24–25.
36. See Mikalson, *Religion in Hellenistic Athens*, 232–324, for a discussion of Aphroditē Hagnē (= Atargatis) on Delos and in Athens. The earliest mention of the cult on Delos is SEG 52:761 (166 BCE), a dedication of a priest and priestess of a shrine adjoining the temple of Sarapis to the "pure goddess," also called the "Syrian goddess." Already in this inscription (and in ID 2225 slightly later) the idea that the goddess has convened (*synagō*) the association is found.
37. Ismard, *La cité des réseaux*, 348–54. See also IG II^2 1335 = GRA I 43, an association devoted to Sabazios, consisting of citizens, foreigner residents of Athens, and slaves.
38. In the first stage of the list, Bithys (Thrace), Botrys (Thrace), Mētrichē (Aegean islands, Crete, Asia), Ammia (northern Greece, Asia), Parnasos (central Greece, Aegean islands, Asia), and Strymon (Thrace).
39. See Arnaoutoglou, "'Ils étaient dans la ville,'" 40; and Fragiadakis, "Attischen Sklavennamen." Bithys, Strymon, and Botrys are clearly Thracian names.
40. Solin, *Die griechischen Personennamen*, 986–95, lists 2 freeborn and 482 slaves and freed slaves bearing this name, and a further 91 bearing the female name Onesimē.
41. Unlike emancipated Roman slaves, who took the praenomen and nomen of their owner, the emancipated slaves of Greek owners retained their slave names only, making it difficult to know whether a person with a servile name is a slave or is emancipated.
42. See GRA I 40 for details. The change in cutter is most visible in column 2, but other changes are visible on the stone itself.
43. Theodotos son of Diodoros was a priest of Aphroditē Hagnē (= Atargatis), a civic administrator on the island of Delos, and is recorded as a proposer of several motions in the Athenian assembly. Josephus (*Ant.* 14.153) mentions that he moved a decree honoring Jonathan Hyrcanus. See Mikalson, *Religion in Hellenistic Athens*, 239, and the comments in GRA I 194–98.
44. Theodotos is named as the priest of Atargatis in ID 2261, 2285 (Delos, 113/112 BCE); again in ID 2228 (Delos, 110/109 BCE); and in ID 1800, 2261, 2626 (Delos, all undated).
45. Mikalson, *Religion in Hellenistic Athens*, 232–33. Mikalson argues that the first evidence of Athenian control came in 112/111 BCE when Theodoros son of Theodoros of Aithalidai became priest (ID 2229); in fact, Diodoros's son Theodotos was priest the previous year (see n. 44 above).
46. ID 2530 = LSCGSup 54 (Delos, late II BCE): "For good fortune. Let them enter (the sanctuary), having been purified from fish for three days; from (eating) pork after

washing; from (intercourse with) a woman, after three days; from childbirth after seven days; from a miscarriage, after forty days; after menstruation, after nine days."

47. Cornthwaite, "Movement and Transmission," has tabulated 217 people connected with the sanctuary of Atargatis on Delos: 25.34 percent from Greece, two from Phoenicia, 10.6 percent with Roman names, 20.73 percent of Syrian origin (all with Greek names), and 42.85 percent of unknown origin.

48. The visualization indicates the familial relationship among Eirēnē, Eirēnaios (priest), and Eirēnaios and between Diodoros of Sounion and his son Theodotos son of Diodoros. It assumes the following: (1) In addition to the several familial relationships, many members were connected to each other apart from their involvement in the cult. But since neither the *album* nor the form of the names provides any clue as to the relationship, for example, between the men in column 1 and the women in column 2, or among the members of either column, the connections that have been drawn between individual members is entirely conjectural. (2) Slaves came to be involved in the association via their owners, although of course the reverse might also have been true. The point is that it is very unlikely that the sole basis for the formation of this association was devotion to Atargatis; other social connections must have existed.

49. Published: P. Chrysostomou, ΑΔ 44–46 (1989–1991), 36–39 (no. 4) (ph. plate γ); Gounaropoulou and Hatzopoulos, Ἐπιγραφές Βεροίας, 130–32, no. 27 (ph.) (SEG 46:737). The eagle surrounded by garlands of oak on the pediment suggests a connection with Theos Hypsistos (on which, see Ustinova, "Thiasoi," 152, and *Supreme Gods*, 248–49).

50. The Furii are an old Roman family attested 258 times in Latin inscriptions and attested in literary sources from the fourth century BCE. A descendant of Q. Furius Valens may have been P. Fur[ius] Pontianus, of senatorial rank and governor of Moesia Inferior in the early third century CE. See Boteva, "On the Cursus Honorum." A funerary dedication to C. Furius Valens is also extant in Moesia Inferior (IGBulg 139), and a Quintus Furius is identified as the father of the deceased in a funerary inscription on Delos (Le Dinahet-Couillard, "Une famille," 648–51, no. 10). Three other Delian inscriptions mention members of the Furian clan. Two are listed in Hatzfeld, "IRD," 37.

51. A lacuna in column 1 presumably includes the trades of three more members.

52. S. Mitchell, "Cult of Theos Hypsistos," provides a catalogue of 293 inscriptions and papyri that refer to Theos Hypsistos, Zeus Hypsistos, or simply Hypsistos, supplemented by a further 83 in S. Mitchell, "Further Thoughts." Another inscription has recently been published by Sharankov, "Надпис," from Nicopolis ad Istrum (Thrace, time of Hadrian), near the current site of Nikyup in modern Bulgaria.

53. *Hypsistos* appears frequently as an epithet of *theos* or *kyrios* or by itself, for example, at Gen 14:18, 19, 20, 22; Num 24:16; Deut 32:8; 2 Sam 22:14; 1 Esd 2:2; 6:30; 8:19, 21; 9:46; Jdt 13:18; Tob 1:4, 13; 4:11; 2 Macc 3:31; 6:2; 3 Macc 7:9, etc.

54. S. Mitchell, "Cult of Theos Hypsistos," 112–13. For example, a dedication on an undecorated block from Akmonia, where a Judean synagogue was located (IJO II 168 =

GRA II 113). SEG 26:1356, "For good fortune: Aurelia Tatis daughter of Onēsimos, along with her husband Onēsimos set this (stone) up from their own resources for Theos Hypsistos."

55. S. Mitchell, "Further Thoughts," 178, 179.
56. The visualization makes the following assumptions: (1) that the six people listed within the wreath occupy (at the time that the inscription was cut) positions of honor or leadership, with Q. Furius Valens as the most prominent; (2) that the several slaves are members in the group by virtue of their owners' memberships (although as stated above apropos of IG II^2 2358 the reverse could be true); (3) that members of the same trade (goldsmiths, stonemasons, nailsmiths) or related trades (fullers, dyers) are also connected to one another outside the guild; (4) that those who share the same patronym (Maximus) or same given name (Epagathos) are also connected; and (5) that some of the freeborn members (Zosas, Epiktetos, Sostratos, Demetrios, and Chresimos) are also connected. These assumptions, of course, are purely hypothetical but are employed to guard against the unlikely scenario that all members are related *solely* by virtue of their devotion to Theos Hypsistos.
57. SB 3:7182 = Scholl, *Corpus der ptolemäischen Sklaventexte*, 1:333–42 (no. 91).
58. Edgar, "Records." The name of the second guest who failed to return is missing in the lacuna, but his patronym is preserved.
59. See chap. 7 below for evidence of differential contributions depending on one's seat at the table.
60. See Perpillou-Thomas, *Fêtes*, on the minor use of animal sacrifice in Egypt and the influence of Greek practices and nomenclature on Egyptian cults.
61. Other instances of "title borrowing" can be seen in the Roman Catholic Church's adoption of the imperial title Pontifex Maximus (the greatest priest) and its application to the bishop of Rome. Much lower down the social ladder, a store-front church in Toronto advertised its two leaders—probably husband and wife—as "archbishop" and "abbess," borrowing (incompatible) titles from both diocesan and monastic organizations.
62. The visualization of SB 3:7182 assumes (1) that in so small a group, all members have antecedent connections with all other members (except the guests), and (2) that one member, Hermias the president, was responsible for the recruiting of both guests, one of whom eventually became a member; hence, there are lines connecting Hermias and Thibron and the associations, but only one line connects [. .]rion son of Horion to the guild, via Hermias.
63. Some later inscriptions record membership lists of Christ groups, for example, Sterrett, EJ no. 89 (Isparta, Phrygia, V CE), a *synodia* of the Holy Georgios with twenty names, most of them without a patronym. But see chap. 4 on the possibility of membership lists among early Christ groups.
64. Epaphroditus/-a: Solin, *Die stadtrömischen Sklavennamen*, 2:281–84 (117 + 65): slaves or freedmen; for Rome, Solin, *Die griechischen Personennamen*, 343–48, lists only 1 freeborn person bearing the name; 181 uncertain occurrences; 16 "probably freedmen"; 120 certainly slaves and freedmen; one son of a freedman; and one *perigrinus*,

for a total of 319 probable slave names. Of common slave names Epaphroditus is the eleventh most frequent, after Hermes (892), Eros (583), Alexander (577), Onesimus (484), Elpis (479), Nice (420), Tyche (413), Eutyches (360), Eutychus (354), and Irene (353) (Solin, *Die griechischen Personennamen*, 1559–1622).

65. In Rome, Syntychē is a name borne by only 1 freeborn woman, 45 *incerti* (people of uncertain status); 6 probable freedwomen, 35 slaves or freedwomen, and 1 daughter of a freedwoman, for a total of 88, plus 10 names for which only the last few letters of the name are extant (e.g., . . .]tyche) (Solin, *Die griechischen Personennamen*, 154, 1447). Eu(h)odus, Euhodas, Euhodianus, Euhodio(n): 1 senator (Euhodianus); 1 freeborn; 34 slaves or freedmen; 65 *incerti* (Solin, *Die griechischen Personennamen*, 923–34); Clement: 30 slaves or freedmen (Solin, *Die stadtrömischen Sklavennamen*, 1:78–79) but many freeborn Romans.
66. See Ascough, *Paul's Macedonian Associations*, 134–35, and the literature cited there.
67. Lydia is another slave name. People bearing names derived from geography (Lydia, Corinthia, Lesbia, Zmyrna, Syra, etc.), especially when found in Rome (or a Roman colony), are usually assumed to be slaves or freedmen/freedwomen (Solin, *Die stadtrömischen Sklavennamen*, 2:363–89).
68. See Horsley, NewDocs 2 (*Review of the Greek Inscriptions*), 25–32. See also Ascough, *Lydia*.
69. The Lukan story in Acts 16:12–40 associates Paul in Philippi with a *proseuchē*, one of the standard terms for a Judean assembly. Yet nothing in Philippians suggests that the assembly included both Judeans and former pagans. Indeed, Paul's warnings in Phil 3:2–9 about those advocating circumcision suggest that the assembly was largely or exclusively non-Judean.
70. Ogereau, *Paul's Koinonia*; Ogereau, "Paul's κοινωνία," developing and nuancing suggestions of Sampley, *Pauline Partnership*, and Fleury, "Une société de fait."
71. Ogereau, "La plus ancienne référence."
72. Fleury, "Une société de fait."
73. Ogereau, "Paul's κοινωνία," 374.
74. CIL 3.633 = GRA I 68.
75. Phil 4:22 indicates that they had a connection with "those of the household of Caesar," probably meaning imperial slaves and freedmen, at Paul's location in Ephesus.
76. *Episkopoi* (supervisors, in the plural!) is not an exclusively Christian term. See IG XII,3 329 (Thera, ca. 200 BCE): Dionysiac *koinon*; I.ScM I 58, line 24 (Istros-Histria [Scythia Minor], II BCE); I.ScM I 59, line 25 (Istros-Histria [Scythia Minor], II BCE); IG XII,1 731, line 8 (Rhodes), where the title (in the plural) appears alongside *epistatai* (supervisors), *hieropoioi* (banquet managers), and a treasurer (*tamias*); IG XII,1 50, line 34 (Rhodes, I BCE); IG XII,1 49, line 42 (Rhodes, II BCE); ASAA 22 (1939/1940) 148, lines 2.3 (Rhodes, II BCE); Clara Rhodos 2 (1932) 193,21, line 8 (Rhodes, II BCE); I.Lindos II 208, line 4 (Lindos [Rhodes], 160 BCE); I.Lindos II 378.ii, line 57 (Lindos [Rhodes] 27 BCE); MAMA VI List 148,159, line 22 (Akmoneia [Phrygia], 85 CE), and many other inscriptions.
77. See Frank, "Race Mixture," 692, and Solin, *Die stadtrömischen Sklavennamen*, 1:95–98 (Fortunatus/-a: 225 occurrences), 152–54 (Tertius/-a: 114 occurrences). Frank's con-

clusions are based on an examination of 13,700 Latin inscriptions in CIL vols. 5, 6, 9, and 14, which yielded more than 5,000 slave names, 2,874 with Greek names and 2,126 with Latin names, of which many are "happy" or "good luck" names.

78. See Nasrallah, "'You Were Bought with a Price,'" on the use of the language of slavery and manumission throughout 1 Corinthians.

79. *Skēnopoioi* are perhaps equivalent to the Latin *tabernacularii*, not tentmakers for the army, which had its own artisans, but those who made the curtains and awnings for atria, gardens, and other private uses. The only *tabernacularii* we know from columbaria inscriptions are all imperial freedmen (CIL 6.5183b; CIL 6.5339, 9053, 9053a, 9054), which is not likely a status enjoyed by Prisca and Aquila.

80. On the social status of *archisynagōgai*, see Rajak and Noy, "*Archisynagogoi*."

81. Pervo, *Dating Acts*, 103, argues that in composing Acts 18 Luke was dependent upon 1 Cor 1:14–16, which has Paul *baptizing* Crispus (v. 14) and the *household* of Stephanas (v. 16). In the conflation of these two characters, Stephanas disappeared, Crispus's household was baptized, and Crispus was promoted to the position of synagogue president. Puzzlingly, Crispus's conversion in Acts 18:8 comes only *after* Paul left the synagogue when he declared that he was now turning to the gentiles (Acts 18:6) and took up residence in the house next door (18:7). It should be added that Crispus is not commonly attested as a Judean name. It appears only in a funerary inscription from Cyrenaica: CJZC 12 (imperial period): *Iosēs Krispou, 4 (years)*, "Yoses son of Crispus, aged 4 years." The feminine form *Crisp(e)ina* is found in JIWE 281, 282 (Rome, III–IV CE). There are no instances of the name in CIIP I–III or IJO I–III. Josephus three times refers to a Crispus (*Vita* 33, 388, 393), evidently a Judean. Lüdemann, *Early Christianity*, 203–4, however, takes the material regarding Crispus in Acts as "probably historical," as do most interpreters of 1 Corinthians, who read the Acts account into 1 Cor 1:14.

82. Last, *Pauline Church*, 62–71. The notion that Gaius as a host goes back to Origen, *Commentariorum in epistolam S. Pauli ad Romanos* 10.41 (PG 14:1289C), where he describes Gaius, as a *vir . . . hospitalis* (hospitable man). Origen reports that an ancient tradition (*traditio maiorum*) had Gaius as the first bishop of the *ekklēsia* at Thessalonica.

83. The fact that one can find a few examples of *xenos* that are ambiguous or that *might* mean "host" does not overturn the fact that the *common meaning* of the term is "stranger" or "guest."

84. Salway, "What's in a Name?" 125. Ninety-nine percent of Roman males in the republican period shared one of seventeen praenomina: Aulus, Appius, Gaius, Gnaeus, Decimus, Lucius, Manius, Marcus, Numerius, Publius, Quintus, Servius, Sextus, Spurius, Titus, Tiberius, and Vibius. Salomies, *Die römischen Vornamen*, 29, estimates that 20 percent of Roman males had Gaius as a praenomen. If we assume that the population of Rome was 1 million (a common estimate) and that about two-thirds of the population were adult and about half of those males, and if we exclude one-third as slaves and foreigners (neither of whom would bear a praenomen), the resulting population of male freeborn and freedmen (with a *tria nomina*) would be about 217,000. The number of Gaii could be as high as 44,000. Assuming a population of Corinth

at 87,000 (Engels, *Roman Corinth*, 82), hence approximately 28,700 adult males, and half of that number represented by male slaves and freeborn Greeks (neither of whom had a praenomen), one might expect that of the approximately 14,300 freeborn males and freedmen with Roman names, 2,900 would have the name Gaius.

85. The Packard Humanities Institute (PHI) database of Greek inscriptions attested "Gaius" in the Peloponnese 211 times in 154 inscriptions.

86. This argument is developed in more detail in Kloppenborg, "Gaius the Roman Guest."

87. Because of its destruction in 146 BCE and the poor state of preservation of its monuments, Corinth is a poor source of information on associations of any kind. AGRW prints only one possible inscription (AGRW 26), which is too fragmentary to be useful. Eckhardt, "Eighteen Associations," doubts there were associations there at all.

88. For example, IG II[2] 1297, lines 3–4 = GRA I 24 (Athens, 236/235 BCE); LSAM 48, lines 3–4 (Miletos, 276/275 BCE); IG II[2] 1343 = GRA I 43 (Athens, 37/36 or 36/35 BCE); IG II[2] 1369, lines 25–26 = GRA I 48 (Liopesi, ca. 100 CE); IG II[2] 1366, line 21 = GRA I 53 (Laurion, ca. 200 CE).

89. SEG 52:761, lines 9–11 = Siebert, "Sur l'histoire du sanctuaire," 360 (Delos, II BCE): "the association of the Syrian *thiasitai* of the twentieth day, whom the goddess has gathered." Similarly, ID 2225 (Delos, end of II BCE): "the *thiasitai* whom she has gathered." See Baslez, "Entre traditions nationales," 242.

90. Dreams (as foundations of cults): Plutarch, *De Iside* 1.28–30; IG X/2.1 255 = GRA I 77 (Thessalonikē, I–II CE); IG XI/4 1299, line 14 (Delos, before 166 BCE); I.MakedD 7 (Edessa, III CE); SEG 42:157 = GRA I 41 (Athens, ca. 116/115–ca. 95/94 BCE); IG II[2] 1365/66 = GRA I 53 (Laurion, ca. 200 CE); Kaunos 23 (found near Küçükkale; no date); TAM V 1539.4 = GRA II 117 (Philadelphia, ca. 100 BCE). Foundations "in accordance with a [god's] command": ID 2080 (Delos, 105–103 BCE); ID 2098 (Delos, after 158/157 BCE); SEG 42:157, lines 7–8 = GRA I 41 (ca. 116/115–ca. 95/94 BCE); IG XI,4 1224, line 3 (Delos, before 166 BCE); IG XI,4 1225, line 2 (Delos, before 166 BCE); IG XI,4 1299, lines 1–2 (Delos, before 166 BCE). See also IG II[2] 1365, lines 7–8/1366, line 2 = GRA I 53; IG X/2.1 255, line 12 = GRA I 77.

91. See Baslez, "Place et rôle des associations," 282–83, and chap. 10 below.

92. *Kaleō*, in reference to divine calling: 1 Thess 2:12, 4:7, 5:24; Gal 1:6, 15; 5:8, 13; Rom 8:30, 9:24; *klēsis*, "calling": Rom 11:29; *klētos/-i*, "called": Rom 1:1, 6, 7; 8:28.

93. *Klētos*, "called": 1 Cor 1:1, 2, 26; *kaleō* (in the passive), "to be called": 1 Cor 1:9; 7:15, 17, 18, 20, 21, 22, 24; *klēsis*, "calling": 1 Cor 1:23.

94. On the connotation of the adjective *kyriaokos/-ē*, see chap. 7, n. 9.

95. See chap. 10, fig. 22.

96. Lucian, *De dea syria*, 14. Lucian refers to the deity as Hera, but her description, especially in §32, and the prohibition of eating fish belong to the cult of Atargatis.

97. I.Smyrna 735 = LSAM 17.

98. See Lytle, "Marine Fisheries," who shows that fishing was a major part of the economy and that Delians consumed fish in considerable quantities.

99. See Joshel, *Work, Identity, and Legal Status*, 4–7, 79–85; and Tran, "*Ars* and *Doctrina*." The funerary monuments erected by freedmen/freedwomen often display the

tools of their profession, evidently with pride. The tomb of Eurysaces at the Porta Maggiore in Rome bears the inscription *est hoc monumentum margei Vergilei Eurysacis pistoris redemptoris*, "This is the monument for Mar‹c›us Vergilius Eurysaces, baker and contractor," and has depictions in the frieze of various aspects of baking (CIL 6.1958a).

100. Thus Kloppenborg, "Φιλαδελφία," 267, and Ascough, "Thessalonian Christian Community," 315, and the authors cited in his n. 20.

101. See Ascough, "Thessalonian Christian Community," 325–28, and the literature discussed there. Even if one renders *skeuos* as "wife" (RSV), the perspective is entirely androcentric.

102. In the Iobakchoi, the *proestōtes* (presiding officers) are distinct from the priest, vice priest, and *archibackchos* (IG II^2 1368, lines 12–13, 30–31 = GRA I 51; Athens, 164/165 CE). *Prostatēs* (president) < *proïstēmi* is found in IG II^2 1369, line 34 = GRA I 49 (Liopesi, ca. 100 CE); SEG 46:800, line 14 = GRA I 72 (Pydna, 250 CE); IK Byzantion 37.7 = GRA I 91 (117–137 CE); I.Sabazios II 6, line 6 (Serdica, ca. 200 CE); BCH 25 (1901) 36 (no. 184) = GRA II 98 (Amastris); and I.CiliciaDF 46, lines 6–7 (I–II CE) and is very widely attested in Egyptian associations.

103. Respectively, IGUR 160 and IG II^2 1368 = GRA I 51.

104. On Marcus Aurelius Prosenes, see chap. 11 below.

105. Bourdieu, "Economy of Symbolic Goods," 102.

106. Bourdieu and Wacquant, *An Invitation*, 191. Elsewhere, Bourdieu ("Forms of Capital," 248–49) is explicit that social capital is derived from membership in a group: "Social capital is the aggregate of the actual or potential resources which are linked to possession of a durable network of more or less institutionalized relationships of mutual acquaintance and recognition—or in other words, to membership in a group—which provides each of its members with the backing of the collectivity-owned capital, a 'credential' which entitles them to credit, in the various senses of the word."

107. Burt, *Brokerage and Closure*, 4.

108. See Coleman, "Social Capital"; and Lin, "Building a Network Theory." Conversely, Robert Putnam has documented the progressive decline in participation in primary associations—churches, synagogues, parent-teacher associations, political associations—in the United States, with the result that more Americans are "bowling alone." They also trust each other less. See Putnam, *Bowling Alone*.

109. MacMullen, *Roman Social Relations*, 75: "A slipper-cobbler in Rome could hardly claim attention from any member of the aristocracy by himself. Hundreds of such were another story."

110. On endowments, see chap. 7. Zuiderhoek, *Politics of Munificence*, offers a brilliant analysis of levels of elite benefactions to cities during the Antonine period, where the mean and median levels of gifts were quite small. Liu, "Economy of Endowments," has shown the same in the case of Latin associations.

111. Coleman, "Social Capital," S102–3.

112. Bourdieu "Forms of Capital," 248–49.

113. Chaniotis ("Rituals Between Norms and Emotions," 229) has drawn attention to the high frequency of *syn-* compounds employed to name those who joined together to

perform ritual actions of sacrificing, singing hymns, participating in a procession, dining, observing a festival, or otherwise acting piously toward the god. This observation applies just as well to the naming of associations, where we find a large number of *syn-* compounds: generic terms such as *synodos, synagōgē, synedrion, synētheia, synētheis, symbiōtai,* and *synoikia;* names that incorporate the names of deities (*Synanoubiastai, Synbakchoi, Synsarapiastai*); and names that indicate particular activities of a group: *synagōnistai, synathlētai, synthytai, synergasia, syntechnia, symmystai, synklitai, synpragmateuomenoi, syssitoi,* and *symposiastai.* See GRA I, index; GRA II, index.

114. Julian, Ep. 22, to Arsacius, high priest of Galatia.

3. VISUALIZING CHRIST ASSEMBLIES

1. See the survey by Runesson, Binder, and Olsson, *Ancient Synagogue.* Unfortunately, no membership lists are extant. The famous Aphrodisias synagogue inscription (I.AphrodJud) is perhaps a version of a membership roster combined with an *epidosis* (contribution list). It was once thought to be third century CE but is now dated to the fourth century at the earliest and more likely from the sixth or seventh century. See Ameling, *Inscriptiones Judaicae Orientis II,* 71–112.
2. Acts 3:11 and 5:12 depict the earliest followers meeting in Solomon's Stoa. Pervo, *Acts,* 135, plausibly suggests that Luke here wishes to represent them as analogous to the Stoics, who met in the Painted Stoa (Diogenes Laertius 7.5).
3. The NRSV translates this as "many thousands," evidently trying to mitigate Luke's gross exaggeration, "how many ten thousands (*posai myriades*) among the Judaeans."
4. For a survey of estimates and for methodological problems, see Goldblatt, "Population Structure."
5. See Pliny, *Ep.* 10.96. Hopkins ("Christian Number," 190–91) argues that "the care with which Pliny claimed to have proceeded at the initial trials (more care, less throughput) and the subsequent single anonymous set of accusations described in the first part of Pliny's letter" are disproportionate to his claim that there were "many of all ages and ranks" in the "towns and villages and countryside." Hopkins suggests that Pliny's Christians numbered in the dozens, not the hundreds, and that the supposed demise of temple life in Bithynia that he reports was either an anomaly or inaccurate, since temples elsewhere continued to flourish.
6. Murphy-O'Connor, *St. Paul's Corinth,* 156–58.
7. De Vos, *Church and Community Conflicts,* 203–4 and n. 98. Similarly, Ebner, *Stadt als Lebensraum,* 85.
8. Welborn, *End to Enmity,* 324.
9. Caragounis, "House Church?," 413.
10. Last, *Pauline Church,* 71: Chloe (1 Cor 1:11), Crispus (1:14), Gaius (1:14), Stephanas (1:16, 16:17), Fortunatus (16:17), Achaicus (16:17), Phoebe (Rom 16:1), Erastos (Rom 16:23). He assumes that Chloe and Phoebe are widows or otherwise unmarried and so posits two unnamed women (i.e., the minimum of women married to nonbelieving spouses implied by 1 Cor 7:12–13). Last considers Gaius of Rom 16:23 to be a

guest rather than a member of the Corinthian assembly. Although 1 Cor 1:16 states that Paul baptized the "household" of Stephanas (Acts 18:8 makes the same claim for Crispus), Last does not consider those spouses to be necessarily members of the Christ assembly, since he argues that marriage did not automatically imply membership in the Christ assembly. Last also omits from his list others named in Acts, 1 Corinthians, and Romans 16 "whom Paul does not describe as members of the Corinthian Christ group": Jason (Rom 16:21), Lucius (Rom 16:21), Sosthenes (1 Cor 1:1), Titus Justus (Acts 18:7), and Tertius (Rom 16:22).

11. For example, Welborn, *End to Enmity*, 245–50, 321–53; Malherbe, *Social Aspects*, 73–74; Theissen, *Social Setting*, 55, 89; and de Vos, *Church and Community Conflicts*, 204. On Gaius as a guest, not a host, see Kloppenborg, "Gaius the Roman Guest."
12. Murphy-O'Connor, *St. Paul's Corinth*, 156–59. Murphy-O'Connor (*Keys to First Corinthians*, 192) faults Horrell for imagining "50 people sitting knee to knee with their food on their laps" in a fifty-square-meter room, but Murphy-O'Connor's own speculation of thirty people eating in a thirty-square-meter atrium (minus one-ninth, to take into account the *impluvium* in the center of the atrium) is even more implausible. Murphy-O'Connor also notes other atria that are larger than that of the Anaploga villa: the Shear villa at Corinth (51.12 m^2), the House of the Vetii at Pompeii (42 m^2), and the Villa of Good Fortune at Olynthus (100 m^2).
13. Beyond the original publication in S. G. Miller, "Mosaic Floor," little has been done on the site, except that the mosaic, once dated to the last quarter of the first century, has been challenged by Salies ("Römische Mosaiken," 278–79). None of this, however, is fatal to Murphy-O'Connor's argument, since, as he later explained, "Even if I was wrong about Anaploga, it cannot be doubted that at the time of Paul Corinth contained houses of that type" (*Keys to First Corinthians*, 191).
14. De Vos, *Church and Community Conflicts*, 204–5.
15. Welborn, *End to Enmity*, 329–35.
16. Welborn, *End to Enmity*, 356–57, 376. This, for Welborn also suggests that Gaius must have belonged to the "upper class," indeed "far up the social scale among the urban elite."
17. Horrell, "Domestic Space," 365, 367. For the original archaeological report, see Williams and Zervos, "Corinth, 1987."
18. Oakes, *Reading Romans in Pompeii*, 70.
19. For arguments that Christ followers were present at Pompeii, see Wayment and Grey, "Jesus Followers"; and Longenecker, *Crosses of Pompeii.*
20. For locations in Pompeii, see the Preface.
21. Oakes, *Reading Romans in Pompeii*, 1–45. The inventory of finds for House 7 can be found online at "Insula of the Menander in Pompeii Vol. III: The Finds in Context: An On-Line Companion," http://www.le.ac.uk/cgi-bin/tab_int/usr/netscape/suitespot/docs/ar/menander/menander?form=tabsrch&operation=psearch&referrer=http%3A%2F%2Fwww.le.ac.uk%2Far%2Fmenander%2Findex.html&s28=F&s3=&Find=Find&max=100000.
22. Balch, *Contested Ethnicities*, chap. 6, figs. 5–7.

23. Balch, "Church Sitting in a Garden," 316, citing DeFelice, "Inns and Taverns," 478. DeFelice (ibid., 483) has surveyed Pompeii and counted ninety-four sites that served food and/or drink (*popinae* or *tabernae*) but that had no facilities for overnight guests and another forty-two that also could accommodate overnight guests.
24. Balch, "Church Sitting in a Garden," 319–29. Visual representations of eating picture guests standing or sitting (not reclining) in an inn (*caupona*) either on individual chairs or on a wooden bench (DeFelice, "Inns and Taverns," 478; Balch, "Church Sitting in a Garden," 317). Balch observes that open gardens in Pompeii could, depending on the size of the open space, accommodate 90–220 diners.
25. D. Smith, "Hospitality," 106; see also Last, *Pauline Church*, 79; and D. Smith, "Revisiting Associations and Christ Groups."
26. D. Smith, "Hospitality," 108.
27. D. Smith, "Hospitality," 108.
28. This model seems to be suggested by the fact that in Rome the building of large basilicas did not predate Constantine. Before that date Christ followers were organized into twenty-five to thirty *tituli* scattered throughout Rome, each centered on neighborhoods, granaries, and small markets. See Petersen, "House-Churches in Rome."
29. Adams, "Placing" and *Earliest Christian Meeting Places.*
30. See fig. 19 below; Adams, *Earliest Christian Meeting Places*, 20–21. See, for example, the *taberae* in Pompeii, *Regio* IX, *Insula* VII, available online at PompeiiinPictures, http://pompeiiinpictures.com/pompeiiinpictures/plans/plan_9_07.htm.
31. See Lefebvre, *Production of Space*, 26–27 and *passim.*
32. Tertullian, *Apol.* 39.15–16. Adams (*Earliest Christian Meeting Places*, 76) thinks that this might mean that by the end of the second century, there were already dedicated church buildings in Carthage with dining spaces.
33. Adams, *Earliest Christian Meeting Places*, chap. 3. See also 2 *Clem.* 17.3, which distinguishes being admonished by the elders and then "returning home" (*eis oikon*).
34. Musurillo, *Acts of the Christian Martyrs*, 44–45.
35. Origen, *Cels.* 3.55.
36. Adams, *Earliest Christian Meeting Places*, 112–33; see also Adams, "Placing."
37. For example, CIL 6.30983, a collegium of Aesculapius and Salus Augusta consisting of fifty-nine men and women and an association of granary workers (CIL 6.338; 159 CE), both meeting in the Horrea Galba (Richardson, *New Topographical Dictionary*, 193), warehouses for grain, wine, oil, other foodstuffs, and marble.
38. While Minucius Felix (*Oct.* 32.1) and Tertullian (*Spect.* 13) in the early Severan period state that Christians have no temples, by the mid-third century there is literary evidence of buildings variously called *oikoi, ekklēsiai, synagoga, curia,* and other terms. See Mohrmann et al., "Les dénominations de l'église." Several churches reported to have been destroyed during the persecution of Diocletian must have been built in the late third century, for example, P.Oxy XXXIII 2673 (304 CE), an *ekklēsia* of the village of Chysis (near Oxyrhynchus). Other late third-century CE churches include one at Panopolis mentioned in a survey of houses (White, *Social Origins*, 1:122) and a now lost inscription of a *synagōgē* from Lebaba (IGLS 2558; 318/319 CE). See the survey of buildings before 400 CE by MacMullen, *Second Church*, 117–41.

39. See Kraeling, *Christian Building;* White, *Social Origins,* 2:n. 36; and Cianca, *Sacred Ritual,* 90–104.
40. Kraeling, *Christian Building,* 19. Similarly, MacMullen, *Second Church,* 3. MacMullen (ibid., 4–9) asks whether the assembly hall (Room 4) could accommodate all of the Christians at Dura and suggests that it could not, with the others gathering in cemeteries.
41. Tepper and Di Segni, *Christian Prayer Hall,* 24–26, 34–42. The centurion's dedication reads, "Gaianus, also called Porphyrius, centurion, our brother, has made the pavement at his own expense as an act of liberality. Brutius has carried out the work." A second inscription concerns the dedication of a "table": "The god-loving Akeptous has offered the table to God Jesus Christ as a memorial."
42. CIL 6.9102 (Rome, I CE): eighty-five names on the *album,* of which thirty-one were still living. On the Agrippinilla inscription, IGUR 160 (Torre Nova, ca. 150 CE), see chap. 1.
43. See Dittmann-Schöne, *Berufsvereine;* and Zimmermann, *Handwerkervereine.*
44. I.Eph 215 (Ephesus, ca. 200 CE). The bakers may not have constituted a guild at all.
45. P.Lond III 1170v.70, 119, 120, 122 (Theadelphia, 259 CE). See Rathbone, *Economic Rationalism,* 146–47.
46. P.Oxy LV 3804, 566 CE.
47. Ruffini, *Social Networks,* 111. For textile workers in Egypt, Wipszycka, *L'industrie textile,* suggested an average size of ten.
48. Fellmeth, "Politische Bewußtsein."
49. On the few exceptions to this, see chap. 6 below.
50. IG II[2] 2358.
51. Epigraphic details can be found in GRA I 194.
52. Original publication: Piccottini, *Mithrastempel in Virunum.*
53. Piccottini, *Mithrastempel in Virunum,* 22–24.
54. Piccottini, *Mithrastempel in Virunum,* 26–28, plate 15; Gordon, "Ritual and Hierarchy."
55. Beck ("'Qui Mortalitatis Causa Convenerunt,'" 336 n. 6) comments that there were normally two *patres* at any given time. The original list contains three, Iulius Secundinus, Trebius Zoticus (Θ), and Atticius Sextus (Θ), the latter perhaps initially designated as a replacement for the deceased Trebius Zoticus. The induction of Trebius Alfius in 184 CE, replacing Atticius Sextus, restored the *patres* to two in number.
56. Piccottini, *Mithrastempel in Virunum,* 28–29, and the tables there.
57. Pliny, *Ep.* 10.96.
58. Estimating the size of Judean assemblies from physical space presents some problems. Spigel, *Ancient Synagogue Seating Capacities,* has calculated the maximum seating capacity of the assembly halls of the archaeological remains of synagogues from ancient Palestine, using 0.70 square meter per seated person and 0.55 square meter per standing person. This results in very high figures for known synagogues: 454–536 for the first-century synagogue in Gamla (320 m^2), 639–741 for the fifth- to eighth-century Capernaum synagogue (397.44 m^2), and 114–142 for the eighth-century synagogue at Jericho (98.88 m^2), for example. This is a measure of the *maximum* capacity and

assumes that most or all available space was occupied. Since we know little of the details of liturgical movements (which would require free space) or sensibilities that would require buffer space for sacred objects (the Torah scrolls) or presiders, it is difficult to calculate what percentage of the space would not have been occupied by congregants. A possible counterindex to the size of a Judean assembly is the presence of *triclinia* in some assembly complexes. The synagogue building at Stobi had one *triclinium* (GRA I 73), which might imply that irrespective of the size of the assembly hall, the congregation was effectively limited to the dining capacity of the *triclinium* (fewer than twenty), unless one supposes that most of the congregation did not engage in communal dining, that they dined in several shifts, or that other spaces were utilized for dining with movable couches.

The mid-fourth-century synagogue at Ostia presents an analogous situation: although the assembly hall (Area D, now Room 14, 185.5 m^2) could accommodate 265–377 people on Spigel's calculus, Area G-B3 (now Room 10) with a mosaic pavement with *klinē* bands indicates a *triclinium* with movable couches. But this room (about 6.2 × 12 m) could not hold more than thirty diners. At a later period, Room 10 became a bakery and Room E (now 18) became the dining room, with about twice as much space as G-B3 (10), but still not able to accommodate the numbers implied by Spigel's formula. (I owe these data to L. Michael White and his ongoing excavations at Ostia.) On the dating of the first phase of the Ostian synagogue, see White, "Reading the Ostia Synagogue"; and Runesson, "Oldest Original Synagogue."

The Herodian-period synagogue at Jericho—if it was a synagogue—had an assembly hall 16.2 by 11.1 meters = 179.82 square meters, which on Spigel's calculus would accommodate 256–326 people. But a small *triclinium* (6.4 × 5.1 m) is attached to the assembly hall, which could have accommodated no more than twenty people. See Netzer, Kalman, and Laureys, "Synagogue from the Hasmonean Period."

All of these data suggest that the area of an assembly hall is probably not a good indication of the effective size of a congregation.

59. For locations in Ostia, see the Preface.
60. Bollmann, *Römische Vereinshäuser*, 304–7: The Temple of the Ship Builders, *Regio* III,II,1–2. The *album* was discovered in front of the temple, probably dating from the beginning of the third century CE (NSA 1953, no. 43). Directly across the street from the Temple of the Ship Builders is the Schola of Trajan (*Regio* IV,V,15), which some have also connected with the ship builders (*fabri navales*). Hermansen, *Ostia*, 72–74, doubts this and thinks instead that it belonged to the sailors (*navicularii*). See the discussion in Bollmann, *Römische Vereinshäuser*, 323–27.
61. Bollmann, *Römische Vereinshäuser*, 284–88, and her fig. 1.
62. CIL 14.4569 (Ostia, 198 CE). This inscription gives the name of the association as *numerus caligatorum* (line 14). CIL 14.160 gives the full name as *numerus caligatorum* | *decuriar(um) XVI* | *colleg(ii) fabrum* | *tignuar(iorum) Ostis(iensium)*.
63. According to Packer (*Insulae*, 67–68, 160) the Caseggiato dei Triclini was originally an *insula* with a ground floor and four upper stories, converted about 119–120 CE for use by the guild. He estimates that before being converted to guild use, it housed about 196 people. The large latrines in Rooms 17 and 23–23A suggest a significant population.

64. Van der Meer, *Ostia Speaks*, 58.
65. Bollmann, *Römische Vereinshäuser*, 288.
66. Bollmann, *Römische Vereinshäuser*, 49. She argues, moreover, that specially constructed masonry couches could be impractical, since they determined the function of the room in a one-sided way. Similarly, Dunbabin, *Roman Banquet*, 94.
67. See Bruneau and Ducat, *Guide de Délos*, 174–79 (no. 57); and Nielsen, *Housing the Chosen*, 146–47.
68. Trümper, "Negotiating Religious and Ethnic Identity," 119–20, quotation at 120.
69. Bizard and Roussel, "Fouilles de Délos."
70. Schwarzer, *Das Gebäude*, 79; Nielsen, *Housing the Chosen*, 119.
71. SEG 29:1264 = I.DionysosJ 92 = GRA II 123.
72. Schwarzer, *Das Gebäude*, 54–61.
73. Schwarzer, *Das Gebäude*, 62–64, figs. 16–17; Nielsen, *Housing the Chosen*, 119–20 and fig. 82B. In the middle of the third century CE the house was redesigned again and the *triclinium* enlarged to the east so that it could accommodate, in Schwarzer's view, up to seventy people (Schwarzer, "Vereinslokale," 232; Schwarzer, *Das Gebäude*, 81; Nielsen, *Housing the Chosen*, 118, fig. 82C).
74. Estimates of the space needed for diners vary. Bakker, *Living and Working*, 114–15, estimated fifty centimeters of lateral space were needed per diner in a mithraeum. White ("Changing Face," 473) recognizes that this would be extremely tight (four people in two linear meters) and so opts for sixty centimeters per person. White, however, notes the narrower the bench, the greater the deviation from perpendicular the diners would have to be. This naturally decreases the number of diners that a bench could accommodate. Thus, at the Mitreo dei Pareti Dipinti (III,I,6), with a bench only one meter deep, diners would need one meter per diner (474). In 2012 ("Associations and Their Meals," 14 n. 35) I suggested considerably more space: about one lateral meter per diner. Since much depends on the depth of the bench, a range of 0.6–1.0 meter is a better metric. The frontispiece picture of Schwarzer (*Das Gebäude*, vii) shows twenty-six men reclining at the west half of the cultic room, which belongs to the seventh building phase, when the room was enlarged and the passage between couches 1 and 2 was removed, creating a sixteen-meter central couch (i.e., 0.61 meter per diner), but this produces very crowded dining.
75. I.Perg 485 = I.DionysosJ 94 = GRA II 110 (Pergamon, I CE).
76. Harland, *Greco-Roman Associations*, 124. The inscription is broken at the bottom, so it is unclear whether the list is complete.
77. The papyrus is broken at the end of the list of names from the first couch, which perhaps suggests that the fragmentary name on line 7 is the *kleitarchēs* of the first couch.
78. Gallazzi et al., *Tebtynis*, 150–52, and Plan 2.
79. SEG 41:1638 (Tebtynis, time of Nero). Bastianini and Gallazzi, "Un'iscrizione inedita di Tebtynis," have argued convincingly that this association was associated with the estate of Claudius Dorophoros, a procurator of Nero, who owned land in the Fayûm.
80. SB 3:7182, Frag. 1.2.11; 1.3.32, Frag. 3.41; Frag. 4.recto.2.45–46; 4.recto.3.60; Frag. 5.recto.75.

81. An Iseion and the *dromos* (sacred way) between the Iseion and the temple of the Dioskouri are mentioned already in P.Cair.Zen II 59168 (Philadelphia 256/255 BCE).
82. TAM V 1539.5–6 = GRA II 117.
83. IGUR 160 (ca. 160 CE).
84. *Oikos* might be a metonymy for "association," as it seems to be in TAM V 1539.23 = GRA II 117 ("no one should cease having goodwill for the *oikos*") although the other occurrences of *oikos* in this inscription clearly refer to a building.
85. SEG 43:59 (Rhamnous, 41/40 BCE) records the membership list of a group of *eranistai*, using at least two *triclinia* and with a membership of at least eleven.
86. Nielsen, *Housing the Chosen*, 118–20.
87. See Nielsen, *Housing the Chosen*, 123–24.
88. SB 10:10278 (Apollonopolite Heptakomia, 98–138 CE).
89. Arzt-Grabner, "Everyday Life," has proposed that both Philemon and Paul might have been weavers and that Philemon's "house" was his workshop.
90. Smit, "Symposiastic Background," and Streett, "Food, Fellowship, and Favoritism." I am grateful to Dr. Streett for a copy of his paper.
91. See Lucian, *Symposion* 13, for a similar scenario: Alcidamas the Cynic arrived at a banquet uninvited, and his host, Aristaenetus, asked him to sit on a chair (rather than recline). Alcidamas objected: sitting on a chair or a stool while the others dined reclining was effeminate. He chose to eat standing up, and if he got tired, he would recline on the floor.
92. Vitruvius, *De architectura* 6.5.1: "For into these rooms nobody has the right to enter except by invitation: bedrooms, *triclinia*, bathrooms, and all others used for similar purposes (*cubicula, triclinia, balneae ceteraque*). The common rooms, however, are those that the uninvited of the population (*invocati . . . de populo*) have the right to enter: that is, entrance courts, *cavaedia*, peristyles, and all intended for the like purpose (*vestibula, cava aedium, peristylia, quaeque eundem habere possunt usum*). Hence, for ordinary people it is unnecessary to have grand vestibules, *tablina*, or atriums built in grand style because such men are more apt to discharge their obligations (*officia*) by going round to others than to have others come to them." (I owe this reference to David Balch.)
93. Again, I am grateful to David Balch for this observation, who refers to Cicero, *Off.* 1.139, who indicates that it was expected that an elite home would be filled with "numerous guests" and "crowds of every sort of person." See Balch, *Roman Domestic Art*, 3–7, 35–38; and Zanker, *Pompeii*, 10–12, 18–19, on the "public" nature of the Roman house.
94. J. A. Weaver, "Re-Examination."
95. Bollmann, *Römische Vereinshäuser*, 113, 382–83, lists several *tabernae* that were likely used by cultic associations. Her catalogue no. A59 is a *taberna* in Herdonia (II CE), a room 4.4 by 8 meters, which was fitted with a podium and marble revetment, suggesting a use other than commercial. Similarly, her no. A62 (Paestum, III CE), a 5.5-by-10.52-meter room with an apse and podium installed also suggests cultic use. See also her nos. A66, A69, and A73.
96. See the discussion on P.Mich V 246 above and Rondot, *Tebtynis II*, 150–52.

97. Radt, *Pergamon*, 196–97.
98. Calza, *La necropoli del Porto*; Graham, "Quick and the Dead"; Braune, *Convivium funebre*.
99. On the use of cemeteries by Christ followers, see MacMullen, *Second Church*, 9–10, 69–94.
100. MacMullen, *Second Church*, 52, 157 n. 4, and MacMullen and Lane, *Paganism and Christianity*, 243.
101. See Dunbabin, *Roman Banquet*, 175–202.
102. Augustine, *Ep.* 22.6 (CSEL 34.1, 59–60) (392 CE). On the distribution of *sportulae* at meals and at funerary commemorations, see chap. 7.

4. BELONGING

1. ILLPRON 610. Piccottini, "Ein römisches Handwerkerkollegium."
2. Flower, *Art of Forgetting*.
3. AE 1929, 161.53, 55, 58, 59, 68, 78, 85, 103 (Trebula Mutuesca, 60 CE): eight (of seventy-eight) erasures; CIL 6.647.iv.1 (Rome): one name; CIL 6.7459 (Rome, II CE): three (of thirty-six) erasures; CIL 6.9102 (Rome, I CE): nine (of eighty-five) erasures; CIL 11.1355a.33 (Luna, II CE): one erasure; CIL 6.33885 (Rome, 117–138 CE): requirement to erase names from the *album;* CIL 14.4569.iv.61, v.1 (Ostia, 198 CE): two erasures; SEG 45:1505 (Aphrodisias, II/III CE): a patron's name erased; IK Apameia 114 (Strobilos [Bithynia], 178–187 CE): a patron's name erased; ILLPRON 610.ii.9, 13; iii.1, 14; iv.1 (Virunum, II CE): five (of fifty-seven) erasures; P.Tebt III/2 894.Frag. 1.v.2.48 [[Eudēmos]] has been erased but the letters are still barely visible.
4. The *damnatio memoriae* of Domitian was largely effective, with many public monuments having his named removed. By contrast, the Senate's wish to issue a *damnatio memoriae* after Hadrian's death was successfully opposed by his successor Antoninus Pius. On the latter, see Flower, *Art of Forgetting*, 272–75.
5. Flower (*Art of Forgetting*, 13) relates the modern example of the fate of Vladimír Clementis, an associate of the communist leader of Czechoslovakia, Klement Gottwald. After his execution in 1952, Clementis's picture was erased from photographs taken in 1948 recording his presence on a balcony with Gottwald. All that remains of Clementis in the photograph is his fur hat, which he had placed on Gottwald's head. A similar fate awaited Nikolai Yezhov, head of the Stalinist NKVD, the forerunner of the KGB, who was active during the "Great Purge" (1936–1938) and involved in the execution of thousands. He was himself executed in 1940, and, having become an "unperson," his picture was erased from photographs where he had been standing beside Joseph Stalin. (I owe this reference to Kiril Lepekhin.)
6. Solin, "Neue Namen," 283. This makes more sense than the suggestion of the editor of ILMN I 124, who proposes D = *decurio.*
7. The sense is not clear. Flambard, "Éléments," 222, renders it "Si quelque membre vient à se mettre en faute, on ne s'occupera plus de lui: si les autres membres ne s'exécutent pas, ils verseront chacun 10 HS [sesterces]."

8. See Schmit Pantel, "Collective Activities," in relation to Greek cities.
9. Lists functioned in associations not only to display their members, but also to shame them. A third-century BCE decree of Athenian *orgeōnes* of the hero Echelos mandates the recording of those who owe dues to the association: "The *orgeōnes* approved. In order that the partnership (*koinōnia*) in the sacrifices be maintained for all time for the association (*koinon*) that is near Kalliphanes's property and that of the hero (5) Echelos, (it was decided) to inscribe (the names) of those who owe anything to the *koinōnia*—both the principal and the interest, as much as each owes—on a stele and set it up by the altar in the temple" (Agora 16:161 = GRA I 14). Similarly, IG II[2] 1361.14–15 = GRA I 4 (Piraeus, 330–324/323 BCE).
10. As Bruno Latour (*Reassembling the Social*, 27–29) observes, the modern emphasis on individuals as isolated, stable agents is more rhetorical than real, and identity continues to be formed in aggregates.
11. Thomas, "Writing, Reading," 32–35, quotation at 34.
12. Van Nijf, "Collegia and Civic Guards," 333.
13. Compare IG II[2] 1297 = GRA I 24, from the same association twelve years later (236/235 BCE), in which the decree is inscribed first, then (in a crown) "The *thiasōtai* (honored) the *archeranistēs* Sophron," and then the membership list (in the nominative case), divided into four columns, men in columns 1–2 and women in columns 3–4.
14. Woolf, "Monumental Writing," 32.
15. Plato, *Resp.* 327AB, 328A. The Bendis procession, revived in the mid-third century, is described in IG II[2] 1283 = GRA I 23 (Piraeus, 240/239 BCE) and represented graphically in an early-fourth-century relief in the British Museum (BM inv. GR 1895, 1028.1) (see chap. 10, fig. 22).
16. *Scriptores historiae Augustae*, Gallienus 8.6; Aurelian 34.4.
17. According to Lydus, *De mensibus* 4.59 (ed. Wünsch 1898, 113), "On the 11th day before the Kalends of April, a pine tree would be carried on the Palatine by the *dendrophori*. The festival was established by the Emperor Claudius."
18. On the *dendrophors* in general, see Salamito, "Les dendrophores."
19. Patterson, "*Collegia*," 235, citing CIL 11.418.
20. Napolitano, "On a Political Economy," discusses the case of a confraternity of El señor de los Milagros, a group of Peruvian immigrants to modern-day Rome who conduct a procession involving an extremely heavy sedan chair, borne through the streets of Rome by groups of men and proceeded by women with special woven clothing. In the understanding of the group, participation in these activities creates a "legality of the soul" for migrants who may not be documented officially by the state and offers a form of masculine labor for migrant males who generally are relegated to feminized forms of labor (caregivers, attendants for the elderly, etc.).
21. Harland, "Christ-Bearers and Fellow Initiates."
22. See, for example, Athenaeus's description of a Dionysiac procession (*Deipn.* 5.197ef; 198b, d, 201a) and Apuleius's description of the procession of Isis (*Metamorphoses* 11.9, 12), where the processional way is spread with aromatic oils, and garlands of roses are carried. I owe this reference to Richard DeMaris.

23. See Kokkinia, "Rosen für die Toten"; Ascough, "A Question of Death," 513–14.
24. See Beck, "Ritual, Myth, Doctrine and Initiation" and "On Becoming a Mithraist."
25. Bremmer, *Initiation into the Mysteries*, 6, 51.
26. On the civic *context* of the baptismal practices of Christ assemblies, see, however, DeMaris, *New Testament*, who argues that the materiality of the baptismal ritual should be seen in the context of the role of water in Roman Corinth, including the use of water in the forum, and other expressions of Rome's control and distribution of water. He argues that baptism was an enactment of symbolic inversion, using water in a way that eluded Roman control and in association with entry into an "alternate society beyond Roman hegemony" (49). The preference expressed in the *Didache* for cold water over warm is perhaps a "muted comment about the Roman bath" (50). Baptism, thus, is a ritual of both mimicry and inversion.
27. The most comprehensive study of *dokimasia* is Feyel, *Dokimasia*, which offers an exhaustive survey of the various types of preliminary examination in Athens and other Greek cities, including the vetting of prospective members in private associations.
28. For example, Aristotle, *Ath. pol.* 55.3; Xenophon, *Mem.* 2.2.13; Dinarchus 2.8–10; and Lysias 31.1.
29. See, for example, IG XII,3 183 (Astypalaea after 300 BCE): "Let not anyone who is not pure (*hagnos*) enter the temple; either to offer (a sacrifice) or to be in the shrine itself."
30. See Kloppenborg, "Moralizing of Discourse."
31. Augustine, *Ep.* 78.4: "For I did not presume to suppress or erase (*supprimere vel delere*) from the roll of his colleagues the name of this presbyter, lest I should seem to insult the Divine Majesty, upon whose arbitration the case now depends, if I were to forestall His decision by any premature decision of mine."
32. SB 3:7182.
33. AM 32 (1907), 295–97 (no. 18), lines 11–12 (Pergamon); IG XII,8 666.1–3 (mid-II BCE); I.Eph 5102 (106/107 CE); I.Delta I 989.20–21 (238 BCE).
34. Similarly, Jub. 36.10. Dan 7:10 and 1 En. 47.3 depict God as sitting in judgment with books in front of him, and 1 En. promises the just that their names will be written "before the glory of the Great One" (104.1) and that the names of sinners will be "blotted out from the Book of Life" (108.3; trans. E. Isaac in James H. Charlesworth, ed., *The Old Testament Pseudepigrapha*, 2 vols. [Garden City, N.Y.: Doubleday, 1983–1985], 1:85, 88). I owe these references to Steven Muir.
35. The idea of God having lists is expanded further in y. Roš Haš 1.3.15–16, where a saying attributed to R. Yoḥanan asserts that God maintains three lists: one for the fully righteous, another for the fully wicked, and a third intermediate one, citing Ps 69:28 as proof.
36. Herm. Vis. 1.3.2; Herm. Sim. 2.1.9.
37. Ascough, "Completion of a Religious Duty."
38. For archaeological evidence, see chap. 3 n. 58 above. Locus 77 at Qumran is routinely identified as a dining hall (Runesson, Binder, and Olsson, *Ancient Synagogue*, no. 41). For literary evidence, see Josephus, *B.J.* 2.128–32 (on the Essenes).

39. Grignon, "Commensality," 23–33, quotation at 29. I am indebted to Richard Ascough for alerting me to Grignon's work. Grignon offers a taxonomy of dining as a set of three contrasting pairs: domestic and institutional commensality, everyday and exceptional commensality, and segregative and transgressive commensality. For our purposes, three of these are of interest: segregative commensality, institutional commensality, and transgressive commensality. Institutional commensality is present when there is an existing hierarchy that determines who eats, where, and with whom: "It appears directly linked to social segregation or even to social repulsion; its concern is not only to keep or to spread a strategic network of acquaintances, but to 'keep up one's position' by sharing in a system of mutual invitations which approves and attests membership of the same level and in the same social world. . . . More precisely, the position held by someone depends on the position of the guests and the invitations he may expect, on the position of those he invites and those who invite him" (26–27). Transgressive commensality plays on oppositions between social groups and the borders between them, temporarily and symbolically transgressing these borders "in the neutralized and ritual parenthesis of a meal"—the factory boss eating with workers, the emperor eating with citizens (30).
40. Donahue, "Toward a Typology," 423–41, quotation at 434.
41. Grignon, "Commensality," 30.
42. For example, I.Prose 40 (Berenike, Egypt, 67–63 BCE), the decision of a guild of farmers to invite their patron, a royal official, to three yearly banquets and to allow him to bring three friends.
43. Ironically, the temporary and fictive eliding of social differences in the end undergirded and sustained social hierarchies. Grignon, "Commensality," 31: "it is by transgressing [social borders] that it contributes to recognizing and maintaining them. Inviting a stranger is a confrontation, a reciprocal challenge, which allows each to test the other, on the basis of shared criteria, with an excessive offer of drink and food, and so to measure the other's value, physically as well as psychologically and morally."
44. CIL 14.2112 (Lanuvium, 136 CE) adds sardines and stipulates "good wine"; CIL 6.33885 (Rome, 117–138 CE) adds laurel cake and dates and Carian figs and pears for the New Year's Day meal, but bread and wine otherwise.
45. See the Glossary.
46. On the nature of ritual as rule-based behavior, see Asad, *Genealogies of Religion*, 62. I am indebted to Vearncombe, "Rituals for Communal Maintenance," for this reference.
47. Bell, *Ritual*, 123. Grimes, *Craft*, 195, defines ritual as "embodied, condensed, and prescribed enactment." Stephenson, "Ritual as Action," 48, stresses the performative nature of ritual, arguing that it "is a different way of framing or paying attention to the connections between what one is doing and what one is thinking or feeling. In ritual, it is the doing of the rite that is primary. Ritual is not an expression of intentions, motivations, feelings, or beliefs; rather, ritual entails engaging in specific, formalized acts not of one's own making." In the case of segregative commensality, a communal meal ritual is a performance of communal belonging (among other things). I am grateful

to Richard DeMaris, one of the editors of the *Oxford Handbook of Early Christian Ritual*, for an advance copy of Stevenson's chapter.

48. Hence, Paul in 1 Cor 11:17–34 intervenes in the Corinthian meal ritual to assert that the meal has been misperformed. It is unclear whether the Corinthians themselves thought that this was the case. On "ritual failure," see in general Grimes, "Infelicitous Performances."
49. For example, IG II^2 1368, line 74 = GRA I 51 (Athens, 164/165 CE).
50. CIL 6.10234 (Rome, 153 CE). The clause "those who at that time happen to be (*qui tunc erunt*) the president (*quinquennalis*) or supervisors (*curatores*) of the above-mentioned association" (lines 21–22) indicates that the offices of president and supervisor were rotating. The term of office for a *curator* is not known, but CIL 14.2112 suggests that it was one year.
51. For the estimate of membership, see Bendlin, "Associations, Funerals, Sociability," 262.
52. P.Mich V 246 (Tebtynis, 43–49 CE). The contributions ranged from 10 to 24 denarii, and members were assigned seats according to the size of the contribution.
53. P.Lond VII 2193.19 (Philadelphia, 69–58? BCE); P.Mich V 243, lines 6–7 (Tebtynis, time of Tiberius); CIL 14.2112, lines 59–60 (Lanuvium, 136 CE); IG II^2 1368, lines 73–74 = GRA I 51 (Athens, 164/165 CE).
54. Pliny, *Ep.* 10.96.7. Justin Martyr (*Apol.* 1.65.5) likewise mentions bread and wine but adds water. A generation later Hippolytus's eucharistic prayers include prayers not only over the bread and wine, but over cheese and olives. See Bradshaw, Johnson, and Phillips, *Apostolic Tradition*, 52–54.
55. Origen, *Cels.* 3.55 (my translation).
56. Walzer, *Galen on Jews and Christians*, 14–15, 68.
57. For example, not repaying evil with evil: 1 Thess 5:15, Rom 12:14; nonconfrontation with outsiders: 1 Thess 4:12–13, Rom 13:1–7, Col 4:5; love toward members: 1 Cor 12:31–3:13; Gal 5:14, 22; Rom 13:8–10; Col 3:14; care for the poor: Jas 2:1–13, 14–26. See also the catalogues of virtues and vices in *Did.* 1–5.
58. MacMullen, "What Difference Did Christianity Make?," 329, points out that the ethical attitudes of Christ followers were very like those of "the everyday sort of Romans, not the aristocracy, [and] among the more severe circles of eastern cities."
59. Hurtado, *Destroyer of the Gods*, chap. 5, emphasizes the distinct nature of the ethics of early Christ devotees, stressing (with Diognetus) the refusal to expose children, avoidance of gladiatorial games and other spectacles, absolute refusal to participate in pagan cults, and a robust sexual ethic. He exaggerates the degree to which the ethic of Christ devotees was unique, in part by dismissing other similar practices as nonreligious and therefore not comparable.
60. Dionysios of Alexandria's letter, cited in Eusebius, *Hist. eccl.* 7.22.7–10. See chap. 11.
61. See Stark, *Rise of Christianity*, 76–94. Stark also cites Julian the Apostate's complaint that during a food shortage, "it is disgraceful that, when no Jew ever has to beg and the impious Galileans (i.e., Christians) support not only their own poor but ours as well, all men see that our people lack aid from us" (*Ep.* 22 to Arsacius, high priest of

Galatia, 362 CE). The authenticity of this letter, however, has been doubted: Van Nuffelen, "Deux fausses lettres."

62. Verbal abuse: SB 3:6319 recto.ii, lines 43–44, P.Lond VII 2193, lines 15–16, BGU XIV 2371, line 6, P.Mich V 243, line 8; physical abuse: BGU XIV 2371, lines 7–8; fighting: SEG 31:122, lines 6–8 = GRA I 50; IG II^2 1368, lines 71, 73, 80–83, 89–90, 94–95 = GRA I 51; IG IX/1^2 670, lines 7–11 = GRA I 61; IG II^2 1369, lines 43–44 = GRA I 49; genealogies: P.Lond VII 2193, line 15; accusations: P.Mich V 243, lines 7–8; seat-stealing: P.Lond VII 2193, line 18, P.Mich V 243, line 7, IG II^2 1368, line 74 = GRA I 51; drunkenness: P.Mich V 243, line 3; interference with conviviality: P.Lond VII 2193, line 18, BGU XIV 2371.4; sordid behavior: SEG 31:122, lines 33–34 = GRA I 50.
63. Obstruction of the president: P.Lond VII 2193, line 20; violation of the bylaws: IG II^2 1328, line 13 = GRA I 34, LSAM 80.
64. P.Cair 30606, lines 11–12, 22; P.Lond VII 2193, lines 11–12; P.Mich V 243, line 4; P.Mich V 244, lines 7–9; P.Mich V 245, lines 35–37; IG II^2 1368, lines 96–99 = GRA I 51; IG IX/1^2 670, lines 13–17 = GRA I 61; CIL 6.10298 (Rome, I CE).
65. P.Lond VII 2193, lines 16–17; BGU XIV 2371, line 2; P.Mich V 243, lines 7–8; P.Mich V 243, lines 7–8; IG II^2 1368, lines 90–94 = GRA I 51.
66. P.Mich V 243 (Tebtynis); P.Mich V 244, lines 16–18 (Tebtynis); AE 1929, 161, lines 13–15 (Trebula Mutuesca, 60 CE); IG II^2 1368, lines 162–63 = GRA I 51 (Athens, 164/165 CE); Philippi II 133/G441, lines 17–21 = GRA I 69 (Philippi, II–III CE).
67. SB 3:6319 recto.ii, lines 45–46; P.Mich V 243, line 8.
68. P.Mich.Zen I 57, line 3; P.Mich V 243, lines 6–9; P.Mich V 244, lines 9–10.
69. Elsewhere I have suggested that the latter advice is not simply a matter of not wanting to "air the dirty laundry of the group in public" but also, and perhaps more importantly, an assertion of the autonomy and sovereignty of the group over its own affairs, critical aspects of identity in Greek cities. See Kloppenborg, "Associations, Christ Groups," 34, and comparable expressions of autonomy in Greco-Roman associations, for example, P.Lond VII 2193, line 17, P.Mich V 243, line 12, and IG II^2 1368, lines 90–94 = GRA I 51.
70. It is commonly supposed that the death of the offender was intended (thus Collins, "Function of 'Excommunication'") because of the use of *olethros*, "ruin, plague, destruction." Forms of *olethr-* appear with some frequency in curses, where it appears to mean "damage," often severe, rather than death. The critical question is whether the purpose clause, "so that the *pneuma* be saved," refers to the offender's "spirit" (so most interpreters and Bible translations) or, more likely, to the *pneuma* of the community that could be contaminated by egregious behavior (Martin, *Corinthian Body*, 169). In 1 Cor 5 Paul seems unconcerned with the fate of humans; he is interested in the purity of the spirit.
71. Papathomas, *Juristische Begriffe*, 65–66, in surveys of Greco-Roman papyri, shows that the principal connotations of *paradidōmi* are (1) to transfer a matter to someone, (2) to hand over a matter to the police, (3) to convey forcibly (e.g., conveying someone to prison), and (4) to hand back the objects of a lease at its conclusion. Paul uses *paradidōmi* in the sense of handing over to a trial at 1 Cor 11:23.

72. For example, P.Mich V 244, lines 16–17 (Tebtynis, 43 CE): "If someone should die . . . and one of the men named below does not defile himself (i.e., attend the funeral) let *such a person* (*ho toioutos*) be fined" (emphasis added); similarly, P.Mich V 244, lines 24–25 (Tebtynis, 47 CE).
73. As Jinyu Liu ("Group Membership") points out, some groups appear to have had very long lifespans: the builder-carpenters of Rome lasted more than 200 years, and those at Ostia, more than 180 years. But others disappeared, perhaps poorer associations, which may not have had the ability to collect dues and fines: "Because the members of such *collegia* were relatively poor, there was a higher chance for them to default on the dues, making it difficult for *collegium* to function properly not to mention participate in civic life" (210). She cites IDR I 31, the association of Jupiter Cernenus in Albernus Maior in Dacia, which dissolved because of a failure of members to contribute dues.
74. CIL 6.10234, lines 16–17 (Rome, 153 CE); IG II^2 1339, lines 13–15 = GRA I 46 (57/56 BCE); IG II^2 1361, lines 19–20 = GRA I 4 (330–324/323 BCE); IG II^2 1368, lines 96–99, 162–63 = GRA I 51 (164/165 CE); IG IX/1^2 670, lines 13–15 = GRA 1 61 (Physkos, mid-II CE); P.Lond VII 2193, line 18 (Philadelpheia, Arsinoites, 69–58 BCE); P.Mich V 243, line 4 (Tebtynis, time of Tiberius); P.Mich V 244, lines 7–9 (Tebtynis, 43 CE).
75. Since IG II^2 1361 = GRA I 4 sets the cost for the members who attend the sacrifice at 2 drachmae, the charge levied on the nonattendees might have been devised in order to ensure that the costs of the sacrificial animal be met; but the fact that there is an implied exclusion for people who are ill suggests that the charge is a penalty for nonattendance.
76. For example, P.Petr III 136 (Arsinoites, 231 BCE).
77. Because of the serious devaluation of Ptolemaic bronze coinage during the second century BCE, 2,200 AE drachmae has an equivalent of 4.5 AR (silver) drachmae; 100 AE drachmae was worth about 0.89 AR drachma.
78. Broekaert, "Partners in Business," 247.
79. In chap. 10 below, I also argue that attendance at the association's internal judicial forum was an exercise of "autonomy" and as such a critical aspect of associative life.
80. See, for example, AM 66 228 no. 4, lines 18–20 (138/137 BCE) (50 drachmae fine); IG II^2 1263, lines 43–45 = GRA I 11 (300/299 BCE) (50 drachmae); IG II^2 1273AB, lines 22–23 = GRA I 18 (265/264 BCE) (50 drachmae); IG II^2 1292, lines 16–17 = GRA I 26 (215/214 BCE) (50 drachmae?); and IG II^2 1297, lines 17–18 = GRA I 24 (236/235 BCE).
81. Sosis, "Religion and Intragroup Cooperation."
82. Sosis and Bressler, "Cooperation and Commune Longevity," 227.
83. Ogilvie, *Institutions and European Trade*. Her larger theoretical interest is whether merchant guilds were in fact economically efficient organizations that benefited the entire economy.
84. Bourdieu, "Forms of Capital," 248–49.
85. Coleman, "Social Capital."

5. CHRIST ASSEMBLIES IN THE URBAN ECONOMY

1. For a recent attempt to describe an ancient "middle class," see Mayer, *Ancient Middle Classes*. The "middle class" in Western sociological theory comprises between one-quarter and two-thirds of the population and is often divided into an upper or professional class of managers and professionals, all with college educations, and other, middle-class ("white-collar") people, most of whom have a college education and who enjoy a comfortable standard of living. By any measure those ancient people with "middling incomes" were very much smaller in number than the middle classes of North Atlantic countries. Moreover, our definitions of "middle class" would hardly apply to those who were positioned between the majority of agricultural workers and the elite. Without any indication of shared consciousness, it is difficult to speak of a "class."
2. All of the quotations in this paragraph are from Kautsky, *Ursprung*; *Foundations*, 329. Kautsky also suggests that Matthew omitted Luke 16:19–31, the rich man and Lazarus.
3. Deissmann, *Licht vom Osten*, translated first in 1910. The standard English translation, published in *Light from the Ancient East*, is based on the fourth German edition (1925). *Das Urchristentum* was based on lectures delivered in June 1908 after the completion of *Licht vom Osten* and was published in English in Deissmann, "Primitive Christianity."
4. Deissmann, *Licht vom Osten*, 173–75; Deissmann, *Das Urchristentum*, 23.
5. Deissmann, *Paul*, 7, 48, 52, 110, 214 (emphasis added).
6. Deissmann, *Paul*, 53, 216–17.
7. Harnack, *Mission and Expansion*, 2:33–36, citing Origen, *Cels.* 1.27; 3.18, 44, 54; Caecilius (cited in Minucius Felix, *Oct.* 5, 8, 12); and Lucian, *Perigr.* 13.
8. For a clear discussion of levels of ancient scribalism, see Kirk, "Scribe as Tradent."
9. Nock, "Vocabulary," 138.
10. The exception to this statement is that by the beginning of the second century CE the curial or aristocratic rank came to be known as the *honestiores*, "more honorable citizens," distinct from commoners, *humiliores*, the "more humble people."
11. See the discussion of this problem in W. V. Harris, "On the Applicability," and Scheidel, "Stratification."
12. Alföldy, *Social History*, 149.
13. Alföldy, *Social History*, 147–48 (emphasis added).
14. Freedmen could serve in minor public offices in some of the Roman colonies: Abbott and Johnson, *Municipal Administration*.
15. Tacitus (*Agr.* 4.1) describes the two grandfathers of his father-in-law, Cn. Iulius Agricola, as *equestris nobilitas*, equestrian nobility, because both had served as imperial procurators.
16. Garnsey and Saller, *Roman Empire*, 118.
17. Cicero, *Off.* 1.150–51; Joshel, *Work, Identity, and Legal Status*, 62–69.
18. P. R. C. Weaver, *Familia Caesaris*.
19. The figures are Scheidel's ("Stratification," 42).

20. Meggitt, *Paul, Poverty and Survival*, 75. See the critical evaluations of Meggitt's argument by Theissen, "Social Structure" and "Social Conflicts," and Martin, "Review Article."
21. Meggitt, *Paul, Poverty and Survival*, 99. Similar "binary" approaches to wealth and poverty are seen in Brunt, *Italian Manpower*, 383; and Garnsey and Saller, *Roman Empire*, 43.
22. Lucas, *Industrial Revolution*. For a critique, see Bowman and Wilson, "Quantifying," 45.
23. Allen, Bengtsson, and Dribe, *Living Standards in the Past*; Jongman, "Gibbon Was Right," 185.
24. On improved nutrition: Kron, "Anthropometry"; Jongman, "Gibbon Was Right," 193–95; Bowman and Wilson, "Quantifying," 44, with some hesitations in Wilson, "Quantifying Roman Economic Performance," 155–56; on iron smelting: Kehoe, "Early Roman Empire," 547–48; Wilson, "Quantifying Roman Economic Performance," 156–57; on fish salting: Wilson, "Fish-Salting Workshops" and "Quantifying Roman Economic Performance," 157–61.
25. Kehoe, "Early Roman Empire," 550, citing Pleket, "Urban Elites" and "Wirtschaft."
26. Rathbone, "Poverty and Population," 106.
27. Brown, *Poverty and Leadership*.
28. Summarizing the analysis of Hanson, "Widows," Rathbone ("Poverty and Population," 104) stated, "Of these 104 [presumed widows], 63 are living with an adult son or other male relation, 39 live in predominantly female households, and only one, or possibly two, seem to have been lodgers in houses with no resident kin, and the one certain solitary had her freedwoman living with her."
29. Rathbone, "Poverty and Population," 108. Rathbone notes that the usual explanation, that tax avoiders simply decamped, "would have been very difficult, for Egypt did not have the uninhabited but liveable wilds known to Europe, and *anachoresis* in fact just denoted absence, mainly of young unmarried men, in the normal expectation that the taxpayer would either be registering and paying in their place of temporary residence, or would settle the arrears on their return, which they were allowed three years to do" (108). See, however, W. V. Harris, "Poverty and Destitution," 36, who is critical of Rathbone, arguing that it is impossible to know whether some avoided paying the poll tax by other means.
30. Wilson, "Machines"; Lo Cascio, "Role of the State"; Jongman, "Rise and Fall"; Temin, *Roman Market Economy*.
31. Scheidel and Friesen, "Size of the Economy."
32. See Hopkins, "Taxes and Trade" and "Rome, Taxes, Rents."
33. Scheidel and Friesen, "Size of the Economy," 82, calculate the elite plus the military population at 3 percent of the total population, but earlier, Scheidel estimated the elite at 350,000–500,000, including family members, and argued that the military consisted of 350,000–400,000 soldiers and 100,000–120,000 veterans ("Stratification," 42 n. 6). These figures would represent only 1.7 percent of the total population of 60 million, 1.4 percent of 70 million. Nevertheless, using 1.7 percent instead of

3 percent (elite plus military income) would affect the Scheidel-Friesen calculations in only a minor way.

34. This figure assumes an average per capita income of about 680 kilograms of grain, factors in 15–30 percent of GDP representing elite income, subtracts the likely level of state expenditures. See also Scheidel, "Stratification," and Temin, "Estimating GDP," who estimate an average per capita income (including elite income) of 614 kilograms of grain. Since Temin's 2006 article, he has revised GDP upward to 50 percent higher than Scheidel and Friesen's estimates, which implies an even larger "middling" group in the empire (*Roman Market Economy*, 259–61).

35. Scheidel and Friesen, "Size of the Economy," 75, 82; compare Hopkins, "Rome, Taxes, Rents," 201, who estimates that the actual GDP was between one-half and one-third higher than minimum subsistence.

36. Rather than distributing the surplus above subsistence evenly, Scheidel and Friesen invoke the Pareto distribution, the statistical observation of an Italian engineer who noted that typical distributions of wealth have the top 20 percent of society controlling 80 percent of the wealth, the next 20 percent controlling 80 percent of the remainder, and so forth. See Persky, "Retrospectives."

37. Scheidel and Friesen, "Size of the Economy," 83–84 (Tables 7, 8, 9).

38. Pleket, "Wirtschaft," 145–46. Using Pleket's estimate, Friesen ("Poverty in Pauline Studies," 342 n. 62) calculates that 6.25 million lived in cities of larger than 10,000 inhabitants. Regional variations meant that in western Asia and around Antioch on the Orontes the urban population may have been as great as 20 percent of the population.

39. Scheidel and Friesen, "Size of the Economy," 90–91.

40. See n. 34 above. Wilson ("Quantifying Roman Economic Performance"), however, remains skeptical that GDP can be calculated, although he does point to various metrics that indicate enhanced per capita income in the early imperial period.

41. Rathbone, "Census Qualification," analyzes the census structure of republican Italy, dividing the population into five categories, those with property declarations of (1) greater than 100,000 sesterces, (2) 75,000 sesterces, (3) 50,000 sesterces, (4) 20,000 sesterces, and (5) 375 sesterces. With an overall population of 525,000 households in Italy, about one-half fell into the third and fourth categories. Kehoe, "Poverty," 190, observes that this would "confirm both the existence of a substantial group of independent property owners who were not members of the elite but were also not in any meaningful sense poor. At the same time there was a large class of people who had little property of their own."

42. A Gini coefficient is generated by dividing a society into population deciles (*x* axis) and plotting the cumulative income or wealth (*y* axis) as one moves from one decile to the next. The resulting line (the Lorenz curve) from bottom left to top right indicates how evenly or unevenly wealth increases to 100 percent. In a situation of equal wealth distribution, the Lorenz curve will match the 45-degree diagonal "line of equality" and results in a Gini coefficient of zero (i.e., the area between the line of equality and the Lorenz curve = 0). This means that 10 percent of the society has 10 percent of ag-

gregate wealth, 30 percent has 30 percent of the wealth, 50 percent has 50 percent of the wealth, and so on. As one or more deciles of the population deviate from the line of equality, the Lorenz curve diverges from the diagonal, and the Gini coefficient increases. The Gini coefficient measures disparities only *within* population groups, not between population groups. Contemporary figures for 2010 put Norway unsurprisingly at 0.257, indicating a relatively high degree of income equality, with Canada at 0.336, the US at 0.404, and Zambia (the highest reported for 2010) at 0.556, showing very high levels of income inequality (see "GINI Index [World Bank Estimate]," World Bank, https://data.worldbank.org/indicator/SI.POV.GINI?year_high_desc=true).

43. Duncan-Jones, *Structure and Scale*, 129–42.
44. Bowman, "Landholding," 151.
45. Bowman, "Landholding," 151.
46. Bagnall, "Landholding in Late Roman Egypt," 130–32, applied the same method to data from several villages, resulting in coefficients of 0.516 (Arsinoë-Krokodilopolis, 216 CE) and 0.638 (Karanis), if one includes the holdings of the metropolitans. If one looks at the holdings of only the villagers, however, the results (0.431) are more equitable (134–36).
47. Kron, "Distribution of Wealth," uses an approach similar to that of Scheidel and Friesen in calculating a Gini coefficient for mid-fourth-century BCE Athens. He calculates the total wealth of Athens at 12,661 talents, given the worth of its three hundred wealthiest estates and its next wealthiest twelve hundred. With about thirty-one thousand male citizens, this results in a mean wealth of 2,451 drachmae and a median of 925 drachmae, but the richest 5 percent of the Athenian population controlled almost 50 percent of Athenian wealth. Kron finds the Gini coefficient (0.708) comparable to that of the wealth of citizens of Florence in 1427 (0.788) and to the US in 1953 (0.71) and more equitable than wealth distribution for England in 1911–1913 (0.95).
48. Wallace-Hadrill, *Houses and Society*, 76.
49. Wallace-Hadrill, *Houses and Society*, 79. I have modified Wallace-Hadrill's table slightly, adding percentages in the second column and the total number of rooms for each range.
50. Wallace-Hadrill, *Houses and Society*, 100–101.
51. That is, the number of rooms (579) divided by the population sample of 1,764.
52. Bagnall and Frier, *Demography*, 68, Table 3.3. The actual average is 4.04 family members per household.
53. Kron, "Comparative Evidence," 122.
54. Wallace-Hadrill, *Houses and Society*, 151–53.
55. Kron, "Comparative Evidence," 127.
56. Jongkind, "Corinth in the First Century AD," 148, compare p. 139.
57. Scheidel and Friesen, "Size of the Economy," 86.
58. Meeks, *First Urban Christians*, 73. Similarly, Kreissig, "Zur sozialen Zusammenhang"; and Stegemann and Stegemann, *Jesus Movement*, 294–96.
59. Theissen, *Social Setting*, esp. 121–43, 145–74; Theissen, "Pauperismus," 119–20.
60. Schleich, "Missionsgeschichte und Sozialstruktur," 279, 288.

61. Celsus (in Origen, *Cels.* 3.49) claimed that Christ groups consisted of "only foolish and low individuals, and persons devoid of perception, and slaves, and women, and children, of whom the teachers of the divine word wish to make converts."
62. Schleich, "Missionsgeschichte und Sozialstruktur," 279 (my translation). Similarly, Kyrtatas, *Social Structure,* who argues that Pauline assemblies recruited not the urban poor, but prosperous freed slaves and artisans.
63. Meeks, *First Urban Christians,* 73.
64. Meeks, *First Urban Christians,* 191. Meeks's observation of a "correlation" has sometimes been understood as implying a *causal* relation, which Meeks was careful to avoid. See further, Meeks, "Taking Stock and Moving On," 138–39.
65. Judge, *Social Pattern,* 60; repr. Judge, *Social Distinctives,* 43.
66. Judge, "Early Christians," 136.
67. Judge, "Early Christians," 130.
68. Judge, "Social Identity" repr., Judge, *Social Distinctives,* 126.
69. Theissen, *Social Setting,* 130–31.

6. THE SOCIAL LEVEL OF CHRIST ASSEMBLIES

1. See Öhler, "Zwischen Elite und Elend," who rightly focuses on the likely economic standing of associations and Christ assemblies as a whole, not individual members.
2. Lampe, *From Paul to Valentinus,* 119: before 300 CE fewer than forty named people of senatorial rank are attested as Christians, two-thirds of them women. See further, chap. 11 below.
3. S. Mitchell, *Anatolia,* 1:151; Christol and Drew-Bear, "Les Sergii Pauli en Antioche." CIL 6.31545 (Rome, 41–47 CE) names five senators, including L. Sergius Paullus, responsible for maintaining the banks of the Tiber (Halfmann, *Die Senatoren,* 101, no. 3). His son was L. Sergius Paullus, a military tribune and *quaestor* attested in AE 2002, 1457. See the full discussion in Weiß, *Soziale Elite,* 66–70.
4. IGRR 3.935.10–11 (Chytri, Cyprus, 14–37 or 37–41 CE): "[Q]uintus Ser[gius——]" is taken by Halfmann (*Die Senatoren,* 101, no. 4) to be Q. Sergius Paul(l)us of Acts 13:7 and perhaps the brother of Q. Sergius Paul(l)us the senator. The original restoration of line 9 proposed in IGRR, "[——Klaudi]iou Kaisaros Sebastou," suggests a date for the inscription of 41–54 CE, consistent with the dating of Paul's visit (according to the traditional chronology of Acts). Mitford ("Roman Cyprus," 1300–1301), however, restores lines 10–11 as "Q Ser | [gius——, proconsul (?)]" and from autopsy argued that line 9 be restored as "[C]aiou Kaisaros Sebastou." This means that the inscription would be dated to the time of Caligula (37–41 CE), not the time of Claudius. However, in his list of procurators, he also lists L. Sergius Paul(l)us as proconsul between 46 and 48 CE, solely on the evidence of Acts 13. More recently Campbell, "Possible Inscriptional Attestation," argues from an examination of the photographs and a squeeze (and following a suggestion of Chaniotis) that "[——Tib]e[r]iou Kaisaros Sebastou" is more probable, which would put the inscription at 14–37 CE. Both of the more recent datings indicate that the conventional chronology of Acts will have to be

revised if this is the (Q.) Sergius Paulus of Acts 13. As Weiß points out, however, the restoration of "Q. Ser[gius Paulus]" is conjectural (*Soziale Elite*, 61). Likewise, Christol and Drew-Bear, "Les Sergii Pauli en Antioche," 188, concluded that it is hazardous to identify the Q. Ser[gius . . .] of the inscription with a person from the principate of Claudius or to identify him with the Sergius Paulus of Acts.

5. Nock, "Paul and the Magus," 187–88, quips: "The proconsul's conversion, which would have been an event of the first importance, is just stated as though it were that of a washerwoman. . . . No Church is said to have been founded at Paphos (contrast the names in 17:34). . . . The conclusion to which one is driven is that Luke has some definite tradition which he has incorporated *tant bien que mal*."
6. Acts 19:31 claims that Paul was friendly with some of the Asiarchs. In the accounts in Acts of Paul's encounter with other Roman officials (the tribune in chap. 23; Felix in 24:22–26; Festus in 25:13–26:32) and with Herod Agrippa (25:23–32), those of high rank treat Paul respectfully. Haenchen, *Acts*, 400, and Eck, "Das Eindringen des Christentums," 391, argue that the clause in 13:12 *ho anthypatos . . . episteusen* is ambiguous and that it could mean "he had confidence in the wonderworker" or that he "became a Christian." Yet Keener, *Acts*, 2:2025, is surely right that the ordinary sense of *pisteuō* in Luke is "become a believer." Keener himself is very cautious; although he credits the story with some historicity, he wonders why Sergius Paulus's "faith" did not lead him to join a Christ group. A better explanation is that Luke's apologetic interests led him to fabricate an encounter with Q. (?) Sergius Paul(l)us and, like his other encounters with those of high rank, to depict the interaction as positive.
7. See Geagan, *Athenian Constitution*, 32–36.
8. Thus Lüdemann, *Early Christianity*, 194; and Pervo, *Acts*, 442. Keener (*Acts*, 3:2677), aware of this problem, replies that as a free city, Athens was not technically a part of Achaia, and he seems to entertain the possibility that Dionysios was "converted" in the absence of a sustaining group in Athens. This, as I argued in chap. 4, presupposes anachronistically a post–Industrial Revolution sense of conversion as principally intellectual and individual.
9. Archon: Agora XVI 295 (Athens, 163/162 BCE); other Erasti: IG II^2 1968 (Athens, 41–54 CE), an *ephebe*; IG II^2 1985 (Athens, mid-I CE), an *ephebe*; IG II^2 1945 (Athens, 45/46 CE), a demesman of Anaphlystos and the *hyperetēs* of a gymnasium; IG II^2 1990 (Athens, 61/62 CE), a *paideutēs* in the gymnasium and a demesman of Besa. Brookins, "(In)Frequency," 509, argues that these four names should be collapsed to two and one of them identified with the Erastus of I.Corinth.Kent 232.
10. Abbott and Johnson, *Municipal Administration*, 407 n. 85.
11. Seventy-five Latin inscriptions record the name Erastus. Solin, *Die griechischen Personennamen*, 953–54, lists thirty-four occurrences of Erastus in Rome where the person named is either a slave or a freedman (with Erastus as a cognomen), more than half of which belong to the period between Augustus and Nero. In other instances, the name appears alone (which could be either a slave name or a cognomen) or with a praenomen and nomen but with no indication of the father's name. Since there are no

instances of the name taking the form, for instance, of M. Ulpius M. f(ilius) Erastus, it is impossible to tell whether the bearer of the name is a freedman or freeborn.

12. Kent, *Corinth—Inscriptions*, 99 n. 232 = AE 1930, 118; AE 1932, 58; AE 1932, 74. Since a slave could not serve as an aedile, the full name must be "[praenomen] [nomen] l. [nomen in the genitive] Erastus." Kent (ibid., 100) notes that praenomen and nomen must have occupied the now-lost slab to the left of the preserved inscription, and that if the second line was placed symmetrically under line 1, the missing slab could have contained only five to six letters: "This must mean that the original text contained no patronymic or tribal abbreviation. Like his contemporary, Cn. Babbius Philinus, Erastus was probably a Corinthian freedman who had acquired considerable wealth in commercial activities."
13. Theissen, *Social Setting*, 80–82; similarly, Meeks, *First Urban Christians*, 58–59, and many others.
14. On municipal administration, see Abbott and Johnson, *Municipal Administration*, 56–68. On the role of the aedile, see Kent, *Corinth—Inscriptions*, 27. See the discussion of the history of this debate in Friesen, "Wrong Erastus." Gill, "Erastus the Aedile," 295–96, points out that other aediles at Corinth were freedmen, and at least one served as one of the *duoviri*.
15. See Friesen, "Wrong Erastus," for a full discussion of the archaeology, including unpublished notes of Williams. Brookins ("[In]Frequency," 507) challenges Friesen's (and Williams's) conclusions and wonders, "Why should we believe that the inscription came into existence at the same time as the pavement?" The simple answer is that the inscription in fact *claims* that Erastus laid the pavement!
16. Kent, *Corinth—Inscriptions*, 99. Similarly, Clarke, "Another Corinthian Erastus Inscription," 150; and Brookins, "(In)Frequency." Brookins offers the most complete catalogue to date of the frequency of the name and argues the case for identity on the grounds that "only some twenty-five date to the first century AD, only four or five of which come from Greece, among which, it has been argued, probably only two or three individuals are actually represented" (515).
17. Meggitt, "Social Status of Erastus," 222: fifty-five in Latin, twenty-three in Greek. Brookins ("[In]Frequency," 500–505) corrects and supplements Meggitt's statistics, reporting 105 instances of the name in Latin and Greek.
18. Mason, *Greek Terms*, 71, listed *oikonomos* as the equivalent for *aedilis coloniae*, but the main evidence for this equivalence is Rom 16:23 and I.Corinth.Kent 232 itself, and hence the argument is circular. Weiß (*Soziale Elite*, 114–15) points out that all of Mason's other examples of *oikonomos* supposedly meaning aedile come from Greek cities and thus cannot be the translation of aedile. Mason, ibid., 19, also lists *agoranomos* as the equivalent for aedile.
19. Theissen, *Social Setting*, 82–83.
20. A funerary inscription from the early second century, I.Corinth.Kent 170, commends a certain Antonius Sospes, who had served as *quaestor*, as military tribune of Legio III Augusta, as the *curator annonae*, as legate of Legio II Adiutrix, as *agonōthetēs*, and finally as one of the *duoviri*. Since the *curator annonae*, in charge of the grain supply,

was normally an aedile, and since the inscription moves from the lesser appointments to the more exalted ones in this *cursus honorum* (which typically alternates between military and civilian posts), it is clear that *quaestor* is junior to aedile (= *agoranomos*) but perhaps equivalent to *oikonomos*.

21. Kent, *Corinth—Inscriptions*, 181 n. 558. A certain Louka, a guardsman (*exkoubitoros*) and probably a slave, is said to have purchased the role of *oikonomos*.
22. Thus Weiß, *Soziale Elite*, 121–39. Goodrich ("Erastus, Quaestor of Corinth") argues on the basis of a late-second-century inscription (SEG 45:418) that *oikonomos* is probably equivalent to *quaestor*, that is, a financial officer subordinate to an aedile. SEG 45:418 is a funerary monument that commends a certain Neikostratos the *oikonomos tēs kolōneias* (manager of the colony [of Patras, northwest of Corinth]), who had served twice as *agonōthetēs* (president of the games), *agoranomos*, and twice as secretary (*grammateus*). Allowing for imprecision and variation in Greek equivalents of Latin titles, this inscription appears to confirm that an *agoranomos* (= aedile) was not equivalent to an *oikonomos*. Goodrich concludes that *oikonomos* must be equivalent to *quaestor*, and although he concedes that Neikostratos was likely a freedman, he claims, rather in a fit of excess, "as the text intimates, the office of *oikonomos* in an Achaean colony, such as Patras, was reserved for accomplished and highly visible *aristocrats*, and was indicative of social, economic, and political achievement" (111, emphasis added). Freedmen should not be confused with aristocrats, whatever their wealth, which was sometimes considerable. Moreover, as Abbott and Johnson showed (*Municipal Administration*, 66), the normal requirement of a free birth for eligibility for magistracies was not observed in some colonies, including Corinth.
23. Weiß, *Soziale Elite*, 138.
24. The earliest inscription that refers to a slave for Weiß (*Soziale Elite*, 129) is IG V/1 40 (Sparta, I/mid-II CE), whereas the earliest inscription in which the *oikonomos* is clearly freeborn is I.Smyrna 761 (I CE?). Weiß excludes as "uncertain" many inscriptions that he acknowledges refer to slaves: SEG 39:1316 (Kyme, I/early II CE), IGRR IV 813; IK Kalchedon 101 (Kalchedon, imperial period); I.CosPH 308 (Kos, I BCE/I CE); I.CosED EF 803 (Cos, imperial period); TAM II 1151 (Olympos, Lycia, imperial period); *JHS* 19 (1899): 124 n. 136 (Galatia, imperial period); SEG 38:710 (Mygdonia, Makedonia imperial period); CIG 6837 (Phrygia, imperial period).
25. Jewett, *Romans*, 982–83.
26. Weiß, *Soziale Elite*, 143–44.
27. For example, I.Smyrna 761, 771, 772; I.Stratonikeia 1103; SEG 26:1044; IG V,1 40; MAMA V Lists I(i):182, line 45; TAM V/3 1463. The full title appears in IGRR IV 813; I.Priene 83, 99, 108, 109, 115.
28. Friesen, "Wrong Erastus," 256, wonders whether instead of considering Erastos as an upwardly mobile Christ follower, we should consider that he was an "exploited slave." This, it seems to me, imports an etic, not an emic analytic framework. *We* might consider a public slave like Erastos to be "exploited," but Paul's identification of him as the "manager of the city" is an assertion of status.
29. On Gaius as a guest, see Kloppenborg, "Gaius the Roman Guest."

30. Fellmeth, "Politische Bewußtsein," esp. 53, and Fellmeth, "Die römischen Vereine und die Politik."
31. CIL 6.10234.
32. On the problematic nature of the terms "religion" and "religious," see the Introduction.
33. (1) The "Dancing Cowherds" (devoted to Dionysos) had a membership that included several Roman citizens (I.DionysosJ 98 = GRA II 124–25) and honored C. Antius Aulus Iulius Quadratus (PIR² J 507), a prominent benefactor of Pergamon (Halfmann, *Die Senatoren*, no. 17), who had been elevated to the senatorial rank by Vespasian and was a close friend of Trajan. Quadratus was *consul ordinarius* (105 CE) and proconsul of Asia (109/110 CE) (Birley, *Hadrian*, 30). (2) The Iobakchoi of Athens (IG II² 1368 = GRA I 51; Athens, 164/165 CE) had co-opted Ti. Claudius Herodes Atticus (PIR² C802) as their patron and chief priest. Herodes Atticus was one of the richest men in the Roman Empire and of consular rank, serving as *consul ordinarius* in 143 CE. (3) The third Dionysiac association had Pompeia Agrippinilla as its patroness (IGUR 160, Torre Nova, Campania, ca. 150 CE). Her husband was M. Gavius Squilla Gallicanus (PIR² G114), a senator and later proconsul of Asia.
34. GRA II 124–25. L. Aninius Flaccus was also a member of the "Hymn Singers" (I.Perg. 374 = GRA II 111).
35. IG II² 1368 = GRA I 51 (Athens, 164/165 CE).
36. IGUR 160 (Torre Nova, Campania, ca. 150 CE), with 402 members.
37. Perry, "*Collegia* and Their Impact," also suggests that patronage served as a way for the elite to exercise control over the subaltern populations by reinforcing the notion of hierarchy as "natural": "the collegium would have served as an institution of control, wielded by the elite to harness the social ambitions of the lower orders. . . . The effect would have been to encourage social mobility, to a point, while not allowing the lower classes—and especially those recently liberated from slavery—to rise so far as to threaten the elite's position" (146).
38. A cult group devoted to Isis (I.Trall 86 = GRA II 145) in the mid-second century CE honored an aristocrat, Iulius Amyntianus, who was likely related to C. Iulius Amyntianus (PIR² I 147), the brother of C. Iulius Severus (PIR² J 573; Halfmann, *Die Senatoren*, no. 62), who was suffect consul in 138 CE and proconsul of Asia in 152–153. The Iuliii Amyntiani were cousins of Gaius Antius Aulus Iulius Quadratus of Pergamon (PIR² J 507) and descendants of the Attalid and Galatian dynasties, including the Attalos II, Deiotaros of Galatia, and Amyntas of Galatia (IGRR III 373; see Harland, *Associations, Synagogues and Congregations*, 140–43). It is unclear, however, whether the honoree of I.Trall 86 had achieved the rank of senator.
39. I.Eph 1267 (Ephesus, II CE): "(Dedicated to) Dionysos Oreios Bakchios, *pro poleōs*, whose priest is Gaius Flavius Furius Aptos." I.Eph 3064 is a dedication by Furius Aptus for his grandfather, T. Flavius Pythion. On Furius Aptos's house, see Krinzinger, *Das Hanghaus 2 von Ephesos*; Thür et al., *Hanghaus 2*; and A. Schäfer, "Dionysische Gruppen."
40. Halfmann, *Die Senatoren*, 23–24; Rathmayr, "Das Haus des Ritters," 307–10.

41. IJO II 168 = GRA II 113 (Akmonia, I/II CE) recorded that the synagogue had been originally constructed by Julia Severa (PIR[2] J 701), high priestess of the imperial cult and director of games for the civic cult of the Sebastoi (Augustan gods) in the mid-first century. She was married to L. Servenius Capito, and her son L. Servenius Cornutus (PIR[1] S 404) became a senator under Nero and served as legate of the proconsul of Asia around 73–77 CE (Halfmann, *Die Senatoren*, no. 5). A relative, C. Iulius Severus (PIR[2] J 573; Halfmann, *Die Senatoren*, no. 62), became suffect consul in 138 CE and proconsul of Asia in 152–153.
42. IJO II 27 (Tralleis, mid-III CE). Claudia Capitolina (PIR[2] C 1085) is called *theosebēs* (pious), for contributing to the building of a synagogue. She was the daughter or sister of Claudius Capitolinus Bassus (PIR[2] C 814), proconsul of Asia, and was married to T. Flavius Stasicles Metrophanes (PIR[2] F 370). Her father-in-law was T. Flavius Kleitosthenes, suffect consul between 220 and 230 CE. Trebilco (*Jewish Communities*, 157–58) takes *theosebēs* to imply that Claudia was a "god fearer" and a "regular attender at the synagogue." This seems an unnecessary conclusion and unlikely given her family connections and involvement with the cult of Zeus Larasios.
43. Judge, *Social Pattern*, 52.
44. For a list of slave names, see Reilly, *Slaves*; Fragiadakis, "Attischen Sklavennamen"; Solin, *Stadtrömischen Sklavennamen*; and Vlassopoulos, "Athenian Slave Names."
45. For example, Friesen, "Poverty in Pauline Studies," 349–50; and Longenecker, *Remember the Poor*, 256.
46. On the meaning of *prolambanō*, see Kloppenborg, "Precedence."
47. Plutarch has one of his characters object to such a meal with the complaint that it "produces many dinners and many diners, but no one dines with anybody else (*oudena de syndeipnon oudenos*)" (Plutarch, *Quaest. conv.* 643A). Martial, *Epigrammata* 3.60, complains of his host, Ponticus, who allots different foods to his guest than what he himself eats: *cur sine te ceno, cum tecum, Pontice, cenem*, "Why Ponticus do I dine without you, while dining with you?"
48. Friesen, "Poverty in Pauline Studies," 350.
49. Longenecker (*Remember the Poor*, 254–55) is careful not to assume that handworkers were below subsistence level but assumes, without any evidence, that they were normally at the subsistence level or only slightly above it.
50. On the designation in Acts of Prisca and Aquila as curtain makers (*skēnopoioi*), see chap. 2, n. 79.
51. I.Kibyra 63.1–5, 5–7 = IGRR IV 907. See also LBW III 656 = Waltzing, *Étude historique*, III 147 = Dittmann-Schöne, *Berufsvereine*, III.5.2 (213) (Philadelphia, after 212 CE): a "sacred *phylē* of leather workers"; and LBW III 648 = Dittmann-Schöne, *Berufsvereine* (Philadelphia, after 212 CE): a "sacred *phylē* of wool-workers," both connected with the city council as "tribes." Linen workers were allotted seats in the stadium in Saittai (Lydia): Labarre and LeDinahet, "Les métiers du textile," 92 n. 45. Van Nijf (*Civic World of Professional Associations*, 20–22) points out that assemblies of Greek cities under Roman rule "remained open to the middle-ranking population" in which handworkers and traders were likely in the majority. See also Cicero's com-

plaint (*Flac.* 17–19, 52–61) that there were "shoemakers and girdle makers" (*sutores et zonarii*) at the civic assembly at Pergamon.

52. See also Labarre and LeDinahet, "Les métiers du textile," 62–67, on textile workers and their associations in Asia, who point out that there is considerable evidence of status hierarchies among textile workers and that those associated with large cities were generally better off than those in smaller villages. Tran, *Les membres* and *Dominus tabernae*, 2–5, points out that occupational guilds were scarcely homogenous in character and certainly were not all poor. He speaks of "plebian euergetism" of handworker guilds as one of the ways to assert the civic status of those groups. Van Nijf, *Civic World of Professional Associations*, 21: "The craftsmen and traders who formed the core of the *demos* were, in an economic sense, spread across a broad band of society. Although many of them were poor *in the eyes of the senatorial elite* (Cicero describes them . . . as *egentes*), they were often, in local terms, relatively well off. At the highest level they merged with the propertied class (that is, with those who could afford to live on the labour of others). Some craftsmen made enough money to secure one of the lower (demotic) public offices, or membership on a board of temple wardens of the *gerousia*" (emphasis original).
53. Longenecker, *Remember the Poor*, 257–58, recognizes the likelihood of Paul's exaggeration.
54. Theissen, *Social Setting*, 73–96; Meeks, *First Urban Christians*, 57–59; Friesen, "Poverty in Pauline Studies," 352–58; Longenecker, *Remember the Poor*, but with varying emphases and results.
55. Friesen, "Poverty in Pauline Studies"; Longenecker, *Remember the Poor*, 44–46.
56. It should be noted that the results of the study by Scheidel and Friesen ("Size of the Economy") cannot be mapped neatly onto Friesen's 2004 categories ("Poverty in Pauline Studies"). At the very least, the PS4 category needs some upward adjustment, especially since Scheidel and Friesen argue that "if some 15 per cent of the total population resided in towns and 'middling' income households were twice as common there as in the countryside, anywhere from one-eighth to one-quarter of the urban populace might have fallen in this 'middling' category" (Scheidel and Friesen, ibid., 90).
57. Edmonson ("Slavery and the Roman Family," 339) points out that it is difficult to generalize about the ownership of slaves by families at each level of Roman society, especially outside of Italy. From the second century BCE onward, Italy can be considered as a slaveowning society, that is, one in which slaveownership was widespread at many levels and where economic production depended in large measure upon slaves. Roman colonies, insofar as they were modeled on Rome, likely also had a large slave population. In the provinces outside of Roman colonies, it is more difficult to assess the degree of slaveownership in subelite families. Justin Martyr in the second century takes for granted that some of his addressees have slaves (2 *Apol.* 12.4).
58. By contrast, Öhler, "Zwischen Elite und Elend," has employed Longenecker's economic scales to locate a variety of cultic associations, but unlike the data from Christ groups, Öhler is able to use data that indicate the monthly dues and other routines

costs associated with the association in order to estimate the economic level of those groups.

59. Longenecker, *Remember the Poor*, 236–49.
60. Longenecker, *Remember the Poor*, 264–76. In contrast, Schmeller, *Hierarchie und Egalität*, 48.
61. Longenecker, *Remember the Poor*, 264, citing Patterson, *Landscapes and Cities*, 255. He also cites Onno van Nijf ("Collegia and Civic Guards," 308–9), who wrote that professional associations "recruited their members mainly from among the upper levels of the urban plebs: craftsmen and traders of at least moderate wealth, . . . a relatively well-off segment of the population. . . . The *collegia* . . . seem to have covered a broad band of society. At the highest level we find individuals who were merging with the ruling order of *decurions*, but most *collegiati* appear to have been men of more moderate means. They occupied the social position for which the Romans used the term *plebs media*."
62. Even among the Roman associations surveyed by Fellmeth ("Die römischen Vereine und die Politik," 56–67), a distinction can be observed between occupational guilds that attracted patrons from among those of the senatorial and equestrian ranks and cultic associations in which high-ranked patrons were unattested.
63. I hasten to add my own generalization from 1996 ("Collegia and *Thiasoi*," 23), when I claimed that associations drew their membership mainly from urban poor, slaves, and freedmen, for which claim Longenecker rightly faults me (*Remember the Poor*, 266 n. 20).
64. Longenecker, *Remember the Poor*, 258: "In general, then, Paul seems to address urban Jesus-groups as if they were comprised primarily of people belonging to ES5 [stable, near subsistence]. At times the rhetorical target is broad enough to incorporate both ES5 and ES6 [subsistence level], but when advice about working with one's hands is combined with exhortations to support others in need, ES5 seems to be most in Paul's sights."
65. Judge, *Social Pattern*, 51, reprinted in Judge, *Social Distinctives*, 36–37. On the other hand Robin Scroggs, writing in the 1980s and reflecting on the relative disappearance of emphases on poverty in Christ groups, asked: "Finally (and here I am perhaps out of place) is there any relation between the 'new consensus' and the change in our society from the more 'revolutionary' period of the 1960s to the more 'conventional' 1970s? Is there a need today to find a more 'respectable' (i.e. middle-class) origin for the church?" ("Sociological Interpretation," 171).
66. See Le Guen, *Les Associations de Technites*; and Aneziri, *Die Vereine der dionysischen Techniten* on the artists associated with Dionysos; on the traveling athletes, see van Nijf, "Global Players."
67. Respectively, I.Eph 22 and P.Lond. III 1178.
68. This assumes that at the time of the writing of 1 Corinthians 16 the assemblies of Galatia and Macedonia had agreed to participate in the collection. But by the time Paul wrote 2 Corinthians and Romans (in which Galatia is no longer mentioned), the Galatian assemblies had either refused to participate or (more likely) withdrawn from

the collection as it was organized by Paul. The tone of Galatians perhaps implies that the Galatian assembly had become a part of a different (non-Pauline) network.

69. Concannon, "Early Christian Connectivity" and *Assembling Early Christianity*.
70. See, for example, Aristotle, *Rhet.* 1.11.16: "Honor (*timē*) and good repute (*eudoxia*) are among the most pleasant things, because everyone imagines that he possesses the qualities of a worthy man, and still more when those whom he believes to be trustworthy say that he does" (trans. LCL).
71. Brennan and Pettit, *Economy of Esteem*, 3, 55–62.
72. Brennan and Pettit, *Economy of Esteem*, 195–221.
73. Hemelrijk, "Patronesses."
74. Van Bremen, *Limits of Participation*, 348–57, on "mothers" and "daughters" of the city; Harland, "Familial Dimensions (II)," on parental language in associations. See also Hemelrijk, "Patronesses," on "mothers of the collegium."
75. Harland, "Familial Dimensions." See also "Associations in the Greco-Roman World," http://philipharland.com/greco-roman-associations/?s=brothers.
76. I.KilikiaBM II 201.b, line 29 (Direvli Kalesi) [Western Rough Cilicia], before Vespasian). See GRA II 415–16.
77. IK Sinope 117.
78. CIRB 1281, line 5; 1283, lines 5–6; 1285, lines 5–6; 1286, line 1 (Tanais, ca. 212–240 CE); compare also CIRB 1282, where one of the members is designated as *patēr synodou*, "father of the association," and CIRB 1284, line 6, restored as "*thias*[*os* of broth]ers."
79. Pauline letters, sixty-four times; 2 Thessalonians, seven times; Hebrews, four times; James, fifteen times; 2 Peter, one time; 1 *Clement*, fifteen times; 2 *Clement*, fifteen times, Ignatius, five times; Hermas, seven times.
80. This is a view that I once espoused in Kloppenborg, "Edwin Hatch, Churches, and *Collegia*," 238, and "Egalitarianism," 259, following Bömer, *Untersuchungen über die Religion*, 172–79.
81. Meeks (*First Urban Christians*), for example, noted that fictive family language was "not unknown in pagan clubs and cultic associations, particularly in Rome and in areas where Roman customs influenced the Greek associations" but thinks that Christ assemblies borrowed their usage from Jews (87, 225 n. 73; similarly, Aasgaard, *My Beloved Brothers*, 111–16). Waltzing, *Étude historique*, 1:329–32, and Bömer, *Untersuchungen über die Religion*, 172–79, treated the use of family language mainly as a Roman phenomenon. Poland, *Geschichte des griechischen Vereinswesens*, 54–55, also acknowledged the use of such language in the West but noted the "adoptive bothers who reverence the Most High God" of Tanais and IK Sinope 117.
82. Harland, "Familial Dimensions." Nock ("Cult-Associations," 105) took for granted that cultic associations were fictive families: "The cult-association is primarily a family. Its head is called 'pater,' not merely by worshipers of Mithras, but also by devotees of Cybele [CIL 14.70, Rome], the Syrian Belela [IG II^2 2361, line 14, Athens], and the Theos Hypsistos in the Bosporus. So a prominent benefactress of the *dendrophori* is given the title *matēr* [IGRR I 604]. The members of these sodalities are brothers: worshipers of Juppiter Dolichenus are called 'fratres carissimi' [CIL 6.406, Rome],

and the term 'fratres' is used to designate members of societies formed to honour Juppiter Beellefarus, Mithras, and Bellona. The Bosporan inscriptions speak of *eispoiētoi adelphoi sebomenoi theon hypsiston:* this phrase is important, since adoption constituted in antiquity as close a tie as blood-relationship. Side by side with it we find as an equivalent *ton idion adelphon* [his own brother]. Further, the body as a whole could be called a *cognatio* [CIL 3.8675], and 'pius in collegio' occurs exactly as 'pius in suos.'"

83. IG II[2] 1368, lines 127–36 (Athens, 164/165 CE) = GRA I 53.
84. P.Mich V 243.5 (Tebtynis, time of Tiberius).
85. For one-year terms, see I.Alex.imp. 46, 90, 92, 94, 96; IGFayum II 122, lines 3–5; IGFayum III 212, lines 7–8; IG II[2] 1298, line 13 = GRA I 20; IG II[2] 1324 = GRA I 32; IG II[2] 1328 = GRA I 34; IG II[2] 1334 = GRA I 45; OGIS I 130; SEG 54:235 = GRA I 47; and others. Roman collegia had terms nominally of five years for *quinquennales*, although as Royden, "Tenure of Office," has shown, the terms ranged from two to five years.
86. Van Nijf, *Civic World of Professional Associations*, 33–34. On funerals and their costs, see chap. 9.
87. On *philadelphia*, see Kloppenborg, "Φιλαδελφία," and the literature cited there.
88. Harrison, "Paul and Ancient Civic Ethics," 105–6. Harrison treats this as an "inversion" of the dominant system of honorific practices, but it can also be a strategy for addressing the tension inherent in associations between the rivalry that honorific practices encouraged and the need for concord (*homonoia*), an issue that all associations also had to address. Paul's suggestion of a strategy might have been unlike those adopted by other associations, but the tension was common to all.
89. For example, Countryman, "Patrons and Officers."
90. MacMullen, "Epigraphic Habit"; Woolf, "Monumental Writing"; Lloris, "Epigraphic Habit."
91. See, for example, SB 22:15460, an honorary decree of an association of imperial slaves (Alexandria, 5 BCE) honoring a former priest.

7. MEALS

1. Pilhofer, "Ökonomische Attraktivität," 207–8. Similarly, Ebel, *Attraktivität*, 217; and Longenecker, *Remember the Poor*, 271.
2. Theissen, *Social Setting*, 145–74.
3. Weiss, *Der erste Korintherbrief*, 281; Lampe, "Das korinthinische Herrenmahl"; Barrett, *First Corinthians*, 263. Winter (*After Paul Left Corinth*, 157) thinks that Paul might have established this custom but erroneously calls this an *asymbolos deipnon* where participants brought their own food. In fact, an *asymbolos deipnon*, as the adjective itself indicates, is a dinner to which participants do *not* contribute. In inscriptions and papyri pertaining to associations, the term *asymbolos* usually designates people who are exempt from paying dues or contributing to a banquet. See n. 72 below.
4. Theissen, *Social Setting*, 148, citing Weiss, *Der erste Korintherbrief*, 293. *Ek tōn idiōn* (or *de suo*) occurs with great frequency in donative and honorific inscriptions and

indicates that a gift to a city or association has been paid for not from public or the association's funds but from the donor's own resources (see GRA I 447, 448). I know of no instances where *ek tōn idiōn* designates a meal practice such as that imagined by Theissen.

5. Theissen, *Social Setting*, 153.
6. See below, n. 18, where various authors complain about the practice of unequal distribution of food at banquets. Martial, *Epigrammata* 3.60, complains of his host, Ponticus, who allots different foods to his guest than what he himself eats: "Why Ponticus do I dine without you, while dining with you?"
7. Theissen, *Social Setting*, 156, 161.
8. Theissen, *Social Setting*, 155.
9. Before Irenaeus and Clement of Alexandria, *kyriakos/-ē/-on* is used in Jewish and Christian literature only to modify *hēmera* (day). In the overwhelming majority of occurrences of the adjective in the imperial period it means "imperial": either the imperial treasury or the imperial *fiscus*. Other occurrences include "imperial service," "imperial needs," and "imperial tax." The imperial usage of the term was already recognized by Deissmann (*Bible Studies*, 217–19), who argued that it was borrowed from imperial usage.
10. On the critique of differential allotments of food and the advocacy of "no difference" among diners, see n. 35 below.
11. *Sportulae*, literally "little baskets," were small gifts, usually of either money or food. Bendlin ("Associations, Funerals, Sociability," 262) suggests that there were forty-eight members, which would imply a gift of 8 sesterces for each of forty-five members, 16 sesterces for the *quinquennalis* (i.e., a double portion), and 12 sesterces each for the secretary and the messenger, for a total of 400 sesterces.
12. The translation of CIL 14.2112 is that of Bendlin, "Associations, Funerals, Sociability" (adjusted slightly), who has also prepared a new edition of the Latin text.
13. Each of the four *magistri* was required to provide 1 *amphora* of wine at a cost of about 61 sesterces or a total per meal of 243 sesterces (= 61 denarii). Two asses of bread added another total of 5.625 denarii (90 asses = 22.5 sesterces), and four sardines (about 225 grams) likely cost another 15.6 denarii, for a total of 82.12 denarii. Divided four ways, this meant about 20.53 denarii per *magister* for each of the six banquets. Duncan-Jones also assumes 61 sesterces for an *amphora* of wine and that wine prices in Rome were higher than those in Campania (*Economy of the Roman Empire*, 364–65). Conison ("Organization of Rome's Wine Trade," 14–19) has shown that prices were actually highly variable, between 2 and 54 sesterces per *amphora* in the previous century and so is loath to fix an average price for the second century. This might mean that the per-*magister* cost of each meal was less than 20 denarii. I have used calculations for wine prices based on the data for CIL 6.10234, on which see below, n. 16.
14. CIL 6.10234 (Rome, 153 CE), trans. AGRW 322. On the identification of this collegium as a group of stonemasons, see Introduction, n. 1.
15. In creating a hypothetical yearly account, I have assumed that there were two *curatores* and four *immunes* (probably previous *quinquennales*). Different numbers would

adjust the final outcome only slightly, since the main expenses of *sportulae* and wine are still those for the *plebs*. My account also assumes between 45 and 56 denarii per *amphora*. Since the endowment seems to be intended to provide for all six meetings, I arrive at this by subtracting from the interest of 750 denarii the aggregate costs of the *sportulae* (282 denarii) and bread (56.25 denarii), which leaves 411.75 denarii, which must account for the cost of between 28 and 36 *amphorae* of wine, that is, between 56 denarii (for 28 *amphorae*) and 45 denarii (for 36 *amphorae*). Duncan-Jones, *Economy of the Roman Empire*, uses a similar method, with slightly different results.

16. This assumes 61 sesterces per *amphora*. The other costs are known exactly, since the bylaws state in monetary terms the size of the *sportulae* and the value of the bread. Duncan-Jones (*Economy of the Roman Empire*, 364–65) assumes a 6 percent draw on income and calculates the price of an *amphora* of wine at 61–88 sesterces. Conison, "Organization of Rome's Wine Trade," argues that the donor likely would not have authorized the purchase of the cheapest wine, but wine prices appear to have been variable. Graffiti from Pompeii and elsewhere suggests that wine prices fell to as low as 15 sesterces per *amphora* owing to the swamping of Italian markets by imported wine (Columella, *Rust*. 3.3.10). Domitian prohibited the growing of wine in the provinces (Suetonius, *Dom*. 7.2, 14.2; Statius, *Silva* 4.3.11–12), which may have led to an increase in prices in the second century, though it is hardly imaginable that Domitian was able to enforce such a ruling.

17. The only other instance of which I am aware is CIL 10.444 (Caposele [Bruttium et Lucania], principate of Domitian), in which a wealthy landowner, L. Domitius Phaon, devoted the income from three of his properties to the support of a cult of Silvanus such that five sacrifices and dinners could be held yearly.

18. The complaints of ancient elite seldom match what is known of association behavior from their bylaws. Varro, *Rust*. 3.2.16, alleges rather incredibly that the number of club dinners (*collegiorum cenae*) had become so great that the price of commodities had risen; Philo (*Ebr*. 20–21, 23; *Flacc*. 4) complains of the immorality of association banquets (*Flacc*. 136); Philo's interests are apologetic: Jewish festivals adopt a different standard of behavior: they are not "associations of banquet-givers or diners, . . . [with] much violence, and sumptuous tables" (*Spec*. 2.193). Cyprian, *Ep*. 67.6, complains of Basilides and Martialis, who participate in "disgraceful and filthy banquets of the Gentiles in their collegium." Tertullian, *Apol*. 39, quips, "And at the smoke of Sarapis's banquet the firefighters will have to get up." Livy 39.8 also suggests that excessive consumption contributed to the Bacchanalia conspiracy.

19. For example, CIL 5.7920: bread, wine, and oil; CIL 5.8251: bread and wine; CIL 11.5215: bread and wine; CIL 11.6033: oil for the bath, and bread and wine; CIL 11.6310: bread and wine. The collegium of ivory and citrus wood dealers (CIL 6.33885) had a meal of bread and wine on most occasions but laurel cake and dates and Carian figs and pears on New Year's Day. See Gutsfeld, "Das Kollegium bei Tisch," 165–66, who comments: "If one sticks to these facts, then one cannot avoid the fact that club banquets were rather frugal, at least as far as the served meals are concerned" (my translation).

20. On association banquets as instances of "public meals," see Dunbabin, *Roman Banquet*, 72–102.
21. See Will, "Banquets et salles de banquet," and Bollmann, *Römische Vereinshäuser.*
22. Respectively, P.Mich V 243 (Tebtynis, time of Tiberius) and P.Mich V 244 (Tebtynis, 43 CE).
23. Grignon, "Commensality," 26–27.
24. Donahue, "Toward a Typology," 423–41 (434).
25. Grignon ("Commensality," 29) observes, "The strong and ideally typical forms of segregative commensality are likely to be found in hierarchised and discontinuous societies, those in which hierarchisation is the very principle of structure and social life, and where this hierarchisation goes with social heterogeneity and repulsion, which render the distances between social universes impassable and the very idea of passing unthinkable." This seems an apt description of the hierarchical and status-conscious character of Roman society.
26. Donahue, *Roman Community at Table*, 128. See the tabulation in Table 6, supplementing Donahue's list.
27. IG XII/3 330 = LSCG 135 = AGRW 243. Sosin, "Perpetual Endowments," 433–39, takes a different view, proposing that the 30,000 denarii and that Epikteta's heirs are to repay the loan in fifteen years plus 5 percent interest, that is, 200 denarii plus 10 denarii interest.
28. I.Eph 3216; Bérard, "Inscriptions de Téménothyrae."
29. CIL 11.126 (Ravenna, III CE).
30. On interest rates, see Duncan-Jones, *Economy of the Roman Empire*, 133–36, ranging from a low of 4.3 percent to a high of 12 percent.
31. The *fabri* in Rome numbered more than thirteen hundred (DeLaine, "Building the Eternal City," 121). The *album* of the guild in Ostia, divided into at least sixteen decuria, with a minimum number of 22 in each decuria, suggests a membership of about 350 members (CIL 14.4569, 198 CE).
32. See Prodromídis, *Another View on an Old Inflation*, and earlier, Duncan-Jones, *Economy of the Roman Empire*; Drexhage, *Preise, Mieten/Pachten, Kosten.*
33. AE 1998, 282 (227–228 CE). Nonnis, "Un patrono dei dendrofori"; Liu, "AE 1998, 282."
34. Grignon, "Commensality," 30.
35. On the complexity of meal performances, see D'Arms, "Roman *Convivium*." The banquet was an expression of *koinōnia/convivia* (fellowship) and *isotēs/aequa libertas*, (equality), but these values were in inevitable tension with competition, seating arrangements, and the need to recognize status differences that existed within and outside the group. Many promoted the ideal of "no differences" (among diners): Xenophon, *Mem.* 3.14.1–3; Musonius Rufus 18B (ed. Hense); Pliny, *Ep.* 2.6.3, 9.5.3; Martial, *Epigrammata* 3.60; Juvenal, *Sat.* 8.177–78; Plutarch, *Quaest. conv.* 1.2.3 (616D); and Lucian, *Sat.* 17. But as D'Arms (ibid., 318) notes: "unlike the practice at the early Greek sympotic gatherings . . . , Roman convivial equality can never have been other than a very fragile kind. Could it have been otherwise in a world where the upper

classes were obsessed with *dignitas* and *existimatio*, where *liberalitas* and *munificentia* were expected components of aristocratic decorum but where convivial *aequalitas* was a temporary *beneficium* which the great man might (or might not) bestow—as Pliny's egalitarian remarks at table . . . clearly show—a world where a patron could order a man *in clientela* to put on a dinner (*cena indicta*), where a host might issue invitations through an intermediary in his employ (the *vocator*), where a principal guest was placed in the *locus consularis* and a freedman in the *locus libertinus*?"

36. Liu, "Economy of Endowments," 231–56 (235).
37. Liu's figures for endowments of private clubs mirror the findings of Zuiderhoek, *Politics of Munificence*, 24–28, who tabulated the sums donated for public buildings in Roman Asia Minor in the second and third centuries CE and reports that while the mean of forty-four donations was 75,369 denarii (skewed by three large donations), the median was only 16,500 denarii (equivalent to 66,000 sesterces) and the mode was 10,000 denarii.
38. Fellmeth, "Politische Bewußtsein."
39. The Seviri Augustales were usually wealthy freedmen who paid for the privilege of the appointment (normally for one year). See Bruun, "True Patriots?"
40. See Andreau, "Fondations privées," 168–69.
41. Andreau, "Fondations privées," 171–72. Andreau's list does not include CIL 14.4557 (Ostia) in which a senator and his freedman provided a one-time banquet for an occupational guild.
42. CIL 10.444 (Caposele [Latium et Campania], time of Domitian). On L. Domitius Phaon, see Bruun, "Name and Possessions of Nero's Freedman Phaon."
43. On geometric versus arithmetic conceptions of equality, see Aristotle, *Eth. nic.* 5.3.6 (1131a): "And there will be the same equality (*isotēs*) between the shares as between the persons, since the ratio between the shares will be equal to the ratio between the persons; for if the persons are not equal, they will not have equal shares; it is when equals possess or are allotted unequal shares, or persons not equal shares equally, that quarrels and complaints arise" (trans. H. Rackham, LCL, p. 269). Plutarch's *Quaest. conv.* 642F–644D reports a debate between Lamprias and Hagias, who argues that the arithmetically equal distribution of food and drink kills sociability (*koinōnia*) and "creates many diners and many (different) diners" (643A), since it distributes "equal portions [of food] to persons who are actually unequal" (643B). Lamprias retorts that unequal distributions antagonize those who eat slowly since others snatch their food (644A) and suggests that sociability perishes when guests have their own portions: "when there is no (arithmetic) equality, for it is not the possession of one's own meal but taking another's and greed for what is in common to all that begins injustice and strife" (644C).
44. For example, Weiss, *Der erste Korintherbrief*, 281.
45. Von Dobschütz, *Christian Life*, 61: "Every man brought his own portion—as opposed to the custom of the Greek guilds, where the cost of the meal was defrayed out of the guild's treasury or by individual members—but the idea was that all the contributions should be put together and then divided equally." The practice of Christ groups

bringing bread and wine to the Eucharist eventually became standard once the Eucharist had ceased to be a real meal and was only the distribution of bread and wine. In the third century Cyprian (*Eleem.* §15) complains of the rich, "You are wealthy and rich; do you suppose that you celebrate the *Dominicum* [Lord's Supper] not having any regard for the offerings of those who come to the *Dominicum* without a sacrifice and yet you take part of the sacrifice that the pauper offers."

46. The god is represented as the one who invites in P.Köln I 57 (Oxyrhynchus, III CE): "the god invites you to the banquet that will happen in the Thoereion tomorrow from the 9th hour." See Koenen, "Einladung."
47. Klauck, *Herrenmahl*, 134, cites Höfler (*Sarapishymnus*, 96): The Sarapis devotees "bring the food as a sacrifice to the temple, dedicate it to the god, and receive it as the gift of the god, perhaps after subtracting the portion intended for Sarapis and his priests" (my translation).
48. Klauck, *Herrenmahl*, 293: "They must have been wealthy members of the assembly, because (a) they could afford to come to the assembly earlier and had more freedom in relation to their time, (b) they owned houses, if one takes the phrase *mē oikias ouk echete* [you have houses don't you?] in a restrictive sense, (c) they had the ability to bring provisions, and besides (d) in v. 22c they are contrasted with the *mē echontes*, those who have nothing" (my translation).
49. Athenaeus 8.64 (362E) derives *eranos* from *syneran*, "to gather together, to pour together": "*eranoi* are assemblies (*synagōgai*) that are constituted from contributions (*symballomena*); (and this name was derived from) each of the guests being friendly together (*apo tou syneran*) and contributing." By the fifth century BCE *eranos* had come to mean "debt" (Aristophanes, *Ach.* 615) or "fund" (Aristophanes, *Lys.* 653). The collective and financial aspect is stressed in Plato: "As far as friendly loans (*eranoi*) are concerned, whoever so wishes may collect as a friend among friends; but if any difference of opinion arises in respect to the collection, they must act on the understanding that in regard to these matters no legal actions are possible" (*Leg.* 11.915E).
50. As a common fund: Vondeling, *Eranos*; Maier, "Eranos als Kreditinstitut"; and Longo, "Eranos." For example, IG II^2 1291, lines 2–7 = GRA I 19 (Piraeus, III BCE): "[the treasurer] managed accurately and fairly the common fund which the *eranistai* had entrusted to him in accordance with the common bylaws of the *eranistai* and the contributors' fund (*eranos*)." As a term for the association itself: IG II^2 1339, lines 13–15 = GRA I 46 (Piraeus, 57/56 BCE); IG II^2 1369, line 40 = GRA I 49 (Liopesi, II CE); SEG 31:122, lines 38, 44 = GRA I 50 (Liopesi, II CE); IG II^2 1366, line 21 = GRA I 53 (Laurion, II/III CE).
51. Homer, *Od.* 1.226–27; Hesiod, *Op.* 722–23.
52. Bdelycleon is trying to persuade his father Philocleon to go out to a symposium and finally calls to the slaves: "But come, we will go and dine at Philoctemon's. Slave! slave! pack our dinner in the basket, Chrysos, we are going on a long binge" (*Wasps* 1250–52, trans. LCL).
53. Lucian, *Lex.* 6: "there was a banquet (composed of) contributions (*to . . . deipnon . . . apo symphorōn*)"; he goes on to detail the various foodstuffs that were brought. This

banquet is interrupted by the appearance of three uninvited guests, who have also brought wine, cheese, and olives (9, 13). Athenaeus, *Deipn.* 8.68 (364F–365D), says that such a banquet is called an *epidosma* or a *deipnon ex epidomatōn* by the Alexandrians, or also a *syndeipnon* or *synagōgion*.

54. Coutsoumpos, *Paul and the Lord's Supper*, 47. Coutsoumpos (46 n. 47) refers to Poland, *Geschichte des griechischen Vereinswesens*, 156–66, which is evidently an error. In fact Poland's discussion is on pp. 258–66, where he says nothing of *eranistic* food practices being typical of associations.
55. Citing a line from Pherecrates (mid-V BCE), "having prepared a dinner for the basket (*deipnon es to spuridion*) he departed to Ophela" (Athenaeus, *Deipn.* 8.68 [365D]), he concludes, "this clearly points to the 'basket dinner' (*to apo spuridos deipnon*) when someone prepares and having put it into a basket goes off to dine with someone." Epictetus (*Diss.* 4.10.21) uses the term *spuris* in connection with dinners (and the "baskets" *distributed* by the host/patron), but he is evidently using the term as an equivalent to *sportula*—that is, not the "baskets" that participants bring but the "baskets" that the patron distributes during the meal. Epictetus mentions this in his conclusion about the futility of striving to be a consul: "And what is the thing that is got? Twelve bundles of rods, to sit three or four times on the tribunal, to exhibit the games in the Circus and to give suppers in small baskets (*dounai kai spurisin deipnisai*)."
56. Athenaeus, *Deipn.* 8.68 [365E], quoting Menander: "'and he finished the *synagogion*.' Probably this is what is also called *to apo symbolōn deipnon*. But what the *symbola* (contributions) are, Alexis [ca. 375–ca. 275 BCE] himself indicates in his 'Angry Woman in Mandragora.'"
57. Lampe, "Eucharist," 39: "In the light of the Greco-Roman potluck custom, I suggest that the Christian situation at Corinth be construed in the following manner. Each Corinthian celebrating the eucharistic dinner party according to the *eranos* custom brought his or her own food but some came early and began eating before the others arrived. Some of the latecomers either had no time or no money to prepare sufficient food baskets for themselves. Because of this, they remained hungry, for when *they* arrived, those who had brought enough for themselves had already eaten most of their own food and thus could no longer share it" (emphasis original).
58. Lampe, "Eucharist," 39: "Not only could everyday dinner parties be organized as an *eranos* but also cultic meals such as the sacrificial meal of the Sarapis cult in the second century CE. . . . Sarapis was considered present at the table both as guest and host. *The participants at the sacrificial meal contributed food.* Sarapis received these contributions and served them out to all who were present—a close parallel to the Eucharist" (emphasis added).
59. Trans. Behr, *P. Aelius Aristides*, 2:266–67 (modified slightly and emphasis added).
60. *Sarapiastai* are attested by IG II^2 1292 = GRA I 26 (Athens, 215/214 BCE); I.Rhamnous II 59 = GRA I 27 (Rhamnous, after 216/215 BCE); IG XII,2 511 (Methymna, Lesbos, I BCE); and IG XII,5 606 (Iulis, Kos).
61. IG II^2 1252 + 999.10–12 = GRA I 6, a late-fourth-century BCE Athenian group of citizen *orgeōnes* of Amynos and Asklepios, speaks of two benefactors being "exempt

(*ateleia*) from 'the heap' (*chous*)": "They shall be exempt from 'the heap' in both temples, both they and their relatives." The meaning of "heap" is uncertain, but it seems to refer either to monetary contributions or to contributions in kind to a banquet. Athenaeus 8.68 (365D): "But the Argives, as Hegesander says in his *Commentaries*, have other words [for contributions to *symposia*]: 'The contribution brought in to the *symposia* by the drinkers is called by the Argives a "heap," while the single share is called a "lot."'" This may be no different from member contributions to a banquet, in which case *ateleia* simply means "dues-exempt." If it refers to food for the banquet, it might be an instance of an *eranos*-type meal.

62. Kloppenborg, "Epigraphy." See earlier, Ziebarth, *Das griechische Vereinswesen*, 156–62.
63. For example, IG II² 1327, lines 13–15 = GRA I 35 (Piraeus, 178/177 BCE); IG XII,5 186 (Paros, III BCE); and I.Knidos 23 (Knidos, Caria, II BCE).
64. I.Perg 374 = GRA II 111 (Pergamon, 129–138 CE).
65. P.Tebt III/2 894 (ca. 114 BCE). See the analysis by Last and Rollens, "Accounting Practices."
66. See Reekmans, "Monetary History" and "Ptolemaic Copper Inflation." To put this into perspective, Reekmans also surveys the subsistence costs in the late second century. Monthly dues in this club would have amounted to 2.5 AR drachmae yearly, assuming monthly meetings, or a little more than one-tenth of yearly subsistence costs. Clearly, membership in this club was not prohibitively expensive.
67. Likewise, Frag. 7.v.2: Epeiph 27 (July 14): "Epeiph 27. 1 *keramion* of wine at 3,400 AE dr.; crowns: 125 dr.; perfumed oil: 50 dr.; (5) lamp-oil: 30 dr., total: 205 dr., grand total: 3,605 dr. (From which funds) we have 2 sacrifice-makers, each (giving) 500 dr., making 1,000 dr. Their names: Onnōphris [. . .] and Herieus son of Peteu[. . .] (10) chief . . . . euris, Pet[. . .]ōn." The cost of wine in the late second century ranged from 3,000 to 4,000 AE drachmae (i.e., 6.25–8.3 AR drachmae) per *keramion*, which suggests that the major expense in mounting a dinner was the cost of the wine. Beer was less expensive but would still have consumed most of the income for each dinner. On the cost of wine, see Maresch, *Bronze und Silber*.
68. See chap. 2 above, and Scholl, *Corpus der ptolemäischen Sklaventexte*, 1:333–42 (no. 91).
69. I owe this observation to Ryan Olfert, who is preparing an edition of P.Mich V 246 for GRA III.
70. CIL 14.2112, lines 12, 23 (Lanuvium, 136 CE): 5 asses (1.25 sesterces) monthly; IG II² 1252 + 999, line 11 = GRA I 6; IG II² 1291 = GRA I 19 (mid-III BCE); IG II² 1298, lines 18–20 = GRA I 20 (248/247 BCE); IG II² 1339, lines 7–9 = GRA I 46 (57/56 BCE); IG II² 1368, lines 46–47 = GRA I 51 (164/165 CE); IG IX/1² 670, lines 5–6 = GRA I 61 (mid-II CE) (14 obols); P.Mich V 243.2 (Tebtynis, early I CE); P.Mich V 244.10 (Tebtynis, 43 CE); P.Tebt I 118, lines 8, 14, 17 (Tebtynis, 112 BCE): 100 AE drachmae (= 0.20 AR drachma); P.Petr III 136 (Arsinoites, 231 BCE): 1 drachma 1 obol; P.Tebt I 224 (Tebtynis, 109/108 BCE): 105 AE drachmae (= 0.22 AR drachma); P.Tebt III/2 894 (Tebtynis, ca. 114 BCE): 100–300 AE drachmae (= 0.21–0.63 AR drachma); SEG

31:122.42 (Liopesi [Attica], ca. 90 CE); SB 3:7182, line 38 (Philadelphia [Fayûm], II/I BCE); IG II[2] 1368, lines 46–47 = GRA I 51 (164/165 CE); Philo, *Ebr.* 20–21.

71. The mathematics is correct in this account when one assumes a 6-obol drachma (rather than a 7-obol drachma). The account indicates that Ktēsippos owes 3 drachmae plus dues of 1 drachma, 1/4 obol (= 1 1/24 drachmae), plus arrears of 11/24 drachma, plus an additional arrears "on account" of 1/24 drachma (1/4 obol), for a total of 4 13/24 drachmae or 4 drachma, 3 1/4 obols.

72. It was common to designate as dues-exempt serving magistrates (but they often had other liturgical responsibilities), donors, former or long-serving magistrates, and others who had shown meritorious service to the association. See ABSA 56 (1961) 5, 5.9 (Cyprus, 114–106 BCE); ASAA 22 (1939/1940) 147, 1.5, 10 (Rhodes, II BCE); CIL VI 10234, line 12 (Rome, 153 CE); ID 1519, line 44 (Delos, 153/152 BCE); I.Prose 40, line 40 (Psenamosis, Egypt; II BCE); I.DionysosJ 7, line 6 = GRA I 60 (141 CE); IK Rhod. Peraia 12 = Rhodian Peraia 110 (Rhodes, III/II BCE); IG II[2] 1361, line 3 = GRA I 4 (330–324/323 BCE); IG II[2] 1368, lines 158–59 = GRA I 51 (164/165 CE) (for the treasurer); IG XII,1 155.II, lines 45, 80, 114 (Rhodes, II BCE); IG XII,7 22, line 9 (Amorgos, III BCE); IG XII,7 241, line 18 (Amorgos, III BCE); P.Tebt I 224 recto r, line 2 (Kerkeosiris, 109/108 BCE); P.Tebt III/2 Frag. 2.r.1, line 4 (Tebtynis, 114 BCE); SB 3:7182, lines 55, 90 (Philadelphia [Fayûm], II/I BCE).

73. At best, the *Didache* (chap. 13) requires that teachers and prophets be supported by the group and that funds also be distributed to the poor (of the group?). There is no indication how the communal banquet is funded.

74. Barclay, "Money and Meetings," 113–28 (120): Because there were no "institutional structures—buildings to construct or maintain," and without a membership fee or annual dues to collect, "there is no reason for the earliest Christians to handle money on any other than an *ad hoc* basis"; Downs, *Offering of the Gentiles*, 101: "There is no evidence that the members of Paul's churches paid monthly or weekly membership dues, or that community funds were used to subsidize the burial expenses of deceased members"; Longenecker, *Remember the Poor*, 271: "There is little to suggest that urban Jesus-groups, unlike other associations, had a membership fee that was paid to the association's treasurer to enhance the goals of the association." There is no evidence *at all* of any financial practices connected to the meal, and so it is odd to single out one silence in the data as an argument for the existence of an alternate practice.

75. For example, MAMA IV 265 (Dionysopolis, Phrygia, I–II CE): contributions ranging from 10 to 30 denarii; I.Knidos 23 (Knidos, Caria, II BCE): contributions to a meal ranging from 5 to 300 denarii; I.Eph. 20 (Ephesus, 54–59 CE): contributions to a building ranging from 5 denarii to large quantities of paving stone and columns.

76. Pilhofer, "Ökonomische Attraktivität"; Ebel, *Attraktivität;* Longenecker, *Remember the Poor*, 271.

77. Pilhofer, "Ökonomische Attraktivität," 206. Similarly, Longenecker, *Remember the Poor*, 271.

78. Pilhofer, "Ökonomische Attraktivität," 206 (emphasis added).

79. Pilhofer, "Ökonomische Attraktivität," 207 (my translation). Similarly, Ebel, *Attraktivität*, 163.
80. Ebel, *Attraktivität*, 217.
81. See, in general, Lendon, *Empire of Honour.*
82. Lambek, *Weight of the Past*, 143, 162. See also Comaroff, *Body of Power*, 235–36.
83. Sosis and Bressler, "Cooperation and Commune Longevity," 227.
84. Last, "Myth of Free Membership," sees the problem in Thessaloniki as one arising from the group allowing certain people not to contribute any dues as the result of some "haggling." The author of 2 Thessalonians (whether Paul or someone writing in his name and using his example) took a less lenient view of dues.
85. See SEG 31:122 = GRA I 50, which first imposes a fine on the free rider, and if it is not paid, then exclusion. IG II^2 1368 = GRA I 51 excludes from the meeting any who have not paid dues.
86. Herm. Sim. 2.1.5. See chap. 10 below.
87. Tertullian, *Apol.* 39, says that Christians bring *stips* (contributions) to each meeting but claims that they were not spent on banquets or drinking but on feeding and burying the poor, supporting orphans, and saving people who had been shipwrecked.
88. For example, Weiss, *Der erste Korintherbrief*, 281: "While some brothers were kept away by their work, [wealthier members] for example, in groups and cliques . . . sat down together and started, if not to feast, then at least to secure their portion" (my translation). Similarly, Klauck, *Herrenmahl*, 291; Lampe, "Eucharist," 39; and Coutsoumpos, *Paul and the Lord's Supper*, 106.
89. Lampe ("Herrenmahl," 197) complicates this picture with a further distinction, between the *mensa prima* and the *mensa secunda*, arguing that if the poorer members appeared only at the beginning of the *mensa secunda*, there likely would be no place for them in the *triclinia* and most of the food would have been consumed by that time. To this suggestion, Schmeller (*Hierarchie und Egalität*, 70) asks: "Why should all the poorer Christians arrive at the break between the main course and the second? One should not presuppose today's German conditions, where there are fixed shop closing times and regulated shift work. Much more likely is that the poorer arrived gradually and that when finally all were there, the Lord's Supper was started."
90. The same assumption is seen in Plautus's depiction of seats at the theater. See Moore, "Seats and Social Status."
91. See Saller, "*Familia*, *Domus* and the Roman Family."
92. E. M. Harris, "Workshop, Marketplace," 71.
93. Kehoe, "Early Roman Empire."
94. Hawkins, "Work in the City," 20, citing A. Smith, *Inquiry*, 119. For example, the *Digest* assumes that a goldsmith might be commissioned to produce jewelry from gold supplied by the buyer (D 19.2.2.1), which implies that employment of the goldsmith is to some extent dependent on the consumer's whim.
95. Treggiari, "Domestic Staff," esp. 243; quotation at 246–47.
96. D 33.9.3.6; Aulus Gellius, *Noct. att.* 4.1.17. Saller, "Women, Slaves and the Economy," 192, notes the related distinction between slaves who had an *artificium*, or skill such as

weaving, and those who had an *officium,* or duty that required no training, such as a litter-bearer, or doorkeeper.

97. Saller, "Women, Slaves and the Economy," 197.
98. IG II^2 1368, lines 63–96; P.Lond VII 2193, lines 12–20; P.Mich V 243, lines 6–7; CIL 14.2112, line 59.
99. Donahue, *Roman Community at Table,* 89.
100. Whereas in 1 Cor 7:1, 25; 8:1; 12:1; and 16:1, 12 Paul is responding to a question raised in the Corinthians' letter, there is no indication in 1 Cor 11:2–16 or 17–34 that the Corinthians have raised a question about either the conduct of women in their assembly or the conduct of their banquet. Paul's intervention seems to be based on rumors or oral reports that he has heard. That the Corinthians would agree with Paul's diagnosis of their "problem" is hence less likely.
101. On the use of *prolambeō,* which can mean either "take beforehand" or "take preferentially," see Kloppenborg, "Precedence."
102. The next sentence, "Don't you have houses in which to eat?," and the later admonition, "If someone is hungry, let them eat at home so that when you do assemble it won't be for condemnation," make sense only if v. 21 describes not the *result* of the banquet but its *initial condition*—hence the advice for those who come hungry to eat at home *before* they gather (*synerchesthai*).
103. Similarly, Klinghardt, *Gemeinschaftsmahl,* 293–94. On Paul's knowledge of association statutes, see Schnöckel, *Ägyptische Vereine,* 376–81.
104. See n. 43 above.
105. For example, Klinghardt, *Gemeinschaftsmahl,* 294.
106. For example, CIL 6.33885.16 (Rome, time of Hadrian), an association of ivory and citrus wood dealers in fact insisted on equality—so that each member of the guilds of ivory and citrus wood dealers would receive "presents (*sportulae*) . . . distributed from the treasury in the amount of 3 denarii, and bread and wine and warm water, without distinction (*passive*)" and that "the *curatores* will supply bread and wine and warm water, without distinction, to those who will dine at the tetrastyle."

8. THE COLLECTION

1. 1 Cor 16:1–4, Gal 2:10, 2 Cor 8–9, Rom 15:25–28.
2. Exceptions are Verbrugge, *Paul's Style*; Downs, *Offering of the Gentiles*; and Longenecker, *Remember the Poor.*
3. Nickle, *The Collection,* 74–99.
4. This assumes that *peri de tēs logeias tēs eis tous hagious* in 1 Cor 16:1 is a letter response formula, referring to a question raised in the Corinthians' letter to Paul. See Hurd, *Origin of 1 Corinthians,* 200–206. Hurd rightly argues that the Corinthians were likely concerned about the nature of the delivery of the collection.
5. Conzelmann, *1 Corinthians,* 296. For similar statements of Barclay, Downs, and Longenecker, see chap. 7 above, n. 76.
6. Downs, *Offering of the Gentiles,* 101.

7. Mackil, *Creating a Common Polity*, 1.
8. On the Lycian *koinon*, see Burrell, *Neokoroi*, 253–58.
9. See, for example, Philo, *Leg.* 156: "Therefore, [Gaius] knew that they had prayer houses (*proseuchē*), and that they gathered in them, especially on the sacred seventh days, when they publicly taught their ancestral philosophy; and he knew also that they collected sacred funds from their first fruits (*chrēmata synagontas apo tōn aparchōn hiera*), sending them to Jerusalem by the hands of those who were to offer the sacrifices."
10. Josephus, *Ant.* 16.162–65 (Augustus), 16.166 (Augustus to Norbanus Flaccus), 16.167–68 (Marcus Agrippa to the magistrates of Ephesus), 16.169–79 (Marcus Agrippa concerning the Judeans of Cyrene), 16.171 (Norbanus Flaccus to the magistrates of Sardis), and 16.172–73 (Julius Antoninus to the magistrates of Ephesus).
11. Harrill, *Paul the Apostle*, 73, however, suggests that Paul's collection was intended to purchase sacrifices for the temple and was *provocative* on Paul's part since it was framed as the offering of "first fruits" of uncircumcised gentiles. It was this act that caused the riot of which Acts speaks and that eventually led to Paul's arrest and execution.
12. The only scholar to note the *epidosis* in connection with the Pauline collection is, as far as I know, Verbrugge, *Paul's Style*, 157–76. Curiously, although Verbrugge concludes that the *epidosis* "does serve as a true parallel to Paul's notion of raising money for the poor in Jerusalem" (157), and after (appropriately) acknowledging that *epidoseis* were typically raised for local needs rather than those of another group, he focuses his attention on the fact that *epidosis* inscriptions "are never used for the actual appeal to make a pledge" (176). This is not true, as SEG 50:1050 illustrates, but it is true that most of the *epidosis* inscriptions are retrospective, the actual appeal having been made orally in the assembly. He concludes that "we have uncovered no example of a letter that asks for donations for a group of needy people" (209) and even *epidoseis* "cannot really be compared to a fund-raising letter seeking to motivate the people to give" (369). This seems an instance of the attempt to find small and irrelevant differences between two *comparanda* to derail comparison. If the call for subscriptions were oral, there would be no need for a letter.
13. Migeotte, *Souscriptions*, is the major collection of public *epidoseis*, but others are also attested. See Chaniotis, "Public Subscriptions"; and Ellis-Evans, "Ideology." Migeotte, "Souscriptions dans les associations," discusses *epidoseis* in private associations and collects more than a dozen subscriptions, mostly for repairs to temples.
14. Chaniotis, "Public Subscriptions," 91.
15. Parker and Obbink, "Aus der Arbeit," 253–65. The English translation is that of Parker and Obbink, modified slightly.
16. Parker and Obbink, "Aus der Arbeit," 262.
17. For example, Plutarch's description of Alcibiades' contribution to an Athenian *epidosis* (*Alc.* 10.1); Ellis-Evans, "Ideology," 109.
18. Migeotte, *Souscriptions*, 93–96 no. 34 (partially reproduced); Béquignon, "Études Thessaliennes," no. 1, face 2.32–38: "they will inscribe on a stele the names of everyone

who has promised (*epaggellamenos*) (a contribution), along with their patronyms, according to what they promised, the first to promise first, and then the others according to the amount."

19. Ellis-Evans, "Ideology," 119, citing SEG 44:1219a, 48:1343; Migeotte, *Souscriptions*, 70.
20. For example, IG II[2] 791, lines 19–20 (Athens, 243 BCE) = Migeotte, *Souscriptions*, no. 17, sets the minimum contribution at 50 drachmae and the maximum at 200. Migeotte (ibid., 316–17) observes apropos of IG II[2] 791 that of the eighty-three legible names, it appears that most gave the maximum. He also suggests that in the absence of specific limits on contributions, minimums and maximums can be derived from the donor list itself. Typical ranges are 10–30, 50–500, 100–300, and 100–500 drachmae, but there are contributions to some *epidoseis* as low as 4 drachmae and one list with no contribution greater than 10 (IG VII 3191–3192; Orchomenos, Boeotia). He also points out that in the case of IG II[2] 2332 (Athens, 183/182 BCE) all the contributions are either 5 or 10 drachmae (presumably the minimum and the maximum, respectively), and that in IG II[2] 2334 (Athens, II BCE), an *epidosis* for the building of a theater in the Piraeus, the contributions are all between 5 and 20 drachmae.
21. For example, Segre, "Tituli Calymnii," 122–27 no. 85 (late III BCE): contributions in the range of 15 ($n = 66$), 20, 30, 40, 50, and 60 drachmae. Chaniotis ("Public Subscriptions," 94–95) suggests that the list was simply determined by the order in which the donations arrived.
22. SEG 48:1103 (Kos, ca. 200 BCE).
23. I.CosPH 387 (late-III BCE): contributions to a temple of Aphroditē, forty donors, each contributing 5 drachmae; I.CosPH 404 (ca. 200 BCE): forty-two donors to an unknown cause, each giving 23 drachmae.
24. SEG 43:212(A) = LSCG 72 (Tanagra, late III BCE/early II BCE) (the last six contributed less than 5 drachmae). Other examples of all-female *epidoseis* are discussed by Ellis-Evans, "Ideology," 111.
25. CJZC 72.
26. Ellis-Evans, "Ideology," 111.
27. Migeotte, *Souscriptions*, no. 50. Similarly, Ioulis (late IV/early III BCE): Migeotte, *Souscriptions*, 56.1–4: male and female citizens, and all the other inhabitants of the city; IG XII,4 94A, lines 17–18 (Halasarna, 250–225 BCE): the demesmen and the other citizens, and the *paroikoi* (those who live nearby); IG XII,4 314, line 2 (III BCE), 320, lines 11–12 (late II BCE); SEG 48:1111 A, lines 48–49; IG II[2] 791, lines 15–17 (Athens, 248–247 BCE).
28. IGRR IV 1431 = I.Smyrna 697 = GRA II 139. On the interpretation of this term, see the discussion in GRA II 314–15.
29. Isaeus 5 (*On the Estate of Dicaeogenes*) 37–38: "Though so many extraordinary contributions for the cost of the war and the safety of the city have been made by all the citizens, Dicaeogenes has never contributed anything, except that after the capture of Lechaeum, at the request of another citizen, he promised in the public assembly a subscription of 300 drachmae, a smaller sum than Cleonymus the Cretan. [38] This

sum he promised but did not pay and his name was posted on a list of defaulters in front of the statues of the Eponymous Heroes, which was headed: 'These are they who voluntarily promised the people to contribute money for the salvation of the city and failed to pay the amounts promised'" (trans. LCL).

30. IG II² 360, lines 8–12 (Athens, 328/327 BCE) = Migeotte, *Souscriptions*, no. 8; IG VII 1719 + 1744 (Thespies, Boeotia, 191–172 BCE) = Migeotte, *Souscriptions*, no. 29; IG XII,5 135 (Paros, early I BCE) = Migeotte, *Souscriptions*, no. 55; IG XII,6 1:172 (Samos, 260 BCE) = Migeotte, *Souscriptions*, no. 62; I.Iasos 244 (Iasos, mid-II BCE); IG XIV 427–30 (Tauromenion, Cyrene, between 110–90 and 46–36 BCE) = Migeotte, *Souscriptions*, no. 87.
31. Hicks, "Iasos," 100–101.
32. Migeotte, "Souscriptions dans les associations": IG II² 1322 (Rhamnous, early III BCE)—repairs to a sanctuary of Amphiaros by twenty-three members; I.ScM III 35 (Kallatis [Scythia Minor], III BCE)—thirty-two donors to a temple of Dionysos giving between 1 gold stater and 10 drachmae; IG XII,1 9 (Rhodes, after 227 BCE)—repair of a necropolis; AD 21 A (1966) 56–61 (Rhodes, III/II BCE)—fragmentary list of donors to the repairs on a necropolis, in amounts ranging from 5 to 30 drachmae; SEG 39:737 (Rhodes, 185 BCE)—thirty-three donors for the repair of a necropolis; ID 2617 (Delos, 100–75 BCE)—donors to the restoration of a reservoir attached to a temple of Sarapis; Migeotte, "Souscriptions dans les associations," 121 (Delos, ca. 160)—reconstruction of a "house"; ID 2627 (Delos, 110/109 BCE)—donor to the decoration of a sanctuary.
33. Kontorini, *Rhodiaka*, 2:73 (no. 10).
34. SEG 31:122 = GRA I 50 = AGRW 9.
35. At a 6 percent draw on the investment, this would represent an endowment of 5,000 drachmae, well within the typical range of endowments (see Sosin, "Perpetual Endowments," *passim*).
36. See the commendations in, for example, IG II² 1256, line 8 = GRA I 5 (two members); IG II² 1263, line 22 = GRA I 11 (a secretary); IG II² 1278, lines 11–12 = GRA I 17 (a treasurer, supervisor, secretary, comptroller, and record-keeper); and IG II² 1284, lines 30–31 = GRA I 22 (a secretary). Whitehead ("Cardinal Virtues," 67–68) notes: "Rendered 'righteousness' by Cynthia Schwenk [*Athens in the Age of Alexander*, 507] and others, *dikaiosynē* is better understood in an epigraphic context as something like 'honesty,' the behavior—financial and otherwise—of someone who has been in a position to feather his own nest but has not (detectably) done so. It was thus a virtue which, unlike some of the ones we examined earlier (such as *eunoia*), was from the outset of its use regarded as at least as suitable for Athenian citizen honorees as for noncitizens, and it was a common choice for both the demos as a whole and its subdivisions to apply to the conduct of those who had discharged service in an official capacity."
37. On disaffiliation in associations, see Kloppenborg, "Disaffiliation."
38. See other examples of the recording of contributions: IG II² 1301, lines 14–16 = GRA I 30: "The supervisors shall inscribe this decree on a stele, on which (are listed) those who have made contributions"; IG II² 1335 = GRA I 43: a list of fifty-one contributors.

39. See Kloppenborg, "Moralizing of Discourse," 216–19, and more generally, Feyel, *Dokimasia.*
40. Holmberg, *Paul and Power,* 38 (emphasis added).
41. Fraud and misappropriation were constant dangers. Thus, a third-century BCE *epidosis* decree from Chios warns that anyone who attempts to alter the purpose of the collection or to divert it to another use will be fined 3,000 drachmae (Robert, "Sur des inscriptions de Chios," 505–17, no. 1.5–9). Five centuries later a former *stratēgos* in Alexandria is told by the emperor that the *epidosis* that he proposed to offer relief for the farmers in Oxyrhynchus who are suffering economically is approved, but its funds cannot be turned to a different use (P.Oxy IV 705.62–63; Oxyrhynchus, 200–202 CE). A little later, an official from Oxyrhynchus reports that the city treasurer has left the city and perhaps Egypt altogether and that only a portion of the *epidosis* that was collected in support of the sacred Capitoline games is available (P.Oxy LXIII 4357.12–13; 317 CE).
42. See Harrill, *Manumission,* 133. I am indebted to Bert Harrill for drawing this to my attention.
43. Munck, *Paul,* 303.
44. Ambassadors normally traveled *ek tōn idiōn:* for example, TAM V/2 1002 (Thyateira, Lydia, undated): "The leather-cutters honored T. Flavius Alexandros son of Metrophanes of the tribe of Quirine, who had served as *agoranomos* for six months in a vigorous and extravagant manner, superintendent (*curator*) of the company (*conventus*) of Romans, ambassador to the emperor in Rome three times acting as an advocate at his own expense (*dapa[nais] idias*) in the matters that were brought concerning Attaleians, and priest of Artemis in a manner displaying piety and love of honor" (GRA II; trans. Harland, modified slightly).
45. On symbolic capital, see chap. 2 above and Bourdieu, "Economy of Symbolic Goods."
46. Similarly, IG II^2 1263, lines 43–45 = GRA I 11 (Piraeus, 300/299 BCE); IG II^2 1273AB, lines 22–23 = GRA I 18 (Piraeus, 265/264 BCE); IG II^2 1292, lines 16–17 = GRA I 26 (Athens or Piraeus?, 215/214 BCE); IG II^2 1297, lines 17–18 = GRA I 24 (Athens, 236/235 BCE).
47. On the public nature of the recognition of contributors to an *epidosis* collection, and the pressure placed upon those who refused, see Chaniotis, "Public Subscriptions."
48. Chaniotis ("Public Subscriptions," 91) observes: "In Greek antiquity there is no such thing as the noble spender who wants to retain his anonymity. Financial contributions for the city were visible, transparent, and, above all, very loud." There is no reason to suppose that members of Christ groups typically favored anonymous donations and cared little for recognition. Of course, Paul cared a great deal for recognition, as Rom 15:25–28, 31 indicates.
49. It should not be assumed too quickly that Paul in fact gained the social capital he expected. In Rom 15:26–31 he seems to anticipate opposition and prays that his "service (*diakonia*) for Jerusalem may be acceptable to the saints." It is uncertain whether this means that the collection was not as large as Paul had initially expected, or whether the scope of the contributions was not as large as initially supposed (Galatia is no

longer mentioned, in contrast to 1 Cor 16), or whether he anticipated opposition to the collection in principle. If the account in Acts is to be credited, Paul was arrested almost as soon as he arrived in Jerusalem, perhaps an indication that the collection had failed to do what Paul had expected.

50. Ellis-Evans, "Ideology," 112.
51. See Migeotte, *Souscriptions*, 402 (index, s.v. *étrangers*).
52. Chaniotis, "Public Subscriptions," 99–104.
53. IG II^2 835 = SEG 19:80. See the comments of Chaniotis, "Public Subscriptions," 103–4. Because of his largesse, Apollas was granted *proxenos* status and the right to buy property (*enktēsis*).
54. A similar instance of a foreigner from Salamis in Cyprus contributing to an Athenian *epidosis* is attested in IG II^2 283, on which, see Walbank, "Notes on Attic Decrees," 63 (no. 5).
55. I.Lindos II 252 (115 BCE) is an *epidosis* list of people who had both promised to contribute and actually contributed to a collection to provide crowns for Athena Lindia, Zeus Polieus, and Nike. The list is mainly the names of individuals, sometimes mentioning wives and sons as associated contributors, but it also lists seven *koina*, all associated with a citizen, Timapolis. Similar lists from Rhodes that combine individual donors and associations (*koina*) are found in Pugliese Carratelli, "Per la storia," 149–50 (no. 4) = I.Kamiros 159a, and Pugliese Carratelli, "Tituli Camirenses," 220–23 = I.KamirosSuppl 157b.
56. Margaret Mitchell ("Paul's Letters to Corinth," 327–33), building on a sensitive reading of rhetorical echoes between 1 Cor 16 and 2 Cor 8, suggested that Paul in 2 Cor 8:22 ("and we are sending with them [Titus and an unnamed 'brother'] whom we have often approved and found eager in many matters") is going back on this undertaking in 1 Cor 16:3 that the Corinthians will be responsible for approving envoys to accompany the collection. She suggests, further, that this change of heart was the cause of anger and distrust, reflected in Paul's defense of himself that he was not "peddling the word of God" (2 Cor 2:17) and that he was in fact behaving in a guiltless way (2 Cor 4:2) (assuming that 2 Cor 2:14–7:4 minus 6:14–7:1 follows 2 Cor 8). Such a change of heart undoubtedly would have caused consternation and distrust, but it is difficult to see how Paul could have blundered into such a counterproductive suggestion given the general anxiety that all had about the security of communally collected funds.
57. I follow Betz, *2 Corinthians 8 and 9*, in thinking that 2 Cor 8 and 2 Cor 9 are separate letters.
58. See Chaniotis, "Public Subscriptions."
59. Ascough, "Completion of a Religious Duty," has shown that Paul's use of *epiteleō* (complete) in 2 Cor 8:1–15 (three times, 6, 11 *bis*) is used in connection with the completion of a cultic duty. Since the verb is frequently connected with the completion of sacrifices and mysteries, Paul is attempting to link the collection with a cultic duty.
60. Brown, *Poverty and Leadership*; Woolf, "Writing Poverty," 84; Brown, *Through the Eye of a Needle*; Silber, "Neither Mauss, nor Veyne"; Cecchet, "Gift-Giving"; Cracco Ruggini, "From Pagan to Christian Euergetism."

61. See Dover, *Greek Popular Morality*, 177; Gottesman, "Beggar and the Clod"; and Aristotle, *Eth. nic.* 4.2 1122a: "the term *megaloprepeia* is not applied to one who spends adequate sums on objects of only small or moderate importance, like the man who said 'I often gave alms to homeless wayfarers' [Hom. *Od.* 17.420]; it denotes someone who spends suitably on great objects. For though the munificent man is liberal, the liberal man is not necessarily munificent" (trans. LCL). But see Parkin, "'You Do Him No Service,'" for a balanced account of charity.
62. For example, IG XII/5 135 (Paros, early I BCE).
63. Bodel, "From *Columbaria* to Catacombs," 231, points out that *tenuis* "refers primarily to social standing rather than to wealth; as used substantively by jurists in its comparative form [as it is in Pliny] it acquires almost the status of a technical term and in the plural defines a category equivalent to that of the *humiliores;* specifically it describes those who do not belong to one of the legally recognized higher *ordines* (senators, knights, and in some contexts municipal magistrates), many of whom certainly possessed sufficient financial means to pay for their own burials and those of their families. . . . not all *tenuiores* were poor, let alone indigent."
64. CIL 14.2112, lines 12–14: *quib*[*us permissum est co*]*nvenire collegiumq*(*ue*) *habere liceat qui stipem menstruam conferre vo* | *len*[*t ad facienda sa*]*cra in it* (!) *collegium coeant neq*(*ue*) *sub specie eius collegi nisi semel in men* | *se c*[*onveniant con*]*ferendi causa unde defuncti sepeliantur*, "These are permitted to assemble, convene, and have a society: those who desire to make monthly contributions [for sacred rites] may assemble in such a society but [they shall] not [convene] in the name of this collegium except once a month for the purpose of [collecting], from which they shall be buried after their demise." The corrected text is that of Bendlin, "Associations, Funerals, Sociability."
65. Contrary to the plain sense of the *senatus consultum*, the club met more than monthly and not simply to collect funds for funerals. The gap between what the *senatus consultum* imagined as the proper function of a collegium and what the collegium actually did may not be very different from a gap between what Trajan assumed apropos of the Amiseni and the actual purposes of their *eranos*. Later jurists invented the idea of the *collegium tenuiorum* (e.g., Aelius Marcianus, D 47.22.3.2), apparently a legal fiction to allow for the continued existence of collegia under the assumption that they only served to support the burial of members.
66. Longenecker, *Remember the Poor*, 292. Longenecker realizes that efforts at the relief of poverty were directed primarily to the poor within Christ groups but cites several texts which suggest that Paul's purview for generosity seems wider: Rom 12:13, "share in the needs of the *hagioi;* show hospitality to strangers"; Gal 6:10, "let us work good for all (*pantes*), especially for those who are of the household of the faith"; 1 Thess 5:15, "but pursue the good always, for each other and for everyone (*pantes*)"; and 2 Cor 9:13, "you glorify God . . . by the simplicity of your sharing with them [the *hagioi*] and with everyone (*pantes*)."
67. Welborn, "'That There May Be Equality,'" 83.
68. The meaning of *isopoliteia* itself is disputed. Mélèze-Modrzejewski, *Jews of Egypt*, argued that in Alexandria it was a quest for citizenship, but Kasher, *Jews in Hellenistic*

and Roman Egypt and *Jews and Hellenistic Cities in Eretz Israel*, 256, thinks that Judeans in Alexandria were pursuing the status of a *politeuma*, a separate and autonomous political body, with rights equal to the polis but not dependent upon it. The goal of *isopoliteia* is even less clear in Caesarea, but the simmering conflict between the Judean and gentile populations of the city was of long standing (see Kloppenborg, "Ethnic and Political Rivalry").

69. Whitehead, "Competitive Outlay."
70. Friesen, "Paul and Economics," 51, argues that Paul's practice "contradicted the normal expectations of patronage" and characterizes it as "redistributive." He cites with approval Downs's conclusion that "Paul's attempt to frame the collection as an act of corporate worship offered in service of God functions to *subvert* the values of patronage and euergetism by depicting an alternate mode of benefaction, one that brings glory, praise and thanksgiving to God rather than to human benefactors" (Downs, *Offering of the Gentiles*, 158, emphasis added). Patronage and euergetism, however, were typically *associated* with the "theological" virtue of *eusebeia* (piety) such that commendation of a patron was never seen to infringe on reverence for the god, and in some instances, it was seen as an imitation of the gods (Seneca, *Ben.* 6.26–32). Moreover, since Paul never forbids acknowledgment of benefactors or those engaged in euergetic activities (Paul himself included), it is difficult to see any "subversion" here (as if Paul were ever to be in a position to subvert a dominant cultural script).
71. Compare Pliny's report of his interrogation of *Christiani* sixty years later (*Ep.* 10.96). Pliny seemed to treat Christian nonparticipation in the imperial cult not as a clear and present danger to the empire but only as a test to determine who was a Christ follower. *Christiani*, in his view, were largely harmless, if benighted: *nihil aliud inveni quiam superstitionem pravam et immodicam.*
72. See especially Harrill, "Paul and Empire," for a compelling critique of the notion that Paul was engaged in a "subversion" of Roman imperialism: "*Transgressive* means violating the cultural norms or rules, whereas *subversive* means actually changing the cultural norms and rules" (292, emphasis original).
73. See Brown, *Poverty and Leadership.*

9. FUNERALS

1. See the comments of Ascough, "Question of Death," 524–25.
2. The same problem arises with the identification of Judean inscriptions, which lack paralinguistic marks (menorah, lulav, etrog, shofar) or distinctively Judean names. See van der Horst, *Ancient Jewish Epitaphs*, 16–18.
3. On Christian names in Egypt, see Bagnall, "Religious Conversion"; and Blumell, *Lettered Christians*, chap. 5.
4. *Dis manibus* famously appears in a Christian inscription of the third century CE (Terme di Diocleziano inv. 67646 = Friggeri, *Terme di Diocleziano*, 568–69 = ICUR II 4246), and it appears along with *in pace* in many other Christian inscriptions.
5. A funerary inscription in the Musée du Louvre, Ancienne collection Campana, inv. Ma 2983 (= ICUR II 4212), commemorates a certain Livia Primitiva, whose name

does not betray Christian identity, but the plaque features an image of the Good Shepherd (center) flanked by two sheep, a fish left, and an anchor right, all characteristically Christian symbols.

6. The Abercius inscription from Hierapolis (ICG 1597 = SEG 30:1479; 175–200 CE), describes the deceased as a "disciple of the holy shepherd," which can refer only to Christ. See also Terme di Diocleziano inv. 67649 (Friggeri, *Terme di Diocleziano*, 570; III CE): "Prōtos who rests in the Holy Spirit"; Terme di Diocleziano inv. 67646 (ibid., 568–69; III CE): an epitaph with two fish, an anchor, and "the fish (*ICHTHYS*) of the living ones"; and NCE 156, probably the oldest funerary inscription (Antonine period, 138–191 CE), which has been identified as Christian on the basis of the phrase "the brothers of the bridal chamber" who praise "the father and the son" (*genetēn kai hiea*), which points to a Christian origin. See the discussion in Snyder, "Second-Century Christian Inscription."
7. ICG 3131 (Thessaloniki, II CE?).
8. See van der Horst, *Ancient Jewish Epitaphs*, 68–72.
9. Öhler, "Graeco-Roman Associations," 87–88.
10. For example, IG II^2 1275.4–7 = GRA I 8 (Athens, 325–275 BCE); IG II^2 1368.159–63 = GRA I 51 (Athens, 164/165 CE).
11. CIL 14.2112, lines 25–34.
12. Bendlin, "Associations, Funerals, Sociability," 254–57, thinks that 250 sesterces contributed by the *cultores* was only a supplement to the cost of the funeral, the full cost of which would be borne by the heirs of the deceased.
13. See the extensive catalogue in Perry, "Death in the *Familia*," chap. 3.
14. The guild of leather workers is well attested in Saittai. They are sometimes called the *synodos* of the leather workers (*skuteis*) (SEG 29:1183; 147/148 CE) or the "sacred tribe (*phylē*)" of leather workers (*skuteis*) (TAM V/3 1491, 1492), and sometimes the "street" of the leather workers (TAM V/1 79 [152/153 CE], 80 [153–154 CE], 81 [173/174 CE], 146 [166/167 CE]). Elsewhere in Lydia they are called the "leather cutters (*skutotomoi*)" (TAM V/2 1002 and SEG 41:1033). In a dedication from Lycia, they are called the "most holy association (*synergasia*) of leather workers (*skutoburseis*)" (I.Kibyra 63; Kibyra, mid-II CE).
15. See also IG VII 685–88 = GRA I 57; SEG 32:488 = GRA I 58; SEG 26:614 = GRA I 59; I.Beroia 372 = GRA I 64; Philippi II 410/G258 = GRA I 67; and TAM V 85 = GRA II 118.
16. For other Latin examples, see Waltzing, *Étude historique*, 4:505–9, 510–18.
17. For example, CIL 3.3583 (Aquincum, Pannonia Inferior): "To the divine spirits. (Dedicated to) Gaius Iulius Filetio, born in Africa, a physician who lived 35 years; Gaius Iulius Filetus and Iulia Euthenia, his parents, made this for their dearest son and for Iulius Athenodorus his brother who lived 35 years. Euthenia set this up. He has been placed here, to whose burial the guild of textile merchants has contributed 300 denarii." Perry, "Death in the *Familia*," 101–34, compiled a much longer list of inscriptions, recording the contributions of collegia to burials.
18. For example, CIL 6.9407 (Rome, I CE): "P(ublius) Cordius [——]dio decurion of the [guild] of builders and carpenters, lived 19 years 10 months, 3 days. P(ublius) Cordius

Pha[——] his father made (this monument) for him [——] and for himself, and for Cordia [——] his mostly holy wife"; CIL 6.9408 (Rome, first half of I CE): "Iulia Arescusa made this monument for herself and for Quintus Haterius Euagogus her husband, well deserving, a decurion of the guild of builders and carpenters, and for her freedmen and freedwomen and their descendants."

19. CIL 14.371 = CCCA 3.423 (Ostia, 161–170 CE) (Musei Vaticani inv. 1195): "To the divine spirits. Gaius Iunius Euhodus of the Palatine tribe, *magister* (and) president (*quinquennalis*) of the guild of builders and carpenters of Ostia in the 21st lustrum made this (sarcophagus) for himself and for Metilia Acte, priestess of the Great Mother of the Gods of the colony of Ostia, his most holy wife."
20. See Perry, "Death in the *Familia*," 134–59, who collects many other instances of collegial graveyards.
21. See Schrumpf, *Bestattung*, 216–19; and Laubry, "Les espaces funéraires," 123. On the method of distributing loculi, see Duinker, "Buried in Collectivity," 69–70.
22. JIWE I 18 (translation modified slightly). The stipulation of the dimensions of the burial ground (18 × 17 feet) is a standard feature of such inscriptions.
23. On the identification of the guild of AE 1937, 161, with CIL 6.10234, see Introduction, n. 1, above.
24. CIL 5.81 = CCCA 4:99 (no. 247) (Pola [Venetia et Histria/*Regio* X], II CE). See Laubry, "Les espaces funéraires," 123, who also cites CIL 6.10237 (Rome, 16 CE), with impressive descriptions of the installations in the tomb, which make clear that it was also used for funerary banquets. See chap. 1 above for a tomb built by a donor for an association of flax workers.
25. CIL 6.7860–77, 37456 (Rome, first half of I CE).
26. CIL 6.339 (Rome, early I CE): another of the Octavianii, M. Octavius Carpus, is listed as one of the *curatores* of the *collegium sagariorum*, also called the collegium of Hercules Salutaris of the first cohort of *sagarii* (cloak manufacturers). See Liu, "Clothing Supply for the Military."
27. Waltzing, *Étude historique*, 4:484–93: professional guilds, 485–87; *collegia domestica:* 487–92; cultic associations: 492–93. Liu, *Collegia Centonariorum*, 167–70, 266–69, discusses the cemetery of 105 square meters controlled by the textile dealers of Picenum (CIL 9.5084). Duinker, "Buried in Collectivity," 66–67, 90, argues that in Rome occupational guilds did not own entire cemeteries (columbaria or catacombs) but sometimes owned a section of a columbarium. Maillot, "Associations and Death," however, assembles evidence from Rhodes for the ownership of cemeteries by associations, mostly immigrant associations.
28. Other inscriptions that name guilds as guardians of a patron's tomb: IMT 1342, 1346: the *hierē technē* of marble masons (*leukourgoi*); IMT 1937: a *synedrion* of porters (*sakkophoroi*); IMT 1801: the most holy *(hierōtatē) synedrion* of the fullers; IMT 1826: the most holy *(hierōtatē) synedrion* of fishermen; IJO II 132 = I.Eph 1677: Judeans in charge of the tomb of a physician and his wife; I.Eph 2304: the *synedrion* of physicians.
29. Patterson, "Patronage, Collegia and Burial," 23.

30. Hopkins, *Death and Renewal*, 201–7; Hope, *Death in Ancient Rome*, 88; Schrumpf, *Bestattung*, 230.
31. Hopkins, *Death and Renewal*, 211. *Chronica urbis Romae* (ed. Mommsen, *Chronica minora*, 146): *Nerva imp. . . . funeraticium plebi urbanae instituit X LXIIS*. "Nerva, . . . instituted a *funeraticium* for the urban *plebs* of 62 denarii (= 250 sesterces)."
32. CIL 8.18162 = 8.3042 (Lambaesis [Numidia]).
33. Saller and Shaw, "Tombstones," 128 and nn. 21, 23. Richard Duncan-Jones (*Economy of the Roman Empire*, 166–71 [nos. 550–636]), offers a comparison with income levels for the army (Table 2, p. 79) in Numidia, where tomb costs relative to yearly salary range from 1 to 1 for centurions (whose pay was high and whose recorded tomb costs were likewise high) to 0.20 to 1 for legionaries. For Italy (Table 3, p. 130) the highest ratio of tomb costs to yearly salary is 1.66 to 1 for a *primiplaris* and the lowest is 0.20 to 1.
34. Schrumpf, *Bestattung*, 233 (my translation). For more limited studies of the costs of columbaria burials, see Hasegawa, *Familia Urbana*, 84, and Duinker, "Buried in Collectivity," 69; and for burial costs in Puteoli and Cumae, see Bodel, "Organization," 159–62.
35. See Calza, *La necropoli del Porto*, 44–46 (figs. 9–10), for examples of funerary urns buried upright in the ground (i.e., outside of any enclosure or funerary monument).
36. Mommsen, *De collegiis et sodaliciis Romanorum*, 87–91. Mommsen, who knew the Lanuvium inscription (later published as CIL 14.2112), connected this with later discussions in the *Digest* (47.22.1), which seemed to authorize as "collegia licita" (licit associations) only under the conditions that they collected monthly contributions (*stips menstrua*) for the burial of the *tenuiores* (poor). Thus he invented the categories of *collegia funeraticia* and *collegia tenuirorum* even though, as Perry (*Roman Collegia*, 29) observes, CIL 14.2112 never refers to its members as *tenuiores*. The category of a "funerary association" was frequently employed with a few modifications by Schiess, *Römischen Collegia Funeraticia*; Waltzing, *Étude historique*; Cracco Ruggini, "Stato e associazioni professionali"; and Flambard, "Éléments," 242.
37. See Ausbüttel, *Untersuchungen zu den Vereinen*, 22–29, 48; Kloppenborg, "Collegia and *Thiasoi*"; Perry, "Death in the *Familia*," chaps. 1–3; Rebillard, *Care of the Dead*, 37–41; and others.
38. Van Nijf, *Civic World of Professional Associations*, 33.
39. See Ascough, "A Question of Death," 510: "Death was inevitable but provided the opportunity for community definition. One did not cease to be a member of an association at death; rather, death was the point at which the association celebrated a person's membership"; Fraser, *Rhodian Funerary Monuments*, 63: "commemorative reunions at the tomb were certainly not only calculated to keep alive the memory of the departed 'friend' or 'brother' but also in general to cement the bonds which linked the members of the *koinon* to each other."
40. For other examples, see GRA II 153.
41. For example, CIL 5.7487 (Industria [Liguria/*Regio* IX], II CE): "The builders (*fabri*), brothers (*fratres*), (buried him)"; CIL 6.7861 (Rome, 44–48 CE): "Lucius Octavius

Secundus Maior freedman of Lucius, president (*quinquennalis*) of the collegium of textile dealers (*centonarii*) during the 11th lustrum, and decurion lived 55 years. Lucius Octavius Primigenius lived 58 years. Lucius Octavius Secundus lived *vacat.* The brothers (*fratres*), summoners of the collegium of textile dealers, (buried them)"; CIL 3.10551 (Aquincum [Pannonia Inferior], 131–230 CE): "To the divine spirits. Gaius Iulius Euritus, from Alexandria, who lived 30 years lies here. The Iulii Crispinus and Lynx his fellow freedmen and brothers (buried him)."

42. See, for example, TAM Supplement III 201 (Rough Cilicia, mid-I CE): "Our tomb belongs to the *koinon;* let no one else bury a body in it. If someone buries someone else, let them pay to Zeus a yoke of oxen and three minas, to Apollo three minas and a yoke of oxen, and three minas to the *demos.*"
43. Cyprian, *Ep.* 67.6.
44. Thus Rebillard, *Care of the Dead,* 50–51. At about the same time (mid-III CE) Commodianus, *Instructiones* 2.29.17, threatens those who attend collegial banquets (*epulae*) with damnation: *cum ipsis et epulas capitis et pascitis ipsos,* "when for yourselves you both receive banquets and feed upon them (you are already entering damnation)."
45. Bodel, "From *Columbaria* to Catacombs," 183: "At the time, Cyprian was quarrelling with Stephen, bishop at Rome, who had previously reinstated both Basilides and Martial to their sees, so his charges against the two Spaniards were hardly disinterested and must be seen as part of a larger polemic with his Roman rival. More importantly, Stephen's actions show that, regardless of Cyprian's opinion, when Martial as bishop had buried his sons according to the practices of a pagan funerary collegium, he did not violate any ecumenical principle serious enough to prevent his subsequent rehabilitation and moreover had done so openly and without fear of retribution. Whatever the currency of Cyprian's views among the Christian community at Carthage, the attitude they represented was parochial and had no authority over or bearing on Christian burial practices in Spain and at Rome."
46. M. J. Johnson, "Pagan-Christian Burial Practices"; Rebillard, *Care of the Dead,* chap. 3; Bodel, "From *Columbaria* to Catacombs," 182: "In fact, early Christian bishops seem to have taken little interest in the funerary behavior of contemporary Christians and evidently exercised only minimal control over cemeteries before the time of Constantine."

10. LIVING IN THE CITY

1. Published by Hicks, "Inscriptions from Eastern Cilicia," 236–37 (no. 1); Dittmann-Schöne, *Berufsvereine,* 243 (no. VI.8.1) = GRA II 153. The inscription was discovered in a tiled pavement in a cottage in modern Kadirli (= Kars-Bazaar) on the river Pyramos. Hicks describes the inscription as "a very handsome tessellated pavement" found in a cottage, but probably from the floor of a church. Hicks described the inscription as "not later than the third century," but Dittmann-Schöne is probably right that it is fourth or fifth century CE.
2. For example, I.HierapJ 40 (undated); I.HierapJ 41 (III CE); I.HierapJ 42 (imperial period); IG II^2 1088 [restored]; IG II^2 1090; IG II^2 1369, line 31 (ca. 100 CE); IG II^2 3625;

I.Miletos 358 (Miletos, imperial period); I.HierapJ 40, lines 1–3 (Hierapolis, imperial period); I.HierapJ 42, lines 5–7 (Hierapolis, imperial period); BCH 2 (1878) 593,1A, lines 5–7 (Lycia).

3. See also ICG 3372: "God (is) helper (?) | Demetrios, the slave of Christ lies here, having lived orderly and piously. . . . if someone should dare (do it), he will not find a defense on the day of the judgement."

4. Other occupational guilds composed of Christian workers are usually identified as such through paralinguistic signs such as a *staurogram* or a chi-rho (⳨). For example, MAMA III 770 = I.KilikiaHW 151 (an association [*systēma*] of linen sellers [*linopōloi*]). Harland (*Greco-Roman Associations*, 440) has argued that I.Perinthos 167–68 (Perinthos, Macedonia; after 212 CE) as well as grave inscriptions that use chi-rhos after the names of the deceased or that refer to the *adelphoi* (brothers) as those who guarantee the inviolability of the grave may be Christian. See chap. 9 above.

5. See later, IG II[2] 13526 (Anavyssos, Attica, V/VI CE) = SEG 37:195; SEG 48:1256(5) (Palermo, Sicilia, 1080/1081 CE): "Nicholaos the most lowly elder."

6. The use of urine as a detergent in the fulling process has been exaggerated. References to fullers in Roman comedy did not focus on the alleged dirtiness of the occupation but on the peculiar jumping movements of fullers in the soaping stalls. See Flohr, *World of the Fullo*, 103–4, 171, 325–28.

7. Mommsen, *De collegiis et sodaliciis Romanorum*, 120; Waltzing, *Étude historique*, 1:357–68, 513; Poland, *Geschichte des griechischen Vereinswesens*, 337–38; Van Nijf, *Civic World of Professional Associations*, 247; Patterson, *Landscapes and Cities*, 256; Gottesman, *Politics and the Street*, 47.

8. Arnaoutoglou, *Thusias heneka kai sunousias*, 141.

9. For example, IG II[2] 2343 = GRA I 1 (Athens, ca. 400 BCE) inscribes the names of sixteen members of an association of devotees (*koino thiasōtōn*), almost certainly demesmen of Kydathenaion devoted to Herakles.

10. For example, IG II[2] 2347 = GRA I 12 (Salamis, ca. 300 BCE): fifteen *thiasōtai*, including three women, all probably *metics* resident in Salamis; IG II[2] 1298 = GRA I 20 (Athens, 248/247 BCE): a decree of the *thiasōtai* of Artemis, with a list of members, six men and five (or six) women, probably *metics*; IG II[2] 1297 = GRA I 24 (Athens, 236/235 BCE): *thiasōtai* devoted to Artemis Kallistē, including thirty-seven men and twenty-one women, including some slaves; IG II[2] 1292 = GRA I 26 (Athens, 215/214 BCE): a decree of *Sarapiastai*, listing a female *proeranistria*, a treasurer, scribe, supervisor, and the remains of several other names, none with a demotic; IG II[2] 2354 = GRA I 30 (Athens, end of III BCE), where none of the twenty-three members is identified with a demotic and (at least) thirteen of these are women; and IG II[2] 2358 = GRA I 40 (Athens, 135 BCE): a cult association, probably for Atargatis, with ninety-four names (forty-six in the original cutting), including only five demesmen but with thirty-two women's names. Several of the names are likely slaves.

11. The term "epigraphic culture" is taken from Gordon et al., "Roman Inscriptions 1986–90," 154.

12. Baslez, "Place et rôle des associations," 282–83, 290–91; Gottesman, *Politics and the Street*, 51.

13. See GRA II index, VII, "Officers and Functionaries Within Associations."
14. Bury, *History of the Later Roman Empire*, 59–60.
15. SB 3:7182.
16. See Abbott and Johnson, *Municipal Administration*, 65.
17. Gordon, "Ritual and Hierarchy," 256.
18. P.Cair 30606 (Tebtynis, 158/157 BCE); P.PragueSatzung = P.Assoc 83–91 (Tebtynis, 137 BCE); P.Lond VII 2193, line 17 (Philadelphia, 69–58 BCE); P.Mich V 243, lines 7–8 (Tebtynis, 14–37 CE); IG II^2 1368, lines 90–94 = GRA I 51 (Athens, 164/165 CE).
19. On *politeumata* in Egypt, see now Kruse, "Ethnic *Koina* and *Politeumata*."
20. De Ste. Croix, *Class Struggle*, 300–326, 518.
21. Festugière, *Études*, 114–28; Ferguson, "Leading Ideas," 35, referred to the "loneliness and helplessness in a vast disintegrating world."
22. Dodds, *Greeks and the Irrational*, 242–43, speaks of "the progressive decay of tradition (which) set the religious man free to choose his own gods" and describes Hellenistic cult associations as giving "their members a real sense of community with a divine patron or protector of their own choice, to replace the inherited local community of the old closed society."
23. Ziebarth, *Das griechische Vereinswesen*, 192 (my translation).
24. Sourvinou-Inwood, "What Is Polis Religion?" For an assessment, see Kindt, "Polis Religion."
25. See, for example, Gordon, "Veil of Power."
26. See Gordon, "Veil of Power"; Sourvinou-Inwood, "What Is Polis Religion?" and "Further Aspects"; and Woolf, "Polis-Religion."
27. On Bendis, see most recently Arnaoutoglou, "Cult Association and Politics"; on the Magna Mater in Rome, see Borgeaud, *La Mère des dieux*.
28. See MacMullen, *Paganism*, 62–72; Price, *Rituals and Power*; Harland, "Declining Polis?"; and Rives, "Graeco-Roman Religion," 250–51, citing Horster and Klöckner, eds., *Civic Priests*.
29. Rüpke, "Antike Großstadtreligion," 18–19: "The discussion of ancient *polis* religion, which stresses the political and social function of ancient religion in the sense of a *theologia civilis*, easily overlooks the fact that along with the *sacra publica*, the official cult, there was something important. This has to do not only with family cults and household religion, but also with a broader realm of cults and religions which represented individual choices, even if, as was often the case, ethnic or occupational identities determined certain preferences" (my translation); Bendlin, "Looking Beyond Civic Compromise," 123: "the normativity attached to the 'civic compromise' proves deficient in accounting for marginal religious groups and individual religious concerns, or when it needs to accommodate the potential or the reasons for change."
30. Rives, *Religion and Authority*, 9, observed apropos of Roman North Africa that the common granting of Roman citizenship to non-Romans "created a radically new political context in which the civic model of religion was increasingly out of place."
31. Scheid, *Introduction to Roman Religion*, 29. Similarly, Harper, *Fate of Rome*, 153–55, on the plague of Cyprian.

32. Thus Rives, *Religion and Authority*, 168–80.
33. N. F. Jones, *Associations of Classical Athens*, 47 and *passim*; and Ober, *Mass and Elite*, 293–307.
34. N. F. Jones, *Associations of Classical Athens*, 47–50. Similarly, for the Latin West, see Verboven, "Les collèges et la romanisation," 16.
35. N. F. Jones, *Associations of Classical Athens*, 305. Yulia Ustinova ("Orgeones in Phratries") has proposed something parallel, but at an earlier stage of Athenian history. Immigrants in the eighth and seventh centuries who were incorporated as citizens into the Athenian demes but not into the clans (the center of cultic activity) formed cultic associations called *orgeōnes*, which after the laws of Solon were fully incorporated into the Athenian state: "Although it was only later that membership in these groups began to bestow real social privileges, from the outset the newly founded corporations were already effective in liberating the immigrants from the sense of inferiority and defenselessness, both in the cultic and the social spheres" (241).
36. See the survey in van Nijf and Alston, "Political Culture." Ma, "Public Speech," has shown from analyses of the speeches of Dio Chrysostom that democratic practices survived into the imperial period. I owe these references to A. C. Miller, *Corinthian Democracy*, 43, 45. Payne, "Spiritual Bodies," chap. 2, has collected 129 civic decrees from Greek cities in the period 1–300 CE and has shown that the *dēmos* continued to exert democratic influence, even though increased oligarchization progressively eroded the power of the citizen assembly. Payne (in a letter) says, "Throughout this period, the *dēmos* actively intervened in many regions of civic life, from determining the shape of local cults or festivals, to resolving issues of municipal finance and regulating public commodities, to holding elections of magistrates and deciding how best to preserve public records." Although about 60 percent of the decrees honor wealthy benefactors, "even a relatively high proportion of honorary decrees need not suggest a decline in the political livelihood of the *dēmos*. Rather, throughout much of this timeframe the *dēmos* continued to exercise ideological hegemony over the *polis* precisely by enforcing a particular image of the ideal citizen through its honorific decrees. In many *poleis* throughout the eastern Mediterranean, both by its more explicit involvement in questions of local governance and by its honorary activity, the Roman-era popular Assembly remained a viable institution for both democratic deliberation and the assertion of collective will."
37. See Horster and Klöckner, eds., *Civic Priests*; and Horster and Klöckner, eds., *Cities and Priests*, for essays illustrating the oligarchization of Greek society and its effects on priestly appointments.
38. Pleket, "Political Culture"; Zuiderhoek, "On the Political Sociology"; and van der Vliet, "Pride and Participation."
39. Vlassopoulos, "Free Spaces," 38. The term had been coined by Evans and Boyte, *Free Spaces*.
40. N. F. Jones, *Associations of Classical Athens*, 290.
41. Kolb, "Vereine 'kleiner Leute,'" argues that for those who did not belong to the curial classes, association membership was practically the *only* way in which the ordinary

person could participate in quasi public life. They voted honors, erected inscriptions, and benefited from the social prestige that came with their connections to the imperial house. She cites CIL 6.30983, CIL 14.4570, and CIL 6.455, all collegia connected with the imperial house.

42. Fellmeth, "Die römischen Vereine und die Politik," 137; Gutsfeld, "Das Vereinigungswesen," 22.
43. Thus Gutsfeld, "Das Vereinigungswesen," 23 (my translation).
44. Thus rightly, Gottesman, *Politics and the Street*, 62.
45. Thus, for example, Arnaoutoglou, "'Ils étaient dans la ville,'" 44, argues that if "private cult associations included a considerable portion of Athenians and free non-Athenians and that collective identity was built and maintained through the corporate functions and demonstrations of collegial solidarity . . . , then one may associate the function of these groups with the creation of an assimilative context for the non-Athenian element. In this context, values were inculcated, organizational principles were put into practice, and a semblance of civic life was emerging."
46. See Millett, "Patronage," and Zelnick-Abramovitz, "Did Patronage Exist?"
47. I.Rhamnous II 59, lines 16–19 = GRA I 27 (Rhamnous, 216/215 BCE). This is evidently a group of citizens, not *metics*, resident in the deme Rhamnous.
48. AM 66:228 no. 4 = GRA I 39 (Athens, 138/137 BCE).
49. Plato, *Resp.* 327AB, 328A.
50. The ritual is described in IG II[2] 1283 = GRA I 23 (240/239 BCE) and represented graphically in a late-fourth-century/early-third-century BCE relief, 26.01 by 18.33 centimeters, in the British Museum (BM inv. GR 1895,1028.1).
51. Trebilco, "Why Did the Early Christians?," offers a scenario in which *ekklēsia* was the choice of the "Hellenists" in Jerusalem and expressed their "theological conviction that their group was in continuity with that assembly of Yahweh" (444); yet these Hellenists used "*ekklēsia* to claim theological continuity with the OT [Old Testament] people of God, *without* thereby saying that other Jews were not the OT people of God" (458, emphasis original). Trebilco asks why Christians adopted *ekklēsia* and not *synagōgē*, especially since they are practically synonymous in the Septuagint (LXX). He concludes: "They adopted *ekklēsia* because the more prominent term in the LXX—*synagōgē*—was already in use" (450) as a designation of both assemblies and buildings for Judeans. "*Ekklēsia* was chosen as an alternative to *synagōgē* and in order to avoid *synagōgē*" (456). See also Beale, "Background."
52. Korner, "Ekklēsia as a Jewish Synagogue Term"; Korner, *Origin and Meaning*, notes that Sirach, Josephus, and Philo all used *ekklēsia* to mean Judean assemblies and argues that Paul employed this term because it was "largely . . . 'free' as a diasporic group designation, and if public *ekklēsiai* in Judea were convened, as Josephus claims, then non-Messianic Jews could have perceived Paul's *ekklēsiai* as being extensions of public Jewish society in the Diaspora. This would have presented Paul's *ekklēsiai* as diasporic 'satellites' in relation to other Judean public *ekklēsiai*. Paul's *ekklēsiai* would then have been viewed as loci for the full expression of all facets of Jewish life, including its ethnoreligious, social, political, economic, and judicial dimensions" (76–77). Korner's argu-

ment is precisely the opposite of Trebilco's, Korner being eager to have Paul demonstrate continuity with Judean practices and Trebilco arguing that early Christ followers wished not to be confused with Judean synagogues. Korner's argument notes, but sidesteps the fact, that *ekklēsia* was the standard term for a citizen assembly in the cities in which Paul worked, which appears to be the more proximate context of Paul's usage.

53. Theissen, "Urchristliche Gemeinden," 226. Van Kooten ("Ἐκκλησία τοῦ θεοῦ") finds Trebilco's efforts to derive *ekklēsia* from the Septuagint problematic and argues that "Paul wishes to contrast the Christian assembly of God with the civic assemblies (*ekklēsiai*) of the Greek cities in the Roman Empire, as a parallel, alternative organization existing alongside the latter" (527). See also Peterson, "Ekklesia"; Ebner, *Stadt als Lebensraum*, 86–87; and Zamfir, "Is the ἐκκλησία a Household?," 514–16.
54. Grieb, *Hellenistische Demokratie*, 42–45 (Athens), 153–57 (Kos), 210–13 (Miletos), and 276–89 (Rhodes).
55. Macedonia: IG X.2/2 1028 (Delos, 230 BCE), referring to the *ekklēsia* of the Thessalonian colony on Delos; I.Beroia 1 (I BCE); SEG 38:662 (400–350 BCE); SEG 43.448, lines 1, 6–7 (Philippi, 200–175 BCE); SEG 39.606 (Krestonia, Macedonia, shortly after 208/207 BCE) (civic decree); SEG 42.578, lines 2–3 (Kalindoia Macedonia, II/I BCE) (honorific decree); SEG 35.744.2–5 (Kalindoia, 1 CE). Corinth and surrounding area: I.Corinth.Meritt 2 (200–150 BCE); I.Corinth.Meritt 3 (200–150 BCE); IG IV 841 (late III BCE), all before the destruction of Corinth; IG IV 757 (Troizen, 146 BCE); IG IV 853 Troizen, 2 CE).
56. Respectively, ID 1519.1, 5 (Delos, 153/152 BCE); IG XII/6 1:133.1–4 (Samos, II BCE); and Robert, *Sanctuaire de Sinuri*, no. 73 (Sinuri [Caria], 350/344 BCE). A few other instances are sometimes cited: OGIS 844 = TAM V/1 222, which refers to the assembly of Philadelphians in the village of Kastello, probably not a private association; IGLAM 1381, 1382 (both from Aspendus [Pamphylia]). In Kloppenborg, "Edwin Hatch, Churches, and *Collegia*," I had reported these as instance of association *names*, which they are not. They are designations of the *meeting* of an association.
57. See GRA I index, s.v. *agora*.
58. Galatia: 1 Cor 16:1, Gal 1:2; Asia: 1 Cor 16:19; Macedonia: 2 Cor 8:1; Judea: Gal 1:22.
59. Mackil, *Creating a Common Polity* and "Greek Koinon."
60. Van Kooten, "Ἐκκλησία τοῦ θεοῦ," 536. Similarly, Ebner, *Stadt als Lebensraum*, 87.
61. Van Kooten ("Ἐκκλησία τοῦ θεοῦ," 524) cites Plato, *Euthyphr.* 3B–C, where Socrates reports that he is laughed at and declared to be crazy "when I say anything in the assembly about divine things and foretell the future to them."
62. Van Kooten, "Ἐκκλησία τοῦ θεοῦ," 546, adds that "Paul's refusal to allow [women] to speak in the *ekklēsia* is in accord with widespread feelings outside the Christian community," including in Greek civic assemblies. But the advice in 1 Cor 14:33–35 collides rather obviously with what is assumed by 1 Cor 11:2–16 and is better treated as an interpolation from the world of the pseudo-Pauline Pastoral letters.
63. Compare Ebner, *Stadt als Lebensraum*, 90.
64. 2 Cor 2:6: *hikanon tō toioutō hē epitimia hautē hē hypo tōn pleionōn*, "the punishment that was imposed by the majority is sufficient for such a one." Associations also drew

attention to the fact that decrees and honors had been approved by the "majority" or by "all present": for example, P.Mich V 243 (Tebtynis, 43 CE); BGU IV 1137 (Alexandria, 6 BCE); I.Prose I 40, lines 47–49 (Psenamosis, 64–67 CE); and I.Prose 49, line 6 (Psenemphaia, 5 BCE).

65. See IG II^2 1368, lines 86–87 = GRA I 51 (Athens, 164/165 CE); and SEG 31:122, line 9 = GRA I 50 (Liopesi, ca. 90 CE) (vote to expel a member).

66. Thus Kloppenborg, "Egalitarianism," 254–56.

67. P.Mich V 243, line 12 (Tebtynis, 14–37 CE). See also IG II^2 1368, lines 90–94 = GRA I 51 (Athens, 164/165 CE) (fines levied if a member resorts to the public courts); P.Lond VII 2193, line 17 (Philadelphia, 69–58? BCE) (sanction on a member taking another to court); and P.Mich V 243, lines 7–8 (Tebtynis, 14–37 CE) (fine for resorting to the court).

68. See I.Iasos 244 (Iasos, mid-II BCE) (see chap. 8 above).

69. See, for example, IG II^2 409 (Athens, 330 BCE); IG II^2 653, lines 43–44 (Athens, 289/288 BCE); IG II^2 687, lines 46–47 (Athens, 266/265 BCE); and IG II^2 1224.Frag. a–c, lines 11–12 (Athens, 166 BCE), plus at least twenty other examples with *cheirotoneō* and *presbeis*.

70. Feyel, *Dokimasia*.

71. Kloppenborg, "Moralizing of Discourse."

72. For example, IG XII/8 186 (Samothrace, I BCE): six *synegdamoi* accompanying the *hieropoioi, mystai, kai epoptai eusebeis* of Rhodes who traveled to Samothrace.

73. Arzt-Grabner, 2. *Korinther*, 409 (my translation). One could add I.Rhamnous II 59, lines 2, 6 = GRA I 27 (Rhamnous, after 216/215 BCE), and IG II^2 1012, line 19 = GRA I 42 (Athens, 112/111 BCE), which use *cheirotoneō* in connection with the election of officials of private associations.

74. Last, "Election of Officers," 379 (emphasis added). Perhaps better rendered, "There need to be elections among you so that the *dokimoi* among you are evident."

75. Thus Brookins, "Supposed Election of Officers." Brookins rejects Last's argument on the grounds that Justin Martyr, *Dial.* 35, attributes a saying to Jesus that speaks of the inevitability of *schismata kai haireseis*, where the two nouns must have roughly the same meaning. This, however, makes Justin's usage determinative of the meaning in 1 Corinthians and attributes to Paul the notion that there is some eschatological necessity to factionalism, a view that he hardly countenances.

76. Arnaoutoglou, *Thusias heneka kai sunousias*, 104–5.

77. Tertullian's complaint against the Marcionites in *Praescr.* 41.8 appears to imply that they have a rotating system of leadership, whereby officers serve for fixed periods of time and are either elected or assigned by rota. Tertullian paints as dire and bizarre a picture as possible: "Thus, one day one person is bishop and another tomorrow; today one is a deacon, and another day a lector; today he is a presbyter who tomorrow will be a layperson" (my translation).

78. Countryman, "Patrons and Officers"; Meeks, *First Urban Christians*, 78. Schmeller, "Gegenwelten," 175, sees honorific practices as replaced by a kind of communal status elevation. Harrison ("Paul's House Churches," 37) argues that Paul's metaphor of the

body "undermines the pecking order of the *cursus honorum* at Rome and in the colonies (1 Cor 12:22–25a)"; it overturns the "entrenched social power of the *kalokagathos* in honoring the socially disenfranchised."

79. For example, SB 22:15460 = P.Berol. inv. 25159 (Alexandria, 5 BCE), an honorific decree of imperial slaves.
80. Harrison, "Paul's House Churches," 38.
81. Van Nijf, *Civic World of Professional Associations*, 119.
82. The same tension is current in modern Greek, where *philotimo*, acting honorably, is encouraged, but *philodoxia*, seeking honor, is discouraged.
83. Brennan and Pettit, *Economy of Esteem*, 195–221.
84. The formula is very common in civic inscriptions and frequent in association inscriptions. See GRA I 133, note on lines 1–6.
85. See Landecker, "Types of Integration."
86. The term has been used extensively by Dunning, "Strangers and Aliens," 4, *Aliens and Sojourners*, 6.
87. *Paroikos, paroikia:* Eph 2:19; 1 Pet 1:1, 17; 2:11; 1 *Clem.* 1.1; 2 *Clem.* 5.1; Pol. *Phil.* 5.1; Mart. Pol. 1.1; Diogn. 5.1–6, 6.8; Apoc. Sedrach 11; Clement of Alexandria, *Paed.* 3.12.85, *Strom.* 4.26. For *parepidēmoi, parepidēmeō*, see Clement of Alexandria, *Strom.* 3.14: "we must conduct ourselves politically as foreigners (*xenoi*) and visitors (*parepidēmounotes*)"; Tertullian, *Exh. cast.* 12.1: "Are not we also wanderers in this world?" See Roldanus, "Références patristiques."
88. See the compilation of texts in Elliott, *1 Peter*, 477.
89. The terms appear to have become a stereotypical way of referring to a church, especially in Eusebius and the earlier letters he cites: Eusebius, *Hist. eccl.* 4.23.5, 5.1.3, 5.22.1, 5.23.3, 5.24.15, 6.2.2, 7.26.3, 7.28.1, 8.13.7, etc.
90. Elliott, *1 Peter*, 476–83. See also Elliott, *Home*, 33–49, who notes how various Bible translations of 1 Pet 1:17 and 2:1 gratuitously offer such translations as "visitors and pilgrims," "strangers and refugees in this world," or "earthly pilgrimage" (39–41).
91. Similarly, Bechtler, *Following in His Steps*, 17: "*paroikos* bore a decidedly negative connotation; the stranger, whether called *paroikos* or *parepidēmois*, was from the standpoint of society a second-class person," citing Feldmeier, *Die Christen als Fremde*, 21.
92. Philo, *Flacc.* 54. Whether Judeans living in Alexandria were in fact citizens (or at least some of them) is controverted. Josephus (*Ant.* 19.281) claims that Judeans living in Alexandria were called "Alexandrians" and that they had obtained *isēs politeias* (equal citizenship) in contrast to Flaccus's claim. On this, see Ben Zeev, *Jewish Rights*, 296–301.
93. Elliott, *Home*, 68–69. Elliott acknowledged that 1 Pet was also addressed to Christ followers in cities.
94. Elliott, *Home*, 24.
95. S. Mitchell, *Anatolia*, 1:176.
96. H. Schäfer, "Paroikoi," 1698; similarly, Bechtler, *Following in His Steps*, 71–73.
97. Text and translation: Reynolds, *Aphrodisias and Rome*, 11–16.

98. See also I.Stratonikeia 172.7–11; I.Stratonikeia 210.7–8 (Sanctuary of Zeus, Panamaros Stratonikeia, Roman period): I.Priene 113.81–84 (Priene, 84–81 BCE). H. Schäfer, "Paroikoi," gives numerous other examples, many from Asia Minor.
99. See Whitehead, "Immigrant Communities," and Demetriou, *Negotiating Identity*. *Metics* in Athens (likely the equivalent of *paroikoi* in other locations) existed in significant numbers in Attica (mainly in the Piraeus). They could not hold office or own land (except by a grant of *enktesis*) but contributed to taxes through the *metoikion* and were expected to contribute to civic life. They could participate in civic rituals through the mediation of a *proxenos*. A *xenos* did not have the rights of a *metic*, but one who had remained in Athens for an unknown amount of time was required to find a *prostatēs* (sponsor) and enlist in an Athenian deme as a *metic*. Athens set up special courts to deal with the legal cases of *metics* and visitors, many of whom were commercial traders; and although they could not avail themselves of Athenian privileges, they required expeditious resolution of lawsuits, etc.
100. See, for example, Baslez, "Communautés d'orientaux," 148.
101. See Elliott, *1 Peter*, 435–38, for a discussion of the translation of this phrase.
102. See Winter, *Seek the Welfare*, 39: "The picture emerges of a positive rôle being taken by rich Christians for the well-being of the community at large and the appropriateness and importance of due recognition by ruling authorities for their contributions. The Christians in Greek cities in the East were exhorted to undertake the same benefactions as their secular counterparts."
103. Balch, *Let Wives*, 81.
104. Balch, "Hellenization/Acculturation."
105. Elliott, *1 Peter*, 501. Achtemeier, *1 Peter*, 188, thinks that the "repetition of the verb *timaō* rather than *phobeomai* in relation to the emperor . . . represents a different, and devalued understanding of imperial authority." Similarly, Goppelt, *Commentary on 1 Peter*, 190. More recently Horrell, "Between Conformity and Resistance," 135, suggests that the author subsumes the role of the emperor under *pasē anthrōpinē ktisei* of 2:13, which implies that he "implicitly denies any claim that the emperor is *theios*."
106. Harland, "Honours and Worship," esp. 326–28. From the time of Augustus onward, Roman collegia used the term *collegia salutare*, which, as Bendlin, "Associations, Funerals, Sociability," 216–23, has shown, reflects "an expression of loyalty to the imperial centre, inseparable from the concept of Salus Augusti, which since the first century was established as a central element of imperial propaganda but reached an apex in the Antonine period" (222).
107. See Dibelius, *Der Hirt des Hermas*, 550, citing Philo, *Agr.* 65: "For in reality every soul of a sage has heaven for its country, and looks upon earth as a foreign land, and considers the house of wisdom his own home; but the house of the body, a lodging-house, on which it proposes to visit for a while" (trans. LCL); *Cher.* 120: "for God, [the wise] are strangers and resident aliens; for each of us comes into the world as to a foreign city, in which he has no share before his birth, and coming there dwells as a resident alien until he has exhausted the period of life that has been assigned" (trans. LCL).
108. Osiek, *Shepherd of Hermas*, 158.

109. Osiek, *Rich and Poor*, 127–32.
110. Woolf, "Food, Poverty and Patronage," 217.
111. Brown, *Through the Eye of a Needle*.
112. That "charity" in the ancient world always expected reciprocation (and therefore was rarely directed outside one's network) is underscored by Hands, *Charities and Social Aid*, 30–31: "The essential point is that there remains basic to the discussion the assumption that the gifts, benefits, or favors in question are to be conferred upon somebody who *can* make a return, so that return, even though it may no longer decently be asked for, is confidently expected" (emphasis original). Only much later does the idea emerge of giving gifts to one who is incapable of reciprocation.
113. A. Robinson, "It Takes One to Know One"; Ginsberg, "Introduction."
114. Jacobs, "Passing," 253, citing A. Robinson, "It Takes One to Know One," 728. I am indebted to Albert Harrill for these references.

11. GETTING IN, FALLING AWAY

1. The text is preserved in Lactantius, *Mort.* 48: "it was proper that the Christians and all others should have liberty to follow that rite which to each of them appeared best (*ut daremus et Christianis et omnibus liberam potestatem sequendi religionem quam quisque voluisset*); so that the God who is seated in heaven might be benign and propitious to us and to every one under our government."
2. The classic study, which forms the starting point for almost all demographers, is Beloch, *Bevölkerung*, 507. Frier ("Demography," 811–12) adjusted the population at the death of Augustus downward to 45 million. For the population at the eve of the Antonine plague, see Frier, "Demography," 813; Scheidel, "Demography," 47: 60–70 million but perhaps as high as 76 million (48). Bang, *Roman Bazaar*, 115, thinks that 80 million is possible.
3. Thus Littman and Littman, "Galen and the Antonine Plague," assuming an empire of 50 million with mortality rates of 13–15 percent in Egypt. Scheidel, "Model," 99–100, points out that more recent epidemiological studies predict a death toll in the range of 25 percent, unevenly distributed, with cities and the army more seriously affected. Bagnall, "Effects of Plague," has expressed some skepticism as to Scheidel's interpretation of some of the papyrological evidence and notes that the evidence in support of claims regarding a decline of the Egyptian population is very slender.
4. Duncan-Jones, "Impact of the Antonine Plague," correlates a series of noteworthy shifts between 165 and 180 that suggest a significant decline in the population: a sharp decline in taxpayers in various Egyptian villages; the disappearance of one- to three-year agricultural leases and dated military diplomas; a decline in dated papyri, dated Roman inscriptions, and imperially financed buildings; and a decline in brick production. Boak, *Manpower Shortage*, argues that the population decline began with the principate of Marcus Aurelius, the result of barbarian invasions, and continued with the plagues of 165–180 and again in 250–270 through malaria, tax policy, and other factors.

5. MacMullen, *Christianizing*, 135 n. 26; and Hopkins, "Christian Number," 195 n. 20, both admitting that this number is hypothetical. Russell ("Late and Medieval Population," 7–8) offers 50 million at the time of Constantine but also notes that these estimates "are unanchored conjectures since demographic information about that Empire is singularly scarce." A. H. M. Jones, *Later Roman Empire*, 1040–45: "it is impossible to calculate what the population of the empire was at any date, or how much it declined, if, as is very probable if not certain, it did decline" (1040). He notes the chronic labor shortages (see Boak, *Manpower Shortage*), less land being under cultivation (resulting in a decline in the food supply), and a declining fertility rate such that peasants could not produce enough children to offset mortality rates.
6. Harnack, *Mission und Ausbreitung*, 2:211–12 n. 4, and *Mission and Expansion*, 2:248 n. 1. A. H. M. Jones, *Later Roman Empire*, 81, argued that in the early fourth century, Christians were "still a tiny minority, especially in the West and they were on the whole people of no importance." Trombley, "Overview," 309, agrees that Christians were a tiny minority in most towns by 300 CE but notes a few places where they might have been dominant: in some towns in Phrygia; at Maiuma, port of Gaza; and in Oxyrhynchus, which already had two churches in 295 CE. However, "estimates of the size of the Christian communities c.300 can only be made by reasoning backwards in time from later, better-documented periods, but this cannot always give satisfactory results" (Trombley, ibid.).
7. For example, Brown, *Poverty and Leadership*, 17. T. A. Robinson (*Who Were the First Christians?*, 14, 18, 24, 26, 32) seems to accept both the 60 million figure for the empire and 10 percent for Christian numbers at the time of Constantine, even though he repeatedly points out that the estimates are arbitrary. His main argument is that, if there were 6 million Christians at the time of Constantine, and if only 10–15 percent of the populace was urban, there must have been rural Christians.
8. Barnes, *Constantine and Eusebius*, 191–92.
9. Stark, *Rise of Christianity*, 6–7.
10. A series of much more complicated models of growth, but equally based on guesswork, has been discussed by Schor, "Conversion by the Numbers," who in the end suggests that network models may better serve the aim of discussing conversion. On network models, see below.
11. Stark, "Why Religious Movements Succeed or Fail," 23, observes that growth rates among Mormons worldwide have ranged from 30 to 50 percent per decade, partly because of higher fertility rates in the US and Britain but also because of conversion.
12. T. A. Robinson, *Who Were the First Christians?*, 250.
13. Cragun and Lawson, "Secular Transition."
14. Concannon, *Assembling Early Christianity*. Similarly Bryant, "Review," 192 n. 97: "It strains all credulity that this or any other religious movement experiences a constant and linear rate of conversion over long periods of socio-historical change."
15. Acts 2:14–41 (preaching to a crowd in Jerusalem); 3:11–26 (in Solomon's portico); 5:25 (preaching in the temple); 14:14–18 (Lystra); 17:17 (agora in Athens), 22–34 (Areopa-

gus); 22:1–21 (steps of the temple). It should be noted that this is not the only way in which Acts depicts recruitment.

16. Mark associates crowds with Jesus's miracle-working activity but mentions crowds in connection with teaching at 2:13 (teaching the crowds), 4:1 (parables discourse), 7:14–17 (on purity), and 11:32–12:12 (parables). Matthew editorially creates crowd scenes: 4:25; 5:1–7:28; 8:1 (the Sermon on the Mount, bracketed by the mention of the "crowds"); 11:7–30 (speech to the "crowds" concerning the Baptist); 13:2, 34, 36 (the parables speech); 15:10–11 (on purity); 19:2 (on divorce); 21:26–46 (parables); 22:33 (the crowd was amazed at his teaching); 23:1–39 (woes against the scribes and Pharisees). Thus also Luke: 3:7, 10 (John's speech to the crowds); 4:42; 5:3 (teaching the crowd); 6:17; 7:24 (speech to the "crowds" concerning the Baptist); 8:4; 11:27, 29; 12:1, 13, 54; 13:14, 17; 14:25, 19:39.
17. Barrett, *Commentary on Romans*, 43.
18. Koester, *History, Culture, and Religion*, 356–57.
19. Cynics were not the only ones to engage in public discourse: Epictetus (2.12.17–25), though he taught in a school in Nicopolis, imagines a street encounter between a Stoic philosopher and a rich man. But this is an imaginary scene, not an ethnographic report. Sophists and rhetoricians spoke in theaters and other public venues, though normally at the invitation of the city.
20. Nock, *Conversion*, 202; Origen, *Cels.* 3.55.
21. Stark and Bainbridge, *Future of Religion*; Stark, *Rise of Christianity*, 18. While many aspects of sociological theories of conversion are still under discussion, there is still widespread agreement that propositional beliefs are of lesser importance in the initial stages of conversion (Gartrell and Shannon, "Contacts, Cognitions, and Conversion," 142; Montemaggi, "Belief, Trust, and Relationality") and that affective bonds and social networks are paramount (Snow and Philipps, "Lofland-Stark Conversion Model"). See further, Gooren, "Reassessing."
22. Stark, *Rise of Christianity*, 20.
23. Stark and Bainbridge, "Networks of Faith"; Welch, "Interpersonal Influence Model."
24. P.Mich VIII 511 (Memphis or Arsinoites, early III CE); published Youtie, "Kline of Sarapis"; Youtie and Pearl, *Papyri and Ostraca*, 2:141–45 (no. 511).
25. Annual subsistence is normally put at 250 kilograms (= 38 *modii*, 8.25 artabae) of wheat equivalent per person per year. See Clark and Haswell, *Economics of Subsistence Agriculture*, 57–59, 175–76. In the early third century, the cost of wheat in the Fayûm ranged between 20 and 24 drachmae per artaba; mid-III CE: 16–24 (mean = 20): Duncan-Jones, "Price of Wheat," and *Structure and Scale*, 152; Drexhage, *Preise, Mieten/Pachten, Kosten*, 16–17. This means that subsistence was about 165 drachmae yearly.
26. For the third century CE, Drexhage, *Preise, Mieten/Pachten, Kosten*, 422–29, reports daily wages of 2–9 drachmae for day laborers (mean = 3), and monthly salaries of 12–128 drachmae, with a mean of 55 and a mode of 40. Assuming that a day laborer did not work more than twenty days per month and not consistently every month, this would probably make membership in the *Sarapiastai* impossible. For a monthly

worker, however, if we take the mean third-century wage, the cost of the meal was less than half of the mean monthly wage; and with the initiation cost added—presumably a one-time cost—it would still be less than the mean monthly salary.

27. Monson, "Ethics and Economics," 228, calculates that in the second century BCE, the yearly contributions to associations of Sobek amounted to about one-quarter of 8–10 artabae of grain needed for subsistence, which implies that members were typically more prosperous than those at the subsistence level.
28. The requirement of wood for sacrifices is also attested in IG XII/5 606.6 (Iulis, Kos); P.Cair.Zen II 59154 (Philadelphia, 256 BCE) (wood for "the festival of *Eisieiōn*"); P.Cair.Zen II 59191.3–4 (Philadelphia, 255 BCE); P.Oxy VIII 1144.15 (Oxyrhynchus, 75–125 CE) (a temple account listing "wood for sacrifice"); and SEG 31:122.42, 45 = GRA I 50 (Liopesi, ca. 90 CE).
29. Tertullian, *Apol.* 39.
30. P.Petaus 40 = P.Mich inv. 6877 (Ptolemais Hormou, Herakleidou meris, Arsinoites, 184–187 CE), published: Hagedorn et al., eds., *Archiv des Petaus*, no. 40.
31. All of the towns and villages mentioned belong to the division of Herakleides, the easternmost division of the Fayûm and the Aphroditopolis on the Nile directly adjacent to the division of Herakleides.
32. The quotation is from Fredriksen, "How Later Contexts," 43. P.VindSal 2.8–9 (Arsinoë, II–III CE) refers to a procession at the Sarapeion in the Hadrianic plaza in Arsinoë-Krokidilopolis on the festival ("day") of the "greatest god Sarapis." Such public events were demonstrations of the "greatness" of the deity in question.
33. The *agoranomos* of an association was an imitation of the civic *agoranomos*. In Egyptian cities he was normally in charge of conduct within the marketplace (Alston, *City in Roman and Byzantine Egypt*, 190–92). During festivals, the *agoranomos* might organize the festival, as he did in SEG 11:923.7–40 (Gytheum, near Sparta, 15 CE). In I.Beroia 22.A3 = GRA I 63) (7 BCE) the *agoranomos* was a liaison between the city and the association for the organization of a festival.
34. P.Mich V 246.3, 5, 21–22 (Tebtynis, ca. 43–49 CE).
35. Clauss, *Cultores Mithrae*, 34–35.
36. See Rainer, "Mithrasverehrung," 110, who notes that the cognomina Callinicus, Hieronimus, Menander, Agatho, Epaphroditus, Ermeros, Hermadio, Criton, Karus, Herakles, Nocomes, and Glyco are all typical of freedmen.
37. For a survey of workshops at Ostia, see Bakker, *Living and Working*, 65–76.
38. CIL 6.33885 (Rome, 117–138 CE).
39. Evers, *Worlds Apart*.
40. Liu, *Collegia Centonariorum*, 196–202.
41. P.Mich V 243 (Tebtynis, 14–27 CE).
42. P.Mich V 244 (Tebtynis, 43 CE).
43. NSA 1953, 244 = CIMRM 1:228. The inscription is on an entablature, probably at the door of the mithraeum. On locations in Ostia, see "A Note on Locations."
44. Hermansen, "*Stuppatores*."
45. CIL 14.4549, 58: *S(tuppatores) R(estiones)*, "Stuppa makers, rope sellers," with the images of a double comb and strands of flax.

46. The mosaics on the floor of the stalls of the Piazzale delle Corporazioni (II,VII,4) suggest the guilds that were represented in each: Statio 43 (*codicarii*), 45–52 (*navicularii*); 53 (upper: grain measurers; lower: Nereid, seahorse, two dolphins, probably shippers); 54 (*navicularii*); 55–56 (*mensores frumentarii*); and 58 (*restiones*).
47. Bakker, *Living and Working*, 66.
48. Arnhold, "Group Settings," 151.
49. Bakker, *Living and Working*, 159, and CIL 14.4530 (215 CE): Coh(ors) VI[I] (centuria) Ost(iensis) imp(erante) | An(tonino) co(n)s(ulibus) L(a)eto et Ce|riale seba(cia)rius | Calpurnius (in the right *ansata*): | X (votis), "Calpurnius, night watchman from the centuria of Ostia, from the seventh cohort, during the principate of Antoninus (Caracalla), in the year that Laetus and Cerialis were consuls, (decennalia)."
50. The inscription dates this as the eighth of the Kalends of the fourth month. The calendar of Roman Asia did not begin with January but with the birthday of Augustus (September 23) so that New Year's Day was in the fourth month, Peritios, which began December 24.
51. IJO II 196 = GRA II 116.
52. See Harland, "Acculturation and Identity," and GRA II 174.
53. Harland, *Associations, Synagogues and Congregations*, 140–42.
54. Sharankov, "Надпис." I am grateful to Stephen Mitchell for alerting me to this inscription and to Mariana Mastagar for translating the article for me.
55. Sharankov, "Надпис," 31.
56. Tačeva-Hitova, "Hypsistos"; S. Mitchell, "Cult of Theos Hypsistos," 131–32 (nos. 60–75); S. Mitchell, "Further Thoughts," 201 (nos. A30–A33).
57. I.ScM II 248 (Tomis, ca. 150–200 CE); I.ScM II 462 (Tomis, II/III CE).
58. S. Mitchell ("Further Thoughts," 178) notes that lavish dedications are largely absent from the cult of Theos Hypsistos and that most point to individuals of modest means. He also notes (ibid., 174) that animal sacrifice did not seem to play a part in the cult of Theos Hypsistos and that while open-air shrines (*naoi*) are attested, temples (*hiera*) are not. This is consistent with the inscription from Nikopolis ad Istrum, which designates the building as a *naos*. We might note that the membership roster of I.Beroia 27 (see chap. 2 above) is poorly and inexpensively made, pointing to a group with very modest resources.
59. Hock, "Workshop as a Social Setting"; Adams, *Earliest Christian Meeting Places*, 138–46.
60. For example, Socrates according to Xenophon, *Mem.* 4.2.1–39 (a saddler's shop); 3.10.1–15 (a painter's shop); Diogenes Laertius 2.122–23 provides a list of topics discussed by Socrates in Simon the cobbler's workshop (*ergastērion*). On this, see Hock, "Simon the Shoemaker."
61. Origen, *Cels.* 3.55.
62. The Leonides archive consists of P.Oxy I 103, P.Oxy II 209 = 𝔓, P.Oxy. XXXI 2585, P.Oxy XLV 3254–3262, and PSI V 469.
63. Luijendijk, "New Testament Papyrus."
64. P.Oxy XXXIII 2673 (304 CE).
65. Price, "Religious Mobility," 8.

66. I.HierapJ 51 (Hierapolis, late I CE): "Titus [Fla]vius Zeuxis, a merchant, having sailed around (Cape) Maleas to Italy seventy-two times, built this tomb for himself and for his children, Flavius Theodoros and Flavius Theudas and for whoever these will concede (access)." See Vearncombe, "Rounding Cape Maleas."
67. North, "Development," 178.
68. Bendlin, "Looking Beyond Civic Compromise," 134.
69. Van Haeperen, "Cohabitation or Competition," found no evidence of competition, at least in relation to the various cults available at Ostia. Steuernagel, "Ancient Harbour Towns," objected to Bendlin's proposal of a "marketplace" on the grounds that there is little or no evidence that associations were established in order to *supply* cultic needs: "While exponents of the market model put individual religious needs as fundamental to the formation or membership of a religious association, it is, I think, necessary to take account of more complex motives. These are determined by individual biographies as well as by social identities, a background from which the market model almost completely prescinds. . . . At any rate, it is not the religious proposal or *supply* which is decisive in the formation of an association" (144, emphasis added). Yet Bendlin makes no claim that associations were *formed* in order to "supply" cultic needs; he claims only that they in fact served to meet demands for cultic "services" while other cults, including some traditional cults, failed to attract adherents and hence languished.
70. Bendlin, "Looking Beyond Civic Compromise," 135 (emphasis added).
71. See Verboven, *Economy of Friends*, who distinguishes different modes of organizing economic transactions through a combination of patronage networks and friend networks.
72. See Bendlin, "Gemeinschaft, Öffentlichkeit und Identität," 33, who also notes the phenomenon of migration and displacement of people, especially unmarried, mainly young, men and says, "the association was a useful alternate space of political, social and religious networking."
73. S. Mitchell, "Cult of Theos Hypsistos," 146 (nos. 283–88).
74. Daniels, "Role of the Roman Army"; Beck, "Mysteries of Mithras."
75. Clauss (*Cultores Mithrae*, 208) reports that in some of the military provinces—Britannia, Germania, Pannonia, Moesia, and Dacia—the percentage of Mithraic dedications by soldiers was only about 40 percent, with dedications by centurions at least as numerous as those by legionaries and auxiliaries. In Italy the number of military dedications was insignificant since legions were not stationed there.
76. Turcan, *Cults of the Roman Empire*, 167; Kuşseven, "Cult of Iupiter Dolichenus," 42, 50; Collar, "Commagene."
77. Stark and Bainbridge, "Networks of Faith," 1378; Snow and Machalek, "Sociology of Conversion," 183.
78. Stark and Bainbridge, "Networks of Faith," 1381, citing Lofland and Stark, "Becoming a World-Saver." Stark, *Rise of Christianity*, 19, also reports that new religious movements "mainly draw their converts from the ranks of the religiously inactive and discontented, and those affiliated with the most accommodated (worldly) religious

communities." The last point is probably irrelevant to antiquity, which lacked a distinction between "religious" and "secular"; and given the pervasive nature of cultic practices, "religiously inactive" is probably not a meaningful term.

79. This can be seen as an instance of "biographical reconstruction," in which the convert's biography is "reconstructed in accordance with the new or ascendant universe of discourse and its attendant grammar and vocabulary of motives" (Snow and Machalek, "Sociology of Conversion," 173).
80. Stark, *Rise of Christianity*, 19–20. For a similar analysis of conversion in contemporary evangelicalism, stressing the relative unimportance of beliefs, see Montemaggi, "Belief, Trust, and Relationality."
81. Monson, "Ethics and Economics."
82. Iannaccone, "Sacrifice and Stigma" (on costs as a way to exclude free riders); Sosis, "Religion and Intragroup Cooperation"; Sosis and Bressler, "Cooperation and Commune Longevity"; Sosis and Alcorta, "Signaling, Solidarity, and the Sacred" (on rule-based behavior and its effect on solidarity and the longevity of elective groups).
83. TAM V 1539.52–54 = GRA II 117 (Philadelphia, Lydia, ca. 100 BCE).
84. Ascough, "Re-Describing the Thessalonians' 'Mission.'" The reference is to IG X/2.1 255 = GRA I 77 (Thessaloniki, I–II CE) (Sarapis's arrival, first to Opus, then Macedonia) and IG XI,4 1299 (Delos, before 166 BCE) (Sarapis's initial arrival on Delos).
85. Frischer, *Sculpted Word*, 197 and his chaps. 2–3, has argued that Epicurus and the Epicureans adopted a purely passive strategy of recruitment and that Epicurus forbade active recruitment. See the review of Frischer by Diskin Clay in *AJP* 105, no. 4 (1984): 484–89.
86. Stark, *Rise of Christianity*, 76–94.
87. Dionysios of Alexandria's letter, cited in Eusebius, *Hist. eccl.* 7.22.7–10.
88. *Ep.* 22 to Arsacius, high priest of Galatia, 362 CE.
89. Eck, "Das Eindringen des Christentums," 388–89, 391–95.
90. Lampe, *From Paul to Valentinus*, 119. He later notes (148) that for the third century CE only at most thirty-two people of senatorial rank can be identified as Christian, twenty-two of them women, and at most six in the first and second centuries.
91. Barnes, "Statistics."
92. Eck, "Das Eindringen des Christentums," 396.
93. Theissen, *Social Setting*, 69; Theissen, "Social Structure," 71; Theissen, "Pauperismus," 119–20. Theissen acknowledged that by the end of the first century some elite women such as Flavia Domitilla may have been attracted to Christ groups, not as members, but as "distanced patronesses" ("Pauperismus," 120), equivalent to my "external patrons."
94. Grant, "Pliny and the Christians." Livy, *Ab urbe condita* 39.8.4, 12.4, 13.9 (nocturnal rites); 39.15.13 (*sacramentum*); 39.18.3 (*carmen*); 39.13.10; 14.8; 16.1, 6 (*flagitia*).
95. Harrill, "Servile Functionaries," 126, comments that Pliny's argument seems to be that "the deeds of this *superstitio* may be 'degenerate,' carried to 'extravagant lengths,' and a 'contagious' disease spreading from the city into the countryside and villages—a threat to society and Roman imperial power, to be sure, leading to the desertion of

temples, the neglect of religious festivals, and a decline in sales of meat sacrificed to a deity. . . , but the name 'Christian' itself *(nomen ipsum)* was not a criminal act (*flagitium*) punishable under the law. Cannibalism, sacrilege, and murder are crimes of an entirely different order, which the touch-stone of torturing the slave *ministrae* proved to Pliny's satisfaction that the Christians did not commit."

96. The dating of James is highly contested, with dates ranging from the mid-60s (or even earlier) to the late second century. For a survey of scholarship on the date and provenance of James, see Allison, *James* 3–32, 94–98. I had earlier proposed a Palestinian provenance for James ("Patronage Avoidance"), but now, agreeing with Allison, I think that Rome is more likely.
97. Cicero, *Verr.* 2.3.76 (§176); Suetonius, *Jul.* 33. For the identification of the man of Jas 2:2–3 as an *eques*, see Reicke, *Diakonie*, 342–43; Judge, *Social Pattern*, 53; Laws, *James*, 98, 105; and Weiß, *Soziale Elite*, 315.
98. For a defense of the scene as a discourse about patronage, see Kloppenborg, "Patronage Avoidance"; Batten, "God in the Letter of James"; and Batten, *Friendship and Benefaction*, 122–44.
99. *1 Clem.* 13.1, 38.2; Lampe, *From Paul to Valentinus*, 85–87.
100. Mikat, *Die Bedeutung der Begriffe*, 34–35.
101. Irenaeus, *Haer.* 4.30.1 (ed. Rousseau, Sources chrétiennes 772).
102. Eusebius, *Hist. eccl.* 5.21.1: By the time of Commodus "many at Rome who were highly distinguished for wealth and birth turned with all their household and relatives unto their salvation."
103. CIL 6.8498 = ILCV 3332 = ICUR 6.17246 (Rome, 217 CE, now in the Villa Borghese): "(Dedicated to) M. Aurelius Prosenes, freedman of the Augusti (Marcus Aurelius and Commodus), (in charge) of the bedchamber, procurator of the treasury, procurator of the imperial estates, procurator of the gladiatorial games (*procurator munerum*), procurator of wine, appointed by the Divine Commodus to the camp; most pious patron, his freedmen furnished this sarcophagus at their own expense; well deserved! (on the side): Prosenes, received by God on the 5th of the nones of May, Sa[me in Cephalle]nia (?), In the year that (C. Bruttius) Praesens and (T. Messius) Extricatus (for the second time) were consuls. He was returned to Rome from the expedition (to Parthia). Ampelius his freedman inscribed this."
104. See Lampe, *From Paul to Valentinus*, 333–34.
105. Lampe, *From Paul to Valentinus*, 122–23.
106. Tertullian, *Apol.* 37.4. He also claims that the North African churches include people of "all ranks" (*omnis dignitatis*): *Nat.* 1.1; *Scap.* 5; *Apol.* 1.4.
107. Tertullian, *Scap.* 4.7.
108. Hippolytus, *Ref.* 9.12.24: "For [Callistus] even permitted unmarried women who were noble (*hai en axia*) . . . and yet were unwilling to abandon their own status by being legally married (*dia tou nomimōs gamēthēnai*) that they might have whoever they would choose as a partner, whether a slave or free, and that a woman, though not legally married, might consider such a companion as a husband." See Ulpian on the *Lex Julia et Papia* (quoted in D 1.9.8: "Women married to men of senatorial (*clarissimi*) rank are included in the term *clarissima*. Daughters of senators do not have the rank

of clarissimae unless they are married to men of senatorial rank (*clarissimi*): husbands (*mariti*) convey senatorial dignity to their wives; but parents do so unless they marry plebians: hence, a woman of senatorial rank (*clarissima femina*) will be such only when married to a senator or any honorable (*clarissimus*) man or if she is divorced from such a man and has not married a man of inferior rank." Ulpian on the *Lex Julia et Papia* (D 23.2.44): "nor shall the daughter of a Senator, or a granddaughter by his son, or a great-granddaughter by his grandson marry a freedman, or a man whose father or mother practices, or has practiced the profession of an actor, whether they do so knowingly, or with malicious intent. Nor can any one of these parties knowingly, or with malicious intent become betrothed to, or marry the daughter of a senator."

109. CIL 6.31731 = ILCV 157: *Luria Ianuaria c(larissima) f(emina) | Caelio Felicissimo v(iro) e(gregio) | coniug(i) ka‹r›iss(imo)*, "Luria Ianuaria, a woman of senatorial rank (built this tomb) for Caelius Felicissimus, equestrian, her most beloved spouse." See Eck, "Das Eindringen des Christentums," 290. Since Ianuaria had married an equestrian, the presumption is that in spite of her self-identification as *clarissima*, her marriage reduced her status to equestrian.

110. Tertullian, *Scap.* 3.5: "L. Claudius Herminianus in Cappadocia, enraged that his wife had become a Christian, had treated the Christians with great cruelty."

111. Hippolytus, *Comm. Dan.* 4.18.

112. Cyprian, *Ep.* 80.1 (CSEL 3.2, 839–40): "bishops and presbyters and deacons should immediately be punished; but that senators, and men of distinction (*egregii viri*), and Roman *equites*, should lose their rank (*dignitas*), and moreover be deprived of their property; and if, when their means were taken away, they should persist in being Christians, then they should also be beheaded; but that matrons should be deprived of their property and sent into exile. Moreover, those of Caesar's household (*Caesariani*), whoever of them had either confessed before, or should now confess, should have their property confiscated and should be sent in chains by assignment to Caesar's estates (*vincti in Caesarianas possessiones*)" (my translation).

113. Fla‹v›ia Alexandria (CIL 6.31991 = ICUR 8.21046 = ILCV 172; Rome, III CE); Cassia Faretria (ICUR 4.10879 = ILCV 158; Rome, III or beginning of IV CE), a woman of senatorial rank but married to an equestrian (Eck, Das Eindringen des Christentums, 389); Varia Octabina (CIL 6.28358 = ILCV 224 = ICUR 1.3340, Rome, late III CE), also a *clarissima femina* probably married to a nonsenatorial man (Eck, Das Eindringen des Christentums, 391); Curtia Catiana (AE 1936, 125; Rome): *clarissima puella* (a girl of senatorial rank); Petronia Auxentia (ICUR 4.10085 = ILCV 159; Rome); Pompeia Octabia Attica Caeciliana (ICUR 4.9431 = ILCV 196; Rome): *clarissima puella* who lived only one month, fifteen days; Acilius Glabrio (CIL 6.31680 = ICUR 9.24836 = ILCV 127; Rome).

114. See Nicols, "Tabulae Patronatus."

115. Trümper, "Negotiating Religious and Ethnic Identity," 119.

116. Zuiderhoek, *Politics of Munificence*, 134.

117. Zuiderhoek, *Politics of Munificence*, 133–38. Zuiderhoek (ibid., 108–9, 128) notes a hungry mob attacking Dio Chrysostom's house (*Or.* 46) and I.Eph 1491 (Ephesus, 145 CE), the latter an example of a local *dēmos* being unappreciative of the forms

of benefaction of Vedius Antoninus, who built public buildings rather than funding distributions and theatrical shows and prizes for the games.

118. Garnsey and Saller, *Roman Empire*, 144.
119. On the *Lex Iulia et Papia Poppaea* of 18 BCE (which may not have been enacted until sometime later), see Lefkowitz and Fant, *Women's Life*, nos. 120–23.
120. Jongman, "Golden Age," 192–94. Already in the first century Garnsey and Saller (*Roman Empire*, 123) note that thirty-nine patrician families known between 70 and 117 CE had disappeared by the time of Hadrian, and another seventeen disappeared in the Antonine period.
121. Zuiderhoek, *Politics of Munificence*, 58–59.
122. See Table 6 above.
123. See chap. 6 above on Pompeia Agrippinilla, C. Antius Aulus Iulius Quadratus, C. Flavius Furius Aptus, and Cl. Herodes Atticus, all patrons of Dionysiac groups, and C. Servilius Diodorus, the patron of a group of *dendrophors* (chap. 7 above).
124. Hemelrijk, "Patronesses," Table 1; chap. 6 above: Julia Severa and Claudia Capitolina, patronnesses of two Judean assemblies.
125. CIL 11.6310 (Pisaurum [*Regio* VI], II CE). The female patron, Blassia Vera, is named along with two male patrons, M. Fremedius Severus and P. Seneca Cornelius, and thirty-seven members.
126. Salvia Marcellina (CIL 6.10234) and Ulpia Cynegis (AE 1937, 161; Rome, Catacombe di Pretestato, II CE).
127. Hemelrijk, "Female Munificence," 73, 79.
128. See the age tables in Saller, *Patriarchy, Property*, 48–65.
129. W. A. Johnson, "Toward a Sociology of Reading," 618.
130. W. A. Johnson, "Toward a Sociology of Reading," 623.
131. Museo Archeologico Nazionale di Napoli (inv. no. 9084).
132. Stock, *Implications of Literacy* and *Listening for the Text*. Bremmer, "Social and Religious Capital," 271, 276, and "Why Did Christianity Attract?," 42–43, also treats the Christian privileging of reading and intellectual practices as reasons for the attraction of educated women to Christ groups.
133. See Bagnall, "Jesus Reads a Book."
134. For further discussion on the development of early Christian book culture, see Hurtado, *Earliest Christian Artifacts*; and Kloppenborg, "Literate Media."
135. Stock, *Listening for the Text*, 25–26.
136. Lampe, *From Paul to Valentinus*, 237–40.
137. Hurtado, *Destroyer of the Gods*, 118–19.
138. See also Bazzana, "'Write in a Book What You See,'" for a discussion of the circulation of ancient books among groups of scribes in Egypt.
139. See Hurtado, *Earliest Christian Artifacts*, 224, citing P.Mich II 130, P.Iand I 4, P.Oxy L 3528, and P.Oxy LXIX 4706, all dated late II/early III CE.
140. Pliny, *Ep.* 10.96.6: *Alii . . . esse se Christianos dixerunt et mox negaverunt; fuisse quidem sed desisse, quidam ante triennium, quidam ante plures annos, non nemo etiam ante viginti*, "Others said that they were Christian but then denied it, saying that they had stopped, some three years ago, others many years ago, some even twenty years ago."

141. First Timothy prescribes rules for the designation of a widow as a "true widow" (*hē ontōs chēra*, 5:5), requiring that she be older than sixty years, which, given normal life expectancy, would limit the pool dramatically.
142. CIL 14.2112.18–19: *tu qui novos*(!) *in hoc collegio*(!) | *intrare vole*[*s p*]*rius legem perlege et sic intra ne postmodum queraris.*
143. SEG 31:122.44–45 = GRA I 50 (Liopesi, Attica, ca. 90 CE).
144. See Kloppenborg, "Disaffiliation," and the literature cited there.
145. I owe this suggestion to Harry Maier.
146. AE 1994, 1334 = Piccottini, *Mithrastempel in Virunum.*
147. IDR I 31 (Alburnus Maior).
148. Thus, Mitrofan, "Antonine Plague."
149. Concannon, *Assembling Early Christianity.* Nine letters of Dionysios are preserved by Eusebius, *Hist. eccl.* 4.23.
150. Concannon, *Assembling Early Christianity*, 209–32.

Bibliography

Aasgaard, Reidar. *"My Beloved Brothers and Sister": Christian Siblingship in Paul.* JSNTSup 265. London: T & T Clark International, 2004.
Abbott, Frank F., and Allan Chester Johnson. *Municipal Administration in the Roman Empire.* Princeton: Princeton University Press, 1926.
Achtemeier, Paul J. *1 Peter: A Commentary on First Peter.* Hermeneia. Minneapolis: Fortress, 1996.
Adams, Edward. *The Earliest Christian Meeting Places: Almost Exclusively Houses?* Library of New Testament Studies 450. London: Bloomsbury T & T Clark, 2013.
———. "Placing the Corinthian Communal Meal." Pages 22–37 in *Text, Image, and Christians in the Graeco-Roman World: A Festschrift in Honor of David Lee Balch.* Edited by Aliou Cissé Niang and Carolyn Osiek. PTMS 176. Eugene, Ore.: Pickwick, 2012.
Alföldy, Géza. *The Social History of Rome.* Rev. ed. Translated by David Braund and Frank Pollock. London: Routledge and Kegan Paul; Baltimore: Johns Hopkins University Press, 1988.
Allen, Robert C., Tommy Bengtsson, and Martin Dribe, eds. *Living Standards in the Past: New Perspectives on Well-Being in Asia and Europe.* Oxford: Oxford University Press, 2005.
Allison, Dale C. *A Critical and Exegetical Commentary on the Epistle of James.* ICC. New York: Bloomsbury, 2013.
Alston, Richard. *The City in Roman and Byzantine Egypt.* London: Routledge, 2002.
Alston, Richard, and Robert. D. Alston. "Urbanism and the Urban Community in Roman Egypt." *JEA* 83 (1997): 199–216.
Ameling, Walter, ed. *Inscriptiones Judaicae Orientis II: Kleinasien.* TSAJ 99. Tübingen: Mohr Siebeck, 2004.
———. "Κοινὸν των Ϲιδωνίων." *ZPE* 81 (1990): 189–99.
Andreau, Jean. "Fondations privées et rapports sociaux en Italie romaine." *Ktema* 2 (1977): 157–209.

Aneziri, Sophia. *Die Vereine der dionysischen Techniten im Kontext der hellenistischen Gesellschaft: Untersuchungen zur Geschichte, Organisation und Wirkung der hellenistischen Technitenvereine.* Historia Einzelschriften 163. Stuttgart: Franz Steiner, 2003.

Ansary, Tamim. *West of Kabul, East of New York: An Afghan American Story.* New York: Farrar, Straus and Giroux, 2002.

Arnaoutoglou, Ilias. "Cult Association and Politics: Worshipping Bendis in Classical and Hellenistic Athens." Pages 25–56 in *Private Associations and the Public Sphere.* Edited by Vincent Gabrielsen and Christian A. Thomsen. Scientia Danica. Series H, Humanistic series 8, no. 9. Copenhagen: Royal Danish Academy of Sciences and Letters, 2015.

———. "'Ils étaient dans la ville, mais tout à fait en dehors de la cité': Status and Identity in Private Religious Associations in Hellenistic Athens." Pages 27–48 in *Political Culture in the Greek City After the Classical Age.* Edited by Onno M. van Nijf and Richard Alston. Groningen-Royal Holloway Studies on the Greek City After the Classical Age 2. Leuven: Peeters, 2011.

———. "Roman Law and *Collegia* in Asia Minor." *RIDA* 49 (2002): 27–44.

———. *Thusias heneka kai sunousias: Private Religious Associations in Hellenistic Athens.* Academy of Athens. Yearbook of the Research Centre for the History of Greek Law, Supplement 37/4. Athens: Academy of Athens, 2003.

———. "Were There Craftsmen Associations in the Hellenistic World?" Paper presented at "Status personnels et main-d'oeuvre en Méditerranée hellénistique," March 17–18, 2016, Clermont-Ferrand.

Arnhold, Marlis. "Group Settings and Religious Experiences." Pages 145–65 in *Memory and Religious Experience in the Greco-Roman World.* Edited by Nicola Cusumano, Valentino Gasparini, Attilio Mastrocinque, and Jörg Rüpke. Alte Geschichte Potsdamer altertumswissenschaftliche Beiträge (PAwB) 45. Stuttgart: Steiner, 2013.

Arzt-Grabner, Peter. "Everyday Life in a Roman Town like Colossae: The Papyrological Evidence." Paper presented at the Annual Meeting of the Centro Italiano di Studi Superiori sulle Religioni, September 28–30, 2017, Bertinoro.

———. *2. Korinther.* Papyrologische Kommentare zum Neuen Testament 4. Göttingen: Vandenhoeck & Ruprecht, 2014.

Asad, Talal. *Genealogies of Religion: Discipline and Reasons of Power in Christianity and Islam.* Baltimore: Johns Hopkins University Press, 1993.

———. "Reading a Modern Classic: W. C. Smith's 'The Meaning and End of Religion.'" *HR* 40.3 (2001): 205–22.

Ascough, Richard S. "Benefaction Gone Wrong: The 'Sin' of Ananias and Sapphira in Context." Pages 91–110 in *Text and Artifact: Religions in Mediterranean Antiquity. Essays in Honour of Peter Richardson.* Edited by Stephen G. Wilson and Michel Desjardins. Studies in Christianity and Judaism 9. Waterloo, Ont.: Wilfrid Laurier University Press, 2000.

———. "The Completion of a Religious Duty: The Background of 2 Cor 8:1–15." *NTS* 42.4 (1996): 584–99.

———. *Lydia: Paul's Cosmopolitan Hostess.* Paul's Social Network: Brothers and Sisters in Faith. Collegeville, Minn.: Liturgical Press, 2009.

——. "Methodological Reflections on Synagogues and Christ Groups as 'Associations': A Response to Erich Gruen." *JJMJS* 4 (2017): 118–26.
——. "Paul, Synagogues, and Associations: Reframing the Question of Models for Pauline Christ Groups." *JJMJS* 2 (2015): 27–52.
——. *Paul's Macedonian Associations: The Social Context of Philippians and 1 Thessalonians.* WUNT 2/161. Tübingen: Mohr Siebeck, 2003.
——. "A Question of Death: Paul's Community-Building Language in 1 Thessalonians 4:13–18." *JBL* 123.3 (2004): 509–35.
——. "Re-Describing the Thessalonians' 'Mission' in Light of Greco-Roman Associations." *NTS* 60.1 (2014): 61–82.
——. "The Thessalonian Christian Community as a Professional Voluntary Association." *JBL* 119.2 (2000): 311–28.
Ausbüttel, Frank M. *Untersuchungen zu den Vereinen im Westen des römischen Reiches.* Frankfurter Althistorische Studien 11. Kallmünz: Michael Laßleben, 1982.
Bagnall, Roger S. "The Effects of Plague: Model and Evidence." *JRA* 15 (2002): 114–20.
——. "Jesus Reads a Book." *JTS* 51.2 (2000): 577–88.
——. "Landholding in Late Roman Egypt: The Distribution of Wealth." *JRS* 82 (1992): 128–49.
——. "Religious Conversion and Onomastic Change." *BASP* 19.3–4 (1982): 105–24.
Bagnall, Roger S., and Bruce W. Frier. *The Demography of Roman Egypt.* Cambridge Studies in Population, Economy, and Society in Past Time 23. Cambridge: Cambridge University Press, 1994.
Bakker, Jan Theo. *Living and Working with the Gods: Studies of Evidence for Private Religion and Its Material Environment in the City of Ostia (100–500 AD).* Dutch Monographs on Ancient History and Archaeology 12. Amsterdam: J. C. Gieben, 1994.
Balch, David L. "The Church Sitting in a Garden (1 Cor 14:30; Rom 16:23; Mark 6:39–40; 8:60 John 6:3, 10; Acts 1:15; 2:1–2)." Pages 311–43 in David L. Balch, *Contested Ethnicities and Images: Studies in Acts and Art.* WUNT 345. Tübingen: Mohr Siebeck, 2015.
——. *Contested Ethnicities and Images: Studies in Acts and Art.* WUNT 345. Tübingen: Mohr Siebeck, 2015.
——. "Hellenization/Acculturation in 1 Peter." Pages 79–101 in *Perspectives on First Peter.* Edited by Charles H. Talbert. National Association of Baptist Professors of Religion. Special Studies Series No. 9. Macon, Ga.: Mercer University Press, 1986.
——. *Let Wives Be Submissive: The Domestic Code in 1 Peter.* SBLMS 26. Chico, Calif.: Scholars Press, 1981.
——. *Roman Domestic Art and Early House Churches.* WUNT 228. Tübingen: Mohr Siebeck, 2008.
Bang, Peter Fibiger. *The Roman Bazaar: A Comparative Study of Trade and Markets in a Tributary Empire.* Cambridge Classical Studies. Cambridge: Cambridge University Press, 2008.
Barclay, John M. D. "Money and Meetings: Group Formation Among Diaspora Jews and Early Christians." Pages 113–28 in *Vereine, Synagogen und Gemeinden im kairserzeitlichen Kleinasiens.* Edited by Andreas Gutsfeld and Dietrich-Alex Koch. STAC 25. Tübingen: Mohr Siebeck, 2006.

Barnes, Timothy D. *Constantine and Eusebius*. Cambridge, Mass.: Harvard University Press, 1981.

———. "Legislation Against the Christians." *JRS* 58 (1968): 32–50.

———. "Statistics and the Conversion of the Roman Aristocracy." *JRS* 85 (1995): 135–47.

Barrett, C. K. *A Commentary of the First Epistle to the Corinthians*. 2nd ed. London: A & C Black; New York: Harper and Row, 1968.

———. *A Commentary on the Epistle to the Romans*. London: A. & C. Black, 1962.

Barton, Carlin A., and Daniel Boyarin. *Imagine No Religion: How Modern Abstractions Hide Ancient Realities*. New York: Fordham University Press, 2016.

Barton, Stephen, and G. H. R. Horsley. "A Hellenistic Cult Group and the New Testament Churches." *JAC* 24 (1981): 7–41.

Baslez, Marie-Françoise. "Les associations à Délos: depuis les débuts de l'indépendance (fin du IVe siècle) à la periode de la colonie athénienne (milieu du IIe siècle)." Pages 227–49 in *Groupes et associations dans les cités grecques (IIIe siècle av. J.-C.–IIe siècle ap. J.-C.)*. Edited by Pierre Frölich and Patrice Hamon. Hautes études du monde gréco-romain 49. Geneva: Librairie Droz, 2013.

———. "Les communautés d'orientaux dans la cité grecque: formes de sociabilité et modèles associatifs." Pages 139–58 in *L'étranger dans le monde grec*. Edited by Raoul Lonis. Travaux et Mémoires. Études anciennes 4. Nancy: Presses Universitaires de Nancy, 1988.

———. "Entre traditions nationales et intégration: les associations sémitiques du monde grec." Pages 235–47 in *La questione delle influenze vicino-orientali sulla religione greca: Stato degli studi e prospettive della ricerca*. Edited by Sergio Ribichini, Maria Rocchi, and Paulo Xella. Monografie Scientifiche. Serie Scienze Umane e Sociali. Rome: Consiglio nazionale delle ricerche, 2001.

———. "Place et rôle des associations dans la cité d'Athènes au IVe siècle." Pages 281–92 in *Le IVe siècle av. J.-C.: Approches historiographiques*. Edited by Pierre Carlier. Études anciennes 15. Paris: Éditions de Boccard, 1996.

Bastianini, Guido, and Claudio Gallazzi. "Un'iscrizione inedita di Tebtynis e la synodos di Doryphorus." *ZPE* 89 (1991): 44–46.

Batten, Alicia. *Friendship and Benefaction in James*. Emory Studies in Early Christianity 15. Blandford Forum, Dorset, UK: Deo Publishing, 2010.

———. "God in the Letter of James: Patron or Benefactor?" *NTS* 50.2 (2004): 257–72.

———. "The Moral World of Greco-Roman Associations." *SR* 36.1 (2007): 135–51.

Baumgarten, Albert I. "Graeco-Roman Voluntary Associations and Ancient Jewish Sects." Pages 93–111 in *Jews in a Graeco-Roman World*. Edited by Martin Goodman. Oxford: Clarendon, 1998.

Bazzana, Giovanni Battista. "'Write in a Book What You See and Send It to the Seven Assemblies': Ancient Reading Practices and the Earliest Papyri of Revelation." Pages 11–32 in *Book of Seven Seals: The Peculiarity of Revelation, Its Manuscripts, Attestation, and Transmission*. Edited by Thomas Kraus. WUNT 363. Tübingen: Mohr Siebeck, 2016.

Beale, G. K. "The Background of ἐκκλησια Revisited." *JSNT* 38.2 (2015): 151–68.

Becatti, Giovanni. *Mosaici e pavimenti marmorei*. Scavi di Ostia 4. Rome: Libreria dello Stato, 1961.

Bechtler, Steven Richard. *Following in His Steps: Suffering, Community, and Christology in 1 Peter.* SBLDS 162. Atlanta: Scholars Press, 1998.

Beck, Roger. "The Mysteries of Mithras: A New Account of Their Genesis." *JRS* 88 (1998): 115–28.

———. "On Becoming a Mithraist: New Evidence for the Propagation of the Mysteries." Pages 175–94 in *Religious Rivalries in the Early Roman Empire and the Rise of Christianity.* Edited by Leif E. Vaage. Studies in Christianity and Judaism 18. Waterloo, Ont.: Wilfrid Laurier University Press, 2006.

———. "'Qui Mortalitatis Causa Convenerunt': The Meeting of the Virunum Mithraists on June 26, A.D. 184." *Phoenix* 52.3/4 (1984): 335–44.

———. "Ritual, Myth, Doctrine and Initiation in the Mysteries of Mithras: New Evidence from a Cult Vessel." *JRS* 90 (2000): 145–80.

Behr, Charles A., ed. and trans. *P. Aelius Aristides: The Complete Works. Vol. 1: Orations 1–16 with an Appendix Containing the Fragments and Inscriptions; Vol. 2: Orations 17–53.* Leiden: Brill, 1981–1986.

Bell, Catherine. *Ritual: Perspectives and Dimensions.* New York: Oxford University Press, 2009.

Beloch, Julius. *Die Bevölkerung der griechisch-römischen Welt.* Leipzig: Duncker & Humblot, 1886.

Ben Zeev, Miriam Pucci. *Jewish Rights in the Roman World.* TSAJ 74. Tübingen: J. C. B. Mohr (Paul Siebeck), 1998.

Bendlin, Andreas. "Associations, Funerals, Sociality, and Roman Law: The *Collegium* of Diana and Antinous in Lanuvium (CIL 14.2112) Reconsidered." Pages 207–96 in *Aposteldekret und antikes Vereinswesen.* Edited by Markus Öhler. WUNT 280. Tübingen: Mohr Siebeck, 2011.

———. "Gemeinschaft, Öffentlichkeit und Identität: Forschungsgeschichtliche Anmerkungen zu den Mustern sozialer Ordnung in Rom." Pages 9–40 in *Religiöse Vereine in der römischen Antike: Untersuchungen zu Organisation, Ritual und Raumordnung.* Edited by Ulrike Egelhaaf-Gaiser and Alfred Schäfer. Tübingen: Mohr Siebeck, 2002.

———. "Looking Beyond the Civic Compromise: Religious Pluralism in Late Republican Rome." Pages 115–35, 167–71 in *Religion in Archaic and Republican Rome and Italy: Evidence and Experience.* Edited by Edward Bispham and Christopher Smith. Edinburgh: Edinburgh University Press, 2000.

Benton, Michael J. "Studying Function and Behavior in the Fossil Record." *PLoS Biology* 8.3 (2010): e1000321; https://doi.org/10.1371/journal.pbio.1000321.

Béquignon, Yves. "Études Thessaliennes: VII. Inscriptions de Thessalie." *BCH* 59 (1935): 36–77.

Bérard, Victor. "Inscriptions de Téménothyrae." *BCH* 19 (1895): 555–60.

Betz, Hans Dieter. *2 Corinthians 8 and 9: A Commentary on Two Administrative Letters of the Apostle Paul.* Hermeneia. Philadelphia: Fortress, 1985.

Birley, Anthony R. *Hadrian: The Restless Emperor.* London: Routledge, 1997.

Bizard, L., and Pierre Roussel. "Fouilles de Délos, exécutées aux frais de M. le Duc de Loubat (1904). Inscriptions (suite)." *BCH* 31 (1907): 421–70.

Blumell, Lincoln. *Lettered Christians: Christians, Letters, and Late Antique Oxyrhynchus.* New Testament Tools, Studies and Documents 39. Leiden: Brill, 2012.

Boak, Arthur E. R. *Manpower Shortage and the Fall of the Roman Empire in the West.* Ann Arbor: University of Michigan Press, 1955.

Board of Cultural Heritage of Pompeii. *A Guide to the Pompeii Excavations.* [Naples]: Board of Cultural Heritage of Pompeii, 2015.

Bodel, John. "From *Columbaria* to Catacombs: Collective Burial in Pagan and Christian Rome." Pages 177–242 in *Commemorating the Dead: Texts and Artifacts in Context. Studies of Roman, Jewish, and Christian Burial.* Ed. Laurie Brink and Deborah A. Green. Berlin: de Gruyter, 2008.

———. "The Organization of the Funerary Trade at Puteoli and Cumae." Pages 147–72 in *Libitina e dintorni: Libitina e i luci sepolcrali: Le leges libitinariae campane, lura sepulcrorum: vecchie e nuove iscrizioni.* Stuttgart: Franz Steiner, 2014.

Bollmann, Beate. *Römische Vereinshäuser: Untersuchungen zu den Scholae der römischen Berufs-, Kult- und Augustalen-Kollegien in Italien.* Mainz: Philipp von Zabern, 1998.

Bömer, Franz. *Untersuchungen über die Religion der Sklaven in Griechenland und Rom.* Akademie der Wissenschaften und der Literatur. Abhandlungen der Geistes- und Sozialwissenschaftlichen Klasse, Jahrg. 1957, Nr. 7, Jahrg. 1960, Nr. 1, Jahrg. 1961, Nr. 4, Jahrg. 1963, Nr. 10. Mainz: Akademie der Wissenschaften und der Literatur, 1958–1963.

Borgeaud, Philippe. *La Mère des dieux: de Cybèle à la Vierge Marie.* Librairie du XXe siècle. Paris: Seuil, 1996.

Boteva, Dilyana. "On the Cursus Honorum of P. Fu. Pontianus (PIR^2 F 496), Provincial Governor of Lower Moesia." *ZPE* 110 (1996): 248–52.

Bourdieu, Pierre. "The Economy of Symbolic Goods." Pages 92–126 in *Practical Reason: On the Theory of Action.* Cambridge: Polity; Stanford, Calif.: Stanford University Press, 1998.

———. "The Forms of Capital." Pages 241–58 in *Handbook of Theory and Research for the Sociology of Education.* Edited by J. Richardson. New York: Greenwood, 1986.

Bourdieu, Pierre, and Loïc J. D. Wacquant. *An Invitation to Reflexive Sociology.* Chicago: University of Chicago Press, 1992.

Bowman, Alan K. "Landholding in the Hermopolite Nome in the Fourth Century A.D." *JRS* 75 (1985): 137–63.

Bowman, Alan, and Andrew Wilson. "Quantifying the Roman Economy: Integration, Growth, Decline?" Pages 3–84 in *Quantifying the Roman Economy: Methods and Problems.* Edited by Alan Bowman and Andrew Wilson. Oxford: Oxford University Press, 2009.

Bradshaw, Paul F., Maxwell E. Johnson, and L. Edward Phillips. *The Apostolic Tradition: A Commentary.* Hermeneia. Minneapolis: Fortress, 2002.

Braune, Sarah. *Convivium funebre: Gestaltung und Funktion römischer Grabtriklinien als Räume für sepulkrale Bankettfeiern.* Spudasmata 121. Hildesheim: Olms, 2008.

Bremmer, Jan N. *Initiation into the Mysteries of the Ancient World.* Münchner Vorlesungen zu antiken Welten 2. Berlin: de Gruyter, 2014.

———. "The Social and Religious Capital of the Early Christians." Pages 269–78 in *Zwischen Kult und Gesellschaft: Kosmopolitische Zentren des antiken Mittelmeerraumes als*

Aktionsraum von Kultvereinen und Religionsgemeinschaften Religionsgemeinschaften. Edited by Inge Nielsen. Hephaistos 24. Augsburg: Camelion, 2006.

———. "Why Did Christianity Attract Upper-Class Women?" Pages 37–47 in *Fructus centesimus: Mélanges offerts à Gerard J. M. Bartelink à l'occasion de son soixante-cinquieme anniversaire.* Edited by A. A. R. Bastiaensen, A. Hilhorst, and C. H. Kneepkens. Instrumenta Patristica 19. Steenbrugge: Kluwer, 1989.

Brennan, Geoffrey, and Philip Pettit. *The Economy of Esteem: An Essay on Civil and Political Society.* Oxford: Oxford University Press, 2004.

Bricault, Laurent. *Recueil des inscriptions concernant les cultes isaiques (RICIS).* Mémoires de l'académie des inscriptions et belles-lettres 31. Paris: Éditions de Boccard, 2005.

Broekaert, Wim. "Partners in Business: Roman Merchants and the Potential Advantages of Being a *collegiatus.*" *Ancient Society* 41 (2011): 221–56.

Brookins, Timothy A. "The (In)Frequency of the Name 'Erastus' in Antiquity: A Literary, Papyrological, and Epigraphical Catalog." *NTS* 59.4 (2013): 496–516.

———. "The Supposed Election of Officers in 1 Cor 11.19: A Response to Richard Last." *NTS* 60.3 (2014): 423–32.

Brown, Peter. *Poverty and Leadership in the Later Roman Empire.* Hanover, N.H.: University Press of New England, 2002.

———. *Through the Eye of a Needle: Wealth, the Fall of Rome, and the Making of Christianity in the West,* 350–550 AD. Princeton: Princeton University Press, 2012.

Bruneau, Philippe, and Jean Ducat. *Guide de Délos.* Sites et Monuments 1. Paris: Éditions de Boccard, 1983.

Brunt, P. A. *Italian Manpower, 255 B.C.–A.D. 14.* Rev. ed. Oxford: Clarendon, 1987.

Bruun, Christer. "The Name and Possessions of Nero's Freedman Phaon." *Arctos* 23 (1989): 41–53.

———. "True Patriots? The Public Activities of the Augustales of Roman Ostia and the Summa Honoraria." *Arctos: Acta Philologica Fennica* 48 (2014): 67–91.

Bryant, Joseph M. "Review of *The Rise of Christianity: A Sociologist Reconsiders History,* by Rodney Stark." *Sociology of Religion* 58.2 (1997): 191–95.

Buckler, William H. "Labour Disputes in the Province of Asia." Pages 27–50 in *Anatolian Studies, Presented to Sir William Mitchell Ramsay.* Edited by William H. Buckler and William M. Calder. Manchester: Manchester University Press, 1923.

Budin, Stephanie L. "A Reconsideration of the Aphrodite-Ashtart Syncretism." *Numen* 51.2 (2004): 95–145.

Buongiorno, Pierangelo. "Senatus consulta: struttura, formulazioni linguistiche, tecniche (189 a.C.–138 d.C.)." *Annali del Seminario Giuridico della Università di Palermo* 59 (2016): 17–60.

Buonocore, Marco. "L'album e la lex della familia Silvani di Trebula Mutuesca. Nuove considerazioni." *Rendiconti della Pontificia Accademia Romana di Archeologia* 75 (2002–2003): 327–94.

Buonocore, Marco, and Olivero Diliberto. "Approfondimenti sull'album e la Lex Familiae Silvani da Trebula Mutuesca." *Minima Epigraphica et Papyrologica* 11 (2006): 211–54.

Burrell, Barbara. *Neokoroi: Greek Cities and Roman Emperors.* Cincinnati Classical Studies 9. Leiden: Brill, 2004.

Burt, Ronald S. *Brokerage and Closure: An Introduction to Social Capital.* Clarendon Lectures in Management Studies Series. Oxford: Oxford University Press, 2005.

Bury, John B. *History of the Later Roman Empire: From the Death of Theodosius I to the Death of Justinian.* New York: Dover, 1958.

Caillet, Jean-Pierre. *L'évergétisme monumental chrétien en Italie et à ses marges: d'après l'épigraphie des pavements de mosaïque (IVe–VIIe s.).* Collection de l'École française de Rome 175. Rome: École française de Rome, 1993.

Calza, Guido. *La necropoli del Porto di Roma nell'Isola Sacra.* Rome: Libreria dello stato, 1940.

Camodeca, Giuseppe, and Pierangelo Buongiorno. "I senatus consulta nella documentazione epigrafica dall'Italia." Paper presented at the seminar "Die Senatus consulta in den epigraphischen, papyrologischen und numismatischen Quellen: Texte und Bezeugungen," Westfälische Wilhelms-Universität, Münster, 2016.

Campbell, Douglas A. "Possible Inscriptional Attestation to Sergius Paul[l]us (Acts 13:6–12), and the Implications for Pauline Chronology." *JTS* 56.1 (2005): 1–29.

Caragounis, Chrys C. "A House Church in Corinth? An Inquiry into the Structure of Early Corinthian Christianity." Pages 1:365–418 in *Saint Paul and Corinth: International Scientific Conference Proceedings, Corinth 23–25 September 2007.* Edited by Constantine J. Belezos. Athens: Psichogios, 2009.

Cecchet, Lucia. "Gift-Giving to the Poor in the Greek World." Pages 157–79 in *Gift-Giving and the "Embedded" Economy in the Ancient World.* Edited by Filippo Carlà and Maja Gori. Akademiekonferenzen (Heidelberger Akademie der Wissenschaften) 17. Heidelberg: Universitätsverlag Winter, 2014.

Chaniotis, Angelos. "Emotional Community Through Ritual: Initiates, Citizens, and Pilgrims as Emotional Communities in the Greek World." Pages 263–90 in *Ritual Dynamics in the Ancient Mediterranean: Agency, Emotion, Gender, Representation.* Edited by Angelos Chaniotis. Heidelberger Althistorische Beiträge und Epigraphische Studien (HABES) 49. Stuttgart: Franz Steiner, 2011.

———. "Public Subscriptions and Loans as Social Capital in the Hellenistic City: Reciprocity, Performance, Commemoration." Pages 89–106 in *Epigraphical Approaches to the Postclassical Polis: Fourth Century BC to Second Century AD.* Edited by Paraskevi Martzavou and Nikolaos Papazarkadas. Oxford Studies in Ancient Documents. Oxford: Oxford University Press, 2013.

———. "Rituals Between Norms and Emotions: Rituals as Shared Experience and Memory." Pages 211–38 in *Ritual and Communication in the Graeco-Roman World.* Edited by Eftychia Stavrianopoulou. Kernos. Supplément 16. Liège: Centre international d'étude de la religion grecque antique, 2006.

Choat, Malcolm. "The City in Roman Egypt: The Evidence of the Papyri." Pages 67–88 in *The First Urban Churches 1: Methodological Foundations.* Edited by James R. Harrison and Larry L. Welborn. Society of Biblical Literature Writings from the Greco-Roman World Supplement Series 7. Atlanta: Society of Biblical Literature, 2015.

Christol, Michel, and Thomas Drew-Bear. "Les Sergii Pauli en Antioche." Pages 178–91 in *Actes du Ier Congrès international sur Antioche de Pisidie.* Edited by Thomas Drew-Bear,

Mehmet Taşlıalan, and Christine M. Thomas. Collection de l'Institut d'archéologie et d'histoire de l'antiquité 5. Lyon: Université Lumière-Lyon 2, 2002.

Christol, Michel, and Michèle Fruyt. "Neptune: étude épigraphique." Pages 104–9 in *César: Le Rhône pour mémoire: vingt ans de fouilles archéologiques dans le fleuve à Arles*. Edited by Luc Long and Pascale Picard. Arles: Musée départemental Arles antique, 2009.

Cianca, Jenn. *Sacred Ritual, Profane Space: The Roman House as Early Christian Meeting Place*. Studies in Christianity and Judaism Series. Montreal: McGill Queen's University Press, 2018.

Clark, Colin, and M. Haswell. *The Economics of Subsistence Agriculture*. 4th ed. London: Macmillan; New York: St. Martin's, 1970.

Clarke, Andrew D. "Another Corinthian Erastus Inscription." *TynBul* 42.1 (1991): 146–51.

Clauss, Manfred. *Cultores Mithrae: Die Anhängerschaft des Mithras-Kultes*. Heidelberger Althistorische Beiträge und Epigraphische Studien 10. Stuttgart: Steiner, 1992.

Clayton, Philip. "Conceptual Foundations of Emergence Theory." Pages 1–31 in *The Re-Emergence of Emergence: The Emergentist Hypothesis from Science to Religion*. Philip Clayton and Paul Davies. New York: Oxford University Press, 2008.

Coleman, James S. "Social Capital in the Creation of Human Capital." *American Journal of Sociology* 94. Supplement: Organizations and Institutions: Sociological and Economic Approaches to the Analysis of Social Structure (1988): S95–S120.

Collar, Anna. "Commagene, Communication and the Cult of Jupiter Dolichenus." Pages 99–109 in *Iuppiter Dolichenus: vom Lokalkult zur Reichsreligion*. Edited by Michael Blömer and Winter Engelbert. Orientalische Religionen in der Antike 8. Tübingen: Mohr Siebeck, 2012.

Collins, Adela Yarbro. "The Function of 'Excommunication' in Paul." *HTR* 73.1/2 (1980): 251–63.

Comaroff, Jean. *Body of Power, Spirit of Resistance: The Culture and History of a South African People*. Chicago: University of Chicago Press, 1985.

Concannon, Cavan W. *Assembling Early Christianity: Trade, Networks, and the Letters of Dionysios of Corinth*. Cambridge: Cambridge University Press, 2017.

———. "Early Christian Connectivity and Ecclesial Assemblages in Ignatius of Antioch." Pages 65–89 in *Across the Corrupting Sea: Post-Braudelian Approaches to the Ancient Eastern Mediterranean*. Edited by Cavan Concannon and Lindsey A. Mazurek. London: Routledge, 2016.

Conison, Alexander. "The Organization of Rome's Wine Trade." PhD diss., University of Michigan, 2012.

Connor, Andrew James. "Temples as Economic Agents in Early Roman Egypt: The Case of Tebtunis and Soknopaiou Nesos." PhD diss., University of Cincinnati, 2014.

Conzelmann, Hans. *1 Corinthians: A Commentary on the First Epistle to the Corinthians*. Hermeneia. Philadelphia: Fortress, 1975.

Cornthwaite, Christopher. "The Movement and Transmission of 'Diaspora' and 'Religion' on the Graeco-Roman Mediterranean." PhD diss., University of Toronto, 2018.

Countryman, L. William. "Patrons and Officers in Club and Church." Pages 135–43 in *Society of Biblical Literature 1977 Seminar Papers*. Edited by Paul J. Achtemeier. SBLSP 11. Missoula, Mont.: Scholars Press, 1977.

———. *The Rich Christian in the Church of the Early Empire: Contradictions and Accommodations.* Lewiston, N.Y.: Edwin Mellen, 1980.

Coutsoumpos, Panayotis. *Paul and the Lord's Supper: A Socio-Historical Investigation.* Studies in Biblical Literature 84. Frankfurt: Peter Lang, 2005.

Cracco Ruggini, Lellia. "From Pagan to Christian Euergetism." Pages 203–12 in *Gift-Giving and the "Embedded" Economy in the Ancient World.* Edited by Filippo Carlà and Maja Gori. Akademiekonferenzen (Heidelberger Akademie der Wissenschaften) 17. Heidelberg: Universitätsverlag Winter, 2014.

———. "Stato e associazioni professionali nell'età imperiale romana." Pages 271–311 in *Akten des VI. Internationalen Kongresses für Griechische und Lateinische Epigraphik, München* 1972. Munich: Beck, 1973.

Cragun, Ryan T., and Ronald Lawson. "The Secular Transition: The Worldwide Growth of Mormons, Jehovah's Witnesses, and Seventh-Day Adventists." *Sociology of Religion* 71.3 (2010): 349–73.

Crook, Zeba A. "BTB Readers Guide: Loyalty." *BTB* 34.4 (2004): 167–77.

———. *Reconceptualising Conversion: Patronage, Loyalty, and Conversion in the Religions of the Ancient Mediterranean.* BZNW 130. Berlin: de Gruyter, 2004.

Cumont, Franz. *The Oriental Religions in Roman Paganism.* Chicago: Open Court, 1911.

Daniels, C. M. "The Role of the Roman Army in the Spread of Mithraism." Pages 2:249–74 in *Mithraic Studies.* 2 vols. Edited by J. R. Hinnells. Manchester: Manchester University Press, 1975.

D'Arms, John H. "The Roman *Convivium* and the Idea of Equality." Pages 308–20 in *Sympotica: A Symposium on the Symposion.* Edited by Oswyn Murray. Oxford: Clarendon; New York: Oxford University Press, 1990.

de Cenival, Françoise. "Comptes d'une association religieuse Thébaine datant des années 29 à 33 du roi Amasis (P. Démot. Louvre E 7840 Bis)." *Revue d'Égyptologie* 37 (1986): 13–29.

———. "Papyrus Seymour de Ricci: Le plus ancien des règlements d'association religieuse (4ème siècle av. J.-C.) (Pap. Bibl. Nationale E 241)." *Revue d'Égyptologie* 39 (1988): 37–46.

de Ste. Croix, G. E. M. *The Class Struggle in the Ancient Greek World.* London: Duckworth; Ithaca, N.Y.: Cornell University Press, 1981.

———. "Why Were the Early Christians Persecuted? A Rejoinder." *P&P* 27 (1964): 28–33.

de Vos, Craig Steven. *Church and Community Conflicts: The Relationships of the Thessalonian, Corinthian, and Philippian Churches with Their Wider Civic Communities.* SBLDS 168. Atlanta: Scholars Press, 1999.

DeFelice, J. "Inns and Taverns." Pages 474–86 in *The World of Pompeii.* John J. Dobbins and Pedar W. Foss. London: Routledge, 2007.

Deissmann, Adolf. *Bible Studies.* Translated by Alexander Grieve. Edinburgh: T & T Clark, 1901.

———. *Das Urchristentum und die unteren Schichten.* Göttingen: Vandenhoeck & Ruprecht, 1908.

———. *Licht vom Osten: Das Neue Testament und die neuentdeckten Texte der hellenistisch-romischen Welt.* Tübingen: Mohr Siebeck, 1908.

———. *Light from the Ancient East: The New Testament Illustrated by Recently Discovered Texts of the Graeco-Roman World.* Translated by Lionel R. Strachan. New York: Harper and Brothers, 1927.

———. *Paul: A Study in Social and Religious History.* Translated by Lionel R. Strachan. New York: Hodder & Stoughton, 1912.

———. "Primitive Christianity and the Lower Classes." *Expositor* 7, 7th ser. (1909): 97–110, 208–24, 352–57.

DeLaine, Janet. "Building the Eternal City: The Construction Industry of Imperial Rome." Pages 119–41 in *Ancient Rome: The Archaeology of the Eternal City.* Edited by Jon Coulston and Hazel Dodge. Oxford University School of Archaeology Monograph 54. Oxford: Oxford University School of Archaeology, 2000.

DeMaris, Richard E. *The New Testament in Its Ritual World.* London: Routledge, 2008.

Demetriou, Denise. *Negotiating Identity in the Ancient Mediterranean: The Archaic and Classical Greek Multiethnic Emporia.* Cambridge: Cambridge University Press, 2012.

Dibelius, Martin. *Der Hirt des Hermas.* Handbuch zum Neuen Testament, Ergänzungsband: Die apostolischen Väter 4. Tübingen: Mohr Siebeck, 1923.

Dittmann-Schöne, Imogen. *Die Berufsvereine in den Städten des kaiserzeitlichen Kleinasiens.* Theorie und Forschung 690. Geschichte 10. Regensburg: Roderer, 2001.

Dodds, E. R. *The Greeks and the Irrational.* Sather Classical Lectures 25. Berkeley: University of California Press, 1951.

Donahue, John F. *The Roman Community at Table During the Principate.* New and expanded ed. Ann Arbor: University of Michigan Press, 2017.

———. "Toward a Typology of Roman Public Feasting." *AJPh* 124.3 [485] (2003): 423–41.

Dorcey, Peter F. *The Cult of Silvanus: A Study in Roman Folk Religion.* Columbia Studies in the Classical Tradition 20. Leiden: Brill, 1992.

Dover, K. J. *Greek Popular Morality in the Time of Plato and Aristotle.* Oxford: Basil Blackwell, 1974.

Downs, David J. *The Offering of the Gentiles: Paul's Collection for Jerusalem in Its Chronological, Cultural, and Cultic Contexts.* WUNT 2/248. Tübingen: Mohr Siebeck, 2008.

Drexhage, Hans-Joachim. *Preise, Mieten/Pachten, Kosten und Löhne im römischen Ägypten bis zum Regierungsantritt Diokletians.* Vorarbeiten zu einer Wirtschaftsgeschichte des römischen Ägypten 1. St. Katharinen: Scripta Mercaturae, 1991.

Dubuisson, Daniel. *The Western Construction of Religion: Myths, Knowledge, and Ideology.* Translated by William Sayers. Baltimore: Johns Hopkins University Press, 2003.

Duinker, Heleen Ellen. "Buried in Collectivity: The Social Context of the Early Imperial Roman Columbaria." MA thesis, University of Groningen, 2015.

Dunbabin, Katherine M. D. *The Roman Banquet: Images of Conviviality.* New York: Cambridge University Press, 2004.

Duncan-Jones, Richard P. *The Economy of the Roman Empire: Quantitative Studies.* 2nd ed. Cambridge: Cambridge University Press, 1982.

———. "The Impact of the Antonine Plague." *JRA* 9 (1996): 108–36.

———. "The Price of Wheat in Roman Egypt Under the Principate." *Chiron* 6 (1976): 241–62.

———. *The Structure and Scale of the Roman Economy.* Cambridge: Cambridge University Press, 1990.

Dunning, Benjamin H. *Aliens and Sojourners: Self as Other in Early Christianity.* Divinations: Rereading Late Ancient Religion. Philadelphia: University of Pennsylvania Press, 2009.

———. "Strangers and Aliens No Longer: Negotiating Identity and Difference in Ephesians 2." *HTR* 99.1 (2006): 1–16.

Ebel, Eva. *Die Attraktivität früher christlicher Gemeinden: Die Gemeinde von Korinth im Spiegel griechisch-römischer Vereine.* WUNT 2/178. Tübingen: Mohr Siebeck, 2004.

Ebner, Martin. *Die Stadt als Lebensraum der ersten Christen.* Das Urchristentum in seiner Umwelt. Das Neue Testament Deutsche—Ergänzungsreihe 1. Göttingen: Vandenhoeck & Ruprecht, 2012.

Eck, Werner. "Das Eindringen des Christentums in den Senatorenstand bis zu Konstantin d. Gr." *Chiron* 1 (1971): 381–406.

Eckhardt, Benedikt. "The Eighteen Associations of Corinth." *GRBS* 56 (2016): 646–62.

———. "Who Thought That Early Christians Formed Associations?" *Mnemosyne* 70.4 (2017): 298–314.

Edgar, C. C. "Records of a Village Club." Pages 369–76 in *Raccolta di scritti in onore di Giacomo Lumbroso (1844–1925).* Pubblicazioni di "Aegyptus." Serie scientifica 3. Milan: Aegyptus, 1925.

Edmonson, Jonathan. "Slavery and the Roman Family." Pages 337–61 in *The Cambridge World History of Slavery. Vol. 1: The Ancient Mediterranean World.* Edited by Keith Bradley and Paul Cartledge. Cambridge: Cambridge University Press, 2011.

Elliott, John H. *1 Peter.* Anchor Yale Bible 37B. New Haven: Yale University Press, 2000.

———. *A Home for the Homeless: A Sociological Exegesis of 1 Peter, Its Situation and Strategy.* Philadelphia: Fortress, 1981.

Ellis-Evans, Aneurin. "The Ideology of Public Subscriptions." Pages 107–25 in *Epigraphical Approaches to the Postclassical Polis: Fourth Century BC to Second Century AD.* Edited by Paraskevi Martzavou and Nikolaos Papazarkadas. Oxford Studies in Ancient Documents. Oxford: Oxford University Press, 2013.

Engels, Donald W. *Roman Corinth: An Alternative Model for the Classical City.* Chicago: University of Chicago Press, 1990.

Erdkamp, Paul. "Grain Funds and Market Intervention in the Roman World." Pages 109–25 in *Feeding the Ancient Greek City.* Edited by Richard Alston and Onno Van Nijf. Groningen-Royal Holloway Studies on the Greek City After the Classical Age 1. Leuven: Peeters, 2008.

Evans, Elizabeth C. *The Cults of the Sabine Territory.* Papers and Monographs of the American Academy in Rome 11. Rome: American Academy in Rome, 1939.

Evans, Sara M., and Harry C. Boyte. *Free Spaces: The Sources of Democratic Change in America: With a New Introduction.* 2nd ed. Chicago: University of Chicago, 1992.

Evers, Kasper Grønlund. *Worlds Apart Trading Together: The Organisation of Long-Distance Trade Between Rome and India in Antiquity.* Archaeopress Roman Archaeology 32. Oxford: Archaeopress, 2017.

Feldmeier, Reinhard. *Die Christen als Fremde: die Metapher der Fremde in der antiken Welt, im Urchristentum und im 1. Petrusbrief.* WUNT 2/64. Tübingen: Mohr Siebeck, 1992.

Fellmeth, Ulrich. "Politische Bewußtsein in den Vereinen der städtlichen Massen in Rom und Italien zur Zeit der Republik und der frühen Kaiserzeit." *Eirene: Studia Graeca et Latina* 27 (1990): 49–71.

———. "Die römischen Vereine und die Politik: Untersuchungen zur sozialen Schichtung und zum politischen Bewußtsein in den Vereinen der städtischen Volksmassen in Rom und Italien." Diss., University of Stuttgart, 1987.

Ferguson, William Scott. "The Leading Ideas of the New Period." Pages 1–40 in *The Hellenistic Monarchies and the Rise of Rome.* Vol. 7 of *The Cambridge Ancient History.* Edited by S. A. Cook, F. E. Adcock, and M. P. Charlesworth. Cambridge: Cambridge University Press, 1928.

Festugière, André J. *Études de religion grecque et hellénistique.* Bibliothèque d'histoire de la philosophie. Paris: Librairie Philosophique J. Vrin, 1972.

Feyel, Christophe. *Dokimasia: la place et le rôle de l'examen préliminaire dans les institutions des cités grecques.* Études anciennes 36. Nancy: Association pour la diffusion de la recherche sur l'antiquité, 2009.

Fitzgerald, Timothy. *Discourse on Civility and Barbarity: A Critical History of Religion and Related Categories.* New York: Oxford University Press, 2007.

Flambard, Jean-Marc. "Éléments pour une approche financière de la mort des les classes populaires du Haut-Empire: analyse du buget de quelques collèges funéraires du Rome et d'Italie." Pages 209–44 in *La Mort, les morts et l'au-dèla dans le monde romain.* Edited by François Hinard. Caen: Université de Caen, 1987.

Fleury, Jean. "Une société de fait dans l'église apostolique (Phil. 4:10 à 22)." Pages 2:41–59 in *Mélanges Philippe Meylan: Recueil de travaux publiés à l'occasion de son soixante dixième anniversaire.* Lausanne: Imprimie centrale de Lausanne, 1963.

Flohr, Miko. *The World of the Fullo: Work, Economy, and Society in Roman Italy.* Oxford Studies on the Roman Economy. Oxford: Oxford University Press, 2013.

Flower, Harriet I. *The Art of Forgetting: Disgrace and Oblivion in Roman Political Culture.* Studies in the History of Greece and Rome. Chapel Hill: University of North Carolina Press, 2006.

Fragiadakis, Charilaos. "Die attischen Sklavennamen von der spätarchaischen Epoche bis in die römische Kaiserzeit: Eine historische und soziologische Untersuchung." PhD diss., Universität Mannheim, 1986.

Frank, Tenney. "Race Mixture in the Roman Empire." *AHR* 21 (1916): 689–708.

Fraser, Peter Marshall. *Rhodian Funerary Monuments.* Oxford: Clarendon, 1977.

Fredriksen, Paula. "How Later Contexts Affect Pauline Content, or: Retrospect Is the Mother of Anachronism." Pages 17–51 in *Jews and Christians in the First and Second Centuries: How to Write Their History.* Edited by Peter J. Tomson and Joshua Schwartz. Compendia Rerum Iudaicarum ad Novum Testamentum 13. Leiden: Brill, 2014.

Frier, Bruce W. "Demography." Pages 787–816 in *The High Empire, AD 70–192.* Vol. 11 of *The Cambridge Ancient History.* 2nd ed. Edited by Alan K. Bowman, Peter Garnsey, and Dominic Rathbone. Cambridge: Cambridge University Press, 2000.

Friesen, Steven J. "Paul and Economics: The Jerusalem Collection as an Alternative to Patronage." Pages 24–54 in *Paul Unbound: Other Perspectives on the Apostle*. Edited by Mark D. Given. Peabody: Hendrickson, 2010.

——. "Poverty in Pauline Studies: Beyond the So-Called New Consensus." *JSNT* 26.3 (2004): 323–61.

——. "The Wrong Erastus: Ideology, Archaeology, and Exegesis." Pages 231–56 in *Corinth in Context: Comparative Studies on Religion and Society*. Edited by Steven J. Friesen, Daniel N. Schowalter, and James C. Walters. NovTSup 134. Leiden: Brill, 2010.

Friggeri, Rosanna. *La collezione epigrafica del Museo nazionale romano alle Terme di Diocleziano*. Milan: Electa, 2001.

——. *Terme di Diocleziano: La collezione epigrafica*. Milan: Electa, 2012.

Frischer, Bernard. *The Sculpted Word: Epicureanism and Philosophical Recruitment in Ancient Greece*. Berkeley: University of California Press, 1982.

Gallazzi, Claudio, Gisèle Hadji-Minaglou, Vincent Rondot, Nikos Litinas, Pascale Ballet, and Anna Południkiewics. *Tebtynis*. Fouilles de l'Institut Français d'Archéologie Orientale du Caire, 42, 50, 55, 56, 68, Publications de l'Institut Français d'Archéologie Orientale du Caire, 853, 918, 970, 971, 1048. Cairo: Institut Français d'Archéologie Orientale, 2000–2012.

Garland, Robert. *Introducing New Gods: The Politics of Athenian Religion*. London: Duckworth, 1992.

——. *The Piraeus: From the Fifth to the First Century B.C.* London: Duckworth, 1987.

Garnsey, Peter, and Richard Saller. *The Roman Empire: Economy, Society and Culture*. London: Duckworth; Berkeley: University of California Press, 1987.

Gartrell, C. D., and Z. K. Shannon. "Contacts, Cognitions, and Conversion: A Rational Choice Approach." *Review of Religious Research* 27 (1985): 32–48.

Geagan, Daniel J. *The Athenian Constitution After Sulla*. Hesperia, Supplement 12. Princeton: American School of Classical Studies at Athens, 1967.

Geertz, Clifford. "From the Native's Point of View: On the Nature of Anthropological Understandings." Pages 221–37 in *Meaning in Anthropology*. Edited by Keith H. Basso and Henry A. Selby. Albuquerque: University of New Mexico Press, 1976.

Gill, David W. J. "Erastus the Aedile." *TynBul* 40 (1989): 293–301.

Gillihan, Yonder Moynihan. *Civic Ideology, Organization, and Law in the Rule Scrolls: A Comparative Study of the Covenanters' Sect and Contemporary Voluntary Associations in Political Context*. Studies on the Texts of the Desert of Judah 97. Leiden: Brill, 2012.

Ginsberg, Elaine K. "Introduction." Pages 1–18 in *Passing and the Fictions of Identity*. Edited by Elaine K. Ginsberg. Durham, N.C.: Duke University Press, 1996.

Goldblatt, David. "Population Structure and Jewish Identity." Pages 102–21 in *The Oxford Handbook of Jewish Daily Life in Roman Palestine*. Edited by Catherine Hezser. Oxford: Oxford University Press, 2010.

Goodrich, John K. "Erastus, Quaestor of Corinth: The Administrative Rank of οἰκονόμος τῆς πόλεως (Rom 16.23) in an Achaean Colony." *NTS* 56.1 (2010): 90–115.

Gooren, Henri. "Reassessing Conventional Approaches to Conversion: Toward a New Synthesis." *Journal for the Scientific Study of Religion* 46.3 (2007): 337–53.

Goppelt, Leonard. A *Commentary on 1 Peter*. Edited by Ferdinand Hahn. Translated by John E. Alsup. Grand Rapids: Eerdmans, 1993.

Gordon, Richard L. "Religion in the Roman Empire: The Civic Compromise and Its Limits." Pages 235–55 in *Pagan Priests: Religion and Power in the Ancient World*. Edited by Mary Beard and John North. Ithaca, N.Y.: Cornell University Press, 1990.

———. "Ritual and Hierarchy in the Mysteries of Mithras." *ARYS* 4 (2001): 245–73.

———. "The Veil of Power: Emperors, Sacrificers, and Benefactors." Pages 199–231 in *Pagan Priests: Religion and Power in the Ancient World*. Edited by Mary Beard and John North. Ithaca, N.Y.: Cornell University Press, 1990.

Gordon, Richard L., Mary Beard, Joyce Reynolds, and Charlotte Roueché. "Roman Inscriptions 1986–90." *JRS* 83 (1993): 131–58.

Gottesman, Alex. "The Beggar and the Clod: The Mythic Notion of Poverty in Ancient Greece." *TAPA* 140.2 (2010): 287–322.

———. *Politics and the Street in Democratic Athens*. Cambridge: Cambridge University Press, 2014.

Gounaropoulou, Loukretias, and Miltiades V. Hatzopoulos, eds. *Ἐπιγραφές Βεροίας. Inscriptiones Beroiae*. In collaboration with P. Nigdeli and G. Souri. Vol. I of *Επιγραφές Κάτω Μακεδονίας (μεταξύ Βερμίου όρους και του Αξιού ποταμού). Inscriptiones Macedoniae Inferioris*. Athens: Hypourgeio politismou Ethnikon Idruma Ereunwn; Paris: Éditions de Boccard, 1998.

Graham, Emma-Jayne. "The Quick and the Dead in the Extra-Urban Landscape: The Roman Cemetery at Ostia/Portus as a Lived Environment." Pages 133–43 in *TRAC 2004: Proceedings of the Fourteenth Annual Theoretical Roman Archaeology Conference*. Edited by J. Bruhn, B. Croxford, and D. Grigoropoulos. Oxford: Oxbow, 2005.

Grant, Robert M. "Pliny and the Christians." *HTR* 41.4 (1948): 273–74.

Grieb, Volker. *Hellenistische Demokratie: Politische Organisation und Struktur in freien griechischen Poleis nach Alexander dem Grossen*. Historia Einzelschriften 199. Stuttgart: Franz Steiner, 2008.

Grignon, Claude. "Commensality and Social Morphology: An Essay of Typology." Pages 23–33 in *Food, Drink and Identity: Cooking, Eating and Drinking in Europe Since the Middle Ages*. Edited by Peter Scholliers. Oxford: Berg, 2001.

Grimes, Ronald L. *The Craft of Ritual Studies*. Oxford: Oxford University Press, 2014.

———. "Infelicitous Performances and Ritual Criticism." Pages 191–209, 205–7 in *Ritual Criticism: Case Studies in Its Practice, Essays on Its Theory*. Edited by Ronald L. Grimes. Studies in Comparative Religion. Columbia: University of South Carolina Press, 1990.

Gruen, Erich S. "Synagogues and Voluntary Associations as Institutional Models: A Response to Richard Ascough and Ralph Korner." *JJMJS* 3 (2016): 125–31.

Guarducci, Margherita. "Iscrizione cristiana del II secolo nei Musei Capitolinin." *Bullettino della commissione archeologica comunale di Roma* 79 (1963–1964): 117–34.

Gutsfeld, Andreas. "Das Kollegium bei Tisch: Überlegungen zum Beitrag der Bankette zur sozialen Kohäsion in paganen Vereinen der frühen Kaiserzeit." Pages 161–83 in *Aposteldekret und antikes Vereinswesen: Gemeinschaft und ihre Ordnung*. Edited by Markus Öhler. WUNT 280. Tübingen: Mohr Siebeck, 2011.

———. "Das Vereinigungswesen und die Städte in der römischen Kaiserzeit." Pages 13–33 in *Gesellschaften im Vergleich: Forschungen aus Sozial- und Geschichtswissenschaften*. Edited by Hartmut Kaelble and Jürgen Schriewer. Komparatistische Bibliothek 9. Frankfurt am Main: Peter Lang, 1999.

Haenchen, Ernst. *The Acts of the Apostles: A Commentary*. Translated by Bernard Noble and Gerald Shinn. Oxford: Basil Blackwell, 1971.

Hagedorn, Ursula, Dieter Hagedorn, L. C. Youtie, and Herbert C. Youtie, eds. *Das Archiv des Petaus*. Abhandlungen der Rheinisch-Westfälischen Akademie der Wissenschaften 4. Cologne: Westdeutscher, 1969.

Halfmann, Helmut. *Die Senatoren aus dem östlichen Teil des Imperium Romanum bis zum Ende des 2. Jahrhunderts n. Chr.* Hypomnemata 58. Göttingen: Vandenhoeck & Ruprecht, 1979.

Hands, A. R. *Charities and Social Aid in Greece and Rome*. London: Thames and Hudson, 1968.

Hanges, James C. "1 Corinthians 4:6 and the Possibility of Written Bylaws in the Corinthian Church." *JBL* 117 (1998): 275–98.

Hansen, Mogens Herman. *Polis: An Introduction to the Ancient Greek City-State*. Oxford: Oxford University Press, 2006.

Hanson, Ann E. "Widows Too Young in Their Widowhood." Pages 149–65 in *I Claudia II: Women in Roman Art and Society*. Edited by Diana E. E. Kleiner and Susan B. Matheson. Austin: University of Texas Press, 2000.

Harland, Philip A. "Acculturation and Identity in the Diaspora: A Jewish Family and 'Pagan' Guilds at Hierapolis." *JJS* 57.2 (2006): 222–44.

———. *Associations, Synagogues and Congregations: Claiming a Place in Ancient Mediterranean Society*. Minneapolis: Fortress, 2003.

———. "Christ-Bearers and Fellow-Initiates: Local Cultural Life and Christian Identity in Ignatius' Letters." *JECS* 11.4 (2003): 481–99.

———. "The Declining Polis? Religious Rivalries in Ancient Civic Context." Pages 21–49 in *Religious Rivalries in the Early Roman Empire and the Rise of Christianity*. Edited by Leif E. Vaage. Studies in Christianity and Judaism 18. Waterloo, Ont.: Wilfrid Laurier University Press, 2006.

———. "Familial Dimensions of Group Identity: 'Brothers' (ἀδελφοί) in Associations of the Greek East." *JBL* 124.3 (2005): 491–513.

———. "Familial Dimensions of Group Identity (II): 'Mothers' and 'Fathers' in Associations and Synagogues of the Greek World." *JSJ* 38.1 (2007): 57–79.

———. *Greco-Roman Associations: Texts, Translations, and Commentary, II: North Coast of the Black Sea, Asia Minor*. BZNW 204. Berlin: de Gruyter, 2014.

———. "Honours and Worship: Emperors, Imperial Cults and Associations at Ephesus (First to Third Centuries C.E.)." *SR/SR* 25.3 (1996): 319–34.

Harnack, Adolf von. *Die Mission und Ausbreitung des Christentums in den ersten drei Jahrhunderten*. 2nd ed. Leipzig: Hinrichs, 1906.

———. *The Mission and Expansion of Christianity in the First Three Centuries*. 2nd ed. New York: Williams and Norgate; London: Putman's Sons, 1908.

Harper, Kyle. *The Fate of Rome: Climate, Disease and the End of an Empire.* Princeton: Princeton University Press, 2017.

Harrill, J. Albert. *The Manumission of Slaves in Early Christianity.* HUT 32. Tübingen: Mohr Siebeck, 1995.

———. "Paul and Empire: Studying Roman Identity After the Cultural Turn." *Early Christianity* 2.3 (2011): 281–311.

———. *Paul the Apostle: His Life and Legacy in Their Roman Context.* Cambridge: Cambridge University Press, 2012.

———. "Servile Functionaries or Priestly Leaders? Roman Domestic Religion, Narrative Intertextuality, and Pliny's Reference to Christian Slave Ministrae (Ep. 10,96,8)." ZNW 97 (2006): 111–30.

Harris, Edward M. "Workshop, Marketplace and Household: The Nature of Technical Specialization in Classical Athens and Its Influence on Economy and Society." Pages 67–99 in *Money, Labour and Land: Approaches to the Economies of Ancient Greece.* Edited by Paul Cartledge, Edward E. Cohen, and Lin Foxhall. London: Routledge, 2002.

Harris, William V. "On the Applicability of the Concept of Class in Roman History." Pages 15–26 in *Rome's Imperial Economy: Twelve Essays.* Oxford: Oxford University Press, 2011.

———. "Poverty and Destitution in the Roman Empire." Pages 27–54 in *Rome's Imperial Economy: Twelve Essays.* Oxford: Oxford University Press, 2011.

Harrison, James R. "Paul and Ancient Civic Ethics: Redefining the Canon of Honour in the Graeco-Roman World." Pages 75–118 in *Paul's Graeco-Roman Context.* Edited by Cilliers Breytenbach. BETL 277. Leuven: Peeters, 2015.

———. "Paul's House Churches and the Cultic Associations." *RTR* 58.1 (1999): 31–47.

Hasegawa, Kinuko. *The* Familia Urbana *During the Early Empire: A Study of Columbaria Inscriptions.* BAR International Series. Oxford: Archaeopress, 2005.

Hatzfeld, Jean. "Les Italiens résidant à Délos." *BCH* 36 (1912): 5–218.

Hawkins, Cameron. "Work in the City: Roman Artisans and the Urban Economy." PhD diss., University of Chicago, 2006.

Hemelrijk, Emily. "Female Munificence in the Cities of the Latin West." Pages 65–84 in *Women and the Roman City in the Latin West.* Edited by Emily Hemelrijk and Greg Woolf. Mnemosyne Supplements 360. Leiden: Brill, 2013.

———. "Patronesses and 'Mothers' of Roman Collegia." *Classical Antiquity* 27.1 (2008): 115–62.

Hermansen, Gustav. *Ostia: Aspects of Roman City Life.* Edmonton: University of Alberta Press, 1982.

———. "The *Stuppatores* and Their Guild in Ostia." *AJA* 86 (1982): 121–26.

Hicks, E. L. "Iasos." *JHS* 8 (1887): 83–118.

———. "Inscriptions from Eastern Cilicia." *JHS* 11 (1890): 236–54.

Hock, Ronald F. "Simon the Shoemaker as an Ideal Cynic." *GRBS* 17.1 (1976): 41–53.

———. "The Workshop as a Social Setting for Paul's Missionary Preaching." *CBQ* 41 (1979): 438–50.

Höfler, Anton. *Der Sarapishymnus des Ailios Aristeides.* Tübinger Beiträge zur Altertumswissenschaft, Heft 27. Stuttgart: W. Kohlhammer, 1935.

Holmberg, Bengt. *Paul and Power: The Structure of Authority in the Primitive Church as Reflected in the Pauline Epistles.* ConB: New Testament Series 11. Lund: Liber Laromedel and C. W. K. Gleerup, 1978.

Hope, Valerie M. *Death in Ancient Rome: A Source Book.* London: Routledge, 2007.

Hopkins, Keith. "Christian Number and Its Implications." *JECS* 6.2 (1998): 185–226.

——. *Death and Renewal.* Sociological Studies in Roman History 2. Cambridge: Cambridge University Press, 1983.

——. "Rome, Taxes, Rents and Trade." Pages 190–230 in *The Ancient Economy.* Edited by Walter Scheidel and Sitta von Reden. Edinburgh Readings on the Ancient World. Edinburgh: Edinburgh University Press; London: Routledge, 2002.

——. "Taxes and Trade in the Roman Empire (200 B.C.–A.D. 400)." *JRS* 70 (1980): 101–25.

——. *A World Full of Gods: The Strange Triumph of Christianity.* New York: Free Press, 1999.

Horrell, David G. "Between Conformity and Resistance: Beyond the Balch-Elliott Debate Towards a Postcolonial Reading of First Peter." Pages 111–43 in *Reading First Peter with New Eyes.* Edited by Robert L. Webb and Betsy Bauman-Martin. Library of New Testament Studies 364. London: T & T Clark International, 2007.

——. "Domestic Space and Christian Meetings at Corinth: Imagining New Contexts and the Buildings East of the Theatre." *NTS* 50.3 (2004): 349–69.

Horsley, G. H. R. *A Review of the Greek Inscriptions and Papyri Published in 1977.* Vol. 2 of *New Documents Illustrating Early Christianity.* North Ryde, N.S.W.: Ancient History Documentary Research Centre, Macquarie University, 1982.

Horster, Marietta, and Anja Klöckner, eds. *Cities and Priests: Cult Personnel in Asia Minor and the Aegean Islands from the Hellenistic to the Imperial Period.* Religionsgeschichtliche Versuche und Vorarbeiten 64. Berlin: de Gruyter, 2013.

——, eds. *Civic Priests: Cult Personnel in Athens from the Hellenistic Period to Late Antiquity.* Religionsgeschichtliche Versuche und Vorarbeiten 58. Berlin: de Gruyter, 2012.

Hurd, John C. *The Origin of 1 Corinthians.* London: SPCK, 1965.

Hurtado, Larry W. *Destroyer of the Gods: Early Christian Distinctiveness in the Roman World.* Waco, Tex.: Baylor University Press, 2016.

——. *The Earliest Christian Artifacts: Manuscripts and Christian Origins.* Grand Rapids: Eerdmans, 2006.

Hutchinson, John R., and Mariano Garcia. "Tyrannosaurus Was not a Fast Runner." *Nature* 415 (2002): 1018–21.

Iannaccone, Laurence R. "Sacrifice and Stigma: Reducing Free-Riding in Cults, Communes, and Other Collectives." *Journal of Political Economy* 100.2 (1992): 271–91.

Ismard, Paulin. *La cité des réseaux: Athènes et ses associations VIe–Ie siècle av. J.-C.* Histoire Ancienne et Médiévale 105. Paris: Publications de la Sorbonne, 2010.

Jacobs, Andrew S. "Passing: Jesus' Circumcision and Strategic Self-Sacrifice." Pages 251–64 in *Ancient Mediterranean Sacrifice.* Edited by Jennifer Wright Knust and Zsuzsanna Várhelyi. Oxford: Oxford University Press, 2011.

Jewett, Robert. *Romans*. Hermeneia. Minneapolis: Fortress, 2007.

Johnson, Mark J. "Pagan-Christian Burial Practices of the Fourth Century: Shared Tombs?" *JECS* 5.1 (1997): 36–58.

Johnson, William A. "Toward a Sociology of Reading in Classical Antiquity." *AJPh* 121.4 (2000): 593–627.

Jones, A. H. M. *The Later Roman Empire: A Social, Economic and Administrative Survey*. Oxford: Basil Blackwell, 1964.

Jones, Nicholas F. *The Associations of Classical Athens: The Response to Democracy*. London: Oxford University Press, 1999.

Jongkind, Dirk. "Corinth in the First Century AD: The Search for Another Class." *TynBul* 52.1 (2001): 139–48.

Jongman, Willem M. "Gibbon Was Right: The Decline and Fall of the Roman Economy." Pages 183–200 in *Crises and the Roman Empire*. Edited by Olivier Hekster, Gerda de Kleijn, and Daniëlle Slootjes. Impact of Empire 7. Leiden: Brill, 2007.

———. "A Golden Age: Death, Money Supply and Social Succession in the Roman Empire." Pages 181–96 in *Credito e moneta nel mondo romano*. Edited by Elio Lo Cascio. Bari: Edipuglia, 2003.

———. "The Rise and Fall of the Roman Economy: Population, Rents and Entitlement." Pages 237–54 in *Ancient Economies, Modern Methodologies: Archaeology, Comparative History, Models and Institutions*. Edited by Peter F. Bang, Mamoru Ikeguchi, and Harmut G. Ziche. Pragmateiai 12. Bari: Edipuglia, 2006.

Joshel, Sandra R. *Work, Identity, and Legal Status at Rome: A Study of the Occupational Inscriptions*. Oklahoma Series in Classical Culture 11. Norman: University of Oklahoma Press, 1992.

Josi, E. "Cimitero di Pretestato. Scavo 1935–1936. Recpero di frammenti di sarcophagi e di iscrizioni." *RAC* 13 (1936): 207–19.

Judge, E. A. "The Early Christians as a Scholastic Community." *JRH* 1 (1960–1961): 4–15, 125–37.

———. *Social Distinctives of the Christians in the First Century*. Edited by David M. Scholer. Peabody, Mass.: Hendrickson, 2008.

———. "The Social Identity of the First Christians: A Question of Method in Religious History." *JRH* 11 (1980): 201–17.

———. *The Social Pattern of Christian Groups in the First Century: Some Prolegomena to the Study of New Testament Ideas of Social Obligation*. London: Tyndale, 1960.

Kasher, Aryeh. *Jews and Hellenistic Cities in Eretz Israel: Relations of the Jews in Eretz-Israel with the Hellenistic Cities During the Second Temple Period (332 BCE—70 CE)*. TSAJ 21. Tübingen: Mohr Siebeck, 1990.

———. *The Jews in Hellenistic and Roman Egypt: The Struggle for Equal Rights*. Rev. English ed. TSAJ 7. Tübingen: Mohr Siebeck, 1985.

Kautsky, Karl. *Der Ursprung des Christentums, eine historische Untersuchung*. Internationale Bibliothek 45. Stuttgart: Dietz, 1908.

———. Foundations of Christianity. Translated by Henry F. Mins. New York: George Allen & Unwin, 1925; reprint, London: Routledge, n.d.

Keener, Craig S. *Acts: An* Exegetical *Commentary*. Grand Rapids: Baker Academic, 2012.

Kehoe, Dennis P. "The Early Roman Empire: Production." Pages 453–569 in *The Cambridge Economic History of the Greco-Roman World.* Edited by Walter Scheidel, Ian Morris, and Richard P. Saller. Cambridge: Cambridge University Press, 2007.

———. "Poverty, Distribution of Wealth, and Economic Growth in the Roman Empire." Pages 183–96 in *Structure and Performance in the Roman Economy: Models, Methods and Case Studies.* Edited by Paul Erdkamp and Koenraad Verboven. Collection Latomus 350. Brussels: Editions Latomus, 2015.

Kent, John Harvey. *Corinth—Inscriptions 1929–1950: Results.* Edited by Harold North Fowler. Corinth: Results of Excavations 8.3. Princeton: American School of Classical Studies at Athens, 1966.

Kindt, Julia. "Polis Religion—A Critical Appreciation." *Kernos: Revue internationale et pluridisciplinaire de religion grecque antique* 22 (2009): 9–34.

Kirk, Alan. "The Scribe as Tradent." Pages 97–115 in *Scribal Practices and Social Structures Among Jesus Adherents: Essays in Honour of John S. Kloppenborg.* Edited by William E. Arnal, Richard S. Ascough, Robert A. Derrenbacker, and Philip A. Harland. BETL 285. Leuven: Peeters, 2016.

Klauck, Hans-Josef. *Herrenmahl und hellenistischer Kult: eine religionsgeschichtliche Untersuchung zum ersten Korintherbrief.* 2nd ed. NTAbh NF 15. Münster: Aschendorff, 1986.

Klinghardt, Matthias. *Gemeinschaftsmahl und Mahlgemeinschaft: Soziologie und Liturgie frühchristlicher Mahlfeiern.* Texte und Arbeiten zum neutestamentlichen Zeitalter 13. Tübingen: Francke, 1996.

Kloppenborg, John S. "Associations and Their Meals." Paper presented at the SBL Meals in the Greco-Roman World Section, 2012 SBL Annual Meeting, November 16–20, 2012, Chicago.

———. "Associations, Christ Groups, and Their Place in the *Polis.*" *ZNW* 108.1 (2017): 1–56.

———. "Collegia and *Thiasoi:* Issues in Function, Taxonomy and Membership." Pages 16–30 in *Voluntary Associations in the Graeco-Roman World.* Edited by John S. Kloppenborg and Stephen G. Wilson. London: Routledge, 1996.

———. "Diaspora Discourse: The Construction of *Ethos* in James." *NTS* 53.2 (2007): 242–70.

———. "Disaffiliation in Associations and the ἀποσυναγωγός of John." *HvTSt* 67 (2011): 159–74.

———. "Edwin Hatch, Churches, and *Collegia.*" Pages 212–38 in *Origins and Method: Towards a New Understanding of Judaism and Christianity: Essays in Honour of John C. Hurd.* Edited by Bradley McLean. JSNTSup 86. Sheffield: JSOT, 1993.

———. "Egalitarianism in the Myth and Rhetoric of Pauline Churches." Pages 247–63 in *Reimagining Christian Origins: A Colloquium Honoring Burton L. Mack.* Edited by Elizabeth Castelli and Hal Taussig. Valley Forge, Pa.: Trinity Press International, 1996.

———. "Epigraphy, Papyrology and the Interpretation of the New Testament: Member Contributions to the Eucharist." Pages 129–53 in *Epigraphik und Neues Testament.* Edited by Thomas Corsten, Markus Öhler, and Joseph Verheyden. WUNT 365. Tübingen: Mohr Siebeck, 2016.

——. "Ethnic and Political Rivalry at Caesarea Maritima." Pages 227–48 in *Religious Rivalries and the Struggle for Success in Caesarea Maritima*. Edited by Terence L. Donaldson. ESCJ 8. Waterloo, Ont.: Wilfrid Laurier University Press, 2000.

——. "Gaius the Roman Guest." *NTS* 63.4 (2017): 534–49.

——. "Literate Media in Early Christian Groups: The Creation of a Christian Book Culture." *JECS* 22.1 (2014): 21–59.

——. "The Moralizing of Discourse in Greco-Roman Associations." Pages 215–28 in *"The One Who Sows Bountifully": Essays in Honor of Stanley K. Stowers*. Edited by Caroline Johnson Hodge, Saul M. Olyan, Daniel Ullucci, and Emma Wasserman. Brown Judaic Studies 256. Providence: Brown Judaic Studies, 2013.

——. "Patronage Avoidance in the Epistle of James." *HvTSt* 55.4 (1999): 755–94.

——. "Precedence at the Communal Meal in Corinth." *NovT* 58.2 (2016): 167–203.

——. "Φιλαδελφία, Θεοδίδακτος and the Dioscuri: Rhetorical Engagement in 1 Thess 4.9–12." *NTS* 39.2 (1993): 265–89.

Koenen, Ludwig. "Eine Einladung zur Kline des Sarapis (P. Colon. inv. 2555)." *ZPE* 1 (1967): 121–26.

Koester, Helmut. *History, Culture, and Religion of the Hellenistic Age*. Vol. 1 of *Introduction to the New Testament*. Hermeneia: Foundations and Facets. Philadelphia: Fortress, 1982.

Kokkinia, Christina. "Rosen für die Toten im griechischen Raum und eine neue ῥοδισμός-Inschrift aus Bithynien." *Museum Helveticum* 56.4 (1999): 204–21.

Kolb, Anne. "Vereine 'kleiner Leute' und die kaiserliche Verwaltung." *ZPE* 107 (1995): 201–12.

Kontorini, Vassa. *Rhodiaka. I: Inscriptions inédites relatives à l'histoire et aux cultes de Rhodes au IIe et au Ier s. av. J.C. II: Anekdotes epigraphes Rodou II, Inscriptions inédites de Rhodes II*. Publications d'Histoire de l'Art et d'Archéologie de l'Université Catholique de Louvain 42. Archaeologia Transatlantica 6. Louvain-la-Neuve: Institut supérieur d'archéologie et d'histoire de l'art, Collège Érasme, 1983–1989.

Korner, Ralph J. "Ekklēsia as a Jewish Synagogue Term: Some Implications for Paul's Socio-Religious Location." *JJMJS* 2 (2015): 53–78.

——. *The Origin and Meaning of Ekklēsia in the Early Jesus Movement*. AJEC 98. Leiden: Brill, 2017.

Kraabel, A. Thomas. "The Diaspora Synagogue: Archaeological and Epigraphic Evidence Since Sukenik." Pages 95–126 in *Ancient Synagogues: Historical Analyses and Archaeological Discovery*. Edited by Dan Urman and Paul V. M. Flesher. SPB 47/1–2. Leiden: Brill, 1995.

——. "Social System of Six Diaspora Synagogues." Pages 79–91 in *Ancient Synagogues: The State of Research*. Edited by Joseph Gutmann. Brown Judaic Studies 22. Chico, Calif.: Scholars Press, 1981.

Kraeling, Carl H. *The Christian Building*. In collaboration with C. B. Welles. The Excavations at Dura-Europos: Final Report 8/2. New Haven: Yale University Press, 1967.

Kreissig, Heinz. "Zur sozialen Zusammenhang der frühchristlichen Gemeinden im ersten Jahrhundert u.Z." *Eirene* 6 (1967): 91–100.

Krinzinger, Friedrich. *Das Hanghaus 2 von Ephesos: Studien zu Baugeschichte und Chronologie.* Denkschriften der Österreichische Akademie der Wissenschaften, Philosophisch-Historische Klasse. Archäologische Forschungen 7. Vienna: Verlag der Österreichischen Akademie der Wissenschaften, 2002.

Kron, Geoffrey. "Anthropometry, Physical Anthropology, and the Reconstruction of Ancient Health, Nutrition, and Living Standards." *Historia* 54.1 (2005): 68–83.

——. "Comparative Evidence and the Reconstruction of the Ancient Economy: Greco-Roman Housing and the Level and Distribution of Wealth and Income." Pages 111–31 in *Long-Term Quantification in Ancient Mediterranean History*. Edited by F. de Callata. Bari: Edipuglia, 2014.

——. "The Distribution of Wealth at Athens in Comparative Perspective." *ZPE* 179 (2011): 129–38.

Kruse, Thomas. "Ethnic *Koina* and *Politeumata* in Ptolemaic Egypt." Pages 270–300 in *Private Associations and the Public Sphere*. Edited by Vincent Gabrielsen and Christian A. Thomsen. Scientia Danica. Series H, Humanistic, Series 8, no. 9. Copenhagen: Royal Danish Academy of Sciences and Letters, 2015.

Kuşseven, Pinar. "The Cult of Iupiter Dolichenus: Origins and Iconography." MA thesis, Bilkent University, Ankara, 2007.

Kyrtatas, Dimitris J. *The Social Structure of the Early Christian Communities*. London: Verso, 1987.

Labarre, Guy, and Marie-Thérèse LeDinahet. "Les métiers du textile en Asie Mineure de l'époque hellénistique à l'époque imperiale." In *Aspects de l'artisanat du textile dans le monde méditerranéen: Egypte, Grèce, monde méditerranée (Égypte, Grèce, Monde romain)*. Collection de l'Institut d'Archéologie et d'Histoire de l'Antiquité 2. Lyon: Lumière-Lyon 2, Institut d'archéologie et d'histoire de l'Antiquité, 1996.

Lambek, Michael. *The Weight of the Past: Living with History in Mahajanga, Madagascar*. Contemporary Anthropology of Religion. New York: Palgrave Macmillan, 2002.

Lampe, Peter. "Das korinthinische Herrenmahl im Schnittpunkt hellenistisch-römischer Mahlpraxis und paulinischer Theologia Crucis [1 Kor 11,17–34]." *ZNW* 82 (1991): 183–212.

——. "The Eucharist: Identifying with Christ on the Cross." *Int* 48.1 (1994): 36–49.

——. *From Paul to Valentinus: Christians at Rome in the First Two Centuries*. Translated by Michael G. Steinhauser. Minneapolis: Fortress, 2003.

Landecker, Werner S. "Types of Integration and Their Measurement." *American Journal of Sociology* 56.4 (1951): 332–40.

Last, Richard. "The Election of Officers in the Corinthian Christ-Group." *NTS* 59.3 (2013): 365–81.

——. "The Myth of Free Membership in Pauline Christ Groups." Pages 495–516 in *Scribal Practices and Social Structures Among Jesus Adherents: Essays in Honour of John S. Kloppenborg*. Edited by William E. Arnal, Richard S. Ascough, Robert A. Derrenbacker, and Philip A. Harland. BETL 285. Leuven: Peeters, 2016.

——. "The Neighborhood (*Vicus*) of the Corinthian *Ekklesia*: Beyond Family-Based Descriptions of the First Urban Christ-Believers." *JSNT* 38.4 (2016): 399–425.

———. *The Pauline Church and the Corinthian Ekklēsia: Greco-Roman Associations in Comparative Context.* SNTSMS 164. Cambridge: Cambridge University Press, 2015.

Last, Richard, and Sarah Rollens. "Accounting Practices in P.Tebt. III/2 894 and Pauline Groups." *Early Christianity* 5.4 (2014): 441–74.

Latour, Bruno. *Reassembling the Social: An Introduction to Actor-Network-Theory.* Clarendon Lectures in Management Studies. Oxford: Oxford University Press, 2005.

Laubry, Nicolas. "Les espaces funéraires des collèges dans l'Italie romaine." Pages 115–35 in *Los espacios de reunión de las asociaciones romanas. Diálogos desde la arqueología y la historia, en homenaje a Bertrand Goffaux.* Edited by Olivia Rodríguez Gutiérrez, Nicolas Tran, and Begoña Soler Huertas. Colección Historia y Geografía 325. Seville: EUS, 2016.

Laws, Sophie. *A Commentary on the Epistle of James.* Black's New Testament Commentaries. London: A. & C. Black, 1980.

Le Dinahet-Couillard, Marie-Thérèse. "Une famille de notables tyriens à Délos." *BCH* 121.2 (1997): 617–66.

Le Guen, Brigitte. *Les Associations de Technites dionysiaques à l'époque hellénistique. Vol. 1, Corpus documentaire. Vol. 2, Synthèse.* Études d'archéologie classique XI–XII. Nancy: Association pour la diffusion de la recherche sur l'Antiquité, 2001.

Lefebvre, Henri. *The Production of Space.* Translated by Donald Nicholson-Smith. Oxford: Blackwell, 1991.

Lefkowitz, Mary R., and Maureen B. Fant. *Women's Life in Greece and Rome.* Baltimore: Johns Hopkins University Press, 1982.

Lendon, J. E. *Empire of Honour: The Art of Government in the Roman World.* Oxford: Clarendon, 1997.

Levine, Lee I. *The Ancient Synagogue: The First Thousand Years.* New Haven: Yale University Press, 2000.

Lévi-Strauss, Claude. *Totemism.* Translated by Rodney Needham. Boston: Beacon, 1963.

Lin, Nan. "Building a Network Theory of Social Capital." *Connections* 22.1 (1999): 28–51.

Littman, R. J., and M. L. Littman. "Galen and the Antonine Plague." *AJP* 94.3 (1973): 243–55.

Liu, Jinyu. "AE 1998, 282: A Case Study of Public Benefaction and Local Politics." Pages 248–62 in *Ancient Documents and Their Contexts: First North American Congress on Greek and Latin Epigraphy (2011).* Edited by John Bodel and Nora Dimitrova. Leiden: Brill, 2014.

———. "Clothing Supply for the Military: A Look at the Inscriptional Evidence." Pages 19–29 in *Wearing the Cloak: Dressing the Soldier in Roman Times.* Edited by Marie-Louise Nosch. Ancient Textiles Series. Oxford: Oxbow Books in association with the Centre for Textile Research, 2011.

———. *Collegia Centonariorum: The Guilds of Textile Dealers in the Roman West.* Columbia Studies in the Classical Tradition 34. Leiden: Brill, 2009.

———. "The Economy of Endowments: The Case of the Roman Collegia." Pages 231–56 in Pistoi Dia Tèn Technèn. *Bankers, Loans and Archives in the Ancient World. Studies in Honour of Raymond Bogaert.* Edited by Koenraad Verboven, Katelijn Vandorpe, and Véronique Chankowski. Studia Hellenistica 44. Leuven: Peeters, 2007.

———. "Group Membership, Trust Networks, and Social Capital: A Critical Analysis." Pages 203–26 in *Work, Labour, and Professions in the Roman World*. Edited by Koenraad Verboven and Christian Laes. Impact of Empire 23. Leiden: Brill, 2017.

———. "Local Governments and Collegia: A New Appraisal of the Evidence." Pages 285–316 in *A Tall Order: Writing the Social History of the Ancient World. Essays in Honor of William V. Harris*. Edited by Jean-Jacques Aubert and Zsuzsanna Várhelyi. Beiträge zur Altertumskunde 216. Munich: K. G. Saur, 2005.

Lloris, Francisco Beltrán. "The Epigraphic Habit in the Roman World." Pages 131–48 in *The Oxford Handbook of Latin Epigraphy*. Edited by Christer Bruun and Jonathan Edmonson. Oxford: Oxford University Press, 2014.

Lo Cascio, Elio. "The Role of the State in the Roman Economy: Making Use of the New Institutional Economics." Pages 217–34 in *Ancient Economies, Modern Methodologies: Archaeology, Comparative History, Models and Institutions*. Edited by Peter F. Bang, Mamoru Ikeguchi, and Harmut G. Ziche. Pragmateiai 12. Bari: Edipuglia, 2006.

Lofland, John, and Rodney Stark. "Becoming a World-Saver: A Theory of Conversion to a Deviant Perspective." *American Sociological Review* 30.6 (1965): 862–75.

Longenecker, Bruce W. *The Crosses of Pompeii: Jesus-Devotion in a Vesuvian Town*. Minneapolis: Fortress, 2016.

———. *Remember the Poor: Paul, Poverty, and the Greco-Roman World*. Grand Rapids: Eerdmans, 2011.

Longo, Oddone. "Eranos." Pages 245–58 in *Mélanges Edouard Delebecque*. Aix-en-Provence: Publications Université de Provence, 1983.

Lucas, Robert E. *The Industrial Revolution: Past and Future: 2003 Annual Report Essay*. Minneapolis: Federal Reserve Bank of Minneapolis, 2004.

Lüderitz, Gert, and Joyce M. Reynolds. *Corpus jüdischer Zeugnisse aus der Cyrenaika*. Beihefte zum Tübinger Atlas des Vorderen Orients. Reihe B, Geisteswissenschaften 53. Wiesbaden: Ludwig Reichert, 1983.

Lüdemann, Gerd. *Early Christianity According to the Traditions of Acts*. Minneapolis: Fortress, 1989.

Luijendijk, Annemarie. "A New Testament Papyrus and Its Documentary Context: An Early Christian Writing Exercise from the Archive of Leonides (*P.Oxy*. II 209/$\mathfrak{P}^{10}$)." *JBL* 129.3 (2011): 575–96.

Lytle, Ephraim. "Marine Fisheries and the Ancient Greek Economy." PhD diss., Duke University, 2006.

Ma, John. "Public Speech and Community in the Euboicus." Pages 108–24 in *Dio Chrysostom: Politics, Letters, and Philosophy*. Edited by Simon Swain. Oxford: Oxford University Press, 2000.

Mackil, Emily. *Creating a Common Polity: Religion, Economy, and Politics in the Making of the Greek Koinon*. Hellenistic Culture and Society 55. Berkeley: University of California Press, 2013.

———. "The Greek Koinon." Pages 305–23 in *The Oxford Handbook of the State in the Ancient Near East and Mediterranean*. Edited by Peter Fibiger Bang and Walter Scheidel. Oxford: Oxford University Press, 2013.

MacMullen, Ramsay. *Christianizing the Roman Empire (A.D. 100–400)*. New Haven: Yale University Press, 1984.

———. "The Epigraphic Habit in the Roman Empire." *AJPh* 103.3 (1982): 233–46.

———. *Paganism in the Roman Empire*. New Haven: Yale University Press, 1981.

———. *Roman Social Relations, 50 B.C. to A.D. 284*. New Haven: Yale University Press, 1974.

———. *The Second Church: Popular Christianity A.D. 200–400*. Society of Biblical Literature Writings from the Greco-Roman World Supplement Series 1. Atlanta: Society of Biblical Literature, 2009.

———. "What Difference Did Christianity Make?" *Historia* 35.3 (1986): 322–43.

MacMullen, Ramsay, and Eugene N. Lane, eds. *Paganism and Christianity, 100–425 C.E. A Sourcebook*. Minneapolis: Fortress, 1992.

Maier, Günther. "Eranos als Kreditinstitut." Inaugural Dissertation. Erlangen: Universität Erlangen–Nürnberg, 1969.

Maillot, Stéphanie. "Associations and Death: Funerary Activities of the Hellenistic Associations." In *Associations in Context: Rethinking Associations and Religion in the Post-Classical Polis*. Edited by Annelies Cazemier and Stella C. Skaltsa. Copenhagen: Royal Danish Academy of Sciences and Letters, forthcoming.

———. "Les associations à Cos." Pages 199–226 in *Groupes et associations dans les cités grecques (IIIe siècle av. J.-C.–IIe siècle ap. J.-C.)*. Edited by Pierre Fröhlich and Patrice Hamon. Hautes études du monde gréco-romain 49. Geneva: Librairie Droz, 2013.

Malherbe, Abraham J. *Social Aspects of Early Christianity*. Baton Rouge: Louisiana State University Press, 1977.

Maresch, Klaus. *Bronze und Silber: Papyrologische Beiträge zur Geschichte der Währung im ptolemäischen und römischen Ägypten biz sum 2. Jahrhundert n. Chr.* Abhandlungen der Nordrhein-Westfalischen Akademie der Wissenschaften, Papyrologica Colonensia 25. Wiesbaden: Westdeutscher, 1996.

Martin, Dale B. *The Corinthian Body*. New Haven: Yale University Press, 1995.

———. "Review Article: Justin J. Meggitt, *Paul, Poverty and Survival*." *JSNT* 84 (2001): 51–64.

Mason, Hugh J. *Greek Terms for Roman Institutions: A Lexicon and Analysis*. American Studies in Papyrology 13. Toronto: Hakkert, 1974.

Mason, Steve, and Philip F. Esler. "Judaean and Christ-Follower Identities: Grounds for a Distinction." *NTS* 63.4 (2017): 493–515.

Mauss, Marcel. "A Category of the Human Mind: The Notion of Person; the Notion of Self." Pages 1–25 in *The Category of the Person: Anthropology, Philosophy, History*. Edited by Michael Carrithers, Steven Collins, and Steven Lukes. Cambridge: Cambridge University Press, 1985.

Mayer, Emanuel. *The Ancient Middle Classes: Urban Life and Aesthetics in the Roman Empire, 100 BCE–250 CE*. Cambridge, Mass.: Harvard University Press, 2012.

McLean, Bradley H. "The Agrippinilla Inscription: Religious Associations and Early Christian Formation." Pages 239–70 in *Origins and Method: Towards a New Understanding of Judaism and Christianity: Essays in Honour of John C. Hurd*. Edited by Bradley McLean. JSNTSup 86. Sheffield: JSOT, 1993.

Meeks, Wayne A. *The First Urban Christians: The Social World of the Apostle Paul.* New Haven: Yale University Press, 1983.

———. "Taking Stock and Moving On." Pages 134–46 in *After the First Urban Christians: The Social-Scientific Study of Pauline Christianity Twenty-Five Years Later.* Edited by Todd D. Still and David G. Horrell. London: T & T Clark International, 2009.

Meggitt, Justin J. *Paul, Poverty and Survival.* Studies of the New Testament and Its World. Edinburgh: T & T Clark, 1998.

———. "The Social Status of Erastus (Rom. 16:23)." *NovT* 38.3 (1996): 218–23.

Meiggs, Russell. *Roman Ostia.* 2nd ed. Oxford: Clarendon, 1973.

Mélèze-Modrzejewski, Joseph. *The Jews of Egypt: From Rameses II to Emperor Hadrian.* Translated by Robert Cornman. Princeton: Princeton University Press, 1997.

Mennella, Giovanni, and Giuseppina Apicella. *Le corporazioni professionali nell' Italia romana. Un aggiornamento al Waltzing.* Quaderni del Dipartimento di scienze dell'antichità, Università degli studi di Salerno 25. Naples: Arte tipografica, 2000.

Migeotte, Léopold. "Les souscriptions dans les associations privées." Pages 113–27 in *Groupes et associations dans les cités grecques (IIIe siècle av. J.-C.–IIe siècle ap. J.-C.).* Edited by Pierre Fröhlich and Patrice Hamon. Hautes études du monde gréco-romain 49. Geneva: Librairie Droz, 2013.

———. *Les souscriptions publiques dans les cités grecques.* Hautes études du monde gréco-romain. Geneva: Librairie Droz; Quebec: Éditions du Sphinx, 1992.

Mikalson, Jon D. *Religion in Hellenistic Athens.* Hellenistic Culture and Society 29. Berkeley: University of California Press, 1998.

Mikat, Paul. *Die Bedeutung der Begriffe Stasis und Aponoia für das Verständnis des 1. Clemensbriefes.* Arbeitsgemeinschaft für Forschung des Landes Nordrhein-Westfalen. Geisteswissenschaften 155. Cologne: Westdeutscher, 1969.

Miller, Anna C. *Corinthian Democracy: Democratic Discourse in 1 Corinthians.* Princeton Theological Monograph Series 220. Eugene, Ore.: Pickwick, 2015.

Miller, Stella Grobel. "A Mosaic Floor from a Roman Villa at Anaploga." *Hesperia* 41.3 (1972): 332–54.

Millett, Paul. "Patronage and Its Avoidance in Classical Athens." Pages 15–47 in *Patronage in Ancient Society.* Edited by Andrew Wallace-Hadrill. Leicester-Nottingham Studies in Ancient Society 1. London: Routledge, 1989.

Mitchell, Margaret M. "Paul's Letters to Corinth: The Interpretive Intertwining of Literary and Historical Reconstruction." Pages 306–38 in *Urban Religion in Roman Corinth: Interdisciplinary Approaches.* Edited by Daniel N. Schowalter and Steven J. Friesen. HTS 53. Cambridge, Mass.: Harvard University Press, 2005.

Mitchell, Stephen. *Anatolia: Land, Men, and Gods in Asia Minor.* Oxford: Clarendon, 1993.

———. "The Cult of Theos Hypsistos Between Pagans, Jews, and Christians." Pages 81–148 in *Pagan Monotheism in Late Antiquity.* Edited by Polymnia Athanassiadi and Michael Frede. Oxford: Clarendon, 1999.

———. "Further Thoughts on the Cult of Theos Hypsistos." Pages 167–208 in *One God: Pagan Monotheism in the Roman Empire.* Edited by Stephen Mitchell and Peter Van Nuffelen. Cambridge: Cambridge University Press, 2010.

Mitford, Terence B. "Roman Cyprus." *ANRW* II 7.2 (1980): 1285–1384.
Mitrofan, Dragoş. "The Antonine Plague in Dacia and Moesia Inferior." *Journal of Ancient History and Archeology* 1.2 (2014): 9–13.
Mohrmann, Christine, Maurice Nédoncelle, B. Botte, L. De Bruyne, André Grabar, R. Marichal, and C. Vogel. "Les dénominations de l'église en tant qu'édifice en grec et en latin au cours des premiers siècles chrétiens." *Revue des sciences religieuses* 36.3–4 (1962): 155–74.
Mommsen, Theodor. *Chronica minora, Saec IV, V, VI, VII*. Monumenta Germaniae Historica 9. Berlin: Weidmann, 1892.
———. *De collegiis et sodaliciis Romanorum. Accedit inscriptio lanuvina*. Kiliae: Libraria Schwersiana, 1843.
Monson, Andrew. "The Ethics and Economics of Ptolemaic Religious Associations." *Ancient Society* 36 (2006): 221–38.
Montemaggi, Francesca E. S. "Belief, Trust, and Relationality: A Simmelian Approach for the Study of Faith." *Religion* 47.2 (2017): 147–60.
Moore, Timothy J. "Seats and Social Status in the Plautine Theatre." *CJ* 90.2 (1995): 113–23.
Morgan, Teresa. "Belief and Practice in Graeco-Roman Religiosity: Plutarch, De Iside and Osiride 379c." Pages 200–213 in *Christianity in the Second Century: Themes and Developments*. Edited by Judith Lieu and James Carleton Paget. Cambridge: Cambridge University Press, 2017.
———. *Roman Faith and Christian Faith: Pistis and Fides in the Early Roman Empire and Early Churches*. Oxford: Oxford University Press, 2015.
Moyer, Ian S. *Egypt and the Limits of Hellenism*. Cambridge: Cambridge University Press, 2011.
Munck, Johannes. *Paul and the Salvation of Mankind*. Translated by Frank Clarke. Richmond, Va.: John Knox, 1959.
Murphy-O'Connor, Jerome. *Keys to First Corinthians: Revisiting the Major Issues*. Oxford: Oxford University Press, 2009.
———. *St. Paul's Corinth: Texts and Archaeology*. Good News Studies 6. Wilmington, Del.: Michael Glazier, 1983.
Musurillo, Herbert Anthony. *The Acts of the Christian Martyrs: Introduction, Texts and Translations*. Oxford Early Christian Texts. Oxford: Clarendon, 1972.
Napolitano, Valentina. "On a Political Economy of Political Theology: *El Señor de los Milagros*." Pages 243–55 in *Anthropology of Catholicism: A Reader*. Edited by Kristin Norget, Valentina Napolitano, and Maya Mayblin. Berkeley: University of California Press, 2017.
Nasrallah, Laura Salah. "'You Were Bought with a Price': Freedpersons and Things in 1 Corinthians." Pages 54–73 in *Corinth in Context: Comparative Studies on Religion and Society*. Edited by Steven J. Friesen, Daniel N. Schowalter, and James C. Walters. NovTSup 134. Leiden: Brill, 2010.
Netzer, Ehud, Ya'akov Kalman, and Rachel Laureys. "A Synagogue from the Hasmonean Period Recently Discovered in the Western Plain of Jericho." *IEJ* 49.3–4 (1999): 203–21.

Nickle, Keith Fullerton. *The Collection: A Study in Paul's Strategy*. SBT 48. London: SCM, 1966.

Nicols, John. "Tabulae Patronatus: A Study of the Agreement Between Patron and Client-Community." *ANRW* II.13 (1980): 535–61.

Nielsen, Inge. *Housing the Chosen: The Architectural Context of Mystery Groups and Religious Associations in the Ancient World*. Contextualizing the Sacred. Turnhout: Brepols, 2014.

Nock, Arthur Darby. *Conversion: The Old and the New in Religion from Alexander the Great to Augustine*. London: Oxford University Press, 1933.

———. "The Historical Importance of Cult-Associations." *CR* 38 (1924): 105–8.

———. "Paul and the Magus." Pages 164–88 in *The Acts of the Apostles*. Vol. 5 of *The Beginnings of Christianity: Additional Notes on the Commentary*. Edited by Kirsopp Lake and Frederick J. Foakes-Jackson. London: Macmillan, 1933.

———. "The Vocabulary of the New Testament." *JBL* 52.2/3 (1933): 131–39.

Nongbri, Brent. *Before Religion: A History of a Modern Concept*. New Haven: Yale University Press, 2013.

———. "Dislodging 'Embedded' Religion: A Brief Note on a Scholarly Trope." *Numen* 55 (2008): 440–60.

Nonnis, David. "Un patrono dei dendrofori di Lavinium: onori e munificenza in un dossier epigrafico di età severiana." *Atti della Pontificia Accademia Romana di Archeologia. Serie III. Rendiconti* 68 (1995–96): 235–62.

North, John. "The Development of Religious Pluralism." Pages 174–93 in *The Jews Among Pagans and Christians in the Roman Empire*. Edited by Judith M. Lieu, John North, and Tessa Rajak. London: Routledge, 1992.

Oakes, Peter. *Reading Romans in Pompeii: Paul's Letter at Ground Level*. Minneapolis: Fortress; London: SPCK, 2009.

Ober, Josiah. *Mass and Elite in Democratic Athens: Rhetoric, Ideology, and the Power of the People*. Princeton: Princeton University Press, 1989.

Ogereau, Julien M. "Paul's κοινωνία with the Philippians: *Societas* as a Missionary-Funding Strategy." *NTS* 60.3 (2014): 360–78.

———. "La plus ancienne référence comptable chrétienne: la signification de l'expression εἰς λόγον δόσεως καὶ λήμψεως (Phil 4 :15)." *Comptabilités* 6 (2014): 2–16.

———. *Paul's Koinonia with the Philippians*. WUNT 2/377. Tübingen: Mohr Siebeck, 2013.

Ogilvie, Sheilagh. *Institutions and European Trade: Merchant Guilds, 1000–1800*. Cambridge: Cambridge University Press, 2011.

Öhler, Markus. "Graeco-Roman Associations, Judean Synagogues and Early Christianity in Bithynia-Pontus." Pages 62–88 in *Authority and Identity in Emerging Christianities in Asia Minor and Greece*. Edited by Cilliers Breytenbach and Julien Ogereau. AJEC 103. Leiden: Brill, 2018.

———. "Zwischen Elite und Elend: Paulinische Gemeinden in Ökonomischer Perspektive." Pages 249–86 in *Réceptions de Paul dans le christianisme naissant: Des origines jusqu'à Irénée*. Edited by Andreas Dettwiler. BZNW. Berlin: de Gruyter, 2018.

Osborne, Michael J., and Sean G. Byrne. *The Foreign Residents of Athens: An Annex to the Lexicon of Greek Personal Names*. Studia Hellenistica 33. Leuven: Peeters, 1996.

Osiek, Carolyn. *Rich and Poor in the Shepherd of Hermas: An Exegetical-Social Investigation*. CBQMS 15. Washington, D.C.: Catholic Biblical Association of America, 1983.

———. *Shepherd of Hermas: A Commentary*. Hermeneia. Minneapolis: Fortress, 1999.

Packer, James E. *The Insulae of Imperial Ostia*. American Academy in Rome, Memoirs 31. Rome: American Academy in Rome, 1971.

Papathomas, Amphilochios. *Juristische Begriffe im ersten Korintherbrief des Paulus: eine semantisch-lexikalische Untersuchung auf der Basis der zeitgenössischen griechischen Papyri*. Tyche Supplementband. Vienna: Holzhausen, 2009.

Parker, Robert, and Dirk Obbink. "Aus der Arbeit der 'Inscriptiones Graecae' VIII. Three Further Inscriptions Concerning Coan Cults." *Chiron* 31 (2001): 253–75.

Parkin, Anneliese. "'You Do Him No Service': An Exploration of Pagan Almsgiving." Pages 60–82 in *Poverty in the Roman World*. Edited by Margaret Atkins and Robin Osborne. Cambridge: Cambridge University Press, 2006.

Patterson, John R. "The *Collegia* and the Transformation of the Towns of Italy in the Second Century AD." Pages 227–38 in *L'Italie d'Auguste à Dioclétien*. Collection de l'École française de Rome 198. Rome: École française de Rome, 1994.

———. *Landscapes and Cities: Rural Settlement and Civic Transformation in Early Imperial Italy*. Oxford: Oxford University Press, 2006.

———. "Patronage, Collegia and Burial in Imperial Rome." Pages 15–27 in *Death in Towns: Urban Responses to the Dying and the Dead, 100–1600*. Edited by Steven Bassett. Leicester: Leicester University Press; New York: St. Martin's, 1992.

Pavolini, Carlo. *Ostia*. 3rd ed. Guide Archeologiche Laterza. Rome: Editori laterza, 1989.

Payne, Steven T. "Spiritual Bodies and the Afterlives of Ancient Democracy in Early Paulinism." PhD diss., Fordham University, 2019.

Pečírka, J. *The Formula for the Grant of Enktesis in Attic Inscriptions*. Acta Universitatis Carolinae. Philosophica et Historica Monographia 15. Prague: Universita Karlova, 1966.

Perpillou-Thomas, Françoise. *Fêtes d'Égypte ptolémaïque et romaine d'après la documentation papyrologique grecque*. Studia Hellenistica 31. Leuven: Peeters, 1993.

Perry, Jonathan S. "*Collegia* and Their Impact on the Constitutional Structure of the Roman State." Pages 137–46 in *The Oxford Handbook of Roman Law and Society*. Edited by Paul J. du Plessis, Clifford Ando, and Kaius Tuori. Oxford Handbooks. Oxford: Oxford University Press, 2016.

———. "Death in the *Familia:* The Funerary Colleges of the Roman Empire." PhD diss., University of North Carolina, 1999.

———. "'L'État intervint peu à peu': State Intervention in the Ephesian 'Bakers' Strike.'" Pages 183–205 in *Private Associations and the Public Sphere*. Edited by Vincent Gabrielsen and Christian A. Thomsen. Scientia Danica. Series H, Humanistic, series 8, no. 9. Copenhagen: Royal Danish Academy of Sciences and Letters, 2015.

———. *The Roman Collegia: The Modern Evolution of an Ancient Concept*. Mnemosyne Supplements 277. Leiden: Brill, 2006.

Persky, Joseph. "Retrospectives: Pareto's Law." *Journal of Economic Perspectives* 6.2 (1992): 181–92.

Persons, W. Scott, and Philip J. Currie. "The Tail of Tyrannosaurus: Reassessing the Size and Locomotive Importance of the M. Caudofemoralis in Non-Avian Theropods." *Anatomical Record* 294 (2011): 119–31.

Pervo, Richard I. *Acts*. Hermeneia. Minneapolis: Fortress, 2009.

———. *Dating Acts: Between the Evangelist and the Apologists*. Santa Rosa, Calif.: Polebridge, 2006.

Petersen, Joan M. "House-Churches in Rome." *VigChr* 23.4 (1969): 264–72.

Peterson, Erik. "Ekklesia: Studien zum altkirchlichen Kirchenbegriff." Pages 9–83 in *Ausgewählte Schriften: Sonderband*. Edited by Barbara Nichtweiss and Hans-Ulrich Weidemann. Würzburg: Echter, 2010.

Petrikovits, Harold V. "Die Spezialisierung des römischen Handwerks." Pages 1:63–132 in *Das Handwerk in vor- und frühgeschichtlicher Zeit: Bericht über die Kolloquien der Kommission für die Altertumskunde Mittel- und Nordeuropas in den Jahren 1977 bis 1980*. Edited by Jankuhn von Herbert. Abhandlungen der Akademie der Wissenschaften in Göttingen. Philologisch-historische Klasse, Folge 3, Nr. 122–23. Göttingen: Vandenhoeck & Ruprecht, 1981.

Picard, Gilbert Charles. "Ostie et la Gaule de l'Ouest." *Mélanges de l'École française de Rome—Antiquité* 93.2 (1981): 883–915.

Piccottini, Gernot. *Mithrastempel in Virunum*. Aus Forschung und Kunst 28. Klagenfurt: Verlag des Geschichtsvereines für Karnten, 1994.

———. "Ein römisches Handwerkerkollegium aus Virunum." *Tyche* 8 (1993): 111–23.

Pilhofer, Peter. "Ökonomische Attraktivität christlicher Gemeinden der Frühzeit." Pages 194–216 in *Die frühen Christen und ihre Welt: Greifswalder Aufsätze 1996–2001*. By Peter Pilhofer. WUNT 2/145. Tübingen: Mohr Siebeck, 2002.

Pleket, H. W. "Political Culture and Political Practice in the Cities of Asia Minor in the Roman Empire." Pages 204–16 in *Politische Theorie und Praxis im Altertum*. Edited by Wolfgang Schuller. Darmstadt: Wissenschaftliche Buchgesellschaft, 1998.

———. "Urban Elites and the Economy of the Greek Cities of the Roman Empire." *Münstersche Beiträge zur antiken Handelsgeschichte* 3 (1984): 3–36.

———. "Wirtschaft." Pages 25–160 in *Handbuch der europäischen Wirtschafts- und Sozialgeschichte. I. Europäische Wirstchafts- und Sozialgeschichte in der römischen Kaiserzeit*. Edited by Friedrich Vittinghoff. Handbuch der europäischen Wirtschafts- und Sozialgeschichte 1. Stuttgart: Ernst Klett and Cotta, 1990.

Poland, Franz. *Geschichte des griechischen Vereinswesens*. Leipzig: Teubner, 1909.

Price, Simon R. F. "Religious Mobility in the Roman Empire." *JRS* 102 (2012): 1–19.

———. *Rituals and Power: The Roman Imperial Cult in Asia Minor*. Cambridge: Cambridge University Press, 1984.

Prodromídis, Pródromos-Ioánnis. *Another View on an Old Inflation: Environment and Policies in the Roman Empire up to Diocletian's Price Edict*. Report of the Centre of

Planning and Economic Research 85. Athens: Centre of Planning and Economic Research, 2006.

Pugliese Carratelli, Giovanni. "Per la storia delle associazioni in Rodi antica." *Annuario della (Regia) Scuola archeologica di Atene* 17–18 (n.s. 1–2) (1939–1940): 147–200.

———. "Tituli Camirenses, Supplementum." *ASAA* 30–32 (n.s. 14–16) (1952–1954): 211–46.

Putnam, Robert D. *Bowling Alone: The Collapse and Revival of American Community.* New York: Simon and Schuster, 2000.

Radt, Wolfgang. *Pergamon: Geschichte und Bauten einer antiken Metropole.* Darmstadt: Wissenschaftliche Buchgesellschaft, 1999.

Rainer, Michael. "Die Mithrasverehrung in Ostia." *Klio* 66.1 (1984): 104–13.

Rajak, Tessa, and David Noy. "*Archisynagogoi*: Office, Title and Social Status in the Greco-Jewish Synagogue." *JRS* 83 (1993): 75–93.

Rathbone, Dominic. "The Census Qualification of the Assidui and the Prima Classis." Pages 121–52 in *De Agricultura: In Memoriam Pieter Willem de Neeve (1945–1990)*. Edited by H. Sancisi-Weerdenburg, R. J. van der Spek, H. C. Teitler, and H. T. Wallinga. Dutch Monographs on Ancient History and Archaeology 10. Amsterdam: J. C. Gieben, 1993.

———. *Economic Rationalism and Rural Society in Third-Century A.D. Egypt: The Heroninos Archive and the Appianus Estate.* Cambridge Classical Studies. Cambridge: Cambridge University Press, 1991.

———. "Poverty and Population in Roman Egypt." Pages 100–114 in *Poverty in the Roman World.* Edited by Margaret Atkins and Robin Osborne. Cambridge: Cambridge University Press, 2006.

Rathmayr, Elisabeth. "Das Haus des Ritters C. Flavius Furius Aptus: Beobachtungen zur Einflussnahme von Hausbesitzern an Architektur und Ausstattung in der Wohneinheit 6 des Hanghauses 2 in Ephesos." *Istambuler Mitteilungen* 59 (2009): 307–36.

Rebillard, Éric. *The Care of the Dead in Late Antiquity.* Translated by Elizabeth Trapnell Rawlings and Jeanine Toutier-Pucci. Cornell Studies in Classical Philology. Ithaca, N.Y.: Cornell University Press, 2009.

Reekmans, Tony. "Monetary History and the Dating of Ptolemaic Papyri." *Studia Hellenistica* 5 (1948): 15–43.

———. "The Ptolemaic Copper Inflation." Pages 61–118 in *Ptolemaica.* E. van 'T Dack and Tony Reekmans. Studia Hellenistica 7. Leiden: Brill; Louvain: E. Nauwelaerts, 1951.

Reicke, Bo I. *Diakonie, Festfreude und Zelos in Verbindung mit der altchristlichen Agapenfeier.* Uppsala Universitets Årsskrift 1951: 5. Uppsala: A.-B. Lundequistska Bokhandeln; Wiesbaden: Otto Harrassowitz, 1951.

Reilly, Linda Collins. *Slaves in Ancient Greece: Slaves from Greek Manumission Inscriptions.* Chicago: Ares, 1978.

Reynolds, Joyce M. *Aphrodisias and Rome: Documents from the Excavation of the Theatre at Aphrodisias Conducted by Professor Kenan T. Erim, Together with Some Related Texts.* Journal of Roman Studies Monographs 1. London: Society for the Promotion of Roman Studies, 1982.

Richardson, Lawrence. *A New Topographical Dictionary of Ancient Rome.* Baltimore: Johns Hopkins University Press, 1992.

Rives, James B. "Graeco-Roman Religion in the Roman Empire: Old Assumptions and New Approaches." *CBR* 8.2 (2010): 240–99.

———. *Religion and Authority in Roman Carthage: From Augustus to Constantine.* Oxford: Clarendon; New York: Oxford University Press, 1995.

Robert, Louis. *Le Sanctuaire de Sinuri près de Mylasa.* Mémoires de l'institut Français d'archéologie de Stamboul 7, Bibliothèque archéologique et historique de l'Institut Français d'archéologie d'Istanbul 8. Paris: Éditions de Boccard, 1945.

———. "Sur des inscriptions de Chios." *BCH* 57 (1933): 505–43.

Robinson, Amy. "It Takes One to Know One: Passing and Communities of Common Interest." *Critical Inquiry* 20.4 (1994): 715–36.

Robinson, Thomas A. *Who Were the First Christians? Dismantling the Urban Thesis.* New York: Oxford University Press, 2016.

Roldanus, Johannes. "Références patristiques au 'chrétien-estranger' dans les trois premier siècles." Pages 27–52 in *Lectures Anciennes de la Bible.* Cahiers de Biblia Patristica 1. Strasbourg: Centre d'analyse et de documentation patristiques, 1987.

Rondot, Vincent. *Tebtynis II: Le temple de Soknebtynis et son dromos.* Fouilles de l'Institut Français d'archéologie orientale du Caire 50 = Publications de l'Institut Français d'archéologie orientale du Caire 918. Cairo: Institut Français d'archéologie orientale, 2000.

Rowlandson, Joan. "Agricultural Tenancy and Village Society in Roman Egypt." Pages 39–158 in *Agriculture in Egypt: From Pharaonic to Modern Times.* Edited by Alan K. Bowman and Eugene Rogan. Proceedings of the British Academy 96. Oxford: Oxford University Press, 1999.

Royden, Halsey L. *The Magistrates of the Roman Professional Collegia in Italy from the First to the Third Century A.D.* Biblioteca di studi antichi 61. Pisa: Giardini Editori e Stampatori, 1988.

———. "The Tenure of Office of the Quinquennalis in the Roman Professional Collegia." *AJPh* 110 (1989): 303–15.

Ruffini, Giovanni Roberto. *Social Networks in Byzantine Egypt.* Cambridge: Cambridge University Press, 2008.

Runesson, Anders. "The Oldest Original Synagogue Building in the Diaspora: A Response to L. Michael White." *HTR* 92.4 (1999): 409–33.

———. *The Origin of the Synagogue: A Socio-Historical Study.* ConB: New Testament Series 37. Stockholm: Almqvist & Wiksell, 2001.

Runesson, Anders, Donald D. Binder, and Birger Olsson, eds. *The Ancient Synagogue from Its Origins to 200 C.E.* AJEC 72. Leiden: Brill, 2007.

Russell, Josiah Cox. "Late Ancient and Medieval Population." *TAPA* 48.3 (1958): 1–152.

Rüpke, Jörg. "Antike Großstadtreligion." Pages 13–30 in *Zwischen Krise und Alltag: antike Religionen im Mittelmeerraum—Conflit et normalité: religions anciennes dans l'espace méditerranéen.* Edited by Christophe Batsch, Ulrike Egelhaaf-Gaiser, and Ruth Stepper. Potsdamer Altertumswissenschaftliche Beiträge 1. Stuttgart: Steiner, 1999.

Salamito, Jean-Marie. "Les dendrophores dans l'empire chrétien: À propos de *Code Théodosien*, XIV, 8, 1 et XVI, 10, 20, 2." *Mélanges de l'École française de Rome—Antiquité* 99 (1987): 991–1018.

Salies, G. Hellenkemper. "Römische Mosaiken im Griechenland." *Bonner Jahrbücher* 186 (1986): 241–84.

Saller, Richard P. "*Familia, Domus*, and the Roman Conception of the Family." *Phoenix* 38 (1984): 336–55.

———. *Patriarchy, Property, and Death in the Roman Family*. Cambridge Studies in Population, Economy, and Society in Past Time 25. Cambridge: Cambridge University Press, 1994.

———. "Women, Slaves and the Economy of the Roman Household." Pages 185–204 in *Early Christian Families in Context: An Interdisciplinary Dialogue*. Edited by David L. Balch and Carolyn Osiek. Grand Rapids: Eerdmans, 2003.

Saller, Richard P., and Brent D. Shaw. "Tombstones and Roman Family Relations in the Principate." *JRS* 74 (1984): 124–56.

Salomies, Olli. *Die römischen Vornamen: Studien zur römischen Namengebung*. Commentationes Humanarum Litterarum 82. Helsinki: Societas Scientiarum Fennica, 1987.

Salway, Benet. "What's in a Name? A Survey of Roman Onomastic Practice from c. 700 B.C. to A.D. 700." *JRS* 84 (1994): 124–45.

Sampley, J. Paul. *Pauline Partnership in Christ: Christian Community and Commitment in Light of Roman Law*. Philadelphia: Fortress, 1980.

Sawyer, R. Keith. "Durkheim's Dilemma: Toward a Sociology of Emergence." *Sociological Theory* 20.2 (2002): 227–47.

Schäfer, Alfred. "Dionysische Gruppen als ein städtliche Phänomen der römischen Kaiserzeit." Pages 161–80 in *Gruppenreligionen im römischen Reich: Sozialformen, Grenzziehungen und Leistungen*. Edited by Jörg Rüpke. STAC 43. Tübingen: Mohr Siebeck, 2007.

Schäfer, Hans. "Paroikoi." *PW* 18.4 (1949): 1695–1707.

Scheid, John. "Community and Community: Reflections on Some Ambiguities Based on the Thiasoi of Roman Egypt." Pages 366–82 in *The Religious History of the Roman Empire*. Edited by John A. North and Simon Price. Oxford: Oxford University Press, 2011.

———. *An Introduction to Roman Religion*. Translated by Janet Lloyd. Edinburgh: Edinburgh University Press, 2003.

Scheidel, Walter. "Demography." Pages 38–86 in *The Cambridge Economic History of the Greco-Roman World*. Edited by Walter Scheidel, Ian Morris, and Richard P. Saller. Cambridge: Cambridge University Press, 2007.

———. "A Model of Demographic and Economic Change in Roman Egypt After the Antonine Plague." *JRA* 15 (2002): 97–114.

———. "Stratification, Deprivation and Quality of Life." Pages 40–59 in *Poverty in the Roman World*. Edited by Margaret Atkins and Robin Osborne. Cambridge: Cambridge University Press, 2006.

Scheidel, Walter, and Stephen J. Friesen. "The Size of the Economy and the Distribution of Income in the Roman Empire." *JRS* 99 (2009): 61–91.

Schiess, Traugott. *Die römischen Collegia Funeraticia nach den Inschriften*. Munich: T. Ackermann königlicher Hof-Buchhandler, 1888.

Schleich, Thomas. "Missionsgeschichte und Sozialstruktur des vorkonstantinischen Christentums." *Geschichte in Wissenschaft und Unterricht* 33 (1982): 269–96.

Schleiermacher, Friedrich. *Die christliche Glaube nach den Grundsätzen der evangelischen Kirch im Zusammenhang dargestellt*. 2nd ed. Berlin: Georg Reimer, 1830.

Schmeller, Thomas. "Gegenwelten: Zum Vergleich zwischen paulinischen Gemeinden und nichtchristlichen Gruppen." *BZ* 47.2 (2003): 167–85.

———. *Hierarchie und Egalität: Eine sozialgeschichtliche Untersuchung paulinischer Gemeinden und griechisch-römischer Vereine*. SBS 162. Stuttgart: Verlag Katholisches Bibelwerk, 1995.

Schmit Pantel, Pauline. "Collective Activities and the Political in the Greek City." Pages 199–213 in *The Greek City from Homer to Alexander*. Edited by Oswyn Murray and S. R. F. Price. Oxford: Clarendon, 1990.

Schnöckel, Karl Heinrich. *Ägyptische Vereine in der frühen Prinzipatszeit: Eine Studie über sechs Vereinssatzungen (Papyri Michigan 243–248)*. Xenia 48. Konstanz: UVK, Universitätsverlag, 2006.

Scholl, Reinhold. *Corpus der ptolemäischen Sklaventexte*. Forschungen zur antiken Sklaverei, Supplement 1. Stuttgart: Franz Steiner, 1990.

Schor, Adam M. "Conversion by the Numbers: Benefits and Pitfalls of Quantitative Modelling in the Study of Early Christian Growth." *JRH* 33.4 (2009): 472–98.

Schrumpf, Stefan. *Bestattung und Bestattungswesen im Römischen Reich: Ablauf, soziale Dimension und ökonomische Bedeutung der Totenfürsorge im lateinischen Westen*. Göttingen: Vandenhoeck & Ruprecht; Bonn: Bonn University Press, 2006.

Schwarzer, Holger. *Das Gebäude mit dem Podiensaal in der Stadtgrabung von Pergamon: Studien zu sakralen Bankettäumen mit Liegepodien in der Antike*. Altertümer von Pergamon XV/4. Berlin: Deutsches Archäologisches Institut, Staatliche Museen zu Berlin, 2008.

———. "Vereinslokale im hellenistischen und römischen Pergamon." Pages 221–51 in *Religiöse Vereine in der römischen Antike: Untersuchungen zu Organisation, Ritual und Raumordnung*. Edited by Ulrike Egelhaaf-Gaiser and Alfred Schäfer. STAC 13. Tübingen: Mohr Siebeck, 2002.

Schwenk, Cynthia J. *Athens in the Age of Alexander: The Dated Laws and Decrees of "The Lykouran Era" 338–322 B.C.* Chicago: Ares, 1985.

Scroggs, Robin. "The Sociological Interpretation of the New Testament: The Present State of Research." *NTS* 26.2 (1980): 164–79.

Segre, Mario. "Tituli Calymnii." *Annuario della scuola archeologica di Atene* 22–23 (n.s. 6–7) (1944–1945): 1–248.

Sharankov, Nicolay. "Надпис за строеж на храм от Никополис ад Иструм." Археология 55.1–2 (2014): 28–48.

Sherwin-White, A. N. "Why Were the Early Christians Persecuted? An Amendment." *P&P* 27 (1964): 23–27.

Siebert, Gérard. "Sur l'histoire du sanctuaire des dieux syriens à Délos." *BCH* 92.2 (1968): 359–74.

Silber, Ilana F. "Neither Mauss, nor Veyne: Peter Brown's Interpretative Path to the Gift." Pages 202–20 in *The Gift in Antiquity*. Edited by Michael L. Satlow. Malden, Mass.: Wiley Blackwell, 2013.

Simms, Ronda R. "Isis in Classical Athens." *CJ* 84 (1988–1989): 216–21.

Smit, Peter-Ben. "A Symposiastic Background to James?" *NTS* 58.1 (2012): 105–22.

Smith, Adam. *An Inquiry into the Nature and Causes of the Wealth of Nations*. New York: Modern Library, 1994.

Smith, Dennis E. "Hospitality, the House Church, and Early Christian Identity." Pages 103–17 in *Mahl und religiöse Identität im frühen Christentum* [Meals and Religious Identity in Early Christianity]. Edited by Matthias Klinghardt and Hal Taussig. TANZ 56. Tübingen: A. Francke, 2012.

———. "Revisiting Associations and Christ Groups." Pages 483–94 in *Scribal Practices and Social Structures Among Jesus Adherents: Essays in Honour of John S. Kloppenborg*. Edited by William E. Arnal, Richard S. Ascough, Robert A. Derrenbacker, and Philip A. Harland. BETL 285. Leuven: Peeters, 2016.

Smith, Jonathan Z. *Drudgery Divine: On the Comparison of Early Christianities and the Religions of Late Antiquity*. Chicago: University of Chicago Press, 1990.

———. *Imagining Religion: From Babylon to Jonestown*. Chicago Studies in the History of Judaism. Chicago: University of Chicago Press, 1982.

———. "Religion, Religions, Religious." Pages 269–84 in *Critical Terms for Religious Studies*. Chicago: University of Chicago Press, 1998.

Snow, David A., and Richard Machalek. "The Sociology of Conversion." *Annual Review of Sociology* 10 (1984): 167–90.

Snow, David A., and C. L. Philipps. "The Lofland-Stark Conversion Model: A Critical Reassessment." *Social Problems* 27.4 (1980): 430–47.Snyder, H. Gregory. "The Discovery and Interpretation of the Flavia Sophe Inscription: New Results." *VigChr* 68.1 (2014): 1–59.

———. "A Second-Century Christian Inscription from the Via Latina." *JECS* 19.2 (2011): 157–95.

Solin, Heikki. *Die griechischen Personennamen in Rom: Ein Namenbuch*. 2nd ed. Corpus Inscriptionum Latinarum, Auctarium Series nova 2. Berlin: de Gruyter, 2003.

———. "Neue Namen und kein Ende. Zu CIL VI 9102." *ZPE* 136 (2001): 279–85.

———. *Die stadtrömischen Sklavennamen: Ein Namenbuch*. Forschungen zur antiken Sklaverei, Supplement 2. Stuttgart: Franz Steiner, 1996.

Sommer, Stefan. *Rom und die Vereinigungen im südwestlichen Kleinasien (133 v. Chr.–284 n. Chr.)*. Pietas 1. Hennef: Buchverlag Marthe Clauss, 2006.

Sosin, Joshua. "Perpetual Endowments in the Hellenistic World: A Case Study in Economic Rationalism." PhD diss., Duke University, 2000.

Sosis, Richard. "Religion and Intragroup Cooperation: Preliminary Results of a Comparative Analysis of Utopian Communities." *Cross-Cultural Research* 34.1 (2000): 77–88.

Sosis, Richard, and Candace Alcorta. "Signaling, Solidarity, and the Sacred: The Evolution of Religious Behavior." *Evolutionary Anthropology* 12 (2003): 264–74.

Sosis, Richard, and Eric R. Bressler. "Cooperation and Commune Longevity: A Test of the Costly Signaling Theory of Religion." *Cross-Cultural Research* 37.2 (2003): 211–39.

Sourvinou-Inwood, Christiane. "Further Aspects of *Polis* Religion." Pages 38–55 in *Oxford Readings in Greek Religion*. Edited by Richard Buxton. Oxford: Oxford University Press, 2001.

———. "What Is Polis Religion?" Pages 13–37 in *Oxford Readings in Greek Religion*. Edited by Richard Buxton. Oxford: Oxford University Press, 2000.

Spera, Lucrezia. *Il paesaggio suburbano di Roma dall'antichità al Medioevo: il comprensorio tra le vie Latina e Ardeatina dalle Mura Aureliane al III miglio*. Bibliotheca Archaeologica 27. Rome: "L'Erma" di Bretschneider, 1999.

Spigel, Chad S. *Ancient Synagogue Seating Capacities: Methodology, Analysis and Limits*. TSAJ 149. Tübingen: Mohr Siebeck, 2012.

Stark, Rodney. "The Rise of a New World Faith." *RRelRes* 26.1 (1984): 18–27.

———. *The Rise of Christianity: A Sociologist Reconsiders History*. Princeton: Princeton University Press, 1996.

———. "Why Religious Movements Succeed or Fail: A Revised General Model." *Journal of Contemporary Religion* 11.2 (1996): 133–46.

Stark, Rodney, and William S. Bainbridge. *The Future of Religion: Secularization, Revival, and Cult Formation*. Berkeley: University of California Press, 1985.

———. "Networks of Faith: Interpersonal Bonds and Recruitment to Cults and Sects." *American Journal of Sociology* 85.6 (1980): 1376–95.

Stegemann, Ekkehard W., and Wolfgang Stegemann. *The Jesus Movement: A Social History of Its First Century*. Translated by O. C. Dean. Minneapolis: Fortress, 1999.

Stephenson, Barry. "Ritual as Action, Performance and Practice." Pages 39–54 in *Oxford Handbook of Early Christian Ritual*. Edited by Risto Uro, Juliette Day, Richard E. DeMaris, Anne Katrine Gudme, and Rikard Roitto. New York: Oxford University Press, 2018.

Steuernagel, Dirk. "Ancient Harbour Towns—Religious Market Places?: Formation and Social Functions of Voluntary Associations in Roman Ostia." Pages 141–51 in *Zwischen Kult und Gesellschaft. Kosmopolitische Zentren des antiken Mittelmeerraums als Aktionsraum von Kultvereinen und Religionsgemeinschaften. Akten eines Symposiums des Archäeologischen Instituts der Universität Hamburg (12.–14. Oktober 2005)*. Edited by Nielsen Inge. Hephaistos 24. Augsburg: Carmelion, 2006.

Stock, Brian. *The Implications of Literacy: Written Language and Models of Interpretation in the Eleventh and Twelfth Centuries*. Princeton: Princeton University Press, 1983.

———. *Listening for the Text: On the Uses of the Past*. Parallax. Baltimore: Johns Hopkins University Press, 1990.

Streett, Daniel R. "Food, Fellowship, and Favoritism: Early Christian Meals as the Setting for James 2:1–9." Paper presented in the Catholic Epistles Section, 2011 Annual Meeting of the Society of Biblical Literature, San Francisco, November 19–22, 2011.

Tačeva-Hitova, Margarita. "Dem Hypsistos geweihte Denkmäler in Trakien. Untersuchungen zur Geschichte der antiken Religionen III." *Thracia* 4 (1977): 271–301.

Teixidor, Javier. "L'assemblée législative en Phénicie d'après les inscriptions." *Syria* 57.2/4 (1980): 453–64.

Temin, Peter. "Estimating GDP in the Early Roman Empire." Pages 31–54 in *Innovazione tecnica e progresso economico nel mondo romano*. Edited by Elio Lo Cascio. Bari: Edipuglia, 2006.

———. *The Roman Market Economy*. Princeton Economic History of the Western World. Princeton: Princeton University Press, 2013.

Tepper, Yotam, and Leah Di Segni. *A Christian Prayer Hall of the Third Century CE at Kefar 'Othnay (Legio): Excavations at the Megiddo Prison 2005*. Jerusalem: Israel Antiquities Authority, 2006.

Theissen, Gerd. "Pauperismus und paulinisches Urchristentum. Zu A. Merz: G. Theißen Beiträge zur Sozialgeschichte." Pages 117–27 in *Von Jesus zur Urchristlichen Zeichenwelt: Neutestamentliche Grenzgange im Dialog*. NTOA 78. Göttingen: Vandenhoeck & Ruprecht, 2011.

———. "Social Conflicts in the Corinthian Community: Further Remarks on J. J. Meggitt, *Paul, Poverty and Survival*." *JSNT* 25.3 (2003): 371–91.

———. *The Social Setting of Pauline Christianity: Essays on Corinth*. Translated by John H. Schütz. Philadelphia: Fortress, 1982.

———. "The Social Structure of Pauline Communities: Some Critical Remarks on J. J. Meggitt, *Paul, Poverty and Survival*." *JSNT* 84 (2001): 65–84.

———. "Urchristliche Gemeinden und antike Vereine. Sozialdynamik im Urchristentum durch Widerspruche zwischen Selbstverstandnis und Sozialstruktur." Pages 221–47 in *In Other Words: Essays on Social Science Methods and the New Testament in Honor of Jerome H. Neyrey*. Edited by Anselm C. Hagedorn, Zeba A. Crook, and Eric Stewart. Social World of Biblical Antiquity 2. Sheffield: Sheffield Phoenix, 2007.

Thomas, Rosalind. "Writing, Reading, Public and Private 'Literacies': Functional Literacy and Democratic Literacy in Greece." Pages 13–45 in *Ancient Literacies: The Culture of Reading in Greece and Rome*. Edited by William A. Johnson and Holt N. Parker. Studies in Book and Print Culture. Oxford: Oxford University Press, 2009.

Thür, Hilke, Ingrid Adenstedt, Sonja Jilek, and Ute Stipanits, eds. *Hanghaus 2 in Ephesos: die Wohneinheit 4: Baubefund, Ausstattung, Funde*. Forschungen in Ephesos VIII/6. Vienna: Verlag der österreichischen Akademie der Wissenschaften, 2005.

Tran, Nicolas. "Les affranchis dans les collèges professionnels du Haut-Empire romain: l'encadrement civique de la mobilité sociale." Pages 389–401 in *Les Régulations sociale dans l'Antiquité: Actes du Colloque d'Angers, 23 et 24 mai 2003*. Edited by Michel Molin. Collection "Histoire." Rennes: Presses Universitaires de Rennes, 2006.

———. "*Ars* and *Doctrina*: The Socioeconomic Identity of Roman Skilled Works (First Century BC–Third Century AD)." Pages 246–61 in *Work, Labour, and Professions in the Roman World*. Edited by Koenraad Verboven and Christian Laes. Impact of Empire 23. Leiden: Brill, 2017.

———. *Dominus tabernae: le statut de travail des artisans et des commerçants de l'Occident romain (Ier siècle av. J.-C.–IIIe siècle ap. J.-C.)*. Bibliothèque des écoles françaises d'Athènes et de Rome 360. Rome: École française de Rome, 2013.

———. *Les membres des associations romaines: le rang social des* collegiati *en Italie et en Gaules, sous le Haut-Empire*. Collection de l'École française de Rome 367. Rome: École française de Rome, 2006.

Trebilco, Paul R. *Jewish Communities in Asia Minor*. SNTSMS 69. Cambridge: Cambridge University Press, 1991.

———. "Why Did the Early Christians Call Themselves ἡ ἐκκλησία?" *NTS* 57.3 (2011): 440–60.

Treggiari, Susan. "Domestic Staff at Rome in the Julio-Claudian Period 27 B.C. to A.D. 68." *Histoire Sociale* 6.12 (1973): 241–55.

Trombley, Frank. "Overview: The Geographical Spread of Christianity." Pages 302–13 in *Origins to Constantine*, Vol. 1 of *Cambridge History of Christianity*. Edited by Margaret M. Mitchell and Frances M. Young. Cambridge: Cambridge University Press, 2006.

Trümper, Monika. "Negotiating Religious and Ethnic Identity: The Case of Clubhouses in Late Hellenistic Delos." Pages 113–40 in *Zwischen Kult und Gesellschaft. Kosmopolitische Zentren des antiken Mittelmeerraums als Aktionsraum von Kultvereinen und Religionsgemeinschaften*. Edited by Nielsen Inge. Hephaistos 24. Augsburg: Camelion, 2006.

———. "Where the Non-Delians Met in Delos. The Meeting-Places of Foreign Associations and Ethnic Communities in Late Hellenistic Delos." Pages 49–100 in *Political Culture in the Greek City After the Classical Age*. Edited by Onno M. van Nijf and Richard Alston. Groningen-Royal Holloway Studies on the Greek City After the Classical Age 2. Leuven: Peeters, 2011.

Tuck, Steven. "Nasty, Brutish, and Short? The Demography of the Roman Imperial Navy." Pages 212–29 in *Ancient Documents and Their Contexts: First North American Congress on Greek and Latin Epigraphy (2011)*. Edited by John Bodel and Nora Dimitrova. Leiden: Brill, 2014.

Turcan, Robert. *The Cults of the Roman Empire*. Translated by Antonia Nevill. Ancient World. Oxford: Blackwell, 1996.

Ustinova, Yulia. "Orgeones in Phratries: A Mechanism of Social Integration in Attica." *Kernos* 9 (1996): 227–42.

———. *The Supreme Gods of the Bosporan Kingdom: Celestial Aphrodite and the Most High God*. Religions in the Graeco-Roman World 135. Leiden: Brill, 1999.

———. "The *Thiasoi* of Theos Hypsistos in Tanais." *HR* 31 (1991): 150–80.

Van Bremen, Riet. *The Limits of Participation: Women and Civic Life in the Greek East in the Hellenistic and Roman Periods*. Dutch Monographs on Ancient History and Archaeology 15. Amsterdam: Gieben, 1996.

van der Horst, Pieter Willem. *Ancient Jewish Epitaphs: An Introductory Survey of a Millennium of Jewish Funerary Epigraphy (300 BCE–700 CE)*. Kampen, Netherlands: Kok Pharos, 1991.

van der Meer, L. Bouke. *Ostia Speaks: Inscriptions, Buildings and Spaces in Rome's Main Port*. Leuven: Peeters, 2012.

van der Vliet, Edward C. L. "Pride and Participation, Political Practice, Euergetism, and Oligarchisation in the Hellenistic *Polis*." Pages 155–84 in *Political Culture in the Greek City After the Classical Age*. Edited by Onno M. van Nijf and Richard Alston. Groningen-Royal Holloway Studies on the Greek City After the Classical Age 2. Leuven: Peeters, 2011.

Van Haeperen, Françoise. "Cohabitation or Competition in Ostia During the Empire." Pages 133–48 in *Religion and Competition in Antiquity*. Edited by David Engels and Peter Van Nuffelen. Collection Latomus 343. Brussels: Éditions Latomus, 2014.

van Kooten, George H. "Ἐκκλησία τοῦ θεοῦ: The 'Church of God' and the Civic Assemblies (ἐκκλησίαι) of the Greek Cities in the Roman Empire: A Response to Paul Trebilco and Richard A. Horsley." *NTS* 58.4 (2012): 522–48.

Van Minnen, Peter. "Urban Craftsmen in Roman Egypt." *Münstersche Beiträge zur antiken Handelsgeschichte* 6.1 (1987): 31–88.

Van Nijf, Onno. *The Civic World of Professional Associations in the Roman East.* Dutch Monographs on Ancient History and Archaeology 17. Amsterdam: Gieben, 1997.

——. "Collegia and Civic Guards: Two Chapters in the History of Sociability." Pages 305–39 in *After the Past: Essays in Ancient History in Honour of H. W. Pleket.* Edited by Willem Jongman and Marc Kleijwegt. Mnemosyne Supplements 233. Leiden: Brill, 2002.

——. "Global Players: Athletes and Performers in the Hellenistic and Roman World." Pages 225–35 in *Zwischen Kult und Gesellschaft: Kosmopolitische Zentren des antiken Mittelmeerraumes als Aktionsraum von Kultvereinen und Religionsgemeinschaften. Akten eines Symposiums des Archäologischen Instituts der Universität Hamburg, 12–14 Oktober 2005.* Edited by Inge Nielsen. Hephaistos 24. Augsburg: Camelion, 2006.

van Nijf, Onno M., and Richard Alston. "Political Culture in the Greek City After the Classical Age: Introduction and Preview." Pages 1–26 in *Political Culture in the Greek City After the Classical Age.* Edited by Onno M. van Nijf and Richard Alston. Groningen-Royal Holloway Studies on the Greek City After the Classical Age 2. Leuven: Peeters, 2011.

Van Nuffelen, Peter. "Deux fausses lettres de Julien l'Apostat (La lettre aux juifs, Ep. 51 [Wright], et la lettre à Arsacius, Ep. 84 [Bidez])." *VigChr* 56.2 (2002): 131–50.

Vearncombe, Erin K. "Rituals for Communal Maintenance." Chap. 5 in *Early Christian Ritual Life.* Edited by Richard DeMaris, Jason Lamoreaux, and Steven C. Muir. London: Routledge, 2017.

——. "Rounding Cape Maleas: The Function of Travel Experience in Paul's Struggle for Status, 2 Corinthians 11:25–26 and Romans 15:19–20." MA thesis, University of St. Michael's College, 2007.

Venticinque, Philip F. *Honor Among Thieves: Craftsmen, Merchants, and Associations in Roman and Late Roman Egypt.* New Texts from Ancient Cultures. Ann Arbor: University of Michigan Press, 2016.

Verboven, Koenraad. "Les collèges et la romanisation dans les provinces occidentales." Pages 13–46 in *Collegia: Le phénomène associatif dans l'Occident romain.* Edited by Monique Dondin-Payre and Nicolas Tran. Scripta Antiqua 41. Bordeaux: Ausonius, 2012.

——. *The Economy of Friends: Economic Aspects of Amicitia and Patronage in the Late Republic.* Collection Latomus 269. Brussels: Latomus, 2002.

——. "Guilds and the Organisation of Urban Populations During the Principate." Pages 173–202 in *Work, Labour, and Professions in the Roman World.* Edited by Koenraad Verboven and Christian Laes. Impact of Empire 23. Leiden: Brill, 2017.

Verbrugge, Verlyn D. *Paul's Style of Church Leadership Illustrated by His Instructions to the Corinthians on the Collection.* San Francisco: Mellen Research University Press, 1992.

Vetter, Emil. "Die familia Silvani in Trebula Mutuesca und die sectores materiarum in Aquileia." Pages 93–119 in *Studi aquileiesi offerti il 7 ottobre 1953 a Giovanni Brusin nel suo 70, compleanno.* Aquileia: Associazione nazionale per Aquileia, 1953.

Vlassopoulos, Kostas. "Athenian Slave Names and Athenian Social History." *ZPE* 175 (2010): 113–44.

———. "Free Spaces: Identity, Experience and Democracy in Classical Athens." *CQ* 57.1 (2007): 33–52.

von Dobschütz, Ernst. *Christian Life in the Primitive Church.* Translated by George Bremner. Theological Translation Library 18. London: Williams and Norgate, 1904.

Vondeling, Johannes. *Eranos.* Proefschrift University of Utrecht. Groningen: Wolters, 1961.

Walbank, Michael B. "Notes on Attic Decrees." *ZPE* 139 (2002): 61–65.

Walker, William O. *Interpolations in the Pauline Letters.* JSNTSup 213. London: Sheffield Academic Press, 2001.

Wallace-Hadrill, Andrew. *Houses and Society in Pompeii and Herculaneum.* Princeton: Princeton University Press, 1994.

Waltzing, Jean Pierre. *Étude historique sur les corporations professionnelles chez les Romains depuis les origines jusqu'à la chute de l'Empire d'Occident.* Louvain: Peeters, 1895–1900.

Walzer, Richard. *Galen on Jews and Christians.* Oxford Classical and Philosophical Monographs. London: Oxford University Press, 1949.

Wayment, Thomas A., and Matthew J. Grey. "Jesus Followers in Pompeii: The *Christianos* Graffito and 'Hotel of the Christians' Reconsidered." *JJMJS* 2 (2015): 102–46.

Weaver, Joel A. "A Re-Examination of 1 Corinthians 14,23–24 in Light of Roman Census Declarations." Pages 817–21 in *Actes du 26e Congrès international de papyrologie, Genève, 16–21 août 2010.* Edited by Paul Schubert. Geneva: Librairie Droz, 2012.

Weaver, P. R. C. *Familia Caesaris: A Social Study of the Emperor's Freedmen and Slaves.* London: Cambridge University Press, 1972.

Weinfeld, Moshe. *The Organizational Pattern and the Penal Code of the Qumran Sect: A Comparison with Guilds and Religious Associations of the Hellenistic-Roman Period.* NTOA 2. Fribourg: Editions Universitaires; Göttingen: Vandenhoeck & Ruprecht, 1986.

Weiß, Alexander. *Soziale Elite und Christentum: Studien zu ordo-Angehörigen unter den frühen Christen.* Millennium-Studien/Millennium Studies 52. Berlin: de Gruyter, 2015.

Weiss, Johannes. *Der erste Korintherbrief.* 9. Primary source ed. Kritisch-exegetischer Kommentar über das Neue Testament. Göttingen: Vandenhoeck & Ruprecht, 1910.

Welborn, Larry L. *An End to Enmity: Paul and the "Wrongdoer" of Second Corinthians.* BZNW 185. Berlin: de Gruyter, 2011.

———. "'That There May Be Equality': The Contexts and Consequences of a Pauline Ideal." *NTS* 59.1 (2012): 73–90.

Welch, Kevin W. "An Interpersonal Influence Model of Traditional Religious Commitment." *Sociological Quarterly* 22.1 (1981): 81–92.

White, L. Michael. *Building God's House in the Roman World: Architectural Adaptation Among Pagans, Jews and Christians.* ASOR Library of Biblical and Near Eastern Archaeology. Baltimore: Johns Hopkins University Press, 1990.

———. "The Changing Face of Mithraism at Ostia." Pages 435–91 in *Contested Spaces: Houses and Temples in Roman Antiquity and the New Testament.* Edited by David L. Balch and Annette Weissenrieder. WUNT 285. Tübingen: Mohr Siebeck, 2012.

———. "Reading the Ostia Synagogue: A Reply to A. Runesson." *HTR* 92.4 (1999): 435–64.

———. *The Social Origins of Christian Architecture. Vol. 1: Building God's House in the Roman World: Architectural Adaptation Among Pagans, Jews, and Christians. Vol. 2: Texts and Monuments for the Christian Domus Ecclesiae in Its Environment.* Harvard Theological Studies 42.1–2. Valley Forge, Pa.: Trinity Press International, 1996–1997.

Whitehead, David. "Cardinal Virtues: The Language of Public Approbation in Democratic Athens." *Classica et Mediaevelia* 44 (1993): 37–75.

———. "Competitive Outlay and Community Profit: φιλοτιμία in Democratic Athens." *Classica et Mediaevelia* 34 (1983): 55–74.

———. "Immigrant Communities in the Classical Polis: Some Principles for a Synoptic Treatment." *L'Antiquité classique* 53 (1984): 47–59.

Will, Ernest. "Banquets et salles de banquet dans les cultes de la Grèce et de l'Empire romain." Pages 353–62 in *Mélanges d'histoire ancienne et d'archéologie offerts à Paul Collart.* Edited by Pierre Ducrey. Cahiers d'archéologie romande de la Bibliothèque historique vaudoise, no. 5. Lausanne: Bibliothèque historique vaudoise, 1976.

Williams, Charles K., and Orestes H. Zervos. "Corinth, 1987: South of Temple E and East of the Theater." *Hesperia* 57.2 (1988): 95–146.

Wilson, Andrew. "Fish-Salting Workshops in Sabratha." Pages 173–81 in *CETARIAE 2005: Salsas y Salazones de Pescado eh Occidente durante la Antigüedad Aetas del Congreso Intemacional (Cádiz, 7–9 de noviembre de 2005).* Edited by L. Lagóstena, D. Bernal, and A. Arevalo. BAR International Series 1686. Cádiz: Universidad de Cádiz, 2007.

———. "Machines, Power, and the Ancient Economy." *JRS* 92 (2002): 1–32.

———. "Quantifying Roman Economic Performance by Means of Proxies: Pitfalls and Potential." Pages 147–67 in *Quantifying the Greco-Roman Economy and Beyond.* Edited by François de Callataÿ. Pragmateia 27. Bari: Edipuglia, 2014.

Winter, Bruce W. *After Paul Left Corinth: The Influence of Secular Ethics and Social Change.* Grand Rapids: Eerdmans, 2001.

———. *Seek the Welfare of the City: Christians as Benefactors and Citizens.* First-Century Christians in the Graeco-Roman World. Grand Rapids: Eerdmans; Carlisle: Paternoster, 1994.

Wipszycka, Ewa. *L'industrie textile dans l'Egypte romaine.* Archiwum Filologiczne 9. Wrocław: Zakład Narodowy imienia Ossolinskich, 1965.

Woolf, Greg. "Food, Poverty and Patronage: The Significance of the Epigraphy of the Roman Alimentary Schemes in Early Imperial Italy." *Proceedings of the British School at Rome* 58 (1990): 197–228.

———. "Monumental Writing and the Expansion of Roman Society in the Early Empire." *JRS* 86 (1996): 22–39.

———. "Polis-Religion and Its Alternatives in the Roman Provinces." Pages 39–54 in *Roman Religion.* Edited by Clifford Ando. Edinburgh: University of Edinburgh Press, 2003.

———. "Writing Poverty in Rome." Pages 83–99 in *Poverty in the Roman World.* Edited by Margaret Atkins and Robin Osborne. Cambridge: Cambridge University Press, 2006.

Youtie, H. C., and O. M. Pearl. *Papyri and Ostraca from Karanis.* Michigan Papyri 6, 8. Ann Arbor: University of Michigan Press, 1944–51.

Youtie, Herbert C. “The Kline of Sarapis.” *HTR* 41.1 (1948): 9–29.

Zamfir, Korinna. “Is the ἐκκλησία a Household (of God)? Reassessing the Notion of οἶκος θεοῦ in 1 Tim 3.15.” *NTS* 60.4 (2014): 511–28.

Zanker, Paul. *Pompeii: Public and Private Life.* Translated by Deborah Lucas Schneider. Cambridge, Mass.: Harvard University Press, 1999.

Zelnick-Abramovitz, Rachel. “Did Patronage Exist in Classical Athens?” *L'Antiquité classique* 69 (2000): 65–80.

Ziebarth, Erich Gustav Ludwig. *Das griechische Vereinswesen.* Stuttgart: S. Hirzel, 1896.

Zimmermann, Carola. *Handwerkervereine im griechischen Osten des Imperium Romanum.* Monographien, Römisch-Germanisches Zentralmuseum Mainz. Forschungsinstitut für Vor- und Frühgeschichte 57. Mainz: Habelt, 2002.

Zuiderhoek, Arjan J. *The Ancient City.* Key Themes in Ancient History. Cambridge: Cambridge University Press, 2017.

———. “Feeding the Citizens: Municipal Grain Funds and Civic Benefactors in the Roman East.” Pages 159–80 in *Feeding the Ancient Greek City.* Edited by Richard Alston and Onno Van Nijf. Groningen-Royal Holloway Studies on the Greek City After the Classical Age 1. Leuven: Peeters, 2008.

———. “On the Political Sociology of the Imperial Greek City.” *GRBS* 48.4 (2008): 417–45.

———. *The Politics of Munificence in the Roman Empire: Citizens, Elites, and Benefactors in Asia Minor.* Greek Culture in the Roman World. Cambridge: Cambridge University Press, 2009.

INDEX OF ANCIENT ASSOCIATIONS

General Index